EU FUNDAMENTAL RIGHTS AS A SPECIAL SOURCE FOR THE EUROPEAN COURT OF HUMAN RIGHTS

European Union Law Series

This series brings together major works in the field of European Union Law. It features a diverse range of publications, including comprehensive handbooks designed to teach European Union Law, treaties for legal practitioners and academics, monographs on specialised topics and some of the best doctoral dissertations from across Europe. Additionally, it includes publications detailing conference proceedings on topical issues, as well as commentaries on major judgments and decisions handed down by the Court of Justice of the European Union.

P. Durand and A. Gilbert-d'Halluin (eds.), *Directive (EU) 2022/2464 as regards Corporate Sustainability Reporting (CSRD)*, 2024.

P. Pailler, *How to Best Regulate Crypto-Assets?. The EU and UAE Perspectives*, 2025.

G. Cavalier, *European R&D Tax Incentives. Contribution to the Emergence of a Concept*, 2025.

G. Marti (ed.), *European Citizenship through the Lens of EU Values*, 2025.

A. Bensoussan, J.Bensoussan, V. Bensoussan-Brulé, *The European AI Act. Summary, Key Points and Article-by-Article Analysis*, 2025.

A. Gridel, *Financial Markets and Instruments in Private International Law*, 2025.

EU FUNDAMENTAL RIGHTS AS A SPECIAL SOURCE FOR THE EUROPEAN COURT OF HUMAN RIGHTS

Victor Davio

INTERSENTIA
LEFEBVRE GROUP

Intersentia
Lefebvre Belgium SA
Avenue Jean Monnet, 4
1348 Louvain-la-Neuve
Belgium
Email: contact@larcier-intersentia.com

Distribution for the UK, Ireland and
Rest of the World (excl. France, Belgium and Luxembourg)
Ingram Publisher Services UK
1 Deltic Avenue, Rooksley
Milton Keynes MK13 8LD
United Kingdom
Tel: +44 1752 202 301 | Fax: +44 1752 202 331
Email: ipsuk.customercare@ingramcontent.com

Distribution for France and Other Countries (excl. Ireland and the UK)
Interforum Editis
92 avenue de France
75013 Paris
France

Distribution for Belgium and Luxembourg (excl. France, Ireland and the UK)
Larcier-Intersentia
Avenue Jean Monnet, 4
1348 Louvain-la-Neuve
Belgium

EU Fundamental Rights as a Special Source for the European Court of Human Rights

ISBN : 978-1-83970-593-9
D/2026/06040/0111
NUR 820

British Library Cataloguing in Publication Data. A catalogue record for this book is available from the British Library

ABSTRACT

This work is part of the RESHUFFLE research project, which explores the growing impact of the European Union's role in the field of fundamental rights. Historically, Europe was split between two systems: the Council of Europe, focused on democracy, the rule of law, and human rights through the European Convention on Human Rights; and the European Union, originally centred on economic integration and the internal market. In the absence of its own fundamental rights regime, the EU—through the Court of Justice of the EU—drew heavily on the ECHR to build its framework.

Over the past few decades, however, the EU has increasingly established its own standards in fundamental rights. Since 2000, the Charter of Fundamental Rights has served as the EU's own Bill of Rights. Legislative action in areas such as equality, data protection, and non-discrimination has further expanded the EU's role. This evolution marks a shift in Europe's fundamental rights landscape: from a position of 'standard-taker', the EU is emerging as a 'standard-setter'. Yet, this transformation and its consequences have received limited academic attention.

This project investigates how EU fundamental rights standards have influenced the case-law of the European Court of Human Rights. The research aims to uncover how the Court has engaged with EU standards, the opportunities these provide, and how it navigates the tensions arising from their use in its case-law.

ACKNOWLEDGMENTS

À tous ceux et celles qui m'ont accueilli lors de mon parcours doctoral,[1]

À tous ceux et celles qui m'ont guidé et épaulé,

À tous ceux et celles qui m'ont ouvert leurs mondes et quotidiens,

À tous ceux et celles avec qui j'ai fait, et je fais encore, chemin de vie,

À tous ceux et celles qui m'ont embrassé de leur affection

Par une accolade, un geste, un regard, une main tendue, un échange, un partage, une aventure, une pensée,

Merci du fond de mon cœur pour ce projet… et pour tout le reste aussi !

1 This book is the outcome of my PhD written in the context of the RESHUFFLE research project hosted by KU Leuven under the direction of Prof. Elise Muir, and supported by the European Research Council (European Union's Horizon 2020 research and innovation programme, grant agreement No. 851621). A more 'targeted' acknowledgment can be found in my PhD thesis where I refer to my different sources of inspiration, including to my supervisor just mentioned, Elise.

LIST OF ABBREVIATIONS

ACHPR	African Charter on Human and Peoples' Rights
ACtHPR	African Court on Human and Peoples' Rights
ACHR	American Convention on Human Rights
CJEU	Court of Justice of the European Union
CEDAW	Convention on the Elimination of All Forms of Discrimination Against Women
ComEDAW	Committee on the Elimination of Discrimination against Women
ComFCNM	Advisory Committee on the Framework Convention for the Protection of National Minorities
Convention 108	Convention for the Protection of Individuals with regard to Automatic Processing of Personal Data
Convention 108+	Modernised Convention for the Protection of Individuals with regard to Automatic Processing of Personal Data
CRPD	Convention on the Rights of Persons with Disabilities
ECHR	European Convention on Human Rights
ECtHR	European Court of Human Rights
EPC	European Political Community
EU	European Union
FCNM	Framework Convention for the Protection of National Minorities
IACHR	Inter-American Court of Human Rights
ICCPR	International Covenant on Civil and Political Rights
Istanbul Convention	Convention on Preventing and Combating Violence Against Women and Domestic Violence
OECD	Organisation for Economic Co-operation and Development
SCEC	Study Committee for the European Constitution
UN HRC	United Nations Human Rights Committee

Je n'ai plus peur de la pluie
Ni même de la nuit
Le noir en toile de fond
Est havre de ma lumière

TABLE OF CONTENTS

PART II
SHIFTING PARADIGM:
THE EU AS A FUNDAMENTAL RIGHTS STANDARD-SETTER

PART III
IN ACTION:
THE USE OF EU FUNDAMENTAL RIGHTS IN PRACTICE

Title 1
THE INFLUENCE OF EU EQUALITY LAW ON ECHR EQUALITY LAW

Title 2
THE INFLUENCE OF EU DATA PROTECTION LAW ON ECHR DATA PROTECTION LAW

PART IV
FUTURE AND RECOMMENDATIONS: A SPECIAL METHOD FOR A SPECIAL SOURCE

FOREWORD

Bridging Two Europes

The story I am about to tell you is that of a photograph. I took this photograph on a Saturday morning in November two years ago. The location of this photo, which you will probably recognise, is Strasbourg. Strasbourg is a city whose structure and architecture speak of our shared past. It was built up in successive waves and layers. If you dare to take a boat tour in Strasbourg, and so did I three times, it will take you to the heart of the conflicts and turmoil of our European history. Not far from Place du Corbeau, the tour begins in the historic district of Strasbourg. As you proceed along the Ill canal, you catch sight of the famous Palais Rohan before noticing a change in the surroundings. The Alsatian architecture with its half-timbered houses gives way to massive buildings constructed from cut stone. You have entered the German imperial quarter, the Neudstadt, which was built following the Treaty of Frankfurt in 1871 when Strasbourg was ceded to the German Empire.

Continuing the visit, you arrive in the European quarter, constructed after the Second World War as a symbol of a new beginning and a commitment to 'never again' on the European continent. This is the place you see in the photograph. On either side of the canal, two buildings are visible. On the right is the Louise Weiss building, where the plenary sessions of the European Parliament are held. To the left, you can catch a glimpse of the Winston Churchill Building, which also belongs to the EU institutions. Just behind this building is the Palais des droits de l'Homme – which cannot be seen on the picture –, home to the Council of Europe, which can be accessed through the Winston Churchill Building. Although both Europes share the purposes of ensuring peace and cooperation between European States, they resemble twins separated at birth.[1] The Council of Europe emerged as the 'Europe of values', upholding democracy, the rule of law, and human rights as its banners. The European Union, known back then as three European Communities, represented the 'Europe of the market', with roots tracing back to Schuman's vision that 'Europe will not be made all at once, or according to a single plan', but will be 'built through concrete achievements which first create a de facto solidarity'.[2]

Within these two Europes, the protection and promotion of human rights, as enshrined in the 1948 Universal Declaration of Human Rights, took divergent paths: central to one, absent in the other. The Council of Europe placed human rights at the heart of its mission. Under its aegis, the European Convention on Human Rights came to birth, along with the European Court of Human Rights, housed in the Palais des Droits de l'Homme, not far from the location in our photograph. The Convention would become one of the most successful and effective human rights instruments in the world, thanks to the supervisory mechanism it puts in place, which operates beyond the national level. In the founding Treaties establishing the European Communities, traces of these rights were scarcely found. But let us not be mistaken. While the absence of human rights may seem like an anomaly, it was the result of historical circumstances. These rights could very well have been at the heart of the Union's architecture from the very beginning too.

Even though the 'young' EU institutions were primarily focused on economic matters, making their impact on human rights not obvious, the issue of their (lack of) protection knocked on the door of the Court of Justice of the European Union, driven by litigants seeking to defend their rights. Although it initially showed some resistance, the EU judiciary – located not in Strasbourg but in Luxembourg – began incorporating these rights through the gateway

---

1 G. Quinn, 'The European Union and the Council of Europe on Human Rights Issues: Twins Separated at Birth', 2001, *McGill Law Journal*, pp. 849–874.

2 Schuman Declaration of 9 May 1950, available at: https://op.europa.eu/en/publication-detail/-/publication/2fa0afe0-9f7c-426d-9933-fca909c50983, p. 17.

of general principles, under increasing pressure from national courts. Lacking sources of inspiration within EU law itself, the CJEU had to look elsewhere. It first turned to the common constitutional traditions to the Member States and then to international treaties, eventually elevating one source as the true *primus inter pares*: the European Convention on Human Rights. The CJEU regarded this as a source of 'particular' or 'special' significance, drawing extensively on both the Convention and Strasbourg case-law, far more than on constitutional traditions, international conventions, or related jurisprudence. The prominent role of ECHR law, endorsed by EU political institutions, led to a situation in which, for a long time, EU fundamental rights were significantly inspired by those of the ECHR.

To express it more vividly and return to our photograph, let us consider, in simplified terms, that the right bank symbolises the EU and EU law, while the left bank represents the Council of Europe and ECHR law. With our picture in mind, one could say that the flow of human rights was unidirectional, crossing the bridge from left to right – from ECHR law to EU law. From right to left, the issue was quite different: it was not about the ECtHR drawing inspiration from EU law, but rather about whether it could oversee measures originating from EU law that might threaten human rights. In this vein, the potential accession of the EU to the ECHR has been in the pipeline since the late 1970s, with the aim of ensuring that acts of EU institutions comply with ECHR law.

The story up to now is well known, but in recent decades, a new chapter seems to be unfolding that could alter its course. This is because, on the right side of the canal, the EU has increasingly adopted fundamental rights standards. One immediately thinks of the Charter of Fundamental Rights, a bill of rights for the Union, which gained the same legal force as the EU Treaties with the Treaty of Lisbon. But that is not all. Although it does not have a general competence in human rights matters, the EU legislator has been granted specific powers since the Treaty of Amsterdam, leading to a burgeoning of legislation that gives flesh to the Charter in areas such as the right to equality and non-discrimination, data protection, and procedural rights, among others.

The wave of EU fundamental rights could modify the flow of traffic between our two banks. The flow from ECHR law to EU law is slowing down: increasingly, the CJEU focuses on the fundamental rights enshrined in the Charter and expressed in secondary legislation, which it tends to interpret autonomously from Strasbourg. A new flow could also emerge, not from left to right, but from right to left, where EU fundamental rights find a place within the ECtHR's case-law. There are solid reasons to believe this may happen: these fundamental rights are highly sophisticated and deeply integrated within the majority of the Council of Europe's States, making them a valuable source of inspiration and a source of law which is part of the background in cases involving EU States. As these rights evolve autonomously from those of the ECHR, there is also a growing need to articulate the EU and ECHR layers.

If this might be true, we should bear in mind that the context in which the flow goes from EU fundamental rights to ECHR law is quite different from the reverse flow. This is because, firstly, all EU States are Parties to the ECHR, whereas not all Convention States are EU States. Moreover, EU law does not enter uncharted territory: the ECtHR has long been open to drawing on international instruments and the practices of European states in shaping its jurisprudence. One might assume that, despite their growing significance in the ECtHR's case-law, EU fundamental rights are just one source among others that the ECtHR takes into account.

So, what impact has the growing role of the EU as a fundamental rights standard-setter had on the other side of the canal? Are EU fundamental rights simply one source among many, or do they hold a special place in ECtHR case-law? At the core of this book lies one central thesis we will unfold: EU fundamental rights are, to some extent, a source of special significance for the ECtHR, a significance that could increase over time. This special significance should be supported by a specific method aimed at strengthening the EU-ECHR fundamental/human rights bridge, which is crucial for upholding our shared European values and advancing the common European project of peace and cooperation, at the very heart of our two Europes.

PART I.

Introduction and Contextualisation: Reshuffling the EU/ECHR Dynamics

CHAPTER 1

SETTING THE SCENE: THE DYNAMICS BETWEEN EU AND ECHR LAWS

That EU and ECHR laws have a special relationship is beyond doubt.[1] While the two European systems are distinct, they are closely interrelated and interdependent. This intertwining is the result of several overlaps between them. *Ratione loci*, both systems apply in the European space, in the Smaller and the Greater Europe respectively. *Ratione personae*, the 27 EU States have acceded to the ECHR, thereby constituting the majority of States Parties to the Convention. *Ratione materiae*, EU and ECHR laws safeguard to a large extent the same fundamental rights.

That the relationship between EU and ECHR laws is a long-standing one is also evident. As early as 1975, the CJEU referred to provisions of the ECHR.[2] In 1989, it acknowledged the particular significance of the ECHR for the advancement of fundamental rights within the EU.[3] One year later, the European Commission of Human Rights decided that it was not competent to examine decisions from organs of the European Communities, but that it could review the actions of States which they had taken to give effect to Community law.[4] Since then, the control of EU measures by the ECtHR is governed by well-established principles such as the *Bosphorus* presumption,[5] which have been applied in many recent judgments.[6]

Given this long-term interplay, the dynamics between EU and ECHR laws appears well-established and settled. Among these dynamics, three stand out. First, ECHR law has been a significant source of inspiration for EU fundamental rights. Second, EU law has often been studied and portrayed as

---

1. Please note that the following two paragraphs stem from V. Davio and E. Muir, 'Introduction. The ECHR in the CJEU's Case-law Post-Charter: A Dual Perspective', *European Papers*, 2023, p. 317.
2. Case C-36/75, *Rutili*, ECLI:EU:C:1975:137, para. 32.
3. Joined Cases C-46/87 and 227/88, *Hoescht*, ECLI:EU:C:1989:337, para. 13.
4. European Commission of Human Rights, *M. & Co. against the Federal Republic of Germany*, no. 13258/87, 9 February 1990.
5. ECtHR, *Bosphorus Hava Yolları Turizm ve Ticaret Anonim Şirketi v. Ireland* [GC], no. 45036/98, §§159–165, 30 June 2005.
6. E.g. ECtHR, *Bivolaru and Moldovan v. France*, nos. 40324/16 and 12623/17, 25 March 2021.

a threat to ECHR rights, and the main question has been whether the ECtHR could oversee the compliance of EU law with ECHR law. Third, a need for coherence between EU and ECHR laws has always been felt as both systems operate within a shared European space.

SECTION I. THE INFLUENCE OF ECHR LAW ON EU LAW

Looking back at the beginning of the EU history, fundamental rights were of secondary importance within the EU's foundational structure, with the Community Treaties remaining almost silent on the matter. These rights emerged timidly within the EU legal order, being recognised as general principles of EU law in the *Stauder* case of 12 November 1969.[7] Their endorsement within the EU Treaties followed, appearing in the preambles of the Single European Act of 1986 and in Article F of the Maastricht Treaty in 1992.[8] For a long period of time, the CJEU was the driving force behind the development of EU fundamental rights. As general principles, these rights were the 'creature of judicial lawmaking'.[9] In the quasi-absence of textual support in EU law,[10] the CJEU drew inspiration from two sources to inform its fundamental rights case-law: the constitutional traditions common to the Member States and international human rights law.[11] Although the latter was the primary source of inspiration, not all international treaties were accorded equal consideration. Among them, the ECHR stood out as a primus inter pares.[12]

---

7 Case C-29/69, *Stauder*, ECLI:EU:C:1969:57, para. 124.

8 In the Single European Act, the Heads of State or Government affirmed their determination to work together to promote democracy 'on the basis of the fundamental rights recognised in the constitutions and laws of the Member States, in the European Convention for the Protection of Human Rights and the European Social Charter, notably freedom, equality and social justice' (para. 3 SEA). Art. F of the Treaty Maastricht provided that: 'The Union shall respect fundamental rights, as guaranteed by the European Convention for the Protection of Human Rights and Fundamental Freedoms signed in Rome on 4 November 1950 and as they result from the constitutional traditions common to the Member States, as general principles of Community law.'

9 The expression is borrowed from K. Lenaerts and J. Gutiérrez-Fons, 'The Place Charter in the EU Constitutional Edifice', in S. Peers, T. Hervey, J. Kenner and A. Ward (eds.), *The EU Charter of Fundamental Rights: A Commentary*, Oxford, Hart Publishing, 2014, p. 1559.

10 As we will see in Part II, Chapter 1, Section I, §1, I. The Limited Traces of Fundamental Rights, there were some limited traces of fundamental rights along two axes: equality and freedom.

11 Case C-11/70, *Internationale Handelsgesellschaft*, 17 December 1970, ECLI:EU:C:1970:114, para. 13.

12 The expression is borrowed from S. Peers, 'Article 52. Scope and Interpretation of Rights and Principles', in S. Peers, T. Hervey, J. Kenner and A. Ward (eds.), *The EU Charter of Fundamental Rights. A Commentary*, Oxford, Hart Publishing, 2014, p. 1462.

The CJEU began referencing the ECHR with some caution in the mid-1970s.[13] About a decade later, the CJEU mentioned that it had 'particular significance' in its fundamental rights case-law.[14] The intensity with which the CJEU referred to the ECHR surpassed by far its references to international instruments,[15] and it seldom diverged from the case-law set by Strasbourg.[16] The choice to draw inspiration from ECHR law unfolded rather naturally given that all EU States were Parties to the Convention.[17]

SECTION II. THE COMPLIANCE OF EU LAW WITH ECHR LAW

EU law has historically not been a source of inspiration for the ECtHR. The primary question relating to EU law in the ECtHR's case-law has long centred on compliance by EU to the ECHR. One of the first instances when Union law reached Strasbourg revolved around whether acts of EU institutions could be subject to Conventional control. The European Commission of Human Rights, in its decision *Confédération française démocratique du travail v. the European Communities* of 10 July 1978, asserted its incompetence to examine the decisions of EU organs.[18] This conclusion, which was reiterated in subsequent case-law,[19] led to a second question: could EU States be held liable under Convention law when they were acting under obligations arising from Union primary and secondary laws?

In the landmark *Matthews v. United Kingdom* case of 18 February 1999, the ECtHR held that States retain responsibility for EU primary law.[20] A similar conclusion was reached for EU secondary law, with the ECtHR considering that States remain responsible for all acts and omissions of their organs, even

---

13 Case C-36/75, *Rutili*, 28 October 1975, ECLI:EU:C:1975:137, para. 32.

14 Joined Cases C-46/87 and 227/88, *Hoescht*, 21 September 1989, ECLI:EU:C:1989:337, para. 13.

15 E.g. I. Butler and O. De Schutter, 'Binding the EU to International Human Rights Law', *Yearbook of European Law*, 2008, pp. 277–320. See further in Part II, Chapter 1, Section III, §2. The Special Significance of ECHR Law.

16 E.g. A. Rosas, 'Fundamental Rights in the Luxembourg and Strasbourg Courts' in C. Baudenbacher, P. Tresselt and T. Orlygsson (eds.), *The EFTA Court: Ten Years On*, Oxford, Hart Publishing, 2005, p. 170. See further in Part II, Chapter 1, Section III, §2. The Special Significance of ECHR Law.

17 In this vein, see the Opinion of Advocate General Maduro of 9 September 2008 in Case C-465/07, *Elgafaji*, ECLI:EU C:2009:94, para. 22.

18 European Commission of Human Rights, *Confédération française démocratique du travail v. European Communities* (dec.), no. 8030/77.

19 E.g. ECtHR, *Bosphorus Hava Yolları Turizm ve Ticaret Anonim Şirketi v. Ireland* [GC], no. 45036/98, § 152, ECHR 2005-VI.

20 ECtHR, *Matthews v. the United Kingdom* [GC], no. 24833/94, §§ 32–35, ECHR 1999-I.

those stemming from compliance with international legal obligations.[21] Yet, the ECtHR introduced the so-called 'Bosphorus presumption', building on the premise that the protection of fundamental rights within the EU legal order was, in principle, equivalent to that provided by the ECHR.[22] Through this presumption, the ECtHR committed to examining the responsibility of EU States only in the presence of a manifest deficiency in so far as they have no margin of manoeuvre when they implement EU law and the full potential of the supervisory mechanism provided for by EU law has been deployed.[23]

The logic of compliance by EU to the ECHR that underpins these various judgments has also manifested in the question of the EU's accession to the ECHR. Already in the late 1970s, the Commission suggested that the EU should accede to the ECHR.[24] Although this idea received support from some EU institutions,[25] accession faced a major obstacle with Opinion 2/94, in which the CJEU held that: 'As Community law now stands, the Community has no competence to accede to the [ECHR].'[26] The Treaty of Lisbon inserted a legal basis and obligation for the accession,[27] which led to new negotiations between the EU and the Council of Europe. However, the CJEU considered that the new draft accession treaty was incompatible with EU law since it conflicted with its autonomy.[28] Even though accession has experienced a tumultuous path, it remains high on the agenda and may be closer to reality than ever before.[29] Accession would mean that the ECtHR can directly control the acts of EU institutions.[30]

The narrative behind the above judgments and the accession's process seems rather straightforward: rather than drawing inspiration from EU law, the gist of the issue is how to prevent deficits in EU States' responsibilities as

---

21 E.g. ECtHR, *Bosphorus Hava Yolları Turizm ve Ticaret Anonim Şirketi v. Ireland* [GC], no. 45036/98, § 153, ECHR 2005-VI.

22 Ibid., §§159–165.

23 See e.g. on the two conditions for the application of the presumption of equivalent protection, ECtHR, *Avotiņš v. Latvia* [GC], no. 17502/07, § 105, 23 May 2016.

24 Memorandum on the accession of the European Communities to the Convention for the protection of Human Rights and Fundamental Freedoms, COM(79) 210 final, 2 May 1979.

25 In particular from the European Parliament, see Resolution of 29 October 1982 embodying the opinion of the European Parliament on the memorandum from the Commission of the European Communities on the accession of the European Communities to the Convention for the Protection of Human Rights and Fundamental Freedoms, [1982] OJ C304/253.

26 Opinion 2/94 of 28 March 1996, ECLI:EU:C:1996:140, para. 36.

27 Article 6(2) TEU provides that: 'The Union shall accede to the European Convention for the Protection of Human Rights and Fundamental Freedoms.'

28 Opinion 2/13 of 18 December 2014, ECLI:EU:C:2014:2454, para. 258.

29 There is a consolidated Draft Accession Agreement as of February 2023, available at: https://rm.coe.int/consolidated-version-of-the-draft-accession-instruments-as-of-2-februa/1680aa3443. We will return in more detail to the potential accession of the EU to the ECHR and its impact on the application of EU fundamental rights in Part IV, Chapter 1, Section III. The Prospect of EU's Accession to the ECHR.

30 Ibid., Preamble 5.

the significance of EU law grows. Before the turn of the millennium, instances where EU law was a source of inspiration could be counted on the fingers of one hand.[31] One of the few examples is *Pellegrin v. France* (1999), in which the ECtHR relied on the notion of employment in the public service, as enshrined in Article 48(6) EEC Treaties, to determine the applicability of the right to a fair trial guaranteed under Article 6(1) ECHR.[32] Overall, interpreting ECHR law in light of EU law was the exception rather than the rule.

SECTION III. THE ARTICULATION BETWEEN EU AND ECHR LAWS

If the interplay between EU and ECHR laws has been driven by the logics of EU law's inspiration from and compliance with ECHR law, their coexistence within a shared European space has raised questions about their articulation. This question is acute for EU domestic judges: when they apply EU law, they must apply ECHR law and vice-versa. They are central actors in making the rights protected under these two sets of laws concrete and effective. As Callewaert explains, '[n]ational judges play an essential role in the protection of fundamental rights today, as they are the ones entrusted with the difficult task of combining and translating into viable solutions the multiple sources of such rights which are being produced by today's complex multipolar and multilayer legal world. They are the ones who, at the end of the day, apply these multiple legal sources to the citizens in the most coherent possible way'.[33]

To implement effectively the rights protected under EU and ECHR laws, a certain coherence between these sets of laws must exist. National judges should be able to determine which rights from which systems must be applied in a given case. To ensure this coherence, the CJEU and the ECtHR are required to display an attitude of openness and dialogue which involves taking into account the law of their counterpart. Failure to do so could lead to inconsistencies and contradictions for EU domestic judges, which could impede

[31] There were some cases which related to the interactions between the proceedings of the CJEU and the ECtHR. For instance, in *Pafitis v. Greece*, the ECtHR held that the length of the proceedings before the CJEU on a preliminary question should not be taken into account in assessing the reasonableness of the length of the domestic proceedings under Article 6(1) ECHR. In this respect, the ECtHR considered that taking this into account would undermine the system of preliminary rulings and the purpose of this system (ECtHR, *Pafitis and Others v. Greece*, 26 February 1998, §95, Reports of Judgments and Decisions 1998-I).

[32] ECtHR, *Pellegrin v. France* [GC], no. 28541/95, § 66, 8 December 1999.

[33] J. Callewaert, 'Convention Control Over the Application of Union Law by National Judges: The Case for a Wholistic Approach to Fundamental Rights', *European Papers*, 2023, p. 332.

the implementation of EU and ECHR rights.[34] The coherence between these rights has long been ensured by the incorporation of ECHR law into CJEU case-law. Even though the CJEU has used ECHR law in a rather unsystematic and selective way, the prevailing attitude was one of deference. This meant that limited divergence emerged between Strasbourg and Luxembourg.[35]

SECTION IV. SHIFTING PARAMETERS

While the dynamics between EU and ECHR laws appeared well-settled and understood, the parameters governing this relationship have experienced shifts over the past decades. One specific element of the EU/ECHR laws equation has evolved: the EU has growingly developed fundamental rights standards at primary and secondary law level.[36] For a long period of the EU history, the EU political institutions[37] maintained a limited presence in fundamental rights matters. Their first collective endorsement of the protection of fundamental rights only took place in 1977.[38] Until the 2000s, they focused on codifying CJEU's case-law within the EU Treaties, and lacked specific competence to enhance the protection of fundamental rights.[39]

We argue collectively that this landscape has undergone a transformation.[40] While the EU can still threaten fundamental rights, and we certainly acknowledge this dimension and do not undervalue its importance, it has become more proactive by developing fundamental rights standards at primary and secondary law level. EU fundamental rights have become a joint undertaking of the EU institutions, where not only the CJEU shapes these rights, but also the EU political institutions.[41]

---

34 V. Davio and E. Muir, 'Introduction. The ECHR in the CJEU's Case-law Post-Charter: A Dual Perspective', *European Papers*, 2023, p. 319.

35 See further in Part II, Chapter 1, Section III, §2. The Special Significance of ECHR Law.

36 E. Muir, 'Reshuffling our understanding of fundamental rights law in Europe: an EU lawyer's research agenda', *European Human Rights Law Review*, 2021, pp. 142–148.

37 In this project, the EU political institutions are defined as institutional actors that have participated in the political process leading to the adoption of EU primary and secondary laws, alongside the EU States. These institutions include the European Commission, the European Parliament, the Council, and the European Council.

38 Joint Declaration by the European Parliament, the Council and the Commission concerning the protection of fundamental rights and the European Convention for the protection of human rights and fundamental freedoms, 27 April 1977, [1977] OJ C103/1.

39 See more in Part II, Chapter 2, Section II, §2. The Fragmented, Yet Increasing Competences of the EU Legislator.

40 This research project is part of the collective, ERC-funded RESHUFFLE research project, which examines the growing role of the EU as a fundamental rights actor (for more information, see: https://www.law.kuleuven.be/eur/en/reshuffle).

41 E. Muir, 'Reshuffling our understanding of fundamental rights law in Europe: an EU lawyer's research agenda', *European Human Rights Law Review*, 2021, pp. 145–146.

At constitutional level, human rights have been enshrined as a value of the Union (Article 2 TEU); fundamental rights have also been fleshed out in the Charter whose legal status is now equivalent to that of the EU Treaties (Article 6(1) TEU). From the outset of its elaboration, a legal discourse has surrounded the Charter according to which the latter does not intend to create anything substantially new, but only to make the protection of fundamental rights more visible in the EU.[42] One needs to be cautious with this discourse. Indeed, we should not underestimate its innovative nature, as we will see.[43]

Another significant phenomenon has unfolded: the development of EU legislative standards on fundamental rights. While the EU lacks a general competence to enact rules on human rights,[44] the EU's legislative mandate has expanded. The EU legislator has been conferred competences to advance specific fundamental rights, notably the right to equality and non-discrimination (Articles 157(3) and 19 TFEU), the right to the protection of personal data (Article 16(2) TFEU), and the procedural rights of individuals involved in criminal procedure (Article 82(2)(2)(b) TFEU). Competences have also been granted in areas sensitive from a fundamental rights perspective, such as those related to asylum and immigration (Article 78(1) TFEU). The EU legislator has shown willingness to rely on these legal bases on multiple occasions, leading to a growing number of EU legislation giving expression to fundamental rights across a broad spectrum of domains, albeit in a somewhat fragmented manner.

If there were already some legislative activities on fundamental rights before the 2000s, there is a blossoming of fields where the EU leaves its significant mark. For instance, consider the domain of equality. The Treaty of Amsterdam inserted Article 13 TEC, empowering the EU legislator to take necessary action to combat discrimination based on sex, racial or ethnic origin, religion or belief, disability, age, or sexual orientation.[45] Relying on this legal basis, the EU legislator has developed a robust anti-discrimination policy – considered by some as the 'first fundamental rights policy of the EU'.[46] Following the entry of a far-right party in the Austrian government, the EU enacted the Racial Discrimination Directive (2000/43/EC)[47] and the Equality Framework

42 For instance, Declaration No. 1 to the TFEU states that the Charter confirms the fundamental rights guaranteed by the ECHR and as they result from the constitutional traditions common to the Member States.

43 We will return to the innovative nature of the Charter in Part II, Chapter 2, Section III, §1. Highly Sophisticated.

44 Opinion 2/94 of 28 March 1996, ECLI:EU:C:1996:140, para. 27.

45 This provision corresponds to the current Article 19 TFEU.

46 E. Muir, *EU Equality Law, The First Fundamental Rights Policy of the EU*, Oxford, Oxford University Press, 2018.

47 Directive 2000/43/EC of 29 June 2000 implementing the principle of equal treatment between persons irrespective of racial or ethnic origin, [2000] OJ L180/22 (hereafter: 'Racial Discrimination Directive (2000/43/EC)).

Directive (2000/78/EC).[48] While the EU had already adopted gender equality directives,[49] these instruments broaden the range of protected grounds. Besides, they are highly specific both in their substantive and procedural dimensions.

The evolving role of the EU in the field of fundamental rights is not a binary or sudden shift between being a standard-taker and a standard-setter, but rather a gradual process marked by changes in intensity and diversity. Diversity in that the EU intervenes in a wide array of fundamental rights-sensitive areas. The past five years have seen legislation emerging in fields such as whistleblower protection[50] and the digital sphere.[51] Intensity as the standards appear steadily more developed. Recent initiatives can be witnessed in fields where the EU legislator had already taken substantial action in the past. This is evident in both the areas of equality and data protection. The EU had already adopted several legislations and implemented substantial reforms over the last decades.[52] In these areas, new laws are being considered to enhance their effective application.[53]

EU fundamental rights, as enshrined in the Charter and given expression in secondary laws, are distinguished by their high level of sophistication. The Charter is a highly innovative instrument: it encompasses several generations of fundamental rights in one single instrument and entails rights which cannot be found in other human rights instruments, such as an autonomous right to data protection (Article 8 Charter). EU secondary laws can define the substance of fundamental rights, how they are to be balanced against competing legitimate interests, as well as some of the modalities for their enforcement.[54] Not only are these instruments highly-developed, but they have matured through CJEU's

---

48 Directive 2000/78/EC of 27 November 2000 establishing a general framework for equal treatment in employment and occupation, [2000] OJ L303/16 (hereafter: 'Equality Framework Directive (2000/78/EC)).

49 E.g. Directive 75/117/EEC of 10 February 1975 on the approximation of the laws of the Member States relating to the application of the principle of equal pay for men and women, [1975] OJ L45/19 (hereafter: 'Equal Pay between Men and Women Council Directive (75/117/EEC)').

50 Directive 2019/1937/EU of 23 October 2019 on the protection of persons who report breaches of Union law, [2019] OJ L305/17 (hereafter: 'Whistleblower Directive (2019/1937/EU)').

51 Regulation 2022/2065/EU of 19 October 2022 on a Single Market For Digital Services and amending Directive 2000/31/EC, [2022] OJ L277/1 (hereafter: 'Digital Services Act (2022/2065/EU)').

52 Think, for instance, of the Regulation 2016/679/EU of 27 April 2016 on the protection of natural persons with regard to the processing of personal data and on the free movement of such data, and repealing Directive 95/46/EC (hereafter: 'GDPR').

53 E.g. Directive 2023/970/EU of 10 May 2023 to strengthen the application of the principle of equal pay for equal work or work of equal value between men and women through pay transparency and enforcement mechanisms, [2023] OJ L132/21 (hereafter 'Pay Transparency Directive (2023/970/EU)').

54 See e.g. E. Muir, 'The Fundamental Rights Implications of EU Legislation: Some Constitutional Challenges', *Common Market Law Review*, 2014, pp. 219–245.

case-law, arguably the 'most effective supranational judicial body in the history of the world',[55] which tends to interpret them autonomously from ECHR law.[56]

If EU fundamental rights become more entrenched within the EU legal framework, they are also deeply integrated within the domestic legal systems of EU States. They benefit from the distinct features of EU law, such as primacy and direct effect, which, as Rizcallah observes, set them apart from traditional international human rights law 'which usually does not directly define how it shall be concretely implemented in national legal systems'.[57] EU fundamental rights are infused into domestic legal systems as they can be relevant within the EU States without the need for cross-border movement and in both vertical and horizontal situations.

SECTION V. RESHUFFLING THE EU/ECHR DYNAMICS

This shifting paradigm, if anything, must be taken seriously. While the EU has traditionally been a 'standard-taker' in the field of fundamental rights, it has turned into a 'standard-setter'. The consequences of this evolution remain uncharted to a large extent. The development of EU standards is not only capable of altering the interactions within the EU legal order;[58] it may also have far-reaching implications beyond that legal order. These standards co-exist, interact and overlap with other sets of norms of fundamental rights, at national, supranational and international level. The central inquiry guiding this research revolves around the growing role of the EU as a standard-setter and its potential to *reshuffle* the dynamics between EU and ECHR laws. EU standards may impact the way the CJEU uses ECHR law as well as the way the ECtHR uses EU law. It is this latter point that is at the core of our research.

---

55 A. Stone Sweet, *The Judicial Construction of Europe*, Oxford, Oxford University Press 2004, p. 1.

56 E.g. R. Tinière, 'The Use of ECtHR Case-law by the CJEU: Instrumentalisation or Quest for Autonomy and Legitimacy', *European Papers*, 2023, pp. 325–336.

57 See C. Rizcallah, *The European Union and Human Rights. Understanding a Singular Regional Player*, Oxford, Hart, forthcoming.

58 See e.g. on the relationship between the EU legislator and the CJEU in the field of fundamental rights, Y. Lorans, *Le juge et le législateur de l'Union européenne. Étude d'une protection collaborative des droits fondamentaux*, PhD thesis, forthcoming.

§ 1. THE USE OF ECHR LAW BY CJEU

Since the Charter became binding, there is a well-documented decline in the use of ECHR law by the CJEU.[59] Not only has the latter made fewer references to it, but these references have been depicted as being sometimes incoherent, random, and selective.[60] This has occurred despite the insertion of the so-called 'homogeneity' or 'equivalence' clause enshrined in Article 52(3) Charter.[61] Scholars have underlined a trend of autonomous development of EU fundamental rights as well as a trend of autonomous interpretation of these rights by the CJEU.[62] In the context of this project, we will use the terms 'autonomisation of EU fundamental rights' to refer to the fact that, on the one hand, the EU political institutions have growingly set fundamental rights, and on the other hand, that these rights have become the focal point of the CJEU. As a corollary, the CJEU takes some judicial distance vis-à-vis ECHR law. This is not to say that EU law diverges much from ECHR law nor that the latter does not play a significant role in EU law anymore.[63] One thing seems rather clear though: the CJEU tends to favour fundamental rights enshrined in the Charter and expressed in EU secondary laws. If the story of EU fundamental rights protection was mainly a Convention law story until recently, this is no longer the case.[64]

§ 2. THE USE OF EU LAW BY ECTHR

While the issue of EU law's compliance with ECHR law remains highly relevant, the evolving setting opens the door to new possibilities for the role

[59] See e.g., S. O'Leary, 'The EU Charter Ten Years On: A View from Strasbourg', in M. Bobek and J. Adams-Prassl (eds.), *The EU Charter of Fundamental Rights in the Member States*, Oxford, Hart Publishing, 2020, 42; G. de Búrca, 'After the EU Charter of Fundamental Rights: The Court of Justice as a Human Rights Adjudicator?', *Maastricht Journal of European and Comparative Law*, 2013, pp. 168–184.

[60] See the Special Issue V. Davio and E. Muir (eds.), *Dialogue on the Way the CJEU Uses ECHR Case-Law* published in *European Papers*, 2023, with the contributions of R. Tinière ('The Use of ECtHR Case-law by the CJEU: Instrumentalisation or Quest for Autonomy and Legitimacy?') and J. Callewaert ('Convention Control Over the Application of Union Law by National Judges: The Case for a Wholistic Approach to Fundamental Rights').

[61] We will come back to Article 52(3) Charter in Part II, Chapter 2, Section III, §1: *Highly sophisticated.*

[62] R. Tinière, 'The Use of ECtHR Case-law by the CJEU: Instrumentalisation or Quest for Autonomy and Legitimacy', *European Papers*, 2023, pp. 325–326; C. Dautricourt, 'A Strasbourg Perspective on the Autonomous Development of Fundamental Rights in EU Law: Trends and Implications', *Jean Monnet Working Paper Series*, 2020.

[63] See further in Part II, Chapter 2, Section III, §1: *Highly sophisticated.*

[64] R. Tinière, 'The Use of ECtHR Case-law by the CJEU: Instrumentalisation or Quest for Autonomy and Legitimacy', *European Papers*, 2023, p. 324.

and place of EU law in ECtHR case-law. EU fundamental rights represent an attractive source of inspiration for Strasbourg. In addition, EU fundamental rights are akin to domestic law for EU States and therefore form part of the background in cases involving these States before the ECtHR. Moreover, these rights create a greater degree of articulation between the EU and ECHR layers. As they are becoming increasingly autonomous from each other, they need to be articulated coherently for the benefit of the shared European fundamental rights space. This coherence, which was long ensured through the CJEU's incorporation of ECHR standards, partly lies in the shared hands of the CJEU and the ECtHR.

For all these reasons, EU fundamental rights can impact the way the ECtHR uses EU fundamental rights. Among other things, the ECtHR can draw inspiration from these rights to enhance the protection of Convention rights, take them into account when dealing with cases involving EU States, or articulate its own standards in relation to them.

I. The Genesis

To initiate our inquiry and acquaint the reader with the topic, let us start at what could be deemed the beginning: the first time the ECtHR referred to the Charter.[65] *Christine Goodwin v. the United Kingdom* and *I. v. the United Kingdom*, both delivered on 7 July 2002 by the Grand Chamber, paved the way.[66] Both cases concern post-operative males to female transsexuals who complained that they could not marry because the law treated them as men.[67] In previous cases, the ECtHR had found that the right to marry (Article 12 ECHR) refers to traditional marriage between persons of opposite biological sex. The inability of transsexuals to marry a person of the sex opposite to their reassigned gender was not found in breach of Article 12.[68] In a departure from its previous case-law, the ECtHR held that the right of a man and a woman to marry is available to post-operative transsexuals.[69] It relied on the fact that there have been social changes in the institution of marriage as well as changes brought about by developments in medicine and science in the field

65 Please note that the genesis may also be situated in references to CJEU judgments or EU secondary laws. We will explore the first references to these in our case studies on equality and non-discrimination, as well as data protection in Part III: In Action. The use of EU fundamental rights in practice.

66 ECtHR, *Christine Goodwin v. the United Kingdom* [GC], no. 28957/95, ECHR 2002-VI; ECtHR, *I. v. the United Kingdom* [GC], no. 25680/94, 11 July 2002.

67 ECtHR, *Christine Goodwin v. the United Kingdom* [GC], ibid. § 95; ECtHR, *I. v. the United Kingdom* [GC], ibid., § 75.

68 ECtHR, *Christine Goodwin v. the United Kingdom* [GC], ibid. § 97; ECtHR, *I. v. the United Kingdom* [GC], ibid., § 77.

69 ECtHR, *Christine Goodwin v. the United Kingdom* [GC], ibid. § 103; ECtHR, *I. v. the United Kingdom* [GC], ibid., § 83.

of transsexuality.[70] It also noted that 'Article 9 of the recently adopted Charter of Fundamental Rights of the European Union departs, no doubt deliberately, from the wording of Article 12 of the Convention in removing the reference to men and women'.[71]

While we will come back to these cases, several points can already be stressed. The ECtHR cites Article 9 Charter at a time when the it was neither legally binding nor mentioned by the CJEU.[72] Even though the EU law reference is not decisive, it stands out as the sole legal source to expand the right to marriage to transsexuals. Article 9 Charter, though suggesting a broad interpretation of marriage rights, seems to lack contextualisation. While it does not specify 'men and women', this provision defers to national laws, a nuance absent in the ECtHR's consideration.[73]

II. Three Examples

These two judgments marked the first time the ECtHR referred to the Charter. Looking at the bigger picture, several cases have shown the growing presence of EU fundamental rights in the ECtHR's case-law since the early 21st century. To give the reader context, three examples will be provided. These, together with the two previously discussed cases, elucidate some of the key issues addressed in this research project. We should underline that these examples are just that: examples. They are not representative of the influence of EU fundamental rights in general which we investigate through our study.

A. Applicability of Article 6(1) ECHR

Our first example concerns two cases related to the applicability of Article 6(1) ECHR which guarantees a right to a fair trial. In *Vilho Eskelinen and Others v. Finland* (2007), the issue concerned whether the functional criterion established in *Pellegrin* to assess whether a dispute involving civil servants fell within the scope of Article 6(1) ECHR should be re-examined.[74] In *Vilho Eskelinen*, the ECtHR considered that there was a need for development and set out new conditions for the applicability of Article 6(1) ECHR.[75]

---

70 ECtHR, *Christine Goodwin v. the United Kingdom* [GC], ibid. § 100; ECtHR, *I. v. the United Kingdom* [GC], ibid., § 80.

71 Ibid.

72 The CJEU mentioned the Charter for the first time in 2006 (Case C-540/03, *Parliament v. Council*, 27 June 2006, ECLI:EU:C:2005:517, para. 38).

73 Article 9 Charter states that 'the right to marry and the right to found a family shall be guaranteed *in accordance with the national laws governing the exercise of these rights*.' Emphasis added.

74 ECtHR, *Pellegrin v. France* [GC], no. 28541/95, § 67, ECHR 1999-VIII.

75 ECtHR, *Vilho Eskelinen and Others v. Finland* [GC], no. 63235/00, §§ 50–62, ECHR 2007-II.

The central argument for this shift is that the functional criterion has not proved fruitful. While the latter was intended to provide a workable concept, this criterion led to anomalous results and difficulties of use in practice.[76] Another argument centred around EU law. The ECtHR mentioned in its relevant legal materials that 'Article 47 is not confined to civil rights and obligations or to criminal matters within the meaning of Article 6 of the Convention' and that 'the Charter codified existing case-law of the Court of Justice of the European Communities'.[77] In its reasoning, the ECtHR observed that:

> *Looking to European law generally, which provides useful guidance* (see Christine Goodwin v. the United Kingdom [GC], no. 28957/95, §§ 43–45, 92 and 100, ECHR 2002 VI; Posti and Rahko v. Finland, no. 27824/95, § 54, ECHR 2002 VII; and Meftah and Others v. France [GC], nos. 32911/96, 35237/97 and 34595/97, § 45, ECHR 2002 VII), the Court notes that Pellegrin sought support in the categories of activities and posts listed by the European Commission and by the Court of Justice of the European Communities in connection with the exception to the freedom of movement [...]. However, the Court would observe that the Luxembourg Court itself applies a wider approach in favour of judicial control, as shown by its landmark judgment in Marguerite Johnston v. Chief Constable of the Royal Ulster Constabulary [...].
>
> This and other case-law in areas having a connection with Community law indicate that the scope of applicability of judicial control in European Union law is wide. If an individual can rely on a material right guaranteed by Community law, his or her status as a holder of public power does not render the requirements of judicial control inapplicable. Moreover, the broad scope of the effective judicial control has been emphasised by the Luxembourg Court's reference to both Articles 6 and 13 of the Convention (see the Marguerite Johnston case, cited above, and the case of Panayotova and Others v. Minister voor Vreemdelingenzaken en Integratie, Case C 327/02, [2004] ECR I-11055, § 27), as well as by the Charter on Fundamental Rights (see above, §§ 29–30).[78]

In *Micallef v. Malta* (2009), the ECtHR was tasked with determining whether Article 6(1) ECHR is applicable to interim measures. Beforehand, the ECtHR held the granting of interim measures did not fall within the scope of Article 6 ECHR.[79] In *Micallef*, the ECtHR decided to overturn this precedent. The ECtHR considered that interim measures can determine the same civil rights or obligations as decisions on the merits of a claim and have the same resulting long-lasting or permanent effects.[80] It also deemed that there was

[76] Ibid., §§ 50–51.
[77] Ibid., § 30.
[78] Ibid., § 60. Emphasis added
[79] ECtHR, *Micallef v. Malta* [GC], no. 17056/06, § 75, ECHR 2009.
[80] Ibid., § 79.

a widespread consensus among Council of Europe States, many of which implicitly or explicitly extend Article 6 guarantees to interim measures. In this respect, the ECtHR noted that 'the European Court of Justice [...] considers that provisional measures must be subject to the guarantees of a fair trial, particularly to the right to be heard.'[81]

These two cases illustrate, first, one of the functions EU fundamental rights can have in ECtHR's case-law: they are used to support a specific interpretation of a Convention's right. Second, they prompt us to consider the legal value attributed to EU fundamental rights in ECtHR case-law. In *Vilho Eskelinen*, the ECtHR referred to EU law as capable of providing 'useful guidance'.[82] Although the terminology varies, one cannot avoid the comparison with the CJEU's description of the ECHR as having 'special significance'. Third, they show the risk of instrumentalisation of EU law. In *Micallef*, the ECtHR relied on the CJEU's case *Bernard Denilauler v. SNC Couchet Frères* of 21 May 1980, where the latter held that provisional measures do not fall within the system of recognition and enforcement of the 1968 Brussels Convention.[83] The ECtHR deemed that this judgment implied that the CJEU considers that provisional measures must be subject to the guarantees of a fair trial.[84] One cannot find such words reflected – at least in explicit terms – in the CJEU's ruling.

B. Indirect Discrimination

Another revealing case is *D.H. v. Czech Republic* [GC](2007). Some of the questions at hand were whether the prohibition of discrimination as guaranteed under Article 14 ECHR applies to cases of indirect discrimination and, if so, whether statistics could be used to prove indirect discrimination. In two previous Chamber cases, the ECtHR had considered that indirect discrimination could be protected but had rendered somewhat contradictory judgments on the issue of statistics.[85] On both aspects, EU law plays a significant role. Concerning the first one, the ECtHR held that:

> The Court has already accepted in previous cases that a difference in treatment may take the form of disproportionately prejudicial effects of a general policy or measure which, though couched in neutral terms, discriminates against a group [...]. *In accordance with, for instance, Council Directives 97/80/EC and 2000/43/*

81 Ibid., § 78.

82 ECtHR, *Vilho Eskelinen and Others v. Finland* [GC], no. 63235/00, § 60, ECHR 2007-II.

83 Case C-125/79, *Bernard Denilauler v. SNC Couchet Frères*, ECLI:EU:C:1980:130, § 18.

84 ECtHR, *Micallef v. Malta* [GC], no. 17056/06, § 78, ECHR 2009.

85 ECtHR, *Hugh Jordan v. the United Kingdom*, no. 24746/94, 4 June 2008; ECtHR, *Hoogendijk v. The Netherlands* (adm. decision), no. 58641/00, 6 January 2005. We will return to these cases in Part III (case study on equality), Chapter 3, Section II, §1, II. Confirmation.

> *EC [...] and the definition provided by ECRI [...], such a situation may amount to 'indirect discrimination', which does not necessarily require a discriminatory intent.*[86]

Concerning the second one, the ECtHR observed that:

> On this point, the Court observes that *Council Directives 97/80/EC and 2000/43/EC* stipulate that persons who consider themselves wronged because the principle of equal treatment has not been applied to them may establish before a domestic authority by any means, including on the basis of statistical evidence, facts from which it may be presumed that there has been discrimination (see paragraphs 82-83 above). The recent case-law of the Court of Justice of the European Communities (see paragraphs 88-89 above) shows that it permits claimants to rely on statistical evidence and the national courts to take such evidence into account where it is valid and significant.[87]

The *D.H.* judgment offers two valuable insights. The first is that, similar to *Vilho Eskelinen* and *Micallef*, the function of EU fundamental rights involves supporting an interpretation of the Convention. However, while in the latter cases, the ECtHR used them to support a new interpretation, in *D.H. v. Czech Republic* (2007), the ECtHR used them to confirm and bolster an existing interpretation of the Convention. In both instances, EU fundamental rights serve as the key aspect of justification for interpreting the ECHR in a certain way. This shows that within one function that EU fundamental rights can play (in this case, interpretative function), there are different nuances, and the weight of EU law in fulfilling this function may vary. The second insight from *D.H.* is that it shows that not only the Charter or CJEU's case-law can influence the ECtHR's case-law, but also EU secondary law. The Burden of Proof Directive (97/80/EC) and the Racial Discrimination Directive (2000/43/EC) appeared central in the ECtHR's reasoning. This prompts us to take a broad approach to the influence of EU fundamental rights, considering standards developed in the Charter and EU secondary laws, as interpreted by the CJEU.

C. Conscientious Objectors

Our last example is *Bayatyan v. Armenia* [GC](2009), where the ECtHR held that Article 9 ECHR could be applicable to conscientious objectors.[88] The ECtHR observed that 'the domestic law of the overwhelming majority of Council of Europe [M]ember States, along with the relevant international instruments, has evolved to the effect that at the material time there was already

86 ECtHR, *D.H. and Others v. the Czech Republic* [GC], no. 57325/00, § 184, ECHR 2007-IV. Emphasis added.

87 Ibid., § 187. Emphasis added

88 ECtHR, *Bayatyan v. Armenia* [GC], no. 23459/03, § 110-111, ECHR 2011.

a virtually general consensus on the question in Europe and beyond.'[89] One of the sources used to establish this consensus was Article 10 Charter:

> In Europe, mention should be made of the proclamation in 2000 of the Charter of Fundamental Rights of the European Union, which came into force in 2009. While the first paragraph of Article 10 of the Charter reproduces Article 9 § 1 of the Convention almost literally, its second paragraph explicitly states that '[t]he right to conscientious objection is recognised, in accordance with the national laws governing the exercise of this right' [...]. Such an explicit addition is no doubt deliberate [...] and reflects the unanimous recognition of the right to conscientious objection by the member States of the European Union, as well as the weight attached to that right in modern European society.[90]

In addition to highlighting that EU fundamental rights can be used when establishing a consensus – a point to which we shall return later on –,[91] *Bayatyan v. Armenia* (2009) allows us to introduce two key elements. First, EU fundamental rights can be a strategic and divisive matter among different actors involved before or within the ECtHR. Before the ECtHR, certain third-party interveners referred to Article 10 Charter to persuade the ECtHR that there was a gradual recognition of the right to conscientious objection.[92] Within the ECtHR, the Armenian judge considered that while Article 10 Charter recognises the right to conscientious objection, its use was not appropriate.[93] This highlights that the influence of EU fundamental rights is not a monolithic process shaped by the ECtHR on its own but rather a process involving multiple actors whose interests and views on EU law may diverge. Second, the ECtHR uses EU fundamental rights in a case involving Armenia, a non-EU State. While Article 10 Charter was one source among others use to establish the consensus,[94] this case highlights that the use of EU fundamental

89 Ibid., § 108.

90 Ibid., § 106.

91 See further in Part IV, Chapter 2, Section II, §2, III. EU Law as Part of a European Consensus.

92 ECtHR, *Bayatyan v. Armenia* [GC], no. 23459/03, , § 86, ECHR 2011.

93 Separate opinion of Judge Gyulumyan in ECtHR, *Bayatyan v. Armenia* [GC], no. 23459/03, § 4, ECHR 2011. The Judge noted in this respect that: 'The Charter of Fundamental Rights of the European Union, adopted in December 2000, which recognises the right to conscientious objection under the right to freedom of thought, conscience and religion, came into force only in December 2009. [...] I would like to stress also that at the time when the applicant was convicted for refusing to serve in the armed forces because of his religious beliefs, there was an explicit case-law according to which the Convention and its Protocols do not guarantee, as such, any right to conscientious objection. The national authorities cannot be blamed for following the existing case-law and not implementing an approach reflecting developments which only came about at a later date.'

94 ECtHR, ibid., §§ 102–110.

rights by the ECtHR can result in these rights being 'imposed' on States that did not participate in the EU deliberative process.

The above examples raise numerous questions: What is the legal value of EU fundamental rights in ECHR law? Have they been used by the ECtHR, and if so, for what purpose? Does the ECtHR use them in cases involving EU or non-EU States? Are there instances where their use appears unsound? Who else than the ECtHR refers to EU fundamental rights?

CHAPTER 2
FRAMING THE DEBATE

Alongside these questions, and taking a wider view, the use of EU fundamental rights by the ECtHR raises four key issues. The first, and probably most important, is whether EU fundamental rights are a source of 'special significance' for the ECtHR. A positive answer suggests not only a new narrative within the European fundamental rights space but also that the other issues can become more pronounced. The second concerns the context of divergences in which EU law is used: although the EU and ECHR systems overlap, they are distinct and propelled by their own dynamics. While these differences suggest that EU law can be a source of learning, they highlight that incorporating EU law should not be taken as a given. The third pertains to the tension between fragmentation and marginalisation: the growing autonomy of EU fundamental rights risks creating fractures within the European landscape. Yet should the ECtHR incorporate EU law and thereby bring convergence, it may weaken its own role and lead to the imposition of EU standards on non-EU States. The fourth concerns the paradox of legitimacy: while the use of EU fundamental rights can contribute to justifying ECtHR's decisions and showing that they are made with full awareness of relevant materials, their use can compromise the legitimacy of ECtHR's decisions if it is not properly justified.

SECTION I. EU FUNDAMENTAL RIGHTS: A SOURCE OF SPECIAL SIGNIFICANCE?

The CJEU has deemed ECHR law as a source of 'special significance' for the development of EU fundamental rights. In its *Rutili* (1975) case, it mentioned ECHR provisions for the first time, but did not attribute any particular meaning to them.[1] After a decade, the CJEU's choice of words changed. In particular in *Marguerite Johnston* (1986), the CJEU pointed out that the requirement of judicial review is a general principle which is laid down in the ECHR, and that 'the principles on which that Convention is based *must be taken into account*

[1] Case C-36/75, *Rutili*, ECLI:EU:C:1975:137, para. 32.

in Community law'.[2] Three years later, in *Hoescht* (1989), it went one step further by affirming that:

> fundamental rights are an integral part of the general principles of law the observance of which the Court ensures, in accordance with constitutional traditions common to the Member States, and the international treaties on which the Member States have collaborated or of which they are signatories. The [ECHR] is of *particular significance* in that regard.[3]

The CJEU has not elaborated on what it means by 'particular significance' or 'special significance'. Its case-law reveals that the expression denotes the distinct influence of ECHR law on its fundamental rights case-law. While the CJEU has expressed its intention to draw on the common constitutional traditions to the Member States and international instruments, the CJEU has predominantly used ECHR law to inform EU fundamental rights. Not only has the CJEU made a modest use of the common constitutional traditions, but it has placed ECHR law in a class of its own compared to international human rights instruments.[4]

The rise of EU fundamental rights prompts the reverse question: does the ECtHR attribute special significance to them? This question arises from a different context than the one in which the CJEU refers to ECHR law. While all EU states are Parties to the ECHR, not all Council of Europe States are EU States. Additionally, the ECHR is dedicated to human rights, whereas EU law covers a broader spectrum, including but not limited to fundamental rights. Lastly, the ECtHR has a long-standing tradition of drawing on international instruments and the practices of European States to inform its judgments.[5] It cannot be excluded that EU fundamental rights, despite their increasing importance, are no more than one source among many others that the ECtHR takes into account. As such, while the ECtHR would use EU fundamental rights, their impact would be part of a broad mosaic of international human rights instruments and practices of European States, which the ECtHR also relies upon.

Certain clues, however, lead us to explore whether the ECtHR has given EU fundamental rights particular importance in its case-law. In a way, the ECtHR has already given a special status to the EU fundamental rights system. Let us recall that, following in the footsteps of the European Commission on Human Rights in *M. & Co* (1990),[6] the ECtHR developed a test of systemic

2 Case C-222/84, *Marguerite Johnston*, ECLI:EU:C:1986:206, para. 18.
3 Joined Cases C-46/87 and 227/88, *Hoescht*, ECLI:EU:C:1989:337, § 13. Emphasis added
4 See further in Part II, Chapter 1, Section III, §2. The Special Significance of ECHR Law.
5 See further in Part I, Chapter 3, Section II, §3. On What: ECtHR's Case-Law.
6 European Commission of Human Rights, *M & Co v. Germany*, no. 13258/87, 9 January 1990.

equivalence: State action taken in compliance with legal obligations flowing from international treaties can be justified 'as long as the relevant organization is considered to protect fundamental rights, as regards both the substantive guarantees offered and the mechanisms controlling their observance, in a manner which can be considered at least equivalent to that for which the Convention provides. […]'.[7] In *Bosphorus v. Ireland* (2005) the ECtHR found that the protection of fundamental rights by EU law could be considered 'equivalent' to that of the ECHR.[8] If the presumption of equivalent protection is not absolute,[9] the EU system is one of the few systems that benefits from it.[10] This is evidenced by the fact that the ECtHR has recently considered that this presumption does not apply (for the time being) when EFTA States implement the European Economic Area Agreement.[11]

In addition, the hybrid nature of EU law makes it a special type of law for the ECHR system. It is a deeply integrated law within the domestic legal systems of 27 States to the Convention. EU law is characterised by the principles of direct effect and primacy, which place national judges at the core of the implementation of Union law.[12] For this reason, EU law may more closely resemble domestic law than international law for the ECtHR.[13] At the same time, EU law has a much broader scale than (other) domestic laws, closer to the scope of some international instruments. As such, EU fundamental rights constitute a valuable source to discern common ground at pan-European level.

A key question is whether the ECtHR has attributed 'special significance' to EU fundamental rights, and if so, in what manner. This necessitates a comparison of the use of EU fundamental rights with other instruments. Specifically, we investigate whether this significance is quantitative (e.g., through more frequent and long-term references) and/or qualitative (e.g., EU fundamental rights having a more profound impact on ECtHR case-law or being used by the ECtHR for functions not performed by other instruments).

---

7 ECtHR, *Bosphorus Hava Yolları Turizm ve Ticaret Anonim Şirketi v. Ireland* [GC], no. 45036/98, § 155, ECHR 2005-VI.

8 Ibid., §§ 159–165.

9 We will discuss the presumption of equivalent presumption in Part IV, Chapter 2, Section I, §2, II. Coherence without Aligning with EU Standards.

10 The ECtHR has applied the presumption to the European Patent Office, which is part of the European Patent Organisation, see ECtHR, *Klausecker v. Germany* (dec.), no. 415/07, § 101, 6 January 2015; European Commission of Human Rights, *Heinz v. The Contracting States Parties to the European Patent Convention* (dec.), no. 21090/92, 10 January 1994.

11 ECtHR, *Norwegian Confederation of Trade Unions (LO) and Norwegian Transport Workers' Union (NTF) v. Norway*, no. 45487/17, §§ 105–108, 10 June 2021. See U. Lattanzi, 'The Inapplicability of the Bosphorus Presumption to the European Economic Area Agreement: A Risk for the Coherence of Legal Systems in Europe', *European Constitutional Law Review*, 2023, pp. 441–461.

12 See further in Part II, Chapter 2, Section III, §2. Deeply Integrated within EU States.

13 In this vein, T. Lock, 'The Influence of EU Law on Strasbourg Doctrines', *European Law Review*, 2016, p. 821.

We also examine whether this significance is evident solely in the ECtHR's use of EU fundamental rights or also in the use by other actors involved prior to, before, or within the ECtHR, such as parties, third parties, domestic judges, as well as judges in separate opinions.

SECTION II. INFLUENCE AMID DIVERGENCE

Although the EU and ECHR fundamental rights systems share similarities and overlap, they are distinct and driven by their own dynamics. These differences provide the context for interactions between the CJEU and ECtHR. While the Courts can learn from each other, integrating the laws and concepts of one system into the other is complex. Each system has distinct objectives, concepts, and approaches, which may not be compatible or desirable in the other framework. Using EU law by the ECtHR can lead to its use out of context or distort the ECHR law's tenets. Whereas we shed light on these differences throughout our research, let us already highlight some of them that are important to keep in mind.

The divergence between the EU and ECHR systems is first manifested in their language: for instance, when one uses 'fundamental rights', the other uses 'human rights'. The interpreters of these languages have different roles and relationships with national judges. The ECtHR seeks to establish a minimum standard for human rights protection across 46 States.[14] The complaint procedure by individuals is the key mechanism by which the ECtHR comes to adjudicate.[15] The CJEU is not only tasked to ensure the protection of fundamental rights but also the uniform interpretation of EU law.[16] The majority of cases are brought by way of preliminary rulings through which national judges seek interpretation and clarification of EU law from the CJEU.[17]

The rationales differ between the EU and ECHR fundamental rights systems. This is noticeable at a general level: whereas the protection of fundamental rights in the EU is distinguished by the coexistence of fundamental rights objectives with other goals related to European integration,[18] ECHR law is

---

14 S. O'Leary, 'The EU Charter Ten Years On: A View from Strasbourg', in M. Bobek and J. Adams-Prassl (eds.), *The EU Charter of Fundamental Rights in the Member States*, Oxford, Hart Publishing, 2020, p. 37.

15 Article 34 ECHR.

16 S. O'Leary, 'The EU Charter Ten Years On: A View from Strasbourg', in M. Bobek and J. Adams-Prassl (eds.), *The EU Charter of Fundamental Rights in the Member States*, Oxford, Hart Publishing, 2020, p. 38.

17 Article 267 TFEU.

18 As the CJEU observed in its Opinion 2/13, if fundamental rights are at the heart of the EU legal structure, their interpretation must be 'ensured within the framework of the structure and objectives of the EU' (Opinion 2/13 of 18 December 2014, ECLI:EU:C:2014:2454,

guided by a human rights logic. This is also noticeable at the level of specific rights: similar rights protected both under EU and ECHR laws are not driven by similar rationale.[19] These divergences in rationale have implications for the scope and content of the rights as protected in EU and ECHR laws.

The structure of the protection systems also diverges. In EU law, while EU fundamental rights are enshrined in the Charter, the legislative framework plays a central role by establishing specific rules that determine case outcomes. EU secondary laws often define the scope, substance, and modalities of enforcement of rights and constitute the core of what the CJEU interprets. In ECHR law, ECHR's rights are broadly formulated and encompass general principles such as legitimacy, lawfulness, and proportionality. This leaves more discretion to the ECtHR to shape these principles and adapt them to the circumstances of each case. The structure of the protection of fundamental rights in EU law is also characterised by distinct features of horizontalisation and proceduralisation. Horizontalisation means that, under certain circumstances, EU fundamental rights can apply in horizontal situations, whereas in ECHR law, this can occur only indirectly through positive obligations. Proceduralisation, on the other hand, refers to how EU law, in certain fields, involves multiple institutional actors responsible for enforcing EU fundamental rights and grants individuals various procedural rights; this type of enforcement framework is not present in the same manner in ECHR law.

In a nutshell, the language, adjudicators, rationales, and structures of the EU and ECHR systems differ. In our research, we delve into how the ECtHR takes these divergences into account when using EU fundamental rights and explore whether it has successfully integrated these rights without compromising the fundamental aspects of its own human rights system.

SECTION III. NAVIGATING BETWEEN FRAGMENTATION AND MARGINALISATION

The growing distance between two systems of fundamental rights within Europe – one encompassing the 27 EU States and the other involving the 46 Council of Europe States – introduces a new line of tension between two poles: the risk of fragmentation on one hand, and the risk of marginalisation on the other.

para. 170) The objectives linked to the European integration can enter into tension with the protection of fundamental rights (see more in C. Rizcallah, *The European Union and Human Rights. Understanding a Singular Regional Player*, Oxford, Hart, forthcoming).

19 This will become clear when we analyze our case studies on equality and data protection in Part III.

The issue of fragmentation of human rights, which has been widely commented upon,[20] is relevant to our context. With the growing autonomy of EU fundamental rights, there arises the potential for a dual phenomenon of fragmentation. The first is between the members of the Council of Europe. The process of autonomisation carries the risk of creating new dividing lines across the European continent, where EU States adhere to one set of standards, while non-EU States follow others.[21] The second is within the EU itself, where both the EU and ECHR layers of rights coexist, making the task of EU domestic judges more complex.

The use of EU fundamental rights by the ECtHR can give rise to a dual phenomenon of marginalisation. The ECtHR could marginalise itself and even become redundant if it were to align systematically with EU standards. For non-EU States, the use of EU standards by the ECtHR entails the risk that they are bound by these standards without having participated in the deliberative process, which points to a danger of majority hegemony.[22] If, from an ECHR perspective, the ECtHR has affirmed that it could use standards from instruments which States have not ratified, it remains a sensitive issue from an institutional balance standpoint.

If divergence between EU and ECHR laws can lead to fragmentation, convergence can lead to marginalisation. The question is how the ECtHR has been able to navigate between these two poles and manage the tension arising from the (non-)use of EU fundamental rights in its case-law.

SECTION IV. THE DOUBLE-EDGED SWORD OF LEGITIMACY

If using EU fundamental rights can contribute to the persuasiveness of ECtHR's decisions and show that they are made with full awareness, such use can be detrimental if it lacks sufficient justification. In other words, while EU fundamental rights can enhance the legitimacy of ECtHR's decisions,

20 E.g. R. Terman and Z.I. Búzás, 'A house divided: Norm fragmentation in the international human rights regime', *International Studies Quarterly*, 2021, pp. 488–499; M. Payandeh, 'Fragmentation within international human rights law', in M. Andenas and E. Bjorge (eds.), *A Farewell to Fragmentation: Reassertion and Convergence in International Law*, Cambridge, Cambridge University Press, 2015, pp. 297–319.

21 E.g. O. de Schutter, 'The two Europes of Human Rights: the Emerging Division of Tasks Between the Council of Europe and the European Union in Promoting Human Rights in Europe', *Columbia Journal of European Law*, 2008, pp. 509–561.

22 In this vein, T. Lock, 'The Influence of EU Law on Strasbourg Doctrines', *European Law Review*, 2016, p. 821. See also C. Dautricourt, 'A Strasbourg Perspective on the Autonomous Development of Fundamental Rights in EU Law: Trends and Implications', *Jean Monnet Working Paper Series*, 2020, pp. 68–69.

there is also a risk that it could have the opposite effect. The acceptability of judgments by the ECtHR which rely on EU law could be called into question if, for example, this law is used in a non-transparent manner, if there is no justification for its use, or if it is not properly contextualised. To address this a priori paradox, we should delve into the concept of legitimacy. From the outset, we should acknowledge that we will not study the concept in detail but rather borrow from one specific approach to guide our research. While this allows us to spend more time on unexplored aspects by drawing from existing work, we must be clear that this is one perspective on legitimacy, and that others could be equally valid.

In ECHR law, legitimacy is often viewed as the capacity of ECtHR judgments to be respected, executed, and obeyed[23] Barkhuysen and van Emmerik define legitimacy as the acceptance of ECtHR's judgments by all the parties involved.[24] According to Dzehtsiarou and Greene, a judgment's legitimacy is anchored in its ability to persuade the civic society that operates under the ECHR and to be recognised as authoritative by those directly affected by the ECtHR's decisions.[25] Dzehtsiarou has further defined legitimacy as the ECtHR's capacity to garner respect and support from the various stakeholders (e.g. State officials, media, applicants, non-governmental organisations or the academic community) that 'the Court will decide cases consistently and in a manner that respects the nature of both the ECHR as a human rights instrument and its jurisdiction as subsidiary and limited, as well as by reference to clear and transparent evidence'.[26]

International tribunals, such as the ECtHR, often operate without the means to enforce their decisions, making the adherence of States to their judgments essential.[27] The traditional source of legitimacy for ECtHR's decisions is State consent.[28] The legitimacy of the ECtHR stems from the fact that all States have ratified the Convention and accepted its jurisdiction.[29] Yet, the ECtHR has gone beyond state consent by developing doctrines such as the dynamic and

---

23 K. Dzehtsiarou, 'Does Consensus Matter? Legitimacy of European Consensus in the Case-law of the European Court of Human Rights', *Public Law*, 2011, p. 535.

24 T. Barkhuysen and M.L. Emmerik, 'Legitimacy of European Court of Human Rights Judgments: Procedural aspects', in N. Huls, M. Adams and J. Bomhoff (eds.), *The legitimacy of Highest Courts' rulings: judicial deliberations and beyond*, The Hague, T.M.C. Asser Press, 2008, p. 437.

25 K. Dzehtsiarou and A. Greene, 'Legitimacy and the Future of the European Court of Human Rights: Critical Perspectives from Academia and Practitioners', *German Law Journal*, p. 1707.

26 K. Dzehtsiarou, *European Consensus and the Legitimacy of the European Court of Human Rights*, Cambridge, Cambridge University Press, 2015, p. 143.

27 K. Dzehtsiarou, 'Does Consensus Matter? Legitimacy of European Consensus in the Case-law of the European Court of Human Rights', *Public Law*, 2011, p. 535.

28 Ibid., p. 536. K. Dzehtsiarou, *European Consensus and the Legitimacy of the European Court of Human Rights*, Cambridge, Cambridge University Press, 2015, p. 149.

29 K. Dzehtsiarou, ibid., p. 154.

evolutive interpretation of the ECHR.[30] State consent is increasingly challenged as a source of legitimacy.[31] This is not to say that consent no longer matters, but rather that other factors are taken into account to assess the legitimacy of ECtHR's decisions.

In this respect, Dzehtsiarou sheds light on the distinction between substantial and procedural legitimacy.[32] Substantial legitimacy presupposes that 'a rule was considered in the light of all relevant data, both objective and attitudinal. This relevant data should not necessarily be binding. It can have a persuasive effect or be merely informative. [...] A substantively legitimate decision, therefore, is one taken by a well-informed decision maker, having consulted available binding and persuasive sources'.[33] Procedural legitimacy refers to the belief that a process is legitimate if it follows established rules and principles. Procedural legitimacy is tied to adherence to certain principles that underpin the fairness and reliability of the legal process. These principles include consistency, coherence, legal certainty, and predictability.[34] In this respect, 'the transparency of the decision-making process enhances the predictability of juridical outcomes. Kumm has argued that political transparency is linked to the accountability of the decision-makers to constituents' concerns. For that reason, the ECtHR describes the reasons for a particular judgment. Each argument the court uses should be transparent and clearly articulated'.[35]

This distinction provides a useful lens to examine the use of EU fundamental rights by the ECtHR and its impact on legitimacy. While using EU fundamental rights can enhance the substantive legitimacy of the ECtHR's decisions by making them more persuasive, it may negatively affect procedural legitimacy if not used properly. The question is whether, through its use of EU fundamental rights, the ECtHR has been able to increase the substantive legitimacy of its decisions without negatively impacting their procedural legitimacy.

---

30 Ibid., pp. 150–152.

31 K. Dzehtsiarou, 'Does Consensus Matter? Legitimacy of European Consensus in the Case-law of the European Court of Human Rights', *Public Law*, 2011, p. 536.

32 Ibid., pp. 537–539.

33 Ibid., p. 539.

34 Ibid., p. 538.

35 Ibid.

CHAPTER 3

WHAT WE LOOK FOR: THE INFLUENCE OF EU FUNDAMENTAL RIGHTS ON ECTHR CASE-LAW

With a view to exploring these four issues, we adopt a broad and systematic perspective. We do so by examining how and to what extent EU fundamental rights have influenced the ECtHR case-law. The aim is to provide a comprehensive overview that covers many dimensions of this influence, whether qualitative or quantitative, in order to address these issues and specifically the special place of EU fundamental rights within ECtHR case-law. The research question guiding this project is: 'How and to what extent have EU fundamental rights influenced the ECtHR case-law?'. In the following lines, we first present the existing research on the subject and explain how our study draws from it, but also distinguishes itself from it. Then, we explain the different components of this research question, which form the backbone of our study.

SECTION I. EXISTING RESEARCH AND DISTINCTIVE FEATURES OF OUR PROJECT

The influence of EU fundamental rights on the ECtHR's case-law remains unexplored to a large extent. Yet, there are three branches of literature which align closely with our approach and form the starting point of our research project. While the first two branches focus on EU and ECHR laws, the third examines their interplay. Our investigation lies at the intersection of these three branches and seeks to embody the continuity of the most recent research in each of these areas.

The first branch analyses the growing role of the EU as a fundamental rights actor. Prior to the 2000s, the literature focused on the emergence of fundamental rights in the EU legal order[1] and on the role of these rights in specific fields.[2] The subject gained momentum when, at the turn of the millennium, and concomitantly with the proclamation of the Charter, a number of scholars questioned the need and desirability of a fundamental rights policy at EU level.[3] In the following years, the Charter attracted a high level of interest.[4] In parallel with the increase of EU fundamental rights competences, research has expanded on the role of the EU legislator. A first pool of researchers has examined the tools developed by the EU political institutions to ensure that they exercise their competences in compliance with fundamental rights.[5] A second pool has reflected on the development of EU legislative fundamental rights. While the initial thrust of the literature was on

---

1 K. Lenaerts, 'Respect for Fundamental Rights as a Constitutional Principle of the European Union', *Columbia Journal of European Law*, 2000, pp. 1–26; H. Schermers, 'The European Communities Bound by Fundamental Human Rights', *Common Market Law Review*, 1990, pp. 249–258; A. Dauses, 'The Protection of Fundamental Rights in the Community Legal Order', *European Law Review*, 1985, pp. 398–419; P. Pescatore, 'The Context and Significance of Fundamental Rights Law of the European Communities', *Human Rights Journal*, 1981, pp. 295–308.

2 E.g. C. Barnard and S. Deakin, 'In Search of Coherence: Social Policy, the Single Market and Fundamental Rights', *Industrial Relations Journal*, 2000, pp. 341–345; S. O'Leary, 'The Relationship Between Community Citizenship and the Protection of Fundamental Rights in Community Law', *Common Market Law Review*, 1995, pp. 519–554.

3 E.g. A. Williams, *EU Human Rights Policies: a Study in Irony*, Oxford, Oxford University Press, 2004; P. Eeckhout, 'The EU Charter of Fundamental Rights and the Federal Question', *Common Market Law Review*, 2002, pp. 945–994; A. Von Bogdandy, 'The European Union as a Human Rights Organization? Human Rights and the Core of the European Union', *Common Market Law Review*, 2000, pp. 1307–1338; P. Alston and J. Weiler, 'An 'Ever Closer Union' in Need of a Human Rights Policy: The European Union and Human Rights', in P. Alston (eds.), *The EU and Human Rights*, Oxford, Oxford University Press, 1999, pp. 3–68.

4 E.g. M. Bobek and J. Adams-Prassl (eds.), *The EU Charter of Fundamental Rights in the Member States*, Oxford, Hart Publishing, 2020; S. de Vries, U. Bernitz and S. Weatherill (eds.), *The EU Charter of Fundamental Rights as a Binding Instrument: Five Years Old and Growing*, Oxford, Hart Publishing, 2015; S. Peers, T. Hervey, J. Kenner and A. Ward (eds.), *The EU Charter of Fundamental Rights: A Commentary*, Oxford, Hart Publishing, 2014; S. Douglas-Scott, 'The EU Charter of Fundamental Rights as a Constitutional Document', *European Human Rights Law Review*, 2004, pp. 1–10; K. Lenaerts and E. de Smijter, 'A "Bill of Rights' for the European Union", *Common Market Law Review*, 2001, pp. 273–300.

5 E.g. J. Morijn, 'Post-Lisbon Civil Rights Protection by the EU's Political Institutions', in S. de Vries, H. de Waele and M.-P. Granger (eds.), *Civil Rights and EU Citizenship*, Cheltenham, Edward Elgar Publishing, 2018, pp. 14–42; M. Dawson, *The Governance of EU Fundamental Rights*, Cambridge, Cambridge University Press, 2017; J.-P. Jacqué, 'La charte des droits fondamentaux et le législateur de l'Union', in P. Iliopoulou and L. Xenou (eds.), *La Charte des droits fondamentaux, source de renouveau constitutionnel européen?*, Brussels, Bruylant, 2020, pp. 139–148; I. Butler, 'Ensuring Compliance with the Charter of Fundamental Rights in Legislative Drafting: The Practice of the European Commission', *European Law Review*, 2012, pp. 397–418.

the dynamics and the competences behind the EU legislative intervention,[6] the most recent research has sought to analyse the phenomenon of EU legislation which gives expression to fundamental rights and its repercussions within the EU legal order.[7]

The second branch examines how the ECtHR has used 'external' law in its case-law.[8] This branch has received considerable attention and echoes the broader literature on why, when and how apex courts rely on comparative human rights law.[9] While many scholars have focused on the use of external sources to establish a consensus on fundamental rights,[10] research has diversified in recent years. Some have, for instance, provided critical assessments of the comparative approach of Strasbourg.[11] The reception of both national and international law has been the subject of significant contributions.[12] The reception of EU law has been explored to a lesser extent. Yet, the topic has

---

6 E.g. E. Dubout, 'The Protection of Fundamental Rights and the Allocation of Competences in the EU. A Clash of Constitutional Logics', in L. Azoulai (ed.), *The Question of Competence in the European Union*, Oxford, Oxford University Press, 2014, pp. 193–212; E. Muir, 'Fundamental Rights: an Unsettling EU Competence', *Human Rights Review*, 2014, pp. 25–37; O. de Schutter, 'Les droits fondamentaux dans le projet européen. Des limites à l'action des institutions à une politique des droits fondamentaux', in O. De Schutter and P. Nihoul (eds.), *Une constitution pour l'Europe. Réflexions sur les transformations du droit de l'Union européenne*, Brussels, Larcier, 2004, pp. 81–117.

7 E.g. Y. Lorans, 'Le législateur européen et la protection des droits fondamentaux dans l'Union : vers une concrétisation législative de la Charte', *Revue trimestrielle de droit européen*, 2021, pp. 59–86; E. Muir, 'The Fundamental Rights Implications of EU Legislation: Some Constitutional Challenges', *Common Market Law Review*, 2014, pp. 219–245.

8 See below Part I, Chapter 4, Section II. Scholarship, Comparative and Quantitative Insights, on the definition of external sources.

9 E.g. A. Müller (ed.), *Judicial Dialogue and Human Rights*, Cambridge, Cambridge University Press, 2017; S. Fredman, 'Foreign Fads or Fashions? The Role of Comparativism in Human Rights Law', *International and Comparative Law Quarterly*, 2015, pp. 631–660; A. Bailleux, 'Human Rights in Network', *Journal européen des droits de l'Homme*, 2014, pp. 293–325; C. Mc Crudden, 'Common Law of Human Rights? Transnational Judicial Conversations on Constitutional Rights', *Oxford Journal of Legal Studies*, 2000, pp. 499–532.

10 E.g. K. Dzehtsiarou, *European Consensus and the Legitimacy of the European Court of Human Rights*, Cambridge, Cambridge University Press, 2015; L. Helfer, 'Consensus, Coherence and the European Convention on Human Rights', *Cornell International Law Journal*, 1993, pp. 133–165.

11 E.g. K. Dzehtsiarou and V. Lukashevich, 'Informed Decision-Making: The Comparative Endeavours of the Strasbourg Court', *Netherlands Quarterly of Human Rights*, 2012, pp. 272–298; M. Ambrus, 'Comparative Law Method in the Jurisprudence of the European Court of Human Rights in the Light of the Rule of Law', *Erasmus Law Review*, 2009, pp. 353–371; P. Carozza, 'Uses and Misuses of Comparative Law in International Human Rights: Some Reflections on the Case-law of the European Court of Human Rights', *Notre Dame Law Review*, 1998, pp. 1217–1238.

12 M. Larché, *Les fonctions du droit international dans la jurisprudence de la Cour européenne des droits de l'Homme*, Paris, Pedone, 2025; M. Forowicz, *The Reception of International Law in the European Court of Human Rights*, Oxford, Oxford University Press, 2010, p. 421; L. Wildhaber, 'The European Convention on Human Rights and International Law', *The International and Comparative Law Quarterly*, 2007, pp. 217–232; P. Mahoney, 'The

gained new impetus recently, with a few researchers who have examined the impact of EU law on the ECtHR case-law, as further explained below.

The third branch explores the interactions between EU and ECHR laws. This subject has attracted the attention of academics long since and remains high on the agenda. Without providing a comprehensive account of the literature, three salient features of the research are worth highlighting. First, the interplay between EU and ECHR laws has primarily been investigated from the perspective of the interactions between the adjudicators of the two legal orders. Extensive research has been carried out on the dialogue between the CJEU and the ECtHR[13] and the way they adjudicate in fundamental rights disputes.[14] Second, the literature has been predominantly unidirectional, in the sense that the focal point has been the reception of ECHR law into the EU legal order.[15] Third, EU law has often been studied and portrayed as a threat to the ECHR. Among the main debates have been the responsibility of EU

Comparative Method in Judgments of the European Court of Human Rights: Reference back to National Law' in G.M. Canivet Andenas and F. Duncan (eds.), *Comparative Law Before the Courts, British Institute of International and Comparative Law*, 2004, pp. 135–150.

13 E.g. A. Frese and H. Olsen, 'Spelling It Out-Convergence and Divergence in the Judicial Dialogue between CJEU and ECtHR', *Nordic Journal of International Law*, 2019, pp. 429–458; S. Morano-Foadi and L. Vickers (eds.), *Fundamental Rights in the EU. A Matter for Two Courts*, Oxford, Hart Publishing, 2015; S. Douglas-Scott, 'A Tale of two Courts: Luxembourg, Strasbourg and the Growing European Human Rights Acquis', *Common Market Law Review*, 2006, pp. 629-665; D. Simon, *Des influences réciproques entre CJCE et CEDH: 'Je t'aime, moi non plus'?*, Pouvoirs, 2001, pp. 31-49; R. Lawson, 'Confusion and Conflict? Divergent Interpretations of the ECHR in Strasbourg and Luxembourg', in R. Lawson and M. de Bloijs (eds.), *The Dynamics of the Protection of Human Rights in Europe*, Nijhoff, 1994, pp. 219–251.

14 E.g. O. Arnadóttir and A. Guðmundsdóttir, 'Speaking the Same Language? Comparing Judicial Restraint at the ECtHR and the ECJ', in O. Arnadóttir and A. Buyse (eds.), *Shifting Centres of Gravity in Human Rights Protection, Rethinking relations between the ECHR, EU and national legal orders*, London, Routledge, 2016, pp. 161–182; S. Gless and J. Martin, 'The Comparative Method in European Courts: A Comparison Between the CJEU and ECtHR?', *Bergen Journal of Criminal Law and Criminal Justice*, 2013, pp. 36–52; S. Greer and A. Williams, 'Human Rights in the Council of Europe and the EU: Towards 'Individual', 'Constitutional' or 'Institutional' Justice?', *European Law Journal*, 2009, pp. 462–481.

15 E.g. J. Krommendijk, 'The Use of ECtHR Case-law by the Court of Justice of the European Union: The View of Luxembourg Insiders', *Maastricht Journal of European and Comparative Law*, 2015, pp. 812–835; J. Murray, 'The Influence of the European Convention on Fundamental Rights on Community Law', *Fordham International Law Journal*, 2011, pp. 1388–1422; B. de Witte, 'The Use of the ECHR and Convention Case-Law by the European Court of Justice', in P.C. Popelier Van de Heyning and P. Van Nuffel (eds.), *Human Rights Protection in the European legal Order: The Interaction Between the European and the National Courts*, Brussels, Intersentia, 2011, pp. 17–34; O. de Schutter, 'L'influence de la Cour européenne des droits de l'homme sur la Cour de justice des Communautés européennes', *CRIDHO Working Paper*, 2007, pp. 3–27.

States before the ECtHR when they implement EU law[16] and the prospect of EU accession to the ECHR.[17] Nonetheless, a recent, albeit limited, pool of researchers departs from these three features. Sparked by the rise of references to EU law in the Strasbourg case-law, they are the ones who paved the way to explore the use of EU law by the ECtHR.[18]

While building on these studies, our research stands out on several fronts. We aim to offer a comprehensive and original understanding of the phenomenon of influence of EU fundamental rights on the ECtHR's case-law through (1) a systematic analysis, (2) an emphasis on EU secondary law next to the Charter and CJEU case-law, (3) and a multifaceted methodology. First, our approach is distinguished by its systematic character. We use a comprehensive dataset to investigate various dimensions of influence which are identified in advance. Second, we place emphasis on the influence of EU legislation giving expression to fundamental rights. While past studies have focused on references to the Charter,[19] the growing importance of EU fundamental rights legislation warrants a thorough scrutiny of its impact. Third, our methodology is multifaceted It combines systematic case-law analysis, supplemented by quantitative and comparative insights, as well as field observations obtained through a research stay within the ECtHR's machinery.

---

16 E.g. T. Lock, 'Beyond Bosphorus: The European Court of Human Rights' Case-law on the Responsibility of Member States of International Organisations under the European Convention on Human Rights', *Human Rights Law Review*, 2010, pp. 529–545. L. Besselink, 'The European Union and the European Convention on Human Rights: From Sovereign Immunity in Bosphorus to Full Scrutiny Under the Reform Treaty?', in I. Boerefijn and J. Goldschmidt (eds.), *Changing Perceptions of Sovereignty and Human Rights, Essays in Honour of Cees Flinterman*, Brussels, Intersentia, 2008, pp. 295–309.

17 E.g. T. Lock, 'The Future of EU Human Rights Law: Is Accession to the ECHR Still Desirable?', *Journal of International and Comparative Law*, 2020, pp. 428–447; S. Peers, 'The EU's Accession to the ECHR: The Dream Becomes a Nightmare', *German Law Journal*, 2015, pp. 213–222; C. Eckes, 'EU accession to the ECHR: between autonomy and adaptation', *The Modern Law Review*, 2013, vol. 76, pp. 254–285.

18 P. Lemmens and M. Piret, 'The Charter of Fundamental Rights of the European Union and the European Convention on Human Rights, from the Perspective of the European Court of Human Rights', *Cahiers de droit européen*, 2021, pp. 183–210; C. Dautricourt, 'A Strasbourg Perspective on the Autonomous Development of Fundamental Rights in EU Law: Trends and Implications', *Jean Monnet Working Paper Series*, 2010, pp. 1–70; A. Nusserberg, 'La prise en compte de la Charte des droits fondamentaux par la Cour européenne des droits de l'homme' in P. Iliopoulou and L. Xenou (ed), *La Charte des droits fondamentaux, source de renouveau constitutionnel européen?*, Brussels, Bruylant, 2020, pp. 69-75; S. O'Leary, 'The EU Charter Ten Years On: A View from Strasbourg', in M. Bobek and J. Adams-Prassl (eds.), *The EU Charter of Fundamental Rights in the Member States*, Oxford, Hart Publishing, 2020, pp. 37–68; T. Lock, 'The Influence of EU law on Strasbourg Doctrines', *European Law Review*, 2016, pp. 804–825; B. Dickson, 'The EU Charter of Fundamental Rights in the Case-law of the European Court of Human Rights', *European Human Rights Law Review*, 2015, pp. 27–40.

19 E.g. A. Nusserberg, ibid., pp. 69–75; B. Dickson, ibid., pp. 27–40.

Our research holds significance for both scientific advancement and societal understanding. The project provides valuable insights for scholars interested in human rights, EU law, ECHR law as well as interactions between legal systems. We offer a new perspective and insights on the dynamics of influence between EU and ECHR laws, and suggest a new narrative within these dynamics, namely that EU fundamental rights are a special source in the ECtHR's case-law. Our project offers side contributions: first, we explore the distinctiveness of the EU and ECHR systems of fundamental rights protection; second, we contribute to the research on EU secondary legislation in the field of fundamental rights. Our research addresses important societal questions, such as understanding how the complex, multi-layered system of fundamental rights in Europe has evolved in light of recent developments at EU level. We shed light on how the ECtHR has reacted to this evolution and whether it has been able to navigate through the various tensions raised by its (non-) use of EU fundamental rights. Through a critical analysis of how the ECtHR uses EU fundamental rights, our project encourages a thoughtful examination of its approach. This sets the stage for future reflections on its practices. We also aim to convey to the reader that the audience for this research project is not limited to academia and the ECtHR: a significant portion of our research is directed towards the use of EU fundamental rights before the ECtHR by practitioners, including parties, national judges, and NGOs. We believe they may find valuable resources in this study.

SECTION II. DELIMITING THE CONTOURS OF OUR INVESTIGATION

As mentioned above, we investigate how and to what extent EU fundamental rights have influenced the ECtHR case-law. The main components of this question deserve to be explained: they highlight the framework and the limitations within which we conducted our research.

§ 1. THE WHAT: INFLUENCE

Using the term 'influence' in our research question was a deliberate, yet not easy, choice. Other expressions could have been used, such as the impact of EU fundamental rights on the ECtHR case-law or the use of EU fundamental rights by the ECtHR. Yet, working with the concept of influence proved fruitful. At first glance, this concept is ambivalent and its contours remain somewhat elusive. In legal scholarship, scholars often do not specify what they mean by 'influence' nor do they explain the methods they use to assess it. Yet, this is not the case for some other social sciences where it is more conceptualised, and from which insights could be gained Not only did this lead us to define the notion of influence for the purposes of our research, but also to delineate the dimensions of influence that we study.

I. An Overlooked Notion in Legal Studies

Influence is a concept that is often used in legal scholarship. Many legal studies are entitled 'The influence of [Law A] on [Law B]' or, alternatively, 'The impact of [Law A] on [Law B]'. The variables A and B differ depending on the study. While the examples diverge in their substance,[20] most of them have in common that they do not provide an answer to the following questions: what do they mean by influence and what are the tools for tracing such influence? Many legal researchers use the concept of influence in an intuitive manner.[21] This does not mean, of course, that their approach is wrong or problematic.[22] However, the 'intuitive' approach leads to the fact that one may have difficulties to understand what the study has covered, which may leave other researchers with questions as to what remain to be studied.

If legal studies are characterised by a lack of specification on influence,[23] there are other social sciences where the conceptualisation of influence is more advanced A good example is the field of arts and literature: many studies have been devoted to examining the influence of an author, artist or movement A on the work of an author, artist or movement B.[24] There are other fields, such as social psychology, where the understanding of the notion of influence is very advanced.[25]

---

20 E.g. on the influence of EU and ECHR laws: T. Van Den Brink, 'The Impact of EU Legislation on National Legal Systems: Towards a New Approach to EU – Member State Relations', *Cambridge Yearbook of European Legal Studies*, 2017, pp. 211–235; P. Giliker, 'The Influence of EU and European Human Rights Law on English Private Law', *International and Comparative Law Quaterly*, 2015, pp. 237–265; H. Keller and A. Stone Sweet, 'Assessing the impact of the ECHR on national legal systems', in H. Keller and A. Stone Sweet (eds.), *A Europe of Rights: The Impact of the ECHR on National Legal Systems*, Oxford, Oxford University Press, 2008, pp. 677–712.

21 M. Meguro, 'Tracing Influence in International Law: Beyond the Antagonism between Doctrine of Law and Social Science', *Amsterdam Law School Research Paper*, 2020, p. 4.

22 As rightly observed by Mannheim, '[m]ethodology seeks but to make explicit in logical terms what is de facto going on in living research', which reminds us that the concept of influence does not always need to be made explicit to be used correctly (K. Mannheim, *Essays on the Sociology of Knowledge*, London, Routledge & Kegan Paul, 1952, p. 37).

23 M. Meguro, 'Tracing Influence in International Law: Beyond the Antagonism between Doctrine of Law and Social Science', *Amsterdam Law School Research Paper*, 2020, p. 5.

24 E.g. G. Hermeren, *Influence in Art and Literature*, Princeton, Princeton University Press, 2015.

25 E.g. R. Cialdini and N. Goldstein, 'Social influence: compliance and conformity', *Annu. Rev. Psychol.*, 2004, pp. 591–621.

While influence is a concept that 'resists an easy or straightforward definition',[26] a common thread throughout various branches of literature is that influence is the ability of one phenomenon to produce an effect on another. A influences B if A produces effects on B. The concept of influence is closely related to that of causality and while the two overlap to some extent, they are often seen as distinct. A can inspire the action of B without necessarily causing it. According to Posner, influence encompasses both causation (the situation in which B would not have occurred if A had not existed) and inspiration (the situation in which an idea is taken from A by B and used by B).[27]

The intention of the actors involved in the influence process is often linked to the notion of influence. Several definitions require that the influencer intends to influence the influencee. Parsons, for example, notes that '[i]nfluence is a way of having an effect on the attitudes and opinions of others through *intentional* (though not necessarily rational) action – the effect may or may not be to change the opinion or to prevent a possible change.'[28] Nagel observes that influence is 'generally understood as an actor's ability to shape a decision in line with her preferences; in other words, a causal relation between the preferences of an actor regarding an outcome and the outcome itself.'[29] Other scholars suggest that the existence of influence depends on the intention of the influencee to be influenced, and whether the latter is free or aware of the influence. Scruton put forward that 'the influenced agent, unlike the agent who is coerced, acts freely. He may choose to ignore those considerations which influence him, and he may himself exert control over the influencing power.'[30]

II. Perimeters of Influence under Scrutiny

What is then the influence that we are investigating? It is first of all a situation of normative influence, in that we examine the effects of legal norms (EU fundamental rights) on other legal norms (ECHR law).[31] This normative influence, we examine it in a broad sense: we do not limit our research to the influence on the interpretation of the Convention's rights. Instead, we explore all effects that EU fundamental rights have had on the ECtHR case-law. We examine how the rise of EU fundamental rights has impacted the ECtHR

---

26 S. Feyen, *Beyond Federal Dogmatics. The Influence of EU Law on Belgian Constitutional Case-law Regarding Federalism*, Leuven, Leuven University Press, 2013, p. 29.

27 R. Posner, 'Bentham's Influence on the Law and Economics Movement', *Current Legal Problems*, 1998, p. 426.

28 T. Parsons, 'On the concept of influence', *Public opinion quarterly*, 1963, p. 38.

29 J. Nagel, *The Descriptive Analysis of Power*, New Haven, Yale University Press, 1975, p. 29.

30 R. Scruton, *A Dictionary of Political Thought*, New York, Macmillan, 1996, p. 432.

31 R. Wessel and S. Blockmans, 'The Legal Status and Influence of Decisions of International Organizations and other Bodies in the European Union', *College of Europe, Research Papers in Law*, 2014, p. 11.

but also other actors who intervene prior to, during, or within the ECtHR proceedings. We look at the influence of EU fundamental rights regardless of the intention of the influencer or the influencee. In line with Duxbury, we consider that the fact that A influences B does not require that A intends to influence B. Similarly, the process of A influencing B does not depend on B being aware of this influence.[32] EU fundamental rights can influence the ECtHR without the EU institutions having intended to influence the ECtHR's case-law[33] or the ECtHR being aware of the process of influence.

We explore five dimensions of this influence:

1) The *quantitative aspects*. We examine the number of times EU fundamental rights have been referred to according to different variables: total number of references, references per type of EU fundamental rights, over time, areas, actors, and respondent States.
2) The *functions* performed by EU fundamental rights when used by the ECtHR. We examine the extent to which these rights play a marginal, limited, notable, or significant role in fulfilling these functions. We explore whether and how other legal sources are used to contribute to the function simultaneously. We look at the sources of EU fundamental rights that are used for the various functions and reflect on whether EU fundamental rights are used to enhance fundamental rights protection when performing their function.
3) The *actors other than the ECtHR* involved prior to, during, or within the ECtHR proceedings which use EU fundamental rights. We examine references by parties, third-party interveners, national judges, and ECtHR judges and analyse to what end they rely on EU fundamental rights.
4) The *respondent States* involved in cases where EU fundamental rights are used. We examine to what extent the ECtHR has used EU fundamental rights in cases involving EU and non-EU States. We analyse whether the ECtHR has developed tools to modulate the influence of these rights depending on the respondent State.
5) The *methodology* when the ECtHR uses EU fundamental rights. We look at the transparency of these references, assessing how openly and clearly

32 As Duxbury notes on this last point, 'the state of being inspired - of B's picking up an idea from A - is not necessarily a conscious one: sometimes, that is, we are influenced by past experiences without being aware of the fact. Influence then, is related but not identical to causality: it occurs where a person's outlook alters as a result of his or her conscious or subconscious noticing of some external stimulus' (N. Duxbury, 'The Dynamics of Influence', in N. Duxbury (ed.), *Jurists and Judges: An Essay on Influence*, Oxford, Hart Publishing, 2001, p. 6).

33 We will not explore whether EU institutions intended to influence the ECtHR's case-law; however, we will observe that, in the field of data protection, there is a clear intention for EU standards to have a global reach (see below Part II, Chapter 2, Section II, §1. The Diverse and Evolving Dynamics behind EU Legislative Action).

the ECtHR engages with EU fundamental rights. We examine if and how the ECtHR justifies and contextualises these references.

Annex I provides an overview of the key questions and sub-questions for each dimension we have investigated in our research.

§ 2. OF WHAT: EU FUNDAMENTAL RIGHTS

For most of the EU's history, fundamental rights have been protected either in specific EU Treaty provisions or as general principles of EU law. Since the beginning of the millennium, new sources of fundamental rights have emerged in EU law: (i) the Charter and an increasing number of (ii) EU legislative instruments that define or relate to fundamental rights. We will study the influence of these two sources as well as (iii) the related CJEU case-law which interprets them. This is prompted by our research angle, which is to examine the repercussions of the growing role of the EU as a standard-setter. This means that other EU fundamental rights, such as the general principles of EU, are outside the scope of this project.[34] This also means that we will not look at how EU law not related to fundamental rights have influenced the ECtHR case-law.[35] Our research uses two case studies: equality and non-discrimination and data protection. We have selected these areas as they represent where the EU has arguably developed its most advanced fundamental rights policies, combining Charter's provisions, robust legislative frameworks, and highly developed CJEU case-law.[36]

34 The influence of general principles of EU law is not examined. While they remain a relevant source of fundamental rights protection, especially when the Charter is not applicable (Case C-166/13, *Mukarubega*, ECLI:EU:C:2014:2336, paras. 44–45), they have tended to become a subsidiary source. The project does not examine the influence of EU Treaty provisions related to fundamental rights, nor the influence of EU soft law instruments on fundamental rights, although both have been referred to by the ECtHR (see for examples on the use of EU soft law instruments, T. Lock, 'The Influence of EU Law on Strasbourg Doctrines', *European Law Review*, 2016, p. 810).

35 The ECtHR has relied upon concepts from EU law to shape in its case-law on a few occasions. In its *Pellegrin v. France* judgment of 8 December 1999, the ECtHR interpreted the scope of Article 6(1) ECHR in the light of the concept of employment in the public administration mentioned in Article 45(4) TFEU, as interpreted by the CJEU (ECtHR, *Pellegrin v. France* [GC], no. 28541/95, §§ 37–41 and 64–66, CEDH 1999-VIII). In *Posti and Rahko v. Finland* of 24 September 2002, the ECtHR referred to the conditions for bringing an action for annulment under Article 263(4) TFEU to determine whether there was a right to challenge legislation that was not directly addressed to applicants (ECtHR, *Posti and Rahko v. Finland*, no. 27824/95, § 54, CEDH 2002-VII). Please note that this footnote stems from V. Davio, 'Le droit de l'Union européenne dans la jurisprudence de la Cour européenne des droits de l'Homme', *Journal de droit européen*, 2023, p. 49. See also T. Lock, *ibid.*, pp. 814–115.

36 We explain the choice of case study in the introduction of Part III: In Action. The Use of EU Fundamental Rights in Practice.

§ 3. ON WHAT: ECTHR'S CASE-LAW

Our research focuses on the way the ECtHR has used EU fundamental rights standards. This means we do not examine the influence of these standards on other Council of Europe instruments,[37] nor do we analyse systematically the reverse influence of ECHR law on EU fundamental rights.[38]

Speaking of the ECtHR, it is important to keep in mind throughout this project that the legitimacy of its decisions remains fragile and is regularly questioned. In 2011, Dzehtsiarou and Greene observed that '[t]he judgments of the ECtHR are fiercely criticized and their legitimacy is repeatedly questioned by the Contracting Parties and media in particular, and by civic society in general. As it stands, the ECtHR is suffocating from the overwhelming number of applications lodged, and even the tiny percentage of these applications that are decided by it face "a barrage of hostile criticism" […].'[39] This observation remains pertinent more than a decade later: even though the ECtHR has

[37] Let us mention briefly that EU and the Council of Europe have a long-standing and close relationship. Today, their cooperation is governed by a 2007 Memorandum which foresees that both organisations 'will develop their relationship in all areas of common interest, in particular the promotion and protection of pluralistic democracy, the respect for human rights and fundamental freedoms, the rule of law, political and legal co-operation, social cohesion and cultural interchange' (Memorandum of understanding between the Council of Europe and European Union, 23 May 2007, point 9) and that they 'will take all the necessary measures to promote their co-operation by exchanging on their respective activities and by preparing and implementing common strategies and programmes for the priorities and areas of shared interest' (ibid., point 11). There are several channels through which the EU can influence and has influenced the standard-setting activities of the Council of Europe. First of all, there is an EU representation in the Committee of Ministers, which allows the Commission to participate in its activities, but without having a vote (Directorate of External Relations of Council of Europe, Co-operation between the Council of Europe and the European Union Overview of arrangements for co-operation between the Council of Europe and the European Union, DER/Inf (2018) 2, 31 May 2018 5). Further, there is an important high-level political dialogue between the EU and the Council of Europe (ibid., 6). In addition, the 2007 Memorandum between the EU and the Council of Europe provides that the two organisations shall consult each other at an early stage of the standard-setting process, including on fundamental rights law, and mentions that both organisations 'will acknowledge each other's experience and standard-setting work, as appropriate, in their respective activities' (Memorandum of understanding between the Council of Europe and European Union, 23 May 2007, point 17).

[38] This means that we will not conduct a systematic review of CJEU's case-law which refers to ECHR law, but we will explore to some extent how ECHR law has influenced EU fundamental rights (Part II, Chapter 1, Section III, §2. The Special Significance of ECHR Law) and consider the interactions between ECHR and EU standards through dialogue between CJEU and ECtHR (Part IV, Chapter 2, Section I, §3. Dialogue), though this is not the primary focus of the project.

[39] K. Dzehtsiarou and A. Greene, 'Legitimacy and the Future of the European Court of Human Rights: Critical Perspectives from Academia and Practitioners', *German Law Journal*, 2011, p. 1707.

implemented mechanisms to address its backlog,[40] the docket remains very high, and its judgments are still frequently contested.[41]

In this context, the ECtHR has shown an increasing openness in its use of external law to support the findings in its decisions. Not only has the ECtHR significantly relied on national laws from a comparative perspective,[42] notably to determine a European consensus,[43] but the ECtHR has also increasingly relied on international law. In this respect, Larché has recently observed that the use of the latter sources has followed a double pattern of intensification and diversification over the last decades.[44] The ECtHR's approach towards the use of external laws has been encapsulated in the well-known *Demir v. Baykara* [GC](2011) case in which it held that: 'in defining the meaning of terms and notions in the text of the Convention, *can and must take into account* elements of international law other than the Convention, the interpretation of such elements by competent organs, and the practice of European States reflecting their common values. The consensus emerging from specialised international instruments and from the practice of Contracting States may constitute a relevant consideration for the Court when it interprets the provisions of the Convention in specific cases.'[45] According to the ECtHR, 'it is not necessary for the respondent State to have ratified the entire collection of instruments that are applicable in respect of the precise subject matter of the case concerned',[46] but that '[i]t will be sufficient for the Court that the relevant international instruments denote a continuous evolution in the norms and principles applied in international law or in the domestic law of the majority of member States of the Council of Europe and show, in a precise area, that there is common ground in modern societies.'[47]

On a broader level, the ECtHR's increased reliance on external sources is part of a larger movement. In recent decades, the law has undergone a profound change, becoming increasingly diverse, varied, hybrid and complex.

---

40 E.g. F. Dehousse, 'The Reforms of the EU Courts (III). The Brilliant Alternative Approach of the European Court of Human Rights', *Egmont Paper*, 2016.

41 See e.g. regarding the non-compliance with ECtHR's interim measures, P. Leach, 'Injunctive relief at the European Court of Human Rights – progress and push-back', in E. Muir, S. Garben and I. Govaere (ed) *Activating the Protection of Fundamental and Human Rights at European Level*, Hart, forthcoming in 2025-2026.

42 P. Mahoney, 'The Comparative Method in Judgments of the European Court of Human Rights: Reference back to National Law', in G.M. Canivet Andenas and F. Duncan (eds.), *Comparative Law Before the Courts, British Institute of International and Comparative Law*, 2004, pp. 135–150.

43 E.g. K. Dzehtsiarou, 'European Consensus: A Way of Reasoning', *UCD Working Papers in Law, Criminology & Socio-Legal Studies Research Paper No. 11/2009*, pp. 9–10.

44 M. Larché, *Les fonctions du droit international dans la jurisprudence de la Cour européenne des droits de l'Homme*, Paris, Pedone, 2025.

45 ECtHR, *Demir and Baykara v. Turkey* [GC], no. 34503/97, § 85, ECHR 2008. Emphasis added.

46 Ibid., § 86.

47 Ibid.

Far from the era of a pyramid-shaped law limited to national legal orders, the Kelsenian model,[48] law has become hybrid, globalised, and the subject of exchanges and dialogues, sometimes legislative, sometimes jurisprudential.[49] If the law has long been a closed system, delimited by rules marked by verticality and hierarchy, the law now appears increasingly open to the world.[50] Today, we speak of a law in network.[51]

Human rights law, the focus of this project, is not immune to this legal revolution, on the contrary. There is a growing porosity between the different legal systems, particularly in the area of fundamental rights protection, to the extent that some speak of a genuine 'judicial commerce' in this area.[52] Dialogue between judges of fundamental rights has become common practice, whether it is orchestrated or unrestrained, or whether it is within a legal order or across borders.[53] As an archetype of this outward-looking movement, the Inter-American Court of Human Rights is known to refer extensively to the case-law of other human rights courts, including in particular the ECtHR.[54]

Studying the use of EU fundamental rights necessitates taking this broader context into account. The increasing reference to and reliance on diverse international instruments by the ECtHR highlights that the use of EU fundamental rights emerges within an already well-established and enriched environment, and that this trend of referring to external instruments is part of a larger trend of increasing interactions between different fundamental rights legal systems.

---

48 H. Kelsen, *Pure theory of law*, University of California Press, 1967.

49 E.g. A. Meuwese and S. Marnix, '"Constitutional Dialogue": An Overview', *Utrecht Law Review*, 2013, pp. 123–140; J. Allard and A. Garapon, *Les juges dans la mondialisation : la nouvelle révolution du droit*, Paris, Le Seuil, 2005; W. Twining, *Globalisation and legal theory*, Cambridge, Cambridge University Press, 2000.

50 L. Burgorgue-Larsen, *Les 3 Cours régionales des droits de l'homme in context. La justice qui n'allait pas de soi*, Paris, Pedone 2020, p. 245.

51 F. Ost and M. Van de Kerchove, *De la pyramide au réseau? Pour une théorie dialectique du droit*, Brussels, Publications des F.U.S.L., 2002.

52 E. Dubout and S. Touze, 'La fonction des droits fondamentaux dans les rapports entre ordres et systèmes juridiques', in E. Dubout and S. Touze (eds.), *Les droits fondamentaux: charnières entre ordres et systèmes juridiques*, Paris, Pedone 2009, p. 12.

53 See e.g. for a classification of the different type of dialogues between judges, L. Burgorgue-Larsen, 'De l'internationalisation du dialogue des juges. Missive doctrinale à l'attention de Bruno Genevois', in *Le Dialogue des juges. Mélanges en l'honneur du Président Bruno Genevois*, Paris, Dalloz, 2009, pp. 95–130.

54 E.g. Inter-American Court of Human Rights, *Last Temptation of Christ Case*, Series C, No. 73 (2001), § 69 which cites ECHR, *Handyside v. the United Kingdom*, 7 December 1976, Series A no. 24; Inter-American Court of Human Rights, *Five Pensioners Case*, Series C, No. 98 (2003), § 30 which cites ECHR, *Gaygusuz v. Austria*, 16 September 1996, Reports of Judgments and Decisions 1996-IV. See also L. Lixinski, 'Treaty interpretation by the Inter-American Court of Human Rights: expansionism at the service of the unity of international law', *European Journal of International Law*, 2010, pp. 585–604; G. Neuman, 'Import, export, and regional consent in the Inter-American Court of Human Rights', *European journal of international law*, 2008, pp. 101–123.

CHAPTER 4
HOW WE LOOK FOR: A MULTIFACETED RESEARCH METHODOLOGY

The methodology developed to study our subject has been diverse and evolved alongside our research. It finds its roots in systematic case-law analysis, which was supplemented by scholarship, comparative and quantitative insights, as well as 'field' observations obtained during a stay within the ECtHR's fabric.

SECTION I. SYSTEMATIC CASE-LAW ANALYSIS

Our study draws inspiration from systemic case-law analysis.[1] Such a methodology is meant to reveal connections, patterns or developments in judgments of judges, arbitrators and other legal dispute resolution bodies in a structured and replicable manner.[2] Under this methodology, the researcher bases the analysis solely or primarily on judicial decisions.[3] The research is descriptive in nature and its purpose is not to comment on the correctness or appropriateness of legal judgments.[4] The systemic case-law analysis implies that data collection takes place in a systematic and transparent manner, so that the method can be repeated by other researchers.[5]

This research project was inspired by several of these characteristics. The analysis highlights patterns in the use of EU fundamental rights by the ECtHR. It is based on a systematic review of ECtHR's judicial decisions. It is primarily descriptive, in that it is meant to shed light on the specific dimensions of

---

1 Such a method has been described as follows: 'a scholar collects a set of documents, such as judicial opinions on a particular subject, and systematically reads them, recording consistent features of each and drawing inferences about their use and meaning' (A. Hall, and W. Ronald, 'Systematic Content Analysis of Judicial Opinions', *California Law Review*, 2008, p. 64).

2 P. Verbruggen, *Methoden van systematische rechtspraakanalyse: Tussen juridische dogmatiek en data science*, Den Haag, Boom juridisch, 2021, p. 1.

3 Ibid., p. 1.

4 Ibid.

5 Ibid., p. 30.

influence discussed above. The collection of data is carried out in a systematic and transparent manner. There is, however, one aspect which is used in some systemic case-law analyses that we do not use: the coding technique.[6] The use of codes is often justified by the large number of cases to be analyzed. However, this approach can lead to a focus on 'counting rather than reading'.[7] The complexity of several dimensions of the influence under consideration led us to opt for a more traditional approach of 'reading rather than counting'.

Citations of EU fundamental rights have been used as a proxy for influence. As Duxbury noted, 'citation counts can be a valuable source of information when endeavouring to assess influence. Even though analyses of citations cannot enable us to measure definitively the influence of a particular work, they can provide some impression of the extent to which that work has been influential'.[8] Citations of EU fundamental rights are one of the most authoritative and traceable indicators of the latter's influence, whether marginal or considerable, on the case-law of the ECtHR. They provide an entry point for a study of the effects of the former on the latter. We looked in particular at judgments from both the Grand Chamber and Chambers of the ECtHR in English which cited EU fundamental rights, as we shall further explain.[9]

SECTION II. SCHOLARSHIP, COMPARATIVE AND QUANTITATIVE INSIGHTS

Looking at the citations can create distortions and leave 'blind spots'. Citations do not necessarily translate into concrete influence and may lead to an excessive focus on certain cases.[10] In our study, focusing on the ECtHR's judgments quickly revealed its limitations. To address this, we supplemented our research with a comprehensive literature review in our case study field, which allowed

---

6 A. Hall and W. Ronald, 'Systematic Content Analysis of Judicial Opinions', *California Law Review*, 2008, p. 80.

7 Ibid., p. 81.

8 N. Duxbury, 'The Dynamics of Influence', in N. Duxbury (ed.), *Jurists and Judges: An Essay on Influence*, Oxford, Hart Publishing, 2001, p. 13. In this vein, Van Der Hagen put forward that 'a mere citation does not necessarily mean that the holding of the cited case was followed, let alone that it was instrumental in the reaching of the verdict of the citing decision. But it does tell us something, namely, that for one reason or another, the citing judge used it to justify his or her decision' (M. Van Der Haegen, 'Building a Legal Citation Network: The Influence of the Court of Cassation on the Lower Judiciary', *Utrecht Law Review*, 2017, p. 67)

9 We will further explain the selection of judgments in the methodology of our case studies (Part III, Chapter 1, Section III. Methodology).

10 N. Duxbury, ibid., p. 22. Duxbury rightly pointed out that 'citations seem generally to be the most reliable and identifiable indicators of influence. But they are not the only indicators. There are other factors on which the research of influence might usefully focus'.

us to identify cases that might have otherwise been overlooked. This was the case, for example, in situations where no English version of the judgment was available[11] or where it concerned (admissibility) decisions which still relevant to capture the influence of EU fundamental rights.[12]

Our methodology was also complemented by quantitative data. It is important to stress that, while quantitative analysis provides insights into the prevalence of references to EU fundamental rights, its capacity to elucidate the 'real' impact of these references is limited. Such analysis offers a preliminary glimpse into the overall trend of influence, rather than a detailed understanding of its effects. While these aspects were not the focal point of our analysis, they proved useful in identifying trends and contextualising elements examined through our qualitative research.

Finally, we gathered comparative insights. We chose to compare systematically the use of EU fundamental rights with international fundamental rights instruments and the outputs of their related bodies.[13] We focused on both general instruments with global reach (such as the International Covenant on Civil and Political Rights (ICCPR)) and regional reach (the African Charter on Human and Peoples' Rights (ACHPR) and the American Convention on Human Rights (ACHR)) as well as specific instruments (e.g., the Convention on the Elimination of All Forms of Discrimination Against Women (CEDAW), the Convention on the Rights of Persons with Disabilities (CRPD) for equality, and Convention 108 for data protection). We refer to EU law and international human rights instruments as sources 'external' to Convention law in the context of this study. It is important to clarify that 'internal' sources refer to the ECHR and the ECtHR case-law, whereas 'external' can include any other sources of law used by the ECtHR, such as EU law, international law or domestic laws.[14]

Our focus on international instruments is driven by the fact that EU law originates from international law, shares certain features with it (such as scope), and the ECtHR has increasingly relied on international law in its jurisprudence.[15] Additionally, international instruments provide an easily identifiable comparator.

However, it should be acknowledged that comparing EU law with international instruments is only one lens of comparison, and others – focusing

[11] E.g. ECtHR, *G.N. and Others v. Italy*, no. 43134/05, 1 December 2009.

[12] E.g. ECtHR, *Peterka v. Czech Republic* (adm. decision), no. 21990/08, 4 May 2010.

[13] Outputs refers to the decisions, rulings, reports, or other official documents produced by judicial or monitoring bodies related to the international instruments.

[14] See for another definition of the terms 'external sources', K. Dzehtsiarou, 'What Is Law for the European Court of Human Rights?', *Georgetown Journal of International Law*, 2017, p. 91.

[15] M. Larché, *Les fonctions du droit international dans la jurisprudence de la Cour européenne des droits de l'Homme*, Paris, Pedone, 2025.

on domestic laws – are equally valid.[16] In fact, EU law is almost akin to domestic law for EU States. While we do not systematically compare EU law with domestic laws (for reasons of feasibility), we will draw comparisons when useful, such as by highlighting instances where the ECtHR treats EU fundamental rights as domestic laws and the consequences of this. Our overall argument is precisely that it is the hybrid nature of EU law, combining characteristics of both domestic and international laws, which makes EU fundamental rights a special source for the ECtHR.

SECTION III. GETTING INTO THE ECTHR'S FABRIC

Last but certainly not least, we spent two months on a research stay at the ECtHR within the Jurisconsult Directorate, focusing on EU law matters. This primarily involves working for and in collaboration with lawyers from the Registry who focus on the relationship between the EU and ECHR laws. Although no formal interviews were conducted, the stay provided opportunities to meet informally with key players involved in the interplay between EU and ECHR laws at the ECtHR. It is not an overstatement to say that this research stay was instrumental in understanding both how EU law is taken into account prior decisions as well as its relevance within the ECtHR's fabric. Three simple yet striking observations emerged from our experience, which we aim to convey throughout our study. First, there is a 'human factor' in the use of EU fundamental rights by the ECtHR. The influence of these rights depends on specific individuals and actors involved before or within the ECtHR. Secondly, there is an 'institutional factor'. The way EU law is used in the ECtHR's judgments depends on the internal organisation and the resources allocated to this issue. The more resources – both human and material – are available, and the better organised the process of integrating EU law within the ECtHR's framework, the more effectively EU law is likely to be applied in its judgments. Thirdly, there is not yet a systematic approach to EU law within the ECtHR; however, this may change in the future due to ongoing shifts in the ECtHR's infrastructure.

---

16 See for a choice to compare the EU fundamental rights with international law: C. Rizcallah, *The European Union and Human Rights. Understanding a Singular Regional Player*, Oxford, Hart, forthcoming. See for a choice to compare the EU fundamental rights regime with the laws of federal States: O. Scarcello, *Contestatory Federalism and Rights: Resisting Incorporation in the US, Canada, and the EU*, Oxford, Oxford University Press, forthcoming.

CHAPTER 5
STRUCTURE

The structure of this book is divided into four parts. Part I, already presented, introduces and contextualises the research project. Part II explores the shifting paradigm through which the EU has evolved from a 'standard-taker' to a 'standard-setter' in the field of fundamental rights, highlighting the impact of this shift on the dynamics between EU and ECHR laws. Part III examines the influence of EU fundamental rights through two case studies – equality and non-discrimination, and data protection – pointing out that EU fundamental rights are a source of special significance in these areas, both quantitatively and qualitatively, not only for the ECtHR but also for other actors. Part IV considers future perspectives, arguing that this special significance could grow and should be accompanied by a method based on guiding principles (complementarity, coherence, and dialogue), methodological principles (transparency, justification, and contextualisation), and an infrastructure that optimises the use of EU fundamental rights within the ECtHR's fabric.

PART II.

Shifting Paradigm: The EU as a Fundamental Rights Standard-Setter

INTRODUCTION

After the turn of the millennium, Quinn affirmed that 'The story of the role of human rights in the construction of the EU is complex, ongoing but compelling. [...] The movement for greater human rights visibility now seems irresistible, and has been described as a train that has left the station but with no obvious destination.'[1] Now, more than twenty years later, while the final destination of the train of EU fundamental rights remains unknown, one thing seems rather certain: this train has moved forward at high speed

In twenty years, the place of fundamental rights in the EU has evolved significantly. They have become explicitly a value on which the EU is founded (Article 2 TEU). Equality between men and women has been included as an objective of the EU (Article 3(3) TEU). A legal basis and obligation for the EU to accede the ECHR has been enshrined in the EU Treaties (Article 6(2) TEU).

But that is not all.

A paradigm shift has unfolded, with significant implications for the dynamics between EU and ECHR laws: from being a fundamental rights 'standard-taker', the EU has evolved into a 'standard-setter'. For a long period in the EU's history, the EU fundamental rights regime followed in the footsteps of ECHR law. Whereas the ECHR came to light under the auspices of the Council of Europe, fundamental rights were almost absent from the founding EU Treaties. It was only in the late 60s that the CJEU integrated them into the EU's legal framework in the form of general principles. Lacking support within EU law, the EU judiciary drew upon several sources to shape EU fundamental rights. Its key source of inspiration was the ECHR to which it gave special significance: its standards were 'taken' or 'absorbed' to shape the EU fundamental rights regime, which was judicially-driven and ECHR-infused. This state of affairs was unaltered by the EU political institutions; on the contrary, they endorsed the development of this type of fundamental rights regime.

A transformation has occurred over the past decades: the EU has developed fundamental rights at primary and secondary law level. These rights have been fleshed out in the Charter whose legal status is now equivalent to that of the EU Treaties. Driven by diverse dynamics and endorsed with specific competences,

[1] G. Quinn, 'The European Union and the Council of Europe on the Issue of Human Rights: Twins Separated at Birth?', *McGill Law Journal*, 2001, pp. 852.

the EU legislator has developed fundamental rights standards. EU legislation giving expression to the Charter has flourished across a wide range of domains.

This evolution does not mean that the EU political institutions did not shape EU fundamental rights at all before the turn of the millennium. However, there has been a noticeable change in both intensity and diversity. Intensity, because EU fundamental rights have become more developed, and diversity, because they now cover areas as varied as equality and non-discrimination, asylum law, data protection, procedural rights in criminal procedure, whistleblowing, and artificial intelligence.

If this shift has impacted the use of ECHR law by the CJEU, it may also impact how the ECtHR uses EU law. EU fundamental rights appears as an attractive source of inspiration due to their highly developed and innovative nature and their shared application within 27 Council of Europe States. Besides, they form part of the background in cases involving EU States before the ECtHR, implying that the ECtHR must take them into account when dealing with such cases. Lastly, the rise of EU fundamental rights creates an increasing need for articulation. The growing autonomy of EU fundamental rights necessitates that the CJEU and the ECtHR articulate the EU and ECHR layers to enable EU domestic judges to apply them effectively which is essential for individuals. Understanding the growing role of the EU as a standard-setter is thus essential to grasp how EU fundamental rights, which have long been shaped by ECHR law, can, in turn, impact ECtHR case-law, introducing a new narrative in the interplay between EU and ECHR laws.

Before shedding light on this transformation, let us express a series of disclaimers. We do not provide an exhaustive history of the protection of fundamental rights in the EU.[2] Rather, we examine this history from a specific perspective: the evolution of the EU from a standard-taker to a standard-setter, with a view to understanding how the dynamics of influence between EU and ECHR laws have evolved. Although we put forward that the EU political institutions have increasingly shaped fundamental rights, we do not claim that the EU has 'a fully-fledged human rights policy'.[3] As the CJEU has pointed out in Opinion 2/94, the EU does not have a general competence to safeguard fundamental rights.[4] This observation is no less true today than it was at the time, even if the EU has gained specific competences. Nor do we argue that the EU has become a 'human rights organisation' or that the CJEU has turned into

---

[2] This endeavour has already been the subject of many substantive publications, e.g. E. Spaventa, 'Fundamental rights in the European Union', in C. Barnard and S. Peers (eds.), *European Union Law*, Oxford, Oxford University Press, pp. 226–254; G. de Búrca, 'The Evolution of EU Human Rights Law', in P. Craig and G. de Búrca (eds.), *The Evolution of EU Law*, Oxford, Oxford University Press, 2011, pp. 465–497.

[3] P. Alston and J. Weiler, 'An Ever Closer Union in Need of a Human Rights Policy', *European Journal of International Law*, 1998, p. 662.

[4] Opinion 2/94 f 28 March 1996, ECLI:EU:C:1996:140, § 27.

a 'second European Court of Human Rights'.[5] Without doubt, the EU plays a more active role in the field of fundamental rights, but this does not entail that its nature and purpose have been reprogrammed. That the EU political institutions have laid down standards does not imply that the protection of fundamental rights has evolved in a coherent manner nor that there is an integrated normative understanding of fundamental rights in the EU.[6]

With all this in mind, it is now time to get on board the EU fundamental rights train!

---

[5] K. Lenaerts, 'EU Values and Constitutional Pluralism: The EU System of Fundamental Rights Protection', *Polish Yearbook of International Law*, p. 137.

[6] See e.g. on criticisms of the EU fundamental rights system, S. Garben, 'Fundamental Rights in EU Copyright Harmonization: Balancing Without a Solid Framework: Funke Medien, Pelham, Spiegel Online ECLI:EU:C:2019:624; and Case C-516/17, Spiegel Online, ECLI:EU:C:2019:625. Judgments of the CJEU (Grand Chamber) of 29 July', *Common Market Law Review*, 2020, 1911; E. Spaventa, 'Should We "Harmonize" Fundamental Rights in the EU? Some Reflections About Minimum Standards and Fundamental Rights Protection in the EU Composite Constitutional System', *Common Market Law Review* 2009, vol. 55, pp. 997–998; P. Alston and J. Weiler, 'An 'Ever Closer Union' in Need of a Human Rights Policy: The European Union and Human Rights', in P. Alston (ed.), *The EU and Human Rights*, Oxford, Oxford University Press, 1999, pp. 3–68; J. Coppel and A. O'Neill, 'The European CJEU: Taking rights seriously?', *Legal Studies*, 1992, pp. 227–245. Still today, one may have difficulties to disagree with Douglas-Scott's claim that the protection of fundamental rights in the EU has evolved in an 'ad hoc, confusing, incremental way and that there is no clear, conceptual underpinning to the rights protected under EU law': see S. Douglas-Scott, 'The European Union and Human Rights after the Treaty of Lisbon', *Human Rights Law Review*, 2011, p. 649.

CHAPTER 1
THE EU AS A FUNDAMENTAL RIGHTS STANDARD-TAKER

For a long period in the EU's history, the EU fundamental rights regime followed in the footsteps of ECHR law. The CJEU incorporated fundamental rights into the EU legal order via the general principles of EU law. Although they were specific to the EU, the CJEU relied heavily on ECHR law, to which it gave 'special significance'. Rather than drafting a bill of rights, the EU political institutions supported the development of the EU regime as a judicially-driven and ECHR-infused system. Before explaining these developments, a step back reveals that a strong place for the ECHR within the EU legal framework dates back to the beginning of the EU's construction: it was envisaged as the source of protection for the project of a European Political Community ('EPC'). However, this project did not come to light, leading to a lack of fundamental rights protection in the early days of the EU's architecture. This contrasts with the Council of Europe, where fundamental rights had a central role from the outset.

SECTION I. A STEP BACK IN TIME: THE EARLY DAYS OF FUNDAMENTAL RIGHTS PROTECTION AT EUROPEAN LEVEL

In Europe, two major organisations were created around 1950, the Council of Europe and what was to become the EU. These two organisations shared a dual purpose: they sought to contribute to the maintenance of peaceful relations between European States and to promote close integration and cooperation between these States.[1] Yet, their means to achieve these goals were

1 This twofold purpose is reflected in the preamble to the Statute of the Council of Europe (*European Treaty Series No. 1*, 5 May 1949), which provides not only that 'the pursuit of peace based upon justice and international co-operation is vital for the preservation of human society and civilisation' (§2), but also that it is necessary to create an organisation 'which will bring European States into closer association' (§5). These objectives are also echoed in the preambles of the founding Treaties of the European Communities, namely the 1951 Treaty establishing the European Coal and Steel Community, the 1957 Treaty establishing

different.[2] The Council of Europe strives for greater unity and peace among its members 'through the organs of the Council by discussion of questions of common concern and by agreements and common action in economic, social, cultural, scientific, legal and administrative matters and in the maintenance and further realisation of human rights and fundamental freedoms.'[3] The founding Treaties establishing the European Communities pursued these objectives through the medium of economic integration, primarily by the establishment of a common market;[4] fundamental rights were largely absent from the original EU edifice.

This initial silence of the Community Treaties has left many observers puzzled.[5] Given the centrality of fundamental rights in post-war Europe, how could they have been left out of these Treaties? How could the Universal Declaration of Human Rights be signed in 1948 and yet no mention of human rights being made in the Treaty of Rome?[6] The silence of the Community Treaties resulted in a kind of division of labour between

---

the European Economic Community and the 1957 Treaty establishing the European Atomic Energy Community. On the objective of peace, see §1, 3 and 4 of the ECSC Treaty; §8 of the EEC Treaty; §1 of the Euratom Treaty. On the objective of European integration, see §3 of the ESC Treaty; §1 of the EEC Treaty. See also in the same vein, e.g. J. Krommendijk and G. de Vries, 'De wisselwerking tussen het HvJ EU en het EHRM: een hernieuwde liefde?', *SEW*, 2021, p. 561; J. Gerards, 'Non-Discrimination, the European Court of Justice and the European Court of Human Rights: Who Takes the Lead?', in T. Giegerich (ed.), *The European Union as Protector and Promoter of Equality,* Springer, 2020, p. 136; C. Dautricourt, 'A Strasbourg Perspective on the Autonomous Development of Fundament Al Rights in EU a Law: Trends and Implications', *NYU Jean Monnet Working Paper*, 2010, p. 10.

2 For this reason, Quinn has described them as 'twins separated at birth', see G. Quinn, 'The European Union and the Council of Europe on the Issue of Human Rights: Twins Separated at Birth?', *McGill Law Journal*, 2001, pp. 850–874. As observed by Quinn, 'two very different paths towards European integration were pursued from the late 1940s: One path, exemplified by the Council of Europe, sought to avoid the excesses of nation-states and the tendency towards self- destruction. It did so by placing a floor beneath which they would not be allowed to fall. This floor was composed of common European standards of human rights. The other path, pursued by the EEC, represented an altogether different model of integration, one that focussed on taming and harnessing economic forces.' (ibid., pp. 855–856).

3 Article 1 of the Statute of the Council of Europe.

4 Article 2 of the EEC Treaty.

5 E.g. A. Bailleux and J. Van Meerbeeck, 'Droits de l'homme, droit pénal et droit communautaire à Luxembourg : Enjeux, difficultés et paradoxes d'un ménage à trois', in Y. Cartuyvels, H. Dumont, F. Ost, M. Van de Kerchove and S. Van Drooghenbroeck (eds.), *Les droits de l'homme, bouclier ou épée du droit pénal?*, Brussels, FUSL, 2007, pp. 114 and following: the authors pointed out that the lack of any reference to fundamental rights in the EEC Treaty was 'one of the greatest mysteries' in the history of European integration.

6 This is even more so as fundamental rights were a keystone of European political regimes after the Second World War. These rights were seen as a *sine qua non* for not reliving the horrors of war, and for building a long-lasting peace on the European continent. At the state level, their protection has been a common feature of the constitutions of all European countries which have experienced authoritarian regimes. See in this vein, F. Fabbrini, *Fundamental Rights in Europe. Challenges and Transformations in Comparative Perspective*, Oxford, Oxford University Press, 2014, p. 7.

a Europe of values, represented by the Council of Europe, and a Europe of economic integration, represented by the EU. Although the centrality of fundamental rights within the Council of Europe framework may have contributed to their absence in the Community Treaties,[7] the protection of fundamental rights was envisaged as a cornerstone of the EU's architecture when the draft Treaty establishing the EPC was under preparation.[8] The latter was abandoned when in 1954, the French National Assembly decided to postpone the ratification of the Treaty establishing the European Defence Community. Afterwards, the approach towards European integration changed and the protection of fundamental rights was no more conceived as a pillar of the EU edifice.

Before turning to the emergence of fundamental rights in EU law, let us have a look back at the intense period in the early 1950s during which fundamental rights were placed at the heart of the EU's architecture. Not only does this retrospective approach highlight that fundamental rights were side-lined in the early EU project, but it shows that the idea of giving a significant role to the ECHR within the EU legal framework dates back to the beginning of the EU's history. The ECHR was developed under the framework of the Council of Europe, where fundamental rights have occupied a central place from the outset.

§ 1. THE LACK OF FUNDAMENTAL RIGHTS PROTECTION UNDER THE EU FRAMEWORK

Looking back in time, the protection of fundamental rights figured prominently in the works of the Study Committee for the European Constitution ('SCEC') and the Ad Hoc Assembly with a view to establishing the EPC. However, fundamental rights were not included in the Community Treaties following the absence of ratification of the Treaty establishing the EPC. Despite this lack of reference to fundamental rights, some traces of fundamental rights could be found along two axes: equality and freedom.

---

7 In this vein, e.g. S. Douglas-Scott, 'The European Union and Human Rights after the Treaty of Lisbon', *Human Rights Law Review*, 2011, p. 648; J. Murray, 'The Influence of the European Convention on Fundamental Rights on Community Law', *Fordham International Law Journal*, 2011, p. 1393; L. Pech and X. Groussot, 'Fundamental Rights Protection in the EU Post Lisbon Treaty', *Foundation Robert Schuman Policy Paper*, 2010, p. 1.

8 G. de Búrca, 'The Road Not Taken: The European Union as a Global Human Rights Actor', *American Journal of International Law*, 2011, pp. 649–693.

I. Aborted Attempts of Fundamental Rights Protection

Two drafting exercises took place with a view to establishing the EPC from 1951 to 1953. The first one consisted of the Resolutions produced by the SCEC.[9] The second one, which drew substantially on the first, was the draft EPC Treaty drawn up by the Ad Hoc Assembly that had been set up with the mission of drafting this Treaty.[10]

Fundamental rights were central in the works of the SCEC and the Ad Hoc Assembly.[11] Both works envisaged entrusting the EPC with a strong intervention role regarding the protection of fundamental rights within Member States.[12] The Resolutions of the SCEC envisioned that the Community could intervene in the event of a human rights crisis in a Member State. This could be when it receives a request to do so from a Member State or without the latter's consent.[13] In contrast, the draft EPC Treaty made Community intervention in a Member State facing a fundamental rights emergency contingent on a request for assistance from the State.[14] Whereas the Resolutions of the SCEC targeted the Member States as potential violators of fundamental rights, the draft EPC

---

9 Resolutions adopted by the Study Committee for the European Constitution (Brussels, November 1952). The SCEC was founded by members of the European Movement, a European federalist movement promoting unity and integration in Europe (see on the European Movement, A. Hick, 'V. The European Movement' in W. Lipgens and W. Loth (ed.), *Transnational Organizations of Political Parties and Pressure Groups in the Struggle for European Union, 1945-1950*, De Gruyter, 2020, pp. 319–435), and was charged with the mission of contributing to the drafting of a constitution for a European Political Community. The SCEC was composed of a group of lawyers, scholars, activists. See G. de Búrca, 'The Road Not Taken: The European Union as a Global Human Rights Actor', *American Journal of International Law*, 2011, p. 654.

10 On 10 September 1952, the six Ministers for Foreign Affairs of the European Coal and Steel Community had decided to establish an Ad Hoc Assembly which would be in charge of drafting the EPC Treaty (Resolution adopted on 10 September 1952 at Luxembourg by the six Ministers for Foreign Affairs). This Assembly was composed of the members of the Common Assembly of the European Coal and Steel Community and several co-opted members. The SCEC and the Ad Hoc Assembly had a close relationship and their membership overlapped to some extent. The SCEC and the Ad Hoc Assembly were both chaired by Paul Henri Spaak.

11 In the first of its nine Resolutions, the SCEC declared that the European Community has the aim 'through establishing a closer bond between the said peoples, of guaranteeing the common well-being, existence and external security of the Member States and of protecting the constitutional order, democratic institutions and fundamental freedoms' (Resolutions adopted by the Study Committee for the European Constitution (Brussels, November 1952) (First resolution, §A). In the same vein, Article 2 of the draft EPC Treaty provided that one of the missions and aims of the European Political Community was to contribute towards the protection of human rights and fundamental freedoms in Member States.

12 See G. de Búrca, 'The Road Not Taken: The European Union as a Global Human Rights Actor', *American Journal of International Law*, 2011, pp. 674–676.

13 First Resolution of the SCEC, point 7.

14 Article 104 Draft EPC Treaty.

Treaty also contemplated that the Community institutions would be subject to compliance with fundamental rights.[15]

If there was divergence regarding the mechanisms and their addresses, a common feature was the source of fundamental rights protection. Both documents proposed that it would be the ECHR.[16] Article 3 of the draft EPC Treaty provided that the ECHR and Protocol No. 1 to the ECHR would form 'an integral part' of the Treaty.[17] The CJEU would be seized of any dispute arising from a decision or measure taken by one of the Community institutions which affected the ECHR.[18] Where a dispute arose which involved a question of principle concerning the ECHR, the CJEU was to renounce judgment until this question had been settled by the judicial organs of the ECHR.[19] All in all, the ECHR would hold a prominent position within the EU edifice, and deference to its mechanisms would be shown.

II. *The Silence of the Community Treaties*

These ambitious plans were confronted with a harsh reality. The ratification process of the draft EPC Treaty was abandoned after the French National Assembly did not ratify the EDC Treaty.[20] At the Messina Conference in 1955, the six Member States of the European Coal and Steel Community decided to relaunch the process of European integration, but the chosen path was different.[21] The integration process was pursued in a more cautious and gradual way. Political integration ambitions were replaced by an economic and sectoral approach.[22] In other words, the European project would focus

15 Article 45 Draft EPC Treaty. See also G. de Búrca, 'The Road Not Taken: The European Union as a Global Human Rights Actor', *American Journal of International Law*, 2011, p. 660.

16 Ibid., pp. 676–680. Interestingly, not all ECSC Member States had yet ratified the ECHR, but the use of the ECHR was seen as a means of facilitating the future accession of other countries to the Community (ibid., p. 655).

17 Article 3 Draft EPC Treaty.

18 Article 45(1) Draft EPC Treaty. De Búrca has interpreted this provision as giving individuals a right of action before the CJEU against the Community institutions for violations of the ECHR (G. de Búrca, 'The Road Not Taken: The European Union as a Global Human Rights Actor', American Journal of International Law, 2011, p. 660).

19 Article 45(3) Draft EPC Treaty.

20 G. de Búrca, 'The Road Not Taken: The European Union as a Global Human Rights Actor', *American Journal of International Law*, 2011, p. 662.

21 Resolution adopted by the Foreign Ministers of the ECSC Member States (Messina, 1 to 3 June 1955).

22 The focus on economic integration was made clear in the Resolution adopted at the Messina Conference: 'The Governments of the German Federal Republic, Belgium, France, Italy, Luxembourg and the Netherlands believe the moment has come to go a step further towards the construction of Europe. In their opinion this step should first of all be taken in the economic field. They consider that the further progress must be towards the setting up of a united Europe by the development of common institutions the gradual merging of

on 'a carefully delimited set of economic concerns' rather than pursuing 'an open-ended political agenda'.[23] The decision was taken that any issues not included in the Messina Resolution would be excluded, meaning that fundamental rights would not be addressed during the negotiations of the Community Treaties as they were in the discussions leading to the draft EPC Treaty.[24]

This new strategy led to the adoption of the more circumscribed EEC Treaty and Euratom Treaty, where the emphasis was on sectoral and economic integration. These priorities were reflected in Article 2 EEC Treaty: the Community's mission was to promote a harmonious development of economic activities, a continuous and balanced expansion, greater stability and an accelerated rise in living standards by the establishment of a common market and by the progressive approximation of the economic policies of the Member States.[25] None of the Community Treaties referred to fundamental rights. They did not contain a catalogue of rights, nor did they refer to fundamental rights as an objective to be pursued. Respect for fundamental rights was not set as a condition for membership of the Community Treaties,[26] although Southern

national economies, the creation of a common market, and the gradual harmonization of their social policies.' (Resolution adopted by the Foreign Ministers of the ECSC Member States (Messina, 1 to 3 June 1955)). See also, S. Smismans, 'Fundamental Rights as a Political Myth of the EU: Can the Myth Survive?', in S. Douglas-Scott (ed.), *Research Handbook on EU Law and Human Rights*, Cheltenham, Edward Elgar Publishing, 2017, p. 17; G. de Búrca, 'The Road Not Taken: The European Union as a Global Human Rights Actor', *American Journal of International Law*, 2011, pp. 665–666. Although in the long-term, economic integration was meant to lead to further political integration (A. Perez, *Conflicts of Rights in the European Union: A Theory of Supranational Adjudication*, Oxford, Oxford University Press, 2009, p. 2). And it was foreseeable that deeper political integration would lead to the emergence of a regime of protection of fundamental rights (G. Quinn, 'The European Union and the Council of Europe on the Issue of Human Rights: Twins Separated at Birth?', *McGill Law Journal*, 2001, p. 870).

23 G. de Búrca, 'The Road Not Taken: The European Union as a Global Human Rights Actor', *American Journal of International Law*, 2011, p. 652.

24 However, no decision was taken as such to exclude any reference to or role for fundamental rights in the envisaged framework (G. de Búrca, ibid., p. 664). It is notable that the idea of including fundamental rights in the Community Treaties were raised during their negotiations. Specifically, the German delegation supported the insertion in the EEC Treaty of a provision that would ensure the protection of individuals against the action of the Communities (G. de Búrca, ibid., p. 665). However, this proposal was rejected due to concerns that Member States would invoke such a provision to limit Community action on the basis of their constitutional requirements, which could ultimately jeopardise Community objectives and the unity of Community law (G. de Búrca, ibid.; M. Zuleeg, 'Fundamental Rights and the Law of the European Communities', *Common Market Law Review*, 1971, pp. 446–447).

25 Article 2(1) EEC Treaty.

26 S. Smismans, 'Fundamental Rights as a Political Myth of the EU: Can the Myth Survive?', in S. Douglas-Scott (ed.), *Research Handbook on EU Law and Human Rights*, Cheltenham, Edward Elgar Publishing, 2017, p. 17.

European countries could de facto not be candidates so long as they were under the control of dictatorial regimes.[27]

III. The Limited Traces of Fundamental Rights

The lack of reference to fundamental rights does not mean that these rights were foreign to the Community Treaties. They contained some traces of fundamental rights, although they were not conceived as such at the time,[28] along two axes: equality and freedom.[29] The Community Treaties contained a wide range of equality and non-discrimination provisions, yet they were not driven by the protection of fundamental rights.[30] Next, the EEC Treaty included 'fundamental' freedoms among which the freedom of movement of goods,[31] the freedom of workers to seek employment in another Member State,[32] the freedom of establishment,[33] the freedom to provide services,[34] and the free movement of capital.[35] The EEC Treaty enshrined the principle of freedom of competition, which implied the prohibition of agreements between companies and the prohibition of abuse of dominant positions.[36] While these freedoms could be seen as the expression of a philosophy of free development of the human person,[37] they were designed as an instrument to achieve the common market.[38] Both the equality and freedom strands of the Community Treaties were driven by economic concerns rather than by a commitment to improving the fundamental rights of individuals.[39]

---

27 C. Leconte and E. Muir, 'Understanding Resistance to the EU Fundamental Rights Policy', *Human Rights Review*, 2014, p. 17.

28 G. Quinn, 'The European Union and the Council of Europe on the Issue of Human Rights: Twins Separated at Birth?', *McGill Law Journal*, 2001, p. 860.

29 See in this vein, P. Pescatore, 'Fundamental rights and freedoms in the system of the European communities', *American Journal of Comparative Law*, 1970, p. 349.

30 See further in Part III (case study on equality), Chapter 2, Section II, §1, I. Fundamental v. Economic.

31 Articles 9 to 39 EEC Treaty.

32 Articles 48 to 51 EEC Treaty.

33 Articles 52 to 58 EEC Treaty.

34 Articles 59 to 66 EEC Treaty.

35 Articles 67 to 73 EEC Treaty.

36 Article 65 to 67 EEC Treaty.

37 P. Pescatore, 'Fundamental rights and freedoms in the system of the European communities', *American Journal of Comparative Law*, 1970, p. 349.

38 O. De Schutter, 'Les droits fondamentaux dans le projet europeen. Des limites à l'action. Des institutions à une politique des droits fondamentaux', in O. De Schutter and P. Nihoul (eds.), *Une Constitution Pour l'Europe. Réflexions sur les transformations du droit de l'Union Européenne*, Brussels, Larcier, 2004, pp. 81–82; G. Quinn, 'The European Union and the Council of Europe on the Issue of Human Rights: Twins Separated at Birth?', *McGill Law Journal*, 2001, p. 859.

39 See more generally on the market based approach to fundamental rights in the EU, e.g. S. Douglas-Scott, 'The European Union and Human Rights after the Treaty of Lisbon', *Human Rights Law Review*, p. 679: 'fundamental rights have functioned epiphenomenally in

In a nutshell, despite the high ambitions at the beginning of the early 1950s, fundamental rights occupied a limited place in the initial EU design. This state of affairs persisted until, at the turn of the 1970s, the CJEU incorporated them as general principles of EU law. The situation at Community level contrasted with the early developments at the level of the Council of Europe. From its inception, the latter anchored fundamental rights at the core of its mission; it is under its auspices that the ECHR came to life. However, the ECHR enforcement machinery was initially restrained.

§ 2. THE PARALLEL DEVELOPMENTS UNDER THE AUSPICES OF THE COUNCIL OF EUROPE

Set in the post-war context, the Council of Europe aims to achieve greater unity between its members by means of agreements and common action in the maintenance and further realisation of human rights and fundamental freedoms.[40] Fundamental rights had a central place in the Council of Europe framework from the outset.[41] More than two hundred conventions have been developed under its framework, including the 1981 Data Protection Convention,[42] the 1995 Framework Convention for the Protection of National Minorities,[43] and the 2011 Istanbul Convention on preventing and combating violence against women and domestic violence.[44]

The most prominent instrument developed under the auspices of the Council of Europe is the ECHR.[45] It has been portrayed as 'almost as a constitutive document of a European federation, a sort of Magna Carta of European political union'[46] and viewed as the 'world's most successful system

the EU, an offshoot of the EU's more central, market led functions.' See also, E. Spaventa, 'Should We "Harmonize" Fundamental Rights in the EU? Some Reflections About Minimum Standards and Fundamental Rights Protection in the EU Composite Constitutional System', *Common Market Law Review*, 2009, p. 1000: '[F]undamental rights have never been entirely absent from the E(E)C/EU discourse but, generally, they have also been instrumental to achieving the internal market.'

40 Article 1(2) Statute of the Council of Europe.

41 Article 3 of the Statute of the Council of Europe states that: 'Every member of the Council of Europe must accept the principles of the rule of law and of the enjoyment by all persons within its jurisdiction of human rights and fundamental freedoms.'

42 Convention for the Protection of Individuals with regard to Automatic Processing of Personal Data, *European Treaty series No. 108*, 28 January 1981.

43 Framework Convention for the Protection of National Minorities, *European Treaty Series No. 157,* 1 February 1995.

44 Convention on preventing and combating violence against women and domestic violence, *European Treaty series No. 210*, 11 May 2011.

45 European Convention for the Protection of Human Rights and Fundamental Freedoms, *European Treaty Series No. 5*, 4 November 1950.

46 R. Beddard, *Human rights and Europe,* Cambridge, Cambridge University Press, 1993, p. 34.

of international law for the protection of human rights'.[47] The ECHR stood out not so much for its catalogue of rights but rather for its system of collective enforcement.[48] The ECHR's core objective was to establish mechanisms beyond state level that could assess whether a State violated the ECHR.[49] In doing so, the Convention sought to 'take the first steps for the collective enforcement of certain of the rights stated in the Universal Declaration'.[50]

If the ECHR became the first translation of the Universal Declaration into a legally binding instrument, individuals had initially limited access to the ECtHR. They had a right of petition before the European Commission on Human Rights.[51] This right was subject to a declaration of recognition of competence[52] and the exhaustion of all domestic remedies.[53] When these conditions were met, the European Commission on Human Rights had to secure a friendly settlement between the parties[54] and, failing such a settlement, draw up a report on the basis of which the Committee of Ministers would decide whether the ECHR had been violated.[55] The ECtHR was only competent when the States or the Commission on Human Rights referred to it.[56] This situation changed with Protocol No. 11 ECHR

---

47 J.P. Flaherty and M.E. Lally-Green, *Fundamental Rights in the European Union*, *Duquesne Law Review*, 1998, p. 249.

48 Preamble, para. 5 ECHR.

49 The establishment of collective enforcement mechanisms was driven by the experience of war, which revealed that the protection of fundamental rights at States level alone could be insufficient. See e.g. F. Fabbrini, *Fundamental Rights in Europe. Challenges and Transformations in Comparative Perspective*, Oxford, Oxford University Press, 2014, p. 13; A. Perez, *Conflicts of Rights in the European Union: A Theory of Supranational Adjudication*, Oxford, Oxford University Press, 2009, p. 28; G. Quinn, 'The European Union and the Council of Europe on the Issue of Human Rights: Twins Separated at Birth?', *McGill Law Journal*, 2001, p. 853. As noted by Fabbrini: 'The memory of the tragedies of the 20th century had made crystal clear to Europe's political elites that the protection of fundamental rights could not be confined solely to the states and that additional norms and institutions beyond the state were necessary to ensure liberty and peace in the European continent.'

50 Preamble, para. 5 ECHR. See e.g. J. Costa, 'On the Legitimacy of the European Court of Human Rights' Judgments', *European Constitutional Law Review*, 201 , p. 177: 'The Convention was drafted as the concrete expression of European states' commitment to rendering some of the provisions of the Declaration effective.' The ECtHR's catalogue of rights was more restricted than the Universal Declaration, since the former contains essentially rights of civil and political nature (see in this vein, N. Jääskinen, 'The Place of the EU Charter within the Tradition of Fundamental and Human Rights', in S. Morano-Foadi and L. Vickers (eds.), *Fundamental Rights in the EU: A Matter for Two Courts*, Oxford, Hart Publishing, 2015, p. 15; J. Murray, 'The Influence of the European Convention on Fundamental Rights on Community Law', *Fordham International Law Journal*, 2011, p. 1391).

51 Article 25 ECHR (original text).

52 Article 25(1) ECHR (original text).

53 Article 26 ECHR (original text).

54 Article 28(b) ECHR (original text).

55 Articles 31 and 32 ECHR (original text). The decisions of the Committee of Ministers were binding (Articles 32(4) ECHR (original text)).

56 Articles 45 and 48 ECHR (original text).

(entered into force in 1998) which made the right of individual application mandatory and ensured that all allegations by individuals were addressed to the ECtHR.[57]

SECTION II. THE BIRTH OF THE PROTECTION OF FUNDAMENTAL RIGHTS AT EU LEVEL

Fundamental rights were not at the forefront of the EU's initial architecture, whereas there were significant developments under the auspices of the Council of Europe. The quasi-silence of the Community Treaties was originally not perceived as a major problem: it was not straightforward to see how the freshly created Community institutions, whose functions were in the economic field, could interfere with fundamental rights.[58] Yet, as early as the 1950s, claimants invoked these rights to contest measures adopted by the Community

---

57 See on Protocol No. 11, e.g. A. Drzemczewski, 'The European Human Rights Convention: Protocol No. 11-Entry into Force and First Year of Application', *Human Rights Law Journal*, 2000, pp. 357–379; N. Rowe and V. Schlette, 'The Protection of Human Rights in Europe and the Eleventh Protocol to the ECHR', *European Law Review*, 1998, pp. 3–16. The European Commission on Human Rights and the European Court of Human Rights were replaced by a new permanent European Court of Human Rights. Article 34 of the ECHR provides that the ECtHR may receive applications from any person, nongovernmental organisation or group of individuals claiming to be the victim of a violation by one of the Parties of the ECHR rights. If following an individual application, the ECtHR finds that a Contracting State has breached ECHR rights, that ruling is binding on this State (Article 46 ECHR).

58 E.g. J.-P. Jacqué, 'La charte des droits fondamentaux et le législateur de l'Union', in P. Iliopoulou and L. Xenou (eds.), *La Charte des droits fondamentaux, source de renouveau constitutionnel européen?*, Brussels, Bruylant, 2020, p. 139; G. Quinn, 'The European Union and the Council of Europe on the Issue of Human Rights: Twins Separated at Birth?', *McGill Law Journal*, 2001, p. 862; P. Pescatore, 'Fundamental rights and freedoms in the system of the European communities', *American Journal of Comparative Law*, 1970, p. 344. For instance, Pescatore claimed in 1970 that: 'In fact, one may even wonder how a problem concerning human rights could possibly arise in an organisation whose tasks are mainly of an economic, social, and technical nature. Experience shows that it is in a quite different sphere of public life that problems relating to human rights and fundamental freedoms normally arise. It is politics and not economics that constitute a real danger zone in this respect.' See also in this vein the Report of the Commission on the protection of fundamental rights, 4 February 1976, COM/1976/037 final, pp. 9–10: 'The frequently asserted danger of massive infringements of fundamental rights by the Community institutions has at no time materialized This must be attributed, first, to the mechanisms adopted by the Community institutions to prevent any conflict between Community legal acts and fundamental rights recognised in the Community legal order and, secondly, to the limited competence of the Community: *the powers of intervention written into the Treaties can by the very nature of things come into conflict only with a relatively limited number of fundamental rights.* The debate about the deficiency of Community law as far as the protection of fundamental rights is concerned has therefore proved to be, to a considerable extent, hypothetical even though the Community institutions awareness of fundamental rights thereby have been considerably increased' Emphasis added.

institutions. At first, the CJEU rejected these claims. This state of affairs changed when, at the end of the 1960s, the CJEU introduced fundamental rights by means of general principles of EU law.[59]

§ 1. THE INITIAL RELUCTANCE OF THE CJEU

The emergence of EU fundamental rights did not happen from one day to the next. Often portrayed in heroic terms for their advancement, the CJEU was initially reluctant to give them a role in Community law.[60] In the 1950s, economic actors challenged the validity of Community acts by putting forward that they undermined their rights protected under their national constitution.[61] Invited to rule on the applicability of fundamental rights to Community acts, the CJEU took a firm negative stand on several occasions

Starting with the *Stork* (1959) judgment, the CJEU rejected that national law could be used as a ground of review for Community law.[62] A German company had sought to overturn a decision of the High Authority of the ECSC and invoked several provisions of the German Basic Law, which guaranteed the free development of the human personality and the free choice of a professional activity.[63] Confronted with this argument, the CJEU replied that the High Authority was not competent to apply the national law of the Member States and that it could itself not rule on the provisions of national law.[64] As a consequence, the High Authority was 'not empowered to examine a ground of complain which maintains that, when it adopted its decision, it infringed principles of German Constitutional Law'.[65]

59 See on the early development of fundamental rights by the CJEU, e.g. J. Weiler, 'Eurocracy and Distrust: Some Questions Concerning the Role of the European Court of Justice in the Protection of Fundamental Human Rights within the Legal Order of the European Communities', *Washington Law Review*, 1986, pp. 1103–1142; A. Drzemczewski, 'Fundamental Rights and the European Communities: Recent Developments', *The Human Rights Review*, 1977, pp. 69–86; P. Pescatore, ibid., pp. 343–351.

60 G. de Búrca, 'The Road Not Taken: The European Union as a Global Human Rights Actor', *American Journal of International Law*, 2011, p. 650.

61 See e.g. S. Smismans, 'Fundamental Rights as a Political Myth of the EU: Can the Myth Survive?', in S. Douglas-Scott (ed.), *Research Handbook on EU Law and Human Rights*, Edward Elgar Publishing, 2017, p. 18; R. Schutze, 'Three "Bills of Rights" for the European Union', *Yearbook of European Law*, 2011,vol 30, pp. 133–134; P. Pescatore, 'Fundamental rights and freedoms in the system of the European communities', *American Journal of Comparative Law*, 1970, pp. 344–345.

62 Case C-1/58, *Stork*, ECLI:EU:C:1959:4.

63 Ibid., para. 23.

64 Ibid., para. 4, 26.

65 Ibid.

The exclusion of national fundamental rights as ground for review was reiterated in the *Geitling* (1960) judgment, which again involved a decision of the High Authority of the ECSC which was contested on the basis of the German Basic Law.[66] The CJEU held that it was not required to assess the legality of the High Authority decisions in light of national law, and this even if the rules at stake were of constitutional nature.[67] The CJEU also mentioned that: 'Community Law, as it arises under the ECSC Treaty, does not contain any general principle, express or otherwise, guaranteeing the maintenance of vested rights'.[68] In the *Sgarlata* (1965) judgment, the CJEU objected that provisions of the EEC Treaty could be overridden by 'fundamental principles governing all the Member States'.[69] All in all, regardless of their domestic or EU origins, the CJEU declined to assess Community measures in light of fundamental rights.

§ 2. THE DISCOVERY OF FUNDAMENTAL RIGHTS AS GENERAL PRINCIPLES

We had to wait a few years before the CJEU recognised fundamental rights as general principles of EU law in *Stauder* (1969).[70] Whereas the above cases originated from applications made by economic actors, the *Stauder* case was brought by a social benefit recipient. The latter challenged a requirement stemming from a decision of the Commission of the European Communities which allegedly made the sale of butter at reduced prices to certain beneficiaries subject to the condition that their names were disclosed to retailers.[71] The referring court did not ask whether the requirement was in line with national law, but whether it was compatible with the general principles of EU law.[72] After having found that Community law did not require the identification of beneficiaries by name,[73] the CJEU held, in probably one of its most important *obiter dicta*, that:

> Interpreted in this way the provision at issue contains nothing capable of prejudicing the fundamental human rights enshrined in the general principles of EU law and protected by the Court.[74]

---

66 Joined Cases C-36, 37, 38–59 and 40–59, *Geitling*, ECLI:EU:C:1960:36.
67 Ibid., para. 438.
68 Ibid., para. 439.
69 Case C-40/64, *Sgarlata*, ECLI:EU:C:1965:36, para. 227.
70 Case C-29/69, *Stauder*, ECLI:EU:C:1969:57.
71 Ibid., para. 1.
72 Ibid.
73 Ibid., para. 6.
74 Ibid., para. 7.

Also advocated by the Advocate General in the *Geitling* case[75] and the then President of the European Commission,[76] this finding marked a key step for the advancement of fundamental rights in EU law. The CJEU asserted that fundamental rights were protected as general principles of EU law and that it would act as its guardian. Including fundamental rights in the EU legal order has been described as a 'perfect example of intense judicial activity',[77] and even as judicial activism.[78] But how to understand this Copernican revolution?[79]

This (r)evolution is best understood against the backdrop of other judicial developments in the mid-1960s.[80] At that time, the CJEU developed the doctrines of direct effect[81] and primacy of EU law.[82] Their emergence was intensely debated by some national constitutional courts. The German and Italian Constitutional Courts expressed concerns that the primacy of EU law could undermine the protection of fundamental rights guaranteed under their domestic system. They declared themselves competent to review the

---

75 Opinion of Advocate General Lagrange of 24 May 1960 in Joined Cases C-36, 37, 38–59 and 40–59, *Geitling*, 15 July 1960, ECLI:EU:C:1960:36, para. 450: [While] it is not for the Court, whose function it is to judge the legality of the authorizations, to apply, or at least to do so directly rules of national law, even constitutional rules, in force in one or other of the Member States. It may allow itself to be influenced by such rules in so far as, where appropriate, it may see in them the expression of a general principle of law which may be taken into consideration in applying the Treaty.'

76 G. de Búrca, 'The Road Not Taken: The European Union as a Global Human Rights Actor', *American Journal of International Law*, 2011, p. 668, fn. 94 This approach was also advocated by the Judge Pescatore (P. Pescatore, 'Les droits de l'Homme et l'intégration européenne', *Cahiers de droit européen*, 1968, pp. 629–673).

77 E. Muir, *EU Equality Law, The First Fundamental Rights Policy of the EU*, Oxford, Oxford University Press, 2018, p. 67.

78 J. Wouters and M. Ovadek, *The European Union and Human Rights. Analysis, Cases, and Materials*, Oxford, 2021, p. 94. Wouters and Ovadek also put forward that there was a lack of resistance by Member States regarding this 'judicial activism' for several reasons: 'First, the process of European integration was market driven, and, in this context, fundamental rights protection was not a main concern. The main goal of the three foundational European Communities was economic integration in specific fields. Secondly, EU rights, at the beginning, were not incorporated against the states but were only binding on EU institutions.'

79 This expression is borrowed from S. Smismans, 'Fundamental Rights as a Political Myth of the EU: Can the Myth Survive?', in S. Douglas-Scott (ed.), *Research Handbook on EU Law and Human Rights*, Cheltenham, Edward Elgar Publishing, 2017, p. 19.

80 E.g. T. Tridimas, 'Fundamental Rights, General Principles of EU Law, and the Charter', *Cambridge Yearbook of European Legal Studies*, 2014, p. 362; J. Wetzel, 'Improving Fundamental Rights Protection in the European Union: Resolving the Conflict and Confusion Between the Luxembourg and Strasbourg Courts', *Fordham Law Review*, 2003, p. 2823; M. Zuleeg, 'Fundamental Rights and the Law of the European Communities', *Common Market Law Review*, 1971, pp. 447–448.

81 Case C-26/62, *Van Gend & Loos*, ECLI:EU:C:1963:1.

82 Case C-6/64, *Costa v. Enel*, ECLI:EU:C:1964:66.

conformity of EU law with their constitutional norms.[83] This is emblemised by *Solange I* (1974), where the German Constitutional Court held that it was entitled to rule on the validity of Community acts as long as the Community lacked a catalogue of fundamental rights and a directly elected parliament with proper legislative powers.[84]

Through its incorporation of fundamental rights, the CJEU sought to guarantee the primacy and integrity of Union law by making sure that national courts would not assess the conformity of EU acts with national laws.[85] As

---

83 As early as 1965, the Italian Constitutional Court set a condition of respect for the fundamental rights of the Italian Constitution (Italian Constitutional Court, *San Michele*, 16 December 1965, n° 98/65). The approach of the Italian Constitutional Court was developed in the 1973 *Frontini* case (Italian Constitutional Court, *Frontini*, 27 December 1973, n° 183/73). See about the approach of the Italian Constitutional Court, e.g. M. Claes, *The National Courts' Mandate in the European Constitution*, Oxford, Hart Publishing, 2006, p. 502; G. Bebr, 'A Critical Review of Recent Case-law of National Courts', *Common Market Law Review*, 1974, pp. 408–431. As regards Germany, Dubout observes that as early as 1968, the Federal Financial Court had already recognised its competence to verify the compatibility of a Community regulation with the fundamental rights protected by the Basic Law (see E. Dubout, *Droit constitutionnel de l'Union européenne*, Brussels, Bruylant, 2021, pp. 393 and references). The particular concern of the German and Italian Constitutional Courts to safeguard their national constitutional rights has been explained by the fact that fundamental rights are the subject of litigation in these States (P. Pescatore, 'Fundamental rights and freedoms in the system of the European communities', *American Journal of Comparative Law*, 1970, p. 344) and the importance of fundamental rights in their post-war constitutional regimes (E. Dubout, *Droit Constitutionnel de l'Union Européenne*, Brussels, Bruylant, 2021, pp. 390–391; M. Zuleeg, 'Fundamental Rights and the Law of the European Communities', *Common Market Law Review*, 1971, p. 448). See also on the reactions of the national Constitutional Courts, e.g. S. Smismans, 'Fundamental Rights as a Political Myth of the EU: Can the Myth Survive?', in S. Douglas-Scott (ed.), *Research Handbook on EU Law and Human Rights*, Edward Elgar Publishing, 2017, p. 19; D. Sarmiento, 'Who's Afraid of the Charter? The Court of Justice, National Courts and the New Framework of Fundamental Rights Protection in Europe', *Common Market Law Review*, 2013, p. 1269; R. Lawson, 'Confusion and Conflict? Divergent Interpretations of the ECHR in Strasbourg and Luxembourg', in R. Lawson and M. de Blois (eds.), *The Dynamics of the Protection of Human Rights in Europe*, Nijhoff, 1994, p. 222; U. Scheuner, 'Fundamental Rights in European Community Law and in National Constitutional Law', *Common Market Law Review*, 1975, pp. 171–191.

84 German Constitutional Court, *Solange I*, 29 May 1974, 37, 271 2 BvL 52/71. See for contemporary comments of this judgment, e.g. J. Darras and O. Pirotte, 'La Cour constitutionnelle fédérale allemande a-t-elle mis en danger la primauté du droit communautaire?', *Revue trimestrielle de droit européen*, 1976, pp. 415–438; C.-D. Ehlermann, 'Primauté du droit communautaire mise en cause par la Cour constitutionnelle fédérale allemande', *R.M.C.*, 1975, p. 10.

85 E.g. E. Dubout, *Droit constitutionnel de l'Union européenne*, Brussels, Bruylant, 2021, p. 389; T. Tridimas, 'Fundamental Rights, General Principles of EU Law, and the Charter', *Cambridge Yearbook of European Legal Studies*, 2014, p. 362; F. Hendrickx, 'Fundamental rights in the EU', R. Blanpain, M. Colucci, E. De Smijter, C. Engels, F. Hendrickx and L. Salas (eds.), *Institutional Changes and European Social Policies after the Treaty of Amsterdam*, The Hague, Kluwer, 1999, pp. 162–165; R. Lawson, 'Confusion and Conflict? Divergent Interpretations of the ECHR in Strasbourg and Luxembourg', in R. Lawson and M. de Blois (eds.), *The Dynamics of the Protection of Human Rights in Europe*, Dordrecht,

previous Judge to the CJEU Mancini has explained, '[r]eading an unwritten Bill of Rights into Community law is indeed the most striking contribution the Court has made to the development of a constitution for Europe'. Yet, 'this statement was forced on the Court by the outside, by the German and, later, the Italian constitutional courts.'[86] If the incorporation of fundamental rights into the EU legal order entailed a positive dimension, in that it contributed to the development of a human rights culture in Europe, it was a rather defensive undertaking.[87] As general principles, fundamental rights fulfilled a negative function. The CJEU introduced them as limits to the Community actions but not as objectives which the Communities should pursue.[88] Fundamental rights were first addressed to the EU institutions[89] and gradually introduced them vis-à-vis EU States.[90] EU fundamental rights would be binding on these States

Nijhoff, 1994, p. 222; J. Weiler, 'Methods of Protection: Towards a Second and Third Generation of Protection', in A. Cassese et al. (ed.), *Human Rights and the European Community: Methods of Protection*, Baden-Baden, Nomos, 1991, p. 581. This strategy was crowned with success since the German Constitutional Court revisited its case-law (German Constitutional Court, *Solange II*, 22 October 1986, 339 2 BvR 197/83). In this ruling, the latter court held that it will no longer review EU law in the light of the fundamental rights contained in the German Basic Law *so long as* the European communities provide effective protection of fundamental rights that is substantially similar to the protection of fundamental rights in the German Basic Law.

86 F. Mancini, 'The Making of a Constitution for Europe', *Common Market Law Review*, 1989, p. 595.

87 See F. Fabrinni, *Fundamental Rights in Europe. Challenges and Transformations in Comparative Perspective*, Oxford, Oxford University Press, 2014, p. 10 and references.

88 O. De Schutter, 'Fundamental Rights and the Transformation of Governance in the European Union', *Cambridge Yearbook of European Legal Studies*, 2007, p. 137.

89 In this way, the transfer of powers to the EU institutions was offset by a guarantee that the exercise of such powers would not undermine fundamental rights, see E. Dubout, *Droit constitutionnel de l'Union européenne*, Brussels, Bruylant, 2021, pp. 425–426.

90 See for early comments on this development, e.g. J. Weiler, 'The European Court at a Crossroads: Community Human Rights and Member State Action', in P. Pescatore and F. Capotorti (eds.), *Du droit international au droit de l'intégration. Liber amicorum Pierre Pescatore*, Baden-Baden, Nomos, 1987, pp. 821–842; K. Lenaerts, 'Le respect des droits fondamentaux en tant que principe constitutionnel de l'Union européenne', in M. Dony and A. de Walsche (eds.), *Mélanges en hommage à Michel Waelbroeck*, Brussels, Bruylant, 1999, pp. 423–457. The CJEU has made clear that it was no competent to examine the compatibility of national rules which do not fall within the scope of EU law (e.g. Case C-12/86, *Demirel*, 30 September 1987, ECLI:EU:C:1987:400, para. 28). It is also worth noting that the evolution of the scope of fundamental rights regarding States has been somewhat different in the EU and the United States. Whereas in the United States most of the rights as contained in the federal Bill of Rights have become binding on all State actions through the Supreme Court's broad interpretation of the Due Process Clause, EU fundamental rights have been – and still are – confined to a limited number of actions by Member States (O. Scarcello, *Contestatory Federalism and Rights: Resisting Incorporation in the US, Canada, and the EU*, Oxford, Oxford University Press, forthcoming; A. Perez, *Conflicts of Rights in the European Union: A Theory of Supranational Adjudication*, Oxford, Oxford University Press, 2009, p. 35).

when they implement EU law ('the *Wachauf* hypothesis')[91] or derogate from it ('the *ERT* hypothesis').[92]

SECTION III. THE JUDICIALLY-DRIVEN AND ECHR-INFUSED EU REGIME

The EU fundamental rights regime thus came into being. Although specific to the EU legal order, the EU regime was heavily influenced by ECHR law. EU fundamental rights mirrored, to a large extent, the standards developed in the Convention and ECtHR case-law. The EU fundamental rights regime was judicially-driven and outward-looking. In the absence of support within primary and secondary laws, the CJEU relied on several sources to shape its fundamental rights case-law. Among these sources, it accorded special significance to ECHR law. This state of affairs was not altered by the EU political institutions; on the contrary, they endorsed the development of the judicially-driven and ECHR-infused regime.

---

91 Case C-5/88, *Wachauf*, 13 July 1989, ECLI:EU:C:1989:321, para. 19. This approach was suggested by the Advocate General, see Opinion of Advocat General Jacobs of 27 April 1989 in Case C-5/88, *Wachauf*, 13 July 1989, ECLI:EU:C:1989:179, para. 22: 'Although the Court' s case-law has hitherto been concerned with respect for property rights by the Community legislator itself, the same principles must in my view apply to the implementation of Community law by the Member States, since it appears to me self-evident that when acting in pursuance of powers granted under Community law, Member States must be subject to the same constraints, in any event in relation to the principle of respect for fundamental rights, as the Community legislator.' The rationale for this doctrine has been that in such a situation, Member States act as agents of the EU and must therefore be bound by EU standards (e.g. E. Spaventa, 'Federalisation versus centralisation: tensions in fundamental rights discourse in the EU', in M. Dougan and S. Currie (eds.), *50 Years of the European treaties: looking back and thinking forward*, Oxford, Hart Publishing, p. 348).

92 Case C-260/89, *ERT*, 18 June 1991, ECLI:EU:C:1991:254, paras. 41–45. More generally in the *ERT* case, the CJEU asserted that 'it has no power to examine the compatibility with the European Convention on Human Rights of national rules which do not fall within the scope of Community law' (para. 42). By contrast, 'where such rules *do fall within the scope of Community law*, and reference is made to the Court for a preliminary ruling, it must provide all the criteria of interpretation needed by the national court to determine whether those rules are compatible with the fundamental rights the observance of which the Court ensures and which derive in particular from the European Convention on Human Rights.' (emphasis added, ibid.) The rationale for the *ERT* hypothesis has been more contested and we defer to the rich literature on the subject (e.g. J.H.H. Weiler, 'Fundamental Rights and Fundamental Boundaries: Common Standards and Conflicting Values in the Protection of Human Rights in the European Legal Space', in R. Kastoryano (ed.), *An Identity for Europe. The Sciences Po Series in International Relations and Political Economy*, Palgrave New York, Macmillan, pp. 91–94).

§ 1. A JUDICIALLY-DRIVEN AND OUTWARD-LOOKING REGIME

The use of general principles as the channel to integrate fundamental rights within EU law was a consequential decision. First, EU fundamental rights would be the 'creature of judicial law-making', which the CJEU would have to develop.[93] Second, the CJEU granted them a Community foundation which meant that these rights would be distinct from national or international fundamental rights[94] and that they could be adapted to the specificities of the European construction.[95] Third, the protection of fundamental rights would evolve in an ad hoc and case-by-case manner, thereby creating potential issues of legal certainty and foreseeability.[96] Lacking textual support in the EU Treaties, the CJEU began to draw on several sources to develop EU fundamental rights. While the CJEU developed rights that were specific to the Union, they became infused with standards enshrined in the common constitutional traditions to the Member States and international fundamental rights instruments.[97]

---

93 The expression is borrowed from K. LENAERTS and J. GUTIÉRREZ-FONS, 'The Place Charter in the EU Constitutional Edifice', in S. PEERS, T. HERVEY, J. KENNER and A. WARD (ed.), *The EU Charter of Fundamental Rights: A Commentary*, Oxford, Hart Publishing, 2014, p. 1559.

94 In this vein, e.g. D. DERO-BUGNY, *Les rapports entre la Cour de justice de l'Union européenne et La Cour européenne des droits de l'Homme*, Brussels, Bruylant, 2015, p. 50. R. SCHUTZE, 'Three "Bills of Rights" for the European Union', *Yearbook of European Law*, 2011, p. 136; G. HARPAZ, 'The European Court Of Justice And Its Relations With The European Court Of Human Rights: The Quest For Enhanced Reliance, Coherence And Legitimacy', *Common Market Law Review*, 2009, p. 107.

95 D. DERO-BUGNY, ibid., p. 50. Already in its *Internationale Handelsgesellschaft* (1970) judgment, to which we shall return, the CJEU stated that the protection of fundamental rights 'must be ensured within the framework of the structure and objectives of the Community' (Case C-11/70, *Internationale Handelsgesellschaft*, ECLI:EU:C:1970:114, para. 4).

96 G. HARPAZ, 'The European Court Of Justice And Its Relations With The European Court Of Human Rights: The Quest For Enhanced Reliance, Coherence And Legitimacy', *Common Market Law Review*, 2009, p. 107; R. LAWSON, 'Confusion and Conflict? Divergent Interpretations of the ECHR in Strasbourg and Luxembourg', in R. LAWSON and M. DE BLOIJS (eds.), *The Dynamics of the Protection of Human Rights in Europe*, Dordrecht, Nijhoff, 1994, p. 228. In its 1979 Memorandum on the accession to the ECHR, the Commission stated that one of the shortcomings affecting the legal order of the Communities through the lack of a written catalogue of fundamental rights is 'the impossibility of knowing in advance which are the liberties which may not be infringed by the Community Institutions under any circumstances.' (Commission, *Memorandum on the accession of the European Communities to the Convention for the protection of Human Rights and Fundamental Freedoms*, COM(79) 210 final, 2 May 1979, p. 6). This is one of the reasons why the Commission proposed accession to the ECHR. According to the Commission, the ECHR could provide an easily accessible written catalogue of rights, which would satisfy the legitimate interest of European citizens in having their rights vis-à-vis the Communities laid down in advance (ibid.).

97 As noted by Besselink, '[a]lthough the CJEU was ostensibly motivated to this incorporation to guarantee the autonomy of the EU legal order which would be threatened by continuous appeals to rights as protected in Member States, this does not diminish the *heteronomy*

The CJEU referred to the common constitutional traditions as a source of inspiration in *Internationale Handelsgesellschaft* (1970). In its preliminary question, the referring court claimed that a deposit system established by Community law was contrary to the German Basic Law and that the latter should take precedence over Community law. The CJEU held that the validity of Community measures 'cannot be affected by allegations that it runs counter to either fundamental rights as formulated by the Constitution of that State or the principle of a national constitutional structure.'[98] Yet, the CJEU stressed that 'respect for fundamental rights forms an integral part of the general principles of law protected by the CJEU'[99] and stated that:

> The protection of such rights, whilst inspired by the constitutional traditions common to the Member States, must be ensured within the framework of the structure and objectives of the Community.[100]

This reference served arguably a strategic purpose. States could be reassured that their constitutional systems would be given due weight when the CJEU would develop its fundamental rights jurisprudence.[101] The intention to use the common constitutional traditions has not translated into practice: the CJEU has made limited use of this source.[102] This may be explained by the complexity of identifying a consensus on fundamental rights among the different national traditions and practices.[103] While the idea is appealing, the differences between

---

of the sources thus incorporated into the general principles of Union law' (L. Besselink, 'Introduction to "The Protection of Fundamental Rights post-Lisbon: The Interaction between the EU Charter of Fundamental Rights, the European Convention on Human Rights (ECHR) and National Constitutions" Reports of the XXV FIDE Congress Tallinn 2012', *Volume 1: The Protection of Fundamental Rights Post-Lisbon*, Tallinn, Tartu University Press, 2012, p. 10).

98 Case C-11/70, *Internationale Handelsgesellschaft*, ECLI:EU:C:1970:114, para. 3.

99 Ibid., para. 4.

100 Ibid.

101 A. Perez, *Conflicts of Rights in the European Union: A Theory of Supranational Adjudication*, Oxford, Oxford University Press, 2009, p. 159.

102 E.g. L. Besselink, 'Introduction to "The Protection of Fundamental Rights post-Lisbon: The Interaction between the EU Charter of Fundamental Rights, the European Convention on Human Rights (ECHR) and National Constitutions" Reports of the XXV FIDE Congress Tallinn 2012', *Volume 1: The Protection of Fundamental Rights Post-Lisbon*, Tallinn, Tartu University Press, 2012, p. 3; J. Murray, 'The Influence of the European Convention on Fundamental Rights on Community Law', *Fordham International Law Journal*, 2011, p. 1394; S. Douglas-Scott, 'The European Union and Human Rights after the Treaty of Lisbon', *Human Rights Law Review*, 2011, p. 669; A. Rosas, 'Fundamental Rights in the Luxembourg and Strasbourg Courts', in C. Baudenbacher, P. Tresselt and T. Orlygsson (eds.), *The EFTA Court: Ten Years On*, Oxford, Hart Publishing, 2005, p. 166.

103 S. Douglas-Scott, ibid., p. 670; U. Scheuner, 'Fundamental Rights in European Community Law and in National Constitutional Law', *Common Market Law Review*, 1975, p. 186.

national conceptions of fundamental rights tend to be significant.[104] In addition, the concern of undermining the primacy of EU law by appearing to rely on a national constitutional provision may have contributed to the limited use of the common constitutional traditions.[105] It is worth underlining that the CJEU has rarely explained its method when it considers that a fundamental right is part of the common constitutional traditions.[106] By contrast, some Advocates General have tried to develop a method to assert whether there exists a general principle flowing from the national constitutional traditions.[107] Most of the time, the CJEU did not make a comparative assessment of the national systems when considering that this was the case.[108]

As a matter of fact, the key source of inspiration were international fundamental rights instruments. This source made its appearance in the *Nold* (1974) judgment. The applicant claimed that trading rules authorised by the Commission violated its rights to property and to free pursuit of business activity as protected under the German Constitution, the constitutions of other Member States and various international treaties. After having held that it is bound to draw inspiration from the common constitutional traditions and that it cannot uphold a measure which is incompatible with the fundamental rights protected by the constitutions of the Member States,[109] the CJEU stated that:

> international treaties for the protection of human rights, on which the Member States have collaborated or of which they are signatories, can supply guidelines which should be followed within the framework of Community Law.[110]

---

104 E.g. Douglas-Scott has put forward that: 'The constitutional traditions of the Member States provide a necessarily incoherent source, given the very different constitutional traditions and practices of those States. The result is that the Court of Justice, in analysing those sources, necessarily forms its own subjective opinion as to whether a right is recognised in common throughout the Member States, and, even if it is recognised, whether it is actually protected in the same way. Indeed, Member State constitutional traditions can prove to be a divisive and fragmenting source, rather than a unifying source, for rights' (S. Douglas-Scott, ibid., p. 669).

105 P. Craig and G. de Búrca, *EU Law: Text, Cases and Materials*, Oxford, Oxford University Press, 2020, p. 422.

106 S. Smismans, 'Fundamental Rights as a Political Myth of the EU: Can the Myth Survive?', in S. Douglas-Scott (ed.), *Research Handbook on EU Law and Human Rights*, Cheltenham, Edward Elgar Publishing, 2017, p. 20.

107 See the Opinion of Advocate General Kokott of 29 April 2010 in Case C-550/07 P, *Akzo Nobel*, ECLI:EU:C:2010:229, paras. 94–95.

108 E.g. Case C-144/04, *Mangold*, ECLI:EU:C:2005:709, paras. 74–75; Case C-387/02, *Berlusconi*, ECLI:EU:C:2005:270, para. 69 (on the principle of retroactive application of the more lenient penalty). There are, however, counter-examples where the CJEU has made a comparative analysis between the constitutional rules and practices of the Member States. See Case C-44/79, *Hauer*, ECLI:EU:C:1979:290, para. 20 and following (on the right to property).

109 Case C-4/73, *Nold*, ECLI:EU:C:1974:51, para. 13.

110 Ibid. See also O. De Schutter, 'L'influence de la Cour européenne des droits de l'homme sur la Cour de justice des Communautés européennes', *CRIDHO Working Paper*, 2007, p. 6. De Schutter put forward that the broad formula can be explained by the timing of France's

Whereas the CJEU uses softer language for the use of international treaties (which could supply guidelines) than for the use of the common constitutional traditions (from which it was bound to draw inspiration), it soon became discernible that international treaties would play a pivotal role. Yet, while international treaties formed the primary source of inspiration, not all received equal attention in the CJEU's case-law. One treaty became a primus inter pares: the ECHR.[111]

§ 2. THE SPECIAL SIGNIFICANCE OF ECHR LAW

To shape its fundamental rights regime, the CJEU has significantly relied on ECHR law, which it deemed of 'special significance'. Although the CJEU has not explained this expression, the special significance highlights the distinctive importance of ECHR law as a source of inspiration for the CJEU's fundamental rights jurisprudence.

The importance of ECHR law has been reflected both linguistically and quantitatively. This is in *Rutili* (1975) that the CJEU mentioned for the first time ECHR provisions, but did not attribute any special significance to them.[112] In *Marguerite Johnston* (1986) the CJEU pointed out that 'the principles on which [the ECHR] is based must be taken into account in Community law'.[113] In *Hoechst* (1989), the CJEU mentioned the 'particular significance' of the ECHR,[114] and has repeatedly used this expression as well as 'special significance'.[115] The CJEU increasingly referred to ECHR law.[116] Between 1974 and 1998, Guild and Lesieur found more than 70 judgments of the CJEU and opinions of Advocates General that included references to the ECHR.[117] From 1998 to 2005, Scheeck noted that the CJEU of the European

ECHR ratification, which took place only after the *Nold* judgment. Such a formula ensured that the ECHR was not excluded as a source of inspiration.

111 The expression is borrowed from S. Peers, 'Article 52. Scope and Interpretation of Rights and Principles', in S. Peers, T. Hervey, J. Kenner and A. Ward (eds.), *The EU Charter of Fundamental Rights. A Commentary*, Oxford, Hart Publishing, 2014, p. 1462.

112 Case C-36/75, *Rutili*, ECLI:EU:C:1975:137, para. 32.

113 Case C-222/84, *Marguerite Johnston*, ECLI:EU:C:1986:206, para. 18.

114 Cases C-46/87 and 227/88, *Hoescht*, ECLI:EU:C:1989:337, para. 13.

115 E.g. Case C-299/95, *Kremzow*, ECLI:EU:C:1997:254, para. 14; Case C-260/89, *ERT*, ECLI:EU:C:1991:254, para. 41.

116 In this vein, see e.g. E. Bribosia and S. Van Drooghenbroeck, 'Emprunts et migrations entre le droit de l'Union européenne et celui du Conseil de l'Europe', in A. Bailleux, Y. Cartuyvels, H. Dumont and F. Ost (eds.), *Traduction et droits européens: enjeux d'une rencontre*, Brussels, FUSL, 2009, point 16.

117 E. Guild and G. Lesieur, *The European Court of Justice on the European Convention on Human Rights*, Brill, 1998 (quoted in E. Bribosia and S. Van Drooghenbroeck, ibid.).

Communities, the Court of First Instance and the Advocates General referred to the ECHR in 287 cases.[118]

The CJEU has placed the ECHR in a class of its own compared to other human rights instruments.[119] The CJEU has referred to the 1961 European Social Charter,[120] the 1966 International Covenant on Civil and Political Rights,[121] the 1996 Revised European Social Charter,[122] and several conventions of the International Labour Organization.[123] Yet, it has only sporadically relied on these instruments, leading Buttler and de Schutter to suggest that the CJEU has 'ignored' other human rights treaties.[124]

---

118 L. Scheeck, 'Le dialogue des droits fondamentaux en Europe, Fédérateur de loyautés, dissolvant de résistances ?', in E. Bribosia, L. Scheeck and A. Ubeda de Torres (eds.), *L'Europe des Cours: loyautés et résistances*, Brussels, Bruylant, 2010, pp. 19–54 (quoted in E. Bribosia and S. Van Drooghenbroeck, ibid.).

119 See e.g. E. Bribosia and S. Van Drooghenbroeck, ibid.; G. Harpaz, 'The European Court Of Justice And Its Relations With The European Court Of Human Rights: The Quest For Enhanced Reliance, Coherence And Legitimacy', *Common Market Law Review*, 2009, p. 109; I. Butler and O. De Schutter, 'Binding the EU to International Human Rights Law', *Yearbook of European Law*, 2008, pp. 277–320.

120 E.g. Case C-24/86, *Blaizot*, ECLI:EU:C:1988:43, para. 10.

121 E.g. Case, C-374/87, *Orkem*, ECLI:EU:C:1989:387, para. 23.

122 E.g. Case T-404/06 P, *Pia Landgren*, ECLI:EU:T:2009:313, para. 69.

123 E.g. Case C-43/75, *Defrenne II*, ECLI:EU:C:1976:56, para. 20 (ILO No. 100); Case C-149/77, *Defrenne III*, ECLI:EU:C:1978:130, para. 28 (ILO No. 111).

124 See e.g. I. Butler and O. De Schutter, 'Binding the EU to International Human Rights Law', *Yearbook of European Law*, 2008, p. 281. In this regard, it has been observed that the 'exclusionary approach towards international human rights instruments other than the ECHR appears to be *a general pattern across all EU policy fields*' (T. Molnar, *The interplay between the EU's Return Acquis and International Law*, Cheltenham, Edward Elgar Publishing, 2021, p. 104, emphasis added). In 2010 *Belgium v. De Fruytier*, the CJEU even rejected reliance on the 1997 Oviedo Convention on Human Rights and Biomedicine on the ground that 'only a small majority of the Member States have actually ratified the convention' (Case C-237/09, *Belgium v. De Fruytier*, ECLI:EU:C:2010:316, para. 27). One notable exception is the UN Convention on the Rights of Persons with Disabilities, to which the EU has become a party in 2011, which the CJEU has increasingly relied upon over the past years. See for an exhaustive analysis, D. Ferri, 'The Unorthodox Relationship between the EU Charter of Fundamental Rights, the UN Convention on the Rights of Persons with Disabilities and Secondary Rights in the Court of Justice Case-law on Disability Discrimination', *European Constitutional Law Review*, 2020, pp. 275–305. For instance, in *HK Danmark*, the CJEU drew on this Convention to define disability within the meaning of the Equality Framework Directive (2000/78/EC) as 'referring to a limitation which results in particular from physical, mental or psychological impairments which in interaction with various barriers may hinder the full and effective participation of the person concerned in professional life on an equal basis with other workers' (Joined Cases C-335/11 and C-337/11, *HK Danmark*, ECLI:EU:C:2013:222, paras. 32–38). Such an interpretation driven by the UN Convention marked a shift in the case-law towards a social model of disability, where the concept of disability is understood as the result of both social barriers and impairments (A. Bailleux and E. Bribosia, 'La protection des droits fondamentaux', in A. Bailleux (ed.) *Actualités du contentieux européen*, Louvain-la-Neuve, Anthemis, 2020, p. 143; M. Bell, 'The Principle of Equal Treatment: Widening and Deepening', in P. Craig and G. De Búrca (eds.), *The Evolution of EU law*, Oxford, Oxford University Press, 2011, p. 673).

The CJEU also made a distinct use of ECtHR case-law. The CJEU referred to the absence of ECtHR case-law to support its position as from the late 1980s.[125] In the mid-1990s, the CJEU started to refer to specific ECtHR judgements.[126] From then on, the CJEU has often drawn on ECtHR case-law.[127] This extensive use contrasted with the limited use of the outputs of other human rights bodies. While the CJEU has referred to other human rights instruments as we have

125 D. Dero-Bugny, *Les rapports entre la Cour de justice de l'Union européenne et La Cour européenne des droits de l'Homme,* Brussels, Bruylant, 2015, p. 25. This was the case, for example, in the (1989) *Hoescht* case, where the CJEU concluded that Article 8 ECHR concerned the development of individual human freedom and could not be extended to commercial premises, relying on the absence of case-law of Strasbourg on this issue (Joined Cases C-46/87 and 227/88, *Hoescht*, ECLI:EU:C:1989:337, para. 18). A similar reasoning could be found in the 1989 *Orkem* case which concerned the right of non self-incrimination, in which the CJEU held that: 'As far as Article 6 of the European Convention is concerned, although it may be relied upon by an undertaking subject to an investigation relating to competition law, it must be observed that neither the wording of that article nor the decisions of the European Court of Human Rights indicate that it upholds the right not to give evidence against oneself' (Case C-374/87, *Orkem*, ECLI:EU:C:1989:387, para. 18).

126 The first time was in the (1996) *P v. S. and Cornwall County Council* judgment, where the CJEU mentioned the (1986) *Rees* ECtHR ruling to interpret the notion of transsexual (Case C-13/94, *P v. S and Cornwall County Council*, ECLI:EU:C:1996:170, para. 16). As observed by Dero-Bugny, this first reference is significant because ECtHR case-law is applied independently from the ECHR which is not mentioned in the judgment (D. Dero-Bugny, *Les rapports entre la Cour de justice de l'Union européenne et La Cour européenne des droits de l'Homme*, Brussels, Bruylant, 2015, pp. 26–27). Remarkably, while the CJEU had mentioned ECHR provisions in 1975, it took more than 20 years for the CJEU to cite specific ECtHR judgments. According to Dero-Bugny, this 'belated reference' can be explained by the evolution of the European context at that time. First, the Maastricht Treaty extended the EU competences in non-economic fields, created a EU citizenship, and codified the CJEU case-law on fundamental rights, a series of elements which implied increasing attention to fundamental rights. (D. Dero-Bugny, ibid., p. 29) Second, the mid-1990s were characterised by the rise in importance of the ECHR judicial system, which resulted from Protocol No. 11 to the ECHR (ibid., p. 31). Third, and more circumstantially, the first judgments of the CJEU referring to ECtHR case-law were adopted shortly after Opinion 2/94 where the CJEU held that the European Community had no competence to accede to the ECHR. The references to specific ECtHR cases have been seen as a 'compensation' for this opinion from the CJEU (ibid., p. 30).

127 E.g. Joined Cases C-402/05 P and C-415/05 P, *Kadi*, ECLI:EU:C:2008:461, paras. 360, 363 and 368; Case C-94/00, *Roquette Frères*, ECLI:EU:C:2002:603, para. 29. See more examples in B. De Witte, 'The Use of the ECHR and Convention Case-law by the European Court of Justice', in P. Popelier, C. Van de Heyning and P. Van Nuffel (eds.), *Human Rights Protection in the European Legal Order: The Interaction between the European and the National Courts*, Brussels, Intersentia, 2011, pp. 17–34. See also G. Harpaz, 'The European Court Of Justice And Its Relations With The European Court Of Human Rights: The Quest For Enhanced Reliance, Coherence And Legitimacy', *Common Market Law Review*, 2009, p. 108. In this vein, Harpaz has suggested that '[t]he evolution of human rights protection in the EU should be attributed […], to a large extent, to the interaction of the Luxembourg Court with the Strasbourg Court'.

noted, it has not, or only to a minor extent, incorporated the interpretative case-law of these instruments.[128]

The material reception of ECHR law has raised questions about the legal status of the ECHR within EU law. The magnitude of the material reception of the ECHR in EU law has even prompted Puissochet, former Judge at the CJEU, to assert in 2000 that 'it is *as if* the European Convention on Human Rights were one of the formal sources of Community law'.[129] The CJEU has long been ambivalent on this issue:[130] it has sometimes referred to the ECHR as if it were integral to EU law,[131] at other times by contrast, suggesting that

---

128 E. Bribosia and S. Van Drooghenbroeck, 'Emprunts et migrations entre le droit de l'Union européenne et celui du Conseil de l'Europe', in A. Bailleux, Y. Cartuyvels, H. Dumont and F. Ost (eds.), *Traduction et droits européens. enjeux d'une rencontre*, Brussels, FUSL, 2009, point 17. In its 1998 *Grant* judgment, for instance, the CJEU expressly rejected a reference to the case-law of the United Nations Human Rights Committee regarding the notion of discrimination on the ground of sex, by asserting that the latter 'is not a judicial institution and whose findings have no binding force in law' (Case C-249/96, *Grant*, ECLI:EU:C:1998:63, para. 46). See on this judgment, E. Bribosia and S. Van Drooghenbroeck, ibid.; O. De Schutter, 'L'influence de la Cour européenne des droits de l'homme sur la Cour de justice des Communautés européennes', *CRIDHO Working Paper*, 2007, p. 11.

129 J.-P. Puissochet, 'La CJCE et les principes généraux du droit', *La protection juridictionnelle des droits dans le système communautaire*, Paris, LGDJ, 2000, p. 9. Translations is ours.

130 The prevalent view in the literature has been that the EU institutions were not as such bound by the ECHR. While some authors have argued that the ECHR was part of Union law, especially after the entry into force of the Maastricht Treaty (see in particular B. De Witte, 'The Use of the ECHR and Convention Case-law by the European Court of Justice', in P. Popelier, C. Van de Heyning and P. Van Nuffel (eds.), *Human Rights Protection in the European Legal Order: The Interaction between the European and the National Courts*, Brussels, Intersentia, 2011, pp. 17–34), most have regarded the ECHR as a material source of primary importance for EU fundamental rights standards but not a formal source of Union law (e.g. A. Rosas, 'Fundamental Rights in the Luxembourg and Strasbourg Courts', in C. Baudenbacher, P. Tresselt and T. Orlygsson (eds.), *The EFTA Court Ten Years On*, Oxford, Hart Publishing, 2005, p. 170; D. Simon, 'Des influences réciproques entre CJCE et CEDH: 'Je t'aime, moi non plus'?', *Pouvoirs*, 2001, p. 36). This standpoint was supported by the fact that there was no formal relationship between the EU and the ECHR, and that the ECtHR itself declined to assess the compatibility of the measures of the EU institutions (Decision of the European Commission of Human Rights of 10 July 1978, *Confédération Française Démocratique du Travail v. the European Communities*, n°8030/77: 'Insofar as the application is directed against the European Communities as such, the Commission § out that the European Communities are not a Contracting Party to the European Convention on Human Rights (Article 66 of the Convention). To this extent, the examination of the complaints of the applicant organisation falls outside the competence of the Commission' (own translation)).

131 E.g. Case C-482/01, *Orfanopoulos*, ECLI:EU:C:2004:262, para. 98; Case C-450/06, *Varec*, ECLI:EU:C:2008:91, para. 44. See for examples of this phenomenon, R. Tinière, 'Le principe d'alignement sur le standard conventionnel pour les droits correspondants', in L. Coutron and C. Picheral (eds.), *Charte des droits fondamentaux de l'Union Européenne et Convention européenne des Droits de l'homme*, Brussels, Bruylant, 2012, p. 3.

the ECHR was not legally binding.[132] Advocates General were more outspoken on the question, either by affirming[133] or denying the binding character of the ECHR.[134] The Court of First Instance of the European Communities rejected forcefully the binding nature of the ECHR in *Mayr-Melnhof* (1998).[135] In the post-Lisbon era, the CJEU has observed that the ECHR 'does not constitute, as long as the [EU] has not acceded to it, a legal instrument which has been formally incorporated into [EU] law.'[136]

Why has ECHR law, if not being binding, been so influential for EU law? As observed by Advocate General Maduro in *Elgafaji* (2008), the CJEU relied on ECHR rights since they could be considered as common European values as all EU States adhere to the ECHR.[137] Besides, the Advocate General rightfully observed that it is important that 'for each existing protection system, while maintaining its independence, to seek to understand how the other systems interpret and develop those same fundamental rights in order not only to minimise the risk of conflicts, but also to begin a process of informal construction of a European area of protection of fundamental rights [...]'.[138] In other words, ECHR law has provided a clear and identifiable point of consensus

---

132 E.g. Case C-185/95 P, *Baustahlgewebe*, ECLI:EU:C:1998:608, para. 29. See for examples of this phenomenon, L. Scheeck, 'Solving Europe's Binary Human Rights Puzzle: The Interaction between Supranational Courts as a Parameter of European Governance', *Questions de recherche/Research Questions, Centre d'études et de recherches internationales Sciences Po*, 2005, p. 23.

133 See e.g. Opinion of Advocate General Jacobs of 30 July 1996 in Case C-84/95 *Bosphorus*, ECLI:EU:C:1996:179, para. 53: 'Although the Community itself is not a party to the Convention, and cannot become a party without amendment both of the Convention and of the Treaty, and although the Convention may not be formally binding upon the Community, nevertheless for practical purposes the Convention can be regarded as part of Community law and can be invoked as such both in this Court and in national courts.'

134 For example, in his Opinion in the 1989 *Orkem* case, Advocate General Darmon asserted that the CJEU had some leeway to interpret the ECHR provisions and was not bound to take systematically into account the interpretation of the ECHR given by the Strasbourg authorities (Opinion of Advocate General Darmon of 18 May 1989, in Case C-374/87, *Orkem*, ECLI:EU:C:1989:207, paras. 139–140).

135 Case T-347/94, *Mayr-Melnhof*, ECLI:EU:T:1998:101, para. 311: 'The Court of First Instance has no jurisdiction to apply the ECHR when reviewing an investigation under competition law, because the ECHR is not itself part of Community law.' See also Case T-112/98, *Mannesmannröhren-Werke*, ECLI:EU:T:2001:61, para. 59; Case T-99/04, *Treuhand*, ECLI:EU:T:2008:256, para. 45.

136 E.g. Case C-510/11, *Kone*, ECLI:EU:C:2013:696, para. 21; Case C-617/10, *Åkerberg Fransson*, ECLI:EU:C:2013:105, para. 44. It is of note that in a qualitative study on the role of the ECHR and the ECtHR case-law in EU law, Krommendijk found that the vast majority of the interviewees – including judges and legal clerks – supported the view that the ECtHR's judgments were not formally legally binding (J. Krommendijk, 'The Use of ECtHR Case-law by the Court of Justice of the European Union: The View of Luxembourg Insiders', *Maastricht Journal of European and Comparative Law*, 2015, pp. 812–835).

137 Opinion of Advocate General Maduro of 9 September 2008 in Case C-465/07, *Elgafaji*, ECLI:EU:C:2008:479, para. 22.

138 Ibid.

on fundamental rights among EU States,[139] and its use has contributed to the coherence of the European fundamental rights architecture.[140] By drawing inspiration from ECHR law, the CJEU has allowed the EU and ECHR systems to coexist in relative harmony. While the CJEU used the ECHR in a rather unsystematic and selective way,[141] at times adjusting it to the structure and objectives of the EU legal order,[142] the prevailing attitude has been one of

---

139 D. Dero-Bugny, *Les rapports entre la Cour de justice de l'Union européenne et La Cour européenne des droits de l'Homme*, Brussels, Bruylant, 2015, p. 27; S. Gless and J. Martin, 'The Comparative Method in European Courts: A Comparison between the CJEU and ECtHR?', *Bergen Journal of Criminal Law and Criminal Justice*, 2013, p. 48; R. Lawson, 'Confusion and Conflict? Divergent Interpretations of the ECHR in Strasbourg and Luxembourg', in R. Lawson and M. de Blois (eds.), *The Dynamics of the Protection of Human Rights in Europe*, Dordrecht, Nijhoff, 1994, pp. 219–251. See already in 1972, P. Pescatore, 'The Protection of Human Rights in the European Communities', *Common Market Law Review*, 1972, p. 79: 'However, these remarks should not in any way be taken as minimizing the magnitude or the difficulties of the task, whose course the Court has set in its recent judgments. Above all, it is to be hoped that the material provisions of the European Convention for the Protection of Human Rights may eventually come to be considered as forming a part of the law common to member States, for this international instrument explicitly represents the best possible combination of their constitutional traditions to which the Court has referred.'

140 In this vein, E. Dubout, *Droit constitutionnel de l'Union européenne*, Brussels, Bruylant, 2021, pp. 392–393. See also T. Lock, *The European Court of Justice and International Courts*, New York, Oxford University Press, 2015, p. 170. Lock observes that the main practical benefit of regular references from CJEU to ECHR law 'is that they help to foster common standards in the protection of fundamental rights. This results in greater legal certainty as far as the precise content of these rights is concerned'. Alongside these explanations, the use of the ECHR has also emerged as a means for the CJEU to legitimise its case-law on fundamental rights. Recourse to ECHR law could reassure national constitutional courts of the level of protection of fundamental rights protected at Union level and encourage the withdrawal of constitutional reserves. The use of ECHR law has also played a legitimising role vis-à-vis the ECtHR itself; it has contributed to the fact that the ECtHR restrained its control over EU States acts that result from Union law. In its *Solange II* judgment, the German Constitutional Court took into account the use of the ECHR and the case-law of the ECtHR to limit its review of Community acts. See for an extensive analysis, D. Dero-Bugny, *Les rapports entre la Cour de justice de l'Union européenne et La Cour européenne des droits de l'Homme*, Brussels, Bruylant, 2015, p. 32.

141 B. De Witte, 'The Use of the ECHR and Convention Case-law by the European Court of Justice', in P. Popelier, C. Van de Heyning and P. Van Nuffel (eds.), *Human Rights Protection in the European Legal Order: The Interaction between the European and the National Courts*, Brussels, Intersentia, 2011, pp. 17–34; S. Douglas-Scott, 'A Tale of two Courts: Luxembourg, Strasbourg and the Growing European Human Rights Acquis', *Common Market Law Review*, 2006, p. 655; L. Scheeck, 'Solving Europe's Binary Human Rights Puzzle: The Interaction between Supranational Courts as a Parameter of European Governance', *Questions de recherche/Research Questions, Centre d'études et de recherches internationales Sciences Po*, 2005, p. 20; D. Simon, 'Des influences réciproques entre CJCE et CEDH: 'Je t'aime, moi non plus'?', *Pouvoirs*, 2001, p. 37.

142 E.g. J. Murray, 'The Influence of the European Convention on Fundamental Rights on Community Law', *Fordham International Law Journal*, 2011, p. 1397; O. De Schutter, 'L'influence de la Cour européenne des droits de l'homme sur la Cour de justice des Communautés européennes, *CRIDHO Working Paper*, 2007, pp. 13–14; R. Lawson,

deference. This attitude has meant that limited divergence has emerged between Strasbourg and Luxembourg.[143]

§ 3. THE ENDORSEMENT OF THE EU REGIME BY THE EU POLITICAL INSTITUTIONS

As we have seen, the development of EU fundamental rights has been driven by the EU judiciary and heavily influenced by ECHR law, forming an EU regime infused with the latter's principles. The EU political institutions have shown an attitude of endorsement toward this system. Rather than developing a bill of rights for the EU, one of their priorities was the EU's accession to the ECHR. Before the turn of the millennium, EU political institutions were not very active in the field of fundamental rights, although there were exceptions in certain areas.

I. *Endorsement of the Regime*

The first collective political endorsement by the EU institutions of the protection of fundamental rights took place almost ten years after the *Stauder* judgment.[144] On 5 April 1977, the European Parliament, the Council and the Commission adopted a Joint Declaration on fundamental rights, in which they stressed 'the prime importance they attach to the protection of fundamental rights, as derived in particular from the constitutions of the Member States and the European Convention for the Protection of Human Rights and Fundamental Freedoms.'[145] They declared their commitment to respect these rights in the exercise of their powers and in the pursuit of the objectives of the European

'Confusion and Conflict? Divergent Interpretations of the ECHR in Strasbourg and Luxembourg', in R. Lawson and M. de Blois (eds.), *The Dynamics of the Protection of Human Rights in Europe*, Dordrecht, Nijhoff, 1994, p. 227.

143 T. Lock, *The European Court of Justice and International Courts*, New York, Oxford University Press, 2015, p. 173; S. Douglas-Scott, 'A Tale of two Courts: Luxembourg, Strasbourg and the Growing European Human Rights Acquis', *Common Market Law Review*, 2006, p. 650; A. Rosas, 'Fundamental Rights in the Luxembourg and Strasbourg Courts', in C. Baudenbacher, P. Tresselt and T. Orlygsson (eds.), *The EFTA Court: Ten Years On*, Oxford, Hart Publishing, 2005, p. 170. In this vein, Judge Rosas put forward the following: 'I find the thesis, often put forward in legal literature, that there is tension or even conflict between Luxembourg and Strasbourg case-law, somewhat exaggerated, to put it mildly. Harmony, rather than conflict, is a much more likely scenario.'

144 It should be noted that the Heads of State or Government of the Member States had already issued a Declaration on National Identity in 1973, in which they affirmed their determination to protect fundamental rights (Declaration on European Identity, 14 December 1973).

145 Joint Declaration by the European Parliament, the Council and the Commission concerning the protection of fundamental rights and the European Convention for the protection of human rights and fundamental freedoms, 27 April 1977,[1977] OJ C103/1, para. 1.

Communities.[146] Far from supporting a proactive role for the EU institutions, this declaration amounted to a political endorsement of the CJEU's case-law.[147]

Fundamental rights made their entrance into the EU Treaties in 1986, with the Single European Act. Their presence would be modest since they were mentioned in its preambles, in which the Heads of State or Government affirmed their determination to work together to promote democracy 'on the basis of the fundamental rights recognised in the constitutions and laws of the Member States, in the European Convention for the Protection of Human Rights and the European Social Charter, notably freedom, equality and social justice.'[148] Fundamental rights had to wait until the Maastricht Treaty to be incorporated into substantive provisions of EU primary law.[149]

---

146 Ibid., para. 2.

147 S. Smismans, 'Fundamental Rights as a Political Myth of the EU: Can the Myth Survive?' in S. Douglas-Scott (ed.), *Research Handbook on EU Law and Human Rights*, Cheltenham, Edward Elgar Publishing, 2017, p. 20. In this respect, the preamble of the Joint Declaration provides that: 'Whereas, as the Court of Justice has recognised, that law comprises, over and above the rules embodied in the treaties and secondary Community legislation, the general principles of law and in particular the fundamental rights, principles and rights on which the constitutional law of the Member States is based' As observed by de Búrca, 'although not legally binding, this declaration had 'symbolic importance in indicating that these institutions supported the Court's 'derivation' of rights from the ECHR and from member states' constitutional principles, and that they were willing, in principle, to respect those rights in conducting their activities' (G. de Búrca, 'The Road Not Taken: The European Union as a Global Human Rights Actor', *American Journal of International Law*, 2011, p. 669). In its report on the protection of fundamental rights of 4 February 1976, the Commission also noted that by adopting this declaration, 'a reply would be given to certain objections directed again the present system, objections which, based on the principle of the separation of powers, take exception to its exclusively judge-made character' (Report of the Commission on the protection of fundamental rights, 4 February 1976, COM/1976/037 final, p. 23).

148 Preamble, para. 3 SEA. While this formulation seems to be inspired by the case-law of the CJEU, it focuses on two specific international fundamental rights treaties. Hence, it appears more reductive than the Luxembourg case-law which refers to all international treaties to which the Member States have collaborated or of which they are signatories. The SEA preambles also mentioned the need to display the principle of respect for human rights on the international scene, which mirrors the central role that fundamental rights have had in the field of external relations from early on (Preamble, para. 4 SEA), to which we shall return in Part II, Chapter 1, Section III, §3, 3. Exception to the Rule: The Example of External Relations.

149 The major innovation came with Article F of the Treaty on European Union, according to which: 'The Union shall respect fundamental rights, as guaranteed by the European Convention for the Protection of Human Rights and Fundamental Freedoms signed in Rome on 4 November 1950 and as they result from the constitutional traditions common to the Member States, as general principles of Community law.' In addition, Article L of the Treaty on the European Union did not give powers to the CJEU to monitor compliance with fundamental rights, an omission which was partially remedied by the Treaty of Amsterdam. Article L of the Treaty on European Union was amended by the Amsterdam Treaty to extend the jurisdiction of the CJEU to control the respect for fundamental rights vis-à-vis the EU institutions, but not vis-à-vis the Member States (see e.g. O. De Schutter, 'L'influence de la Cour européenne des droits de l'homme sur la Cour de justice des Communautés

II. Accession to the ECHR

Alongside this codification exercise, one of the main priorities of the EU political institutions was the accession to the ECHR. This ambition was reflected in the works of the Commission of the European Communities from the late 1970s. If in 1976 the Commission expressed that it was not necessary for the Community to become a party to the ECHR,[150] it reversed its position three years later.[151] It identified a 'need to reinforce the protection of fundamental rights at Community level' considering the increasing direct interactions between the Community and individuals.[152] According to the Commission, 'the best way of replying to the need to reinforce the protection of fundamental rights at Community level [...] consists in the Community formally adhering to the [ECHR].'[153] Such an approach was not meant to prevent the elaboration of an EU catalogue of rights.[154] However, this prospect was not considered foreseeable 'because of the differences of opinion which exist between the Member States on the definition of economic and social rights'.[155] At that time, the political will to adopt an overarching and legally binding document on fundamental rights was limited, except on the side of the European Parliament.[156] The latter endorsed the accession to the ECHR and requested the Commission to submit to the Council a formal proposal

---

européennes', *CRIDHO Working Paper*, 2007, p. 10; K. Lenaerts, 'Respect for Fundamental Rights as a Constitutional Principle of the European Union', *Columbia Journal of European Law*, 2000, p. 5).

150 The Commission considered that the fundamental rights set out in the ECHR were recognised as binding under Community law without the need of further constitutive act, see Report of the Commission on the protection of fundamental rights, 4 February 1976, COM/1976/037 final, p. 17.

151 Memorandum on the accession of the European Communities to the Convention for the protection of Human Rights and Fundamental Freedoms, COM(79) 210 final, 2 May 1979.

152 Ibid., p. 1.

153 Ibid.

154 Ibid., p. 2.

155 Ibid.

156 K. Lenaerts and E. de Smijter, 'A "Bill of Rights" for the European Union', *Common Market Law Review*, 2001, p. 277. On 12 April 1989, the latter adopted a Declaration on fundamental rights and freedoms, which was conceived as a Bill of Rights for the EU (Resolution adopting the Declaration of fundamental rights and freedom, [1989] OJ C120/51, pp. 51–57). The latter was composed of 28 articles and contained not only civil and political rights, but also economic and social rights, such as a right to social welfare (ibid., Article 15). The same year, all Member States of the European Communities, except for Great Britain, signed the Community Charter of Fundamental Social Rights of Workers, which was to be implemented through the Social Charter Action Programme (Communication from the Commission concerning its Action Programme relating to the Implementation of the Community Charter of Basic Social Rights for Workers, COM (89) 568 final, 29 November 1989).

on the accession of the Community to the ECHR.[157] In 1990, the Commission issued a Communication on Community accession to the ECHR in which it put forward that the time had come to make a formal request for Community accession to the ECHR.[158] With a view to accession, the Commission asked the Council to approve the request for the Community's accession to the ECHR and to authorise the Commission to negotiate this accession.[159] In 1994, the Council decided to seek the opinion of the CJEU on whether the Community's accession to the ECHR was compatible with the provisions of the EC Treaty.

This political will was curbed by Opinion 2/94 which marked a halt in the accession process: the CJEU held that '[a]s Community law now stands, the Community has no competence to accede to the [ECHR].'[160] The CJEU rejected that the flexibility clause could be used as a legal basis for the accession.[161] Given the constitutional importance of the accession, a Treaty amendment was deemed necessary.[162] The Treaty of Lisbon inserted a legal basis and obligation for the accession.[163] In parallel, Protocol No. 14 ECHR enabled the EU to accede to the ECHR.[164] Accession was negotiated between the Council of Europe and the EU from 2010 to 2013. This led to a second step from the CJEU. In its Opinion 2/13, the CJEU concluded that the draft accession Treaty was incompatible with EU law because it conflicted with its autonomy.[165]

157 Resolution of 29 October 1982 embodying the opinion of the European Parliament on the memorandum from the Commission of the European Communities on the accession of the European Communities to the Convention for the Protection of Human Rights and Fundamental Freedoms, [1982] OJ C304/253.

158 Communication from the Commission on Community accession to the European Convention for the Protection of Human Rights and Fundamental Rights, SEC(90) 2087 final, 19 November 1990

159 Ibid., p. 5

160 Opinion 2/94 of 28 March 1996, ECLI:EU:C:1996:140, para. 36.

161 Ibid., para. 34.

162 Ibid., para. 35.

163 Article 6(2) TEU provides that: 'The Union shall accede to the European Convention for the Protection of Human Rights and Fundamental Freedoms.'

164 Protocol No. 14 to the Convention for the Protection of Human Rights and Fundamental Freedoms, amending the control system of the Convention, *European Treaty Series* No. 194, 13 May 2005.

165 Opinion 2/13 of 18 December 2014, ECLI:EU:C:2014:2454, para. 258. See more in D. Halberstam, 'It's the Autonomy, Stupid! A Modest Defense of Opinion 2/13 on EU Accession to the ECHR, and the Way Forward', *German Law Journal*, 2015, pp. 105–146; T. Lock, 'Walking on a tightrope: the draft ECHR accession agreement and the autonomy of the EU legal order', *Common Market Law Review*, 2011, pp. 1025–1054.

Negotiations for accession have resumed in 2020 and made considerable progress in recent times.[166]

III. Exception to the Rule: The Example of External Relations

The limited role of the EU political institutions in the early years of European integration deserves, however, to be nuanced. There were areas where a level of activity related to fundamental rights could be observed: equality and non-discrimination, data protection and external relations. While we will come back to the first two in our case studies, let us briefly touch upon the latter. The field of EU external relations is one area where human rights have figured prominently from early on. Already in 1970, the Davignon Report, whose aim was to foster cooperation in foreign policy between Member States of the European Communities, provided that: 'A united Europe should be based on a common heritage of respect for the liberty and rights of man and bring together democratic States with freely elected parliaments.'[167] At the 1973 Copenhagen European Summit, the concept of European identity was introduced. The Heads of State or Government of the Community States affirmed that the fundamental elements of this identity include 'the principles of representative democracy, the rule of law, social justice – which is the goal of economic progress – and respect for human rights'.[168] Several declarations and resolutions were adopted in the 1980s and 1990s in which the EU institutions and States reiterated their commitment to respect fundamental rights in external policies.[169] The Maastricht Treaty made respect for human rights an objective in the field of development

166 A draft Accession Agreement is available as from 2 January 2023 (https://rm.coe.int/consolidated-version-of-the-draft-accession-instruments-as-of-2-februa/1680aa3443). We will return in more detail to the potential accession of the EU to the ECHR and its impact on the application of EU fundamental rights in Part IV, Chapter 1, Section III. The Prospect of EU's Accession to the ECHR.

167 Report by the Foreign Ministers of the Member States on the problems of political unification ('Davignon Report'), 27 October 1970.

168 Declaration on European Identity (Copenhagen, 14 December 1973).

169 In 1991, the Council issued its Declaration on Human Rights in which it stated that 'respecting, promoting and safeguarding human rights is an essential part of international relations and one of the cornerstones of European cooperation and of relations between the Community and its Member States and other countries' (Council Declaration of 28 June 1991 on fundamental rights, Bull EC 6–1991, point I.45.) The same year, the Council and representatives of the Member States meeting in the Council adopted a Resolution on human rights, democracy and development whose objective was 'to formulate concrete guidelines, procedures and lines of action' to promote human rights and democracy in developing countries (Council Resolution en Representatives of the Governments of the Member States of 28 November 1991 on human rights, democracy and development, Bull EC 11–1991, §1.3.67 and 2.3.1.).

cooperation[170] and foreign and security policy.[171] All in all, fundamental rights had long occupied a significant place in the external relations of the EU, which contrasted with the limited development of fundamental rights for the EU internal action.[172]

170 Article 130u TEC.

171 Article J.1 of the TEU.

172 The emphasis on the promotion of fundamental rights in the EU external policies has attracted criticism. Several authors have argued that the EU has developed double standard of fundamental rights between its internal and external policies. See in particular A. Williams, *EU Human Rights Policies. A Study in Irony*, Oxford, Oxford University Press, 2004. See also, e.g. G. de Búrca, 'The Road Not Taken: The European Union as a Global Human Rights Actor', *American Journal of International Law*, 2011, pp. 680–685. Today, this asymmetry is reflected in the objectives of the EU. Regarding the EU internal policies, the promotion of fundamental rights is not expressly identified as an objective. Article 3(3) TEU refers to a series of objectives related to certain fundamental rights, but does not encompass a general clause on fundamental rights. In comparison, Article 3(5) TEU refers to the protection of human rights as an objective of the external policies of the EU. Moreover, Article 21 TEU mentions that the Union's action on the international scene shall be guided by the principle of 'the universality and indivisibility of human rights and fundamental freedoms'. This provision also provides that the Union shall define and pursue common policies and actions, and shall work for a high degree of cooperation in all fields of international relations, to consolidate and support democracy, the rule of law, human rights and the principles of international law.

CHAPTER 2
THE EU AS A FUNDAMENTAL RIGHTS STANDARD-SETTER

For a long period in EU history, the EU political institutions maintained a modest presence in fundamental rights matters. However, over the past decades, they have taken an increasingly proactive stance These institutions, together with the EU States, have developed fundamental rights at both primary and secondary law level. These rights have been fleshed out in the Charter, which emerged from a unique decision-making process and whose legal status is now equivalent to that of the EU Treaties. The EU legislator has not only developed tools to ensure that fundamental rights are taken into account within the decision-making process but has also developed EU legislative standards on fundamental rights. While the EU lacks general competence to enact fundamental rights, the EU legislator has been given specific competences to advance particular rights. It has relied on these legal bases, leading to a growing body of EU legislation that gives expression to fundamental rights. EU fundamental rights, as enshrined in the Charter and expressed in secondary laws, are distinguished by their high level of sophistication and integration within the domestic legal systems of EU States.

SECTION I. THE EMERGENCE OF THE CHARTER AND EU FUNDAMENTAL RIGHTS LEGISLATION

The past decades have witnessed the emergence of the Charter and a growing body of EU legislation in the field of fundamental rights. The first instrument came into being through a unique decision-making process. Following the 1999 Report of the Expert Group on Fundamental Rights appointed by the Commission,[1] the European Council decided that the fundamental rights applicable at EU level should be consolidated in a Charter and established an ad hoc Convention tasked with drawing up a draft Charter [2] The establishment

---

1 Affirming fundamental rights in the European Union. Time to act. Report of the Expert Group on Fundamental Rights, February 1999.

2 Conclusions of the Presidency, Bull. EU 6–1999, §I.18.44-I.18.45 and I.64.

of the Convention was unprecedented in the EU history: it was remarkable in both its composition and method of work.[3] The Convention was predominantly composed of members of the EU and national parliaments,[4] and was carried out with a high degree of openness and transparency.[5] These procedural features gave a high degree of legitimacy to the Charter and, according to some, contributed to its 'constitutional' dimension.[6]

---

3 F. Debusseré, 'Het Handvest van de grondrechten van de Europese Unie', *Jura Falconis*, 2001, p. 60.

4 At the Tampere Summit on 15 and 16 October 1999, the European Council reached an agreement on the composition, method of work and practical arrangements of the Convention (Conclusions of the Presidency, Bull. EU 10–1999, §I.2 and annex). Regarding its composition first, the European Council decided that the Convention was to be composed of 62 members, namely fifteen representatives of the Heads of State or Government of Member States, one representative of the President of the European Commission, sixteen members of the European Parliament, thirty members of national parliaments with two from each national parliament. The status of observers was given to two representatives of the CJEU and two representatives of the Council of Europe, including one from the ECHR. The Tampere Conclusions also specified that the Economic and Social Committee, the Committee of the Regions and the Ombudsman should be invited to give their views and that an appropriate exchange of views should be held with the applicant States. Social groups and experts could be invited by the Convention to give their views. The strong presence of parliamentarians was aimed at ensuring a more direct representation of European citizens than that provided by national governments (M. Maduro, 'The Double Constitutional Life Charter of Fundamental Rights of the European Union', in T. Hervey and J. Kenner (eds.), *Economic and Social Rights under the EU Charter of Fundamental Rights – A Legal Perspective*, Oxford, Hart Publishing, 2003, p. 273). Furthermore, the involvement of members of the Judiciary, the civil society and applicants States was unparalleled (F. Debusseré, 'Het Handvest van de grondrechten van de Europese Unie', *Jura Falconis*, 2001, p. 61).

5 S. Douglas-Scott, 'The EU Charter of Fundamental Rights as a Constitutional Document', *European Human Rights Law Review*, 2004, p. 4; F. Debusseré, 'Het Handvest van de grondrechten van de Europese Unie', *Jura Falconis*, 2001, p. 62.

6 S. Douglas-Scott, 'The EU Charter of Fundamental Rights as a Constitutional Document', *European Human Rights Law Review*, 2004, p. 3. See in this vein, M. Maduro, 'The Double Constitutional Life Charter of Fundamental Rights of the European Union', in T. Hervey and J. Kenner (eds.), *Economic and Social Rights under the EU Charter of Fundamental Rights – A Legal Perspective*, Oxford, Hart Publishing, 2003, pp. 272–273: 'It may not to be an overstatement to say that the most important constitutional dimension Charter stems from its process of deliberation. Though ultimately adopted simply as a declaration from the EU institutions, the Charter was the result of a drafting process that constituted a kind of constitution-making experiment for the EU. Instead of being subject to the traditional inter-governmental process, the drafting Charter was the product of a different kind of process: the Convention. the EU. Instead of being subject to the traditional inter-governmental process, the drafting Charter was the product of a different kind of process: the Convention.' Along these lines, in his Opinion in the 2001 *Hautala* case, Advocate General Léger observed that: 'As the solemnity of its form and the procedure which led to its adoption would give one to assume, the Charter was intended to constitute a privileged instrument for identifying fundamental rights. It is a source of guidance as to the true nature of the Community rules of positive law.' (Opinion of Advocate Général Léger, 10 July 2001 in Case C-353/99 P, *Council of the European Union v. Hautala*, ECLI:EU:C:2001:392, para. 83)

From the work of the Convention, a (draft) Charter emerged,[7] but its legal status remained uncertain for a long time. Whereas it was proclaimed by the European Parliament, the Council, and the Commission in 2000,[8] the CJEU was reluctant to engage with the Charter.[9] It is only with the Treaty of Lisbon that this ambiguity was clarified: the Charter was elevated to the rank of primary law, having the same legal value as the EU Treaties.[10] With its binding legal status, the Charter took on a new dimension within the CJEU's case-law,[11] giving rise to what has been called 'Charter centrism': namely, the decline in the use of ECHR law by the CJEU, correlated with its growing use of the Charter.[12]

The early 2000s saw the growing integration of fundamental rights within the decision-making process of the EU institutions.[13] The Commission was the first to show keen interest in ensuring that its proposals and documents took fundamental rights into account. It developed a series of instruments, including a 'fundamental rights checklist', to ensure the compliance of its proposals with

---

7 Bull. EU 10–2000, §1.2.1.

8 Conclusions of the Presidency, Bull. EU 12–2000, §1.2.2.

9 When the Charter was proclaimed, the Court of First Instance and several Advocates General started to refer to the Charter, e.g. Case T-112/98, *Mannesmannröhren-Werke*, ECLI:EU:T:2001:61, para. 76; Case T-177/01, *Jégo-Quéré*, ECLI:EU:T:2002:112, para. 42; Opinion of Advocate General Tizanno of 8 February 2001 in Case C-173/99, *The Queen and Secretary of State for Trade and Industry/Broadcasting, Entertainment, Cinematographic and Theatre Union (BECTU)*, ECLI:EU:C:2001:81, para. 27. The CJEU appeared more cautious and only mentioned the Charter for the first time in 2006 (Case C-540/03, *Parliament v. Council*, ECLI:EU:C:2005:517, para. 38). See on the reasons behind the reluctance of the CJEU to use the Charter before the entry into force of the Treaty of Lisbon, e.g. M. Maduro, 'The Double Constitutional Life Charter of Fundamental Rights of the European Union', in T. Hervey and J. Kenner (eds.), *Economic and Social Rights under the EU Charter of Fundamental Rights – A Legal Perspective*, Oxford, Hart Publishing, 2003, pp. 283–284. See also S. Sánchez, 'The Court and the Charter: The impact of the entry into force of the Lisbon Treaty on the CJEU's approach to fundamental rights', *Common Market Law Review*, 2012, pp. 1569–1573.

10 Article 6(1) TEU.

11 S. Iglesias Sánchez, 'The Court and the Charter: the impact of the entry into force of the Lisbon Treaty on the CJEU's approach to fundamental rights', *Common Market Law Review*, 2012, pp. 1565–1611.

12 E.g. G de Búrca, 'After the EU Charter of Fundamental Rights: The Court of Justice as a Human Rights Adjudicator?, *Maastricht Journal of European and Comparative Law*, 2013, p. 168. See for an empirical study of the reasons behind this trend, J. Krommendijk, 'The Use of ECtHR Case-law by the Court of Justice of the European Union: The View of Luxembourg Insiders', *Maastricht Journal of European and Comparative Law*, 2015, pp. 830–833.

13 J. Morijn, 'Post-Lisbon Civil Rights Protection by the EU's Political Institutions', in S. de Vries, H. de Waele and M.-P. Granger (eds.), *Civil Rights and EU Citizenship*, Edward Elgar Publishing, 2018, pp. 14–42; J. Morijn, 'Kissing Awake a Sleeping Beauty? The Charter of Fundamental Rights in EU and Member States' Policy Practice', in V. Kosta, N. Skoutaris and V. Tzevelekos (eds.), *EU Accession to the ECHR*, Oxford, Hart Publishing, 2014, pp. 123–139.

fundamental rights.[14] The European Parliament[15] and the Council[16] each, in turn followed by adopting various tools to ensure that fundamental rights are taken into account in their activities. While these mechanisms have contributed to a culture of fundamental rights in the EU and have helped reinforce upstream the compatibility of acts with fundamental rights, they have not been fully

---

14 In 2005, the Commission presented a methodology for compliance with the Charter of Commission legislative proposals (Communication from the Commission - Compliance with the Charter of Fundamental Rights in Commission legislative proposals - Methodology for systematic and rigorous monitoring, COM/2005/0172 final). In 2010, the Commission adopted its 'Strategy for the effective implementation Charter of Fundamental Rights by the European Union' with the goal of strengthening the culture of fundamental rights at all stages of the procedure that lead to the adoption of legislative or non-legislative acts (Commission Communication – Strategy for the effective implementation of the Charter of Fundamental Rights by the European Union, COM/2010/0573 final). In this context, the Commission elaborated operational guidance addressed to its departments to ensure that fundamental rights are taken into account throughout the decision-making process. This operational guidance seeks primarily to reinforce the assessment of the impact of draft proposals on fundamental rights. The Commission also developed a 'fundamental rights check-list' which lists a series of questions that the Commission services have to take into account when examining the impact of draft legislative proposals on fundamental rights (Commission Staff Working Paper – Operational Guidance on taking account of Fundamental Rights in Commission Impact Assessments, SEC(2011) 567 final). More recently, the Commission has reaffirmed its willingness to check the compliance with the Charter of all key commission initiatives that may have a major impact on the Charter rights from the preparatory stage of the initiative (Communication from the Commission – Strategy to strengthen the application Charter of Fundamental Rights in the EU, COM/2020/711 final).

15 The Council has elaborated methodological guidelines on fundamental rights compatibility checks for the Council's preparatory bodies. Adopted in 2011 and updated in 2014, these non-legally binding guidelines are meant to help these bodies 'to take the methodological steps necessary to identify and deal with fundamental rights issues arising in connection with the proposals under discussion at the relevant Council preparatory bodies.' (Guidelines on methodological steps to be taken to check fundamental rights compatibility at the Council preparatory bodies, 20 January 2015, 5377/15) The guidelines are addressed to all the Council's bodies. In case of doubt, the guidelines suggest to consult the Council Legal Service, use national expertise of national experts, and inform the FREMP Working Party or other preparatory body specialising in a specific fundamental right (ibid., 9). In these guidelines, the Council develops a 'fundamental rights check-list' which is relatively similar to the check-list of the Commission.

16 The European Parliament has adopted a rule of procedure to ensure the compliance of legislative proposals with fundamental rights. Rule 39 of the Rules of Procedure foresees that where the committee responsible for the subject matter, a political group or members reaching at least the low threshold believe that a proposal for a legislative act does not comply with the fundamental rights of the European Union, they can refer the matter to the committee responsible for the protection of fundamental rights, namely the Committee on Civil Liberties, Justice and Home Affairs.

satisfactory in ensuring the compliance of EU acts with fundamental rights[17] and have failed to serve as tools for promoting fundamental rights.[18]

If the approach under these mechanisms tends to be rather passive, focusing on ensuring the compliance of EU acts with fundamental rights, the EU legislator has also adopted a more active stance. EU legislative standards that elaborate on, or relate to, fundamental rights have proliferated. Driven by diverse and evolving dynamics and equipped with specific legal bases, the EU legislator has enacted a growing number of legislations giving expression to fundamental rights.

SECTION II. ZOOMING IN ON EU FUNDAMENTAL RIGHTS LEGISLATION

The EU legislator has acted in the field of fundamental rights under diverse and evolving dynamics: while its intervention used to be related to objectives linked to the realisation of a common European space, these have gradually given way to complementary rationales. For legislative action in the field of fundamental rights to gain momentum, it was necessary to wait for the Treaty

---

17 The Commission's impact assessments represent one the main tools to screen horizontally all major EU policy initiatives in the light of specific interests including fundamental rights. However, criticism has been expressed regarding the way fundamental rights have been taken into account in the Commission's impact assessments. E.g. L. Guilloud-Colliat, 'La charte des droits fondamentaux et les actes législatifs', in R. Tinière et C. Vial (eds.), *Les dix ans de la Charte des droits fondamentaux de l'Union européenne, Bilan et perspectives*, Brussels, Larcier, 2020, p. 212; O. De Schutter, 'The Implementation Charter of Fundamental Rights in the EU Institutional Framework', *Study for the AFCO Committee*, 2016, p. 8. Besides, fundamental rights are not the subject of a separate category for the impact assessments but have been integrated into existing categories, namely the categories of economic, social and environmental impacts (I. Butler, 'Ensuring Compliance with the Charter of Fundamental Rights in Legislative Drafting: The Practice of the European Commission', *European Law Review*, 2012, p. 405). Last but not least, the mechanisms put in place by the EU institutions remain for the most part internal procedures (L. Guilloud-Colliat, ibid., p. 213).

18 Criticisms have been voiced that the ex-ante mechanisms are primarily intended to ensure that Union acts comply with fundamental rights, but have not been the vehicle for a fundamental rights policy at EU level. See e.g. the Report on the implementation of the Charter of Fundamental Rights of the European Union in the EU institutional framework (2017/2089(INI)) 30 January 2019, in particular explanatory statement: 'Notwithstanding relevant progresses made by the EU institutions to integrate the Charter into the legislative and decision-making processes, it still appears to be an under-evaluated instrument, not exploited to its full potential. The general tendency is that of focusing on avoiding its violation rather than on maximising its potential, despite the fact that the duty of promoting its application is clearly spelled out in the Charter itself (article 51(1)). Compatibility checks and impact assessments - the main tools at the Commission's disposal to evaluate, ex ante, the compliance of its proposals with fundamental rights, hence with the Charter - follow that path, highlighting a passive attitude toward the Charter rather than a proactive one.'

of Amsterdam, which initiated a process of granting specific powers to the EU legislator to flesh out fundamental rights. This does not mean, however, that the EU was unable to adopt measures in the field of fundamental rights before this Treaty. Nevertheless, the EU's action faced significant resistance from EU States and was based on general competences not specifically tailored for fundamental rights. With the expansion of specific fundamental rights competences, the EU legislator has developed sectoral legislation shaping particular fundamental rights. Concurrently, the CJEU has increasingly recognised that specific legislation 'gives expression' to a fundamental right protected at the level of EU primary law.

§ 1. THE DIVERSE AND EVOLVING DYNAMICS BEHIND EU LEGISLATIVE ACTION

The intervention of the EU legislator in the realm of fundamental rights has historically been driven by aims connected to the establishment and proper functioning of a common European space – firstly, the internal market, and subsequently, the Area of Freedom, Security, and Justice. Regulating fundamental rights at EU level may be essential for the realisation of this common space. National regulation of fundamental rights can create barriers to the formation of this space, thus prompting the EU to act to harmonise fundamental rights.[19] The harmonisation has also been envisaged as a means for achieving the common European space grounded in the principles of mutual recognition and mutual trust. Mutual recognition has been heralded as 'the cornerstone of judicial cooperation in both civil and criminal matters within the Union.'[20] Mutual trust has increasingly been developed as a foundation

[19] In this vein, national fundamental rights can limit the freedoms of movement enshrined in the EU Treaties. The CJEU has acknowledged that the protection of fundamental rights may justify a restriction of the freedoms of movement (Case C-112/00, *Schmidberger*, ECLI:EU:C:2003:333, para. 82), even if the national conception of fundamental right does not correspond to a conception shared by all EU States (Case C-36/02, *Omega Spielhallen*, ECLI:EU:C:2004:614, para. 37). The reliance on national fundamental rights can thus lead to a fragmentation of the internal market. The adoption of common EU fundamental rights standards allows the obstacles to be overcome. Hence, the EU legislator has adopted several instruments aimed at contributing to free movement which have harmonised fundamental rights. This dynamic has been particularly prominent regarding the adoption of common standards for the processing of personal data. This dynamic linked to the removal of obstacles to free movement has been reflected in the data protection legislative instruments. The 1995 Data Protection Directive (95/46/EC), the first EU instrument on data protection, explicitly pursues the aim of preventing EU States from restricting the free flow of personal data between Member States, by ensuring that EU States could not adopt more protective measures for the protection of personal data (Article 1(2)).

[20] Presidency Conclusions of the Tampere European Council, 15 and 16 October 1999, point 33.

and prerequisite for the principle of mutual recognition.[21] To strengthen mutual trust among EU States, common minimum rules on a set of procedural fundamental rights in criminal matters were established at EU level.[22] The concern of a regulatory 'race to the bottom' has also prompted the adoption of EU fundamental rights to prevent the erosion of national fundamental rights within the common European space.[23]

Alongside these dynamics, new dynamics have surfaced in recent years. The EU has regulated the fundamental right to equality and non-discrimination with a logic that goes beyond the market paradigm: equality appears more and more as an objective in and of itself of the EU legislator. The generation of equality directives which were adopted as from the 2000s, such as the Race Equality Directive (2000/43/EC) and the Equality Framework Directive (2000/78/EC), appear to be motivated by the ambition to enhance equality among the peoples of Europe.[24] Equality and non-discrimination are conceived as an end in and of themselves rather than for ensuring fair competition between EU States or removing obstacles to free movement. [25] The directives are also accompanied by a much more pronounced fundamental rights narrative than in the past,[26] and are relevant within EU States without the need for cross-border movement.[27]

If the objectives for the adoption of EU fundamental rights used to be internal, these objectives have been accompanied by external motives for data protection. The objective of ensuring the free movement of data has been and remains an important driver for the intervention of the EU

21 F.-X. Millet, 'The Protection of Fundamental Rights within the AFSJ: Through or Against Mutual Trust and Mutual Recognition?', in S. Iglesias Sánchez and M. González Pascual (eds.), *Fundamental Rights in the EU Area of Freedom, Security and Justice*, Cambridge, Cambridge University Press, pp. 57–74.

22 We will come back to the EU procedural rights directives in Part IV, Chapter 1, Section I. More EU Fundamental Rights.

23 For instance, the harmonisation of social fundamental rights standards was deemed desirable to avoid EU States lowering their social rights standards to attract companies, see M. Beijer, *Limits of Fundamental Rights Protection by the EU: The Scope for the Development of Positive Obligations*, Brussels, Intersentia, 2017, p. 216.

24 E. Muir, *EU Equality Law, The First Fundamental Rights Policy of the EU*, Oxford, Oxford University Press, 2018, p. 4.

25 E. Muir, ibid., p. 4.

26 The recitals to the new directives are permeated with references to fundamental rights (e.g. Recitals 1, 4, 5 Equality Framework Directive (2000/78/EC). Some of these directives state explicitly that their purpose is to put into effect the principle of equal treatment in the Member States (Articles 1 Racial Discrimination Directive (2000/43/EC) and Equality Framework Directive (2000/78/EC).

27 E. Muir, *EU Equality Law, The First Fundamental Rights Policy of the EU*, Oxford, Oxford University Press, 2018, p. 4.

legislator.[28] Increasingly, this internal motivation is coupled with an external motivation, i.e. that EU data protection standards serve as a benchmark for global standards.[29] As Bradford observed, the EU's internal objectives for data protection have made room for a more multifaceted set of goals, both internal and external. The internal objectives have not disappeared altogether. The external motivation seems to complement rather than replace the internal agenda of the EU institutions in this area.[30]

§ 2. THE FRAGMENTED, YET INCREASING COMPETENCES OF THE EU LEGISLATOR

EU's action in the field of fundamental rights has been subject to significant resistance at Member States level. If some resistances already existed at the beginning of the European integration process, they have become more pronounced from the 1990s.[31] These resistances are reflected in several Treaties provisions, which aim to restrict the scope of EU competence in this area.[32] The limited EU competences in fundamental rights matters has been used an alibi for inaction.[33] This could be witnessed, for instance, in the area

28 For instance, the recitals of the GDPR (2016/679/EU) mention that it seeks to remove obstacles to the flow of personal data within the Union by developing a consistent and homogeneous application of the rules for the fundamental right to the protection of personal data (Recital 10).

29 In the 2009 Stockholm Programme for instance, the European Council stressed that: 'On a broader front, the Union must be a driving force behind the development and promotion of international standards for personal data protection, based on relevant EU instruments on data protection and the 1981 Council of Europe Convention, and in the conclusion of appropriate bilateral or multilateral instruments.' (Stockholm Programme - An open and secure Europe serving and protecting the citizens, December 2009, 14449/09 JAI 679, 19)

30 A. Bradford, *The Brussels Effect: How the European Union Rules the World*, Oxford, Oxford University Press, 2020, p. 137.

31 C. Leconte and E. Muir, 'Understanding Resistance to the EU Fundamental Rights Policy', *Human Rights Review*, 2014, p. 19.

32 Article 6 TFEU provides, on the one hand, that the accession of the EU to the ECHR 'shall not affect the Union's competences as defined in the Treaties' (paragraph 2) and, on the other hand, that the Charter 'shall not extend in any way the competences of the Union as defined in the Treaties' (paragraph 1). The latter aspect is echoed in Article 51(2) Charter according to which '[t]he Charter does not extend the field of application of Union law beyond the powers of the Union or establish any new power or task for the Union, or modify powers and tasks as defined in the Treaties.' Its preambles further indicate that the Charter reaffirmed existing fundamental rights 'with due regard for the powers and tasks of the Union and for the principle of subsidiarity'.

33 In this vein, P. Alston and J. Weiler, 'An "Ever Closer Union" in Need of a Human Rights Policy: The European Union and Human Rights', in P. Alston (ed.), *The EU and Human Rights*, Oxford, Oxford University Press, 1999, p. 678: 'The issue of competences is of particular importance in this context, not only because of the extent to which it has underpinned the resistance to an EU human rights policy on the part of some states but perhaps more importantly because it has been the preferred excuse invoked by those who

of equality and non-discrimination. Although there have been calls for EU action on a wider range of discrimination grounds than gender equality and nationality non-discrimination during the 1990s, they were dismissed due to the EU's alleged lack of legal competence for other forms of discrimination.[34]

This does not mean, however, that the EU was not able to adopt measures in the field of fundamental rights: the EU relied on general competences for doing so.[35] The EU legislator has relied on the flexibility clause, which allows the EU to take measures necessary to achieve a EU objective even without explicit competence, to give effect to certain fundamental rights.[36] This was, for example, the case regarding several directives in the field of equality and non-discrimination.[37] The clause was also used to establish the EU Fundamental Rights Agency.[38] Besides, the EU legislator has relied on the internal market harmonisation clause to flesh out fundamental rights.[39] It made considerable use of this clause to regulate certain non-economic values, under the guise of the proper functioning and completion of the internal market.[40] The clause has been used to adopt measures in the fields of equality[41] and data protection.[42] However, neither the flexibility clause nor the internal market one is the panacea to act in the field of fundamental rights: both are surrounded by stringent procedural and substantive limitations.[43] In addition to these two

do not want such a policy for very different reasons. Those reasons range from a simplistic belief that the Union can and should confine itself to a narrow range of economic aspects of integration to a more general sense that human rights just get in the road of efforts to build a strong and wealthy new Europe. Whatever the motivation it is essential to put the issue of competences into perspective so that the debate over the real issues can move ahead.'

34 M. Bell, 'The Principle of Equal Treatment: Widening and Deepening' The Evolution of EU Law, in P. Craig and G. De Búrca (eds.), *The Evolution of EU law*, Oxford, Oxford University Press, 2011, p. 618.

35 See also Y. Lorans, 'Le législateur européen et la protection des droits fondamentaux dans l'Union : vers une concrétisation législative de la Charte', *Revue trimestrielle de droit européen*, 2021, pp. 59–86.

36 Article 352 TFEU (ex-Article 235 EEC Treaty).

37 This was for example the case regarding the Employment Equal Treatment Between Men and Women Council Directive (76/207/EEC) and the Social Security Equal Treatment Between Men and Women Council Directive (79/7/EEC).

38 Article 2 Council Regulation (168/2007/EC) of 15 February 2007 establishing a European Union Agency for Fundamental Rights, [2007] OJ L53/1.

39 Article 114 TFEU (ex-Article 100 CEE).

40 See E. Muir, V. Davio and L. Van der Meulen, 'The Horizontal Clauses (arts 8 & 10 TFEU) and Their Contribution to the Course of EU Equality Law: Still an Empty Vessel', *European Papers*, pp. 1386 and references.

41 This was for example the case for the adoption of the Equal Pay Between Men and Women Council Directive (75/117/EEC).

42 This was for example the case for the adoption of the Data Protection Directive (95/46/EC).

43 Regarding the flexibility clause, a major procedural obstacle is that it requires unanimity in the Council (Article 352(1) TFEU). On the substance, this clause can only be used if EU action is necessary to attain one of the objectives of the Union (ibid.); if there is no provision in the Treaty for action to attain the objective (*ibid.*); and if it does not entail harmonisation of the laws or regulations of the Member States in cases where the Treaties

clauses, there were also specific provisions in the EU Treaties governing areas close to fundamental rights, such as social rights[44] and citizenship.[45]

The Amsterdam Treaty signalled an important step forward for the EU's ability to intervene in the field of fundamental rights. It granted the EU legislator specific powers to protect fundamental rights, particularly in the fields of equality and data protection. The Lisbon Treaty marked a further step in terms of EU fundamental rights competences. It strengthened the EU's competences in the field of data protection, and extended EU fundamental rights competences to new areas such as the procedural rights of individuals involved in criminal procedures.[46] Even though these two Treaties have increased the range of specific legal bases, the EU's competence remains fragmented There is no legal basis for the EU institutions to take general action in the field of fundamental rights.[47]

---

exclude such harmonisation (Article 352(3) TFEU). In its Opinion 2/94, the CJEU pointed out that the flexibility clause could not be used as a legal basis for the Union's accession, see Opinion 2/94 of 28 March 1996, ECLI:EU:C:1996:140, para. 29 and following. According to the CJEU, '[t]hat provision, being an integral part of an institutional system based on the principle of conferred powers, cannot serve as a basis for widening the scope of Community powers beyond the general framework created by the provisions of the Treaty as a whole and, in particular, by those that define the tasks and the activities of the Community. On any view, Article 235 cannot be used as a basis for the adoption of provisions whose effect would, in substance, be to amend the Treaty without following the procedure which it provides for that purpose.' Regarding the internal market clause, while it can be relied upon to regulate non-economic values, the CJEU had made it clear that measures adopted on this basis must genuinely have as its object the improvement of the conditions for the establishment and functioning of the internal market (Case C-376/98, *Tobacco Advertising*, ECLI:EU:C:2000:544, para. 84). Besides, the internal market clause may not be used as a legal basis to circumvent the express exclusion of harmonisation laid down in the EU Treaties (ibid., para. 84).

44 Regarding social rights, the SEA included a legal basis for the adoption of minimum requirements in the field of social policy, namely Article 118a of the EEC Treaty. Several measures were adopted on this basis to promote the improvement of working conditions, such as the Safety and Health of Workers at Work Council Directive (89/391/EEC)(Council Directive 89/391/EEC of 12 June 1989 on the introduction of measures to encourage improvements in the safety and health of workers at work, [1989] OJ L183/1).

45 Regarding EU citizenship, the Maastricht Treaty provided a legal basis to facilitate the right of EU citizens to move and reside freely within the territory of the Member States (Article 8a(2) TEC). The second paragraph of Article 8e TEC also granted the Union a general competence to legislate in the field of EU citizenship. The latter provision provided that 'without prejudice to the other provisions of this Treaty, the Council, acting unanimously on a proposal from the Commission and after consulting the European Parliament, may adopt provisions to strengthen or to add to the rights laid down in [the Part Two - Citizenship of the Union].'

46 Considering our case studies, we focus on competences in the fields of equality and non-discrimination and data protection. We will briefly return to the competences for the adoption of the EU procedural rights directives in Part IV, Chapter 1, Section I. More EU Fundamental Rights.

47 Opinion 2/94 of 28 March 1996, ECLI:EU:C:1996:140, para. 27.

Focusing on the fields of our case studies, the Amsterdam Treaty is a turning point for equality and non-discrimination competences. In the past, the EU's competence was confined to discrimination on grounds of nationality.[48] With this Treaty, new competences were granted to the EU legislator. The most significant novelty stems from the insertion of Article 13 TEC which allows to take legislation action to combat discrimination based on sex, racial or ethnic origin, religion or belief, disability, age or sexual orientation.[49] Next, Article 119(3) TEC empowers the Council, acting in accordance with the co-decision procedure and after consulting the Economic and Social Committee, to adopt measures to ensure the application of the principle of equal opportunities and equal treatment of men and women in matters of employment and occupation, including the principle of equal pay for equal work or work of equal value.

The Treaty of Amsterdam also brought competences in the field of data protection. First, Article 286 TEC which dealt with the processing of personal data by the EU institutions and bodies.[50] Second, Article 30(1)(b) TEU which related to police cooperation in criminal matters.[51] The two legal bases had limitations as to the addressees of data protection measures (Article 286 EC Treaty referred to EU institutions and bodies) and as to the areas in which such measures could be adopted (Article 30(1)(b) EU Treaty was limited to the area of police cooperation). The Treaty of Lisbon strengthened the mandate of the EU legislator in the field of data protection with Article 16 TFEU. This provision constitutes a comprehensive legal basis for data protection: it allows for the adoption of data protection rules applicable to private parties and public authorities, including both the EU States and the EU institutions.[52] Furthermore, it may be used for adopting measures in all areas of EU law, except in the area of CFSP.[53]

---

48 See further in Part III (case study on equality), Chapter 2, Section I, §1. The Emergence of the Highly Developed EU Equality System.

49 Article 13(1) TEC (current Article 19(1) TFEU).

50 It called for the adoption of measures for the protection of personal data that would be applicable to the EU institutions and bodies (Article 286(1) TEC). It also provided a legal basis for the Council, according to the co-decision procedure, to adopt these measures and to establish an independent supervisory body to monitor the application of these measures (Article 286(2) TEC).

51 Article 30(1)(b) TEU required that the collection, storage, processing, analysis and exchange of relevant information in the field of police cooperation in criminal matters is subject to appropriate provisions on the protection of personal data.

52 C. Docksey and G. Zanfir-Fortuna, 'Article 16 [Protection of Personal Data] (ex-Article 286 TEC)', in H.-J. Blank and S. Mangiameli (eds.), *Treaty on the Functioning of the European Union – A Commentary, Volume I: Preamble, Articles 1-89*, Cham, Springer, 2021, p. 421.

53 Regarding the latter, Article 39 TEU provides for a specific legal basis by which the Council shall adopt rules relating to the protection of individuals with regard to the processing of personal data by the Member States when they carry out CFSP activities and the rules relating to the free movement of such data.

The EU legislator has significantly relied on the specific EU competences to enact legislations regulating equality and data protection. In equality law, the EU has adopted gender equality directives as early as the 1970s on the basis of general competences.[54] At the turn of the millennium, this arsenal was completed by a handful of instruments targeting other grounds of discrimination, including the Racial Discrimination Directive (2000/43/EC) and the Equality Framework Directive (2000/78/EC), which were adopted on the basis of Article 13 TEC.[55] In the field of data protection, the main legislation before the 2000s was the Data Protection Directive (95/46/EC), which was adopted on the basis of internal market clause. Article 286 TEC and Article 30(1)(b) TEU served as legal bases for the adoption of several additional legislations which strengthened the EU data protection framework.[56] Article 16 TFEU is the legal basis used for the 'Copernican' reform of EU data protection law, to which we will return.[57]

§ 3. UNVEILING EU LEGISLATION AS 'GIVING EXPRESSION' TO FUNDAMENTAL RIGHTS[58]

With the expansion of specific fundamental rights competences, the EU legislator has developed a series of legislation shaping specific fundamental rights by defining their scope, their content, balancing them against competing legitimate interests, as well as specifying some of the modalities for their enforcement.[59] In a concomitant manner, the CJEU has increasingly often recognised that (elements of such) specific EU legislation actually 'give(s) expression' to a fundamental right protected at the level of EU primary law.

[54] See further in Part III (case study on equality), Chapter , Section I, §1. The Emergence of the Highly Developed EU Equality System.

[55] Article 13 TEC was also used for the adoption of the Gender Equality Goods and Services Directive (2004/113/EC) which extended the scope of sex discrimination to the area of goods and services.

[56] Article 286 TEC was used to adopt the EU Institutions Data Protection Regulation (45/2001/EC) which concerned the protection of individuals with regard to the processing of personal data by the Community institutions and bodies and on the free movement of such data. Article 30 TEU was used to adopt the Law Enforcement Data Protection Framework Decision (2008/977/JHA).

[57] See further in Part III (case study on data protection), Chapter , Section II, §2, I.A. EU Data Protection Law as A Rule-Based System.

[58] It should be noted that this section is partly derived from a joint work in progress with E. Muir and Y. Lorans on EU legislation in the field of fundamental rights. Further information can be provided on this project.

[59] E. Muir, 'The fundamental rights implications of EU legislation: some constitutional challenges', *Common Market Law Review*, 2014, pp. 219–245; Y. Lorans, 'Le législateur européen et la protection des droits fondamentaux dans l'Union : vers une concrétisation législative de la Charte', *Revue trimestrielle de droit européen*, 2021, pp. 59–86.

For that purpose, the CJEU uses several formulas such as 'giving expression', 'concretising', or 'giving effect'. The CJEU has identified the existence of a special relationship between (provisions of) legislative acts and fundamental rights in fields as varied as: equality,[60] data protection,[61] procedural rights in criminal matters,[62] social policy,[63] intellectual property right[64] and asylum.[65] The CJEU, however, does not clarify how it identifies the relevant elements of EU legislation that give expression to a fundamental right, nor does it specify the consequences of the special relationship established between these provisions or acts and the Charter.

In the context of our study, we aim to investigate the influence of EU legislation 'giving expression' to fundamental rights on the ECtHR's case-law in our case studies. Hence, we will try to flesh out some criteria to identify this type of EU legislation and demarcate them from EU 'ordinary' legislation.[66] Our focus is here on the *identification* of EU legislation 'giving expression to fundamental rights', rather than on the consequences of this identification. We first show how the CJEU has increasingly identified legislation as giving expression to fundamental rights, as well as the limits of this identification. We then reflect on a set of criteria for identifying legislation giving expression to a fundamental right, with a view to selecting them in a series of areas. This allows us to analyze their influence on the ECtHR case-law, and more generally, to highlight the impact of the growing role of the EU as a standard-setter on Strasbourg case-law.

I. *The Growing, Yet Limited Recognition of EU Legislation as Giving Expression to Fundamental Rights*

The CJEU has early on identified provisions of EU secondary law as giving expression to fundamental rights. Already in the *Rutili* (1975) case, the CJEU held that certain legislative provisions on the free movement of workers were 'a specific manifestation of the more general principle, enshrined in Articles 8, 9, 10 and 11 of the [ECHR], and in Article 2 of protocol No. 4 of the [ECHR].'[67]

60 E.g. Joined Cases C-804/18 and C-341/19, *WABE*, ECLI:EU:C:2021:594, para. 62.

61 E.g. Case C-131/12, *Google Spain*, ECLI:EU:C:2014:317, para. 69; Joined Cases C-511/18, 512/18 and C-520/18, *La Quadrature du Net and Others*, ECLI:EU:C:2020:791, para. 109.

62 E.g. Case C-467/18, *Rayonna prokuratura Lom*, ECLI:EU:C:2019:765, para. 37; Case C-242/22 PPU, *Criminal proceedings against TL*, ECLI:EU:C:2022:611, para. 42.

63 Case C-55/18, *Federación de Servicios de Comisiones Obreras*, ECLI:EU:C:2019:402, para. 31; Case C-174/16, *H.*, ECLI:EU:C:2017:637, para. 44.

64 Case C-264/19, *Constantin Film*, ECLI:EU:C:2020:542, para. 35.

65 Case C-465/07, *Elgafaji*, ECLI:EU:C:2009:94, para. 28; Joined Cases C-924/19 PPU and 925/19 PPU, *FMS and Others*, ECLI:EU:C:2020:367, para. 192.

66 EU 'ordinary' legislation is defined negatively in the context of this project, namely as EU legislation that does not give expression to a fundamental right.

67 Case C-36/75, *Rutili*, ECLI:EU:C:1975:137, para. 32.

Similarly, the CJEU has recognised that some provisions of EU secondary law on gender equality either reflected a general principle underlying the common constitutional traditions of the Member States and specific articles of the ECHR,[68] or provided 'further details regarding certain aspects of the material scope' of equality law provisions enshrined in primary law (Article 119 TEEC).[69] A normative connection has also been identified between national legislation and fundamental rights. In *Hauer* (1979), the CJEU acknowledged that national laws could constitute a 'concrete expression' of fundamental rights.[70] If the CJEU has identified a special relationship between EU primary and secondary laws in matters of fundamental rights from the mid-1970s, this recognition was infrequent and without explanation.

While the CJEU's recognition of (provisions of) EU legislation as giving expression to fundamental rights has for long existed, the scale of this recognition has changed significantly over the past years. This recognition takes place in a much broader range of fields covered by new areas of legislative action, as we have seen above. As Lorans observed, there is a steady increase in references to EU legislative instruments giving expression to fundamental rights starting from the 2010s, thus when the legal effects of the Charter start co-existing with emerging EU legislation in these fields. If there were only two cases where the CJEU identified legislative instruments as giving expression to a fundamental right in 2010, more than 30 occurrences to (provision of a) legislation giving expression to fundamental rights between 2011 and 2019 could be spotted, and almost 50 occurrences since 2020.[71]

Whereas the CJEU increasingly recognised legislation as giving expression to fundamental rights, the methods and terminology used to identify this type of legislation as well as its role in relation to primary law remain often blurred. First, the CJEU does not use a consistent terminology to identify such legislation; it uses a broad range of terms to bridge between EU legislative acts and EU fundamental rights protected by primary law, without explaining or distinguishing between the different terms it uses. The CJEU has qualified a (provision of) legislative act as giving 'specific expression',[72] 'specific form',[73] 'concrete form'[74] to a Charter's right or which 'corresponds'[75] to such a fundamental right. Second, the CJEU sometimes considers that EU legislation

68 Case C-222/84, *Johnston*, ECLI:EU:C:1986:206, para. 18.
69 Case C-43/75, *Defrenne*, ECLI:EU:C:1976:56, para. 54.
70 Case C-44/79, *Hauer*, ECLI:EU:C :1979:290, para. 20.
71 Y. Lorans, *Le juge et le législateur de l'Union européenne. Etude d'une protection collaborative des droits fondamentaux*, PhD thesis, forthcoming.
72 E.g. Case C-414/16, *Egenberger*, ECLI:EU:C:2018:257, para. 47.
73 E.g. Case C-589/19, *Academia de Studii Economice din București Judgment*, ECLI:EU:C:2017:637, para. 37.
74 Cases C-924/19 PPU and 925/19 PPU, *FMS*, ECLI:EU:C:2020:367, para. 192.
75 Case C-465/07, *Elgafaji*, ECLI:EU:C:2009:94, para. 28.

as a whole is an expression of a fundamental right,[76] sometimes that a specific and isolated provision of legislation is such an expression.[77] Third, the CJEU does not have a systematic and clear methodology for identifying (provisions of) EU legislation giving expression to fundamental rights. Fourth, the CJEU's case-law remains somewhat blurry regarding the implications of identifying EU legislation as giving expression to fundamental rights.[78]

II. Identifying Legislation as Giving Expression to Fundamental Rights

The identification of EU legislation that gives expression to fundamental rights, while growing, remains somewhat unclear. How, then, can we identify legislation as giving expression to fundamental rights? Let us seek some clues in primary and secondary law, as well as in CJEU case-law, before attempting to develop a set of criteria for identifying legislation that expresses fundamental rights, with a view to selecting them in the areas of our case studies.

Neither the Charter nor EU secondary legislation explicitly identifies legislation as giving expression to fundamental rights. However, they provide useful guidance for identifying such legislation in two ways. First, the explanations to the Charter highlight the close relationship between Charter provisions and EU secondary legislation. The explanations' added value to identify legislation as an expression of a fundamental right is, however, limited. This is because they do not systematically point out the connection between Charter provisions and secondary legislation. When they do so, the explanations remain succinct and are rarely explicit about the nature of this connection.[79] Sometimes, the explanations are slightly more explicit about this relationship: they indicate that the Charter's provisions are based on or draw inspiration from EU secondary legislation.[80]

---

76 E.g. Case C-414/16, *Egenberger*, ECLI:EU:C:2018:257, para. 47.

77 Case C-350/20, *O.D.*, ECLI:EU:C:2021:659, para. 46.

78 One of the key questions is whether there is a 'priority rule' that applies in the field of EU fundamental rights, whereby the CJEU uses EU secondary legislation instead of the EU Charter when assessing the compliance of domestic measures. For further discussion on the priority rule in the context of the free movement of goods, see E. Ní Chaoimh, *The Legislative Priority Rule and the EU Internal Market for Goods. A Constitutional Approach*, Oxford, Oxford University Press, 2022.

79 For instance, the explanations on Article 30 Charter (protection in the event of unjustified dismissal) refers to two directives on the protection of employees, but fails to explain the relationship between this Charter provision and these directives.

80 This is the case, for example, regarding Articles 11 (freedom of expression and information), 23 (equality between men and women), 31 (fair and just working conditions), 32 (prohibition of child labour and protection of young people at work) and 33 (family and professional life) of the Charter. One exception where the explanations are more elaborate on the relationship between Charter provision and secondary EU law pertains to Article 8 (protection of personal data). The explanations indicate that EU data protection legislation, specifically the Data Protection Directive (95/46/EC) and the EU Institutions Data Protection Regulation

Second, EU secondary laws increasingly express their intention to promote or give effect to specific fundamental rights. This intention is reflected in the titles of EU secondary legislation, which are steadily more explicit about their implications for fundamental rights.[81] It is also apparent in the 'subject matter' or 'object' provisions of EU secondary legislation.[82] The recitals to EU secondary legislation have become increasingly explicit in expressing the legislative intent to promote fundamental rights.[83] However, fundamental rights recitals are sometimes used in legislation with a limited impact on fundamental rights, while they are absent in other legislation with significant repercussions on these rights.[84]

Even if the CJEU lacks a systematic methodology, some insights can be gleaned from its practice of identifying legislation as giving expression to fundamental rights. The CJEU has relied on a literal interpretation of legislative texts to find, both from the title of the directive and from the wording of the legislative provisions in question, that the latter concretises a fundamental

---

(45/2001/EC), has been a source of inspiration for the design of the fundamental right to data protection. Besides, the explanations indicate that these laws flesh out certain aspects of the right to data protection; according to the explanations, these laws 'contain conditions and limitations for the exercise of the right to the protection of personal data.' While such a clear statement on the relationship between the Charter provision and EU secondary legislation is relevant to identify legislation giving flesh to a fundamental right, it remains an isolated case.

81 This is well illustrated with the Presumption of Innocence Directive (2016/343/EU) [2016] OJ L65/1, which lays down common minimum rules concerning certain aspects of the presumption of innocence and the right to be present at the trial in criminal proceedings, whose title is Directive on the *strengthening* of certain aspects of the presumption of innocence and of the right to be present at the trial in criminal proceedings.

82 For example, the Racial Discrimination Directive (2000/43/EC) and the Equality Framework Directive (2000/78/EC) indicate that they aim to lay down a general framework for combating discrimination – respectively on the grounds of racial or ethnic origin and on the grounds of religion or belief, disability age or sexual orientation as regards employment and occupation – with a view to putting into effect in the Member States the principle of equal treatment (Article 1 Racial Discrimination Directive (2000/43/EC) and Article 1 Equality Framework Directive (2000/78/EC)).

83 E.g. Recital 41 Right to Information Directive (2012/13/EU), [2012] OJ L142/1, 1 June 2012: 'This Directive respects fundamental rights and observes the principles recognised by the Charter. In particular, this Directive seeks to promote the right to liberty, the right to a fair trial and the rights of the defence.'

84 R. Tinière, 'Le discours sans la méthode, les droits fondamentaux dans les actes de droit dérivé de l'Union européenne', *Revue DLF*, 2013, pp. 1–13. It is of note that the practice of including fundamental rights recitals results from a 2001 Memorandum on the application of the Charter (Commission Memorandum: Application of the Charter of Fundamental Rights of the European Union, SEC(2001)380/3). The latter provided that legislative proposals or draft instruments which have a specific link with fundamental rights must incorporate the following recital as a formal statement of compatibility: 'This [act] respects the fundamental rights and observes the principles recognised in particular by the Charter'. In case where certain rights or principles of the Charter were specifically involved, a second sentence could be added to state that the act seeks to ensure full respect and or promote the application of the specific Charter rights or principles.

right.[85] The CJEU has also drawn on a contextual interpretation, referring to the context of the legislative norms, such as their legal basis[86] or the overall framework of the legislative text and its provisions.[87] One criterion that seems to predominate is the intention of the legislator. The CJEU relies sometimes on the intention of institutions as expressed in the article devoted to the purpose of the legislative act[88] or in the preambles,[89] and even at times in the preparatory works.[90] Conversely, the CJEU does not appear to attach importance to the fact that the secondary legislation predates the enshrinement of the fundamental right in the Charter or that the secondary legislation was adopted on a legal basis which is not specific to fundamental rights.[91]

In legal scholarship, Muir has proposed a set of three criteria for distinguishing EU legislation giving expression to fundamental rights from ordinary EU legislation, namely:

1) A fundamental right protected by EU constitutional law;
2) EU legislation that gives substance to the identified fundamental right;
3) An organic relationship between the legislation and the constitutional right.[92]

These are the criteria which we use to identify legislation as giving expression to the fundamental rights studied in our case studies, which allows us to examine their influence on the ECtHR case-law. In this research, the first two criteria are required in any case to identify legislation as an expression of fundamental rights, while the third is facultative, but reinforcing. The organic relationship may be evidenced either by the legal basis on which the EU legislation has been adopted or by the intention of the EU legislator to promote or flesh out a fundamental right.[93]

The legal basis can play a role in identifying legislation as an expression of a fundamental right, but it should be approached with caution. Although the EU legislator has been granted more competences in the field of fundamental rights, these competences remain fragmented and limited. As a result, the EU

---

85 E.g. Case C-282/19, *MIUR*, ECLI:EU:C:2022:3, paras. 59–60.

86 E.g. Case C-507/18, *Associazione Avvocatura per i diritti LGBTI*, ECLI:EU:C:2020:289, paras. 34–38, in particular para. 35.

87 E.g. Case C-242/22 PPU, *Criminal proceedings against TL*, ECLI:EU:C:2022:611, paras. 37–42.

88 E.g. Case C-414/16, *Egenberger*, ECLI:EU:C:2018:257, para. 47.

89 E.g. Case C-467/18, *Rayonna prokuratura Lom*, ECLI:EU:C:2019:765, para. 37.

90 E.g. Joined Cases C-511/18, 512/18 and C-520/18, *La Quadrature du Net and Others*, ECLI:EU:C:2020:791, para. 106.

91 In its (2014) *Google Spain* for instance, the CJEU asserted that Article 8(2) and (3) Charter (protection of personal data) was implemented by the 1995 Data Protection Directive (95/46/EC), which was adopted before the drafting of the Charter on the basis of the general internal market clause. See Case C-131/12, *Google Spain*, ECLI:EU:C:2014:317, para. 69.

92 E. Muir, *EU Equality Law, The First Fundamental Rights Policy of the EU*, Oxford, Oxford University Press, 2018, p. 124.

93 Ibid.

has had (and will have) recourse to general legal bases, such as the internal market clause and the flexibility clause, to flesh out fundamental rights.[94] Similarly, the EU legislator's intention to flesh out fundamental rights may serve as an indicator, yet one must be cautious with this enhanced visibility, as we have seen above. Conversely, there are instances where the EU legislator does not express an intention to give flesh to a fundamental right, and yet the legislation has been identified as such.[95]

While some legislation will clearly express a fundamental right[96] and others will not,[97] grey areas will inevitably remain. The criteria may be seen as necessarily imperfect, given the great diversity of legislative acts that give expression to fundamental rights, which do not lend themselves to a 'mathematical' approach. In cases of doubt, we will adopt a flexible and pragmatic approach, constantly bearing in mind the final objective of this project, namely to examine the impact of the growing role of the EU as

---

94 See above, Part II, Chapter 2, Section II, §2. The fragmented, Yet Increasing Competences of the EU Legislator.

95 This is the case, for example, with the Working Time Directive (2003/88/EC), which does not contain any reference to fundamental rights although some of its provisions on paid annual leave have been deemed as an expression of Article 31(2) Charter (the right to paid annual leave) (E.g. Case C-589/19, *Academia de Studii Economice din București Judgment*, ECLI:EU:C:2017:637, para. 37 (Working Time Directive (2003/88/EC)).

96 By way of illustration, we may refer to the Racial Discrimination Directive (2000/43/EC) and the Equality Framework Directive (2000/78/EC). Regarding these directives, there is a clear overlap between the equality charter rights and the substantive provisions of these directives (criteria 1 and 2); they were adopted on the basis of a specific fundamental right legal basis, namely Article 13 TEC (criterion 3); they aim to lay down a general framework for combating discrimination with a view to putting into effect in the Member States the principle of equal treatment (criterion 3). Another example can be found with the GDPR (2016/679/EU). The latter instrument gives concrete expression to the fundamental right to data protection enshrined in Article 8 Charter (criteria 1 and 2), was adopted on the basis of a specific fundamental right legal basis, namely Article 16 TFEU (criterion 3), and aims, *inter alia*, to protect the fundamental rights and freedoms of natural persons and in particular their right to the protection of personal data (criterion 3).

97 The criteria also enable certain legislation to be excluded from the category of EU legislation that gives expression to a fundamental right. This applies to EU legislation which is linked to a certain EU policy and which contains isolated clauses relating to fundamental rights, for example relating to equality or the right to an effective remedy. Such is the case with certain directives which aim to protect atypical workers, namely workers other than those subject to the classic permanent full-time contract, which includes isolated equality clauses. For instance, Article 5 of the Temporary Agency Work Directive (2008/104/EC), [2008] OJ L327/9, provides that '[t]he basic working and employment conditions of temporary agency workers shall be, for the duration of their assignment at a user undertaking, at least those that would apply if they had been recruited directly by that undertaking to occupy the same job.' This type of legislation is excluded since the EU legislation does not, as a whole, give substance to a fundamental right protected at constitutional level (criterion 2); that it has been adopted on a legal basis which is not specific to fundamental rights, namely Article 137(2) TEC (criterion 3); that the intention of the legislator is to ensure the protection of temporary agency workers and to improve the quality of temporary agency and not to flesh out the equality Charter rights (criterion 3).

a standard-setter on ECtHR case-law. EU legislation that gives expression to the fundamental rights of equality and non-discrimination, as well as data protection is identified in Annexes II and IV.

SECTION III. SPECIFIC FEATURES OF EU FUNDAMENTAL RIGHTS

EU fundamental rights, as enshrined in the Charter and expressed in secondary laws, are distinguished by their high level of sophistication and integration within the domestic legal systems of EU States. While EU legislation giving expression to these rights is notable for its comprehensiveness and specificity in shaping the contours of the fundamental rights it protects, the Charter stands out for its highly developed and innovative nature. Both the Charter and legislative standards have also matured in CJEU case-law, with the CJEU increasingly providing these standards with an autonomous interpretation. These standards benefit from the distinct features of EU law, such as primacy and direct effect, which place national judges at the core of the implementation of Union law. EU fundamental rights, which these judges guarantee, are highly infused into domestic legal systems, as they can be relevant within the EU States without the need for cross-border movement and in both vertical and horizontal situations.

§ 1. HIGHLY SOPHISTICATED

EU fundamental rights legislations stand out due to their comprehensiveness and specificity in shaping the contours of the fundamental rights they protect. Not only do they define their scope and content, but they can also outline how these rights should be balanced against competing legitimate interests. Additionally, they can provide procedural tools to ensure that the fundamental right is made effective.

As we will revisit these aspects in our case studies, let us focus here on the Charter. From the outset of its elaboration, a legal discourse has surrounded the Charter according to which the latter does not intend to create anything substantially new, but only to make the protection of fundamental rights more visible in the EU.[98] One needs to be cautious with this discourse. Indeed, we should not underestimate its highly developed and innovative nature.

---

98 For instance, Declaration No. 1 to the TFEU states that the Charter confirms the fundamental rights guaranteed by the ECHR and as they result from the constitutional traditions common to the Member States. See in this vein, M. Maduro, 'The Double Constitutional

Unlike the ECHR, the Charter is a comprehensive instrument that encompasses several generations of fundamental rights. The Charter breaks new ground by combining different traditions of rights into a single, legally binding instrument, covering not only civil and political rights but also social, economic, and environmental rights, among others.[99] Its comprehensiveness arises from the diverse range of sources that inspired its drafters. The ECHR has been one of the key sources,[100] along with the Community Charter of the Fundamental Social Rights of Workers and the Council of Europe Social Charters.[101] Other human rights instruments also inspired the Charter.[102] Some provisions are based on the EU Treaties and CJEU's case-law,[103] while others

---

Life Charter of Fundamental Rights of the European Union', in T. Hervey and J. Kenner (eds.), *Economic and Social Rights under the EU Charter of Fundamental Rights – A Legal Perspective*, Oxford, Hart Publishing, 2003, p. 272.

99 In so doing, the Charter embraces the principle of indivisibility of fundamental rights reflected in the Universal Declaration of Human Rights, which sees fundamental rights as an indivisible whole; fundamental rights are conceived as a system in which all rights are interdependent, indivisible and interrelated (S. Douglas-Scott, 'The EU Charter of Fundamental Rights as a Constitutional Document', *European Human Rights Law Review*, 2004, p. 3). The indivisibility of fundamental rights is echoed in the preambles to the Charter, which refer to the values of the Union as indivisible and universal, and in Article 21(1) TEU, which states that the Union's action on the international scene shall be guided by the principle of universality and indivisibility of human rights. O'Leary observed that while the Court of First Instance has repeatedly referred to the indivisibility and universality of fundamental rights in CFSP asset freezing cases, the CJEU has not done so yet (S. O'Leary, 'The EU Charter Ten Years On: A View from Strasbourg', in M. Bobek and J. Adams-Prassl (eds.), *The EU Charter of Fundamental Rights in the Member States*, Oxford: Oxford, Hart Publishing, 2020, p. 41).

100 In this vein, at the first meeting of the Convention in 1999, Judge Fischbach of the ECtHR, who was one of the observers for the Council of Europe, stated that with regard to civil and political rights, 'the Charter should build on the European Convention on Human Rights. The rights and freedoms contained in the Convention and its additional protocols are worded in such a way that they could be incorporated stock and barrel into Community law' (see for the reference, P. Lemmens, 'The Relations between the Charter of Fundamental Rights of the European Union and the European Convention on Human Rights Substantive Aspects', *Maastricht Journal of European and Comparative Law*, 2001, p. 50). Notably, the Charter provisions included in Chapter I (Dignity), Chapter II (Freedoms) and Chapter VI (Justice) are largely derived from the ECHR.

101 Most provisions in Chapter IV (Solidarity) and several provisions in Chapter II (Freedoms) and Chapter III (Equality) have their basis in these instruments.

102 For instance, the principles of Article 3 Charter (the right to the integrity of the person), which includes *inter alia* the prohibition of the reproductive cloning of human being, were guided by the 1997 Oviedo Convention on Human Rights and Biomedicine and its additional Protocols. In a similar way, the 1989 New York Convention on the Rights of the Child inspired Article 24 Charter (Convention for the protection of Human Rights and Dignity of the Human Being with regard to the Application of Biology and Medicine: Convention on Human Rights and Biomedicine, *European treaty Series*, 4 April 1997, No. 164).

103 The case-law of the CJEU has informed *inter alia* Articles 1 (human dignity), 3 (right to the integrity of the person) and 16 (freedom to conduct a business) Charter. Regarding the EU Treaties, this is in particular the case of the provisions of Chapter V (Citizens'

are rooted in EU secondary laws[104] or inspired by the common constitutional traditions of the Member States.[105]

The Charter is also, to some extent, an enriched and updated version of the ECHR. Where Charter provisions draw inspiration from the ECHR, they often introduce innovations. Notable are the modifications in the wording of Charter provisions compared to their ECHR equivalents. Examples include Article 47 Charter compared to Articles 6 and 13 ECHR,[106] Article 7 Charter compared to Article 8 ECHR,[107] and Article 9 Charter compared to Article 12 ECHR.[108] Beyond changes in wording, several Charter provisions have been enriched and updated in comparison to the ECHR. This is the case of Article 10 Charter

---

rights), where the explanations to the Charter indicate that each provision of the Charter finds echo in these Treaties. Other provisions of the Charter inspired by the EU Treaties include Articles 18 (right to asylum), 21 (non-discrimination), 24 (the rights of the child), 37 (environmental protection), 38 (consumer protection).

104 For instance, the explanations to the Charter refer to the Data Protection Directive (95/46/EC) and the EU Institutions Data Protection Regulation (45/2001/EC) as sources of inspiration for the conception of the autonomous fundamental right to data protection enshrined in Article 8 Charter. This is also the case for several provisions in Chapter IV (Solidarity): for instance, Article 31(2) Charter (the right to paid annual leave) is based on the 1993 Working Time Directive (93/104/EC).

105 The explanations to the Charter indicate that this is the case for Articles 13 (freedom of the arts and sciences), 14 (right to education), 17 (right to property), 37 (environmental protection), 49 (principles of legality and proportionality of criminal offences and penalties).

106 Article 47 of the Charter guarantees the right to an effective remedy before a court in the event of an alleged violation of rights and freedoms, whereas the corresponding Article 13 ECHR provides for a remedy before a national authority. The second paragraph of Article 47, which guarantees the right to a fair trial before an independent and impartial tribunal established by law, has a broader scope than its ECHR equivalent: Article 6 of the ECHR applies where civil rights and obligations are involved or where a criminal charge is at issue, whereas Article 47 contains no such restriction. See e.g. on the scope of application of Article 6 ECHR, P. Lemmens, 'The right to a fair trial and its multiple manifestations. Article 6(1) ECHR. Shaping Rights in the ECHR', in E. Brems and J. Gerards (eds.), *The Role of the European Court of Human Rights in Determining the Scope of Human Rights*, Cambridge, Cambridge University Press, 2013, pp. 294–314.

107 While the latter guarantees to everyone the right to respect for his private and family life, his home and his correspondence, Article 7 replaces the word correspondence with the broader and more modern concept of communication.

108 While the latter mentions that the rights to marry and found a family belong to *men and women of marriageable age*, the latter reference is deleted in favour of a broader and more neutral formulation: 'The right to marry and the right to found a family shall be guaranteed in accordance with the national laws governing the exercise of these rights.

vis-à-vis Article 9 ECHR,[109] Article 11 Charter vis-à-vis Article 10 ECHR,[110] and Article 49(1) Charter vis-à-vis Article 7(1) ECHR.[111] The Charter also lays down certain rights closely connected to ECHR provisions in a separate way. This is particularly the case for the autonomous fundamental right to data protection, which is enshrined in Article 8 Charter.[112]

The highly-sophisticated nature of the Charter and legislative standards is also due to their maturation in CJEU case-law. Since the Treaty of Lisbon, the Charter has played a key role in CJEU case-law.[113] In some fields, legislation has been part of case-law for decades,[114] while in other areas, case-law has 'exploded' in recent years.[115] The CJEU has increasingly provided these standards with an autonomous interpretation. They have become the focal point of the CJEU, which tends to interpret them autonomously from ECHR law.[116] As shown by Tinière, the CJEU has progressively replaced references to ECHR law with EU-centered references.[117] The movement towards autonomy

---

109 Whereas the first paragraphs of these two articles are almost identical, the second paragraph of Article 10 Charter recognises the right to conscientious objection, which is not the case with Article 9 ECHR. In an article published 2001, Lemmens observed that at the time it was settled case-law that the right of conscientious objection to military service and alternative service was not guaranteed by the ECHR. See P. Lemmens, 'The Relations between the Charter of Fundamental Rights of the European Union and the European Convention on Human Rights Substantive Aspects', *Maastricht Journal of European and Comparative Law*, 2001, p. 50.

110 The second paragraph of Article 11 Charter adds a specific paragraph related to the respect for the freedom and pluralism of the media.

111 Article 49(1) Charter, as Article 7(1) ECHR, enshrines the prohibition of retroactive application of criminal law. Unlike the latter ECHR provision, the Charter provision provides for the application of the more lenient criminal law.

112 Article 8 ECHR provides for the right to respect for private and family life, but not (explicitly) for the right to data protection. Yet, the ECtHR has ruled on multiple data protection issues, most often from the perspective of Article 8 ECHR, as we shall see below in our case study on data protection in Part III.

113 S. Iglesias Sánchez, 'The Court and the Charter: the impact of the entry into force of the Lisbon Treaty on the CJEU's approach to fundamental rights', *Common Market Law Review*, 2012, pp. 1565–1611.

114 An example is the field of equality law where the CJEU has already rendered key judgments in the 1970s, such as the *Defrenne* cases (Case C-80/70, *Defrenne I*, ECLI:EU:C:1971:55; Case C-43/75, *Defrenne II*, ECLI:EU:C:1976:56; Case C-149/77, *Defrenne III*, ECLI:EU:C:1978:130).

115 This seems to be the case in the field of data protection where there is an increase of cases over the past few years as explained in Part IV, Chapter 1, Section I. More EU Fundamental Rights.

116 E.g. C. Rizcallah, *The European Union and Human Rights. Unlocking the opportunities and challenges of a singular regional player*, forthcoming.

117 R. Tinière, 'The Use of ECtHR Case-law by the CJEU: Instrumentalisation or Quest for Autonomy and Legitimacy', *European Papers*, 2023, pp. 325–326.

is not limited to the Charter: the CJEU has also interpreted EU fundamental rights legislation autonomously from ECHR law.[118]

The CJEU has scarcely provided justification for its autonomous interpretation of EU fundamental rights.[119] It has, however, increasingly made references to the autonomy of EU law and of the CJEU in the field of fundamental rights.[120] Advocates General have suggested that the CJEU can interpret Charter rights that correspond to ECHR rights in an autonomous way, insofar as this interpretation results in a higher level of protection than that guaranteed by the ECHR.[121] While an autonomous interpretation of the Charter cannot lower the level of protection guaranteed by the ECHR,[122] such an interpretation could lead to a higher level of protection even when a Charter right corresponds to an ECHR right.[123]

The autonomous interpretation of EU fundamental rights should not lead us to conclude that ECHR law has lost its relevance within CJEU's case-law. Numerous examples demonstrate the significant role ECHR law continues to play in the CJEU case-law. It is important to note that the Charter includes a principle which guarantees a certain harmony with the ECHR, namely Article 52(3) Charter. Its first sentence includes a principle of 'homogeneity' or

118 As we will explain below, in the context of the judicial saga on detention in the Hungarian transit zones, the CJEU relied on EU secondary law and interpreted it autonomously from ECHR law to depart from ECtHR case-law (Part IV, Chapter 2, Section I, §3, I.A.Missed Judicial Dialogue). See V. DAVIO, 'Detention in the Hungarian Transit Zones: A Case of Higher Fundamental Rights Protection by EU Law vis-à-vis the ECHR', *European Law Review*, 2022, p. 400.

119 Please note that this paragraph is inspired by V. DAVIO, ibid., pp. 404–405.

120 J. CALLEWAERT, 'Do we still need Article 6(2) TEU? Considerations on the absence of EU accession to the ECHR and its consequences', *Common Market Law Review*, 2018, pp. 1699–1700. The CJEU has made a growing number of references to the explanations relating to Article 52(3) Charter according to which: 'Paragraph 3 is intended to ensure the necessary consistency between the Charter and the ECHR [...]. This means in particular that the legislator, in laying down limitations to those rights, must comply with the same standards as are fixed by the detailed limitation arrangements laid down in the ECHR, which are thus made applicable for the rights covered by this paragraph, *without thereby adversely affecting the autonomy of Union law and of that of the Court of Justice of the European Union*.' Emphasis added

121 Opinion of Advocate General PIKAMÄE, 23 April 2020 in Joined Cases C-924/19 PPU and 925/19 PPU, *FMS and Others*, ECLI:EU:C:2020:294, paras. 149–150; Opinion of Advocate General Campos SANCHEZ-BORDONA, 12 September 2017 in *Menci*, Case C-524/15, ECLI:EU:C:2017:667, paras. 74–75.

122 The explanations relating to Art. 52(3) Charter provides that: 'The last sentence of the paragraph is designed to allow the Union to guarantee more extensive protection. *In any event, the level of protection afforded by the Charter may never be lower than that guaranteed by the ECHR*.' Emphasis added

123 J. CALLEWAERT, 'Do we still need Article 6(2) TEU? Considerations on the absence of EU accession to the ECHR and its consequences', *Common Market Law Review*, 2018, p. 1699.

'equivalence' with the ECHR,[124] according to which the Charter rights shall have the same meaning and scope as those of the corresponding rights guaranteed by the ECHR. The explanations to the Charter indicate that the reference to the ECHR covers the ECHR and its Protocols, and that the meaning and the scope of the guaranteed rights are determined not only by the text of these instruments, but also by ECtHR case-law.[125] The first sentence of Article 52(3) Charter is therefore an important channel through which the ECHR and the ECtHR case-law continues to influence the shape of EU fundamental rights and has allowed considerable harmony between EU fundamental rights and the ECHR.[126] There are numerous areas where ECHR law has been used significantly in recent years, such as procedural rights in criminal procedure,[127] the rule of law,[128] and the ne bis in idem principle.[129] Moreover, there has been not only a substantial alignment with ECHR law but also (arguably) a methodological one.[130]

§ 2. DEEPLY INTEGRATED WITHIN EU STATES

EU fundamental rights, defined at both the primary and secondary law levels, have become highly developed within the EU legal framework. They are also deeply integrated into the domestic legal systems of the EU States. EU fundamental rights benefit from the distinct features of EU law, such as primacy

---

124 S. O'Leary, 'The EU Charter Ten Years On: A View from Strasbourg', in M. Bobek and J. Adams-Prassl (eds.), *The EU Charter of Fundamental Rights in the Member States*, Oxford, Hart Publishing, 2020, p. 42.

125 Explanation on Article 52 – Scope and interpretation of rights and principles.

126 See for recent examples of the use of the first sentence of Article 52(3) Charter, e.g. Case C-564/19, *IS*, ECLI:EU:C:2021:949, para. 101 and following; Case C-336/19, *Centraal Israëlitisch Consistorie van België and Others*, ECLI:EU:C:2020:1031, para. 56 and following; Joined Cases C-511/18, 512/18 and C-520/18, *La Quadrature du Net and Others*, ECLI:EU:C:2020:791, para. 124 and following. See also e.g., J. Krommendijk and G. de Vries, 'De wisselwerking tussen het HvJ EU en het EHRM: een hernieuwde liefde?' *SEW*, 2021, p. 570 where the authors even suggested that '[d]espite, or perhaps even thanks to, the EU's failure to accede to the ECHR, the [Court of Justice and the ECtHR] seem to have moved closer to each other again in the last five years. After a brief separation after Opinion 2/13, love seems to have been rekindled' (translation is ours); J. Callewaert, 'Do we still need Article 6(2) TEU? Considerations on the Absence of EU Accession to the ECHR and its Consequences', *CMLR*, 2018, p. 1693.

127 See below Part IV, Chapter 1, Section I. More EU Fundamental Rights.

128 See below Part IV, Chapter 2, Section I, §3, I.B. Virtuous Circles.

129 See below Part IV, Chapter 2, Section I, §2, II. Coherence without Aligning with EU Standards.

130 See e.g. Case C-336/19, *Centraal Israëlitisch Consistorie van België and Others*, ECLI:EU:C:2020:1031, where the CJEU refers to the doctrines of margin of appreciation and consensus (paras. 67–68) as well as the living instrument doctrine (para. 77) with references to ECtHR case-law.

and direct effect. EU law takes precedence over national law, regardless of whether the national law predated or postdated EU law, and this applies even over the highest norms of the EU States.[131] It confer rights and obligations to individuals which may be enforced directly at domestic level.[132] As Rizcallah observed, these distinctive features, which also concern EU fundamental rights, set them apart from traditional international human rights law.[133] While both primacy and direct effect are not foreign to public international law, States are usually afforded the discretion to determine the methods by which they fulfil their international commitments.[134]

These specific features place national judges at the heart of the implementation of Union law. Let us recall that 'national courts, in collaboration with the [CJEU], fulfil a duty entrusted to them both of ensuring that in the interpretation and application of the Treaties the law is observed'.[135] They are the primary guarantors of the effectiveness of Union law.[136] National judges must, in particular, set aside any national provision that conflicts with a provision of EU law with direct effect[137] and interpret national rules in conformity with EU law.[138]

EU fundamental rights, which national judges guarantee, are highly infused into domestic legal systems. First, they can be relevant within the EU States without the need for cross-border movement. This is the case for instance with the set of procedural rights directives which have been adopted on the basis of Article 82(2)(b) TFEU. While these directives are intended to enhance cross-border cooperation between EU States, they are also applicable in purely

131 Case C-11/70, *Internationale Handelsgesellschaft*, ECLI:EU:C:1970:114, para. 3.

132 See on recent developments on primacy and direct effect in light of *Polawski II* (Case C-573/17, *Polawski II*, ECLI:EU:C:2019:530), D. Miasik and M. Szwarc, 'Primacy and direct effect - still together: Poplawski II', *Common Market Law Review*, 2021, pp. 571–590.

133 See C. Rizcallah, *The European Union and Human Rights. Understanding a Singular Regional Player*, Oxford, Hart, forthcoming.

134 Ibid.

135 Please note that this paragraph is inspired by C. Rizcallah and V. Davio, 'L'article 19 du Traité sur l'Union européenne : sésame de l'Union de droit - Analyse de la jurisprudence récente de la Cour de justice de l'Union européenne relative à l'indépendance des juges nationaux', *Revue trimestrielle des droits de l'homme*, 2009, pp. 155–185. Opinion 1/09 of 8 March 2011, ECLI:EU:C:2011:123, para. 69. See also Case C-64/16, *Associação Sindical dos Juíes Portugueses*, ECLI:EU:C:2018:117, para. 34.

136 B. Smulders, 'De verknochtheid tussen de rechtsstaat, de EU en haar lidstaten', in B.-J. van Etterkoven a.o. (ed.), *Rechtsorde en bestuur : liber amicorum aangeboden aan Piet Hein Donner*, Den Haag, Boom Juridische uitgevers, 2018, p. 457.

137 Case C-573/17, *Polawski II*, ECLI:EU:C:2019:530, para. 61; Case C-106/77, *Simmenthal*, ECLI:EU:C:1978:49, para. 24.

138 Case C-14/83, *Von Colson*, ECLI:EU:C:1984:153.

national situations. They apply to all criminal proceedings conducted in Member States without requiring a transnational element.[139]

Second, EU fundamental rights can apply in both vertical and horizontal situations. A notable feature of the EU system is the horizontal applicability of some fundamental rights, allowing private parties to invoke these rights against other private parties.[140] Some EU fundamental rights legislations imposed obligations on individuals which may be invoked by individuals either by relying on their national transposition or directly on these instruments.[141] The CJEU has recognised that fundamental rights either expressed in general principle or the Charter could benefit from horizontal direct effect.[142]

---

139 In this respect, see I. Wieczorek, 'The emerging role of the EU as a primary normative actor in the EU Area of Criminal Justice', *European Law Journal: Review of European Law in Context*, 2023, pp. 378–407.

140 See generally on the topic E. Frantziou, *The Horizontal Effect of Fundamental Rights in the European Union. A Constitutional Analysis*, Oxford, Oxford University Press, 2019.

141 This is for instance the case of the GDPR which can be relied upon by private parties against other private parties.

142 E.g. Case C-144/04, *Mangold*, ECLI:EU:C:2005:709, paras. 76–78; Case C-414/16, *Egenberger*, ECLI:EU:C:2018:257, para. 76. See on an attempt to capture the dynamics of the CJEU case-law in this field, E. Muir, 'The Horizontal Effects of Charter Rights given expression to in EU Legislation, from Mangold to Bauer', *Review of European Administrative Law*, 2020, pp. 185–215.

CONCLUSION: THE EVOLVING EUROPEAN HOUSE OF FUNDAMENTAL RIGHTS

The metaphor of the crowded house is probably one of the most well-known among EU fundamental rights lawyers.[1] Coined by former Advocate General Villalón, it conveys the idea that within Europe – a relatively small geographical area – there exists a significant number of fundamental rights adjudicators and a diverse array of sources for fundamental rights protection. Villalón's powerful image highlighted three key sources of protection: national constitutions, the ECHR, and the Charter. He pointed out that the Charter entered a room that was 'already crowded'.

Yet, EU fundamental rights have been fleshed out not only in the Charter but also through secondary legislation, with an expanding body of sectoral legislative instruments that further define these rights. The emergence of standards at EU primary and secondary law levels raises significant questions: Has the European house become overcrowded? What new balances have emerged within this house?

The evolving role of the EU as a standard-setter carries the potential to alter the dynamics between EU and ECHR laws. Historically, the EU's fundamental rights regime closely followed the ECHR law. However, with the Charter and secondary legislation taking centre stage, EU fundamental rights are increasingly distinguishing themselves from ECHR law. These EU-specific standards have become the primary focus of the CJEU, leading to a noticeable decline in the reliance on ECHR law by the CJEU. While EU fundamental rights could for long be almost equated to ECHR standards, they can now impact ECtHR case-law.

This shifting paradigm presents both a curse and a blessing for the ECHR legal system. A curse, firstly, because the autonomous nature of EU fundamental rights increases the risk of tensions and inconsistencies with the ECHR legal system. As the EU and ECHR layers become increasingly distinct from one another, they must be articulated coherently for the benefit of the shared European fundamental rights space. This coherence, long maintained

[1] P. Villalon, 'Rights in Europe: The Crowded House ?' *KCL Working Papers in European Law*, 2020, pp. 1–20.

through the CJEU's incorporation of ECHR standards, rests partly in the hands of the CJEU and the ECtHR. This coherence is crucial for national judges in EU States who are required to apply both layers of rights. A lack of coherence could undermine the effectiveness of these rights, ultimately affecting individuals.

A blessing then, as, in the words of Villalón, '[t]he crowed house offers all kind of opportunities: for interaction, for adversial discourses, even for trial and error. [...] A reduce space facilitates cross fertilisation in a larger measure than other situations do.'[2] Indeed, one should not only see the development of EU fundamental rights as a threat to the ECHR system. These rights can be a highly attractive source of inspiration for the ECtHR. They are a potential source of enrichment for ECHR law, which can enrich, refine, or clarify its case-law in light of the innovative EU fundamental rights.

How has the ECtHR responded to the EU's increasing role as a standard-setter? Let us now delve into this question, particularly within the realms of equality and non-discrimination, as well as data protection. Let us step into a specific room within the evolving European house of fundamental rights.

---

2 Ibid., p. 20.

PART III.

In Action: The Use of EU Fundamental Rights in Practice

INTRODUCTION

To examine the influence of EU fundamental rights on the ECtHR case-law, we use two case studies: equality and non-discrimination, and data protection. For non-EU fundamental rights lawyers, this choice might not seem immediately obvious, as these two rights have not much in common at first glance. They have experienced different historical developments. Equality has been discussed since ancient Greece, whereas data protection is a quintessentially contemporary fundamental right, emerging in the 1970s with the advent of the digital age. These rights are perceived in different ways by the public. Equality often raises sensitive and controversial issues, such as the wearing of headscarves or transgender rights. Data protection, in contrast, is rather a technical and complex field.

If there are other areas where EU fundamental rights – and EU law in general – have influenced the ECtHR's case-law,[1] equality and data protection seem particularly well-suited for studying the impact of the growing role of the EU as a standard-setter on Strasbourg case-law. The EU has long been committed to protecting these two rights. Equality has been present since the early days of European integration and legislative measures on gender equality were adopted from the 1970s. It was in the wake of the first data protection instruments that the EU legislator developed a robust data protection policy from the mid-1990s. These two rights have undergone successive waves of legislative interventions. Initially, they were limited in scope, based on the EU's general competences, and closely tied to economic objectives. Later waves expanded in scope, were based on specific competences, and were driven by complementary rationales. Both fields are examples of where the EU has enacted legislation that gives expression to fundamental rights. Next, the Charter, with legally binding status since the Lisbon Treaty, marked a momentum for the protection of these two rights. First, it enshrines an autonomous fundamental right to data protection. Second, it dedicates a specific title with a series of general and specific equality provisions. The long-standing presence of these rights in secondary laws and the Charter means they have had time to mature in CJEU case-law. The CJEU have interpreted directives such as the Race Equality Directive (2000/43/EC) and the Equality Framework Directive (2000/78/EC)

1 Consider, for example, the fields of asylum and migration, mutual recognition, *ne bis in idem*, the rule of law, international child abduction, ritual slaughter, and fundamental rights in competition proceedings.

for more than twenty years, whereas a surge of data protection cases can be observed over the past years.

This combination of legislative acts, Charter provisions and CJEU case-law makes equality and data protection (among) the most sophisticatedly fundamental rights protected in EU law. They are highly elaborated not only at substantive level, with specific definitions, principles, and rights enshrined in EU instruments, but also at procedural level. There is a high degree of proceduralisation in both areas, with the establishment of enforcement institutions aimed at ensuring the effectiveness of these rights. Equality and data protection are also deeply integrated into the domestic legal systems of the EU States. Proof of this is that these two rights can be applied within these States without the requirement of a cross-border element and that they apply in both vertical and horizontal situations.

If equality and data protection are probably the areas of fundamental rights where the EU has developed its most advanced policies, they operate in distinct normative environments when we take a step back from EU law.

This is first evident when we examine the protection of these rights within the ECHR system. The protection of equality has historically been considered inadequate or subordinate, particularly due to the accessory nature of Article 14 ECHR. It is only recently that we see a process of autonomisation and enrichment of ECHR equality law. In contrast, although the ECHR does not enshrine a fundamental right to data protection, the ECtHR has developed extensive case-law on data protection since the late 1980s under Article 8 ECHR.

This also holds true when we consider the protection of these rights by international human rights instruments. The protection of equality is fleshed out in numerous general and specific conventions, most of which focus on one specific ground of discrimination, such as disability, gender or ethnic minorities. For data protection, there are fewer binding international instruments, but there is the landmark Convention 108 from the Council of Europe which entered into force in 1985 whose principles have served as the foundation for many national and European legislations.

It goes without saying that our case studies need to be used with caution. They are areas where the influence of EU fundamental rights is particularly likely; they may thus present a picture of influence that is more significant than it would be for other areas. It is thus important not to overstretch the conclusions drawn from the case studies. Nevertheless, they are illustrative of dynamics that are occurring or will occur in other fields where fundamental rights policies or instruments are developed at EU level. Contextual factors within each field need to be carefully considered. We will show that while the dynamics of influence overlap in both fields, there are differences in the way EU equality and data protection laws have left an imprint on ECHR law. The distinct normative environments which we have just introduced are key to understanding the specific dynamics in each field.

TITLE 1

THE INFLUENCE OF EU EQUALITY LAW ON ECHR EQUALITY LAW

CHAPTER 1
INTRODUCTION

In Europe, there exist two distinct, but closely related and interdependent, systems of protection against discrimination, namely that of the EU and of the ECHR. These two systems are marked by considerable differences and are driven by their own dynamics. The fact that they operate separately and are not identical does not mean that they do not interact with each other, quite the contrary. There are often mutual interactions and influences between the two equality law systems, and this is even more true in recent years. These interactions can be fruitful for the protection and promotion of equality at European level. Recently, Gerards has pointed out that: 'one advantage of the coexistence of the two [equality law] systems is that the [CJEU] and the [ECtHR] can learn from each other and make use of each other's expertise by adopting each other's doctrines and embedding them in their own [case-law]. There are numerous examples of this in practice, with sometimes the CJEU taking the lead and sometimes the ECtHR. This mutual learning can ultimately contribute to a further development and refinement of the [case-law] on non-discrimination in each of the two systems, and perhaps ultimately [...] to convergence'.[1]

SECTION I. THE INTERACTIONS BETWEEN EU AND ECHR EQUALITY LAW: AN UNDER-RESEARCHED AREA

Despite the importance of these interactions to improve and ensure the coherence of the European multi-layered equality architecture, the latter topic has received limited coverage. This is in contrast to the increasing research attention paid to the equality protection mechanisms at European supranational level. The last two decades have seen a burgeoning literature on equality protection at EU level. This is particularly the case since the insertion of Article 13 EC Treaty into the Treaty of Amsterdam, a legal basis which

[1] J. Gerards, 'Systeemverklaringen voor verschillen tussen de gelijkebehandelingsrechtspraak van het HvJ EU en het EHRM', *SEW*, 2021, p. 581. The translation is ours.

has been used for the adoption of the so-called 'next generation' equality directives.[2] The protection of equality at ECHR level has received renewed attention in the literature. The revived interest was driven by the adoption in 2000 and the entry into force in 2005 of Additional Protocol No. 12 ECHR, which contains a general prohibition of discrimination.[3] The coexistence of two equality law systems at European level and the growing attention they receive has prompted researchers to compare and contrast them.[4]

Although these topics have garnered attention, the interactions between the EU and ECHR equality law systems remain under-researched. The influence of EU equality law on ECHR equality law has not been thoroughly examined. Although scholars have highlighted that EU law has had a strong impact on the ECtHR equality case-law,[5] this issue has been addressed peripherally.

This observation may not be so surprising after all: the influence of EU equality law on ECHR law is not an obvious avenue of research. The ECHR has had, and still has, an extensive impact on the development of EU fundamental

[2] The expression 'next generation equality directives' is borrowed from M. Bell, 'The Principle of Equal Treatment: Widening and Deepening', in P. Craig and G. De Búrca (eds.), *The Evolution of EU law*, 2011, p. 618. It refers to the directives, such as the such as the Race Equality Directive (2000/43/EC) and the Equality Framework Directive (2000/78/EC), which were adopted as from the 2000s. E.g. E. Muir, *EU Equality Law: The First Fundamental Rights Policy of the EU*, Oxford/OSO, Oxford University Press USA, 2018; R. Xenidis, 'Shaking the Normative Foundations of EU Equality Law: Evolution and Hierarchy between Market Integration and Human Rights Rationales', 2017, EUI Department of Law Research Paper No. 2017/04; M. Bell, *Anti-Discrimination Law and the European Union*, Oxford, Oxford University Press, 2002.

[3] E.g. S. Fredman, 'Emerging from the Shadows: Substantive Equality and Article 14 of the European Convention on Human Rights', *Human Rights Law Review*, 2016, pp. 273–301; O.M. Arnardóttir, 'The differences that make a difference: recent developments on the discrimination grounds and the margin of appreciation under Article 14 of the European Convention on Human Rights', *Human Rights Law Review*, 2014, pp. 647–670; J. Gerards, 'The Discrimination Grounds of Article 14 of the European Convention on Human Rights', *Human Rights Law Review*, 2013, pp. 99–124.

[4] E.g. M. Möschel, 'Comparing the activist claim between Strasbourg and Luxembourg in the field of non-discrimination', in B. de Witte, M. Dawson and E. Muir (eds.), *Revisiting Judicial Politics in the European Union*, Cheltenham, Edward Elgar Publishing, 2024, pp. 334–351; J. Gerards, 'Systeemverklaringen voor verschillen tussen de gelijkebehandelingsrechtspraak van het HvJ EU en het EHRM', *SEW*, 2021, pp. 571–581; E. Dubout, 'Une approche comparative du principe de non-discrimination dans le cadre européen : Convention européenne des droits de l'homme et droit de l'Union européenne', in M. Balboni (ed.), *The European Convention of Human Rights and the Principle of Non-Discrimination*, Naples, Editoriale Scientifica, 2017, pp. 63–120.

[5] E.g. S. Fredman, 'Emerging from the Shadows: Substantive Equality and Article 14 of the European Convention on Human Rights', *Human Rights Law Review*, 2016, p. 274; M. Bell, 'The principle of equal treatment: widening and deepening', in P. Craig and G. de Búrca (eds.), *The evolution of EU law*, Oxford, Oxford University Press, 2011, p. 638; S. Besson, 'Gender Discrimination under EU and ECHR Law: Never Will the Twain Meet?', *Human Rights Law Review*, 2008, pp. 649–650.

rights.[6] Hence the focal research point has been on the reception of ECHR law in EU law and not the opposite. EU law has often been studied and portrayed as a threat to the ECHR rights rather than a source of inspiration.[7] At first glance, it is thus not self-evident that the ECtHR would draw upon the doctrines and concepts of EU law to shape its case-law.

That being said, the EU's fundamental rights landscape has undergone significant changes, which may have important consequences beyond the confines of the EU legal order. Historically, the EU has played a relatively minor role in the realm of fundamental rights, with the EU judiciary being the primary actor. Yet, as we have shown in Part II of this project, this situation is changing, as evidenced by the proclamation of the Charter in 2000, which became binding in 2009. In addition, the EU's legislative activity in the field of fundamental rights has grown over the past three decades. The EU legislature has begun to develop a body of fundamental rights standards, which clarify the meaning, scope, and limits of specific rights. EU fundamental rights tend to emancipate themselves from ECHR law, which used to constitute the main source of inspiration for these rights.

The field of equality and non-discrimination is not foreign to these developments. The EU has developed a strong anti-discrimination policy, which has been portrayed as the 'first fundamental rights policy of the EU',[8] inter alia by adopting a series of legislative instruments covering a considerable number of protected grounds.[9] In contrast, the protection of equality in the ECHR system has long been perceived as one of its 'Achilles' heels'. This is primarily due to the fact that the provision of this Convention devoted to equality, namely its Article 14, has a so-called 'accessory' character, which means that it must be invoked in conjunction with another provision of the ECHR.

This atypical situation, with (prima facie) strong protection of a fundamental right at EU level and limited protection at ECHR level, have led authors to consider that the relationship between EU and ECHR laws should be turned upside down: while the CJEU has generally to adapt its interpretations and definitions to the ECtHR case-law, the situation may be the other way around in the equality field.[10] Whereas the ECtHR has increasingly developed its equality doctrines over the last decades, they are still evolving, and as a result,

---

[6] See above Part II, Chapter 1, Section III, §2. The Special Significance of ECHR Law.

[7] See above Part I, Chapter 3, Section I. Existing Research and Distinctive Features of Our Project.

[8] See E. Muir, *EU Equality Law, The First Fundamental Rights Policy of the EU*, Oxford, Oxford University Press, 2018.

[9] E.g. A. Bailleux and E. Bribosia, 'La protection des droits fondamentaux', in A. Bailleux (ed.), *Actualités du contentieux européen*, Louvain-la-Neuve, Anthemis, 2020, p. 134.

[10] J. Gerards, 'The Discrimination Grounds of Article 14 of the European Convention on Human Rights', *Human Rights Law Review*, 2013, p. 102.

the ECtHR may be inclined to draw from the sophisticated EU equality law framework to enrich or refine its case-law.

The overlap between the EU and ECHR equality regimes prompts the need for articulation between the two systems. There are numerous instances where the CJEU and the ECtHR are dealing with similar questions on equality, sometimes involving the same (EU) States. This overlap stems from analogous factual circumstances or from the similarity of the equality concepts at stake, exemplified by matters involving indirect discrimination[11] or discrimination by association.[12] Judicial dialogue between the ECtHR and the CJEU is therefore crucial to ensure the coherence of equality protection in Europe. This is particularly important for domestic judges in EU States, who must apply both EU and ECHR equality laws.

SECTION II. MAIN RESEARCH QUESTION AND RELEVANCE

We will seek to address the main research question of this project, which is, 'How and to what extent have EU fundamental rights influenced the ECtHR case-law?' in the field of equality law. This translates into: 'How and to what extent has EU equality law influenced ECHR equality law?'. Exploring the influence of EU equality law is not only timely, as more than twenty years have passed since the adoption of significant directives such as the Race Equality Directive (2000/43/EC) and the Equality Framework Directive (2000/78/EC), but it is relevant from both a scholarly perspective and a societal perspective. The scientific relevance is evidenced by the gap in the literature. The societal relevance flows from the fact that the influence of EU equality law may have far-reaching consequences for individuals.

A short example may be useful. In *Guberina v. Croatia* (2016), the applicant was denied tax relief for the purchase of a new house to provide his disabled child with accommodation more suited to his needs. The ECtHR embraced for the first time the concept of discrimination by association, which covers cases where a person is treated less favourably based on the status of another person's protected characteristic. As a result, the ECtHR was able to find that the tax authorities had not sufficiently taken into account the special needs of the disabled child when considering tax relief and found a violation of Article 14

---

11 E.g. at CJEU level: Case C-83/14, *CHEZ*, ECLI:EU:C:2015:480 and Case C-303/06, *S. Coleman v. Attridge Law and Steve Law*, ECLI:EU:C:2008:415; E.g. at ECtHR level: ECtHR, *D.H. and Others v. the Czech Republic* [GC], no. 57325/00, ECHR 2007-IV.

12 E.g. at CJEU level: Case C-223/19, *YS v. NK*, ECLI:EU:C:2020:753; E.g. at ECtHR level: ECtHR, *Molla Sali v. Greece* [GC], no. 20452/14, § 134, 19 December 2018; ECtHR, *Guberina v. Croatia*, no. 23682/13, 22 March 2016.

ECHR.[13] The influence of EU equality law in embracing discrimination by association was perceptible, yet the ECtHR did not acknowledge it in its reasoning, as we will explain below.[14] This example highlights that while the ECtHR's use of EU equality law may benefit individuals, the methodological approach used by the ECtHR may require some improvements.

The impact of EU equality law on ECHR law raises a series of important questions: How has EU equality law contributed to shape the equality doctrines at ECHR level? Has this led to a greater protection and convergence of equality at European level? Are there areas in which more influence can be seen? Who are the actors who play a role in the influence process? Who are the States involved when the ECtHR uses EU equality law? Does the ECtHR develop a method when it refers to EU equality law?

SECTION III. METHODOLOGY

Our methodology involves a systematic analysis of ECtHR equality case-law that refer to EU equality law under scrutiny – (i) EU legislation giving expression to the equality fundamental rights,[15] (ii) the Charter[16] and (iii) related CJEU case-law[17] – using the Hudoc database.[18] We found 32 cases for legislative instruments, 22 cases for the Charter and 29 cases for related CJEU case-law. The cumulative cases led to a total of 52 cases for EU equality law.[19]

To provide comparative insights, we examined ECtHR judgments on equality that refer to international instruments and related bodies.[20] We selected

13 ECtHR, *Guberina v. Croatia*, no. 23682/13, §§ 98–100, 22 March 2016.

14 See further below, Part III (case study on equality), Chapter 2, Section II, §1, I. New Interpretation.

15 For legislative instruments, we use the specific identifier of the instrument (e.g., '2000/43/EC'), which was the indicator that yielded the most results.

16 We use 'Charter of Fundamental Rights of the European Union' and the title of each of the Charter's provisions in the Equality Title (e.g., 'Article 21 - Non-discrimination'). We selected the cases where the Charter was used in the equality reasoning of the ECtHR or where the ECtHR uses an equality Charter provision.

17 We use the terms 'Court of Justice of the European Union', 'Court of Justice of the European Communities', and 'European Court of Justice'. We selected cases where the CJEU interpreted EU legislation giving expression to equality rights or Charter equality rights.

18 We analyse judgments from both the Grand Chamber and Chambers of the ECtHR in English, considering cases up until 1 February 2024. For all our categories, we use the Hudoc keywords 'prohibition of discrimination (Article 14)' and 'general prohibition of discrimination (P12-1)' to limit our research to ECtHR case-law on equality and non-discrimination.

19 We added the cases where there are references to EU legislation, the Charter, or CJEU case-law, withdrawing duplicate cases.

20 We examined judgments from both the Grand Chamber and Chambers of the ECtHR in English, using the HUDOC keywords 'prohibition of discrimination (Article 14)' and 'general prohibition of discrimination (P12-1)'.

cases referring to specific equality instruments, in particular the Framework Convention for the Protection of National Minorities (FCNM)(32 cases), the Convention on the Elimination of All Forms of Discrimination Against Women (CEDAW)(28 cases), the Convention on the Rights of Persons with Disabilities (CRPD)(16 cases), and the Convention on Preventing and Combating Violence Against Women and Domestic Violence (Istanbul Convention)(11 cases). We examined references to one general international human rights instrument, the International Covenant on Civil and Political Rights (ICCPR),[21] with 16 cases. We also looked at references to some related bodies, including the United Nations Human Rights Committee (UN Human Rights Committee)(28 cases), the Committee on the Elimination of Discrimination against Women (ComEDAW)(17 cases) and the Advisory Committee on the Framework Convention for the Protection of National Minorities (ComFCNM)(12 cases). We also analysed cases from regional human rights bodies, particularly the Inter-American Court of Human Rights (2 cases) and the African Court on Human and Peoples' Rights (no case).[22]

Examining the influence of EU equality law on ECHR law is challenging due to the diffuse or implicit nature of such influence in some cases. For this reason, we conducted a literature review on four themes, namely EU equality law,[23]

---

[21] We selected cases where these instruments were used in the equality reasoning of the ECtHR or where equality provisions of these instruments were mentioned by the ECtHR.

[22] We selected cases where their decisions were related to equality or where their decisions had an influence on the equality reasoning of the ECtHR.

[23] E.g. E. Muir, *EU Equality Law: The First Fundamental Rights Policy of the EU*, Oxford/OSO, Oxford University Press USA, 2018; E. Muir, 'Procedural rules in the service of the 'transformative function' of EU equality law: bringing the prohibition of nationality discrimination along', *Review of European Administrative Law*, 2015, pp. 151–173; E. Muir, 'The transformative function of EU equality law', *European Review of Private Law*, 2013, pp. 1231–1254; M. Bell, 'The principle of equal treatment: widening and deepening', in P. Craig and G. de Búrca (eds.), *The evolution of EU law*, Oxford, Oxford University Press, 2011, pp. 611–639; B. de Witte, 'From a "Common Principle of Equality" to "European Antidiscrimination Law"', *American Behavioral Scientist*, 2010, pp. 1715–1730; M. Bell, *Anti-Discrimination Law and the European Union*, Oxford, Oxford University Press, 2002; L. Waddington and M. Bell, 'Reflecting on Inequalities in European Equality Law', *European Law Review*, 2003, pp. 349–369; G. More, 'The Principle of Equal Treatment: From Market Unifier to Fundamental Right?', in P. Craig and G. De Burca (eds.), *The Evolution of EU law*, 1st ed., Oxford, Oxford University Press, 1999, pp. 517–553.

ECHR equality law,[24] comparative equality law,[25] and comparative EU-ECHR equality law,[26] with a view to complementing our analysis of the explicit references to EU equality law.

The research methodology is a combination of qualitative and quantitative approaches. It involves a systemic case-law analysis along with a statistical analysis to investigate various aspects of the influence, such as the evolution of the influence of the EU equality standards over the years and their prominence in certain fields. The quantitative analysis is meant to serve the qualitative analysis of the judgments. Whilst the quantitative approach facilitates the observation of certain patterns, the qualitative approach enables us to shed light on the actual use of EU law by the ECtHR.

---

24 M. Möschel, 'European Convention of Human Rights/Council of Europe', in M. Mercat-Bruns, D. Oppenheimer and C. Sartorius (eds.), *Comparative Perspectives on the Enforcement and Effectiveness of Antidiscrimination Law. Ius Comparatum - Global Studies in Comparative Law*, 2018; S. Fredman, 'Emerging from the Shadows: Substantive Equality and Article 14 of the European Convention on Human Rights', *Human Rights Law Review*, 2016, pp. 273–301; O.M. Arnardottir, 'Cross-fertilisation, Clarity and Consistency at an Overburdened European Court of Human Rights - the Case of the Discrimination Grounds under Article 14 ECHR', *Nordic Journal of Human Rights*, 2015, pp. 220–242; O.M. Arnardóttir, 'The differences that make a difference: recent developments on the discrimination grounds and the margin of appreciation under Article 14 of the European Convention on Human Rights', *Human Rights Law Review*, 2014, pp. 647–670; J. Gerards, 'The Discrimination Grounds of Article 14 of the European Convention on Human Rights', *Human Rights Law Review*, 2013, pp. 99 124; O.M. Arnardottir, *Equality and non-discrimination under the European Convention on Human Rights*, The Hague, Nijhoff, 2003.

25 G. De Burca, 'The Trajectories of European and American Antidiscrimination Law', *The American Journal of Comparative Law*, 2012, pp. 1–22; M. Bell, *Cases, materials and text on national, supranational and international non-discrimination law*, Oxford, Hart Publishing, 2007.

26 M. Möschel, 'Comparing the activist claim between Strasbourg and Luxembourg in the field of non-discrimination', in B. de Witte, M. Dawson and E. Muir (eds.), *Revisiting Judicial Politics in the European Union*, Cheltenham, Edward Elgar Publishing, 2024, pp. 334–351; J. Gerards, 'Systeemverklaringen voor verschillen tussen de gelijke behandelingsrechtspraak van het HvJ EU en het EHRM', *SEW*, 2021, pp. 571 581; J. Gerards, 'Non-Discrimination, the European Court of Justice and the European Court of Human Rights: Who Takes the Lead?', in T. Giegerich (ed.), *The European Union as Protector and Promoter of Equality. European Union and its Neighbours in a Globalized World*, Cham, Springer, pp. 135–153; E. Dubout, 'Une approche comparative du principe de non-discrimination dans le cadre européen : Convention européenne des droits de l'homme et droit de l'Union européenne', in M. Balboni (ed.), *The European Convention of Human Rights and the Principle of Non-Discrimination*, Naples, Editoriale Scientifica, 2017, pp. 63–120; C. McCrudden and S. Prechal, *The Concepts of Equality and Non-Discrimination in Europe: A Practical Approach*, Oxford Legal Studies Research Paper No. 4/2011.

SECTION IV. LIMITS

As is clear from above, the focus is on the influence of EU equality law on ECHR equality law, which has several implications. First, we do not look at the influence of EU law on other instruments of the Council of Europe. Second, we do not explore the other way around, namely the influence of ECHR equality law on EU law. Third, the focus is on the influence of specific EU equality standards, although we also shed light on the influence of other related EU standards but in an ancillary manner. Among the EU equality standards, we focus on the influence of EU legislation which gives expression to the equality fundamental rights, the Charter and related CJEU case-law.[27]

SECTION V. STRUCTURE

Chapter 2 illustrates the divergent historical development of the EU and ECHR equality systems. The EU system has evolved into a highly sophisticated and integrated framework, while the ECHR legal system was previously regarded as underdeveloped. In recent decades, ECHR equality law has undergone a process of autonomisation and enrichment. Despite the overlap between the two systems, they remain distinct and are driven by different dynamics. This asymmetry in their development, along with their overlapping yet distinct approaches, explains some of the dynamics of EU equality law's influence on ECHR law, which are further elaborated in Chapter 3.

First, EU equality law is the most prominent external source used by the ECtHR in its equality case-law. Second, the ECtHR has notably drawn from EU equality law to shape some of the key principles of its equality case-law. Third, EU equality law has been used in ECtHR judgments for other purposes. These include cases where EU equality law serves as informative material, as a source the ECtHR seeks to distinguish from ECHR law, as part of the assessment of the justification of States' interferences, and as a source relied upon by many actors prior to or before the ECtHR.

---

27 The identification of the legislation has been carried out in accordance with the criteria established in Part II (Chapter 2, Section II, §3, II. Identifying Legislation as Giving Expression to Fundamental Rights). The legislative instruments giving expression to equality fundamental rights are identified in Annex II.

CHAPTER 2
EU AND ECHR EQUALITY LAWS: DIVERGENT DEVELOPMENT FOR OVERLAPPING, YET DISTINCT SYSTEMS

To understand the dynamics of the influence of EU equality law on ECtHR case-law, it is essential to highlight that the two equality systems have developed differently. The EU equality system has rapidly evolved into a highly sophisticated and integrated framework, whereas the ECHR system has historically been regarded as underdeveloped. Yet, a recent process of autonomisation and enrichment within ECHR equality law has emerged. Although there are overlaps between the two equality systems, they are distinct and driven by different dynamics. It is of note that, for the reader's convenience in reading this section, a table that summarises the comparison between EU and ECHR equality laws is available in Annex III.

SECTION I. THE DIVERGENT DEVELOPMENT OF THE TWO EQUALITY SYSTEMS

The principle of equality has held a central position in the EU legal order since its inception. This stands in contrast with the ECHR legal system where equality protection has historically been deemed underdeveloped. Shedding light on the above is key to understanding why the ECtHR seeks to draw inspiration from other equality systems to enrich its equality law system, and why EU law appears as a highly attractive source of inspiration.

§ 1. THE EMERGENCE OF THE HIGHLY DEVELOPED EU EQUALITY SYSTEM

Equality has been widely acknowledged as a driving force of the EU integration process. Its importance is reflected by its inclusion in the EU Treaties since the very beginning. Even though the Community Treaties did not initially refer to fundamental rights, they contained numerous equality and non-discrimination provisions. The EEC Treaty included two noteworthy provisions. First, Article 7 which prohibited any discrimination on grounds of nationality and which empowered the Council to adopt any regulations with a view to prohibiting such discrimination.[1] Second, Article 119 which required each State to ensure the application of the principle of equal pay for male and female workers for equal work.[2] The EEC Treaty also contained a plethora of non-discrimination provisions which were meant to ensure the free movement of persons, services and capital[3] and the proper functioning of common policies, such as agriculture[4] and transport.[5] The ECSC Treaty encompassed a general non-discrimination clause in the context of the common market for coal and steel[6] as well as specific non-discrimination provisions.[7] Several provisions related to equality could also be found in the Euratom Treaty.[8] In the 1970s and 1980s, the European Economic Community adopted legislative measures related to the principle of equal treatment between men and women.

The CJEU has also been a key actor behind the development of EU equality law.[9] The EU judiciary shaped key concepts of the principle of equal treatment, including indirect discrimination,[10] the reversal of the burden of proof,[11] the exclusion of upper limits on compensation,[12] and the horizontal and direct effect of Article 119 EEC Treaty.[13]

The combination of Treaty equality provisions, legislative measures, and CJEU case-law has led to a highly developed EU equality system. Over the last decades, the principle of equality has gained even greater prominence and can

---

1 Article 7 EEC Treaty.
2 Article 119 EEC Treaty.
3 E.g. Article 48(2) EEC Treaty on the prohibition of discrimination on grounds of nationality between workers within the Community.
4 Articles 40(2), 44(1), 45(1)(2) EEC Treaty.
5 Article 79(1) EEC Treaty.
6 Article 4(b) ECSC Treaty.
7 E.g. the prohibition of discriminatory tariff practices (Article 60 ECSC Treaty) or the prohibition of restrictions based on nationality in employment in the coal and steel industries (Article 69(1) ECSC Treaty).
8 E.g. Article 52(4) Euratom Treaty.
9 M. Bell, 'The Principle of Equal Treatment: Widening and Deepening', in P. Craig and G. De Búrca (eds.), *The Evolution of EU Law*, Oxford, Oxford University Press, 2011, pp. 611; See also E. Muir, *EU Equality Law, The First Fundamental Rights Policy of the EU*, Oxford, Oxford University Press, 2018, p. 79 and following.
10 E.g. Case C-170/84, *Bilka*, ECLI:EU:C:1986:204, paras. 24–31.
11 E.g. Case C-127/92, *Enderby*, ECLI:EU:C:1993:859, paras. 13–19.
12 E.g. Case C-271/9, *Marshall*, ECLI:EU:C:1993:335, paras. 27–32.
13 Case C-43/75, *Defrenne II*, ECLI:EU:C:1976:56, paras. 24 and 39. See for an analysis of this case, e.g. R. Cichowski, *The European Court and Civil Society. Litigation, Mobilization and Governance*, Cambridge, Cambridge University Press, 2009, pp. 96 and following.

be considered ubiquitous in the EU legal system.[14] Combatting discrimination and promoting equality between men and women are objectives of the Union (Article 3(3), para. 1, TEU), and equality is a value on which the EU is founded and which is common to the EU States (Article 2 TEU). The EU has gained competence to flesh out EU equality policies, independently from the dynamics of the internal market.[15] Equality and non-discrimination are fundamental rights in the EU legal order.[16] Equality and non-discrimination are also covered by two horizontal clauses which aim to ensure that equality concerns are taken into account in all activities of the EU institutions.[17] The EU has ratified in 2010 an international treaty related to equality, namely the CRPD, which has played an important role in the CJEU case-law.[18]

The EU legislator has relied on the above-mentioned competences to enact several legislative instruments. While we will discuss these instruments below, it is already noteworthy that they are highly specific: they determine, for instance, the forms of discrimination that are banned, the admissible grounds of justification, and the procedural tools that should be implemented to ensure their effectiveness. They also contribute to a significant change in the scope of protection offered by EU equality law. Whereas the protection of equal treatment was limited to the areas of gender equality and nationality non-discrimination until the Treaty of Amsterdam, these instruments extended the scope of EU equality law to encompass additional grounds such as race, religion, and disability. The scope of EU equality law stands in contrast with international instruments in the field of equality, most of which are focused on one specific ground of discrimination, such as disability or gender.[19]

---

14 This paragraph is inspired by E. Muir, V. Davio and L. Van der Meulen, 'The Horizontal Clauses (arts 8 & 10 TFEU) and Their Contribution to the Course of EU Equality Law: Still an Empty Vessel?', *European Papers*, 2023, pp. 1381–1403.

15 Articles 19 and 157(3) TFEU

16 Article 20 provides for equality before the law, Article 21 Charter provides for a non-discrimination clause on the basis of an open-ended list of grounds. There are also several other Charter provisions that deal with specific forms of discrimination, such as gender equality or disability, and which have been described as a 'véritable pot-pourri of rights' (see M. Bell, 'The principle of equal treatment: widening and deepening', in P. Craig and G. de Búrca (eds.), *The Evolution of EU Law*, Oxford, Oxford University Press, 2011, p. 629).

17 Namely Article 8 TFEU on equality between men and women and Article 10 TFEU on discrimination based on sex, racial or ethnic origin, religion or belief, disability, age or sexual orientation. For a recent assessment of the contribution of the horizontal equality clauses to the course of EU equality law, see E. Muir, V. Davio and L. Van der Meulen, 'The Horizontal Clauses (arts 8 & 10 TFEU) and Their Contribution to the Course of EU Equality Law: Still an Empty Vessel?', *European Papers*, 2023, pp. 1381–1403.

18 See D. Ferri, 'The Unorthodox Relationship between the EU Charter of Fundamental Rights, the UN Convention on the Rights of Persons with Disabilities and Secondary Rights in the Court of Justice Case-law on Disability Discrimination', *European Constitutional Law Review*, 2020, pp. 275–305.

19 For instance, the CEDAW and Istanbul Convention relate to discrimination against women, whereas the CRPD tackles discrimination on grounds of disability.

§ 2. FROM A MARGINAL TO A MORE PROMINENT PLACE IN ECHR LAW

The protection of equality in the ECHR legal system has historically been considered inadequate or subordinate. Article 14 ECHR has been described with various terms such as 'insipid',[20] 'parasitic',[21] 'a Cinderella provision',[22] and 'second-class',[23] while the ECtHR approach to equality has been deemed 'less than satisfactory'.[24] This negative appraisal is related to the accessory nature of Article 14 ECHR.[25] This provision does not prohibit discrimination as such, but only discrimination in the enjoyment of the 'rights and freedoms set forth in the Convention'. The guarantee provided by Article 14 has been regarded as having no independent existence.[26] In practice, the ECtHR examines Article 14 in conjunction with another substantive provision of the Convention. As a result, the scope of Article 14 is narrower than that of standalone equality provisions found in other legal systems, such as Article 26 of the International Covenant on Civil and Political Rights or Article 15 of the Canadian Charter of Rights and Freedoms.[27] The early ECtHR case-law seemed to imply that Article 14 could only be triggered if there was a breach of another substantive provision, rendering it superfluous.[28] It has now been clarified that it is sufficient that the issue falls within the ambit of another ECHR provision, as we will see below. Yet, the ECtHR sometimes chooses not to address a case under Article 14 when it has already determined a violation of another Convention's provision.[29] In addition to its accessory nature, the ECHR equality law regime has been subject to criticism due to the ECtHR's limited development of its equality doctrines; the latter's approach was

20 S. Fredman, 'Emerging from the Shadows: Substantive Equality and Article 14 of the European Convention on Human Rights', *Human Rights Law Review*, 2016, p. 273.
21 Ibid., p. 273.
22 R. O'Connell, 'Cinderella Comes to the Ball: Art 14 and the Right to Non-discrimination in the ECHR', *Legal Studies*, 2009, p. 212.
23 Ibid.
24 Ibid.
25 J. Gerards, 'The Discrimination Grounds of Article 14 of the European Convention on Human Rights', *Human Rights Law Review*, 2013, p. 100.
26 E.g. ECtHR, Case "relating to certain aspects of the laws on the use of languages in education in Belgium", (merits), 23 July 1968, §32, Series A no. 6. 2.
27 R. O'Connell, 'Cinderella Comes to the Ball: Art 14 and the Right to Non-discrimination in the ECHR', *Legal Studies*, 2009, p. 212.
28 S. Fredman, 'Emerging from the Shadows: Substantive Equality and Article 14 of the European Convention on Human Rights', *Human Rights Law Review*, 2016, p. 275.
29 R. O'Connell, 'Cinderella Comes to the Ball: Art 14 and the Right to Non-discrimination in the ECHR', *Legal Studies*, 2009, p. 212.

considered as timid until the 2000s.[30] This approach was characterised by a focus on a formal conception of equality.

Yet, there has been a process of autonomisation and enrichment of ECHR equality law in recent years.[31] The autonomisation can be observed in two distinct ways. First, the ECtHR has clarified that Article 14 ECHR does not require the violation of another substantive ECHR right.[32] Second, Article 1 Additional Protocol No. 12 ECHR extends the scope of protection against discrimination to 'any right set forth by law', introducing a self-standing prohibition of discrimination.[33] As of October 2024, this Protocol has been ratified by 20 States.[34]

A process of enrichment of ECHR equality law is evidenced by an increasingly sophisticated approach taken by the ECtHR. Whereas the ECtHR prohibited only direct and overt discrimination,[35] it has developed and used a range of new concepts and doctrines, such as indirect discrimination and discrimination by association, thereby allowing for a more substantive approach to equality. We will show that the ECtHR has significantly drawn from EU equality law to shape the key principles of its equality case-law. This seems to result from two main elements: on the one hand, the willingness of the ECtHR to enrich its system of equality protection, and on the other hand, the fact that EU equality law appears as a highly attractive source of inspiration.

30 M. Möschel, 'Comparing the activist claim between Strasbourg and Luxembourg in the field of non-discrimination', in B. de Witte, M. Dawson and E. Muir (eds.), *Revisiting Judicial Politics in the European Union*, Cheltenham, Edward Elgar Publishing, 2024, pp. 334–351.

31 J. Gerards, 'The Discrimination Grounds of Article 14 of the European Convention on Human Rights', *Human Rights Law Review*, 2013, p. 100; R. O'Connell, 'Cinderella Comes to the Ball: Art 14 and the Right to Non-discrimination in the ECHR', *Legal Studies*, 2009, p. 228. This shift is reflected in the increasing amount of litigation related to Article 14 ECHR, which was previously rarely invoked before the ECtHR (G. De Burca, 'The Trajectories of European and American Antidiscrimination Law', *The American Journal of Comparative Law*, 2012, p. 9).

32 ECtHR, *Carson and Others v. the United Kingdom* [GC], no. 42184/05, § 63, ECHR 2010; ECtHR, *E.B. v. France* [GC], no. 43546/02, § 47, 22 January 2008

33 ECtHR, *Sejdić and Finci v. Bosnia and Herzegovina* [GC], nos. 27996/06 and 34836/06, § 53, ECHR 2009.

34 ECtHR, ibid., § 55. The ECtHR has considered that the notion of 'discrimination' enshrined in Article 1 of the Additional Protocol No. 12 to the ECHR is identical to that in Article 14 ECHR.

35 R. O'Connell, 'Cinderella Comes to the Ball: Art 14 and the Right to Non-discrimination in the ECHR', *Legal Studies*, 2009, p. 219.

SECTION II. TWO OVERLAPPING YET DISTINCT SYSTEMS PROPELLED BY THEIR OWN DYNAMICS

The EU and ECHR equality systems, while significantly overlapping, are distinct and driven by different dynamics. While we shed light on the overlaps, our focus is on the differences between the two systems, as these are key to understanding the influence of EU equality law on ECtHR case-law. These differences underscore the need for coherent articulation between the two legal systems. The distinct features of the EU system also help explaining why it is a highly attractive source of inspiration. Lastly, these differences show that integrating elements of EU law into the ECHR framework is a complex endeavour.

§ 1. RATIONALE

The equality systems of the EU and the ECHR are propelled by rationales that are distinct to some extent. While EU equality law involves a co-existence of market and fundamental rights rationales, ECHR equality law is driven by a fundamental rights logic. Additionally, EU law appears to be predominantly driven by a non-discrimination rationale, while ECHR law is guided by an equality rationale, which may be evolving. Finally, both systems are increasingly promoting a substantive version of equality, although this shift is more recent in ECHR law. Highlighting these rationales is key to understanding how the two systems protect equality and the differences between them. It is also important to understand the extent to which some of the EU equality rationales have impacted ECHR rationales.

I. Fundamental v. Economic

The development of equality in the EU was initially motivated by a market-driven rationale. While the Community Treaties were infused with equality provisions, these were not driven by the protection of fundamental rights. Their rationale was of an economic nature: equality and non-discrimination were conceived as a means to removing obstacles to free movement, with a view to contributing to the development of a common market in the fields of the Communities.[36] The legislative acts implemented to promote gender equality

[36] A. Bailleux and E. Bribosia, 'La protection des droits fondamentaux' in A. Bailleux (ed), *Actualités du contentieux européen*, Louvain-la-Neuve, Anthemis, 2020, p. 133; M. Bell, 'The Principle of Equal Treatment: Widening and Deepening', in P. Craig and G. De Búrca

in the EU were also informed by market integration rationale, as reflected in their preambles.[37]

Despite the fact that the principle of equal treatment had its origins in market-related concerns, it has gradually begun to shake off its market-oriented shackles.[38] The CJEU has played a pivotal role in shaping the social and fundamental rights discourse surrounding the principle of equal treatment.[39] Likewise, the equality directives adopted as from the 2000s have been accompanied by a stronger emphasis on fundamental rights than was the case in the past. Whereas the preambles to the gender equality directives of the 1970s mentioned that they aimed to improve the internal market, as mentioned

(eds.), *The Evolution of EU Law*, Oxford, Oxford University Press, 2011, p. 611; G. Quinn, 'The European Union and the Council of Europe on the Issue of Human Rights: Twins Separated at Birth?', *McGill Law Journal*, 2001, p. 861; G. More, 'The Principle of Equal Treatment: From Market Unifier to Fundamental Right?', in P. Craig and G. De Búrca (eds.), *The Evolution of EU Law*, Oxford, Oxford University Press 1999, pp. 517–553. The main clauses of the Treaty of Rome, specifically Articles 7 and 119 TEC, were initially driven by a market integration rationale. Similarly, the principle of equal pay for men and women was originally motivated by economic considerations. Some Member States, which had implemented this principle, were concerned that their companies would face economic disadvantages compared to those operating in Member States where this principle was not as rigorously enforced (e.g. R. Cichowski, *The European Court and Civil Society. Litigation, Mobilization and Governance* Cambridge, Cambridge University Press, 2009, p. 73).

37 The preambles to the gender equality legislative measures were largely silent on the social or fundamental rights dimensions of equality and non-discrimination On the contrary, the preambles of the Equal Pay between Men and Women Council Directive (75/117/EEC) mentioned, for instance, that: 'the implementation of the principle that men and women should receive equal pay contained in Article 119 of the EEC Treaty is an integral section of the establishment and functioning of the common market.'

38 G. More, 'The Principle of Equal Treatment: From Market Unifier to Fundamental Right?', in P. Craig and G. De Burca (eds.), *The Evolution of EU Law*, 1st ed., Oxford, Oxford University Press, 1999, p. 517.

39 An example relates to the narrative of Article 119 EEC, which the CJEU began to revisit with the (1976) *Defrenne II* case. In the latter ruling, it held that this provision pursued a double economic and social aim. On the one hand, this provision aims 'to avoid a situation in which undertakings established in States which have actually implemented the principle of equal pay suffer a competitive disadvantage in intra-Community competition as compared with undertakings established in States which have not yet eliminated discrimination against women workers as regards pay'. On the other hand, it forms part of the social objectives of the Community, which is not merely an economic union, but is at the same time intended, by common action, to ensure social progress and seek the constant improvement of the living and working conditions of their peoples (Case C-43/75, *Defrenne II*, ECLI:EU:C:1976:56, paras. 9-10). The CJEU took a significant step towards shaping the fundamental rights discourse of Article 119 EEC Treaty with its (1996) *Schröder* case. In this case which concerned the exclusion of part-time workers from an occupational pension scheme, the CJEU held that the economic aim '*was secondary to the social aim* pursued by [Article 119 EEC Treaty], which constitutes the expression of a fundamental right.' (Case C-50/96, *Schröder*, ECLI:EU:C:2000:72, para. 57. Emphasis added). See for an analysis of the *Schröder* case, E. Muir, *EU Equality Law, The First Fundamental Rights Policy of the EU*, Oxford, Oxford University Press, 2018, p. 10.

above, the preambles to the new directives are permeated with references to fundamental rights.[40]

EU equality law reflects thus a coexistence of two narratives: one based on economic integration and the other on human rights concerns. This interplay creates a certain degree of tension within EU equality law.[41] This tension is evident in the material scope of equality directives such as such as the Race Equality Directive (2000/43/EC) and the Equality Framework Directive (2000/78/EC). Although motivated by fundamental rights considerations, these directives are mainly applicable within the economic sphere.[42]

ECHR equality law is guided by a fundamental rights rationale. Article 14 ECHR is not linked to any market or economic objectives. This is reflected in its material scope which is not limited to the economic sphere. The question is whether, through the influence of EU equality law, the ECtHR integrates an economic rationale within ECHR law. As we will see, the ECtHR has primarily used EU equality law to enhance the protection of equality within ECHR law, without integrating an economic rationale.

II. Equality v. Non-Discrimination

Equality regimes may be driven by equality or non-discrimination rationale. A regime is considered to have an equality rationale when it prohibits all forms of unjustified unequal treatment whether based on certain specific characteristics or not.[43] A regime is said to have a non-discrimination rationale when it focuses on protecting particular groups with specific characteristics.[44]

---

40 E.g. Recitals 1, 4, 5 Equality Framework Directive (2000/78/EC).

41 R. Xenidis, 'Shaking the Normative Foundations of EU Equality Law: Evolution and Hierarchy between Market Integration and Human Rights Rationales', 2017, *EUI Department of Law Research Paper* No. 2017/04, p. 14.

42 See below Part III (case study on equality), Chapter 2, Section II, §4, I. Material Scope.

43 In this perspective, the principle of equality emerges as an 'empty legal principle', without any moral content and is mainly instrumental or procedural (J. Gerards, 'The Discrimination Grounds of Article 14 of the European Convention on Human Rights', *Human Rights Law Review*, 2013, p. 115). In other words, any difference in treatment must be evaluated for its reasonableness and fairness, and the grounds of discrimination is irrelevant to both the applicability of the test and the justification itself (ibid.).

44 As observed by Gerards, 'it can be held to be unacceptable if legislation or decisions are based on grounds that cannot be influenced by individuals, either because they concern innate and immutable personal characteristics (race, gender, disability, age) or because they are clearly within the range of individual autonomy (religion, political opinion).' (ibid.) The prohibition of discrimination on 'suspect' grounds serves as a clear expression of societal disapproval towards acts that are driven by irrational motives. By prohibiting discrimination, the aim is to ensure that significant social benefits such as employment and services are allocated based on rational criteria, rather than on irrelevant grounds or deeply entrenched stereotypes and subjective biases (ibid).

A regime may exhibit characteristics of both rationales, as can be seen in both EU and ECHR equality laws. In the EU context, the dominant rationale is non-discrimination, although this varies with specific provisions. For instance, Article 20 Charter, which guarantees equality before the law, aligns closely with an equality rationale. Other Charter provisions address specific groups, such as people with disabilities, the elderly, and children. Similarly, various equality directives protect specific grounds like race, religion, and gender.

Ambiguity arises when determining the rationale that governs ECHR equality law. Historically, the ECtHR applied Article 14 regardless of the protected grounds, suggesting an equality rationale. Recently, however, it has adopted a more restrictive approach, limiting Article 14's scope to grounds related to certain personal characteristics.[45] Additionally, the ECtHR has developed a 'suspect grounds' model, permitting differences in treatment based on suspect grounds only in exceptional circumstances, which leans towards a non-discrimination rationale. We will revisit this issue, considering the potential influence of EU law on the shift towards a non-discrimination rationale.

§ 2. FORMAL V. SUBSTANTIVE

Equality regimes can promote a formal or substantive version of equality. The former is limited to verifying that the law does not create unjustified differences in treatment, while the latter consider the effects of the law and address issues of systematic disadvantage and oppression.[46] Both the EU and ECHR legal regimes have evolved towards a more substantive version of equality. This shift is reflected in the ECtHR and CJEU case-law, which have addressed issues such as positive obligations, reasonable accommodation, and indirect discrimination. EU equality law has contributed to promote a more substantive approach in ECHR equality law, as we will see below.

§ 3. RULE-BASED V. PRINCIPLE-BASED

While the EU Treaties and Charter include equality provisions, the legislative framework plays a central role by establishing specific rules that determine

---

45 O.M. Arnardottir, 'Cross-fertilisation, Clarity and Consistency at an Overburdened European Court of Human Rights – the Case of the Discrimination Grounds under Article 14 ECHR', *Nordic Journal of Human Rights*, 2015, pp. 220–242. See also J. Gerards, 'The Discrimination Grounds of Article 14 of the European Convention on Human Rights', *Human Rights Law Review*, 2013, pp. 104–113.

46 R. O'Connell, 'Cinderella Comes to the Ball: Art 14 and the Right to Non-discrimination in the ECHR', *Legal Studies*, 2009, p. 213.

whether there is any impermissible difference in treatment. In this sense, the EU's equality regime can be characterised as 'rules-based'. When the ECtHR assesses potential equality violations, its approach is more 'principle-based', in that the protection of equality is not contingent on specific rules but rather is governed by Article 14 ECHR, which is formulated as a general principle. This distinction is important to highlight the highly developed nature of EU equality law as well as the higher level of flexibility that the ECtHR enjoys when dealing with equality cases.

I. EU Equality Law as a Rule-Based System

The legislative framework represents the cornerstone of the EU equality regime. This framework determines the scope of the protection, the forms of justification that are prohibited, and the types of justification that are permissible. Legislation aimed at promoting equality is not a recent phenomenon in the EU since directives on equality between men and women were already adopted in the 1970s.[47] These instruments were followed in the 1980s and 1990s by additional directives on gender equality.[48] The adoption of EU equality legislation was channelled through the general internal market clause or the flexibility clause.[49]

At the turn of the 21st century, there was a marked increase in the intensity and diversity of EU equality legislation.[50] This development was made possible by the inclusion of new legal bases in the Amsterdam Treaty. The most significant novelty stems from the insertion of Article 13 TEC, the current Article 19 TFEU, which makes it possible for the EU legislator to take appropriate action to combat discrimination based on sex, racial or ethnic origin, religion or belief, disability, age or sexual orientation. In the wake of the entry of a far-right party into the Austrian government,[51] the EU enacted the Racial Discrimination Directive (2000/43/EC) and the Equality Framework Directive (2000/78/EC).[52]

---

47 In the 1970s the European Economic Community enacted the Equal Pay between Men and Women Council Directive (75/117/EEC), the Employment Equal Treatment Between Men and Women Council Directive (76/207/EEC), and the Social Security Equal Treatment Between Men and Women Council Directive (79/7/EEC).

48 This includes the Occupational Social Security Schemes Equal Treatment Between Men and Women (86/378/EEC) and the Burden of Proof Council Directive (97/80/EC).

49 See above Part II, Chapter 2, Section II, §2. The Fragmented, Yet Increasing Competences of the EU Legislator.

50 M. Bell, 'The principle of equal treatment: widening and deepening', in P. Craig and G. de Búrca (eds.), *The Evolution of EU Law*, Oxford, Oxford University Press, 2011, pp. 611–639.

51 Ibid., p. 618.

52 Article 13 TEC was subsequently used for the adoption of the Gender Equality Goods and Services Directive (2004/113/EC) which extended the scope of sex discrimination to the area of goods and services Council Directive 2004/113/EC of 13 December 2004

Next to Article 13 TEC, the Treaty of Amsterdam inserted Article 119(3) TEC, the current Article 157(3) TFEU, which empowers the Council, acting in accordance with the co-decision procedure and after consulting the Economic and Social Committee, to adopt measures to ensure the application of the principle of equal opportunities and equal treatment of men and women in matters of employment and occupation, including the principle of equal pay for equal work or work of equal value. This legal basis gave rise to the Equal Treatment Between Men and Women Recast Directive (2006/54/EC), which co-ordinates and strengthens six previous directives that had been grounded on the flexibility or the internal market harmonisation clauses.[53]

The wave of equality legislation has brought about three important changes, which are explored above and below. Firstly, there has been a broadening of the scope of the protected grounds. Whereas previously, equal treatment protection was restricted to the areas of gender equality and non-discrimination on the grounds of nationality, the more recent EU equality laws encompass additional grounds such as race, religion, or disability. Secondly, these directives have been accompanied by a more pronounced fundamental rights discourse. Finally, there has been a transformation in the substantial and procedural elements of EU equality law, with the incorporation of new concepts, definitions and procedural tools.

The Charter, which was adopted in 2000 and entered into force in 2009, contains a series of provisions aimed at promoting equality. These provisions do not undermine the central role of equality legislation. The practical significance of the equality Charter provisions appears to be relatively limited EU equality legislations are used as lex specialis by the CJEU for the Charter equality provisions. The CJEU favours an assessment based on the specific provisions of the directives, while the Charter serves mainly as a guideline for interpretation.[54]

II. ECHR Equality Law as a Principle-Based System

The ECHR equality law appears more of a 'principle-based' system. This stems from the open formulation of Article 14, which states that the enjoyment of the rights and freedoms in the ECHR shall be secured without discrimination on any ground such as sex, race, colour, language, religion, political or other

implementing the principle of equal treatment between men and women in the access to and supply of goods and services.

53 Prbl 1 Equal Treatment Between Men and Women Recast Directive (2006/54/EC).

54 J. Gerards, 'Systeemverklaring voor verschillen tussen de gelijkebehandelingsrechtspraak van het HvJ EU en het EHRM', *SEW*, 2021, p. 574; S. Greer, J. Gerards and R. Slowe, *Human Rights in the Council of Europe and the European Union. Achievements, Trends and Challenges*, Cambridge, Cambridge University Press, 2018, p. 345.

opinion, national or social origin, association with a national minority, property, birth or other status. This provision articulates a broad principle of non-discrimination without providing specific delineation of the prohibited forms of discrimination and the corresponding justifications. As explained below, the ECtHR has used a general proportionality test that is likewise framed in a principled manner. While the CJEU evaluates whether a specific situation falls under the scope of EU equality legislative instruments and identifies if the situation corresponds to a type of discriminatory conduct prohibited by said instruments, subsequently determining admissible justifications for such behaviour as prescribed by these instruments, the ECtHR benefits from a greater degree of flexibility to balance various factors.[55]

§ 4. SCOPE

The material scope, scope of protected grounds and horizontal applicability of the ECHR and EU equality systems differ. This is partly due to the distinct rationales of the two systems. Highlighting these differences allows us to emphasise the EU's broadening scope of application as well as the integrated nature of EU equality law with domestic legal systems which are both significant to understand some of the dynamics of influence on ECHR equality law.

I. Material Scope

The various EU equal treatment directives have a precise and well-defined scope. While the equality directives adopted as from the 2000s have broadened the material scope of legislative instruments, most of them are primarily relevant in the economic sphere, either in employment or in the access to and supply of goods and services. The Equal Treatment Between Men and Women Recast Directive (2006/54/EC), which co-ordinates and strengthens six previous directives, outlaws different treatment of men and women in the field of employment and occupation.[56] While the Gender Equality Goods and Services Directive (2004/113/EEC) extended this principle of equal treatment

---

[55] As explained by Arnardottir, 'the EU non-discrimination directives provide rules with a low level of generality that are enacted at the level of secondary law and provide specific norms of behaviour which are either fulfilled or not. In contrast, Article 14 and Protocol 12 ECHR have a high level of generality and are enacted in a document of a higher, some might say constitutional, standing. They also provide a more flexible standard of behaviour depending on the justification for different treatment that may exist in a given case.' (O.M. Arnardottir, 'Cross-fertilisation, Clarity and Consistency at an Overburdened European Court of Human Rights – the Case of the Discrimination Grounds under Article 14 ECHR', *Nordic Journal of Human Rights*, 2015, p. 235)

[56] Article 1 Equal Treatment Between Men and Women Recast Directive (2006/54/EC).

to the field of goods and services, the prohibition of sex discrimination in EU secondary law remains confined to the economic sphere. By contrast, the Racial Discrimination Directive (2000/43/EC) applies not only to employment but also to social protection, including social security and health care, social advantages, education, and access to and supply of goods and services available to the public, including house.[57] The differences between the various directives have led some authors to suggest that there exists a hierarchy among them.[58]

Article 14 ECHR is distinct in that it has a potentially unlimited material scope, but it is limited by the requirement that it only applies in connection with another Convention right. Since the *Belgian Linguistics* (1968) case, the ECtHR has emphasised that the violation of another substantive provision is not a requirement for Article 14's application.[59] This provision is applicable when the facts of a case fall within the ambit of another substantive provision of the Convention or its Protocols.[60] The ECtHR has adopted a broad approach towards the meaning of the 'ambit' of a right.[61] Moreover, the ECtHR has held that the prohibition of discrimination applies to other rights falling within the general scope of an article of the Convention, for which the State has voluntarily chosen to provide protection.[62] Although the ECtHR has broadened the ambit of ECHR rights, it has not disregarded the requirement of ambit. There are

57 Articles 3(1) Racial Discrimination Directive (2000/43/EC).

58 E.g. R. Xenidis, 'Shaking the Normative Foundations of EU Equality Law: Evolution and Hierarchy between Market Integration and Human Rights Rationales', 2017, EUI Department of Law Research Paper No. 2017/04, p. 23; B. de Witte, 'From a "Common Principle of Equality" to "European Antidiscrimination Law"', *American Behavioral Scientist*, 2010, p. 1719.

59 E.g. ECtHR, Case 'relating to certain aspects of the laws on the use of languages in education in Belgium', (merits), 23 July 1968, §8, Series A no. 6.

60 E.g. ECtHR, *Carson and Others v. the United Kingdom* [GC], no. 42184/05, § 63, ECHR 2010; ECtHR, *E.B. v. France* [GC], no. 43546/02, § 47, 22 January 2008

61 For instance, by interpreting the right to respect for property under Article 1 of the first additional Protocol to the ECHR expansively, the ECtHR has extended protection against discrimination to entitlements to certain social benefits, see E. Dubout, 'Une approche comparative du principe de non-discrimination dans le cadre européen : Convention européenne des droits de l'homme et droit de l'Union européenne', in M. Balboni (ed.), *The European Convention of Human Rights and the Principle of Non-Discrimination*, Naples, Editoriale Scientifica, 2017, see point §1, A, 1.1.

62 E.g. ECtHR, *Carson and Others v. the United Kingdom* [GC], no. 42184/05, § 63, ECHR 2010. The case of (2008) *E.B. v. France* provides an illustration of this principle, where the ECtHR dealt with discrimination against a homosexual woman seeking to adopt a child. The ECtHR held that while Article 8 did not expressly provide a single person with the right to adopt a child, it nevertheless fell within the scope of Article 8. Thus, a State that has created such a right by exceeding its obligations under Article 8 may not discriminate in its application, as per Article 14 ECtHR, see ECtHR, *E.B. v. France* [GC], no. 43546/02, § 48, 22 January 2008.

certain areas that still fall outside the reach of Article 14.[63] Besides, a complaint under Article 14 ECHR that does not identify the corresponding substantive right will be dismissed as being manifestly ill-founded.[64]

II. Horizontal Applicability

The equality principle in EU law has undergone a process of 'horizontalisation'. This principle has transitioned from being an infrastructural principle to becoming an instrument for transforming European societies by directly intervening in private relations. This transformation has arisen due to a multifaceted interaction between political institutions and judicial law-making.[65] The process of horizontalisation was initiated by the CJEU through the *Defrenne II* (1976) case, in which it established that the current Article 157 TFEU has horizontal direct effect.[66] Along with judicial advancements, a political trend has emerged that has recognised the role of EU law as a tool for transformation, leading to the integration of equality norms into interpersonal relations.[67] The various equality directives have extended the scope of equal treatment obligations horizontally, thereby imposing through implementing measures at national level a duty of non-discrimination on private persons in addition to the public authorities in areas covered by the directives.[68] The CJEU has also acknowledged that the general principle of non-discrimination on the grounds of age and certain equality provisions of the Charter have direct horizontal effects.[69]

In ECHR law, discrimination claims must be directed against State authorities.[70] Article 34 ECHR provides that individual applications must be filed against one of the High Contracting States; 'horizontal' cases must thus

63 See more in E. Dubout, 'Une approche comparative du principe de non-discrimination dans le cadre européen : Convention européenne des droits de l'homme et droit de l'Union européenne', in M. Balboni (ed.), *The European Convention of Human Rights and the Principle of Non-Discrimination*, Naples, Editoriale Scientifica, 2017, see point §1, A, 1.2.

64 R. O'Connell, 'Cinderella Comes to the Ball: Art 14 and the Right to Non-discrimination in the ECHR', *Legal Studies,* 2009, p. 217.

65 E. Muir, 'The transformative function of EU equality law', *European Review of Private Law*, 2013, p. 1252.

66 Case C-43/75, *Defrenne II*, ECLI:EU:C:1976:56, paras. 24 and 39.

67 E. Muir, 'The transformative function of EU equality law', *European Review of Private Law*, 2013, p. 1238.

68 B. de Witte, 'From a "Common Principle of Equality" to "European Antidiscrimination Law"', *American Behavioral Scientist*, 2010, p. 1722.

69 E. Muir, 'The Horizontal Effects of Charter Rights given Expression to in EU Legislation, from Mangold to Bauer', *Review of European Administrative Law*, 2020, pp. 185–215.

70 M. Möschel, 'European Convention of Human Rights/Council of Europe', in M. Mercat-Bruns, D. Oppenheimer, and C. Sartorius (eds.), *Comparative Perspectives on the Enforcement and Effectiveness of Antidiscrimination Law. Ius Comparatum - Global Studies in Comparative Law*, Cham, Springer, 2018, p. 534.

be 'verticalised' to be admissible. This implies that a private entity who has first filed a case against another private entity in the national courts must, in its ECHR's application, contest the State's (in)action.[71] The ECtHR has extended the protection of Convention rights in relations between private entities by enforcing horizontal positive obligations on Contracting States.[72] In the sphere of equality, the ECtHR has, for example, ruled procedural violations of Articles 2 and 3 in conjunction with Article 14, indicating that the State did not investigate effectively if violence was racially motivated or prosecute the perpetrators of the violence.[73]

§ 5. CONTENT

Regarding their substantive and procedural elements, notable differences exist between the two equality regimes. Whereas the substantive components of the two systems exhibit resemblance, the most prominent divergence lies in the procedural aspects. Both the substantive and procedural aspects shed light on the highly sophisticated EU equality system, which is one of the factors that might make it attractive as a source of inspiration for the ECtHR.

I. Substantive Elements

In EU equality law, the EU equality legislative instruments ascertain both the forms of discrimination that are banned and the admissible grounds of justification. The legislative instruments enumerate the prohibited forms of discrimination, which are common in the most recent versions of equality directives, albeit with slight variations.[74] They forbid direct and indirect discrimination, as well as harassment, with each of these behaviours being

---

71 C. Loven, '"Verticalised" cases before the European Court of Human Rights unravelled: An analysis of their characteristics and the Court's approach to them', *Netherlands Quarterly of Human Rights*, 2020, pp. 246–263.

72 The ECtHR extended for the first time the concept of positive obligations to relations between private actors in the case *X and Y v. the Netherlands*, 26 March 1985, § 23, Series A no. 91.

73 ECtHR, *Abdu v. Bulgaria*, no. 26827/08, § 44, 11 March 2014; ECtHR, *Milanović v. Serbia*, no. 44614/07, § 90, 14 December 2010. Nonetheless, even in such situations, the State and its agents remain the ultimate addressee. M. Möschel 'European Convention of Human Rights/Council of Europe', in M. Mercat-Bruns, C. Oppenheimer and C. Sartorius (eds.), *Comparative Perspectives on the Enforcement and Effectiveness of Antidiscrimination Law. Ius Comparatum - Global Studies in Comparative Law*, Cham, Springer, 2018, p. 535.

74 See more in L. Waddington and M. Bell, 'More Equal than Others: Distinguishing European Union Equality Directives', *Common Market Law Review*, 2001, pp. 587–612.

defined within the directives.[75] The inclusion of harassment as a prohibited form of discrimination in the equality directives adopted as from the 2000s represents a significant advancement, and this concept has been phrased broadly.[76] Regarding positive action,[77] the CJEU adopted a narrow perspective on the scope of positive action in the *Kalanke* (1995) case, emphasising that such measures constituted an exception to the prohibition of discrimination between individuals.[78] The Amsterdam Treaty introduced a new provision in the EC Treaty, namely Article 141(4), which authorises positive actions. In equality directives such as the Race Equality Directive (2000/43/EC) and the Equality Framework Directive (2000/78/EC), Member States have the possibility of introducing positive actions.[79]

The justification and the level of scrutiny of a difference in treatment vary depending on the equality provisions and the forms of discrimination at stake.[80] In principle, direct discrimination can only be justified on the basis of specific grounds that are listed in the relevant EU legislative instruments. In contrast, indirect discrimination can be justified if it can be shown that it is objectively justified by a legitimate aim and the means of achieving that aim are appropriate and necessary.[81]

---

75 For instance, Article 2(2)(a) of the Racial Discrimination Directive (2000/43/EC) reads: 'Direct discrimination will be taken to occur where one person is treated less favourably than another is, has been or would be treated in a comparable situation on grounds of racial or ethnic origin', while Article 2(2)(b) provides that: 'Indirect discrimination will be taken to occur where an apparently neutral provision, criterion or practice would put persons of a racial or ethnic origin at a particular disadvantage compared with other persons, unless that provision, criterion or practice is objectively justified by a legitimate aim and the means of achieving that aim are appropriate and necessary.'

76 Article 2(3) of the Racial Discrimination Directive (2000/43/EC) reads as follows: 'Harassment will be deemed to be discrimination within the meaning of paragraph 1, when an unwanted conduct related to racial or ethnic origin takes place with the purpose or effect of violating the dignity of a person and of creating an intimidating, hostile, degrading, humiliating or offensive environment. In this context, the concept of harassment may be defined in accordance with the national laws and practice of the Member States.'

77 See more on positive actions in L. Waddington and M. Bell, 'Exploring the Boundaries of Positive Obligation Under EU Law: A Search for Conceptual Clarity', *Common Market Law Review*, 2011, pp. 1503–1526.

78 Case C-450/93, *Kalanke*, ECLI:EU:C:1995:322, para. 21.

79 Article 5 of the Racial Discrimination Directive (2000/43/EC) states for instance that 'with a view to ensuring full equality in practice, the principle of equal treatment will not prevent any Member State from maintaining or adopting specific measures to prevent or compensate for disadvantages linked to racial or ethnic origin'. Article 7(2) of the Equality Framework Directive (2000/78/EC) offers additional protection in relation to individuals with disabilities.

80 J. Gerards, 'Systeemverklaringen voor verschillen tussen de gelijkebehandelingsrechtspraak van het HvJ EU en het EHRM', *SEW*, 2021, pp. 576–577.

81 *Ibid.* There is one exception to the general rule regarding justification and direct discrimination, which pertains specifically to discrimination on the basis of age. Article 6(1) of the Equality Framework Directive (2000/78/EC) establishes that 'differences of treatment on grounds of age will not constitute discrimination, if, within the context of national

Article 14 ECHR provides that the enjoyment of rights must be ensured 'without discrimination' on the specified grounds, without further elucidation.[82] The ECHR took initially a rather formalistic approach and restricted its purview to direct discrimination. Since then, it has shifted towards a more substantive definition of equality. This is evidenced by the *Thlimmenos* (2000) case in which the ECtHR held that: 'The Court has so far considered that Article 14 is violated when States treat differently persons in analogous situations without providing an objective and reasonable justification. [Article 14] is also violated when States without an objective and reasonable justification fail to treat differently persons whose situations are significantly different.'[83] Over time, the ECtHR has incorporated additional forms of discrimination, such as discrimination by association or indirect discrimination, into its case-law. In relation to positive action, Article 14 ECHR does not prohibit a State from treating groups differently if the aim is to rectify 'de facto inequalities' between them. In some situations, the failure to address such inequalities through differentiated treatment may lead to a violation of Article 14.[84]

Regarding justification, the ECtHR examines whether there is a difference in treatment and assesses whether it has an objective and reasonable justification. This involves determining if the difference in treatment pursues a legitimate aim and if there is a reasonable relationship of proportionality between the means employed and the aim sought to be realised[85] The ECtHR uses the margin of appreciation doctrine, which affords States greater latitude in situations where the ECtHR deems it ill-placed to second guess the national judgment.[86] The margin varies depending on the grounds of protection in question: a narrow margin of appreciation will usually be applied to forms of discrimination linked to inherent personal traits or fundamental choices that have a substantial impact on an individual's identity and existence, while a broader margin and less stringent review is used for other forms of

---

law, they are objectively and reasonably justified by a legitimate aim, including legitimate employment policy, labour market and vocational training objectives, and if the means of achieving that aim are appropriate and necessary'. This provision is further supported by a non-exhaustive list of examples of situations where direct age discrimination may be justified

82 S. Fredman, 'Emerging from the Shadows: Substantive Equality and Article 14 of the European Convention on Human Rights', *Human Rights Law Review*, 2016, p. 278.

83 ECtHR, *Thlimmenos v. Greece* [GC], no. 34369/97, § 38, ECHR 2000-IV.

84 E.g. ECtHR, *Taddeucci and McCall v. Italy*, no. 51362/09, § 81, 30 June 2016; ECtHR, *Sejdić and Finci v. Bosnia and Herzegovina* [GC], nos. 27996/06 and 34836/06, § 44, ECHR 2009.

85 ECtHR, *Vallianatos and Others v. Greece* [GC], nos. 29381/09 and 32684/09, § 76, ECHR 2013.

86 R. O'Connell, 'Cinderella Comes to the Ball: Art 14 and the Right to Non-discrimination in the ECHR', *Legal Studies*, 2009, p. 224.

discrimination.[87] The ECtHR has adopted an approach whereby some grounds of discrimination are considered 'suspect' and are less likely to be justified. The ECtHR has formulated a specific 'very weighty reasons' test in instances of discrimination based on sex and gender, 'illegitimate' birth outside of marriage, nationality and disability. Even in cases where the very serious reasons test is not used, discrimination based on race or ethnic origin has also demonstrated a significantly reduced margin of appreciation, as is the case for discrimination on the grounds of sexual orientation and religion.[88]

II. Procedural Elements

The EU equality framework places emphasis on the establishment of special procedures and remedies to ensure the effective implementation of substantive equality rules.[89] Although procedural provisions have been present in EU equality legislation for some time, their importance has increased since the Amsterdam Treaty.[90] The 'proceduralisation' of EU equality law is the result of a combination of legislative and judicial initiatives, but with significant influence from legal innovation through legislative law-making.[91] As observed by Muir, ensuring the effectiveness of the right to equal treatment is a prerequisite for setting in motion the policy's substance and its transformative and societal function. Therefore, the procedural rules are designed to support private claimants to engage in vertical and horizontal litigation.[92] Despite being dispersed throughout the various EU equality directives and not always identical, the procedural elements present in the EU equality directives adopted as from the 2000s are comparable. They involve not only procedural rights for victims of discrimination but also the establishment of institutions aimed at supporting victims of discrimination. There is no such procedural system in ECHR equality law. In recent years, there have been changes in certain aspects of ECHR procedural equality law, such as for the burden of proof and evidence. Some of these changes have been influenced by EU law, as we will see below.[93]

---

87 O.M. Arnardóttir, 'The differences that make a difference: recent developments on the discrimination grounds and the margin of appreciation under Article 14 of the European Convention on Human Rights', *Human Rights Law Review*, 2014, p. 655.

88 O.M. Arnardottir, 'Cross-fertilisation, Clarity and Consistency at an Overburdened European Court of Human Rights – the Case of the Discrimination Grounds under Article 14 ECHR', *Nordic Journal of Human Rights*, 2015, p. 227.

89 B. de Witte, 'From a "Common Principle of Equality" to "European Antidiscrimination Law"', *American Behavioral Scientist*, 2010, p. 1721.

90 E. Muir, 'Procedural rules in the service of the 'transformative function' of EU equality law: bringing the prohibition of nationality discrimination along', *Review of European Administrative Law*, 2015, p. 153.

91 Ibid., p. 175.

92 Ibid., p. 166.

93 See in particular Part III (case study on equality), Chapter 3, Section II, §1, II. Confirmation.

CHAPTER 3
THE INFLUENCE OF EU EQUALITY LAW UNDER SCRUTINY

In this section, we investigate five dimensions to understand the influence of EU equality law on the ECtHR's equality case-law. Firstly, we conduct a statistical analysis to determine the quantitative significance of EU equality law in the ECtHR case-law. Next, we examine the functions performed by EU equality law. We highlight, in particular, four functions. The first is interpretative: the ECtHR uses EU equality law to support the interpretation of the meaning and scope of ECHR (equality) provisions. The second is justification: the ECtHR uses EU equality law during its evaluation of the justification for an interference by a national measure or practice. The third is distinguishing: the ECtHR distinguishes its stance from that of EU equality law. The fourth is information: the ECtHR uses EU equality law as relevant information either in the context of its judgments or in its related legal materials. Afterwards, we look at how several other actors – including parties, third-party interveners, national courts, and specific judges within the ECtHR – engage with EU equality law. Next, we focus on the respondent States involved in cases where EU equality law is used, particularly examining whether EU equality law is applied in cases involving non-EU States. Finally, we analyze the methodology of the ECtHR when it uses EU equality law, focusing on three aspects: transparency, justification, and contextualisation. For each dimension, we systematically compare the use of EU equality law with the use of several relevant international instruments. We also shed light on situations where the ECtHR appears to treat EU fundamental rights as domestic laws. The key questions and sub-questions for each dimension that we seek to examine are laid out in Annex I.

SECTION I. QUANTITATIVE ANALYSIS

We begin with the quantitative analysis. This analysis is introductory and is meant to highlight some general patterns, which are further investigated in our qualitative analysis. We show that EU equality law is the most prominent external source used by the ECtHR in its equality case-law from a quantitative point of view. The ECtHR has consistently referred to EU equality law over a long period across various domains in a notable proportion of its equality case-law. The ECtHR has referred to it more frequently than international instruments and related bodies' outputs. In contrast to our data protection case study, where the ECtHR primarily refers to EU data protection law and Convention 108 law but very limitedly to other sources, the ECtHR refers to several international instruments in the field of equality in a more balanced manner.

§ 1. FREQUENCY PER STANDARDS

Let us begin with how often the ECtHR has cited EU equality standards.[1] We highlight that there is a diversified use of EU equality law, similar to our data protection case study. The ECtHR engages with the various facets of EU equality law in a balanced manner, yet there are significant disparities in references among the various legal instruments or provisions. There is a prevalence of references to EU equality law over international instruments and related bodies' outputs.

Reference per category of EU equality standards

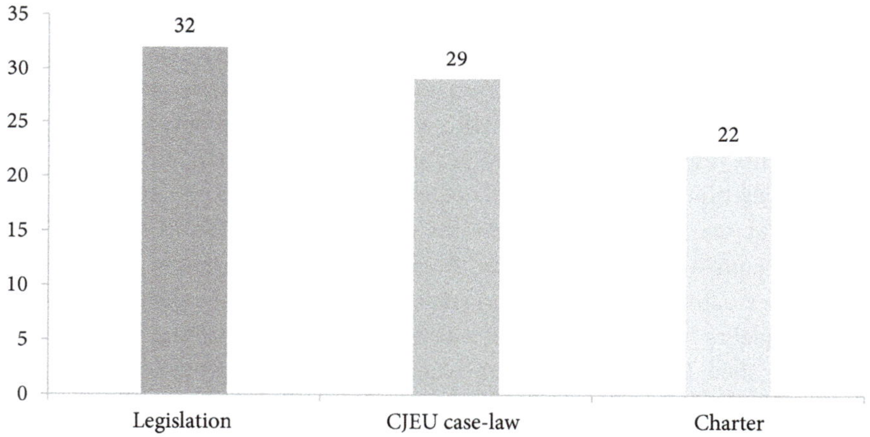

The bar chart displays the frequency of references to the three categories of EU equality standards. EU legislation is the most frequently cited, appearing in 32 cases. This is followed by 29 references to CJEU case-law, and 22 references to the Charter. The ECtHR engages with the various facets of EU equality law in a balanced way and EU legislation is cited more often than other categories,

1 By frequency of references, we mean the number of ECtHR's cases where the ECtHR refers to the EU equality standards.

as in our data protection case study. Yet, the ECtHR refers most of the time to EU secondary legislation together with CJEU related case-law; it is the latter that most often plays a decisive role in the ECtHR's reasoning, as we will show below.[2]

If we examine the references to specific legislative instruments and Charter provisions, we observe significant disparities, similar to our findings in the data protection case study.

Reference per EU legislation

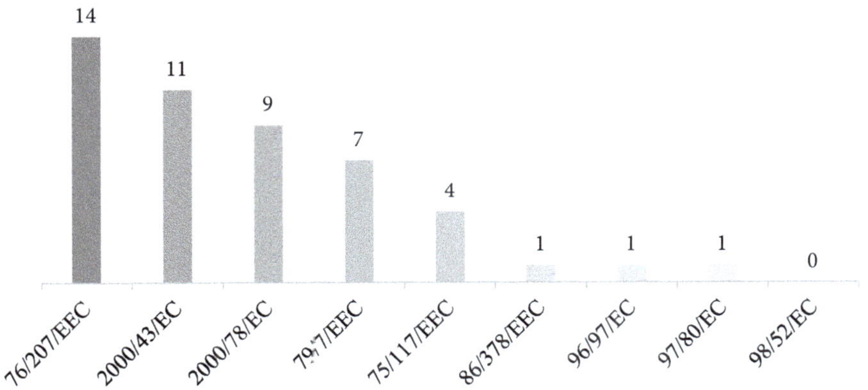

This bar chart shows the frequency of references to EU legislation that gives expression to the fundamental right to equality. Significant disparities exist between the EU equality legislative instruments The Employment Equality between Men and Women Directive (76/207/EEC) was mentioned in 14 cases. The Race Equality Directive (2000/43/EC) and the Equality Framework Directive (2000/78/EC) are frequently cited by the ECtHR, with 11 and 9 mentions. The ECtHR has rarely mentioned some instruments, if at all. The entry into force of the legislative instruments, although it may explain the high level of references to certain instruments,[3] is not necessarily correlated with the number of references. Some recent directives are among the most cited,[4] while older ones have been less referenced.[5] The scope of the directives and the number of references appear correlated. Instruments with limited scope tend to

2 See in particular the conclusion of Part III: Are EU Fundamental Rights A Source of Special Significance?

3 This may partly explain the high number of references to the Employment Equality between Men and Women Directive (76/207/EEC).

4 This is the case of the Racial Discrimination Directive (2000/43/EC) and the Equality Framework Directive (2000/78/EC).

5 This is the case of the Equal Pay between Men and Women Council Directive (75/117/EEC).

be referred less frequently,[6] whereas instruments with broad scope have more references.[7] The profile of Strasbourg cases is another factor that may explain the disparity among the instruments: some instruments have been referred significantly due to the closeness between the nature of ECtHR's cases and these instruments.[8]

Reference per Charter's provision

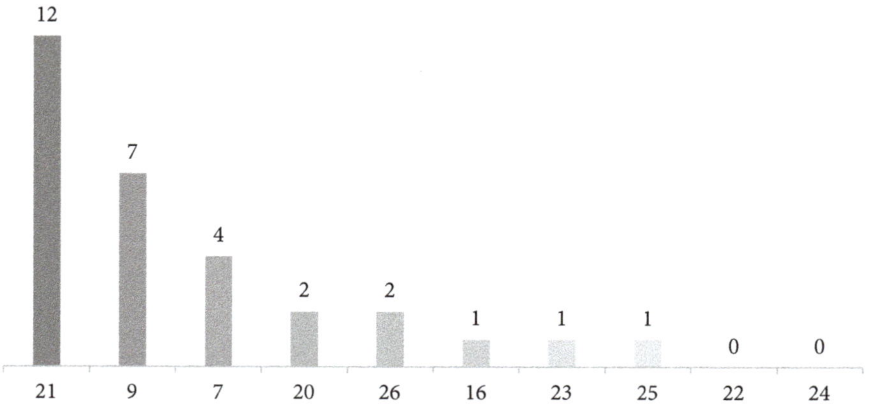

This bar chart presents the frequency with which the ECtHR has referred to Charter's provisions. As for the legislative instruments, there exist significant discrepancies, with some provisions being more prevalent, as in our data protection case study. Article 21 Charter which entails a prohibition of discrimination on several grounds, has been referred to the most, with a total of 12 cases.[9] Although some of these references have no impact on the ECtHR's

---

6 This is the case of the Burden of Proof Directives (97/80/EC and 98/52/EC).

7 This is the case of the Racial Discrimination Directive (2000/43/EC) and the Equality Framework Directive (2000/78/EC).

8 This is the case of the Social Security Equal Treatment Between Men and Women Council Directive (79/7/EEC) where there are a series of cases which relate to a specific provision of this instrument, namely Article 7, and the related interpretative CJEU's case-law: ECtHR, *Stec and Others v. the United Kingdom* [GC], nos. 65731/01 and 65900/01, §§ 17–19, 39–41, 45, 48, 56–58, ECHR 2006-VI; ECtHR, *Walker v. the United Kingdom*, no. 37212/02, §§ 19–20, 34–36, 22 August 2006; ECtHR, *Pearson v. the United Kingdom*, no. 8374/03, §§ 12–13, 17, 22 August 2006; ECtHR, *Barrow v. the United Kingdom*, no. 42735/02, § 30, 36, 22 August 2006.

9 We may recall that the first paragraph of this provision explicitly prohibits discrimination and reads as follows: 'Any discrimination based on any ground such as sex, race, colour, ethnic or social origin, genetic features, language, religion or belief, political or any other opinion, membership of a national minority, property, birth, disability, age or sexual orientation will be prohibited.'

reasoning,[10] the ECtHR has used Article 21 Charter to delimit the scope of the protected grounds as we will see.[11] A high number of references can be witnessed for Article 9 Charter – which concerns the right to marry and the right to found a family – with 7 references. The ECtHR has mentioned this provision in cases concerning the rights of same-sex partners[12] and transsexuals.[13] The ECtHR has made limited references to the equality Charter's provisions which refer to specific categories of the population, such as children, the elderly and persons with disability. While Article 26 (integration of persons with disabilities) was referred to 2 times, Articles 23 (equality between men and women) and 25 (the rights of the elderly) only once. Article 22 (cultural, religious and linguistic diversity) and 24 (the rights of the child) were not referred to at all. In all the cases, the ECtHR has referred to these specific provisions in passing.[14]

The above data sheds light on the diversified use of EU equality law, highlighting significant disparities in references among legal instruments and provisions. Placing this data in a comparative perspective provides insights into the relative importance of EU equality law in the ECtHR's case-law.

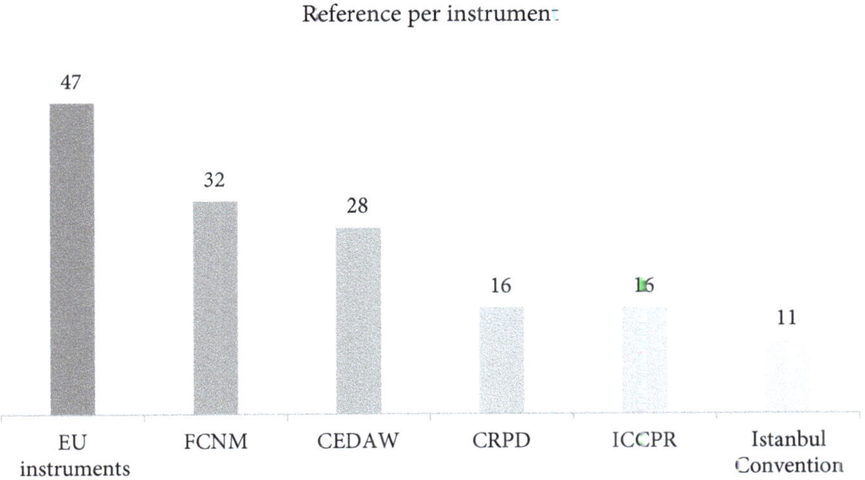

10 E.g. ECtHR, *Molla Sali v. Greece* [GC], no. 20452/14, § 57, 19 December 2018; ECtHR, *Guberina v. Croatia*, no. 23682/13, § 40, 22 March 2016; ECtHR, *Vallianatos and Others v. Greece* [GC], nos. 29381/09 and 32684/09, §§ 31–32, ECHR 2013 (extracts).

11 See below Part III (case study on equality), Chapter 3, Section II, §1, II. Confirmation.

12 ECtHR, *Taddeucci and McCall v. Italy*, no. 51362/09, § 46, 30 June 2016; ECtHR, *Vallianatos and Others v. Greece* [GC], nos. 29381/09 and 32684/09, §§ 31–32, ECHR 2013 (extracts).

13 ECtHR, *Christine Goodwin v. the United Kingdom* [GC], no. 28957/95, § 100, ECHR 2002-VI; ECtHR, *I. v. the United Kingdom* [GC], no. 25680/94, § 80, 11 July 2002.

14 ECtHR, *Jivan v. Romania*, no. 62250/19, § 22, 8 February 2022. For instance, in the *Jivan v. Romania* (2022) case, which involved the deprivation of a personal assistant to an elderly person due to an inadequate assessment of his disability's severity, the ECtHR referred to Article 25 of the Charter (rights of the elderly) and Article 26 (integration of persons with disabilities), but merely as part of the applicable legal framework and not in the ECHR's reasoning.

The bar chart displays the frequency of references to EU equality instruments alongside several international instruments.[15] The data reveals that EU instruments are referred to the most, with a total of 47. Subsequently, three specific instruments, the Framework Convention for the Protection of National Minorities (FCNM), the Convention on the Elimination of All Forms of Discrimination Against Women (CEDAW) and the Convention on the Rights of Persons with Disabilities (CRPD) are cited with decreasing frequency, recording 32, 28, and 16 references. The International Covenant on Civil and Political Rights (ICCPR) garners 16 references. The ECtHR seems to refer more to specific instruments than the general one in the equality field. An exception is the Convention on Preventing and Combating Violence Against Women and Domestic Violence (Istanbul Convention) which is referenced 11 times, which may be explained by the fact that the Convention was adopted more recently.[16] There is thus a prevalence of references to EU equality law over other instruments; yet if the discrepancy between EU and other instruments is notable, it is not significant. The prevalence of EU equality law can also be seen when comparing the outputs of related bodies.

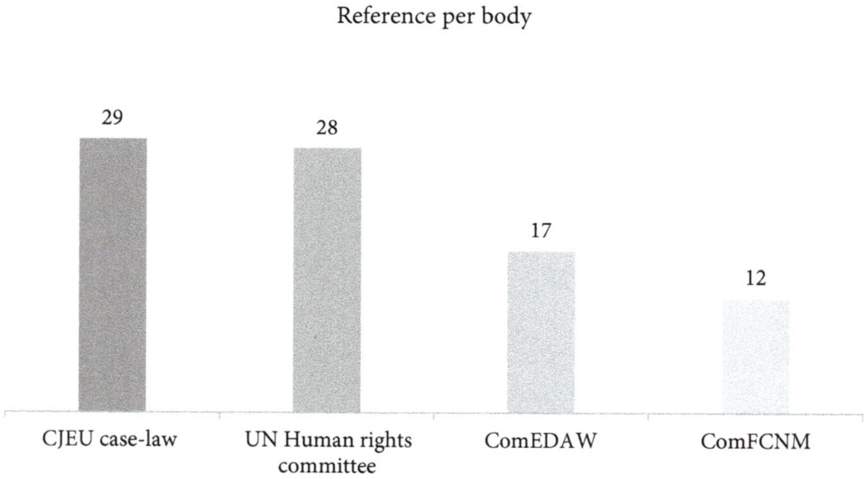

The bar chart shows the frequency of references to CJEU case-law alongside the outputs of bodies related to international equality instruments. There is a prevalence of references to CJEU case-law (29 cases), yet the discrepancy is limited, particularly vis-à-vis the United Nations Human Rights Committee

15 These data are compared with the cumulative references to the Charter and legislation giving expression to the fundamental right to equality. We added the cases where there are references to EU legislation and the Charter, withdrawing duplicate cases.

16 The Istanbul Convention was adopted in 2011.

(UN HRC)(28 cases). There is a notable number of references to the Committee on the Elimination of Discrimination against Women (ComEDAW)(17 cases) and the Advisory Committee on the Framework Convention for the Protection of National Minorities (ComFCNM)(12 cases). Thus, there are more references to the body related to a general instrument than to bodies related to specific equality instruments. While not included in the graph, there are two references to the IACHR and no references to the ACtHPR. The fact that there are numerous references to the outputs of the UN HRC, the ComEDAW, and the ComFCNM can be in part attributed to the fact that the ECtHR often uses them as evidence in equality cases, as we will see below. The high number of references to these instruments contrasts with our data protection case study, where there are very few references to the Consultative Committee of Convention 108.

A final aspect to consider is the total number of equality-related cases handled by the ECtHR. The data shows that there are 981 Chamber cases and 84 Grand Chamber cases concerning equality and non-discrimination.[17] EU equality law is cited in approximately 4.88% of discrimination cases (52 out of 1,065). Notably, out of these 52 cases referring to EU equality law, 15 are Grand Chamber cases. This means that EU equality law is referenced in 17.86% (15 out of 84) of Grand Chamber cases, as opposed to 3.77% (37 out of 981) in Chamber cases. EU equality law is more frequently present in Grand Chamber cases, which may be linked to the tendency of the Grand Chamber of the ECtHR to refer more to external sources.[18] The proportion of cases referencing EU equality law is more limited than references to EU law in our data protection case study.

§ 2. FREQUENCY OVER TIME

We now explore the evolution over time of references to EU equality law.[19] The data shows a consistent use of EU equality law over almost 25 years, with a slight intensification around 2015, which aligns with our findings in our data protection case study. Compared to international instruments, we observe that they follow a similar pattern.

---

[17] We use the keywords 'prohibition of discrimination (Article 14)' and 'general prohibition of discrimination (P12-1)' on Hudoc until May 2024.

[18] M. Larché, *Les fonctions du droit international dans la jurisprudence de la Cour européenne des droits de l'Homme*, Paris, Pedone, 2025.

[19] By frequency over time, we mean the number of time of ECtHR cases where the ECtHR refers to EU equality law per year.

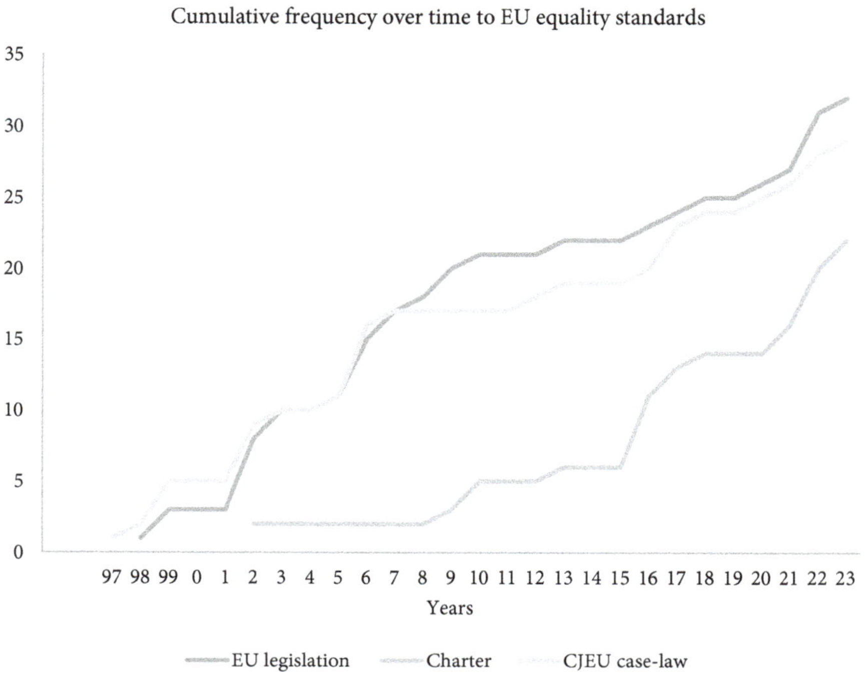

The line chart illustrates the cumulative frequency over time of the three categories of EU equality law standards by the ECtHR. The first reference is to CJEU case-law in 1997,[20] followed by references to EU legislation in 1998,[21] and the Charter in 2002.[22] There is a consistent referral to these three instruments, highlighting a referencing practice spanning approximately 25 years. This provides some perspective on the overall frequency of references to EU equality law, which amounts to 52 cases, equating to roughly two cases per year over a quarter-century – a figure which is similar as in our data protection case study. We observe a strong correlation between the references to EU legislation and CJEU case-law, which is due to the fact that the ECtHR refers most often to both sources together. Despite occasional fluctuations, the curves of EU legislation and CJEU case-law remain stable. The Charter follows a distinct pattern: there is a surge in references from 2017. While there were six references from 2002 until 2016, the period between 2017 and 2023 saw 14 references. The late increase can be partly attributed to its entry into force,

[20] ECtHR, *X, Y and Z v. the United Kingdom*, 22 April 1997, §§ 38–39, *Reports of Judgments and Decisions* 1997-II.

[21] ECtHR, *Sheffield and Horsham v. the United Kingdom*, 30 July 1998, §§ 33–34, *Reports of Judgments and Decisions* 1998-V.

[22] ECtHR, *Christine Goodwin v. the United Kingdom* [GC], no. 28957/95, § 100, ECHR 2002-VI; ECtHR, *I. v. the United Kingdom* [GC], no. 25680/94, § 80, 11 July 2002.

suggesting a growing presence in the ECtHR's rulings as the Charter solidified its place within EU law.

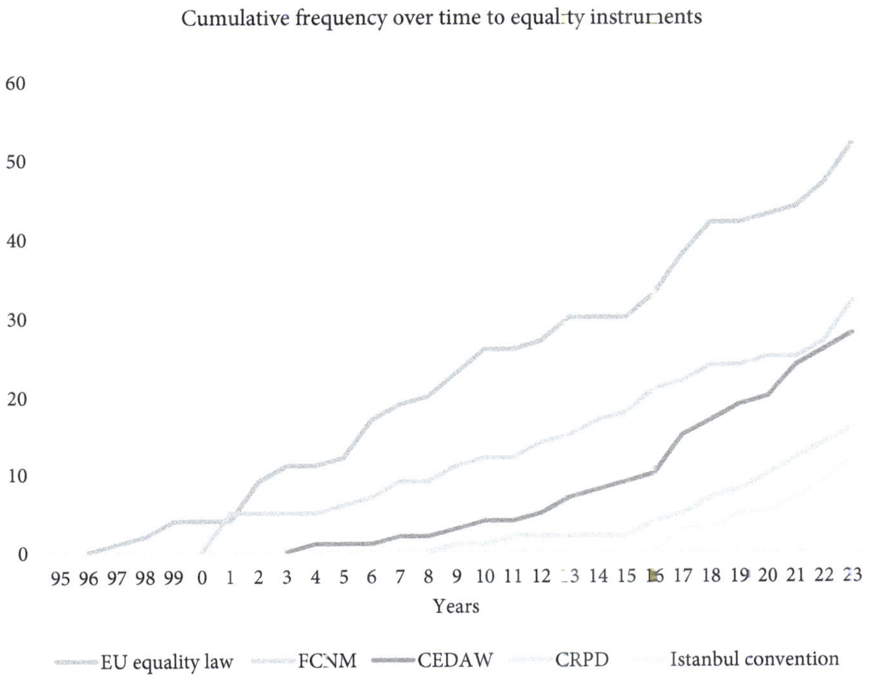

The line chart presents the cumulative frequency over time to EU equality law, FCNM, CEDAW, CRPD, and Istanbul Convention. EU equality law was the first to be referenced, beginning in 1997.[23] The FCNM started to be referenced after the turn of the century in 2001, with CEDAW following in 2004. References to the CRPD began in 2009, and the Istanbul Convention was cited in 2017. All instruments display a constant evolution. An intensification around 2015 can be seen for EU equality law: from 1997 to 2015 (over 18 years), there were 30 references, and from 2016 to 2023 (over 7 years), there were 22 references. An intensification can be observed for CEDAW, CRPD and Istanbul Convention around the same period. For instance, there were 10 references to the CEDAW from 2003 to 2016 (13 years), and 18 references from 2017 to 2023 (6 years). The increase in references to EU equality law around 2015 can be attributed to several factors. The EU framework on equality has evolved: the Charter, which includes several equality rights, became binding

23 Please note that the data are not exhaustive and not entirely comparable (i.a. because we only look at the international instruments and not at related outputs from their respective monitoring body). Yet they still provide us with valuable insights into the use of EU equality law and international instruments over time.

with the Lisbon Treaty, and EU equality legislative instruments have matured in CJEU case-law. Furthermore, this increase should be seen in the context of the ECtHR's trend of referring increasingly to external instruments.[24] It is also worth noting that this intensification occurs in the post-CJEU'S Opinion 2/13, and although more speculative, it may have contributed to an increase in references by the ECtHR in order to foster dialogue with the CJEU.

§ 3. FREQUENCY PER AREA

We conclude with a statistical analysis of the frequency of references to EU equality law per area. The ECtHR refers to EU equality law in diverse areas, with some being referenced more frequently than others. There is also significant diversity in the areas where CEDAW is used, with a prevalence in areas related to its purpose and scope.

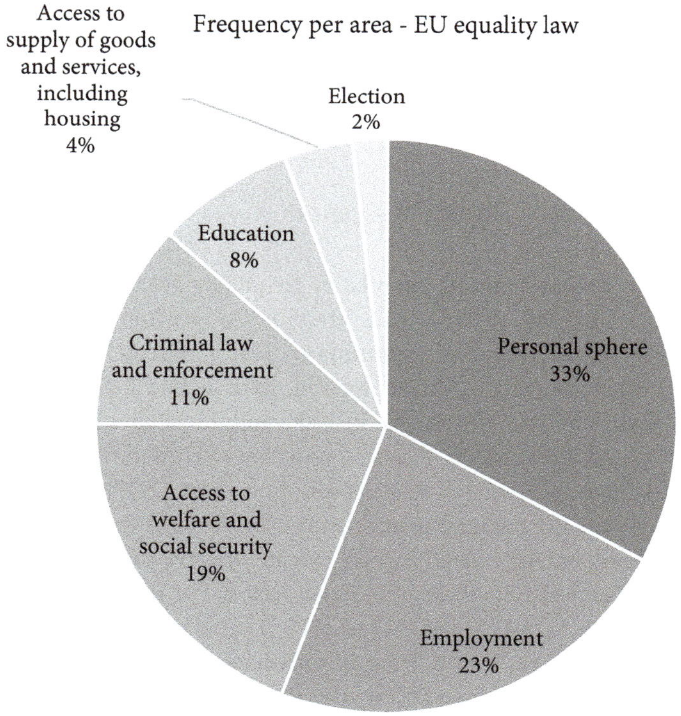

[24] The data did not suggest that the rising number of equality cases adjudicated by the Strasbourg court each year is directly correlated with increased references to EU equality law. We found no significant rise in the number of cases per year post-2015 compared to previous years. For instance, 2022 had 28 cases and 2021 had 24 cases, yet earlier years such as 2013 saw 31 cases, and 2009 had as many as 40 cases.

This pie chart shows the frequency of references to EU equality law per area. The data highlight the significant diversity of fields in which the ECtHR refers to EU equality law, as in our data protection case study. 23% of the cases are related to employment, with for instance cases of dismissal[25] or change of diplomatic post.[26] Access to welfare and social security make up 17.5% of the cases, with a significant number relating to pensions.[27] The use of EU equality law extends beyond the economic sphere. The personal sphere accounts for the largest share of cases at 37.5%. This includes matters related to the legal recognition of transsexuals,[28] same-sex partners,[29] and family reunification.[30] The ECtHR refers to EU equality law in relation to criminal and enforcement law matters (11%).[31] There are some cases related to access to the supply of goods and services, including housing, which constitute 4% of the total, as well as one case pertaining to elections.[32]

The ECtHR tends to refer to EU equality law in areas corresponding to the scope of application of the relevant EU legal instruments. Certain EU directives have only been mentioned in cases related to their scope of application.[33] When

---

25 E.g. ECtHR, *Perkins and R. v the United Kingdom*, nos. 43208/98 and 44875/98, 22 October 2002; ECtHR, *Beck and Others v. the United Kingdom*, nos. 48535/99 and 2 others, 22 October 2002; ECtHR, *Lustig-Prean and Beckett v. the United Kingdom*, nos. 31417/96 and 32377/96, 27 September 1999; ECtHR, *Smith and Grady v. the United Kingdom*, nos. 33985/96 and 33986/96, ECHR 1999-VI.

26 ECtHR, *Napotnik v. Romania*, no. 33139/13, 20 October 2020.

27 ECtHR *Aldeguer Tomás v. Spain*, no. 35214/09, 14 June 2016; ECtHR, *Stec and Others v. the United Kingdom* [GC], nos. 65731/01 and 65900/01, ECHR 2006-VI; *Barrow v. the United Kingdom*, no. 42735/02, 22 August 2006; *Pearson v. the United Kingdom*, no. 8374/03, 22 August 2006.

28 ECtHR, *Christine Goodwin v. the United Kingdom* [GC], no. 28957/95, ECHR 2002-VI; ECtHR, *Van Kück v. Germany*, no. 35968/97, ECHR 2003-VII; ECtHR, *I. v. the United Kingdom* [GC], no. 25680/94, 11 July 2002; ECtHR, *Sheffield and Horsham v. the United Kingdom*, 30 July 1998, Reports of Judgments and Decisions 1998-V; ECtHR, *X, Y and Z v. the United Kingdom*, 22 April 1997, *Reports of Judgments and Decisions* 1997-II.

29 ECtHR, *Fedotova and Others v. Russia* [GC], nos. 40792/10 and 2 others, 17 January 2023; ECtHR, *Oliari and Others v. Italy*, nos. 18766/11 and 36030/11, 21 July 2015; ECtHR, *Vallianatos and Others v. Greece* [GC], nos. 29381/09 and 32684/09, ECHR 2013 (extracts); ECtHR, *Schalk and Kopf v. Austria*, no. 30141/04, ECHR 2010.

30 ECtHR, *Biao v. Denmark* [GC], no. 38590/10, 24 May 2016; ECtHR, *Pajić v. Croatia*, no. 68453/13, 23 February 2016.

31 E.g. ECtHR, *Muhammad v. Spain*, no. 34085/17, 18 October 2022 (identity control); ECtHR, *Basu v. Germany*, no. 215/19, 18 October 2022 (identity control); ECtHR, *Khamtokhu and Aksenchik v. Russia* [GC], nos. 60367/08 and 961/11, 24 January 2017 (life sentences).

32 ECtHR, *Sejdić and Finci v. Bosnia and Herzegovina* [GC], nos. 27996/06 and 34836/06, ECHR 2009.

33 See regarding the Social Security Equal Treatment Between Men and Women Council Directive (79/7/EEC), e.g. ECtHR, *Barrow v. the United Kingdom*, no. 42735/02, § 30, 36, 22 August 2006; ECtHR, *Pearson v. the United Kingdom*, no. 8374/03, §§ 12 13, 17, 22 August 2006; ECtHR, *Walker v. the United Kingdom*, no. 37212/02, §§ 19–20, 35, 22 August 2006, ECtHR *Stec and Others v. the United Kingdom* [GC], nos. 65731/01 and 65900/01, §§ 17–19, 39-41, 45, 48, 56-58, ECHR 2006-VI.

references are made to EU law in areas that are arguably outside its scope, there is often a substantive link between the subject matter of the case and the content of an EU law provision. For example, the ECtHR has referred to Article 9 Charter, which concerns the right to marry and found a family, in cases concerning same-sex relationships, even though these cases have no link to EU law and therefore arguably fall outside the scope of EU law (and the Charter).[34]

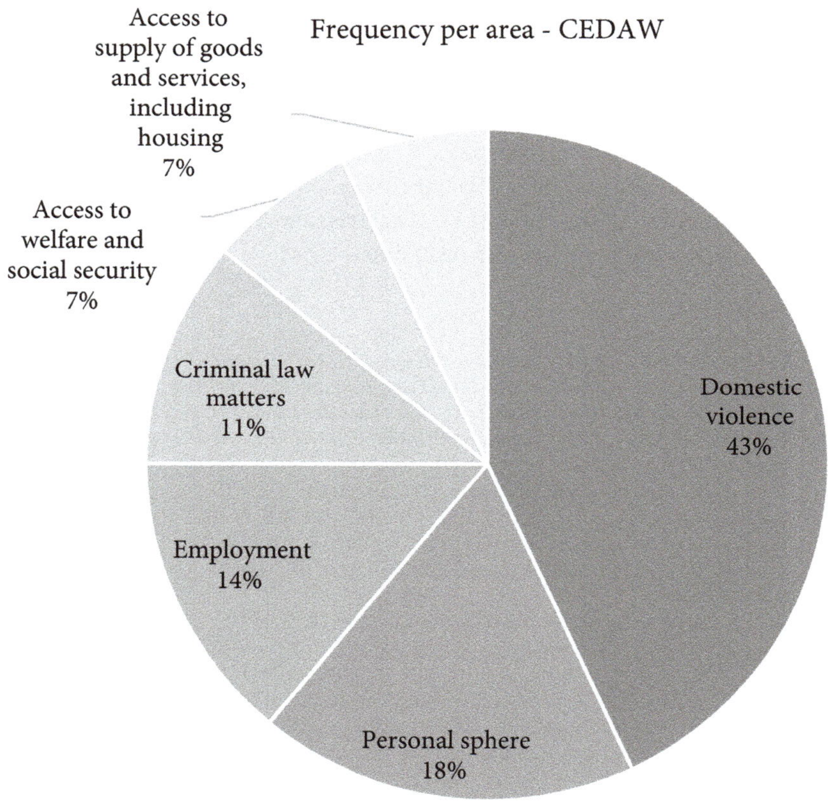

This pie chart shows the frequency of references to CEDAW across various areas.[35] Two points can be made. First, the data shows a significant diversity of areas where the instrument is used. Second, CEDAW is most frequently

[34] E.g. ECtHR, *Vallianatos and Others v. Greece* [GC], nos. 29381/09 and 32684/09, §§ 31–32, ECHR 2013 (extracts); ECtHR, *Schalk and Kopf v. Austria*, no. 30141/04, §§ 55, 57, 60–61, ECHR 2010.

[35] We offer some perspective by showing the references per area to one particular equality instrument, namely CEDAW. This more limited comparative approach is deliberate, as here it seems less relevant to examine all the international instruments because comparing domains does not really add value.

referenced in cases of domestic violence, aligning with its focus on gender-specific issues. This illustrates that the area in which specific international instruments are referenced is often closely related to the purpose and scope of the instrument.

SECTION II. FUNCTIONS

We now move to the qualitative study and examine the functions of EU equality law in ECtHR case-law.[36] Our qualitative analysis reflects our quantitative findings: EU equality law is the most prominent external source used by the ECtHR in its equality case-law. EU equality law has played a wide variety of functions (interpretation, justification, distinguishing, and information) in the ECtHR case-law and has often had a significant or notable impact in performing them. International instruments perform similar functions to those in EU equality law, albeit to a lesser extent. They either play a less significant role in performing these functions or do not perform certain function at all. However, there is one function performed by international instruments that is not performed by EU equality law: the evidentiary function.

§ 1. INTERPRETATION

EU equality law has played a notable role in supporting the interpretation of the meaning and scope of ECHR equality provisions and, to a lesser extent, other Convention's provisions. It has been used to perform a variety of sub-functions: supporting a new interpretation, confirming and bolstering an existing interpretation, and finding a consensus for interpreting Convention's provisions. It has impacted all dimensions of ECHR equality law, including its scope, substantive and procedural elements. The interpretation supported by EU equality law has brought important transformations to ECHR law.

I. *New Interpretation*

The ECtHR has notably used EU equality law to support or refute new interpretations of the meaning and scope of ECHR equality provisions and other Convention provisions, resulting in substantial changes to ECHR law.

The impact of Union law is first and foremost visible concerning the types of discrimination prohibited under ECHR equality law. Despite its historical

36 It is worth noting that in any one case before the ECtHR, EU equality law may perform several functions. It can be used to perform an informative function and, at the same time, another function, such as the interpretation of the Convention.

emphasis on formal equality protection, the ECtHR operated a shift around the 2000s. It embraced a more substantive definition of equality by protecting new forms of discrimination. The ECtHR has used EU equality law to confirm and bolster that indirect discrimination is safeguarded under ECHR equality law, as we will see below. The role of EU law in shaping the interpretation of the ECHR's forms of discrimination is not limited to indirect discrimination. The ECtHR has relied on EU equality law to support a new interpretation of Article 14 ECHR, under which the concept of discrimination by association is protected.

In *Guberina v. Croatia* (2016), the applicant had purchased a new house more suitable for the needs of his disabled child and applied for a tax exemption that could be provided to people who needed a different house to address their needs. His application was refused on the grounds that the flat he had sold met his family's needs. The applicant did not allege discriminatory treatment related to his own disability, but rather unfavourable treatment because of the disability of his child, with whom he lives and cares for.[37] The question arose whether Article 14 ECHR covered situations of discrimination by association. The ECtHR answered that the said provision covers cases where a person is treated less favourably on the basis of the protected status or characteristics of another person.[38]

To assess whether discrimination by association was covered by Article 14, the ECtHR examined whether the disability of the applicant's child could bring the applicant's situation within the term 'other status' in the said provision. The ECtHR stressed that the words 'other status' have been given a wide meaning in its case-law, and that their interpretation has not been limited to characteristics which are personal in the sense that they are innate or inherent. It relied on one previous case, *Efe v. Austria* (2014), to illustrate that the ECtHR has accepted cases of discrimination where the applicants' status was determined in relation to their family situation, namely the children's place of residence.[39]

While there is no mention of EU equality law, there is, arguably, an implicit influence of the latter source. In its relevant legal materials, the ECtHR mentioned two CJEU cases, *CHEZ Razpredelenie Bulgaria AD* (C-83/14) and *S. Coleman v. Attridge Law and Steve Law* (C-303/06), in which the CJEU held that the Racial Discrimination Directive (2000/43/EC) and the Equality Framework Directive (2000/78/EC) benefit persons who, although not themselves possessing the protected characteristic, suffer less favourable treatment because they are associated with a person with the protected

[37] ECtHR, *Guberina v. Croatia*, no. 23682/13, § 77, 22 March 2016.
[38] Ibid., § 78.
[39] Ibid.

characteristic.[40] These two judgments are the only legal sources which are mentioned by the ECtHR that refer to discrimination by association. Even if it remains somewhat speculative, one may argue that they played a role in supporting the integration of discrimination by association into the ECHR equality palette.[41]

In *Molla Sali v. Greece* [GC](2018), the ECtHR confirmed that discrimination by association is protected under ECHR equality law. The ECtHR provided a similar type of reasoning as in *Guberina v. Croatia* (2016).[42] It did not refer to EU equality law in its reasoning, but referred to the two CJEU judgments in the relevant legal materials.[43] The difference with *Guberina* is that the ECtHR mentioned (also in the relevant legal materials) the 2018 General Comment No. 6 on equality and non-discrimination from the CRPD, according to which discrimination includes discrimination by association with a person with a disability.[44]

Not only has the ECtHR used EU equality law to support the inclusion of new forms of discrimination, but it has used it to support that a specific difference in treatment should be considered a specific type of discrimination. This approach can be seen in *Napotnik v. Romania* (2020), which involved the termination of the applicant's diplomatic posting to Slovenia due to her pregnancy. The ECtHR relied on CJEU case-law – via the technique of 'use by reference' which we will explain below[45] – to support that a difference in treatment on grounds of pregnancy amounts to direct discrimination on grounds of sex. The ECtHR observed that: '(...) women can be treated differently on grounds of pregnancy, and for this reason such a difference in treatment will amount to direct discrimination on grounds of sex if it is not justified *On this point, the Court cannot but note that a similar approach has also been taken by the CJEU in its case-law (see paragraphs 44 and 46 above)*, and that the approach is consistent with domestic law (see paragraph 31 above) and practice (see paragraphs 34 to 36 above).'[46] CJEU case-law is used to support the conclusion reached by the ECtHR, by pointing out that a similar approach is used in EU law.

---

40 Ibid., §§ 41–42. Case C-83/14, *CHEZ*, ECLI:EU:C:2015:480, para. 56 and Case C-303/06, *S. Coleman v. Attridge Law and Steve Law*, ECLI:EU:C:2008:415, para 56.

41 See in this vein, S. O'Leary, 'The EU Charter Ten Years On: A View from Strasbourg', in M. Bobek and J. Adams-Prassl (eds.), *The EU Charter of Fundamental Rights in the Member States*, Oxford, Hart Publishing, 2020, pp. 53–54.

42 ECtHR, *Molla Sali v. Greece* [GC], no. 20452/14, § 134, 19 December 2018.

43 Ibid., §§ 78–81.

44 Ibid., § 69.

45 See below Part III (case study on equality), Chapter , Section V. Methodology of the ECtHR when Using EU Equality Law.

46 ECtHR, *Napotnik v. Romania*, no. 33139/13, § 77, 20 October 2020. Emphasis added

EU equality law has been influential not only in defining the types of discrimination but also in supporting an extension of the scope of the protected grounds under Article 14 ECHR. This occurred in *G.N. and Others v. Italy* (2009), in which the ECtHR had to determine whether discrimination based on a genetic disorder fell under Article 14 ECHR. The ECtHR stated that Article 14 does not mention health status, genetic characteristics, or disabilities as prohibited grounds of discrimination, but observed that the list of grounds stated in Article 14 is not exhaustive. It highlighted that the possibility of genetic characteristics being a factor of prohibited discrimination among individuals is corroborated by external sources to the Convention, such as the Charter. In particular, Article 21 Charter forbids, among other things, discrimination based on genetic characteristics or disabilities.[47] In light of this, the ECtHR concluded that Article 14 ECHR covers discrimination on grounds of genetic disorders.[48] In other words, the ECtHR support its new interpretation of Article 14 ECHR by relying on the scope of the protected grounds under the Charter.

If the impact of EU equality law is first and foremost felt on the equality provisions of the Convention, it has also been influential in interpreting the scope of other provisions of the Convention. This has occurred in cases where the issues raised under these provisions were linked to equality concerns. This is the case with regard to the right of marriage enshrined in Article 12 ECHR. The first relevant cases are *Christine Goodwin v. the United Kingdom* and *I. v. the United Kingdom*, both delivered on 7 July 2002 by the Grand Chamber of the ECtHR.[49] Both cases concern post-operative males to female transsexuals. The applicants complained that they could not marry because the law treated them as men.[50] In previous cases, the ECtHR had found that the right to marry guaranteed by Article 12 ECHR refers to the traditional marriage between persons of opposite biological sex. The inability of transsexuals to marry a person of the sex opposite to their reassigned gender was not found in breach of Article 12.[51] In a departure from its previous case-law, the ECtHR held that the right of a man and a woman to marry would also be of avail to post-operative transsexuals under certain circumstances.[52]

47 ECtHR, *G.N. and Others v. Italy*, no. 43134/05, § 126, 1 December 2009.

48 Ibid., § 127.

49 ECtHR, *Christine Goodwin v. the United Kingdom* [GC], no. 28957/95, ECHR 2002-VI; ECtHR, *I. v. the United Kingdom* [GC], no. 25680/94, 11 July 2002. Please note that these cases were introduced in Part I of this research project (Chapter 1, Section V, §2, I. The Genesis).

50 ECtHR, *Christine Goodwin v. the United Kingdom* [GC], ibid. § 95; ECtHR, *I. v. the United Kingdom* [GC], ibid., § 75.

51 ECtHR, *Christine Goodwin v. the United Kingdom* [GC], ibid. § 97; ECtHR, *I. v. the United Kingdom* [GC], ibid., § 77.

52 ECtHR, *Christine Goodwin v. the United Kingdom* [GC], ibid. § 103; ECtHR, *I. v. the United Kingdom* [GC], ibid., § 83.

To reach this conclusion, the ECtHR relied predominantly on the fact that there have been social changes in the institution of marriage as well as changes brought about by developments in medicine and science in the field of transsexuality.[53] The ECtHR also noted that 'Article 9 of the recently adopted Charter of Fundamental Rights of the European Union departs, no doubt deliberately, from the wording of Article 12 of the Convention in removing the reference to men and women' without further elucidation.[54] The wording of Article 9 Charter is used to support a novel interpretation of the terms 'right of a man and woman to marry', thereby expanding the protection provided by Article 12 ECHR. While the reference to EU equality is not the sole argument brought forward by the ECtHR, it stands out as the sole legal source to justify its departure from established case-law.

In *Schalk and Kopf v. Austria* (2010), the ECtHR relied on Article 9 Charter in the context of a new interpretation of Article 12 ECHR. The applicants alleged that they were discriminated against as, being a same-sex couple, they were denied the possibility to marry or to have their relationship otherwise recognised by law.[55] The use of Article 9 Charter is two-fold in this case. First, it is used to refuse to give a new interpretation to Article 12 ECHR according to which the latter would guarantee a right to same-sex marriage. In this respect, the ECtHR mentioned that:

> Turning to the comparison between Article 12 of the Convention and Article 9 of the Charter, the Court has already noted that the latter has deliberately dropped the reference to "men and women" (see *Christine Goodwin*, cited above, § 100). The Commentary of the Charter, which became legally binding in December 2009, confirms that Article 9 is meant to be broader in scope than the corresponding Articles in other human rights instruments (see paragraph 25 above). At the same time, the reference to domestic law reflects the diversity of national regulations, which range from allowing same-sex marriage to explicitly forbidding it. By referring to national law, Article 9 of the Charter leaves the decision whether or not to allow same-sex marriage to the States. In the words of the Commentary: "... it may be argued that there is no obstacle to recognise same-sex relationships in the context of marriage. There is, however, no explicit requirement that domestic laws should facilitate such marriages".[56]

The ECtHR highlighted that Article 9 Charter leaves discretion to the States whether or not to allow same-sex marriage. This is one of the arguments to refuse to interpret Article 12 ECHR as imposing an obligation to grant access

53 ECtHR, *Christine Goodwin v. the United Kingdom* [GC], ibid. § 100; ECtHR, *I. v. the United Kingdom* [GC], ibid., § 80.
54 Ibid.
55 ECtHR, *Schalk and Kopf v. Austria*, no. 30141/04, § 3, ECHR 2010.
56 Ibid., § 60.

to marriage to same-sex couples.[57] The ECtHR also used Article 9 Charter to support a new interpretation of Article 12 ECHR according to which the right to marry is not limited to marriage between persons from the opposite sex: 'Regard being had to Article 9 of the Charter, therefore, the Court would no longer consider that the right to marry enshrined in Article 12 must in all circumstances be limited to marriage between two persons of the opposite sex. Consequently, it cannot be said that Article 12 is inapplicable to the applicants' complaint. [...]'.[58] EU equality law is here the sole argument and legal source which is mentioned by the ECtHR.

II. Confirmation

The ECtHR has used EU equality law to confirm and support an interpretation of the ECHR equality provisions as well as related procedural elements. As hinted above, the ECtHR has done so for the types of discrimination covered under Article 14 ECHR, in particular for indirect discrimination in *D.H. v. Czech Republic* [GC](2007).[59]

If the CJEU had early on extended protection against such types of discrimination,[60] this notion has long remained unaddressed in ECHR equality law. This can be attributed to the fact that Article 14 ECHR encompasses an open prohibition of discrimination, allowing for the possibility to challenge all manifestations of unequal treatment. As Gerards noted, a change occurred when the ECtHR established its very weighty reasons doctrine, making it attractive for applicants to demonstrate that a 'neutral' case of unequal treatment disproportionately affects a group defined by suspect characteristics.[61] Whereas

---

57 There were other arguments used by the ECtHR, such as a textual argument: ibid., § 55: 'The applicants argued that the wording did not necessarily imply that a man could only marry a woman and vice versa. The Court observes that, looked at in isolation, the wording of Article 12 might be interpreted so as not to exclude the marriage between two men or two women. However, in contrast, all other substantive Articles of the Convention grant rights and freedoms to "everyone" or state that "no one" is to be subjected to certain types of prohibited treatment. The choice of wording in Article 12 must thus be regarded as deliberate. Moreover, regard must be had to the historical context in which the Convention was adopted In the 1950s marriage was clearly understood in the traditional sense of being a union between partners of different sex.'

58 Ibid., § 61.

59 Please note that this case was introduced in Part I of this research project (Chapter 1, Section 5, §2, II.B. Indirect Discrimination).

60 E. Dubout, 'Une approche comparative du principe de non-discrimination dans le cadre européen : Convention européenne des droits de l'homme et droit de l'Union européenne', in M. Balboni (ed.), *The European Convention of Human Rights and the Principle of Non-Discrimination*, Naples, Editoriale Scientifica, 2017, point §2, A, 1.2.

61 J. Gerards, 'Non-Discrimination, the European Court of Justice and the European Court of Human Rights: Who Takes the Lead?', in T. Giegerich (ed.), *The European Union as Protector and Promoter of Equality. European Union and its Neighbours in a Globalized World*, Springer, 2020, p. 141.

the ECtHR had begun to accept the concept of indirect discrimination, it was not until *D.H. v. Czech Republic* that it wholeheartedly endorsed the doctrine.[62]

Roma children were being disproportionately assigned to 'special' schools due to the way in which educational tests were formulated and administered. The applicants argued that they were being discriminated against as they were treated less favourably than other children in comparable situations because of their race or ethnic origin.[63] The question at hand was whether Article 14 ECHR covers cases of indirect discrimination. The ECtHR responded in the positive:

> The Court has already accepted in previous cases that a difference in treatment may take the form of disproportionately prejudicial effects of a general policy or measure which, though couched in neutral terms, discriminates against a group (see Hugh Jordan, cited above, § 154, and Hoogendijk, cited above). In accordance with, for instance, Council Directives 97/80/EC and 2000/43/EC (see paragraphs 82-84 above) and the definition provided by ECRI (see paragraph 60 above), such a situation may amount to "indirect discrimination", which does not necessarily require a discriminatory intent.[64]

Two legislative equality instruments were used to confirm and support one specific interpretation of Article 14 ECHR that had already been used by the ECtHR. The latter only referred to its previous case-law and the EU instruments as well as one definition from the European Commission against Racism and Intolerance to incorporate indirect discrimination. Equally noteworthy is that the ECtHR referred in the relevant legal materials to various provisions in EU equality legislation that incorporate and define indirect discrimination.[65]

In *D.H. v. Czech Republic*, EU equality law is also used to confirm and support the interpretation of a related procedural aspect, namely whether statistics could be used to prove indirect discrimination. In previous cases, the ECtHR had issued somewhat contradictory Chamber's judgments. Whereas in *Hugh Jordan v. The United Kingdom* (2001), the ECtHR did not consider that statistics could in themselves disclose a practice which could be classified as discriminatory,[66] in *Hoogendijk v. The Netherlands* (2005), the ECtHR had deemed that 'where an applicant is able to show, on the basis of undisputed official statistics, the existence of a prima facie indication that a specific rule – although formulated in a neutral manner – in fact affects a clearly higher percentage of women than men, it is for the respondent Government to show that this is the result of objective factors unrelated to any discrimination on

---

62 Ibid.

63 ECtHR, *D.H. and Others v. the Czech Republic* [GC], no. 57325/00, § 124, ECHR 2007-IV.

64 Ibid., § 184.

65 Ibid., § 81–91.

66 ECtHR, *Hugh Jordan v. the United Kingdom*, no. 24746/94, § 154 4 June 2008.

grounds of sex.'[67] In *D.H. v. Czech Republic*, the ECtHR held that statistical evidence could be used to raise a presumption of discrimination and noted:

> On this point, the Court observes that *Council Directives 97/80/EC and 2000/43/EC* stipulate that persons who consider themselves wronged because the principle of equal treatment has not been applied to them may establish before a domestic authority by any means, including on the basis of statistical evidence, facts from which it may be presumed that there has been discrimination (see paragraphs 82-83 above). *The recent case-law of the Court of Justice of the European Communities* (see paragraphs 88-89 above) shows that it permits claimants to rely on statistical evidence and the national courts to take such evidence into account where it is valid and significant.[68]

EU legislative instruments and CJEU case-law are used to confirm one of the previous interpretations given by the ECtHR. The ECtHR relied on its previous case-law, EU equality law, as well as the fact that 'the information furnished by the third-party interveners' shows 'that the courts of many countries and the supervisory bodies of the United Nations treaties habitually accept statistics as evidence of indirect discrimination in order to facilitate the victims' task of adducing prima facie evidence.'[69] EU equality law emerges as the legal source to which the ECtHR referred with greater depth and precision to endorse the use of statistical data to prove indirect discrimination.

Lastly, EU equality law has been used to confirm and support the interpretation of the scope of the protected grounds in *Peterka v. Czech Republic* (2008) and *Moraru v. Romania* (2022). In the latter, the ECtHR referred to Article 21 Charter, as sole legal source and argument, to confirm that genetic feature falls within the list of prohibited ground for discrimination set out in Article 14 ECHR, thereby supporting its extensive jurisprudence established in *G.N. v. Italy* (2009).[70] In the former case, the ECtHR used Article 21 Charter to support its restrictive line of case-law on the scope of protected grounds. Even though it is 'only' a decision of admissibility, the *Peterka* case deserves some elaboration as it sheds light on the potential influence of EU law in restricting the scope of protected grounds under ECHR equality law.

The *Peterka* case concerned an applicant who alleged discrimination on the basis of the type of employment contract. Since this criterion is not listed in Article 14, the ECtHR had to determine whether it falls within the scope of

67 ECtHR, *Hoogendijk v. The Netherlands* (adm. decision), no. 58641/00, pp. 21-22, 6 January 2005.

68 ECtHR, *D.H. and Others v. the Czech Republic* [GC], no. 57325/00, § 187, ECHR 2007-IV. Emphasis added

69 Ibid.

70 ECtHR, *Moraru v. Romania*, no. 64480/19, § 32, 8 November 2022.

the provision's 'any other status' phrase.[71] The ECtHR noted that while the list of grounds for discrimination in Article 14 is indicative, it cannot be said that the provision prohibits all forms of discrimination, regardless of the criterion on which it is based. The term 'any other status' is intended to cover only analogous or similar criteria to those explicitly listed, relating to a personal characteristic.[72] This could encompass grounds that reflect individual personality traits, such as religion, political opinion, sexual orientation, and gender identity, or grounds relating to personal characteristics over which one has no control, such as sex, race, disability, and age.[73] In this respect, the ECtHR observed that:

> […] [T]he grounds listed in Article 21(1) of the Charter of Fundamental Rights of the European Union, in addition to those listed in the Convention, may also be covered by Article 14, namely ethnic origin, genetic characteristics, convictions, disability, age or sexual orientation.[74]

The ECtHR concluded that criteria such as the duration of the employment contract or the fact of being temporarily employed or self-employed, which do not appear to reflect any personal characteristics or beliefs do not fall within the expression 'any other status' referred to in Article 14 ECHR.[75]

While considering both the *Moraru v. Romania* judgment and *Peterka v. Czech Republic* decision, they have in common that the ECtHR refers to Article 21 Charter in relation to the scope of protected grounds. Yet, it is important to distinguish the two cases. In *Moraru*, the ECtHR relies on this provision to support an extensive interpretation of the scope of Article 14 ECHR. In *Peterka*, the ECtHR uses Article 21 Charter to endorse its restrictive line of case-law according to which the scope of Article 14 ECHR is confined to personal characteristics.

As pointed out above, there is arguably a shift from an open equality model in ECtHR case-law, in which all types of discrimination grounds are protected, to a closed model that covers only specific protected grounds.[76] This trend is epitomised by *Carlson v. United Kingdom* (2010), in which the ECtHR held that: 'only differences in treatment based on a personal characteristic (or 'status')

---

71 ECtHR, *Peterka v. Czech Republic* (adm. decision), no. 21990/08, 4 May 2010.
72 Ibid., p. 5.
73 Ibid., p. 6.
74 Ibid.
75 Ibid.
76 O.M. Arnardottir, 'Cross-fertilisation, Clarity and Consistency at an Overburdened European Court of Human Rights – the Case of the Discrimination Grounds under Article 14 ECHR', *Nordic Journal of Human Rights*, 2015, pp. 231–233; J. Gerards, 'The Discrimination Grounds of Article 14 of the European Convention on Human Rights', *Human Rights Law Review*, 2013, pp. 104–113.

by which persons or groups of persons are distinguishable from each other are capable of amounting to discrimination within the meaning of Article 14'.[77] In this judgment and also subsequent ones,[78] the ECtHR indicated that the scope of protected grounds is limited to those explicitly listed in Article 14 ECHR, and those based on a personal characteristic. However, the ECtHR's position lacks clarity and consistency.[79]

One question is whether EU equality law has played a role in the shift from an open to a closed system of protected grounds. Arnardottir has suggested that EU equality law may have had a diffuse influence:

> The tendencies towards narrowing the scope of protection of [A]rticle 14 [...] reflect a development that can be conceptualised in terms of a move from the open model non-discrimination clause to the closed model. As such, they reflect how the Strasbourg [case-law] is partly moving towards a closer resemblance with the model underpinning the Luxembourg [case-law] under the EU non-discrimination directives. This cross-fertilisation (or cross-contamination) effect is supported by the fact that these directives have been implemented in the law of the EU member states and that lawyers from these countries have become accustomed to thinking about non-discrimination in the terms of EU law over and above the terms of the ECHR.[80]

The emphasis on personal characteristics and the narrowing interpretation of Article 14 ECHR would thus, in part, be attributed to the influence of EU equality law. While the latter may have exerted some influence, only the *Peterka* decision illustrates an explicit use in supporting a restrictive interpretation of the scope of Article 14 ECHR. Assessing the precise impact of EU law is challenging, to say the least. Taking a complementary perspective between EU and ECHR equality law, there are compelling reasons for the ECtHR to uphold an open model for the protected grounds, as will be argued in Part IV.[81]

III. Consensus

The ECtHR has used EU equality law to determine whether there is a consensus with a view to interpreting Convention's provisions. It has only happened in *Fedotova v. Russia* (2023), with a limited role for EU law. The ECtHR found

[77] ECtHR, *Carson and Others v. the United Kingdom* [GC], no. 42184/05, § 70, ECHR 2010.

[78] E.g. ECtHR, *Clift v. the United Kingdom*, no. 7205/07, 13 July 2010.

[79] O.M. Arnardottir, 'Cross-fertilisation, Clarity and Consistency at an Overburdened European Court of Human Rights – the Case of the Discrimination Grounds under Article 14 ECHR', *Nordic Journal of Human Rights*, 2015, p. 233; J. Gerards, 'The Discrimination Grounds of Article 14 of the European Convention on Human Rights', *Human Rights Law Review*, 2013, pp. 103 and following.

[80] O.M. Arnardottir, ibid., p. 234.

[81] See below Part IV, Chapter 2, Section I, §1, I. Preserving.

that there was a clear ongoing trend on the protection of same-sex couples in Council of Europe States, which allowed it to interpret Article 8 ECHR as imposing a positive obligation on States to provide a legal framework allowing same-sex couples to be granted adequate recognition and protection of their relationship.[82] The ECtHR observed that 'several Council of Europe bodies have stressed the need to ensure legal recognition and protection for same-sex couples within the member States (see paragraphs 48-56 above). *The Court also takes note of developments at international level* (see, in particular, paragraphs 46 and 61 above). Lastly, it observes that the Inter-American Court of Human Rights, in its advisory opinion no. OC-24/17, expressed the view that the States Parties to the American Convention on Human Rights were required to ensure access to all the legal institutions existing in their domestic laws in order to guarantee the protection of the rights of families composed of same-sex couples, without discrimination in relation to families constituted by different-sex couples (see paragraph 64 above).'[83] EU equality standards, in particular Charter's provisions and CJEU case-law, are part of the international developments mentioned in above excerpt.[84] EU equality law is only one source among many used by the ECtHR – as the excerpt shows, the IACHR's opinion plays a more influential role.[85]

IV. Intermediary Conclusions

EU equality law has played a notable role in supporting the interpretation of the meaning and scope of ECHR equality provisions and, to a lesser extent, other Convention's provisions. First, it has been used to perform a variety of sub-functions: supporting a new interpretation,[86] confirming and supporting an existing interpretation,[87] and finding a consensus for interpreting Convention's provisions,[88] albeit with notable differences, with the use for consensus being the least frequent. When EU equality law is used to interpret Convention's

---

82 ECtHR, *Fedotova and Others v. Russia* [GC], nos. 40792/10 and 2 others, § 178, 17 January 2023.

83 Ibid., § 177. Emphasis added.

84 Ibid., §§ 57–62.

85 Ibid., § 177.

86 E.g. ECtHR, *D.H. and Others v. the Czech Republic* [GC], no. 57325/00, §§ 184 and 187, ECHR 2007-IV; ECtHR, *Moraru v. Romania*, no. 64480/19, § 32, 8 November 2022.

87 E.g. ECtHR, *Moraru v. Romania*, no. 64480/19, § 32, 8 November 2022; ECtHR, *D.H. and Others v. the Czech Republic* [GC], no. 57325/00, §§ 184 and 187, ECHR 2007-IV.

88 ECtHR, *Fedotova and Others v. Russia* [GC], nos. 40792/10 and 2 others, §§ 177-188, 17 January 2023.

provisions, it is most often either the Charter[89] or CJEU case-law.[90] Legislative instruments have rarely been used for this purpose.[91] Second, EU equality law has impacted all dimensions of ECHR equality law, including its scope,[92] substantive[93] and procedural elements.[94] Third, the interpretation supported by EU equality law brings important transformations to ECHR equality law. This is evident, for example, in the recognition of indirect discrimination[95] and discrimination by association,[96] as well as in the recognition of the right to marriage for transsexuals.[97] Fourth, EU equality law is often the sole argument used to support a new interpretation of Convention's provisions or to confirm and support an interpretation already used by the ECtHR.[98] There are few cases where EU equality law is used as one argument among others in its reasoning.[99] Fifth, EU equality law is often the sole legal source on which the ECtHR relies to interpret the Convention.[100] In some cases, a plurality of legal sources is mentioned in the relevant legal materials, but only EU equality law pertains to the specific issue being interpreted by the ECtHR.[101] Sixth, EU

89 ECtHR, *Moraru v. Romania*, no. 64480/19, § 42, 8 November 2022; ECtHR, *G.N. and Others v. Italy*, no. 43134/05, §§ 125–126, 1 December 2009; ECtHR, *Schalk and Kopf v. Austria*, no. 30141/04, §§ 55, 57, 60–61, ECHR 2010; ECtHR, *Peterka v. Czech Republic*, no. 21990/08, 4 May 2010; ECtHR, *Christine Goodwin v. the United Kingdom* [GC], no. 28957/95, § 100, ECHR 2002-VI; ECtHR, *I. v. the United Kingdom* [GC], no. 25680/94, § 80, 11 July 2002.

90 ECtHR, *Napotnik v. Romania*, no. 33139/13, §§ 77–78, 20 October 2020; ECtHR, *Molla Sali v. Greece* [GC], no. 20452/14, §§ 78–81, 19 December 2018; ECtHR, *Guberina v. Croatia*, no. 23682/13, §§ 41–42, 22 March 2016.

91 An exception is ECtHR, *D.H. and Others v. the Czech Republic* [GC], no. 57325/00, §§ 184 and 187, ECHR 2007-IV.

92 E.g. ECtHR, *Moraru v. Romania*, no. 64480/19, § 32, 8 November 2022; ECtHR, *Peterka v. Czech Republic* (adm. decision), no. 21990/08, p. 6, 4 May 2010; ECtHR, *G.N. and Others v. Italy*, no. 43134/05, § 126, 1 December 2009.

93 E.g. ECtHR, *Molla Sali v. Greece* [GC], no. 20452/14, §§ 78–81, 134, 19 December 2018; ECtHR, *Guberina v. Croatia*, no. 23682/13, §§ 41–42, 78, 22 March 2016; ECtHR, *D.H. and Others v. the Czech Republic* [GC], no. 57325/00, § 184, ECHR 2007-IV.

94 ECtHR, *D.H. and Others v. the Czech Repubblic*, ibid., § 187.

95 Ibid., § 184.

96 E.g. ECtHR, *Molla Sali v. Greece* [GC], no. 20452/14, §§ 78–81, 134, 19 December 2018; ECtHR, *Guberina v. Croatia*, no. 23682/13, §§ 41–42, 78, 22 March 2016.

97 ECtHR, *Christine Goodwin v. the United Kingdom* [GC], no. 28957/95, § 100, ECHR 2002-VI; ECtHR, *I. v. the United Kingdom* [GC], no. 25680/94, § 80, 11 July 2002.

98 E.g. ECtHR, *Schalk and Kopf v. Austria*, no. 30141/04, § 61, ECHR 2010 (on the point that right to marry is not limited to marriage between persons from the opposite sex).

99 ECtHR, ibid., e.g. § 55, ECHR 2010 (on the point that ECHR law does not guarantee a right to same-sex marriage).

100 ECtHR, *Moraru v. Romania*, no. 64480/19, § 42, 8 November 2022; ECtHR, *G.N. and Others v. Italy*, no. 43134/05, §§ 125–126, 1 December 2009; ECtHR, *Peterka v. Czech Republic*, no. 21990/08, 4 May 2010; ECtHR, *D.H. and Others v. the Czech Republic* [GC], no. 57325/00, § 187, ECHR 2007-IV; ECtHR, *Christine Goodwin v. the United Kingdom* [GC], no. 28957/95, § 100, ECHR 2002-VI; ECtHR, *I. v. the United Kingdom* [GC], no. 25680/94, § 80, 11 July 2002 .

101 ECtHR, *Guberina v. Croatia*, no. 23682/13, §§ 40–42, 22 March 2016.

equality law has most often been used to enhance the protection of equality. Notably, it has been mobilised with regard to the recognition of indirect discrimination,[102] discrimination by association,[103] difference in treatment on grounds of pregnancy as direct discrimination,[104] the right to marriage for transsexuals,[105] genetic features as a ground of discrimination,[106] and the use of statistical tools to prove indirect discrimination.[107] There are two exceptions: it has been used once to support that there is no right to marriage for same-sex couples[108] and once to support a restrictive line of case-law according to which protected grounds are limited to personal characteristics.[109] Overall, our equality case study differs markedly from our data protection case study, where the interpretative function is very limited.

§ 2. JUSTIFICATION

The ECtHR has notably relied on EU equality law during its evaluation of the justification of an interference by a national measure or practice. EU equality law has been mobilised to assess the legitimacy of the aim of a difference in treatment, its proportionality, as well as the margin of appreciation.

I. Legitimacy

EU equality law has been used on several occasions to assess whether a difference of treatment is based on an objective and reasonable justification. The ECtHR has relied upon it either to support or oppose that an objective pursued by a respondent State is a legitimate one. This occurred in *Valiullina and others v. Latvia* (2021) which concerned a reduction in the use of minority languages as languages of instructions in Latvian schools. The ECtHR held that the need to protect and strengthen the Latvian language was a legitimate

102 ECtHR, *D.H. and Others v. the Czech Republic* [GC], no. 57325/00, § 184, ECHR 2007-IV.

103 ECtHR, *Molla Sali v. Greece* [GC], no. 20452/14, §§ 78–81, 134, 19 December 2018; ECtHR, *Guberina v. Croatia*, no. 23682/13, §§ 41–42, 78, 22 March 2016.

104 ECtHR, *Jurčić v. Croatia*, no. 54711/15, § 69, 4 February 2021; ECtHR, *Napotnik v. Romania*, no. 33139/13, § 77, 20 October 2020.

105 ECtHR, *Christine Goodwin v. the United Kingdom* [GC], no. 28957/95, § 100, ECHR 2002-VI; ECtHR, *I. v. the United Kingdom* [GC], no. 25680/94 § 80, 11 July 2002.

106 ECtHR, *Jurčić v. Croatia*, no. 54711/15, § 69, 4 February 2021; ECtHR, *G.N. and Others v. Italy*, no. 43134/05, §§ 125–126, 1 December 2009.

107 ECtHR, *D.H. and Others v. the Czech Republic* [GC], no. 57325/00, § 187, ECHR 2007-IV.

108 ECtHR, *Schalk and Kopf v. Austria*, no. 30141/04, § 55, 57, 60–61, ECHR 2010.

109 ECtHR, *Peterka v. Czech Republic*, no. 21990/08, 4 May 2010.

aim.[110] The ECtHR observed that 'it is relevant to note that the CJEU – in its preliminary ruling concerning the language of instruction in universities in Latvia – held that the objective of promoting and encouraging the use of one of the official languages of a member State must be regarded as being a legitimate objective in respect of the freedom of establishment as enshrined in EU law (see paragraph 70 of the CJEU judgment, quoted in paragraph 94 above).'[111] The ECtHR referred to various arguments, including historical circumstances and other legal documents, such as an opinion by the Venice Commission regarding Latvia, to support the view that the protection and strengthening of the Latvian language was a legitimate aim.[112]

In *Jurcic v. Croatia* (2021), the reverse phenomenon occurred. The applicant was denied insured employee status and a work-related benefit on the grounds that her employment was considered fictitious due to her pregnancy. The Government argued that the decision to revoke the applicant's insurance status pursued the legitimate aim of protecting public resources from fraudulent use and ensuring the overall stability of the healthcare system.[113] The ECtHR observed that 'a woman's pregnancy as such cannot be considered fraudulent behaviour. Furthermore, the Court considers that the financial obligations imposed on the State during a woman's pregnancy cannot by themselves constitute sufficiently weighty reasons to justify a difference in treatment on the basis of sex (see paragraph 65 above; *see also the CJEU's case-law in relation to the employment of pregnant women, cited at paragraphs 35-41 above*, and the relevant ILO standards, cited at paragraph 43 above).'[114] As can be seen, both CJEU case-law and ILO standards are used to support the view that financial obligations imposed on a State cannot serve as a legitimate interest.

II. Proportionality

The ECtHR has relied upon EU equality law either to support or oppose that a difference in treatment is proportionate in several notable cases. On one hand, EU equality law has been deemed of strong persuasive value to consider that a difference in treatment was reasonably and objectively justified. On the other hand, the ECtHR took into account the lack of engagement by national

---

110 ECtHR, *Valiullina and Others v. Latvia*, nos. 56928/19 and 2 others, § 200, 14 September 2023. The CJEU's case related to whether Articles 49 and 56 TFEU and Article 16 Charter must be interpreted as precluding legislation of an EU State which, in principle, obliges higher education institutions to provide teaching solely in the official language of that Member State (ibid., § 91).

111 Ibid., § 199.

112 Ibid., §§ 199–200.

113 ECtHR, *Jurčić v. Croatia*, no. 54711/15, § 73, 4 February 2021.

114 Ibid. Emphasis added.

authorities with EU equality law to support its conclusion that the differences in treatment were not based on a reasonable or objective justification.

A. Supportive

The ECtHR has used EU equality law to support that a difference in treatment is proportionate. There is one key case, the *Stec v. United Kingdom* (2006) judgment, whose circumstances and legal background are relatively complex. The claimants were all victims of accidents at work and received Reduced Earnings Allowance (REA) as a result. They all received retirement benefits when they reached the age at which they were entitled to a retirement pension which differed between women and men. For all the claimants, this resulted in a reduction of income that they would not have had if they had been of the opposite sex and subject to the other retirement age.

In the course of the national proceedings, the domestic court referred a preliminary question to the CJEU which held that the termination of the REA was not incompatible with the Social Security Equal Treatment Between Men and Women Council Directive (79/7/EEC). The CJEU interpreted an exception to the principle of equal treatment between men and women in social security matters which is contained in Article 7(1)(a) of that directive. This provision provides that 'the Directive is to be without prejudice to the right of Member States to exclude from its scope the determination of pensionable age for the purposes of granting old-age and retirement pensions and the possible consequences thereof for other benefits'. The CJEU held that this exception applied to differences in treatment linked to pensionable age where they could jeopardise the financial balance of the social security system or undermine the coherence between the retirement pension scheme and the other benefits scheme.[115] In the applicants' case, the CJEU held that it had been objectively necessary to introduce different age conditions based on sex for the REA to maintain coherence between the State retirement pension scheme and other benefit schemes.[116] In other words, the CJEU did not examine whether the measures in question were disproportionate but rather whether they fell within the scope of the exception to the principle of equality between men and women in matters of social security.

In *Stec*, the ECtHR reasoned on the justification of the difference in treatment between men and women as follows. First, it pointed out that a single cut-off age would not have achieved the same level of consistency with the State pension scheme, which is based on a notional 'end of working

115 Case C-196/98, *Hepple*, ECLI:EU:C:2000:278, §§ 31–34.

116 ECtHR, *Stec and Others v. the United Kingdom* [GC], nos. 65731/01 and 65900/01, § 41, ECHR 2006-VI.

life' at 60 for women and 65 for men.[117] Second, it observed that questions of administrative economy and coherence generally fall within the margin of appreciation of States.[118] Third, it noted that:

> [I]t finds it significant that, in the present applicants' case, the ECJ found that since REA was intended to compensate people of working age for loss of earning capacity due to an accident at work or occupational disease, it was necessary, in order to preserve coherence with the old-age pension scheme, to link the age limits (see paragraph 41 above). While it is true that Article 7(1)(a) of the Directive provides an express exception to the general prohibition on discrimination in social security (see paragraph 38 above), the ECJ was called upon, in deciding whether the case fell within the Article 7 exception, to make a judgment as to whether the discrimination in the REA scheme arising from the link to differential pensionable ages was objectively necessary in order to ensure consistency with the pension scheme. In reaching a conclusion on this issue which, while not determinative of the issue under Article 14 of the Convention, is nonetheless of central importance, *particular regard should be had to the strong persuasive value of the ECJ's finding on this point.*[119]

Based on these observations, the ECtHR considered 'that both the policy decision to stop paying REA to persons who would otherwise have retired from paid employment, and the decision to achieve this aim by linking the cut-off age for REA to the notional 'end of working life', or State pensionable age, pursued a legitimate aim and were reasonably and objectively justified'.[120] The ECtHR then assessed whether the underlying difference in treatment between men and women in the State pension scheme was acceptable – an aspect that will not be investigated here.[121]

EU equality law played a decisive role in supporting that the measures adopted by the Government were proportionate. The CJEU's finding that the different age conditions based on sex for the REA were necessary to maintain coherence between the State retirement pension scheme and other benefit schemes was deemed of 'strong persuasive value'. The coherence argument was used to consider both that the difference in treatment pursued a legitimate aim and was reasonably and objectively justified. The *Stec* case had also a number of follow-ups. In subsequent cases, the ECtHR was confronted with differences in treatment on the basis of sex related to the loss of benefit schemes when the pension age was reached. In these cases, the coherence argument, which

---

117 Ibid., § 56.
118 Ibid., § 57.
119 Ibid., § 58. Emphasis added
120 Ibid., § 59.
121 Ibid., §§ 60–65.

is based on CJEU's judgments, was used as a key argument to justify the proportionality of the difference in treatment.[122]

B. Dismissive

EU equality law has also been used when the ECtHR refuted the proportionality of a difference in treatment. This occurred in *Moraru v. Romania* (2022) and *Moraru and Marin v. Romania* (2022) in which the ECtHR took into account the lack of engagement by national authorities with EU equality law to support its conclusion that the differences in treatment were not based on a reasonable or objective justification. It should be emphasised that these are two recent judgments which, while potentially significant, are chamber rulings pronounced each time against the same respondent State. One should thus refrain from drawing too hasty conclusions about the wider impact of these judgments.

The first is the *Moraru v. Romania* case of 8 November 2022. The applicant alleged that the refusal of the Romanian authorities to allow her to sit the entrance examination to study military medicine because her height and weight were below certain thresholds was contrary to Article 14 ECHR read in conjunction with Article 2 of Protocol No. 1 ECHR. The anthropometric limits set by law were different for male and female candidates. The applicant relied on EU law, and especially on the *Kalliri* judgment of 2017 in which the CJEU deemed that the Employment Equal Treatment Between Men and Women Council Directive (76/207/EEC) should prevail over a law of Greece which made candidates' admission to a competition for entry into a policy academy, whatever their sex, subject to a requirement that they be of a physical height of at least 1.70 metres.[123] Domestic courts – at first instance and appeal levels – rejected the EU law argument as they considered that in *Kalliri* the CJEU had examined an allegation of indirect discrimination against female candidates, which was not applicable to the present situation.[124]

The ECtHR started its reasoning by considering that there was a difference in treatment based on a genetic feature, size – and not on the basis of sex.[125] It then examined if there was any objective and reasonable justification for the difference in treatment. The ECtHR observed that it is within the purview of the State authorities to set the criteria for the selection of candidates for military educational institutes and that it would not substitute itself for the national authorities in the issue of recruitment to and organisation of the armed

122 ECtHR, *Walker v. the United Kingdom*, no. 37212/02, §§ 19–20, 34–36, 22 August 2006; ECtHR, *Barrow v. the United Kingdom*, no. 42735/02, § 36, 22 August 2006.

123 Case C-409/16, *Kalliri*, ECLI EU:C:2017:767.

124 ECtHR, *Moraru v. Romania*, no. 64480/19, §§ 11–13, 8 November 2022.

125 Ibid., §§ 42–44.

forces unless these criteria are 'manifestly without reasonable foundation.'[126] The ECtHR considered that the national authorities did not show that there was necessarily a link between the criteria selected by the legislature (the size of candidates) and the justification given for those restrictions (the need to determine each candidate's strength).[127] It noted that:

> The applicant expressly noted that point during the domestic proceedings [...], and relied on the findings of the CJEU in Kalliri to lend force to her argument [...]. The domestic courts, however, contested her assertions, including her reliance on Kalliri. In doing so, they limited their examination and regarded the CJEU judgment exclusively from the standpoint of indirect discrimination based on sex.
>
> It is not for this Court to interpret European Union law as such. That said, the Court cannot but note that by summarily deeming Kalliri to be irrelevant to the facts of the case, *the domestic courts failed to engage meaningfully with that judgment of the CJEU and to examine its ramifications highlighted by the applicant in her arguments before the court.*[128]

The ECtHR reiterated afterwards that the domestic courts did not provide any justification concerning the connection between a candidate's height and his or her strength and, on this basis primarily, concluded there was a violation of Article 14 ECHR.[129]

Before analysing the references to EU equality law, let us present the second case, *Moraru and Marin v. Romania* (2022). The case pertains to women who wanted to work until the retirement age for men. The applicants complained that by not being allowed to continue work after they had reached the retirement age for women, they had been discriminated against on grounds of sex. The first applicant relied on the Equal Treatment Between Men and Women Recast Directive (2006/54/EC) and compared her situation to that examined in the *Kleist and Marwill* cases from the CJEU who concerned women who wanted to work until the retirement age for men.[130] The Court of Appeal held that 'Directive 2006/54/EC [...] did not apply to the facts of the case, which were instead governed by Directive 79/7/CEE [...]' and that 'Article 7 of Directive 79/7/CEE allowed member States to exclude from its scope the determination of retirement age for the purposes of granting old-age and retirement pensions.'[131]

126 Ibid., § 40.
127 Ibid., § 53.
128 Ibid., § 54. Emphasis added.
129 Ibid., §§ 55–58.
130 ECtHR, *Moraru and Marin v. Romania*, nos. 53282/18 and 31428/20, § 10, 20 December 2022.
131 Ibid., § 12.

After having found that there was a difference of treatment on grounds of sex, the ECtHR noted that very weighty reasons should be put forward for such a type of difference of treatment and that there was a narrow margin of appreciation.[132] The ECtHR found a violation of Article 1 of Protocol No. 12 to the Convention based on several arguments, including the fact that the difference in treatment entailed a stereotypical view of gender roles[133] and that it had not been shown that the measure sought by the applicant would entail significant costs for society or a systemic change of the pension system in place.[134] One of the key arguments is based on EU law:

> In the present case, the applicants' employers were public authorities whose acts engaged the State's responsibility under the Convention. The Court cannot but observe that neither those public authorities nor the domestic courts which examined the applicants' cases offered any explanation as to how their decisions not to allow the applicants to continue to work were compatible with the Convention or the applicable EU law. In this respect, the Court observes that in her domestic action, the first applicant explicitly argued that the termination of her employment had been contrary to the applicable EU law, and to that effect she relied on the CJEU's judgments in *Marwill* and *Kleist* (see paragraphs 10, 71 and 75 above). *The Galați Court of Appeal however failed to engage meaningfully with those judgments of the CJEU and to examine their ramifications highlighted by the applicant in her arguments before the court.*[135]

In both *Moraru and Moraru and Marin*, the ECtHR considered that domestic authorities failed to engage meaningfully with CJEU case-law and take it into account to consider that the differences in treatment were disproportionate. This line of jurisprudence is potentially significant since it implies that the failure of a national authority to engage with EU law is considered when assessing the proportionality of a measure at ECHR level. This constitutes a substantial argument that applicants can use before the ECtHR. Furthermore, this jurisprudence contributes to the effectiveness of EU law, as the ECtHR indirectly sanctions the poor application of EU law. However, this line of cases remains unclear at this stage.

First, the causal link between the lack of engagement with EU law and the finding of non-proportionality is not clear. In both cases, the ECtHR takes into account the engagement by national authorities to highlight a lack of satisfactory justification, but this is one (albeit important) argument among others to which the ECtHR refers. It is likely that the ECtHR could have reached the same conclusion even if national authorities had engaged with EU

---

132 Ibid., § 116.
133 Ibid., § 118.
134 Ibid., § 120.
135 Ibid., § 119. Emphasis added.

equality law. Conversely, it seems plausible that ECtHR could consider that, despite a lack of engagement with EU law, a measure could be justified. At this stage, we can observe at best that the lack of engagement with EU equality law reinforces the ECtHR's argumentation in favour of an unsatisfactory justification, leading to a violation of the Convention.

Second, it is not clear what the ECtHR considers as a failure to engage meaningfully with EU equality law. It is not about a complete lack of engagement with EU law. In these cases, the domestic courts did engage with EU equality law: domestic courts deemed that EU equality law was not applicable. It is about the fact that engagement is insufficient. Yet, the ECtHR does not specify whether this insufficiency is procedural or substantive – that is, whether it concerns the manner in which EU equality law is taken into account by national authorities or the fact that these authorities do not correctly apply the standards of EU equality law. The first approach seems the most likely since the ECtHR does not, in principle, rule on the interpretation of EU law. If it is a procedural obligation, it is not clear from these judgments what the threshold is for a national authority to satisfy engagement with EU equality law.

To sum up, the ECtHR case-law on the engagement by national authorities with EU equality law is still limited and there are many unknowns at this stage, yet it may have significant repercussions. We can observe that the lack of engagement can play an important role in supporting that differences in treatment in ECHR equality law are not justified, without integrating the substance of the former. EU equality law was the sole source mentioned by the ECtHR regarding the way national authorities engaged with it. The use of EU equality law can be considered positive for enhancing the protection of equality at Convention's level, but also more generally at European level. It allows for finding a violation of Article 14 ECHR and articulates the relationship between EU equality law and that of the ECHR without integrating the substance of EU law.

These two judgments appear as part of a wider trend in which the ECtHR has taken into account whether national authorities engage with EU law when assessing their compliance with the Convention.[136] In our data protection case study, we show that the ECtHR demonstrates a certain degree of deference when national authorities engage with EU data protection law.[137] This particular trajectory of legal cases, by which the ECtHR takes into account States' compliance with EU law when assessing the compliance to Convention

---

[136] J. Krommendijk, 'Straatsburg als hoeder van het EU-recht', *Nederlands Juristenblad*, 2023, pp. 2462–2471.

[137] Part III (case study on data protection), Chapter 3, Section II, §2, II. Lawfulness.

obligations, may carry considerable significance. Therefore we will revisit this matter at a later stage.[138]

C. Margin of Appreciation

A last aspect where EU equality law was used for the justification relates to the margin of appreciation. This occurred in *Biao v. Denmark* (2016) case, where the ECtHR referred to EU law on family reunification, among several other sources, to consider that there is a very narrow margin of appreciation on indirect discrimination between a State's own nationals based on ethnic origin.[139] Another instance is *Napotnik v. Romania* (2020), where, as we have seen, the ECtHR deemed that a difference of treatment on grounds of pregnancy is – direct – discrimination on grounds of sex by relying (inter alia) on CJEU case-law.[140] This has a bearing on the margin of appreciation. As the ECtHR observed, 'where a difference in treatment is based on sex, the margin of appreciation afforded to the State is narrow, and in such situations the principle of proportionality does not merely require that the measure chosen should in general be suited to the fulfilment of the aim pursued, but it must also be shown that it was necessary in the circumstances.'[141]

III. Intermediary Conclusions

To conclude this section, we may observe that the justification function of EU equality law is notable. The ECtHR has relied upon it in several cases either to support[142] or refute[143] that a difference in treatment is based on an objective and reasonable justification. EU equality law has been mobilised to assess the

138 Part IV, Chapter 2, Section I, §1, II. Contributing to the Effectiveness.
139 ECtHR, *Biao v. Denmark* [GC], no. 38590/10, §§ 131–138, 24 May 2016.
140 ECtHR, *Napotnik v. Romania*, no. 33139/13, § 77, 20 October 2020.
141 Ibid., § 75.
142 ECtHR, *Valiullina and Others v. Latvia*, nos. 56923/19 and 2 others, §§ 199–200, 14 September 2023; ECtHR, *Stec and Others v. the United Kingdom* [GC], nos. 65731/01 and 65900/01, §§ 58–59, ECHR 2006-VI; ECtHR, *Barrow v. the United Kingdom*, no. 42735/02, § 36, 22 August 2006; ECtHR, *Walker v. the United Kingdom*, no. 37212/02, §§ 34–36, 22 August 2006.
143 ECtHR, *Moraru v. Romania*, no. 64480/19, §§ 53–55, 8 November 2022; ECtHR, *Moraru and Marin v. Romania*, nos. 53282/18 and 31428/20, § 119, 20 December 2022; ECtHR, *Jurčić v. Croatia*, no. 54711/15, § 73, 4 February 2021; ECtHR, *Napotnik v. Romania*, no. 33139/13, §§ 77–78, 20 October 2020; ECtHR, *Biao v. Denmark* [GC], no. 38590/10, §§ 134–135, 24 May 2016.

legitimacy of the aim of a difference in treatment,[144] its proportionality,[145] as well as the margin of appreciation.[146] In some cases, the ECtHR uses it as a central argument,[147] whereas in others, it is one argument among many to support the ECtHR's reasoning.[148] When it is used, EU equality law is often the sole legal source.[149] All references to EU equality law at the stage of the justification are CJEU case-law.[150] EU equality law has most often been used in a way that is favourable to the fundamental rights – especially the protection of equality – of the applicants. EU equality law has been used to assess that there was a limited margin of appreciation,[151] that certain aims could not be considered legitimate,[152] or that the difference in treatment was not proportionate.[153] The main exception relates to the *Stec* saga, where CJEU case-law was used to consider that the difference in treatment was based on a legitimate aim and justified.[154]

---

[144] ECtHR, *Valiullina and Others v. Latvia*, nos. 56928/19 and 2 others, §§ 199–200, 14 September 2023; ECtHR, *Jurčić v. Croatia*, no. 54711/15, § 73, 4 February 2021.

[145] ECtHR, *Moraru v. Romania*, no. 64480/19, §§ 53–55, 8 November 2022; ECtHR, *Moraru and Marin v. Romania*, nos. 53282/18 and 31428/20, § 119, 20 December 2022; ECtHR, *Stec and Others v. the United Kingdom* [GC], nos. 65731/01 and 65900/01, §§ 58–59, ECHR 2006-VI; ECtHR, *Walker v. the United Kingdom*, no. 37212/02, §§ 34–36, 22 August 2006; ECtHR, *Barrow v. the United Kingdom*, no. 42735/02, § 36, 22 August 2006.

[146] ECtHR, *Napotnik v. Romania*, no. 33139/13, §§ 75, 77–78, 20 October 2020; ECtHR, *Biao v. Denmark* [GC], no. 38590/10, §§ 134–135, 24 May 2016.

[147] ECtHR, *Moraru v. Romania*, no. 64480/19, §§ 53–55, 8 November 2022; ECtHR, *Moraru and Marin v. Romania*, nos. 53282/18 and 31428/20, § 119, 20 December 2022; ECtHR, *Stec and Others v. the United Kingdom* [GC], nos. 65731/01 and 65900/01, §§ 17–19, 58–59, ECHR 2006-VI; ECtHR, *Walker v. the United Kingdom*, no. 37212/02, §§ 34–36, 22 August 2006; ECtHR, *Barrow v. the United Kingdom*, no. 42735/02, § 36, 22 August 2006.

[148] ECtHR, *Valiullina and Others v. Latvia*, nos. 56928/19 and 2 others, §§ 199–200, 14 September 2023; ECtHR, *Biao v. Denmark* [GC], no. 38590/10, §§ 134–135, 24 May 2016.

[149] ECtHR, *Moraru v. Romania*, no. 64480/19, §§ 53–55, 8 November 2022; ECtHR, *Moraru and Marin v. Romania*, nos. 53282/18 and 31428/20, § 119, 20 December 2022; ECtHR, *Stec and Others v. the United Kingdom* [GC], nos. 65731/01 and 65900/01, §58-59, ECHR 2006-VI; ECtHR, *Walker v. the United Kingdom*, no. 37212/02, §§ 34–36, 22 August 2006; ECtHR, *Barrow v. the United Kingdom*, no. 42735/02, § 36, 22 August 2006.

[150] E.g. ECtHR, *Valiullina and Others v. Latvia*, nos. 56928/19 and 2 others, §§ 199–200, 14 September 2023; ECtHR, *Jurčić v. Croatia*, no. 54711/15, § 73, 4 February 2021; ECtHR *Stec and Others v. the United Kingdom* [GC], nos. 65731/01 and 65900/01, §§ 58–59, ECHR 2006-VI.

[151] ECtHR, *Napotnik v. Romania*, no. 33139/13, §§ 75, 77–78, 20 October 2020; ECtHR, *Biao v. Denmark* [GC], no. 38590/10, §§ 134–135, 24 May 2016.

[152] ECtHR, *Jurčić v. Croatia*, no. 54711/15, § 73, 4 February 2021.

[153] ECtHR, *Moraru v. Romania*, no. 64480/19, §§ 53–55, 8 November 2022; ECtHR, *Moraru and Marin v. Romania*, nos. 53282/18 and 31428/20, § 119, 20 December 2022.

[154] ECtHR, *Stec and Others v. the United Kingdom* [GC], nos. 65731/01 and 65900/01, §§ 58–59, ECHR 2006-VI; ECtHR, *Walker v. the United Kingdom*, no. 37212/02, §§ 34–36, 22 August 2006; ECtHR, *Barrow v. the United Kingdom*, no. 42735/02, § 36, 22 August 2006.

§ 3. DISTINGUISHING

The ECtHR has also at times distinguished its stance from that of EU equality law. It has highlighted that EU equality law was not applicable or that there were not yet cases from the CJEU on the matter. It has also pointed out that there were factual or contextual differences between its case-law and that of the CJEU, which could explain differences in legal solutions. If the distinguishing references are limited, EU equality law is (almost) the sole legal source used in this perspective, as in our data protection case study.

The ECtHR has indicated that EU equality law is not applicable in a given case. This can be seen in cases concerning dismissal from the military based on sexual orientation, where the ECtHR has mentioned CJEU's rulings according to which the Equal Pay between Men and Women Council Directive (75/117/EEC) did not apply to discrimination based on sexual orientation. These references are, however, brief and form part of the context.[155] The ECtHR is not explicit that it seeks to differentiate EU equality law from ECHR equality law. In other cases, the ECtHR mentions the scope of application of provisions of EU equality law as part of its relevant legal materials, implying that they are not applicable in the cases at hand. In *Nachova v. Bulgaria* (2005), the ECtHR referred to specific paragraphs of Article 8 of Directive the Racial Discrimination Directive (2000/43/EC) and Article 10 of Equality Framework Directive (2000/78/EC) on the applicability of the reversal of the burden of proof and does not return to it. Yet the facts of the case suggest that these provisions were not applicable.[156] The ECtHR's approach is limited in that it does not itself highlight the difference between EU and ECHR equality laws nor is it explicit that it seeks to distinguish the two sets of laws.

The ECtHR has pointed out that the CJEU has not yet ruled on the issue with which the ECtHR is dealing. This occurred in Judge O'Leary's separate opinion in *Ebrahim v. France* (2015), which pertains to the wearing of the veil at work. The Judge highlighted that France is an EU State and is subject to the Equality Framework Directive (2000/78/EC), which prohibits direct and indirect discrimination on the grounds of religion and belief. The Judge noted that: 'The Court of Justice of the European Union has not yet dealt with a preliminary reference or infringement action concerning the wearing of religious symbols at work. It remains to be seen whether it would follow a 'functional' approach (as the terms of Article 4 § 1 might suggest) or whether,

[155] ECtHR, *Beck and Others v. the United Kingdom*, nos. 48535/99 and 2 others, § 42, 22 October 2002; ECtHR, *Smith and Grady v. the United Kingdom*, nos. 33985/96 and 33986/96, § 40, ECHR 1999-VI.

[156] ECtHR, *Nachova and Others v. Bulgaria*, nos. 43577/98 and 43579/98, § 80, 6 July 2005. The case concerns alleged discrimination of persons of Roma origins in the context of criminal investigations.

on the basis of the broader terms of Article 2 § 5 of the Directive, which to a large extent resembles Article 9 § 2 of the Convention, an approach akin to that of the present judgment would pass muster.'[157] This reference is made in a footnote, showing that it is ancillary.

The ECtHR has shed light on the differences between the cases handled by the ECtHR and the CJEU, with a view to explaining the differences between the legal solutions adopted under the two systems. The ECtHR has distinguished the facts of its case from those in a CJEU case. This situation occurred in *Napotnik v. Romania* (2020), where the ECtHR differentiated the specifics of the case from those previously considered by the CJEU. The case concerned a change of a diplomatic post rather than a dismissal, which had been the subject of earlier rulings by the CJEU. Having drawn this distinction, the ECtHR found that there was no violation of Article 1 Protocol No. 12 ECHR:[158]

> In this vein the Court notes that although her working conditions changed because of the early termination of her posting abroad, *the applicant was not dismissed from her post as a diplomat in the MFA (see, in contrast, the case-law of the CJEU, quoted in paragraphs 43 to 48 above)*. That change in circumstances cannot be equated with a loss of employment (see also, for reference, the domestic case-law referred to in paragraph 35 above).
>
> The Court therefore considers it established that the consequences for the applicant of the early termination of her posting abroad were not of the same nature as those expressly prohibited by the domestic equal opportunity laws (see paragraphs 31-32 above) and the State's international commitments in the field of protection of pregnancy and maternity (see paragraphs 39-42 and 49 above).[159]

By stressing that it is not a dismissal but a change of diplomatic post, the ECtHR justifies that there can be a difference between the legal solutions adopted under ECHR law (no violation of the ECHR in the case of change of post) and EU law (where a dismissal on grounds of pregnancy led to a violation of EU law). The ECtHR's approach is limited: it mentions EU equality law briefly and does not state that the factual difference explains a possible difference in outcome. It observes that the consequences of the early termination of posting abroad (which is not a dismissal) were not of the same nature as what is prohibited by domestic and international law; the articulation is therefore not limited to EU equality law.

The ECtHR has pointed out contextual differences between its case-law and CJEU case-law in *Hobbs v. United Kingdom* (2006) which concerned

157 Separate opinion of Judge O'Leary in ECtHR, *Ebrahimian v. France*, no. 64846/11, ECHR 2015, fn.°16.

158 ECtHR, *Napotnik v. Romania*, no. 33139/13, § 82, 20 October 2020.

159 Ibid., §§ 82–83. Emphasis added.

compensation for the discriminatory refusal to grant bereavement allowance to widower. The applicants argued that they were entitled to compensation in the amount that they would have received if they had been widows. They argued that this approach is consistent with the CJEU case-law 'which had on a number of occasions addressed the remedy for unlawful discrimination and concluded that it should be by way of 'levelling up' – that is, treating the complainant in the same way as the favoured group – rather than 'levelling down' – giving no compensation on the basis that neither class should have received the benefit'.[160] Replying to this argument, the ECtHR noted that the CJEU's cases 'relied on by the applicants were not relevant, and the context in which questions of compensation for discriminatory treatment arose before the [CJEU] was quite different, as was the impact of a decision to 'level up'. In the present cases, the advantage provided to widowed women did not provide the only, or even an appropriate, reference point for measuring the treatment which should properly be afforded to widowed men, who were in the same position as all other tax-payers. *Darby v. Sweden* and *P.M. v. the United Kingdom* were not comparable to the present cases since each had concerned a discriminatory failure to extend to the applicant a justifiable tax relief or exemption.'[161] The ECtHR distinguishes the CJEU's judgments, but in a brief manner: it neither explains why they are not relevant nor why the context is different.

All in all, the ECtHR has distinguished its stance from that of EU equality law in a restricted manner. The ECtHR has highlighted that EU equality law was not applicable or that there were not yet cases from the CJEU on the matter. It has also pointed out that there were factual or contextual differences between its case-law and that of the CJEU. However, the references are limited. They are brief[162] and often made in a peripheral manner.[163] The ECtHR is sometimes not explicit about the differences between EU and ECHR equality

160 ECtHR, *Hobbs, Richard, Walsh and Geen v. the United Kingdom*, nos. 63684/00 and 3 others, § 62, 14 November 2006.

161 Ibid, § 66.

162 ECtHR, *Napotnik v. Romania*, no. 33139/13, §§ 82–83, 20 October 2020; ECtHR, *Hobbs, Richard, Walsh and Geen v. the United Kingdom*, nos. 63684/00 and 3 others, § 66, 14 November 2006; ECtHR, *Beck and Others v. the United Kingdom*, nos. 48535/99 and 2 others, § 42, 22 October 2002; ECtHR, *Smith and Grady v. the United Kingdom*, nos. 33985/96 and 33986/96, § 40, ECHR 1999-VI.

163 E.g. Separate opinion of Judge O'Leary in ECtHR, *Ebrahimian v. France*, no. 64846/11, ECHR 2015, fn. 16.

laws.[164] It is rarely explicit that it seeks to distinguish between EU equality law and ECHR law.[165]

If the distinguishing function remains limited, EU equality law is almost the sole source from which the ECtHR seeks to differentiate ECHR equality law. Most often, this distinguishing occurs in relation to CJEU case-law. In so doing, the ECtHR seems to aim to articulate its approach with CJEU case-law to ensure coherence, as can also be seen in our data protection case study.

§ 4. INFORMATION

EU equality law serves a significant informative function: the ECtHR uses it as relevant information either in the context of its judgments or in its relevant legal materials.[166] EU equality law is frequently cited as the primary legal source (alongside domestic laws) in relevant legal materials.

The ECtHR refers to EU equality law in the context of its cases.[167] EU equality law plays a limited contextual role in numerous cases: the ECtHR refers to the fact that either the applicants have mentioned EU equality law as part of their argumentation before national courts[168] or that national courts have referred to it.[169] In a few cases, EU equality law takes a significant place in the background of ECtHR cases. This occurs when key legal questions and debates at the national level revolve around the interpretation and compliance with EU equality law.[170] The significance of EU equality law sometimes stems

164 ECtHR, *Napotnik v. Romania*, no. 33139/13, §§ 82-83, 20 October 2020; ECtHR, *Hobbs, Richard, Walsh and Geen v. the United Kingdom*, nos. 63684/00 and 3 others, § 66, 14 November 2006; ECtHR, *Nachova and Others v. Bulgaria*, nos. 43577/98 and 43579/98, §80, 6 July 2005.

165 ECtHR, *Napotnik v. Romania*, no. 33139/13, §§ 82–83, 20 October 2020; ECtHR, *Beck and Others v. the United Kingdom*, nos. 48535/99 and 2 others, § 42, 22 October 2002; ECtHR, *Smith and Grady v. the United Kingdom*, nos 33985/96 and 33986/96, § 40, ECHR 1999-VI.

166 Note that EU equality law may afterwards be used in the reasoning to serve other functions (for example, to interpret the Convention or to analyse the proportionality of a difference in treatment), but this is not always the case.

167 Here, we refer in particular to references to EU equality law in the 'Background or Context' section of the ECtHR's judgments, which precedes the 'Relevant Legal Framework' section, where the ECtHR outlines the relevant legal standards.

168 ECtHR, *Saltynite v. Lithuania*, no. 32934/19, § 5, 26 October 2010.

169 ECtHR, *Hoppen and trade union of AB Amber Grid employees v. Lithuania*, no. 976/20, § 128, 17 January 2023; ECtHR, *Orlandi and Others v. Italy*, nos. 26431/12 and 3 others, § 170, 14 December 2017; ECtHR, *Aldeguer Tomás v. Spain*, no. 35214/09, § 45, 14 June 2016; ECtHR, *Muñoz Díaz v. Spain*, no. 49151/07, § 14, ECHR 2009; ECtHR, *Wessels-Bergervoet v. the Netherlands*, no. 34462/97, § 24, ECHR 2002-IV.

170 This occurs in *Moraru v. Romania* (2022) and *Moraru and Marin v. Romania* (2022) where the question of whether equality law is applicable is an important aspect of the debate at national level, see above Part III (case study on equality), Chapter 3, Section II, §2, II.B. Dismissive.

from the fact that a preliminary question was asked to the CJEU in a case related to the one before the ECtHR.[171] In all cases where EU equality law has a significant role as part of the context, it is most often CJEU cases that are at stake – for example, rulings from preliminary questions to the CJEU[172] or the debate on the interpretation of these judgments at national level.[173]

EU equality law is often used as relevant legal standards information. The ECtHR describes the relevant legal standards of EU equality law in its relevant legal materials in more than twenty cases. The ECtHR increasingly presents relevant EU equality law in an exhaustive, precise, and up-to-date manner. The sources of EU equality law referred to are diverse: it is sometimes the Charter,[174] EU legislative instruments,[175] CJEU cases,[176] or a combination of different sources.[177] EU equality law is often mentioned as the sole legal source (next to domestic laws) in the relevant legal materials.[178] In other cases, while other sources are mentioned, the ECtHR describes EU equality law in greater depth than other sources.[179] It is rare that at the stage of providing information, EU equality law is only one source among others.[180]

171 ECtHR, *Stec and Others v. the United Kingdom* [GC], nos. 65731/01 and 65900/01, §§ 17–19, 39–41, 45, 48, 56–58, ECHR 2006-VI; ECtHR, *Smith and Grady v. the United Kingdom*, nos. 33985/96 and 33986/96, §§ 4–6, ECHR 1999-VI; ECtHR, *Perkins and R. v. the United Kingdom*, nos. 43208/98 and 44875/98, 22 October 2002; ECtHR, *Beck and Others v. the United Kingdom*, nos. 48535/99 and 2 others, § 43, 22 October 2002; ECtHR, *Lustig-Prean and Beckett v. the United Kingdom*, nos. 31417/96 and 32377/96, § 4, 27 September 1999.

172 E.g. ECtHR, *Stec and Others v. the United Kingdom* [GC], nos. 65731/01 and 65900/01, §§ 17–19, 39–41, 45, 48, 56–58, ECHR 2006-VI.

173 E.g. ECtHR, *Moraru v. Romania*, no. 64480/19, §§ 8, 11–13, 8 November 2022; ECtHR, *Moraru and Marin v. Romania*, nos. 53282/18 and 31428/20, §§ 10–13, 20 December 2022.

174 ECtHR, *Peterka v. Czech Republic*, no. 21990/08, 4 May 2010; ECtHR, *G.N. and Others v. Italy*, no. 43134/05, § 52, 1 December 2009.

175 ECtHR, *Nachova and Others v. Bulgaria*, nos. 43577/98 and 43579/98, § 80, 6 July 2005.

176 ECtHR, *Van Kück v. Germany*, no. 35968/97, §§ 36–37, ECHR 2003-VII; ECtHR, *Lustig-Prean and Beckett v. the United Kingdom*, nos. 31417/96 and 32377/96, §§ 38–41, 27 September 1999.

177 E.g. ECtHR, *Moraru and Marin v. Romania*, nos. 53282/18 and 31428/20, §§ 10–13, 20 December 2022; ECtHR, *Jurčić v. Croatia*, no. 54711/15, § 69, 4 February 2021; ECtHR, *Napotnik v. Romania*, no. 33139/13, §§ 41–48, 20 October 2020; ECtHR, *Vallianatos and Others v. Greece* [GC], nos. 29381/09 and 32684/09, §§ 31–37, ECHR 2013 (extracts); ECtHR, *Christine Goodwin v. the United Kingdom* [GC], no. 28957/95, § 100, ECHR 2002-VI; ECtHR, *I. v. the United Kingdom* [GC], no. 25680/94, § 80, 11 July 2002.

178 E.g. ECtHR, *Moraru v. Romania*, no. 64480/19, §§ 22–26, 8 November 2022; ECtHR, *Walker v. the United Kingdom*, no. 37212/02, §§ 19–20, 22 August 2006; ECtHR *Pearson v. the United Kingdom*, no. 8374/03, §§ 12–13, 22 August 2006.

179 E.g. ECtHR, *Napotnik v. Romania*, no. 33139/13, §§ 41–48, 20 October 2020; ECtHR, *Vallianatos and Others v. Greece* [GC], nos. 29381/09 and 32684/09, §§ 31–37, ECHR 2013 (extracts); ECtHR, *D.H. and Others v. the Czech Republic* [GC], no. 57325/00, §§ 81–88, ECHR 2007-IV.

180 E.g. ECtHR, *Fedotova and Others v. Russia* [GC], nos. 40792/10 and 2 others, §§ 57–61, 17 January 2023.

In several recent cases, the ECtHR has extensively referenced EU equality law. The ECtHR meticulously lays out the relevant legal provisions, their preambles, and summarises the relevant CJEU's case-law, leaving one quite impressed by the level of detail provided. In *Napotnik v. Croatia* (2020) for instance, the ECtHR dedicated a specific section to the 'Law and practice of the European Union', referring to Directive 2006/54/EC and Council Directive 92/85/EEC (discussing their preambles and relevant provisions). Additionally, the ECtHR summarises several CJEU cases on discrimination on grounds of pregnancy and highlights specific paragraphs.[181] This engagement underscores the ECtHR's commitment to obtain a comprehensive overview of EU equality law to inform its equality decisions, as in our data protection case study. More generally, the prominent role of EU equality law as part of the context or relevant legal materials can be understood by the fact that EU law provides the backdrop in cases involving EU States.

§ 5. COMPARATIVE INSIGHTS

An analysis of the functions of international instruments[182] show that they perform similar functions to those in EU equality law, albeit to a lesser extent. International instruments either play a less significant role in performing functions such as interpretation, justification, and information or do not perform certain functions at all, such as distinguishing. However, there is one function performed by these instruments that is not performed by EU equality law: the evidentiary function. Reports from monitoring bodies are used as evidence to substantiate the factual situation in the respondent State.

Starting with the interpretative function, the international equality instruments have played a limited, yet noteworthy role in supporting the interpretation of the Conventions' provisions. Compared with EU equality law, these instruments have had a less significant impact in performing this function. Some of the instruments or the outputs from the related monitoring bodies have been used to support a new interpretation of the Conventions' provisions. The cases are relatively limited, however.

One of the key cases is *Opuz v. Turkey* (2009), in which the ECtHR interpreted the meaning of 'discrimination' in the context of domestic violence.[183] The ECtHR stated that it should 'have regard to the provisions

181 ECtHR, *Napotnik v. Romania*, no. 33139/13, §§ 40–48, 20 October 2020.

182 We have looked at the functions performed by the FCNM, the CEDAW, the CRPD, and the Istanbul Convention.

183 The CEDAW was also used to interpret the scope of the State's positive obligation to prevent the risk of domestic violence under Article 3 ECHR. In *Luca v. the Republic of Molodova* (2023), the ECtHR relied on the CEDAW's committee and the GREVIO – which is the

of more specialised legal instruments and the decisions of international legal bodies on the question of violence against women.'[184] The ECtHR referred to both the definition of discrimination against women under the CEDAW and the CEDAW committee's position according to which domestic violence constitutes a form of discrimination against women.[185] While the ECtHR also mentioned other legal sources,[186] the CEDAW plays a decisive role to support the ECtHR's interpretation that a State's failure to protect women against domestic violence can breach their right to equal protection of the law, regardless of whether this failure is intentional.[187]

The ECtHR has used the CRPD to support its interpretation of the meaning of 'reasonable accommodation' under Article 14 ECHR. In *Cam v. Turkey* (2016), the ECtHR observed that this provision 'must be read in the light of the requirements of those texts regarding reasonable accommodation – understood as 'necessary and appropriate modification and adjustments not imposing a disproportionate or undue burden, where needed in a particular case'– which persons with disabilities are entitled to expect in order to ensure 'the enjoyment or exercise on an equal basis with others of all human rights and fundamental freedoms' (Article 2 of the Convention on the Rights of Persons with Disabilities...).'[188]

The ECtHR has used international instruments to confirm and bolster an interpretation of the Convention. Most often, these are cases where the ECtHR refers to one of the instruments to confirm an interpretation of the Convention that had found support in these instruments. This is the case regarding the fact that violence against women is discrimination against women[189] or the meaning of reasonable accommodation under ECHR equality provisions.[190] The ECtHR has very limitedly used international instruments to determine a consensus with a view to interpreting the Convention. It has relied on the FCNM to point out that 'there is an emerging international consensus among the Contracting States of the Council of Europe recognising the special needs of minorities and an obligation to protect their security, identity, and lifestyle'[191] or on the CRPD to affirm that there is a 'European and worldwide consensus on the

group of experts monitoring the Istanbul Convention – to consider that this scope covers psychological violence (ECtHR, *Luca v. the Republic of Moldova*, no. 55351/17, §§ 72, 78–79, 17 October 2023).

184 ECtHR, *Opuz v. Turkey*, no. 33401/02, § 185, ECHR 2009.

185 Ibid., §§ 187–188.

186 Ibid., §§ 189–190.

187 Ibid., § 191.

188 ECtHR, *Çam v. Turkey*, no. 51500/08, § 65, 23 February 2016.

189 E.g. ECtHR, *Bălşan v. Romania*, no. 49645/09, § 79, 23 May 2017

190 E.g. ECtHR, *Toplak and Mrak v. Slovenia*, nos. 34591/19 and 42545/19, § 114, 26 October 2021.

191 ECtHR, *Muñoz Díaz v. Spain*, no. 49151/07, § 60, ECHR 2009.

need to protect people with disabilities from discriminatory treatment'.[192] Yet, these references do not lead to an evolutive interpretation of the Convention.

Moving to the functions of justification and information, EU equality law appears to have played a more significant role for both functions. First, international instruments have rarely been used when evaluating the justification of an interference. When it has been the case, the ECtHR has mostly referred to them to support that a difference in treatment is not proportionate.[193] Second, whereas the ECtHR has frequently used international instruments as relevant sources within the context of its judgments and relevant legal materials, this appears less significant compared to EU equality law. The ECtHR has used international equality instruments in the context number of cases, as they are part of the reasoning of domestic courts[194] or the applicants,[195] or both.[196] It is rare that the instruments take centre stage in the context of the case.[197] The ECtHR has also mentioned these instruments as part of the relevant legal materials.[198] There is a high degree of precision in references to the legal standards: the ECtHR often refers to specific provisions of these instruments,[199] explanatory reports of these conventions,[200] comments,[201] general recommendations,[202] or communications[203] made by related bodies. The ECtHR has also referred to information that can be termed as evidentiary, meaning that the ECtHR does not refer (only) to the relevant legal standards in international law but to reports from the monitoring bodies on the factual situation in the respondent State.[204]

192 ECtHR, *Glor v. Switzerland*, no. 13444/04, § 53, ECHR 2009.

193 ECtHR, *Jurčić v. Croatia*, no. 54711/15, § 83, 4 February 2021 (CEDAW); ECtHR, *Beeler v. Switzerland* [GC], no. 78630/12, § 113, 20 October 2020 (CEDAW).

194 E.g. ECtHR, *Muñoz Díaz v. Spain*, no. 49151/07, § 19, ECHR 2009 (FCNM); ECtHR, *Valiullina and Others v. Latvia*, nos. 56928/19 and 2 others, § 52, 14 September 2023 (FCNM).

195 ECtHR, *Beganović v. Croatia*, no 46423/06, § 13, 25 June 2009 (FCNM).

196 E.g. ECtHR, *Caamaño Valle v. Spain*, no. 43564/17, §§ 7, 9, 13–14, 11 May 2021 (CRPD).

197 See in particular ECtHR, *Caamaño Valle v. Spain*, no. 43564/17, §§ 7, 9, 13–14, 11 May 2021 (CRPD).

198 The ECtHR has done so on approximately ten occasions for the FCNM and the CRPD, five times for CEDAW, and a bit less for the Istanbul Convention.

199 E.g. ECtHR, *Jurčić v. Croatia*, no. 54711/15, § 45, 4 February 2021 (CEDAW); ECtHR, *Guberina v. Croatia*, no. 23682/13, §§ 34–35, 22 March 2016 (CRPD and Istanbul Convention).

200 E.g. ECtHR, *Molla Sali v. Greece* [GC], no. 20452/14, §§ 67–68, 19 December 2018 (FCNM).

201 ECtHR, *Arnar Helgi Lárusson v. Iceland*, no. 23077/19, §§ 25–27, 31 May 2022 (CRPD).

202 E.g. ECtHR, *A.E. v. Bulgaria*, no. 53891/20, §§ 47–48, 23 May 2023 (CEDAW); ECtHR, *Volodina v. Russia*, no. 41261/17, §§ 51–56, 9 July 2019 (CEDAW).

203 ECtHR, *Volodina v. Russia*, ibid.

204 ECtHR, *A.E. v. Bulgaria*, no. 53891/20, § 49, 23 May 2023 (CEDAW); ECtHR, *Volodina v. Russia*, ibid., § 54.

This leads us to our final observation: the reports of monitoring bodies of international instruments have served an evidentiary function that is not performed by EU equality law. The ECtHR has relied on these reports as evidence of the factual situation in the respondent State. The ECtHR has not only made extensive use of these reports, particularly those from the ComFCNM,[205] but has also developed some guiding principles on how and when they can be used before the ECtHR.[206]

SECTION III. ACTORS

Not only does the ECtHR engage with EU equality law, but also several other actors, including parties, third-party interveners, national courts, and specific judges within the ECtHR. We will now focus on these actors, showing that their engagement with EU equality law is more pronounced than with international instruments. There are strong similarities in how actors use both EU equality and data protection laws, with a key difference being the stronger engagement with the latter in separate opinions.

§ 1. QUANTITATIVE OVERVIEW

Let us begin by examining some quantitative data on the frequency of references per actor in order to contextualise the qualitative analysis.[207] Our data highlights a notable engagement with EU equality law by different actors, as is the case in our data protection case study. The data shows a stronger engagement by various actors with EU equality law compared to international instruments, yet not for all actors.

205 E.g. ECtHR, *Talpis v. Italy*, no. 41237/14, § 57, 2 March 2017 (CEDAW); ECtHR, *D.H. and Others v. the Czech Republic* [GC], no. 57325/00, § 66–76, 192-195, ECHR 2007-IV (FCNM).

206 ECtHR, *Y and Others v. Bulgaria*, no. 9077/18, § 122, 22 March 2022. In *Y and others v. Bulgaria* (2022), the ECtHR observed that the evidence that the reports of international observers - such as the CEDAW - can be used as prima facie evidence to establish that domestic violence affects women disproportionately, leading to a burden of shift on the State.

207 We looked specifically at the number of ECtHR cases in which a given actor has referred to EU equality law and international instruments.

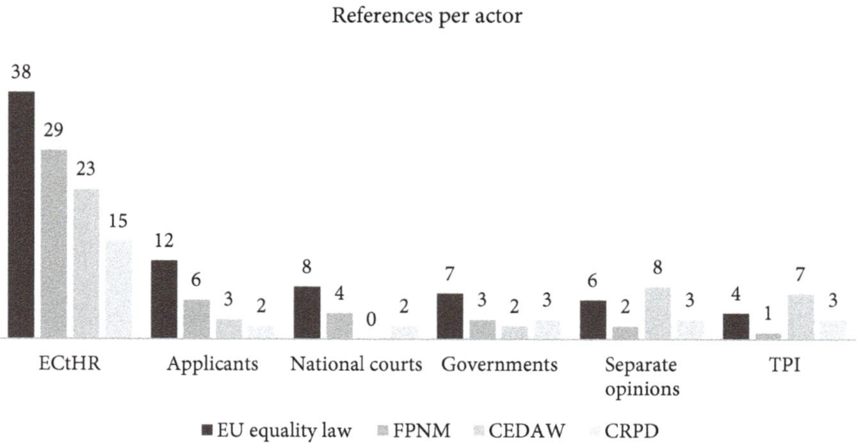

The bar chart displays the frequency with which different actors have referred to EU equality law and international equality instruments.[208] An important point to clarify: when the ECtHR refers to EU equality law, we mean all instances where it mentions EU equality law, which cannot be attributed to another actor. It might be that the references made by the ECtHR are based on those made by parties and national courts, either before national courts or the ECtHR itself. It might also be that some references to EU law by parties, third-parties and national judges at domestic or ECHR level are not mentioned in the judgment. We should thus be careful when interpreting these data.

Focusing on EU equality law, the ECtHR stands out as the main actor, referencing EU equality law in 38 instances. Applicants demonstrate notable engagement, invoking EU equality law in 12 cases. National courts, governments, and judges in separate opinions refer to EU equality law in 8, 7, and 6 instances. Third-party interveners contribute to a lesser extent, with 4 references. This underscores the diverse engagement with EU equality law among different actors, similar to our data protection case study.

When we compare these data with those from international instruments, two main observations emerge. First, the diversity of engagement is not unique to EU equality law: all actors refer to nearly all instruments. Second, EU equality law is distinguished by the high number of references across categories of actors. This is noticeable for the applicants, where there are 12 references to EU equality law versus 6 (FCPNM), 3 (CEDAW), and 2 (CRPD); and for national courts, where there are 8 references to EU equality law versus

208 We examine here both EU equality law and three specific international instruments, namely the FCNM, CEDAW, and CRPD. Although the data are not exhaustive and not entirely comparable (i.a. because we only look at the international instruments and not at related outputs from their respective monitoring body), they still provide us with valuable insights into the use of EU equality law and international instruments by the actors.

4 (FCPNM), 2 (CRPD), and 0 (CEDAW). This is not the case for judges in separate opinions and third-party interveners, where CEDAW is the most cited (8 and 7 references), and there are less references to EU equality law (6 and 4 references). This contrasts with our data protection case study where there is a prevalence of references to EU data protection law for each actor.[209]

It is important to put in perspective the engagement by these actors by considering the overall number of cases on equality, which totals 1,065. While there is indeed a higher number of references to EU equality law than to international instruments, the overall frequency of these references remains relatively limited when viewed in the context of the total caseload. Yet, it is possible that some references made by parties do not ultimately find their way into the judgments, making it challenging to draw definitive conclusions from the data.

§ 2. ZOOMING IN ON THE ACTORS

These data show that various actors engage with EU equality law: parties, third-party interveners, national judges, and judges at the ECtHR have relied on EU equality law, although judges at the ECtHR have done so to a lesser extent. Let us now examine why these actors refer to EU equality law and begin with the perspective of the parties and third parties, for which EU law is used as an argumentative resource.

I. *Applicants*

For applicants, EU equality law is akin to a 'sword': they mention it in to challenge the legality of a national practice or measure. The detail and centrality of EU-law arguments in the applicants' claims can vary. In some instances, they make vague references arguing that national measures or practices are inconsistent with EU equality law.[210] In other cases, EU equality law is a central element of the parties' argumentation.[211] Applicants invoke EU equality law before various jurisdictions, whether at domestic level or before the ECtHR.[212] It is common for applicants to allege a breach of EU equality law before national courts but refrain from using this argument before the ECtHR. In *Moraru v. Marin* (2022) and *Moraru and Marin v. Romania* (2022),

209 Part III (case study on data protection), Chapter 3, Section III, §1. Quantitative Overview.

210 E.g. ECtHR, *Biao v. Denmark* [GC], no. 38590/10, § 73, 24 May 2016.

211 E.g. ECtHR, *Moraru v. Romania*, no. 64480/19, §§ 8–13, 8 November 2022; ECtHR, *Stec and Others v. the United Kingdom* [GC], nos. 65731/01 and 65900/01, §§ 17–19, 39-41, 45, 48, 56–58, ECHR 2006-VI.

212 E.g. ECtHR, *Moraru v. Romania*, ibid., § 8 (before national courts).

the applicants relied on specific instruments of EU law and related CJEU's cases before national courts.[213] The latter ruled that EU equality law was not applicable, because either the instrument or CJEU's decisions were deemed irrelevant.[214] This led the applicants to present fresh arguments before the ECtHR, showing that it can be a forum to change their legal strategy. Although applicants may abandon references to EU equality law before the ECtHR, its use at national level can impact the ECtHR's reasoning, as we will see below.

There are two main types of arguments used by the applicants: those aimed at neutralising EU equality law that is unfavourable to them, and those aimed at reinforcing their position by relying on aspects of EU equality law that support their claims. An illustration of the former is found in *Stec v. United Kingdom* [GC](2006). The CJEU had reached a conclusion adverse to the applicants: it held that the relevant EU equality law was not applicable.[215] The applicants use a series of neutralising arguments before the ECtHR:

> Although the ECJ had decided against them, the applicants emphasised that it had been adjudicating on a different question, namely whether the amendments fell within the scope of the Article 7 exception to the non-discrimination provisions of the Directive. In particular, the ECJ did not have to decide whether there was a proportionate justification for the discrimination, but was instead construing the phrase 'the possible consequences thereof for other benefits' in Article 7. The applicants did not consider that a finding in their favour would have wider implications for the case-law of the ECJ under Article 7, since the impact would be limited to other cases where there was no financial necessity to maintain the link between the benefit in question and pensionable age, and no compelling reason to do so. Moreover, the mere fact that a measure which discriminated on grounds of sex nonetheless fell outside the European Union's limited restrictions upon social security discrimination did not prevent this Court from examining for itself the issue of justification.[216]

First, there is an argument of differentiation: the applicants pinpoint that what the CJEU has decided upon (the extent of an exception within a directive) does not cover what they have left undetermined (whether there is a proportionate justification), which is the issue the ECtHR needs to address. Second, there is an argument of minimisation: they highlight the limited effect that a decision in their favour would exert on the CJEU's case-law. Third, there is an argument on the role of the ECtHR: they suggest that being outside the remit of EU law

---

[213] ECtHR, *Moraru and Marin v. Romania*, nos. 53282/18 and 31428/20, § 12, 20 December 2022 and ECtHR, *Moraru v. Romania*, no. 64480/19, § 8, 8 November 2022.

[214] ECtHR, *Moraru and Marin v. Romania, ibid.*; *Moraru v. Romania*, ibid., § 11.

[215] ECtHR, *Stec and Others v. the United Kingdom* [GC], nos. 65731/01 and 65900/01, § 41, ECHR 2006-VI.

[216] Ibid., § 45.

does not strip the ECtHR of its jurisdiction to scrutinise the justification of the measures.

Next to defensive arguments, applicants use EU equality law that is advantageous to them. Commonly, they draw parallels with developments in EU equality law and, implicitly, suggest that the ECtHR should likewise apply them.[217]

The impact of the applicants' arguments on the ECtHR's reasoning is complex to trace. However, we can discern instances of both direct and indirect incorporation of applicants' arguments, as well as explicit and implicit rejections. In *D.H. v. Czech Republic* [GC](2007), the applicants argued that statistical data should be considered as a valid form of evidence for discrimination. They stressed that the Racial Discrimination Directive (2000/43/EC) allows for indirect discrimination to be established 'by any means, including on the basis of statistical evidence.'[218] The ECtHR incorporated this argument into its reasoning, affirming that 'Council Directives 97/80/EC and 2000/43/EC stipulate that persons who believe they have been victims of the non-application of the principle of equal treatment may, before a domestic authority, establish by any means, including on the basis of statistical evidence, facts from which it may be presumed that there has been discrimination.'[219] The incorporation of parties' arguments can also be more indirect, in that the ECtHR may draw upon arguments based on EU law that were invoked before national jurisdictions. This is the case in *Moraru v. Romania* (2022) and *Moraru and Marin v. Romania* (2022), where, as mentioned earlier, the ECtHR relied on the lack of engagement of national courts with EU equality law to find that the interferences were disproportionate.[220] Cases of incorporation allows us to highlight the 'human factor' in the influence of EU equality law. When certain individuals or actors mobilise EU equality law before the ECtHR, it can impact its use by the ECtHR. This highlights the relevance of EU law as a persuasive tool within the ECtHR's deliberations.

Regarding the rejection of applicants' arguments, there are explicit and implicit situations. On the implicit side, the *Sejdic v. Serbia* (2009) case is a good example. The applicant pointed out that a difference in treatment based on race or ethnicity was not capable of justification and constituted direct discrimination, in accordance with EU law.[221] The ECtHR considered that when a difference in treatment is based on race or ethnicity, the notion of

217 ECtHR, *Jurčić v. Croatia*, no. 54711/15, § 56, 4 February 2021; ECtHR, *Sejdić and Finci v. Bosnia and Herzegovina* [GC], nos. 27996/06 and 34836/06, § 32, ECHR 2009; ECtHR, *D.H. and Others v. the Czech Republic* [GC], no. 57325/00, § 136, ECHR 2007-IV

218 ECtHR, *D.H. and Others v. the Czech Republic* [GC], no. 57325/00, § 136, ECHR 2007-IV.

219 Ibid., § 187.

220 Part III (case study on equality), Chapter 3, Section II, §2, II.B. Dismissive.

221 ECtHR, *Sejdić and Finci v. Bosnia and Herzegovina* [GC], nos. 27996/06 and 34836/06, § 32, ECHR 2009.

objective and reasonable justification must be interpreted as strictly as possible, although some exceptions may exist, without referring to the EU law-based argument.[222] On the explicit side, let us mention *Stec v. United Kingdom* [GC] (2006), where the ECtHR, although recognising the argument of differentiation (namely that the CJEU ruled on a different matter), still affords significant weight to the CJEU's reasoning.[223]

II. Governments

If we look at how governments use EU equality law, this law serves a 'shield' function: they refer to it in defending against alleged ECHR's violations. Similar as the applicants, they use arguments either to neutralise EU equality law when it is unfavourable or to mobilise it when it is favourable. In the first category, examples are rare. In *X, Y and Z v. United Kingdom* (1997), which concerns transsexuals, the government sought to dismiss the relevance of the *P. v. S.* (1996) CJEU's ruling,[224] on the grounds that it did not pertain to the extent to which a State was obliged to recognise a person's change of sex for legal purposes.[225] In the second category, where the approach is to mobilise EU equality law positively, the most common argument is that of legality or compatibility: governments emphasise that their policies or measures are legal or conform to EU equality law. In so doing, they suggest that legality under EU law equates to or contributes to legality under ECHR law. Governments sometimes mention in a general manner that they act in accordance with EU equality law.[226]

Beyond this compliance argument, there are two other types of arguments. First, the argument of coherence, which aims to demonstrate that if the ECtHR were to deem a practice or measure illegal while it is legal under EU law, this could lead to inconsistencies.[227] Second, the argument of discretion, which highlights that EU law grants EU States discretionary power to regulate the issue. This argument is repeatedly invoked in relation to Article 9 Charter,

222 Ibid., § 44.

223 ECtHR, *Stec and Others v. the United Kingdom* [GC], nos. 65731/01 and 65900/01, § 58, ECHR 2006-VI.

224 Case C-13/94,, *P. v. S.*, ECLI:EU:C:1996:170.

225 ECtHR, *X, Y and Z v. the United Kingdom*, 22 April 1997, § 97, *Reports of Judgments and Decisions* 1997-II.

226 ECtHR, *I.B. v. Greece*, no. 552/10, § 57, ECHR 2013.

227 ECtHR, *Stec and Others v. the United Kingdom* [GC], nos. 65731/01 and 65900/01, § 48, ECHR 2006-VI. In *Stec v. United Kingdom* (2006), the Government argued that: 'If the Court were to find a violation in the present case, it would create considerable confusion: the domestic legislation would be lawful under a Directive specifically concerned with sex discrimination in social security, but unlawful under the more general provisions of the Convention.'

asserting that this provision allows States the discretion to regulate the rights to marry and to found a family based on the wording of this provision.[228]

III. Third-Party Interveners

It is not solely the parties that uses EU equality law as an argumentative resource; third-party interveners also strategically use EU equality law. The use of EU equality law hinges on the interests they seek to safeguard. For example, in the case of *Biao v. Denmark* (2016), the AIRE Centre, a UK-based NGO dedicated to advocating for and safeguarding human rights throughout Europe, invoked EU law on family reunification to contend that there was a violation of the Convention.[229] The use of EU equality law by third-party interveners is less developed and less frequent compared to applicants and governments; indeed, cases where they mention EU equality law are sparse and its use is limited.[230] One exception featuring more sophisticated argumentation is in *Biao v. Denmark* (2016), where the AIRE Centre argued that by virtue of Article 53 ECHR, the ECtHR cannot provide a more restrictive interpretation of ECHR law than EU law. In other words, to the extent that EU law applied, the Convention could not be interpreted in a way that would offer less generous protection to family (and private) life than that guaranteed by the relevant EU law provisions.[231]

IV. National Judges

Turning to the use of EU equality law by judges at domestic level, there is a noticeable number of references to EU equality law by national courts, which is either in their reasoning or in dissenting opinions.[232] The relatively high number of references result from the simple fact that these courts often adjudicate on EU equality law before the case reaches the ECtHR.[233]

---

228 E.g. ECtHR, *Orlandi and Others v. Italy*, nos. 26431/12 and 3 others, § 170, 14 December 2017; ECtHR, *Schalk and Kopf v. Austria*, no. 30141/04, § 24, ECHR 2010.

229 ECtHR, *Biao v. Denmark* [GC], no. 38590/10, § 87, 24 May 2016.

230 E.g. ECtHR, *Khamtokhu and Aksenchik v. Russia* [GC], nos. 60367/08 and 961/11, § 51, 24 January 2017; ECtHR, *Guberina v. Croatia*, no. 23682/13, § 64, 22 March 2016.

231 ECtHR, *Biao v. Denmark* [GC], no. 38590/10, § 87, 24 May 2016.

232 ECtHR *Aldeguer Tomás v. Spain*, no. 35214/09, § 45, 14 June 2016.

233 E.g. ECtHR, *Muñoz Díaz v. Spain*, no. 49151/07, § 14, ECHR 2009. In the cases under scrutiny, national courts most often ruled on its applicability and often concluded that it was not applicable, see ECtHR, *Hoppen and trade union of AB Amber Grid employees v. Lithuania*, no. 976/20, § 130, 17 January 2023; ECtHR, *Moraru and Marin v. Romania*, nos. 53282/18 and 31428/20, § 12, 20 December 2022; ECtHR, *Moraru v. Romania*, no. 64480/19, § 13, 8 November 2022; ECtHR, *Wessels-Bergervoet v. the Netherlands*, no. 34462/97, §§ 24 and 31, ECHR 2002-IV.

V. *Judges in Separate Opinions*

As for ECtHR's judges of the ECtHR, it is rare that EU equality law is discussed in separate opinions in depth. This contrasts with the robust engagement with EU data protection law by ECtHR's judges in separate opinions. Nevertheless, three types of references can be distinguished and are argumentative in nature. Some references are used to oppose or diverge from the approach adopted by the ECtHR.[234] Others aim to demonstrate that EU equality law is used in a decontextualised manner.[235] Finally, some references are meant to support and contribute to the findings of the majority.[236]

§ 3. COMPARATIVE INSIGHTS

As is shown by our quantitative analysis, the use of international instruments by the actors has been less frequent than the use of EU equality law, yet not for all actors. The use of international instruments by applicants and governments is similar as for EU equality law, yet their use is less frequent and less developed. As for the governments, they have sought to neutralise international instruments when it is unfavourable to them, emphasising that they act in compliance with instrument, whether this compliance is substantive[237] or formal,[238] or that the instrument leaves them a certain discretion.[239] As for the applicants, there are some arguments not found in our analysis on EU equality law. There is the consensus argument: they highlight how the international instrument contributes to a certain consensus on the legal interest in question.[240] There is the evidence argument: they rely on the findings of bodies related to international instruments to substantiate their claim.[241] Sometimes, the applicants mention the legal value that the ECtHR must give to the international instruments, which was not found for EU equality law.[242]

---

234 Separate opinion of Judges Sicilianos, Mose, Lubarda, Mourou-Vikstrom and Kucksko-Stadlmayer in *Khamtokhu and Aksenchik v. Russia* [GC], nos. 60367/08 and 961/11, § 11, 24 January 2017.

235 Separate opinion of Judge Pavli in ECtHR, *Basu v. Germany*, no. 215/19, § 5, 18 October 2022.

236 Separate opinion of Judges Elosegui and Serghides in ECtHR, *Muhammad v. Spain*, no. 34085/17, § 3, 18 October 2022.

237 ECtHR, *Enver Şahin v. Turkey*, no. 23065/12, § 52, 30 January 2018 (CRPD).

238 ECtHR, *Volodina v. Russia*, no. 41261/17, § 104, 9 July 2019 (CEDAW).

239 Ibid., § 105.

240 ECtHR, *Chapman v. the United Kingdom* [GC], no. 27238/95, § 87, ECHR 2001-I (FCNM).

241 ECtHR, *Valiullina and Others v. Latvia*, nos. 56928/19 and 2 others, § 121, 14 September 2023 (FCNM).

242 ECtHR, *Caamaño Valle v. Spain*, no. 43564/17, § 38, 11 May 2021 (CRPD).

As for third-party interveners, the trend is reversed: there is a more frequent and developed use of international instruments than EU equality law. Often third-party interveners rely on the findings of the monitoring bodies of international conventions, whether decisions,[243] general recommendations,[244] or reports,[245] to substantiate the factual situation in the respondent State.

Regarding national judges, we see a less frequent but similar use compared to EU equality law. National judges rule on aspects such as the compatibility of national measures or practices with conventions,[246] or the interpretation of rights within these conventions.[247] Regarding judges in separate opinions, we observe more frequent and detailed references than for EU equality law, particularly with CEDAW.[248]

SECTION IV. STATES

We now examine the respondent States involved in cases where EU equality law is used. Our specific focus on this aspect is linked to the fact that the use of EU standards by the ECtHR carries the risk of non-EU States being bound by those standards without having participated in the deliberative process, as explained in Part I of our project.[249] We therefore specifically investigate whether EU equality law has been used in cases involving non-EU States.

EU equality law has been mentioned in cases concerning a diverse range of States, most frequently EU States. EU law is more commonly used than other international instruments in EU cases. There is very limited use – either direct or indirect – of EU equality law against non-EU States, yet this limited use is implicit. Overall, our findings align closely with those from our data protection case study.

243 ECtHR, *Opuz v. Turkey*, no. 33401/02, § 121, ECHR 2009 (CEDAW).

244 ECtHR, *Valiullina and Others v. Latvia*, nos. 56928/19 and 2 others, § 121, 14 September 2023 (FCNM).

245 ECtHR, *Tapayeva and Others v. Russia*, no. 24757/18, § 98, 23 November 2021 (CEDAW).

246 ECtHR, *Caamaño Valle v. Spain*, no. 43564/17, § 10, 11 May 2021 (CRPD).

247 ECtHR, *Valiullina and Others v. Latvia*, nos. 56928/19 and 2 others, § 52, 14 September 2023 (FCNM).

248 E.g. Separate opinion of Judge Lemmens in ECtHR, *Caamaño Valle v. Spain*, no. 43564/17, §§ 4–10, 11 May 2021 (CRPD); Separate opinion of Judge Pinto de Albuquerque in ECtHR, *Volodina v. Russia*, no. 41261/17, §§ 3, 4, 8, 12, 13, 15, 16, 9 July 2019 (CEDAW); Separate opinion of Judge Eicke in ECtHR, *Talpis v. Italy*, no. 41237/14, §§ 13–15, 2 March 2017 (CEDAW and Istanbul Convention); Separate opinion of Judges Sicilianos, Mose, Lubarda, Mourou-Vikstrom and Kucksko-Stadlmayer in *Khamtokhu and Aksenchik v. Russia* [GC], nos. 60367/08 and 961/11, §§ 5, 8–13, 24 January 2017 (CEDAW).

249 See above Part I, Chapter 2, Section III. Navigating between Fragmentation and Marginalisation.

§ 1. QUANTITATIVE OVERVIEW

Examining the frequency of references per respondent State, we find that references to EU equality law span a diverse range of States. There are notable disparities, with references being much more frequent in cases involving EU States, as in our data protection case study.

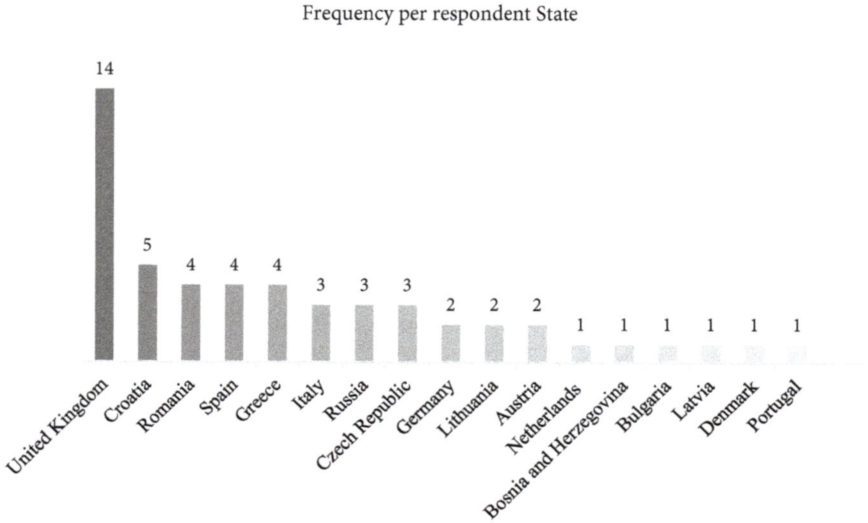

The data provided is a bar chart showing the distribution of ECtHR cases that refer to EU equality law per respondent State. The United Kingdom is by far the country most frequently involved in cases where the ECtHR refers to EU equality law (14 cases out of 52). Cases against the UK often involve similar issues (especially cases on dismissal from the military on the grounds of sexual orientation,[250] gender reassignment,[251] and pensions[252]) in which the ECtHR reiterates a specific reference to EU equality law. Croatia, Romania, Spain and Greece follow, each with 4 to 5 cases. A larger number of States have only 1 or 2 references. Concerning the distinction between EU and non-EU States, there

[250] E.g. ECtHR, *Beck and Others v. the United Kingdom*, nos. 48535/99 and 2 others, 22 October 2002; ECtHR, *Smith and Grady v. the United Kingdom*, nos. 33985/96 and 33986/96, ECHR 1999-VI; ECtHR, *Lustig-Prean and Beckett v. the United Kingdom*, nos. 31417/96 and 32377/96, 27 September 1999.

[251] ECtHR, *Christine Goodwin v. the United Kingdom* [GC], no. 28957/95, ECHR 2002-VI; ECtHR, *I. v. the United Kingdom* [GC], no. 25680/94, 11 July 2002; ECtHR, *Sheffield and Horsham v. the United Kingdom*, 30 July 1998, Reports of Judgments and Decisions 1998-V.

[252] E.g. ECtHR, *Stec and Others v. the United Kingdom* [GC], nos. 65731/01 and 65900/01, ECHR 2006-VI; ECtHR, *Barrow v. the United Kingdom*, no. 42735/02, 22 August 2006.

are 4 cases in total, 3 against Russia[253] and 1 against Bosnia-Herzegovina[254] – all UK cases date from when the UK was an EU State. This means that there are 7.69% of cases against non-EU States and 92.21% against EU States.

Respondent EU States

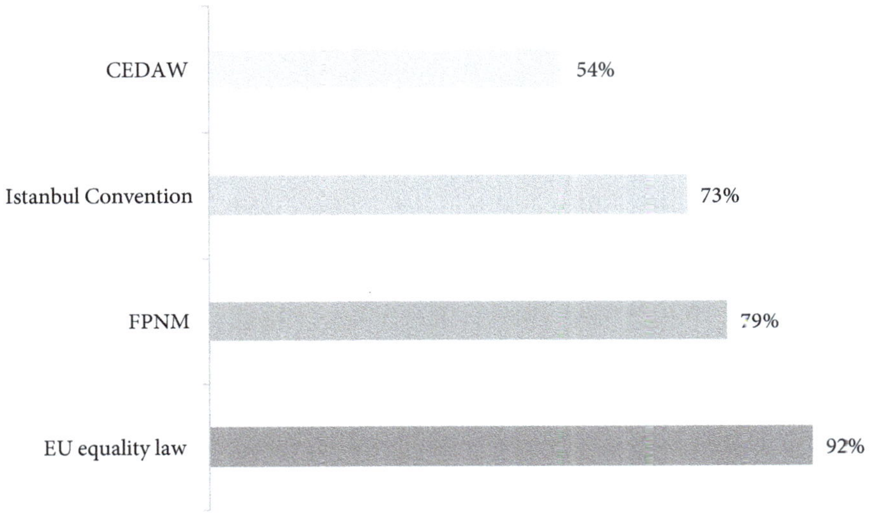

The graph indicates the percentage of cases involving EU respondent States for cases referencing EU equality law and international instruments. The data shows notable differences: 92% of the cases referencing EU equality law involve EU States, indicating a high correlation between references to EU equality law and the respondent States being from the EU. This is followed by the FCNM, where 79% of the cases involve EU States, and the Istanbul Convention with 73%. For the CEDAW, the proportion drops to 54%. EU equality law is thus the most frequently referenced in cases involving EU States, which can partly be explained by the fact that it is deeply integrated within the domestic legal systems of EU States and therefore forms part of the legal context of the cases for these States. The higher rate for international instruments involving non-EU States may be linked to the fact that they have ratified these instruments.

253 ECtHR, *Fedotova and Others v. Russia* [GC], nos. 40792/10 and 2 others, 17 January 2023; ECtHR, *Khamtokhu and Aksenchik v. Russia* [GC], nos. 60367/08 and 961/11, 24 January 2017; ECtHR, *Konstantin Markin v. Russia* [GC], no. 30078/06, §§ 65–70, ECHR 2012.

254 ECtHR, *Sejdić and Finci v. Bosnia and Herzegovina* [GC], nos. 27996/06 and 34836/06, ECHR 2009.

§ 2. QUALITATIVE ANALYSIS

The impact of EU equality law on the ECtHR's reasoning in cases involving non-EU States is very limited, as in our data protection case study. In *Khamotku v. Russia* (2017), EU equality law is mentioned in passing in the dissenting opinion to argue for a restrictive interpretation of an exception for pregnant women.[255] In *Sejdic v. Turkey* (2009), EU equality law is mentioned by the applicant to argue that there is a direct discrimination on racial grounds which cannot be justified; the ECtHR did not incorporate this argument in its reasoning.[256] In *Fedotova v. Russia* (2023), the ECtHR mentioned EU equality law to determine that there is a growing tendency among States of the Council of Europe to establish a legal framework that allows same-sex couples to receive adequate recognition and protection of their relationship. EU equality law is one source among many others to which the ECtHR relied upon.[257] In *Konstantin Markin v. Russia* (2012), the ECtHR referred to CJEU's cases on parental leave in its relevant legal materials.[258]

When the ECtHR references EU equality law in cases against EU States, it does not explicitly state that this law binds the respondent State. This contrasts with the ECtHR's use of international equality instruments, where it often notes in its judgments that the respondent State has ratified the instrument and specifies the time of ratification.[259] The ECtHR have noted when the respondent States have not ratified the instrument, and even taken into account a lack of ratification.[260] The ECtHR mentions sometimes all States that have and have not ratified a specific international equality instrument.[261]

The question arises whether the use of EU equality law in cases involving EU States can have indirect impact in cases involving non-EU respondent

255 Separate opinion of Judges Sicilianos, Mose, Lubarda, Mourou-Vikstrom and Kucksko-Stadlmayer in *Khamtokhu and Aksenchik v. Russia* [GC], nos. 60367/08 and 961/11, § 11, 24 January 2017.

256 ECtHR, *Sejdić and Finci v. Bosnia and Herzegovina* [GC], nos. 27996/06 and 34836/06, § 44, ECHR 2009.

257 ECtHR, *Fedotova and Others v. Russia* [GC], nos. 40792/10 and 2 others, § 178, 17 January 2023.

258 ECtHR, *Konstantin Markin v. Russia* [GC], no. 30078/06, §§ 65–70, ECHR 2012. Please note that this case was included, although it is not strictly related to a legislation that gives expression to fundamental equality rights in the sense developed in this project.

259 E.g. ECtHR, *Beeler v. Switzerland* [GC], no. 78630/12, § 30, 20 October 2020 (CEDAW); ECtHR, *Jurčić v. Croatia*, no. 54711/15, § 42, 4 February 2021 (CEDAW); ECtHR, *Toplak and Mrak v. Slovenia*, nos. 34591/19 and 42545/19, § 54, 26 October 2021 (CRPD).

260 E.g. ECtHR, *A.E. v. Bulgaria*, no. 53891/20, § 123, 23 May 2023: In *A.E. v. Bulgaria* (2023), the ECtHR observed that 'the refusal of the Bulgarian authorities to ratify the Istanbul Convention [...] can still be seen as indicative of the level of their commitment to effectively fighting domestic violence'.

261 ECtHR, *Valiullina and Others v. Latvia*, nos. 56928/19 and 2 others, § 85, 14 September 2023 (FCNM).

States through precedents.[262] The ECtHR has developed a system of *de facto* precedents.[263] In the words of the ECtHR, '[i]t is true that [...] the Court is not bound by its previous judgments; indeed, this is borne out by Rule 51 para. 1 of the Rules of Court. However, it usually follows and applies its own precedents, such a course being in the interests of legal certainty and the orderly development of the Convention case-law. Nevertheless, this would not prevent the Court from departing from an earlier decision if it was persuaded that there were cogent reasons for doing so. Such a departure might, for example, be warranted in order to ensure that the interpretation of the Convention reflects societal changes and remains in line with present-day conditions.'[264] As explained by Judge Wojtyczek, following precedents is the default rule, while deviating from precedents is a permissible exception that requires a 'good reason'.[265]

We have traced the influence of three elements where there was an influence of EU equality law on ECtHR case-law in cases involving EU States: the recognition of indirect discrimination (*D.H. v. Czech Republic* (2007)), the recognition of discrimination by association (*Guberina v. Croatia* (2016); *Molla Sali v. Greece* (2018)), and the use of statistical evidence to prove prima facie indirect discrimination (*D.H. v. Czech Republic* (2007)).

There are several cases where the ECtHR mentions these elements in cases involving non-EU States. This is the case in *Memedova v. North Macedonia* (2023) concerning the use of statistics, where it mentioned that 'statistics which appear on critical examination to be reliable and significant will be sufficient to constitute the prima facie evidence the applicant is required to produce. This does not, however, mean that indirect discrimination cannot be proved without statistical evidence (see *D.H. and Others v. the Czech Republic* [GC], no. 57325/00, § 188, ECHR 2007-IV). Reliable national or international reports can also be used to that effect (see, mutatis mutandis, *D.H. and Others v. the Czech Republic*, cited above, § 113, and Y and Others v. Bulgaria, no. 9077/18, § 122, 22 March 2022).'[266] This is also the case concerning the concept of indirect discrimination, which is mentioned in cases against Turkey[267] and

---

262 T. Lock, 'The Influence of EU Law on Strasbourg Doctrines', *European Law Review*, 2016, p. 822.

263 E.g. K. Wojtyczek, 'Precedent in the system of the European Convention on Human Rights', in M. Florczak-Wątor (ed.), *Constitutional Law and Precedent*, London, Routledge, 2022, pp. 234–252.

264 ECtHR, *Cossey v. The United Kingdom*, no. 10843/84, § 35, 27 September 1990.

265 K. Wojtyczek, 'Precedent in the system of the European Convention on Human Rights,' in M. Florczak-Wątor (ed.), *Constitutional Law and Precedent*, London, Routledge, 2022, p. 240.

266 ECtHR, *Memedova and Others v. North Macedonia*, nos. 42429/16 and 2 others, § 88, 24 October 2023. See also e.g. ECtHR, *Tapayeva and Others v. Russia*, no. 24757/18, § 109, 23 November 2021.

267 ECtHR, *Duğan v. Türkiye*, no. 84543/17, § 50, 7 February 2023.

Bosnia and Herzegovina.[268] What is common to the various cases is that the ECtHR does not acknowledge EU equality law as having played an influential role in subsequent cases. This contrasts with international equality instruments, where the ECtHR often mentions in subsequent cases that the instrument is the source of the influence for a given interpretation of the Convention.[269]

A final element of inquiry is whether the ECtHR uses techniques which allow to modulate the influence of EU equality law according to the respondent State. In other words, does the ECtHR rely on certain elements (either textual in the Convention or interpretation techniques) that ensure that the use of EU equality law is limited to cases involving EU States? This could be, for instance, by using the technique of margin of appreciation (which could be limited in cases where there is EU equality law that regulates the topic), the term 'law' which is enshrined in several provisions of the Convention,[270] or Article 53 ECHR.[271] We found no use of specific techniques to modulate the influence of EU equality law. As noted above, the AIRE Centre argued in *Biao v. Denmark* (2016) that under Article 53 ECHR, the ECtHR cannot provide a more restrictive interpretation of ECHR law than EU law.[272] The argument was not addressed by the ECtHR. Yet the use of EU equality law is sometimes limited to the specific circumstances of the cases. This is the case in *Moraru v. Romania* (2022) and *Moraru and Marin v. Romania* (2022) in which the ECtHR took into account the lack of engagement by national authorities with EU equality law to support its conclusion that the differences in treatment were not proportionate.

SECTION V. METHODOLOGY OF THE ECTHR WHEN USING EU EQUALITY LAW

Alongside the increasing significance of EU equality law in ECtHR case-law, there has been an overall improvement in the ECtHR's methodological use of the former, as in our data protection case study. However, certain areas still need enhancement, be it in terms of transparency, justification or contextualisation. The methodological approach is more developed with regard to international instruments than for EU equality law, despite the fact that the latter is the most prominent external source used by the ECtHR in in its equality case-law.

---

268 ECtHR, *Pinkas and Others v. Bosnia and Herzegovina*, no. 8701/21, § 62, 4 October 2022.

269 See below Part III (case study on equality), Chapter 3, Section V, §4. Comparative Insights.

270 See further in Part IV, Chapter 2, Section II, §2, II. EU Law as A Condition For Lawfulness.

271 See further in Part IV, Chapter 2, Section II, §2, I. Article 53 ECHR.

272 ECtHR, *Biao v. Denmark* [GC], no. 38590/10, § 87, 24 May 2016.

§ 1. TRANSPARENCY

There are several situations where the ECtHR exhibits limited transparency in its use of EU equality law. A first concern relates to the phenomenon that can be termed as 'use by reference'. The ECtHR uses EU equality law in its reasoning in a summary manner and refers to the relevant legal materials where EU equality law is described in detail. This situation is highly present in the ECtHR's equality case-law. In *Napotnik v. Croatia* (2020), the ECtHR provided detailed references to relevant EU secondary law and CJEU's case-law related to discrimination due to pregnancy in its relevant legal materials.[273] When the ECtHR uses this case-law to support the interpretation that a difference in treatment constitutes direct discrimination on the grounds of sex, the reasoning is, to say the least, limited.[274] Another example relates to *Moraru v. Romania* (2022) and *Moraru and Marin v. Romania* (2022), in which the ECtHR considered that the national judges had not engaged meaningfully with the CJEU's case-law. The ECtHR provides a lengthy description of the CJEU cases in its relevant legal materials,[275] but offers limited explanation when it assesses that national courts had not engaged meaningfully with EU equality law.[276]

The technique of 'use by reference' presents advantages: it may enhance the clarity and conciseness of the ECtHR's reasoning. Nevertheless, it can become particularly problematic when it leads to erroneous use of EU equality law. *D.H. v. Czech Republic* [GC](2007) is a good example. As observed above, the ECtHR uses EU equality law to support its interpretation that statistics may be used to establish a presumption of indirect discrimination.[277] The ECtHR assumes that the relevant EU directives give a right to individuals to use statistical evidence:

273 ECtHR, *Napotnik v. Romania* no. 33139/13, §§ 40–48, 20 October 2020.

274 Ibid., § 77. Empasis added See also ECtHR, *Jurčić v. Croatia*, no. 54711/15, § 69, 4 February 2021.

275 ECtHR, *Moraru v. Romania*, no. 64480/19, §§ 22–26, 8 November 2022.

276 ECtHR, ibid., §§ 53–54, 8 November 2022. In particular, the ECtHR held that: 'The applicant expressly noted that point during the domestic proceedings (see paragraph 8 above), and relied on the findings of the CJEU in *Kalliri* to lend force to her argument (see paragraphs 8 and 12 above). The domestic courts, however, contested her assertions, including her reliance on *Kalliri*. In doing so, they limited their examination and regarded the CJEU judgment exclusively from the standpoint of indirect discrimination based on sex (see paragraphs 11 and 13 above). […] Admittedly, it is not for this Court to interpret European Union law as such. That said, the Court cannot but note that by summarily deeming *Kalliri* to be irrelevant to the facts of the case, the domestic courts failed to engage meaningfully with that judgment of the CJEU and to examine its ramifications highlighted by the applicant in her arguments before the court.'

277 See above Part III (case study on equality), Chapter 3, Section II, §1, II. Confirmation.

> Council Directives 97/80/EC and 2000/43/EC stipulate that persons who consider themselves wronged because the principle of equal treatment has not been applied to them may establish before a domestic authority by any means, including on the basis of statistical evidence, facts from which it may be presumed that there has been discrimination.[278]

However, the directives mention (in their preambles) that:

> The appreciation of the facts from which it may be inferred that there has been direct or indirect discrimination is a matter for national judicial or other competent bodies, in accordance with rules of national law or practice. Such rules *may* provide in particular for indirect discrimination to be established by any means including on the basis of statistical evidence.[279]

The directives allow national authorities to authorise the use of statistical evidence, but they are not required to do so. The ECtHR suggests that under EU equality law, the use of statistical evidence is always permissible, whereas the directives state that the use of statistical evidence is permissible provided that national procedural law allows for it. The use of EU law has significant implications, as the reliance on the EU equality directives is a key argument to justify the ECtHR's stance that statistical evidence may be used to establish a presumption of indirect discrimination. Through the technique of 'use by reference', the ECtHR seems to distort EU equality law.

Another example relates to the cases of *Christine Goodwin v. United Kingdom* (2002) and *I. v. United Kingdom* (2002), where the ECtHR relied on Article 9 Charter in the following way: 'The Court would also note that Article 9 of the recently adopted Charter of Fundamental Rights of the European Union departs, no doubt deliberately, from the wording of Article 12 of the Convention in removing the reference to men and women (see paragraph 41 above).'[280] The ECtHR does not cite the Charter's provisions but makes a cross-reference to it, which is included in the relevant legal materials.[281] This provision provides that the right to marry will be guaranteed in accordance with national laws; however, this aspect of deference to national levels, crucial for understanding the scope of this provision, is omitted in the reasoning. Nonetheless, the ECtHR considered this dimension in subsequent cases, as we will explain below.

278 ECtHR, *D.H. and Others v. the Czech Republic* [GC], no. 57325/00, § 187, ECHR 2007-IV.

279 Ibid., § 83. Emphasis added.

280 ECtHR, *Christine Goodwin v. the United Kingdom* [GC], no. 28957/95, § 100, ECHR 2002-VI; ECtHR, *I. v. the United Kingdom* [GC], no. 25680/94, § 80, 11 July 2002.

281 ECtHR, *Christine Goodwin v. the United Kingdom* [GC], ibid., § 58; ECtHR, *I. v. the United Kingdom* [GC], ibid., § 41.

Another concern is that the ECtHR often refers to EU equality law only within the relevant legal materials. Such types of references are not, in themselves, an issue as EU equality law then serves an informative function. However, there are situations where one might suspect an 'implicit' influence of EU equality law on the ECtHR's case-law. EU law appears to have impacted the ECtHR's reasoning but it is only mentioned in the relevant legal materials. A good example relates to the recognition of the concept of discrimination by association in ECHR law, as we have seen above in *Guberina v. Croatia* (2016) and *Molla Sali v. Greece* [GC](2018).[282]

A last concern relates to situations where there is no reference to EU equality law. If it is not the role of the ECtHR to be an EU law court, and it cannot be expected to cite EU law, references to EU law may appear necessary or desirable in certain instances. They are necessary when EU equality law plays a role in the ECtHR's reasoning[283] and desirable when the ECtHR is faced with comparable or analogous cases as the CJEU. The ECtHR seems increasingly inclined to do so. Such an approach is valuable for national judges – who are tasked with applying both EU and ECHR laws – and ultimately individuals as we will revisit later.[284]

§ 2. JUSTIFICATION

The ECtHR almost never mentions what justifies its reference to EU equality law. EU equality law is most often used without any explanation. This is noticeable in cases that mention the Charter,[285] EU legislative instruments,[286] or CJEU case-law.[287] One of the exceptions where the ECtHR substantiates why it refers to EU equality law is in *Stec v. United Kingdom* (2006). As we have seen above, the ECtHR mentioned that: 'In reaching a conclusion on this issue, which, while not determinative of the issue under Article 14 of the Convention, is nonetheless of central importance, particular regard should be had to the

---

282 See above Part III (case study on equality), Chapter 3, Section II, §1, I. New Interpretation.

283 See above Part III (case study on equality), Chapter 3, Section II, §1, II. Confirmation.

284 Part IV, Chapter 2, Section II, §1. Transparency.

285 ECtHR, *Peterka v. Czech Republic*, no. 21990/08, 4 May 2010, p. 6 ECtHR, *G.N. and Others v. Italy*, no. 43134/05, § 126, 1 December 2009; ECtHR, *Christine Goodwin v. the United Kingdom* [GC], no. 28957/95, § 100, ECHR 2002-VI; ECtHR, *I. v. the United Kingdom* [GC], no. 25680/94, § 80, 11 July 2002.

286 ECtHR, *D.H. and Others v. the Czech Republic* [GC], no. 57325/00, §§ 184 (re. indirect discrimination) and 187 (re. use of statistics), ECHR 2007-IV.

287 ECtHR, *Moraru v. Romania*, no. 64480/19, § 54, 8 November 2022; ECtHR, *Moraru and Marin v. Romania*, nos. 53282/18 and 31428/20, § 119, 20 December 2022; ECtHR, *Jurčić v. Croatia*, no. 54711/15, § 69, 4 February 2021; ECtHR, *Napotnik v. Romania*, no. 33139/13, § 77, 20 October 2020.

strong persuasive value of the ECJ's finding on this point.'[288] The justification is rather limited: it is the persuasive value that would justify the ECtHR's use of the CJEU's case-law without further explanation.[289]

The ECtHR uses very rarely its methods of interpretation, such as contextual interpretation, dynamic and evolutive interpretation, or the European consensus, to justify its use of EU equality law. Only two exceptions could be found. In *Biao v. Denmark* (2016), the ECtHR referred to EU law on family reunification, among other sources, to demonstrate that there is a narrow margin of appreciation.[290] In *Fedotova v. Russia* (2023), the ECtHR mentioned EU equality law among other sources to determine that there is a growing tendency among States of the Council of Europe to establish a legal framework that allows same-sex couples to receive adequate recognition and protection of their relationship.[291]

§ 3. CONTEXTUALISATION

A final point concerns whether and how the ECtHR contextualises EU equality law, which means in the context of this project whether the ECtHR takes into account the context and limits of EU equality law. There is a discernible trend toward increased contextualisation in particular from a material point of view, but there are instances where this remains limited. Regarding the temporal and geographical dimensions, the ECtHR most often does not mention the temporal dimension of EU equality law (for example, when it comes into force, when it is binding, whether it has been repealed) or the geographical dimension (for example who EU equality law applies to, whether the respondent State is bound by EU equality law). Examples in this regard are plentiful,[292] and there are only a few exceptions.[293]

---

288 ECtHR, *Stec and Others v. the United Kingdom* [GC], nos. 65731/01 and 65900/01, § 58, ECHR 2006-VI.

289 See also other cases where the ECtHR reiterated this point, e.g. ECtHR, *Walker v. the United Kingdom*, no. 37212/02, § 35, 22 August 2006; ECtHR, *Barrow v. the United Kingdom*, no. 42735/02, § 36, 22 August 2006.

290 ECtHR, *Biao v. Denmark* [GC], no. 38590/10, § 138, 24 May 2016.

291 ECtHR, *Fedotova and Others v. Russia* [GC], nos. 40792/10 and 2 others, § 178, 17 January 2023.

292 E.g. ECtHR, *Basu v. Germany*, no. 215/19, § 16, 18 October 2022; ECtHR, *Molla Sali v. Greece* [GC], no. 20452/14, §§ 78–81, 19 December 2018; ECtHR, *Guberina v. Croatia*, no. 23682/13, §§ 40–42, 22 March 2016; ECtHR *Walker v. the United Kingdom*, no. 37212/02, §§ 19–20, 22 August 2006; *Pearson v. the United Kingdom*, no. 8374/03, §§ 12–13, 22 August 2006.

293 From a temporal point of view, there are a few brief mentions in the case of *Moraru v. Romania* (2022), which notes that 'Directive 2006/54/EC repealed Directive 76/207/EEC' (ECtHR, *Moraru v. Romania*, no. 64480/19, § 32, 8 November 2022) and in the case of *Moraru and Marin* (2022), which mentions that 'Council Directive 76/207/EEC of 9 February 1976'

From a material point of view, one can observe strong signs of improvement over the past few years: the ECtHR increasingly presents the relevant EU equality law in its judgments in an exhaustive, precise, and up-to-date manner.[294] In earlier judgments where it referred to EU equality law, the ECtHR often mentioned it briefly without presenting the broader context of EU equality law.[295] Several examples attest to a change in its approach. In *Christine Goodwin* [GC](2002) and *I. v. United Kingdom* [GC](2002), the ECtHR mentioned Article 9 Charter to justify that the right to marriage could also apply to transgender individuals; yet the ECtHR did not refer to the national discretion that this provision allows in this matter.[296] By contrast, in *Schalk and Kopf* (2010), the ECtHR took more account of the context of Article 9 Charter. It referred to the Commentary of the Charter and observed that Article 9 Charter leaves the decision whether or not to allow same-sex marriage to the States.[297]

There are cases, although not very frequent, where the ECtHR fails to consider or acknowledge the material limits of EU equality law. We have already observed an instance of distortion in the case of *D.H. v. Czech Republic* (2007),[298] but there are also situations of inadequate transplants, by which the ECtHR uses one aspect of EU equality law to inform a different aspect of ECHR equality law. *Stec v. United Kingdom* [GC](2006) provides a good example, where, as we have seen, the ECtHR relied on an exception to the application of the Social Security Equal Treatment Between Men and Women Council Directive (79/7/EEC) to develop its reasoning on the justification of interference with Article 14 ECHR.[299] While this approach prevents a certain coherence, it is problematic in that the specific context and objectives of the

---

was 'in force until 14 August 2009' (ECtHR, *Moraru and Marin v. Romania*, nos. 53282/18 and 31428/20, § 68, 20 December 2022).There is also a very limited mention in the cases *Christine Goodwin v. United Kingdom* (2002) that the Charter had been 'recently adopted' without stating that it was not binding at the time (ECtHR, *Christine Goodwin v. the United Kingdom* [GC], no. 28957/95, § 100, ECHR 2002-VI). A slight improvement in this regard can be seen in the case of *Schalk and Kopf* (2010), where the ECtHR mentions that the Charter was signed on 7 December 2000 and came into force on 1 December 2009 (ECtHR, *Schalk and Kopf v. Austria*, no. 30141/04, § 24, ECHR 2010). There is one case where the ECtHR pays more attention to the temporal dimension of EU law, namely *Biao v. Denmark* (2016), to which we will return in Part IV, Chapter 2, Section II, §3. Contextualisation.

294 See above Part III (case study on equality), Chapter 3, Section II, §4. Information.

295 In several cases adopted at the turn of the 2000s, the ECtHR merely noted that the CJEU held that the Equal Pay between Men and Women Council Directive (75/117/EEC) did not apply to discrimination based on sexual orientation (e.g. ECtHR, *Beck and Others v. the United Kingdom*, nos. 48535/99 and 2 others, § 42, 22 October 2002; ECtHR, *Smith and Grady v. the United Kingdom*, nos. 33985/96 and 33986/96, § 40, ECHR 1999-VI).

296 See above Part III (case study on equality), Chapter 3, Section II, §1, I. New Interpretation.

297 ECtHR, *Schalk and Kopf v. Austria*, no. 30141/04, § 60, ECHR 2010.

298 See above Part III (case study on equality), Chapter 3, Section V, §1. Transparency.

299 See above Part III (case study on equality), Chapter 3, Section II, §2, II.A. Supportive.

EU directive may differ from those of ECHR law and risk lowering the level of protection for equality in ECHR law.

§ 4. COMPARATIVE INSIGHTS

Looking at the methodology used for international equality instruments, the ECtHR's methodological approach appears more developed with regard to these instruments than for EU equality law. We observed increased transparency and justification as well as stronger contextualisation from both temporal and geographical perspectives.

Starting with transparency, the ECtHR frequently uses the technique of 'use by reference'. This technique can be seen both when the ECtHR uses the instruments as such[300] or the conclusions and reports of monitoring bodies.[301] It is rare for the ECtHR to state the provisions of the instruments or the outputs of these bodies in its reasoning.[302] Where a notable difference can be observed vis-à-vis EU equality law is that the ECtHR, on one hand, expresses more clearly when it uses an international instrument and, on the other hand, it recognises the influence this instrument has had in subsequent cases.

A good example is *Opuz v. Turkey* (2009), where the ECtHR discussed the meaning of discrimination in the context of domestic violence. It noted that it must consider the international context, and particularly having regard to the provisions of more specialised legal instruments and the decisions of international legal bodies on the question of violence against women.[303] It mentioned the definition of discrimination under the CEDAW as well as observations from the ComEDAW according to which violence against women, including domestic violence, is a form of discrimination against women.[304] Based on these elements, among others, the ECtHR concluded that the State's failure to protect women against domestic violence breaches their right to equal protection of the law and that this failure does not need to be intentional.[305] What is remarkable is that the ECtHR recognises the influence of CEDAW in subsequent judgments. In *Talpis v. Italy* (2017) for instance, the ECtHR observed that 'it was in its landmark judgment in *Opuz v. Turkey* (no. 33401/02, § 191, ECHR 2009), that this Court, drawing inspiration from

---

300 E.g. ECtHR, *Jurčić v. Croatia*, no. 54711/15, § 83, 4 February 2021 (CEDAW); ECtHR, *Guberina v. Croatia*, no. 23682/13, § 73, 22 March 2016 (CRPD).

301 ECtHR, *Carvalho Pinto de Sousa Morais v. Portugal*, no. 17484/15, § 54, 25 July 2017 (CEDAW).

302 See for an exception, ECtHR, *Volodina v. Russia*, no. 41261/17, §§ 113 and 117, 9 July 2019 (CEDAW).

303 ECtHR, *Opuz v. Turkey*, no. 33401/02, §§ 184–185, ECHR 2009 (CEDAW).

304 Ibid., §§ 186–187.

305 Ibid., § 191.

the terms of CEDAW and the work of the CEDAW Committee, first recognised that a State's failure to protect women against domestic violence is capable of breaching their right to equal protection of the law irrespective of whether this failure is intentional or not.'[306]

A similar approach can be seen with regard to the definition of reasonable accommodation under ECHR law. In *Cam v. Turkey* (2016), the ECtHR considered that Article 14 ECHR should be read in the light of the requirements of those texts regarding reasonable accommodation, and in particular Article 2 CRPD.[307] In *Arnar Helgi Lárusson v. Iceland* (2016), the ECtHR mentioned that: 'In previous cases concerning the rights of people with disabilities, the Court, referring to the CRPD, has found that Article 14 of the Convention has to be read in the light of the requirements of those texts regarding "reasonable accommodation" [...].'[308]

Where the contrast becomes even more pronounced compared to EU equality law is in terms of justification. Although it sometimes occurs that the ECtHR does not justify the use of international equality instruments,[309] it often provides strong justification when referring to them or places this use in the context of its interpretation techniques. We see the frequent use of instruments when the ECtHR is deciding on the existence of a consensus, whether it concerns the need to protect people with disabilities from discriminatory treatment,[310] the need to protect the security, identity and lifestyle of minorities,[311] or the obligation to teach in minority languages.[312] The ECtHR has also referred to international equality instruments after having discussed its doctrines of effectiveness and/or on interpreting the Convention in light of international

306 ECtHR, *Talpis v. Italy*, no. 41237/14, § 14, 2 March 2017. See also ECtHR, *Volodina v. Russia*, no. 41261/17, § 110, 9 July 2019.

307 ECtHR, *Çam v. Turkey*, no. 51500/08, § 65, 23 February 2016.

308 ECtHR, *Arnar Helgi Lárusson v. Iceland*, no. 23077/19, § 59, 31 May 2022. See also ECtHR, *Toplak and Mrak v. Slovenia*, nos. 34591/19 and 42545/19, § 111, 26 October 2021. This approach of stating the influence of an international equality instrument in subsequent jurisprudence can also be seen regarding the FCNM. See ECtHR, *Bakirdzi and E.C. v. Hungary*, nos. 49636/14 and 65678/14, § 54, 10 November 2022: 'In *Partei Die Friesen v. Germany*, the Court observed that the Council of Europe's Framework Convention, while acknowledging the margin of appreciation enjoyed by the State in electoral matters, put an emphasis on the participation of national minorities in public affairs (see Article 15 of the Framework Convention in paragraph 17 above).'

309 E.g. ECtHR, *Beeler v. Switzerland* [GC], no. 78630/12, § 113, 20 October 2020.

310 ECtHR, *Glor v. Switzerland*, no. 13444/04, § 53, ECHR 2009.

311 ECtHR, *Muñoz Díaz v. Spain*, no. 49151/07, § 60, ECHR 2009; ECtHR, *Chapman v. the United Kingdom* [GC], no. 27238/95, § 93, ECHR 2001-I.

312 ECtHR, *Valiullina and Others v. Latvia*, nos. 56928/19 and 2 others, § 134, 14 September 2023 (FCNM).

law.[313] The ECtHR has also explained that reports from monitoring bodies could be used to establish prima facie justification of domestic violence.[314]

There are also notable differences with EU equality law for the contextualisation. The ECtHR contextualises more frequently the temporal and geographical dimensions of international equality instruments.[315] *Ratione materiae*, the ECtHR refers more and more exhaustively to the material context of the instruments, by mentioning the outputs of monitoring bodies or the general context of the instruments.[316] As for EU equality law, the use of these instruments can be subject to criticism. We refer to key separate opinions on this matter, which highlight distinct views on the (lack of) use of international equality instruments.[317]

---

313 A good illustration is provided by *Arnar Helgi Larusson v. Iceland* (2022), where the ECtHR noted that 'the Convention should, as far as possible, be interpreted in harmony with other rules of international law of which it forms part' (ECtHR, *Arnar Helgi Lárusson v. Iceland*, no. 23077/19, § 57, 31 May 2022) and that therefore, 'the provisions regarding the rights of people with disabilities set out in the CRPD should [...] be taken into consideration.' (*ibid.*) The ECtHR observed that 'in its General Comment No. 2 the CRPD Committee noted that the denial of access of people with disabilities to, inter alia, facilities and services open to the public should be viewed within the context of discrimination.' (*ibid.*) Another interesting case is *Caamano Valle v. Spain* (2021) where the ECtHR observed that the 'Convention is an international treaty that is to be interpreted in accordance with the relevant standards and principles of public international law' and that the Court must 'take into account any relevant rules and principles of international law applicable in relations between the Contracting Parties', in line with its consistent case-law (ECtHR, *Caamaño Valle v. Spain*, no. 43564/17, § 52, 11 May 2021). The ECtHR mentioned that other instruments can offer wider protection than the Convention and that it is not bound by interpretations given to similar instruments by other bodies (ibid., § 54). Only after recalling these principles did the ECtHR observed that it is not for the ECtHR 'to express an opinion on whether Article 29 of the CRPD imposes stricter obligations on the States that are parties to that convention.' (ibid., § 59).

314 See ECtHR, *Volodina v. Russia*, no. 41261/17, § 113, 9 July 2019: 'the Court has referred to reports by international and local human-rights organisations, periodic reports by the CEDAW Committee, and statistical data from the authorities and academic institutions to establish the existence of a prima facie indication that domestic violence affects mainly women and that the general attitude of the local authorities - such as the manner in which the women are treated at police stations when they report domestic violence and judicial passivity in providing effective protection to victims - creates a climate that is conducive to domestic violence.'

315 See above Part III (case study on equality), Chapter 3, Section IV, §2.Qualitative Analysis.

316 E.g. ECtHR, *Volodina v. Russia*, no. 41261/17, §§ 51–52, 9 July 2019 (CEDAW).

317 See Separate opinion of Judges Sicilianos, Mose, Lubarda, Mourou-Vikström and Kickso-Stadlmayer in ECtHR, *Khamtokhu and Aksenchik v. Russia* [GC], nos. 60367/08 and 961/11, §§ 5–12, 24 January 2017 (on the use of the CEDAW); see Separate opinion of Judge Lemmens in ECtHR, *Caamaño Valle v. Spain*, no. 43564/17, §§ 3–11 (on the use of the CRPD).

CHAPTER 4
INTERMEDIARY CONCLUSION

The general conclusions for our two case studies are detailed at the end of the case studies. However, it may be helpful to recap some of the findings from our equality case study at this point.

Section 2 demonstrated that the EU and ECHR equality systems have experienced divergent developments. While the EU equality system has evolved into a highly sophisticated framework, equality protection under the ECHR legal system has historically been viewed as underdeveloped. Although these two systems have significant overlap and operate within a shared space, they are distinct and driven by different dynamics. The asymmetry in their development and their overlapping yet distinct approaches are crucial elements in understanding the influence of EU equality law on ECtHR case-law, which we have explored in Section 3.

EU equality law is the most prominent external source referenced by the ECtHR in its equality case-law. The ECtHR has referred to EU equality law more frequently than to international instruments and has consistently applied it across various domains in a notable proportion of its equality-related judgments. While both EU equality law and international instruments serve similar functions, international instruments either play a less significant role in performing these functions (interpretation, justification, and information) or do not perform certain functions at all (distinguishing). However, one function performed by international instruments that is not served by EU equality law is the evidentiary function.

EU equality law has played a notable role in supporting the interpretation of the Convention's provisions and has shaped some of the key principles of the equality ECtHR's case-law. Additionally, EU equality law has served an important justification function in the ECtHR's case-law. The ECtHR has also, at times, sought to distinguish its stance from that of EU equality law. Furthermore, EU equality law has provided a valuable informative function, with the ECtHR referencing it as a relevant contextual or legal standard.

Apart from the ECtHR itself, EU equality law has seen strong engagement from various actors, including parties, third parties, and national judges. EU equality law has been predominantly used in cases involving EU States, with very limited use against non-EU States. Alongside the growing importance of EU equality law in ECtHR case-law, there has been a noticeable improvement in the ECtHR's methodological use of this law. However, certain areas still require enhancement.

TITLE 2

THE INFLUENCE OF EU DATA PROTECTION LAW ON ECHR DATA PROTECTION LAW

CHAPTER 1
INTRODUCTION

The protection of personal data is a highly topical subject.[1] Whether it concerns the data retention obligations imposed on electronic communications service providers, the restrictions placed on data transfers from Europe to the United States or the strong concerns expressed regarding data processing by public authorities during the COVID-19 crisis, examples abound.

While the issue of personal data holds a prominent place in the public debate, its legal protection is recent. The right to the protection of personal data emerged in the second half of the 20th century in response to major societal changes. The shift toward the digital age started at the beginning of the 20th century. Characterised by the transition from a traditional industry to an economy based on information and communication technologies, this era became possible with the deployment of various technologies starting in the 1950s. While the rise of these technologies opened up numerous optimistic prospects, it led to an unprecedented increase in the volume of data being created and circulated.[2]

In response to this proliferation of data, the first legal instruments emerged in Europe in the early 1970s, initially at national level and then at European and international levels. Under the auspices of the Council of Europe, one of the landmark instruments in the field of data protection was developed, namely Convention 108 for the Protection of Individuals with regard to Automatic Processing of Personal Data, adopted in 1981. This instrument marked a milestone in the emergence of the fundamental right to data protection, with its principles serving as the foundation for many national and European legislations. Several decades later, the right to data protection is safeguarded by a complex and significant web of protections through several intertwined legal systems.

1 Some paragraphs in this introduction are inspired by or stem from V. Davio, 'Le droit fondamental à la protection des données personnelles : illustrations, principes et limites' in B. Docquir (ed.), *Le RGPD dans la pratique : un exercice d'équilibre*, Brussels, Larcier, 2021, pp. 9–40.

2 R. Tinière, 'Article 8. Protection des données à caractère personnel', in F. Picod, C. Rizcallah and S. Van Drooghenbroeck (eds.), *Charte des droits fondamentaux de l'Union européenne. Commentaire article par article*, 2nd ed., Brussels, Larcier, 2020, p. 213.

At European supranational level, two major legal systems coexist to protect personal data, both of which have some of their roots in Convention 108. First, the EU system, which includes an autonomous fundamental right to data protection under Article 8 Charter. Since the mid-1990s, the EU has developed a plethora of legislative instruments in this field, and data protection has become increasingly prominent in the CJEU's case-law. Second, the ECHR system, while not guaranteeing such a fundamental right per se, has seen the ECtHR address unjustified interferences with personal data since the 1970s, developing a highly advanced and mature system for the protection of personal data. The ECtHR has ruled on multiple data protection issues, most often from the perspective of the right to privacy.

Applying to some extent to the same actors and within the same geographical territory – with the 27 EU States being part of the ECHR – these two systems are closely related and interdependent. While they overlap, these systems exhibit notable differences in the way they protect personal data: their normative foundations, scope, and content are distinct.[3] The proximity of these two systems is an opportunity to enhance data protection on a European scale. The CJEU and the ECtHR can learn from each other in the context of the changing technological landscape that demands innovative legal responses.

Their coexistence also goes with its challenges. Their interdependent and intricate relationship requires careful articulation. The latter is necessary for national judges who must apply both EU and ECHR laws. For them, it is important to know the sources they should apply in a given case. This is also important for private and public authorities seeking to understand their rights and obligations. This is not only a matter of legal certainty but also of effectiveness, as clarity in obligations ensures that rights are well safeguarded. As interpreters of EU and ECHR laws, the CJEU and the ECtHR share part of the responsibility of articulating their sources.[4] Through interactions and dialogue between their bodies of case-law, a harmonious and fruitful coexistence is conceivable.

---

[3] J. Kokott and C. Sobotta, 'The distinction between privacy and data protection in the jurisprudence of the CJEU and the ECtHR', *International Data Privacy Law*, 2013, p. 228; P. de Hert and S. Gutwirth, 'Data Protection in the Case-law of Strasbourg and Luxemburg: Constitutionalisation in Action', in S. Gutwirth et al.(ed.), *Reinventing Data Protection*, Dordrecht, Springer, 2009, p. 9.

[4] See further in V. Davio and E. Muir, 'Introduction. The ECHR in the CJEU's Case-law Post-Charter: A Dual Perspective', *European papers*, 2023, p. 319.

SECTION I. THE INTERACTIONS BETWEEN EU AND ECHR DATA PROTECTION: AN AREA OF LIMITED RESEARCH

The existence of these two European systems safeguarding personal data raises important questions: How have the CJEU and the ECtHR articulated their case-law? Have they interacted with each other in this field? These questions, despite their significance, have attracted limited academic attention. In recent years, both data protection at EU and ECHR levels have garnered increasing interest. This is especially true for EU law since the introduction of Article 8 Charter.[5] This is also true at ECHR level, where the primary focus has long been on privacy, but a growing interest in data protection can be observed.[6] The co-existence of these two European protection systems have led to comparisons highlighting their similarities and differences.[7]

Yet, the interactions between EU and ECHR data protection laws have been underexplored. The topic has only caught the attention of a few researchers; some of them have focused on the impact of ECtHR case-law on EU data protection law.[8] A question that remains uncharted is the opposite question: the influence of EU data protection law on ECHR data protection law. Whereas

---

5 E.g. O. Lynskey, *The foundations of EU data protection law*, Oxford, Oxford University Press, 2015; G. Gonzalez Fuster, *The Emergence of Personal Data Protection as a Fundamental Right of the EU*, Cham, Springer, 2014.

6 See e.g. the Guide to the Case-law of the of the European Court of Human Rights on Data Protection, prepared by the Registry and updated on 28 February 2023, available here: https://ks.echr.coe.int/documents/d/echr-ks/guide_data_protection_eng; E. Psychogiopoulou, 'The European Court of Human Rights, Privacy and Data Protection in the Digital Era', in E. Psychogiopoulou and S. de la Sierra (eds.), *Courts, Privacy and Data Protection in the Digital Environment*, 2017, pp. 32–62.

7 E.g. E. Psychogiopoulou, 'Judicial Dialogue and Digitalization: CJEU Engagement with ECtHR Case-law and Fundamental Rights Standards in the EU', *JIPITEC*, 2022, pp. 1–18; B. van der Sloot, 'Wij zijn twee vriendjes, jij en ik: De innige tango van de twee Europese hoven op het gebied van privacy en gegevensbescherming', *S.E.W*, 2021, pp. 582–594; J. Kokott and C. Sobotta, 'The distinction between privacy and data protection in the jurisprudence of the CJEU and the ECtHR', *International Data Privacy Law*, 2013, pp. 222–228.

8 M.-L. Deftou, *Exporting the European Convention on Human Rights*, Oxford, Hart Publishing, 2022, pp. 20–29; E. Psychogiopoulou, 'Judicial Dialogue and Digitalization: CJEU Engagement with ECtHR Case-law and Fundamental Rights Standards in the EU', *JIPITEC*, 2022, pp. 1–18.

the impact of the latter on national[9] and international law[10] have been explored, the same cannot be said for its influence on the ECHR's legal framework.

Tracing the influence of EU data protection law on the ECHR is not a straightforward research path. As we observed above, EU law has been examined and depicted as posing a threat to Convention's rights rather than serving as a source of inspiration. The prevailing question revolves around whether EU States, when applying EU law, comply with the Convention. Recent examples show that this issue arises in the context of data protection.[11]

SECTION II. MAIN RESEARCH QUESTION AND RELEVANCE

Why, then, would one delve into the topic of the influence of EU data protection on ECHR law? To begin with, EU law has been portrayed as the 'lighthouse' for privacy rights in Europe.[12] First, the autonomous fundamental right to data protection, distinct from the right to privacy, is a distinctive feature of the EU legal framework.[13] Second, the EU legislator has developed a robust data protection policy, which started in the mid-90s and has seen further elaboration over the past decade. This is an example of an area where the EU legislator has adopted legislative measures that give effect to Article 8 Charter. There is an opportunity for the ECtHR to glean insights from the highly sophisticated data protection rules developed in Brussels and interpreted in Luxembourg.

Next, the influence of EU data protection law has extended beyond its boundaries.[14] Bradford has shown that the 'Brussels effect' – where both private and public entities uses EU laws outside the EU legal order – is present in the realm of data protection.[15] As summarised by Lynskey, 'data protection is one of the rare fields in which the EU could be said to exercise global regulatory supremacy; the EU rules have now been used as a blueprint for regulatory regimes across the Western world […]. Alternatives to the EU's comprehensive regime are fast disappearing at international level. For this reason, the EU

9 O. Lynskey, 'Article 8: The Right to Data Protection', in M. Bobek and J. Adams-Prassl (eds.), *The EU Charter of Fundamental Rights in the Member States*, Oxford, Hart Publishing, 2020, pp. 353–370.

10 O. Lynskey, 'Extraterritorial Impact in Data Protection Law through an EU Law Lens', *Brexit Institute Working Paper Series - No 8/2020*, available here: https://papers.ssrn.com/sol3/papers.cfm?abstract_id=3674413.

11 E.g. ECtHR, *Willems v. the Netherlands* (dec.), no. 57294/16, 9 November 2021.

12 See Separate opinion of Judge Pinto de Albuquerque in *Big Brother Watch and Others v. the United Kingdom* [GC], nos. 58170/13 and 2 others, § 59, 25 May 2021.

13 H. Kranenborg, 'Article 8', in S. Peers, T. Hervey, J. Kenner and A. Ward (eds.), *The EU Charter of Fundamental Rights. A Commentary*, Oxford, Hart Publishing, 2014, p. 228.

14 A. Bradford, 'The Brussels Effect', *Northwestern University Law Review*, 2012, p. 23.

15 Ibid.

regime can be said to be an influential one.'[16] This global reach demonstrates the relevance of the EU data protection framework as a source of influence.

Lastly, the CJEU and ECtHR encounter similar legal issues in their bodies of case-law. These encompass data surveillance,[17] the right to be forgotten,[18] international data transfers,[19] the retention of biometric data,[20] the publication of tax data,[21] the collection of data in the context of door-to-door activities of Jehovah's Witnesses[22] and the transmission of data between administrative authorities.[23] To ensure the coherence of data protection in Europe, a strong judicial dialogue between the two courts is of utmost importance. As observed by Psychogiopoulou, '[t]he pace of technology's evolution creates numerous hurdles for judges with particularly complex questions of both facts and law permeating judicial decision-making.'[24] In this respect, 'judicial dialogue can help address the novelty of the factual and legal context and also bring broader benefits to the fore, in particular adjudicative coherence, which is imperative in fundamental rights disputes'.[25]

---

16 O. Lynskey, *The foundations of EU data protection law*, Oxford, Oxford University Press, 2015, p. 41. Emphasis added See also O. Lynskey, 'Extraterritorial Impact in Data Protection Law through an EU Law Lens', *Brexit Institute Working Paper Series - No 8/2020*, available here: https://papers.ssrn.com/sol3/papers.cfm?abstract_id=3674413.

17 E.g. at ECtHR level: *Big Brother Watch and Others v. the United Kingdom* [GC], nos. 58170/13 and 2 others, 25 May 2021; *Centrum för rättvisa v. Sweden* [GC], no. 35252/08, 25 May 2021; e.g. at CJEU level: Case C-623/17, *Privacy International*, ECLI:EU:C:2020:790; Joined Cases C-511/18, 512/18 and C-520/18, *La Quadrature du Net and Others*, ECLI:EU:C:2020:791; Joined Cases C-293/12 and C-594/12, *Digital Rights Ireland*, ECLI:EU:C:2014:238. See on the comparison between the ECtHR and CJEU case-law on surveillance: S. O'Leary, 'Balancing Rights in a Digital age', *Irish Jurist*, 2018, pp. 59–92.

18 E.g. at ECtHR level: *Hurbain v. Belgium* [GC], no. 57292/16, 4 July 2023; *M.L. and W.W. v. Germany*, nos. 60798/10 and 65599/10, 28 June 2018; e.g. at CJEU level: Case C-136/17, *GC and others*, ECLI:EU:C:2019:773; Case C-507/17, *Google*, ECLI:EU:C:2019:772; Case C-131/12, *Google Spain*, ECLI:EU:C:2014:317.

19 At ECtHR level: *Big Brother Watch and Others v. the United Kingdom* [GC], nos. 58170/13 and 2 others, 25 May 2021; at CJEU level: Case C-311/18, *Schrems II*, ECLI:EU:C:2015:650; Case C-362/14, *Schrems I*, ECLI:EU:C:2015:650.

20 At ECtHR level: *Willems v. the Netherlands* (dec.), no. 57294/16, 9 November 2021; *S. and Marper v. the United Kingdom* [GC], nos. 30562/04 and 30566/04, ECHR 2008; at CJEU level: Case C-291/12, *Schwarz*, ECLI:EU:C:2013:670.

21 At ECtHR level: *L.B. v. Hungary* [GC], no. 36345/16, 9 March 2023; *Satakunnan Markkinapörssi Oy and Satamedia Oy v. Finland* [GC], no. 931/13, 27 June 2017; at CJEU level: Case C-73/07, *Tietosuojavaltuutettu v. Satakunnan Markkinapörssi Oy and Satamedia Oy*, ECLI:EU:C:2008:727.

22 At ECtHR level: *Jehovah's Witnesses v. Finland*, no. 31172/19, 9 May 2023; at CJEU level: Case C-25/17, *Jehovan todistajat*, ECLI:ECLI:EU:C:2018:551.

23 At ECtHR level: *Benedik v. Slovenia*, no. 62357/14, 24 April 2018; at CJEU level: Case C-582/14, *Breyer*, ECLI:EU:C:2016:779.

24 E. Psychogiopoulou, 'Judicial Dialogue and Digitalization: CJEU Engagement with ECtHR Case-law and Fundamental Rights Standards in the EU' *JIPITEC*, 2022, p. 147.

25 Ibid.

We aim to address the main research question of this project: 'How and to what extent have EU fundamental rights influenced ECtHR case-law?' in the field of data protection. This translates to: 'How and to what extent has EU data protection law influenced ECHR data protection law?' We examine, among other things, the functions of EU data protection law in ECtHR case-law, the actors involved in the influence process, the methodology of the ECtHR when it uses EU data protection law, and the areas where this influence is perceivable. To use a metaphor, let us refer to the separate opinion of Judge Pinto de Albuquerque in the *Big Brother Watch and Others v. United Kingdom* [GC] (2021) case, where EU law is likened to a lighthouse guiding data protection in Europe.[26] Here the question is: How bright is the EU lighthouse? How far has its light reached within the ECtHR case-law?

SECTION III. METHODOLOGY

Our methodological approach is similar to that developed for the equality case study.[27] It involves a systematic analysis of ECtHR judgments that refer to the EU data protection standards under scrutiny – (i) EU legislation giving expression to the data protection fundamental right,[28] (ii) the Charter[29] and (iii) related CJEU case-law[30] – using the Hudoc database.[31] We found 45 cases for legislative instruments, 19 cases for the Charter and 26 cases for related CJEU case-law. The cumulative cases led to a total of 46 cases for EU data protection law.[32]

To provide comparative insights, we examined ECtHR judgments that refer to international instruments and related bodies.[33] Compared to the field of equality, there are fewer specific international binding instruments on data

26 See Separate opinion of Judge Pinto de Albuquerque in *Big Brother Watch and Others v. the United Kingdom* [GC], nos. 58170/13 and 2 others, § 59, 25 May 2021.

27 See above Part III (case study on equality), Chapter 1, Section III. Methodology.

28 For legislative instruments, we use the specific identifier of the instrument (e.g., '95/46/EC'), which was the indicator that yielded the most results.

29 We selected the cases where the Charter was used in the data protection reasoning of the ECtHR.

30 We use the terms 'Court of Justice of the European Union', 'Court of Justice of the European Communities', and 'European Court of Justice'. We selected cases where the CJEU interpreted EU legislation giving expression to data protection rights or the Charter's data protection right.

31 We examine judgments from both the Grand Chamber and Chambers of the ECtHR in English, considering cases up until 1 April 2024. For all our categories, we use the Hudoc keyword 'data protection' to limit our research to ECtHR case-law on data protection.

32 We added the cases where there are references to EU legislation, the Charter, or CJEU case-law, withdrawing duplicate cases.

33 We examined judgments from both the Grand Chamber and Chambers of the ECtHR in English, using the HUDOC keyword 'data protection'.

protection. We selected the Convention 108 instruments: Convention 108 itself (38 cases), Additional Protocol to the Convention (6 cases), and Convention 108+ (4 cases). We included one general international instrument, the ICCPR (6 cases),[34] and one non-binding instrument, the 1980 Organisation for Economic Co-operation and Development (OECD) Privacy Guidelines (2 cases), which, as we will observe below, has played a notable role in the development of data protection. We examined references to the outputs of the bodies related to the international instruments, specifically including outputs from the Consultative Committee on Convention 108 (1 case) and the UN Human Rights Committee (related to the ICCPR) (3 cases).[35] We looked at the references to the African Convention on Human and Peoples' Rights and the Inter-American Convention on Human Rights and their related bodies, but this yielded only one result.[36]

A literature review was conducted, focusing on five main themes: EU data protection law,[37] ECHR data protection law,[38] comparative EU/ECHR data

[34] We selected cases where this instrument was used in the data protection reasoning of the ECtHR or where the ECtHR used ICCPR provisions related to data protection.

[35] We selected the cases where their decisions were related to data protection or where their decisions influenced the data protection reasoning of the ECtHR.

[36] ECtHR, *S. and Marper v. the United Kingdom* [GC], nos. 30562/04 and 30566/04, §§ 60–63, ECHR 2008.

[37] R. Tinière and C. Vial, *Manuel de droit de l'Union européenne des droits fondamentaux*, Brussels, Larcier, 2023, pp. 13–31; O. Lynskey, 'Article 8: The Right to Data Protection', in M. Bobek and J. Adams-Prassl (ed), *The EU Charter of Fundamental Rights in the Member States*, Oxford, Hart Publishing, 2020, pp. 353–370; O. Lynskey, Extraterritorial Impact in Data Protection Law through an EU Law Lens, *Brexit Institute Working Paper Series - No 8/2020*; R. Tinière, 'Article 8. Protection des données à caractère personnel', in F. Picod, C. Rizcallah and S. Van Drooghenbroeck (eds.), *Charte des droits fondamentaux de l'Union européenne. Commentaire article par article*, 2nd ed., Brussels, Larcier, 2020 ; F. Hendrickx, 'Article 8 - Protection of Personal Data', in F. Dorssemont, K. Lörcher, S. Clauwaert and M. Schmitt (eds.), *The Charter of Fundamental Rights of the European Union and the Employment Relation*, Oxford, Hart Publishing, Oxford, 2019, pp. 249–272; Y. McDermott, 'Conceptualising the right to data protection in an era of Big Data', *Big Data & Society*, 2017; O. Lynskey, *The foundations of EU data protection law*, Oxford, Oxford University Press, 2015; G. Gonzalez Fuster, *The Emergence of Personal Data Protection as a Fundamental Right of the EU*, Springer, 2014; H. Kranenborg, 'Article 8', in S. Peers, T. Hervey, J. Kenner and A. Ward (eds.), *The EU Charter of Fundamental Rights. A Commentary*, Oxford, Hart Publishing, 2014, pp. 228–265; O. Lynskey, 'Deconstructing data protection: the 'added-value' of a right to data protection in the EU legal order, *International and Comparative Law Quarterly*, 2013, pp. 569–597; G. González Fuster and S. Gutwirth, 'Opening up personal data protection: A conceptual controversy', *The Computer Law and Security Report*, 2013, pp. 531–539; G. Gonzalez Fuster and R. Gellert, 'The Fundamental Right of Data Protection in the European Union: In Search of an Uncharted Right', *International Review of Law, Computers & Technology*, 2012, pp. 73–82.

[38] J. Walter, 'La Convention 108, un complément nécessaire à l'article 8 de la CEDH à l'heure du numérique' *Civitas Europa*, 2023, pp. 251–261; S. Turgis, 'La Convention européenne des droits de l'homme et la protection des droits et libertés à l'ère du numérique', *Civitas Europa*, 2023, p. 263; E. Psychogiopoulou, 'The European Court of Human Rights,

protection law,[39] data protection law theory,[40] and influence of EU law on the ECHR.[41] As for our equality case study, the research methodology encompasses a systemic case-law analysis, supplemented by a statistical analysis to explore various aspects of influence that were more suited for this type of analysis (such as the areas of influence and the evolution of influence). We should stress that the quantitative analysis is meant to serve the qualitative analysis of the judgments.

SECTION IV. LIMITS

A small disclaimer before getting into the substance: our focus is on the influence of EU legislation that gives expression to the fundamental right to

Privacy and Data Protection in the Digital Era', in E. Psychogiopoulou and S. de la Sierra (eds.), *Courts, Privacy and Data Protection in the Digital Environment*, Cheltenham, Edward Elgar Publishing, 2017, pp. 32–62; G. Nardell, 'Levelling up: Data Privacy and the European Court of Human Rights', in S. Gutwirth, Y. Poullet and P. De Hert (eds.), *Data Protection in a Profiled World*, Dordrecht, Springer, 2010, pp. 43–52; T. Moonen, 'Special Investigation Techniques, Data Processing and Privacy Protection in the Jurisprudence of the European Court of Human Rights', *Pace International Law Review Online Companion*, 2010, pp. 97–136.

39 M.-L. Deftou, *Exporting the European Convention on Human Rights*, Oxford, Hart Publishing, 2022, pp. 20–29; V. Mitsilegas et al., 'Data retention and the future of large-scale surveillance: The evolution and contestation of judicial benchmarks', *European Law Journal*, 2022, pp. 1–36; E. Psychogiopoulou, 'Judicial Dialogue and Digitalization: CJEU Engagement with ECtHR Case-law and Fundamental Rights Standards in the EU', *JIPITEC*, 2022, pp. 145–159; E. Psychogiopoulou and S. de la Sierra (eds.), *Digital Media Governance and Supranational Courts: Selected Issues and Insights from the European Judiciary*, Cheltenham, Edward Elgar Publishing, 2022; B. van der Sloot, 'Wij zijn twee vriendjes, jij en ik: De innige tango van de twee Europese hoven op het gebied van privacy en gegevensbescherming', *SEW*, 2021, pp. 582–594; S. O'Leary, 'Balancing Rights in a Digital age', *Irish Jurist*, 2018, pp. 59–92; J. Kokott and C. Sobotta, 'The distinction between privacy and data protection in the jurisprudence of the CJEU and the ECtHR', *International Data Privacy Law*, 2013, pp. 222–228; P. de Hert and S. Gutwirth, 'Data Protection in the Case-law of Strasbourg and Luxemburg: Constitutionalisation in Action', in S. Gutwirth et al. (ed.), *Reinventing Data Protection*, Dordrecht, Springer, 2009, pp. 3–44.

40 R. Gellert and S. Gutwirth, 'The legal construction of privacy and data protection', *The Computer Law and Security Report*, 2013, pp. 522–530; S. Rodota, 'Data Protection as a Fundamental Right', in S. Gutwirth et al. (ed.), *Reinventing Data Protection*, Dordrecht, Springer, 2009, pp. 77–83.

41 P. Lemmens and M. Piret, 'The Charter of Fundamental Rights of the European Union and the European Convention on Human Rights, from the Perspective of the European Court of Human Rights', *Cahiers de droit européen*, 2021, pp. 183–210; S. O'Leary, 'The EU Charter Ten Years On: A View from Strasbourg', in M. Bobek and J. Adams-Prassl (eds.), *The EU Charter of Fundamental Rights in the Member States*, Oxford, Hart Publishing, 2020, pp. 37–68; T. Lock, 'The Influence of EU law on Strasbourg Doctrines', *Edinburgh School of Law Research Paper series*, 2017, pp. 1–29; B. Dickson, 'The EU Charter of Fundamental Rights in the Case-law of the European Court of Human Rights', *European Human Rights Law Review*, 2015, pp. 27–40.

data protection,[42] the Charter and related CJEU case-law. This implies that we do not investigate the influence of EU law on other instruments of the Council of Europe, such as Convention 108. This approach also means that we do not examine the influence of ECHR law on EU data protection law. We do not look at all ECtHR cases but focus specifically on its case-law related to data protection.

SECTION V. STRUCTURE

The EU and ECHR data protection frameworks are both well-established and highly developed, sharing common roots in Convention 108. Despite their strong proximity and overlap, these systems are driven by different rationales (Chapter 2). The existence of Convention 108 and the fact that each framework is highly developed, yet driven by distinct approaches, explains some of the dynamics of influence of EU data protection on ECtHR case-law (Chapter 3).

First, both EU data protection law and Convention 108 are the two primary external sources used by the ECtHR in its data protection cases. Second, the ECtHR has rarely drawn from EU data protection law to shape the key principles of its data protection case-law. Third, despite this, EU data protection law has been notably used in ECtHR judgments as informative material, as a source the ECtHR seeks to distinguish from ECHR law, as part of the assessment of the justification of States' interferences, and as a source relied upon by many actors prior to, before and within the ECtHR.

42 The identification of the legislation has been carried out in accordance with the criteria established in Part II (Chapter 2, Section II, §3, II. Identifying Legislation as Giving Expression to Fundamental Rights). The legislative instruments giving expression to data protection fundamental rights are identified in Annex IV.

CHAPTER 2

EU AND ECHR DATA PROTECTION LAWS: COMMON ROOTS FOR OVERLAPPING, YET DISTINCT SYSTEMS[1]

To understand the dynamics of influence of EU data protection law on ECtHR case-law, it is key to highlight that both the EU and ECHR systems are well-established and highly developed, partially originating from common roots in Convention 108. Despite their strong proximity and overlap, the systems are driven by different dynamics: the EU is guided by a data protection-focused approach, whereas the ECHR is guided by a privacy-centred approach. It is of note that, for the reader's convenience in reading this section, a table that summarises the comparison between EU and ECHR data protection laws is available in Annex V.

SECTION I. TWO WELL-ESTABLISHED AND HIGHLY DEVELOPED SYSTEMS WITH COMMON ROOTS

The EU and ECHR data protection systems have been strongly influenced by one instrument adopted by the Council of Europe in the early 1980s: Convention 108. Before discussing this instrument, which serves as the shared foundation of EU and ECHR data protection laws, let us recall how personal data came to be protected in Europe and show how the EU and ECHR systems emerged. Shedding light on the above is key to understanding why, in the field of data protection, both EU data protection law and Convention 108 are the two primary external sources used by the ECtHR. It is also useful to explain why the ECtHR rarely draws from EU data protection law to shape

[1] Some paragraphs in this section are inspired by or derived from V. Davio, 'Le droit fondamental à la protection des données personnelles : illustrations, principes et limites', in B. Docquir (ed.), *Le RGPD dans la pratique : un exercice d'équilibre*, Brussels, Larcier, 2021, pp. 9–40.

the principles of its data protection case-law. It finally highlights how EU law, being deeply integrated within domestic legal systems, differs from Convention 108, which may account for its differentiated use by the ECtHR.

§ 1. THE EMERGENCE OF DATA PROTECTION IN EUROPE

Starting in the early 1970s, various European countries began introducing legal instruments to regulate the processing of personal data. It was in Germany that personal data was first protected. The iconic starting point for data protection was the adoption of the Data Protection Act by the German federal state of Hesse in 1970.[2] In 1977, Germany became the first Member State of the European Communities to adopt specific legislation on data protection.[3] At constitutional level, the first European country to incorporate a specific provision on data processing into its constitutional standards was Portugal.[4]

The early 1980s witnessed the emergence of personal data protection in European and international texts. Three international organisations stood out: the OECD, the Council of Europe, and the EU. The OECD was one of the first organisations to respond to the growing concerns regarding data protection. It adopted guidelines governing the protection of privacy and cross-border flows of personal data in 1980 whose purpose is twofold. They aim to contribute to the safeguarding of human rights, particularly the protection of the right to privacy. In addition, they seek to prevent disruptions to international data flows by contributing to the harmonisation of national legislations regarding privacy protection.[5]

§ 2. THE EMERGENCE OF DATA PROTECTION AT EU AND ECHR LEVELS

At European supranational level, both the EU and the Council of Europe are distinguished by their early commitment to protecting against data abuses. The Council of Europe has played a significant role in developing the fundamental right to data protection through two channels: Convention 108 (which we will discuss below) and ECtHR case-law.

---

2 Hessisches Datenschutzgesetz, 7 October 1970. G. Gonzalez Fuster, *The Emergence of Personal Data Protection as a Fundamental Right of the EU*, Cham, Springer, 2014, p. 56.

3 Gesetz zum Schutz vor mißbrauch personenbezogener Daten bei der Datenverarbeitung, 27 January 1977; G. Gonzalez Fuster, ibid., pp. 59–60.

4 Article 35 of the Portuguese Constitution of 2 April 1976.

5 OECD Guidelines on the Protection of Privacy and Transborder Flows of Personal Data, 23 September 1980, §§ 2–3 of the preambles of the OECD Guidelines.

The ECtHR has early on developed significant case-law on data protection, establishing clear and well-defined principles in this area. Although the ECHR does not enshrine a fundamental right to data protection, the ECtHR has opposed unjustified interferences with personal data since the late 1980s under Article 8 ECHR (right to private life). Its expansive interpretation of private life led the ECtHR to assert that Article 8 ECHR encompasses 'the right to a form of informational self-determination, allowing individuals to rely on their right to privacy as regards data which, albeit neutral, are collected, processed and disseminated collectively and in such a form or manner that their Article 8 rights may be engaged'.[6]

As underscored by the former President of the ECtHR, Siofra O'Leary, the Strasbourg Court 'has a long record of cases dealing with data protection and continues to develop it, thereby responding to technological progress, institutional developments and present-day conditions in digitalised societies which have to deal with organised and cybercrime and the threat of terrorism. As such, it has laid down standards for lawful and human-rights compatible surveillance practices which have in turn influenced, at least in part, the CJEU.'[7]

At EU level, data protection also emerged early on. The rationale was to ensure the free movement of data, which could be hindered by differing domestic laws on data protection. Already in a 1981 Commission Recommendation on the automatic processing of personal data, the Commission observed that:

> Divergent data protection law in the EC Member States creates disparate conditions for data processing. The establishment and functioning of the common market in data processing calls for extensive standardisation of the conditions obtaining in relation to data processing and, therefore, to data protection at European level. Approximation of data protection is desirable so that there can be free movement of data and information across frontiers and in order to prevent unequal conditions of competition and the consequent distortion of competition in the common market.[8]

This dynamic led to the adoption of the first data protection legislative instruments by the EU from the mid-1990s. They aimed not only at protecting personal data but also at preventing States from restricting the free flow of

---

6 ECtHR, *Satakunnan Markkinapörssi Oy and Satamedia Oy v. Finland* [GC], no. 931/13, § 137, 27 June 2017.

7 Ibid. See also G. Malgieri and P. De Hert, 'European Human Rights, Criminal Surveillance, and Intelligence Surveillance: Towards "Good Enough" Oversight, Preferably but Not Necessarily by Judges', *Brussels Privacy Hub Working Paper*, 2017, pp. 1–24.

8 Commission Recommendation of 29 July 1981 (81/679/EEC) relating to the Council of Europe Convention for the protection of individuals with regard to automatic processing of personal data.

personal data.[9] The EU also enshrined a distinct fundamental right to data protection in the Charter, as we will see.

§ 3. CONVENTION 108, AN INFLUENTIAL EUROPEAN MODEL

Both the ECHR and EU data protection systems have been significantly influenced by Convention 108, which was developed under the auspices of the Council of Europe. This instrument came into force on 1 October 1985 and has been ratified by all EU States. In contrast to the OECD guidelines and EU law which pursue a double economic and fundamental rights objective, Convention 108 has a single objective: the protection of data from the perspective of fundamental rights.[10] This instrument marked a pivotal milestone in the emergence of the fundamental right to data protection: its principles have served as the foundation for numerous national and European legislations.[11]

Convention 108's influence was pronounced in both ECHR and EU data protection laws. While we will delve into its impact on ECtHR case-law in detail later, let us already highlight that the ECtHR turned to Convention 108 early on as a source of inspiration in cases involving the processing of personal data.[12] In *Satakunnan v. Finland* [GC](2017), the ECtHR acknowledged its practice of referring to Convention 108: 'in the particular context of data protection, the Court has, *on a number of occasions*, referred to the Data Protection Convention, which itself underpins the Data Protection Directive applied by the domestic courts in the present case.'[13] The ECtHR has significantly drawn upon its key principles to develop its safeguards to avoid data abuses.[14] The significance of Convention 108 is notable to the extent that Hustinx noted

---

9 See below Part III (case study on data protection), Chapter 2, Section II, §1, I. Fundamental v. Economic.

10 See Article 1 of Convention 108 : 'The purpose of this Convention is to secure in the territory of each Party for every individual, whatever his nationality or residence, respect for his rights and fundamental freedoms, and in particular his right to privacy, with regard to automatic processing of personal data relating to him.'

11 G. Gonzalez Fuster, *The Emergence of Personal Data Protection as a Fundamental Right of the EU*, Cham, Springer, 2014, pp. 92–93.

12 J. Walter, 'La Convention 108, un complément nécessaire à l'article 8 de la CEDH à l'heure du numérique', *Civitas Europa*, 2023, p. 255 ; S. O'Leary, 'Balancing Rights in a Digital age', *Irish Jurist*, 2018, p. 66.

13 ECtHR, *Satakunnan Markkinapörssi Oy and Satamedia Oy v. Finland* [GC], no. 931/13, § 133, 27 June 2017. Emphasis added.

14 See below Part III (case study on data protection), Chapter 3, Section II, §5. Comparative Insights.

that, according to the ECtHR, Article 8 ECHR likely encompasses the duty to uphold the fundamental principles outlined in Convention 108.[15]

While Convention 108 has had a significant impact on ECtHR case-law, it has also played an influential role in shaping EU data protection law. The key concepts and principles found in EU legislative instruments originate from Convention 108 and are further developed in EU data protection law. As noted in the preamble of the Data Protection Directive (95/46/EC), the 'principles of the protection of the rights and freedoms of individuals, notably the right to privacy, which are contained in this Directive, give substance to and amplify those contained in the Council of Europe Convention of 28 January 1981 for the Protection of Individuals with regard to Automatic Processing of Personal Data.'[16] EU secondary laws are closely intertwined with Convention 108, with both exerting mutual influence.[17] This is exemplified by the recent efforts to modernise Convention 108,[18] where the draft explanatory report mentions that: 'With regard to the EU data protection reform package in particular, the works ran in parallel and utmost care was taken to ensure consistency between both legal frameworks. [...].'[19] Regarding the Charter, its Explanations point out that Convention 108 has inspired the autonomous fundamental right to data protection.[20]

While Convention 108 shares a distinctive proximity with EU law, it does not possess the same status for EU States. The Convention is not directly applicable: it is the responsibility of each State party to the Convention to enact measures to implement the fundamental principles for data protection enshrined in the Convention.[21] EU data protection law, which is more detailed than Convention 108, is deeply integrated within domestic legal systems: it enjoys primacy and direct effect and is applicable in both vertical and horizontal

15 P. de Hert and S. Gutwirth, 'Data Protection in the Case-law of Strasbourg and Luxemburg: Constitutionalisation in Action', in S. Gutwirth et al. (ed.), *Reinventing Data Protection*, Dordrecht, Springer, 2009, p. 27.

16 Recital 11.

17 See e.g. Recital 105 of the GDPR.

18 A modernised Convention 108 (known as Convention 108 +) has been adopted on 18 May 2018 by the Committee of Ministers (Protocol amending the Convention for the Protection of Individuals with regard to Automatic Processing of Personal Data (CETS No. 223)). It will enter into force once 38 Parties to Convention 108 have ratified the Protocol.

19 Article 4 of Convention 108.

20 See Explanations of the Charter of Fundamental Rights on Article 8 – Protection of personal data: 'This Article has been based on Article 286 of the Treaty establishing the European Community and Directive 95/46/EC of the European Parliament and of the Council on the protection of individuals with regard to the processing of personal data and on the free movement of such data ([1995] OJ L281/ 31) as well as on Article 8 of the ECHR and on the Council of Europe Convention of 28 January 1981 for the Protection of Individuals with regard to Automatic Processing of Personal Data, which has been ratified by all the Member States.'

21 Article 4 Convention 108.

settings. This may explain some of the dynamics of influence, such as why the ECtHR relies heavily on EU data protection law in an informative way or as part of the justification of interferences. EU data protection forms part of the background in cases involving EU States, as we will explain.

SECTION II. TWO OVERLAPPING YET DISTINCT SYSTEMS PROPELLED BY THEIR OWN DYNAMICS

The above shows that Convention 108 has played a significant role in shaping EU and ECHR data protection laws, which explain the proximity of these two systems. If the two systems overlap, they are driven by different dynamics. The main difference relates to the rationales of each system: the EU is guided by a data protection approach with a dual focus on fundamental rights and economic objectives, whereas the ECHR is guided by a privacy-centred approach with an exclusive focus on fundamental rights. These divergent rationales explain some of the differences in the scope and content of both systems. As observed in the context of the equality case study, another difference is that the EU is a 'rule-based' system, whereas the ECHR is a 'principle-based' system.

§ 1. RATIONALE

The EU and ECHR data protection systems are propelled by distinct rationales. While the EU system is driven by a focus on data protection, the ECHR system places an emphasis on privacy. This distinction influences how these two systems safeguard personal data. In addition, they diverge in the sense that the EU system encompasses not only a fundamental rights objective but also an economic one.

I. Fundamental v. Economic

EU data protection law has been characterised by a dual objective since its inception. Article 1 of the Data Protection Directive (95/46/EC) outlined these objectives: firstly, to safeguard the fundamental rights and freedoms of natural persons, especially their right to privacy, and secondly, to facilitate the free flow of personal data between EU States without unjustified restrictions linked to the protection of fundamental rights. The fundamental rights and economic aims are interconnected EU data protection legislation serves to standardise national laws, thereby ensuring a consistent level of rights protection across all

EU States. This harmonisation, in turn, eliminates objections to cross-border data transfers on the grounds of fundamental rights.[22]

In the past, the CJEU tended to prioritise market integration over fundamental rights.[23] However, there has been a shift, with these objectives now being treated as equally important.[24] This evolution has been attributed to the entry into force of the Treaty of Lisbon, which introduced a comprehensive legal basis for data protection and made the Charter legally binding.[25] This transformation is evident in the CJEU's approach, which has considered that measures, whether adopted at national or European level, breach the autonomous right to data protection enshrined in the Charter.[26]

ECHR data protection law is guided by a fundamental rights rationale. The ECHR does not encompass an economic rationale but seeks to protect individuals against abuses in the processing of their personal data. While EU data protection law aims to harmonise national laws to facilitate cross-border data flows, ECHR data protection is focused on protecting the right to privacy of individuals. This explains that the ECHR legal regime does not seek, per se, to harmonise national laws on data protection. Instead, it allows leeway for national authorities through the margin of appreciation.[27] The question is whether, through the influence of EU data protection law, the ECtHR integrates an economic rationale within ECHR law – the answer appears to be no, as we will see below.

II. Data Protection v. Privacy

Perhaps the most important distinction between EU and ECHR data protection laws relates to their core rationale: data protection versus privacy. Distinguishing between these two concepts has posed significant challenges, both within

---

22 O. Lynskey, *The foundations of EU data protection law*, Oxford, Oxford University Press, 2015, p. 47.

23 Ibid., pp. 57–58. See also P. de Hert and S. Gutwirth, 'Data Protection in the Case-law of Strasbourg and Luxembourg: Constitutionalisation in Action', in S. Gutwirth et al. (ed.), *Reinventing Data Protection*, Cham, Springer, 2009, p. 8.

24 Ibid., p. 62.

25 Ibid.

26 For instance, in the *Volker and Eifert* (2009) case, which was issued one year after the Charter became binding, German farmers contested the publication of their personal data on the website of the Federal Office for Agriculture and Food. The CJEU, in the context of a preliminary ruling on the validity of this publication requirement in light of fundamental rights, found that while transparency in fund use is a legitimate public interest, the obligation to publish personal data of all recipients without relevant distinctions was disproportionately infringing on their right to privacy and data protection, as guaranteed by Articles 7 and 8 Charter, see Joined Cases C-92/09 and C-93/09, *Volker and Eifert*, ECLI:EU:C:2010:662, para. 80.

27 See below Part III (case study on data protection), Chapter 2, Section II, §4, I. Substantive Elements.

the case-law of the two European Courts and scholarly discourse.[28] There is a considerable degree of overlap between them which makes it difficult to draw a clear line.[29] Both share the common purpose of enabling individuals to exercise their rights in democratic societies without fear of repercussions.[30] Lynskey has shown that there are three main conceptions of the relationship between data protection and privacy: (i) data protection and privacy are distinct yet complementary rights; (ii) data protection is a subset of the right to privacy; (iii) data protection is an independent right serving multiple functions, including, but not limited to, the safeguarding of privacy.[31]

It is the third model that seems to be prevalent in the EU. According to this model, 'data protection overlaps considerably with the right to privacy, as they both ensure informational or data privacy, but data protection serves a number of purposes that privacy does not and vice versa.'[32] At EU level, data protection is an autonomous fundamental right enshrined in the Charter. Looking back in time, no political explanations were provided for its introduction as a distinct right.[33] This lack of clarity left the CJEU grappling with the relationship between data protection and privacy for an extended period, during which it often merged the two rights.[34] In recent times, the CJEU has demonstrated a greater inclination to emphasise the autonomy of the right to personal data

---

28 E.g. G. González and S. Gutwirth, 'Opening up personal data protection: A conceptual controversy', *The Computer Law and Security Report*, 2013, pp. 531–539; O. Lynskey, 'Deconstructing data protection: the 'added-value' of a right to data protection in the EU legal order, *International and Comparative Law Quarterly*, 2013, pp. 569–597; R. Gellert and S. Gutwirth, 'The legal construction of privacy and data protection. The Computer Law and Security Report', 2013, pp. 522–530; S. Rodota, 'Data Protection as a Fundamental Right', in S. Gutwirth et al. (ed.), *Reinventing Data Protection, Springer*, 2009, pp. 77–83.

29 O. Lynskey, 'Deconstructing data protection: the 'added-value' of a right to data protection in the EU legal order', *International and Comparative Law Quarterly*, 2013, p. 587.

30 Ibid.

31 O. Lynskey, *The foundations of EU data protection law*, Oxford, Oxford University Press, 2015, pp. 94, 101 and 103.

32 Ibid., p. 103.

33 Ibid., p. 93.

34 O. Lynskey, 'Deconstructing data protection: the 'added-value' of a right to data protection in the EU legal order, *International and Comparative Law Quarterly*, 2013, p. 574. The difficulty in clearly distinguishing these two rights is reflected in the case-law of the CJEU. As an illustration, in the *Österreichischer* judgment of 20 May 2003 (Cases C-465/00, C-138/01, and C-139/01, ECLI:EU:C:2003:294), the CJEU had to rule on the validity of national regulation in light of the right to privacy and the Data Protection Directive (95/46/EC). In its decision, the CJEU considered that, to the extent that the national regulation was not compatible with this fundamental right, it could de facto not meet the requirements of Directive 95/46/EC. However, as noted by Kranenborg, the CJEU did not specify the applicable solution if it had reached the opposite conclusion, namely if Article 8 of the ECHR had been respected (H. Kranenborg, 'Article 8', in S. Peers, T. Hervey, J. Kenner and A. Ward (eds.), *The EU Charter of Fundamental Rights. A Commentary*, Oxford, Hart Publishing, 2014, p. 230).

protection, albeit acknowledging its close connection to the right of privacy.[35] This approach aligns with the views of numerous scholars who advocate for the recognition of data protection as an independent right.[36] The data protection rationale has implications for the scope and content of personal data protection within the EU legal system. Personal data is considered as such regardless of its direct link to an individual's privacy. Additionally, the EU legal system safeguards certain rights that aim not solely to protect individuals' privacy but to grant individuals greater control over their data, as exemplified by the right to data portability.[37]

The protection of personal data is not a distinct, standalone right within the array of rights encompassed by the ECHR. Article 8 is the principal avenue through which personal data finds protection within the Convention system, even though considerations related to this protection may arise under other provisions of the ECHR and its Protocols.[38] Data protection is often treated as a subset to the right to privacy.[39] In this vein, the ECtHR has observed that: 'The protection of personal data is of fundamental importance to a person's enjoyment of his or her right to respect for private and family life, as guaranteed by Article 8 of the Convention.'[40] While it would go beyond the scope of this

35 R. Tinière, 'Article 8. Protection des données à caractère personnel', in F. Picod, C. Rizcallah and S. Van Drooghenbroeck (eds.), *Charte des droits fondamentaux de l'Union européenne. Commentaire article par article*, 2nd ed., Brussels, Larcier, 2020, p. 228; Cases C-92/09 and C-93/09, *Volker and Eifert*, ECLI:EU:C:2010:662, para. 47: 'In this regard, Article 8(1) of the Charter states that '[e]veryone has the right to the protection of personal data concerning him or her'. That fundamental right is closely connected with the right to respect of private life expressed in Article 7 of the Charter.'

36 E.g. Y. McDermott, 'Conceptualising the right to data protection in an ea of Big Data', *Big Data & Society*, 2017, p. 2; O. Lynskey, 'Deconstructing data protection: the 'added-value' of a right to data protection in the EU legal order, *International and Comparative Law Quarterly*, 2013, p. 588; G. Gonzalez Fuster and R. Gellert, 'The Fundamental Right of Data Protection in the European Union: In Search of an Uncharted Right', *International Review of Law, Computers & Technology*, 2012, p. 78; P. de Hert and S. Gutwirth, 'Data Protection in the Case-law of Strasbourg and Luxemburg: Constitutionalisation in Action', in S. Gutwirth et al. (ed.), *Reinventing Data Protection*, Dordrecht, Springer, 2009, p. 12; S. Rodota, 'Data Protection as a Fundamental Right', in S. Gutwirth et al. (ed.), *Reinventing Data Protection*, Dordrecht, Springer, 2009, pp. 79-80; P. de Hert and S. Gutwirth, 'Data Protection in the Case-law of Strasbourg and Luxemburg: Constitutionalisation in Action', in S. Gutwirth et al. (ed.), *Reinventing Data Protection*, Dordrecht, Springer, 2009, p. 10. Ibid., pp. 2–3.

37 O. Lynskey, ibid., p. 591.

38 See the Guide to the Case-law of the of the European Court of Human Rights on Data Protection, prepared by the Registry and updated on 28 February 2023, available here: https://ks.echr.coe.int/documents/d/echr-ks/guide_data_protection_eng, p. 7.

39 E. Psychogiopoulou, 'The European Court of Human Rights, Privacy and Data Protection in the Digital Era', in E. Psychogiopoulou and S. de la Sierra (eds.), *Courts, Privacy and Data Protection in the Digital Environment*, 2017, p. 33

40 E.g. ECtHR, *Satakunnan Markkinapörssi Oy and Satamedia Oy v. Finland* [GC], no. 931/13, § 137, 27 June 2017.

project to delve into the right to privacy,[41] the protection of personal data under Article 8 of the ECHR influences both the scope and substance of this safeguard. We will see that the privacy-focus of the ECHR system has not changed under the influence of EU data protection law.

§ 2. RULE-BASED V. PRINCIPLED-BASED

While an autonomous EU data protection right exists, it is fleshed out in legislative instruments, which play a pivotal role in determining case outcomes. In this sense, the EU's data protection regime can be characterised as 'rule-based'. Data protection under ECHR law does not rely on detailed rules, at least at the level of the Convention's text. When the ECtHR assesses potential violations of the Convention, its approach is more 'principle-based', drawing on broad principles of lawfulness, legitimacy, and proportionality. Yet, the ECtHR has developed data protection safeguards under these criteria.

I. EU Data Protection Law as a Rule-Based System

The autonomous fundamental right to data protection did not emerge within a legal vacuum at EU level. Since the mid-1990s, the EU has established a range of instruments aimed at data protection. The Data Protection Directive (95/46/EC) was the primary legal framework for many years.[42] Subsequently, Directive (2002/58/EC) on privacy and electronic communications complemented the Data Protection Directive (95/46/EC), primarily by harmonising EU States' legislation concerning the right to privacy in electronic communications.[43] Three additional instruments were adopted in the early 2000s.[44] One decade ago, the EU's legislative framework for data protection underwent a substantial

[41] Regarding the right of privacy in the case-law of the ECtHR, see e.g. the Guide to the Case-law of the of the European Court of Human Rights on the right to private life, prepared by the Registry and updated on 9 April 2024, available here: https://ks.echr.coe.int/documents/d/echr-ks/guide_art_8_eng.

[42] It was adopted on the basis of the general harmonization clause of the internal market, the current Article 114 TFEU. It pursued a dual objective. On the one hand, it aimed to protect the fundamental freedoms and rights of natural persons regarding the processing of personal data. On the other hand, it sought to prevent Member States from restricting the free movement of personal data between Member States, ensuring that they could not adopt more protective measures for the protection of personal data (Article 1).

[43] Directive 2002/58/EC of the European Parliament and of the Council of 12 July 2002 concerning the processing of personal data and the protection of privacy in the electronic communications sector (hereafter: 'Directive (2002/58/EC) on privacy and electronic communications').

[44] First, the Data Retention Directive (2006/24/EC), which was later repealed following its annulment by the CJEU in the *Digital Rights Ireland* [GC](2014) case. Second, Regulation (45/2001/EC) concerning the protection of individuals with regard to the processing of

overhaul. In 2016, the EU adopted the GDPR alongside Directive (2016/680/EU) in the field of criminal matters.[45] Lastly, the EU adopted Regulation (2018/1725/EU) on personal data protection by EU institutions.[46] This new wave of instruments has been hailed as a 'Copernican revolution' in the realm of data protection, marking significant advancements towards the empowerment of individuals in data protection.[47]

The legislative instruments maintain a special relationship with the Charter's fundamental right to data protection. As revealed by the Charter's explanations, legislative instruments have been a major source of inspiration for the autonomous right to data protection.[48] To some extent, they embody certain aspects of Charter's right to data protection by regulating in detail how it should be understood and balanced with other interests.[49] The CJEU has acknowledged the specific link between Article 8 Charter and data protection legislation.[50] Generally, the CJEU assesses the compliance of national rules with data protection through the prism of legislative instruments. In other

---

personal data by Community institutions and bodies and on the free movement of such data. Third, Council Framework Decision (2008/977/JHA) on the protection of personal data processed in the context of police and judicial cooperation in criminal matters.

45 Directive 2016/680/EU of the European Parliament and of the Council of 27 April 2016 on the protection of natural persons with regard to the processing of personal data by competent authorities for the purposes of the prevention, investigation, detection or prosecution of criminal offences or the execution of criminal penalties, and on the free movement of such data, and repealing Council Framework Decision 2008/977/JHA (hereafter: 'Directive (2016/680/EU) in the field of criminal matters').

46 Regulation 2018/1725/EU of the European Parliament and of the Council of 23 October 2018 on the protection of natural persons with regard to the processing of personal data by the Union institutions, bodies, offices and agencies and on the free movement of such data, and repealing Regulation (EC) No 45/2001 and Decision No 1247/2002/EC (hereafter: 'Regulation (2018/1725/EU) on personal data protection by EU institutions').

47 C. Kuner, 'The European Commission's Proposed Data Protection Regulation: A Copernican Revolution in European Data Protection Law', *Bloomberg BNA Privacy and Security Law Report*, 2012, pp. 1–15.

48 See Explanations of the Charter of Fundamental Rights on Article 8 - Protection of personal data: 'This Article has been based on Article 286 of the Treaty establishing the European Community and Directive 95/46/EC of the European Parliament and of the Council on the protection of individuals with regard to the processing of personal data and on the free movement of such data ([1995] OJ L281/31) as well as on Article 8 of the ECHR and on the Council of Europe Convention of 28 January 1981 for the Protection of Individuals with regard to Automatic Processing of Personal Data, which has been ratified by all the Member States.'

49 An example that comes to mind is Article 17 GDPR, which governs the right to be forgotten in detail.

50 Case C-131/12, *Google Spain*, ECLI:EU:C:2014:317, para. 69. In its judgment *Google Spain* of 13 May 2014, the CJEU affirmed that: 'Article 7 of the Charter guarantees the right to respect for private life, whilst Article 8 of the Charter expressly proclaims the right to the protection of personal data. Article 8(2) and (3) specify that such data must be processed fairly for specified purposes and on the basis of the consent of the person concerned or some other legitimate basis laid down by law, that everyone has the right of access to data which have been collected concerning him or her and the right to have the data rectified,

words, the legislative framework serves as a 'lex specialis' when evaluating national laws.[51]

II. ECHR Data Protection Law as a Principle-Based System

The protection of personal data, as – most often – safeguarded under the right to privacy, is not governed by specific, detailed provisions at least if one looks at the text of the Convention. Article 8 is couched in an open-textured manner. Its first paragraph provides that everyone has the right to respect for their private and family life, their home, and their correspondence. Its second paragraph provides that there shall be no *interference* by a public authority with the exercise of this right except as is *in accordance with the law* and is *necessary* in a democratic society for reasons of national security, public safety, the economic well-being of the country, the prevention of disorder or crime, the protection of health or morals, or the protection of the rights and freedoms of others.

Due to the open-ended nature of Article 8 ECHR, the ECtHR enjoys a significant degree of flexibility in shaping the overarching principles of legitimacy, lawfulness, and proportionality. This adaptability distinguishes the ECtHR from the CJEU, which interprets specific rules laid down in EU legislative instruments. Under the lawfulness and necessity criteria, the ECtHR has developed specific data protection safeguards. Convention 108, rather than EU law, has played an influential role in the development of these safeguards, as we will see below.

§ 3. SCOPE

The material scope and horizontal applicability of ECHR and EU data protection regimes differ significantly. In both regards, EU law provides a wider scope of protection for personal data. This is partly due to the EU framework not being solely centred on privacy.

---

and that compliance with these rules is to be subject to control by an independent authority. *Those requirements are implemented inter alia by Articles 6, 7, 12, 14 and 28 of Directive 95/46.*' Emphasis added.

51 See e.g. Case C-507/17, *Google*, ECLI:EU:C:2019:772, para. 45 and following where the CJEU has used the provisions of the 1995 Data Protection Directive (95/46/EC) and the GDPR (2016/679/EU) as the normative reference in its reasoning instead of Article 8 Charter.

I. *Material Scope*

If both EU and ECHR laws have extensive coverage, EU law offers a broader scope in terms of the types of data and the actions related to data that it protects.[52] This is because the EU framework is not solely driven by privacy considerations. The scope of EU law is very extensive as is evidenced by the concepts of 'personal data' and 'processing of personal data' which are key to assess whether the EU data protection framework is applicable. Personal data is defined as 'any information relating to an identified or identifiable natural person'.[53] This concept was intentionally defined to encompass any data that could be linked to an individual.[54] The material scope of personal data protection applies regardless of the technology used and is not contingent on whether the personal data are sensitive or non-sensitive private or public.[55] The CJEU has provided a broad interpretation of personal data.[56] Processing of personal data is defined as 'any operation or set of operations which is performed on personal data or on sets of personal data, whether or not by automated means.'[57] Lynskey has noted that it is challenging to conceive of any operation in electronic commerce involving personal data that would not fall under this definition.[58] While EU secondary legislation foresees exceptions to the application of EU data protection law, the CJEU has interpreted them narrowly.[59]

The material scope of data protection in ECHR law has a strong connection with the provision under which data are most often protected, Article 8 ECHR. Whereas EU data protection applies whenever personal data undergo processing, privacy comes into play when the ECtHR deems that the processing

---

52 O. Lynskey, *The foundations of EU data protection law*, Oxford, Oxford University Press, 2015, p. 582.

53 Article 4(1) GDPR.

54 H. Kranenborg, 'Article 8', in S. Peers, T. Hervey, J. Kenner and A. Ward (eds.), *The EU Charter of Fundamental Rights. A Commentary*, Oxford, Hart Publishing, 2014, p. 243.

55 Ibid.

56 For instance, in the *Breyer* case of 19 October 2016, the CJEU held that a dynamic IP address recorded by an online media services provider during a website visit could be considered personal data if the provider had legal means to identify the individual using additional information held by the internet service provider (Case C-582/14 *Breyer*, 19 October 2016, ECLI:EU:C:2016:779, para. 49). Even though dynamic IP addresses, unlike static ones, do not allow immediate user identification, the CJEU ruled that their combination with supplementary information justified classifying them as personal data, emphasising that all identifying information need not be held by a single entity (ibid. para. 43).

57 Article 4(2) GDPR.

58 O. Lynskey, 'Deconstructing data protection: the "added-value" of a right to data protection in the EU legal order', *International and Comparative Law Quarterly*, 2013, p. 587.

59 P. de Hert and S. Gutwirth, 'Data Protection in the Case-law of Strasbourg and Luxemburg: Constitutionalisation in Action', in S. Gutwirth et al. (ed.), *Reinventing Data Protection*, Dordrecht, Springer, 2009, p. 30.

activity infringes upon an individual's right to privacy.[60] The ECtHR has, however, provided a broad interpretation of the right to private life, relying at times on the definition of personal data under Convention 108.[61] This broad interpretation has led to many situations falling with the scope of Article 8 ECHR, such as the processing of publicly available data[62] or data processing within a professional context.[63]

The ECtHR does not only examine the nature of the data, determining whether it qualifies as personal data, but consider other elements. The ECtHR takes into account whether the data is systematically stored, delving into the depth of the processing activities[64] or whether the applicant had any expectations concerning their private life.[65] In other words, the processing of personal data does not trigger the application of Article 8 ECHR, as would in principle be the case in EU law. We will see that the privacy-focused scope of ECHR data protection law has not changed under the influence of EU law.

II. Horizontal Applicability

The right to data protection under EU law is primarily intended to protect natural persons. The GDPR, for example, states that it applies only to natural persons.[66] However, the question remains open as to whether legal entities, not just natural persons, can exercise the right to data protection through Article 8 Charter.[67] This right applies to both public and private actors. EU law has a specific feature of horizontal applicability in that it can be invoked by private parties against other private parties.[68] The extent to which individuals

60 R. Gellert and S. Gutwirth, 'The legal construction of privacy and data protection', *The Computer Law and Security Report*, 2013, p. 526.

61 E.g. ECtHR, *Amann v. Switzerland* [GC], no. 27798/95, § 65, ECHR 2000-II.

62 ECtHR, *Satakunnan Markkinapörssi Oy and Satamedia Oy v. Finland* [GC], no. 931/13, § 134, 27 June 2017.

63 E. Psychogiopoulou, 'The European Court of Human Rights, Privacy and Data Protection in the Digital Era', in E. Psychogiopoulou and S. de la Sierra (eds.), *Courts, Privacy and Data Protection in the Digital Environment*, Cheltenham, Edward Elgar Publishing, 2017, p. 51.

64 ECtHR, *Uzun v. Germany*, no. 35623/05, § 51, ECHR 2010.

65 ECtHR, *Benedik v. Slovenia*, no. 62357/14, §§ 115–118, 24 April 2018.

66 Article 4(2) GDPR.

67 F. Hendrickx, 'Article 8 - Protection of Personal Data.', in F. Dorssemont, K. Lörcher, S. Clauwaert and M. Schmitt (eds.), *The Charter of Fundamental Rights of the European Union and the Employment Relation*, Oxford, Hart Publishing, 2019, p. 258.

68 See in this vein, Y. McDermott, 'Conceptualising the right to data protection in an era of Big Data', *Big Data & Society*, 2017, p. 2: 'Indeed, the framing of data protection as a right appears to have imposed much greater obligations on private actors than most other human rights - it is difficult, for example, to think of another human right that product designers must take into account when developing new products, as is required under the GDPR.'

can rely on data protection rules depends on specific provisions and whether they meet the conditions for direct effect.[69]

Article 8 ECHR can only be invoked against public bodies.[70] Yet, it can still be used in disputes between private parties via the doctrine of positive obligations. These positive obligations, with their roots dating back to the landmark *Marckx v. Belgium* (1979),[71] compel national authorities to take 'reasonable and adequate measures to protect the rights of individuals'.[72] While negative obligations require states to refrain from interference, positive obligations call for active measures by the States.[73] We will see that the personal scope of ECHR law has not changed under the influence of EU data protection law.

§ 4. CONTENT

When it comes to the substantive and procedural elements, notable differences exist between the two data protection regimes. While the substantive components of the two systems exhibit similarities, a strong divergence lies in the procedural aspects. The substantive components show that both systems are highly developed, and the procedural components shed light on one of the specificities of EU data protection law, namely its high degree of proceduralisation.

I. *Substantive Elements*

Article 8 Charter elaborates on the substance of the right to data protection. It provides that data must be processed fairly for specified purposes and on the basis of the consent of the person concerned or some other legitimate basis laid down by law. It grants to everyone the right of access to data which has been collected concerning him or her, and the right to have it rectified These rights and principles are largely fleshed out in EU secondary legislation.

The legislative instruments are highly sophisticated and often give flesh to the principles enshrined in Convention 108. First, they identify the situations in which data processing is considered lawful. For example processing is lawful when the data subject has given consent, when processing is necessary to fulfil

---

69 O. Lynskey, *The foundations of EU data protection law*, Oxford, Oxford University Press, 2015, pp. 119 and following.

70 Articles 33 and 34 ECHR.

71 ECtHR, *Marckx v. Belgium*, 13 June 1979, § 31, Series A no. 31.

72 ECtHR, *López Ostra v. Spain*, 9 December 1994, § 51, Series A no. 303-C.

73 ECtHR, *X and Y v. the Netherlands*, 26 March 1985, § 23, Series A no. 91; J. Kokott and C. Sobotta, 'The distinction between privacy and data protection in the jurisprudence of the CJEU and the ECtHR', *International Data Privacy Law*, 2013, p. 226.

a legal obligation, or when it is required for the performance of a task carried out in the public interest or in the exercise of official authority vested in the controller.[74] Second, they provide a series of principles, forming the backbone of data protection law.[75] These principles encompass lawfulness, fairness, and transparency; purpose limitation; data minimisation; accuracy; storage limitation; and integrity and confidentiality.[76] Third, they include provisions for sensitive data, which generally cannot be processed.[77] Fourth, they grant specific rights to individuals, such as the right to be informed, the right to access their data, the right to rectify and erase data, the right to data portability, and protection against automated decision-making.[78]

The test for evaluating the legality of an interference in light of Article 8 ECHR is three-fold. First, the interference must be 'in accordance with the law'. This implies that the interference must have a basis in domestic legislation and that the law is accessible and foreseeable for individuals.[79] Second, the interference must serve a legitimate purpose, as outlined in Article 8(2) ECHR. These purposes include national security, public safety, the economic well-being of the country, prevention of disorder or crime, protection of health or morals, and the protection of the rights and freedoms of others. Third, the interference must be necessary in a democratic society. This means there should be a careful balance of interests, and the restriction should be essential for the functioning of a democratic society.[80] National authorities are also granted a margin of appreciation, the extent of which depends on various factors.[81] The ECtHR has developed specific principles tailored to the data protection context. The ECtHR has developed specific safeguards in the context of mass and secret surveillance under the lawfulness criterion. It has also developed a set of adequate safeguards that States must respect in the context of the use of personal data under the necessity criterion. These safeguards overlap to a large extent with some of the principles enshrined in EU law. However, it is not under the influence of EU law that they were developed in ECHR law, but under the influence of Convention 108, as we will see.

---

74 Article 6 GDPR.

75 O. Lynskey, *The foundations of EU data protection law*, Oxford, Oxford University Press, 2015, p. 35.

76 Article 5 GDPR.

77 Article 9 GDPR.

78 Articles 13 to 22 GDPR.

79 ECtHR, *S. and Marper v. the United Kingdom* [GC], nos. 30562/04 and 30566/04, § 95, ECHR 2008.

80 T. Moonen, 'Special Investigation Techniques, Data Processing and Privacy Protection in the Jurisprudence of the European Court of Human Rights', *Pace International Law Review Online Companion*, 2010, p. 114.

81 Ibid., p. 115; J.Kokott and C. Sobotta, 'The distinction between privacy and data protection in the jurisprudence of the CJEU and the ECtHR', *International Data Privacy Law*, 2013, p. 225.

II. Procedural Elements

A specific feature of the EU data protection framework is its strong procedural orientation.[82] While Convention 108 calls for the establishment of appropriate sanctions and remedies to enforce data protection principles, EU secondary legislation takes a more comprehensive and concrete approach.[83] The EU has created an extensive enforcement machinery designed to protect effectively personal data.[84] This system combines various institutional actors responsible for enforcing data protection laws and provides individuals with several procedural rights. EU law establishes data protection authorities responsible for ensuring compliance with EU data protection standards.[85] The procedural rights encompass the right to file a complaint with a supervisory authority, the right to pursue an effective judicial remedy against a controller or processor, as well as the right to seek compensation and establish liability.[86]

There is no similar enforcement structure with specific mechanisms and institutions dedicated to guaranteeing the effective protection of personal data in ECHR law. Yet, the ECtHR has provided a broad interpretation of the right to an effective remedy in data protection matters.[87] In the context of data protection cases, the ECtHR has fleshed out the following general principles: (i) the right to an effective remedy encompasses the right to have a remedy before a national authority to have his or her claim decided and, if appropriate, to obtain redress; (ii) the authority referred to in Article 13 ECHR need not be a judicial authority but, if it is not, the powers and the guarantees which it affords are relevant in determining whether the remedy before it is effective; (iii) even if no single remedy may itself entirely satisfy the right to an effective

---

82 See more on the 'proceduralisation' of EU data protection law in A. GALETTA and P. DE HERT, 'The Proceduralisation of Data Protection Remedies under EU Data Protection Law: Towards a More Effective and Data Subject-oriented Remedial System?', *Review of European Administrative Law*, 2015, pp. 125–151. See also on the use of the term 'proceduralisation', in M. ELIANTONIO and E. MUIR, 'Legitimacy, rationale and extent of the incidental proceduralisation of EU Law, *Review of European Administrative Law*, 2015, pp. 175–204.

83 H. KRANENBORG, 'Article 8', in S. PEERS, T. HERVEY, J. KENNER and A. WARD (eds.), *The EU Charter of Fundamental Rights. A Commentary*, Oxford, Hart Publishing, 2014, p. 263.

84 R. TINIÈRE and C. VIAL, *Manuel de droit de l'Union européenne des droits fondamentaux*, Brussels, Larcier, 2023, pp. 429–430.

85 See further in F. HENDRICKX, 'Article 8 – Protection of Personal Data', in F. DORSSEMONT, K. LÖRCHER, S. CLAUWAERT and M. SCHMITT (eds.), *The Charter of Fundamental Rights of the European Union and the Employment Relation*, Oxford, Hart Publishing, 2019, p. 270; O. LYNSKEY, *The foundations of EU data protection law*, Oxford, Oxford University Press, 2015, p. 26.

86 Articles 78, 79 and 82 GDPR.

87 A. GALETTA and P. DE HERT, 'The Proceduralisation of Data Protection Remedies under EU Data Protection Law: Towards a More Effective and Data Subject-oriented Remedial System?', *Review of European Administrative Law*, 2015, p. 133.

remedy, can be fulfilled, the aggregate of remedies provided for under domestic law may do so.[88] We will see that EU law had no impact on the procedural components of ECHR data protection law.

[88] E.g. ECtHR, *Leander v. Sweden*, 26 March 1987, § 77, Series A no. 116.

CHAPTER 3
THE INFLUENCE OF EU DATA PROTECTION LAW UNDER SCRUTINY

In this section, we explore the influence of EU data protection law on ECHR data protection case-law. First, we carry out a statistical analysis to evaluate the quantitative importance of EU data protection law in ECtHR case-law. Following that, we investigate the various functions played by EU data protection law. As in our equality case study, we identify four key functions of EU data protection law: interpretative, justification, distinguishing, and informative. Subsequently, we examine how other actors – including parties, third-party interveners, national courts, and individual judges within the ECtHR – engage with EU data protection law. We then turn our attention to the respondent States in cases where EU data protection law is used, with a particular focus on whether it is used in cases involving non-EU States. Finally, we examine the ECtHR's methodology when engaging with EU data protection law, paying special attention to transparency, justification, and contextualisation.

For each dimension, we systematically compare the use of EU data protection law with that of various relevant international instruments, most importantly Convention 108. Additionally, we highlight instances where the ECtHR appears to treat EU data protection law as domestic law for the purpose of ECHR law. The key questions and sub-questions for each dimension are detailed in Annex I.

SECTION I. QUANTITATIVE ANALYSIS

Let us start with the quantitative analysis. Our analysis reveals that there are two key external sources the ECtHR references in its data protection case-law: EU data protection law and Convention 108. The ECtHR has referred to them significantly more often than other instruments and has used them consistently over a long period of time across various domains in a significant proportion of its data protection case-law. Where EU law stands out is in its multifaceted use. The ECtHR not only refers to the Charter and legislative instruments but also significantly to the CJEU's case-law.

§ 1. FREQUENCY PER STANDARDS

We start with a statistical analysis of how often EU data protection standards are cited We show that there is a diversified use of EU data protection law, relatively similar to what we observe in our equality case study. However, a difference emerges with the latter case study. In the ECtHR's data protection case-law, two sources stand out: EU data protection law and Convention 108. In the equality case study, the ECtHR referred to a plurality of international instruments in a less differentiated manner. Vis-à-vis Convention 108, the use of EU data protection law is distinguished by the fact that the ECtHR refers much more significantly to the CJEU's case-law than to the outputs of the Consultative Committee of Convention 108.

Reference per category of EU data protection standards

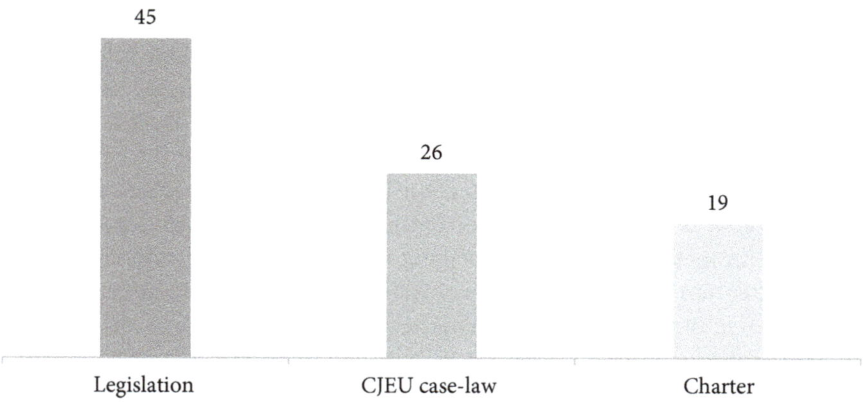

The bar chart displays the frequency of references to the three categories of EU data protection standards under scrutiny.[1] EU legislation is the most frequently cited, appearing in 45 cases, followed by 26 references to CJEU case-law, and 19 references to the Charter. Similar to our equality case study, there is evident engagement with all aspects of data protection law and EU legislation is cited more frequently than the other sources. The prevalence of legislation is even more pronounced than in the equality case study.[2] There are no cases where CJEU case-law is cited alone. That being said, it is the latter source that plays the most significant role in the ECtHR's reasoning, as we will see.[3]

1 For each category, we counted the number of ECtHR cases that mention the category of standards.
2 See above Part III (case study on equality), Chapter 3, Section I, §1. Frequency Per Standards.
3 See in particular the conclusion of Part III: Are EU Fundamental Rights a Source of Special Significance?

If we examine the references to specific legislative instruments and Charter provisions, we notice significant disparities, similar to our findings in the equality case study.

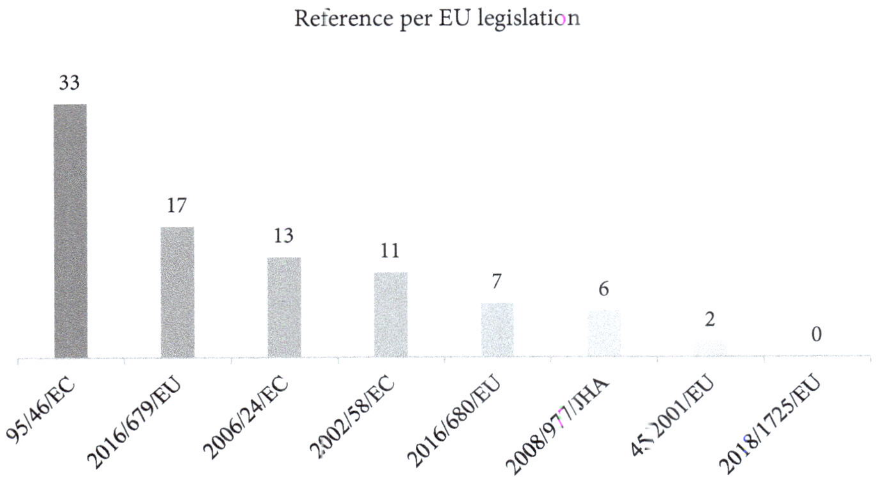

This bar chart displays the frequency of references to EU legislation that gives expression to the fundamental right to data protection. Significant disparities exist among the different legislative instruments. The most frequently cited is the Data Protection Directive (95/46/EC), with 34 references, followed by the GDPR (2016/679/EU), with 18 references, and the Data Retention Directive (2006/24/EC), with 13 references. These are followed by sector-specific instruments, namely the Directive (2002/58/EC) on privacy and electronic communications, with 11 references, and the Law Enforcement Data Protection Directives (2016/680/EU and 2008/977/JHA), with 7 and 6 references. There are very few references to the data protection instruments applicable to EU institutions (45/2001/EU and 2018/1725/EU). As in our equality case study, instruments of general application, the Data Protection Directive (95/46/EC) and the GDPR (2016/679/EU), are cited more frequently than those with a specific scope.[4] The entry into force of legislative instruments appears to play a role in the frequency of references, as illustrated by the high number of citations to the Data Protection Directive (95/46/EC). Yet, recent instruments are sometimes quoted more often than their older equivalents, as is the case regarding the Law Enforcement Data Protection Directives.

---

4 See above Part III (case study on equality), Chapter 3, Section I, §1. Frequency Per Standards.

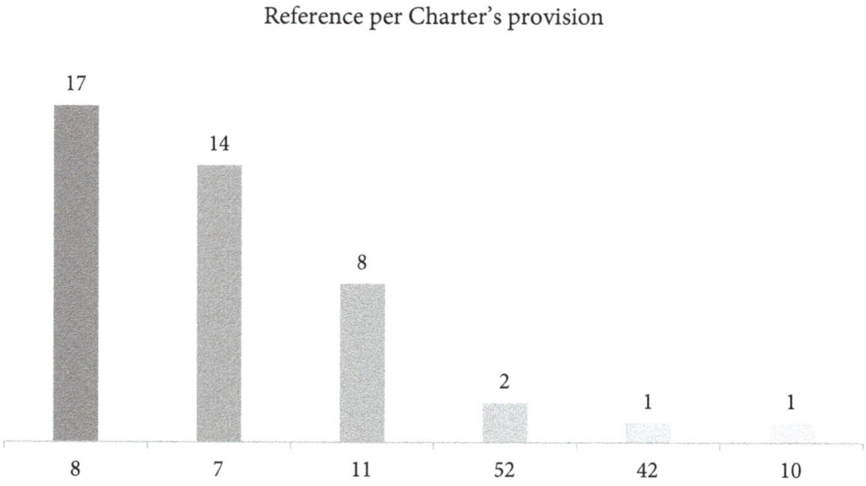

This bar chart shows the frequency with which the ECtHR has referred to Charter provisions in its data protection cases. As for legislative instruments, there are significant discrepancies. Three specific provisions are most frequently cited: the right to data protection (Article 8 Charter), the right to privacy (Article 7 Charter), and the right to freedom of expression (Article 11 Charter), with 17, 14 and 8 references. The ECtHR often mentions these three provisions together.[5] As in our equality case study, certain Charter provisions are thus more prevalent. A notable difference is that, unlike equality Charter provisions, which have influenced the ECtHR's reasoning,[6] the Charter provisions have not done so in its data protection case-law. The ECtHR has referred to these provisions only in an informative manner.[7]

The data presented above highlights the diversified use of EU data protection law by the ECtHR, revealing also significant disparities in references among various legal instruments and provisions. Placing these data in a comparative perspective highlights the relative importance of EU data protection law in the ECtHR's case-law.

---

5 E.g. ECtHR, *Hurbain v. Belgium* [GC], no. 57292/16, § 67, 4 July 2023.

6 See above Part III (case study on equality), Chapter 3, Section I, §1. Frequency Per Standards.

7 E.g. ECtHR, *Hurbain v. Belgium* [GC], no. 57292/16, § 67, 4 July 2023.

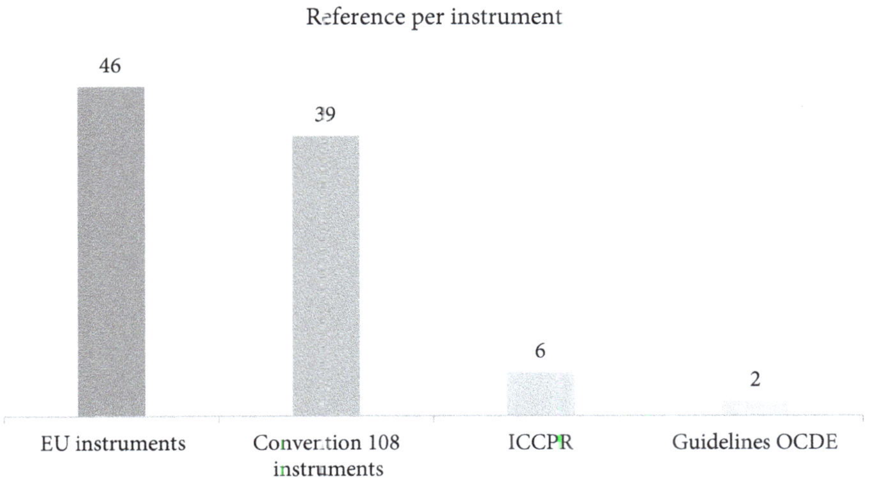

The bar chart displays the frequency of references to EU data protection instruments alongside several international instruments.[8] As observed in our equality case study, there is a notable prevalence of references to EU data protection instruments. However, unlike the equality case study, where there was a relatively balanced distribution of references to various instruments, the field of data protection shows sharper disparities. EU instruments and Convention 108 instruments are in a distinct category. Where there is a significant difference between the references to EU data protection law and Convention 108 law is in references to the outputs of the related bodies: there is a strong prevalence of references to CJEU's case-law when compared to the references to outputs of the Consultative Committee of Convention 108.

8 The data on international instruments are compared with the cumulative references to the Charter and legislation giving expression to the fundamental right to data protection (we have added the cases for the two categories and withdrawn the duplications).

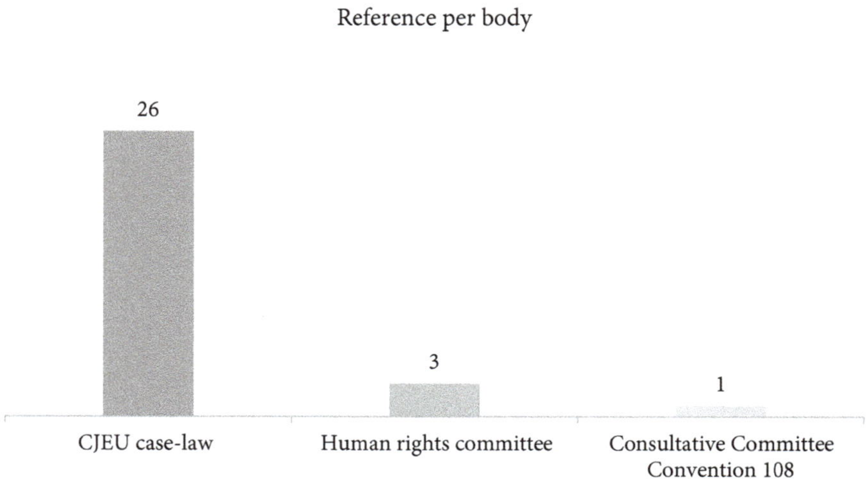

The bar chart shows the frequency of references to CJEU case-law alongside the outputs of bodies related to international – data protection – instruments. The data reveals that CJEU case-law is referenced 26 times, whereas the Human Rights Committee and the Consultative Committee on Convention 108 are referenced only three and one times in the field of data protection. EU data protection law stands out due to the significant use of the CJEU case-law. This is a notable difference from our equality law case study, where, although there were more references to CJEU case-law than to the outputs of other bodies, there was still a considerable number of references to their outputs.

If we compare the number of cases that refer to EU data protection law to the total number of data protection cases handled by the ECtHR, EU data protection law is present in a significant proportion of cases. Out of 22 Grand Chamber cases, 11 refer to EU data protection law (50%). Among 99 Chamber cases, 35 mention EU data protection law (33%). This contrasts with our equality case study, where the proportion of equality cases referencing EU equality law was more limited.

§ 2. FREQUENCY OVER TIME

Let us now examine the evolution over time of references to EU data protection law.[9] The data highlights a consistent use of EU data protection law over almost twenty years, with a notable intensification around 2015, which aligns with our findings in the equality case study. Compared to references to Convention

9 We have looked at the number of ECtHR cases where the ECtHR refers to EU data protection law per year.

108, we observe that if the latter was cited before EU data protection law and followed a similar pattern of evolution over time, EU data protection has now surpassed Convention 108.

Cumulative frequency over time to EU data protection standards

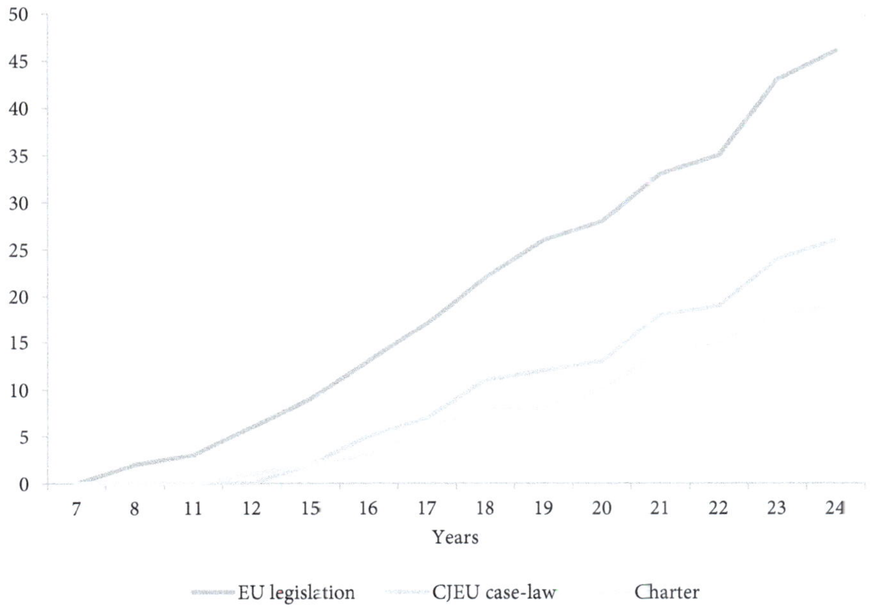

The line chart illustrates the cumulative frequency over time of the three categories of EU data protection standards. The ECtHR referred for the first time to EU data protection legislation in 2008 in the Grand Chamber's case *S and Marper v. United Kingdom* and the Chamber's case *K.U. v. Finland*.[10] The first reference to the Charter occurred in 2012 in the case of *M.M. v. the United Kingdom*,[11] whereas the first reference to CJEU case-law occurred in 2015 in the *Satakunnan v. Finland*.[12] There is a consistent referral to these three instruments over the years, highlighting a referencing practice spanning almost 20 years. This offers perspective on the overall frequency of references to EU data protection law. With 46 cases over nearly twenty years, this equates to roughly two cases per year – a figure comparable to our findings in the equality case study.

---

[10] ECtHR, *S. and Marper v. the United Kingdom* [GC], nos. 30562/04 and 30566/04, § 50, ECHR 2008; ECtHR, *K.U. v. Finland*, no. 2872/02, § 30, 2 December 2008.

[11] ECtHR, *M.M. v. the United Kingdom*, no. 24029/07, § 144, 13 November 2012.

[12] ECtHR, *Satakunnan Markkinapörssi Oy and Satamedia Oy v. Finland*, no. 931/13, §§ 68–70, 21 July 2015.

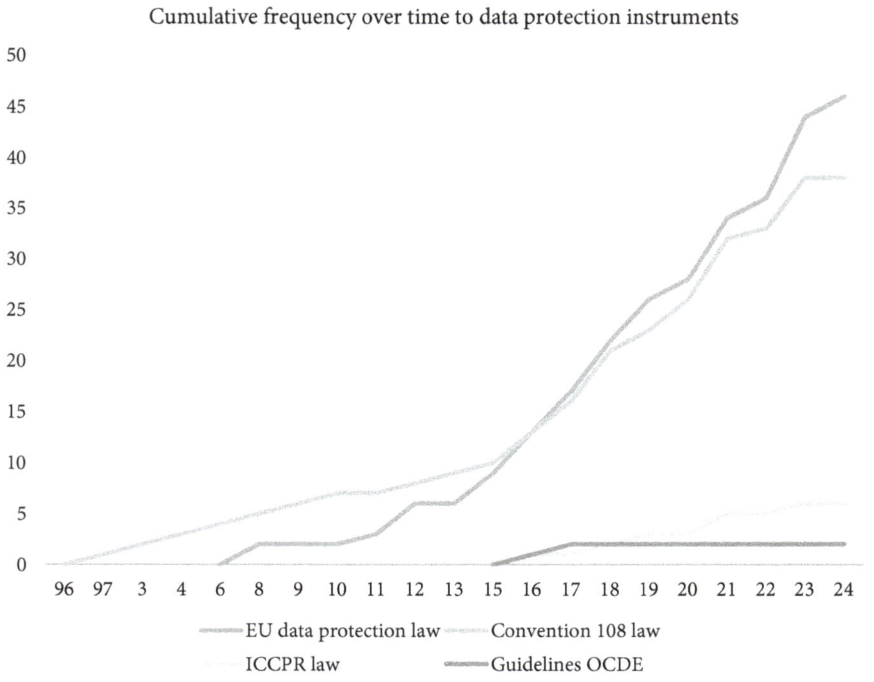

The line chart presents the cumulative frequency over time of references to EU data protection law, Convention 108 law, ICCPR law and OECD guidelines. Convention 108 law was first referenced in 1997 (unlike for our equality case study, where EU equality law was referenced first before international instruments), followed by EU data protection law in 2008, and much later, ICCPR law and OECD guidelines in 2016. The curves for EU data protection law and Convention 108 law intersect in 2016. Before this, there were more references to Convention 108 law, and after this, more to EU data protection law. From around 2015, there is an intensification of references to EU data protection law, as in our equality case study. From 2008 to 2014 (6 years), there were 6 references; from 2015 to 2024 (9 years), there were 41 references. An intensification can also be observed for Convention 108 law: from 1996 to 2014, there were 9 references; from 2015 to 2024, there were 29 references. The intensification is stronger for EU data protection law. For ICCPR law and OECD guidelines, the first references occurred around the same period but remained low.

Why is there an increase in references to EU data protection law around 2015? The answer is likely multifactorial as in our equality case study. The EU framework on data protection has become more developed: there is an increasing number of EU data protection legislative instruments; the Charter, which includes the autonomous right to data protection, became binding with the Lisbon Treaty; and data protection law has matured in CJEU case-law.

A related factor that is more challenging to account for objectively, but may be of importance, is the growing awareness of EU data protection law within the ECtHR. As this legal area becomes more sophisticated and firmly anchored in EU law, staffs working at the ECtHR and ECtHR judges may become more conscious of it. An important factor is the growing number of data protection cases dealt with by the ECtHR. From 1996 to 2014 (8 years), there were 43 cases, whereas from 2015 to 2024 (9 years), there are 78 cases. The more cases the ECtHR deals with on data protection, the more likely it is to reference EU data protection law. There is also a trend whereby the ECtHR increasingly refers to international instruments that may play a role.[13]

§ 3. FREQUENCY PER AREA

We conclude our quantitative analysis by providing a statistical analysis of the frequency of references to EU data protection law per area. Our analysis shows that EU data protection law has been referenced across a diverse array of areas, with some areas being referenced more frequently than others. The ECtHR has referred to Convention 108 law in a similar manner, which is partly explained by the fact that the ECtHR often references both EU data protection law and Convention 108 law in the same cases.

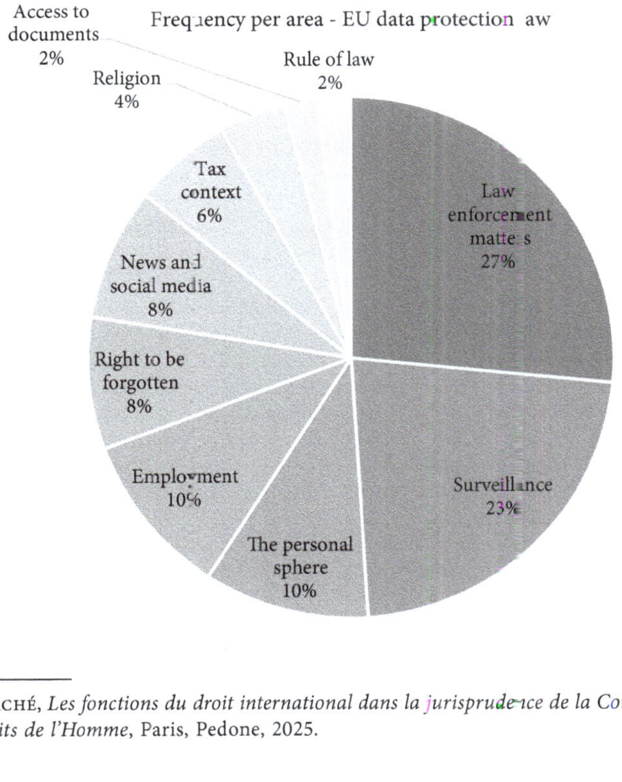

[13] M. Larché, *Les fonctions du droit international dans la jurisprudence de la Cour européenne des droits de l'Homme*, Paris, Pedone, 2025.

This pie chart displays the frequency of references to EU data protection law per area. As in our equality case study, the data shows a great diversity of fields in which the ECtHR refers to EU data protection law. Its use encompasses cases ranging from news and social media,[14] religion,[15] tax context,[16] employment[17] and the personal sphere.[18] Within this diverse set of references, specific domains emerge as fertile grounds. Law enforcement matters take the lead with the highest percentage (27%).[19] Following closely is the area of surveillance (23%), which is also prolific.[20] There are also fields in which there are much less references, such as in relation to access to documents[21] and the rule of law.[22]

Similar as in our equality case study, there is a broad tendency for the ECtHR to refer to EU data protection law in areas corresponding to the scope of application of the EU instruments. Specific legislative instruments are used in contexts that align with their scope of application within EU law. For example, Council Framework Decision (2008/977/JHA) is often referenced in

[14] E.g. ECtHR, *Sanchez v. France* [GC], no. 45581/15, §§ 74–78, 15 May 2023; ECtHR, *Delfi AS v. Estonia* [GC], no. 64569/09, §§ 50–57 and 147, ECHR 2015.

[15] E.g. ECtHR, *Jehovah's Witnesses v. Finland*, no. 31172/19, §§ 39–41 and §§ 85–87, 9 May 2023.

[16] ECtHR, *L.B. v. Hungary* [GC], no. 36345/16, §§ 39–41 and 85–87, 9 March 2023; ECtHR, *Satakunnan Markkinapörssi Oy and Satamedia Oy v. Finland* [GC], no. 931/13, §§ 55–79, 133, 149–151, 158–159, 188, 193, 197 and 212, 27 June 2017.

[17] E.g. ECtHR, *López Ribalda and Others v. Spain* [GC], nos. 1874/13 and 8567/13, §§ 63–66, 17 October 2019; ECtHR, *Bărbulescu v. Romania* [GC], no. 61496/08, §§ 44–51, 5 September 2017.

[18] E.g. ECtHR, *Jessica Marchi v. Italy*, no. 54978/17, § 30, 27 May 2021 (on termination of pre-adoption foster placement); Separate Opinion of Judge Koskelo in ECtHR, *Orlandi and Others v. Italy*, nos. 26431/12 and 3 others, § 21, 14 December 2017 (on the refusal to register same-sex marriages contracted abroad); ECtHR, *Mosley v. the United Kingdom*, no. 48009/08, § 64, 10 May 2011 (on the absence of any legal requirement for newspapers to give advance notice before publishing details of a person's private life).

[19] E.g. ECtHR, *Margari v. Greece*, no. 36705/16, §§ 12 and 59, 20 June 2023; ECtHR, *Benedik v. Slovenia*, no. 62357/14, §§ 53–62, 95, and 107, 24 April 2018.

[20] ECtHR, *Ekimdzhiev and Others v. Bulgaria*, no. 70078/12, §§ 230–245 and 419, 11 January 2022; ECtHR, *Centrum för rättvisa v. Sweden* [GC], no. 35252/08, §§ 92–130, 25 May 2021; ECtHR, *Big Brother Watch and Others v. the United Kingdom* [GC], nos. 58170/13 and 2 others, §§ 202–241, 25 May 2021; ECtHR, *Szabó and Vissy v. Hungary*, no. 37138/14, §§ 23, 25, 68, 70 and 73, 12 January 2016; ECtHR, *Roman Zakharov v. Russia* [GC], no. 47143/06, §§ 145–147 and 269, ECHR 2015.

[21] ECtHR, *Magyar Helsinki Bizottság v. Hungary* [GC], no. 18030/11, §§ 55–59 and 144, 8 November 2016.

[22] ECtHR, *Baka v. Hungary* [GC], no. 20261/12, § 70, 23 June 2016.

cases related to criminal matters,[23] whereas Directive (2002/58/EC) on privacy and electronic communications is cited in the context of surveillance cases.[24]

The significance of EU data protection in certain domains can at times be attributed to the CJEU positioning itself at the forefront of these areas. A good example relates to the right to be forgotten, where the CJEU has been particularly active since its judgment *Google Spain* of 14 May 2014.[25] A few years later, the ECtHR dealt with the issue and took note of the developments at CJEU level.[26] In its more recent judgments, the ECtHR systematically refers to EU law on the right to be forgotten, which sometimes lead to influencing its reasoning, as we will see.[27]

There are domains where the ECtHR had already left its mark for an extended period, but following the emergence of CJEU case-law, the ECtHR now references EU law. Regarding data surveillance, the ECtHR established a set of specific safeguards against abuses as early as 1978.[28] The question of the legality of surveillance systems arose in EU law much later with the *Digital Rights Ireland* case in 2014.[29] From there on, the CJEU has delivered a series of significant judgments.[30] In the context of this influx of EU law judgments, the ECtHR has mentioned the EU law's perspective into its decisions, although most often in an informative way.[31] This highlights a distinctive responsiveness to developments at EU level. The ECtHR demonstrates a high level of flexibility that allows it to consider and integrate the implications of EU data protection law changes into its decisions.

---

23 ECtHR, *Gluhkin v. Russia*, no. 11519/20, § 38, 4 July 2023; ECtHR, *Catt v. the United Kingdom*, no. 43514/15, § 69, 24 January 2019; ECtHR, *Benedik v. Slovenia*, no. 62357/14, §§ 57–59, 24 April 2018.

24 ECtHR, *Ekimdzhiev and Others v. Bulgaria*, no. 70078/12, § 230, 11 January 2022; ECtHR, *Centrum för rättvisa v. Sweden* [GC], no. 35252/08, § 96, 25 May 2021; ECtHR, *Big Brother Watch and Others v. the United Kingdom* [GC], nos. 58170/13 and 2 others, § 206, 25 May 2021.

25 Case C-131/12, *Google Spain*, ECLI:EU:C:2014:317.

26 ECtHR, *M.L. and W.W. v. Germany*, nos. 60798/10 and 65599/10, §§ 57–63 and 97, 28 June 2018.

27 ECtHR, *Hurbain v. Belgium* [GC], no. 57292/16, §§ 67–87 and 83, 4 July 2023; ECtHR, *Biancardi v. Italy*, no. 77419/16, §§ 18–29, 53 and 67, 25 November 2021.

28 ECtHR, *Klass and Others v. Germany*, 6 September 1978, § 50, Series A no. 28.

29 Joined Cases C-293/12 and C-594/12, *Digital Rights Ireland*, ECLI:EU:C:2014:238.

30 Case C-623/17, *Privacy International*, 6 October 2020, ECLI:EU:C:2020:790; Joined Cases C-511/18, 512/18 and C-520/18, *La Quadrature du Net and Others*, 6 October 2020, ECLI:EU:C:2020:791.

31 See below, Part III (case study on data protection), Chapter 3, Section II, §4. Information.

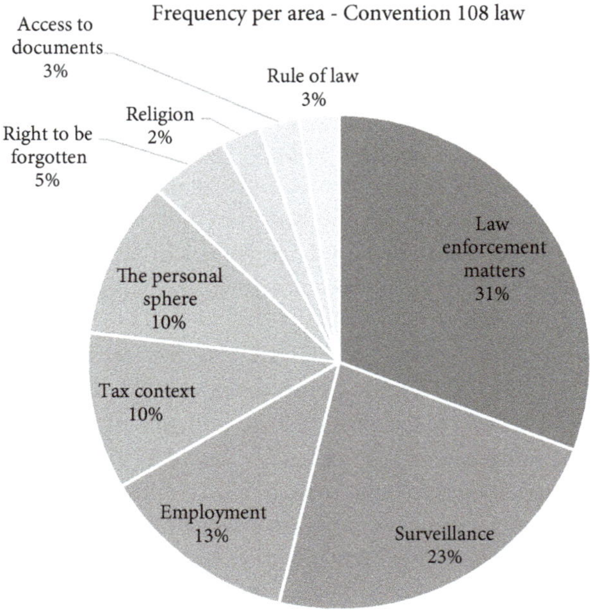

The pie chart illustrates the distribution of references to Convention 108 law across various areas. The highest frequency is in law enforcement matters, accounting for 31% of the references.[32] Surveillance is the second most referenced area at 23%.[33] Employment issues account for 13% of the references,[34] while both the personal sphere and tax context each comprise 10%.[35] The remaining references are distributed among various other areas with smaller percentages. The use of Convention 108 law is relatively similar to the use of EU data protection law: Convention 108 law, like EU data protection law, is applied broadly across various similar contexts with comparable distribution patterns. This is in part due to the fact that in many data protection cases the ECtHR refers to both EU data protection law and Convention 108 law.[36]

---

32 E.g. ECtHR, *Benedik v. Slovenia*, no. 62357/14, §§ 46, 102 and 107, 24 April 2018.

33 E.g. ECtHR, *Big Brother Watch and Others v. the United Kingdom* [GC], nos. 58170/13 and 2 others, §§ 192–193, 25 May 2021.

34 E.g. ECtHR, *López Ribalda and Others v. Spain* [GC], nos. 1874/13 and 8567/13, § 60, 17 October 2019.

35 E.g. in the personal sphere: ECtHR, *Z v. Finland*, 25 February 1997, § 95, Reports of Judgments and Decisions 1997-I; in the tax context: ECtHR, *L.B. v. Hungary* [GC], no. 36345/16, § 42, 9 March 2023.

36 For instance, almost ECtHR's cases which refer to Convention 108, and are mentioned in this sub-section on frequency by area, refer to EU data protection law.

SECTION II. FUNCTIONS

We now start the qualitative analysis and look at the functions of EU data protection law in the ECtHR's case-law. Our qualitative analysis aligns with our quantitative findings: EU data protection law and Convention 108 are the two primary external sources in the ECtHR's case-law. While their functions overlap in some cases, particularly in information and interpretation, there are noteworthy differences. Only EU law has been used from a distinguishing perspective, and in terms of justification, they perform different sub-functions, though the impact is notable in both cases.

The ECtHR has rarely drawn upon EU data protection law to shape the key principles of its data protection case-law. It had a minimal impact on the interpretation of the Convention's provisions and played a very limited role in developing the ECtHR's safeguards to prevent abuse of personal data. The ECtHR has significantly relied on the principles enshrined in Convention 108 in shaping these safeguards.

That being said, the ECtHR has notably used EU data protection law in various ways. First, EU data protection law has played a notable justification function in ECtHR case-law, particularly in assessing whether an interference was lawful and necessary in a democratic society. Second, the ECtHR has sought to distinguish its stance from that of EU data protection law. Third, EU data protection law serves a significant informative function, with the ECtHR referencing it as relevant contextual or legal standards. Some of these functions are done exclusively by EU data protection law or are more performed by the latter than Convention 108.

§ 1. INTERPRETATION

The influence of EU data protection law on the interpretation of the ECHR's provisions has been very limited. The former has only been used concerning the material scope of ECHR data protection law. The ECtHR has relied upon EU law to assess whether a data related situation falls within the scope of 'private life' for the purposes of Article 8 ECHR. EU data protection law has been used to support a broad interpretation of private life in the context of personal data.

One of the key cases is *Benedik v. Slovenia* (2018), which involved a situation where the police requested subscriber information related to a dynamic IP address from an Internet service provider in the context of criminal proceedings. Unlike static IP addresses, dynamic IP addresses do not allow for the identification of the user. The Internet service provider has additional information that, when combined with the IP address, allows for user identification. The CJEU had ruled in its *Breyer* (2016) judgment that a dynamic IP address could constitute personal data, especially when there is a possibility of identifying an individual through additional information.[37]

As a preliminary observation in the *Benedik* case, the ECtHR observed 'the particular context of the present case, which concerns the disclosure of subscriber information associated with a dynamic IP address'[38] and took note:

> *of the extensive legislation and of the case-law concerning personal data protection and privacy of electronic communication within the European Union* and will rely on them and on other relevant comparative-law material in assessing some of the technical matters applicable to the present case. It will also have regard, where appropriate, to the legal doctrines established therein.[39]

While the ECtHR indicated its intention to give weight to EU law, its impact is confined to determining whether the matter falls within private life. The ECtHR observed, concerning the nature of the data, that '[t]he Government did not dispute that the subscriber information in principle concerned personal data [...]. Such a conclusion also follows from the definitions contained in the 1981 Convention, *the legislation of the European Union*, as well as domestic legislation aimed at their implementation.'[40] EU law is used among other sources to consider that the data at stake are personal data, without the ECtHR relying on the CJEU's *Breyer* case. The ECtHR looked beyond the nature of the data to assess whether the situation fell within the purview of Article 8 ECHR. The classification of the data as personal data, in itself, did not bring it within the scope of private life. It is only one argument among others in this assessment. The ECtHR's approach remains 'privacy-centered', prioritising privacy over a focus on personal data.

EU data protection law has been used to support that other data related situations fall within the ambit of private life. Regarding the retention of DNA profiles, in *S. and Marper v. United Kingdom* (2008), the ECtHR noted that '[t]he possibility the DNA profiles create for inferences to be drawn as to ethnic origin makes their retention all the more sensitive and susceptible of affecting the right to private life. This conclusion is consistent with the principle laid down in the Data Protection Convention and reflected in the *Data Protection Act* that both list personal data revealing ethnic origin among the special categories of sensitive data attracting a heightened level of protection.'[41] While EU data protection law is not mentioned, the ECtHR referred to the Data

---

37 ECtHR, *Breyer v. Germany*, no. 50001/12, § 49, 30 January 2020.

38 ECtHR, *Benedik v. Slovenia*, no. 62357/14, §§ 95 and 107, 24 April 2018.

39 Ibid. Emphasis added.

40 Ibid., § 107. Emphasis added.

41 ECtHR, *S. and Marper v. the United Kingdom* [GC], nos. 30562/04 and 30566/04, § 76, ECHR 2008. Emphasis added.

Protection Act which incorporates its principles – we will revisit this situation of influence 'through the national backdoor' later on.[42]

Regarding monitoring computer use in the employment context, in *Bărbulescu v. Romania* [GC](2016), the ECtHR stated that '[t]he Court must therefore determine whether, in view of the general prohibition imposed by his employer, the applicant retained a reasonable expectation that his communications would not be monitored In this regard, the Court takes notice that the Data Protection Convention sets up clear principles applying to automatic data processing in order to enable an individual to establish the existence of an automated personal data file and its main purposes. *The relevant EU law goes in the same direction, notably in the field of surveillance of electronic communications in the workplace.*'[43]

In these two cases, there are other legal sources, particularly Convention 108, as well as other arguments, which are used to assess whether the situation falls within the purview of Article 8 ECHR.[44]

Another related instance where the ECtHR has relied on EU law is to bolster its interpretation that data in the public domain can be protected under Article 8 ECHR. In *Jehova's Witness v. Finland* (2023), the ECtHR affirmed that the mere presence of data in the public domain neither diminishes the expectation of privacy of the applicants nor implies a lesser need for protection of such data.[45] Relying on EU law to support this affirmation, the ECtHR highlighted that:

> In the case Satakunnan Markkinapörssi Oy and Satamedia Oy (C-73/07 […]), the Grand Chamber of the CJEU held that 'a general derogation from the application of the [Data Protection Directive] in respect of published information would largely deprive the directive of its effect' and that '[i]t would be sufficient for the Member States to publish data in order for those data to cease to enjoy the protection afforded by the directive' […]. This finding was confirmed and reinforced in the case Google Spain and Google (C-131/12 […]), in which the CJEU argued that 'the operations referred to in Article 2(b) of Directive 95/46 [had to] also be classified as [data] processing where they exclusively concern[ed] material that [had] already been published in unaltered form in the media'[…).[46]

It is noteworthy that the ECtHR uses EU law not when determining whether the matter fall within the scope of Article 8 ECHR but when assessing whether

---

42 Ibid., § 30. See below Part III (case study on data protection), Chapter 3, Section V, §1. Transparency.

43 ECtHR, *Bărbulescu v. Romania* [GC], no. 61496/08, § 42 5 September 2017. Emphasis added.

44 Ibid., § 44; ECtHR, *S. and Marper v. the United Kingdom* [GC], nos. 30562/04 and 30566/04, § 75, ECHR 2008.

45 ECtHR, *Jehovah's Witnesses v. Finland*, no. 31172/19, § 94, 9 May 2023.

46 Ibid.

the interference is necessary in a democratic society (in other words, when assessing the proportionality of the interference). A similar reasoning occurred in *Satakunnan v. Finland* [GC](2017). When assessing whether the situation fell within private life, the ECtHR stressed that information already in the public domain does not necessarily forfeit the protection afforded by Article 8 ECHR; for this purpose, the ECtHR relied on Convention 108 and its own case-law.[47] At a later point, the ECtHR mentioned that 'the CJEU has made clear – not least in Satakunnan Markkinapörssi Oy, § 48; and Google Spain, § 30 – that the public character of data processed does not exclude such data from the scope of the Data Protection Directive and the guarantees the latter lays down for the protection of privacy'.[48] Again such a statement is done when the ECtHR assessed whether the interference was 'necessary in a democratic society'.

All in all, the ECtHR has only used EU data protection law to determine whether certain situations fall within the scope of Article 8 ECHR or to bolster its interpretation that data in the public domain can be protected under Article 8 ECHR. When EU law is mentioned, it is not used as the sole argument or legal source; instead, Convention 108 often plays a more significant role. As shown below, Convention 108 has played a more notable, albeit limited, interpretative function. The ECtHR has relied on this instrument to define the notion of personal data. To some extent this can explain the limited role of EU data protection law: the ECtHR has given priority to Convention 108, relying on it either exclusively or in conjunction with EU law. When the latter is used, sources of EU law are diverse, including EU legislation and, most often, CJEU case-law. The use of EU law has been 'data protection-friendly', as all cases have bolstered that data related matters fall within the scope of Article 8 ECHR. The interpretative function of EU data protection law has not changed the dynamics of ECHR law. This is illustrated by the fact that the categorisation of data as personal data is not sufficient to fall within the scope of Article 8 ECHR. Overall, our data protection case study differs markedly from our equality case study, where the interpretative function of EU equality law was more diverse, impacted various elements, and had some transformational effects on the dynamics of ECHR equality law.

§ 2. JUSTIFICATION

The ECtHR has strongly relied on EU data protection law during its evaluation of the justification of an interference by a national measure or practice. EU

---

47 ECtHR, *Satakunnan Markkinapörssi Oy and Satamedia Oy v. Finland* [GC], no. 931/13, §§ 134–138, 27 June 2017.

48 Ibid., § 188.

law has been used to assess whether an interference pursued a legitimate aim, whether it was lawful, and whether it was necessary in a democratic society. Compared to the impact of Convention 108, the latter appears to have had a distinct, yet more significant impact on the necessity condition, as the ECtHR heavily relied upon it to shape its safeguards to avoid abuses in the context of personal data. Yet, this instrument has not been used to assess the legitimacy of an interference and only limitedly to assess its lawfulness.

I. Legitimate Aim

The impact of EU law on the condition of legitimate purpose has been restricted. In two cases, the ECtHR referred to the purposes of EU data protection to support that the interference pursued a legitimate aim. In the case of *Jehovah's Witnesses v. Finland* (2023) to which we will come back[49] which addressed whether Jehovah's Witnesses need to obtain consent when collecting personal data during door-to-door preaching, the ECtHR reasoned as follows: 'Taking into account the aims of the Personal Data Act [...] and the Data Protection Directive as interpreted by the CJEU [...], as well as the established case-law of the Court [...], it is clear that the interference with the applicant community's right to freedom of religion pursued the legitimate aim of protecting 'the rights and freedoms of others', data subjects in the present case, within the meaning of Article 9 § 2 of the Convention.'[50]

A similar line of reasoning is present in *Satakunnan v. Finland* [GC](2017), which dealt with the publication of tax data by private companies to which we will also come back.[51] The ECtHR referred to the aims of EU data protection law to conclude that the interference with the applicant companies' right to freedom of expression pursued the legitimate aim of protecting 'the reputation or rights of others', as outlined in Article 10(2) ECHR.[52] The applicants had argued that while privacy could be a legitimate aim, there was no real threat to privacy.[53] In response, the ECtHR focused primarily on the objectives of EU law – as laid down in EU data protection legislation, interpreted by the CJEU, and transposed into domestic laws – to conclude that the interference pursued a legitimate aim, also noting that privacy is at the heart of EU legislation.[54]

The two cases share a noteworthy commonality: the ECtHR relies on the objectives set forth by EU data protection law to support the legitimacy

---

49 See below Part III (case study on data protection), Chapter 3, Section II, §2, II. Lawfulness.

50 ECtHR, *Jehovah's Witnesses v. Finland*, no. 31172/19, §§ 39–41 and 89, 9 May 2023.

51 See below Part III (case study on data protection), Chapter 3, Section II, §2, II. Lawfulness.

52 ECtHR, *Satakunnan Markkinapörssi Oy and Satamedia Oy v. Finland* [GC], no. 931/13, §§ 158–159, 27 June 2017.

53 Ibid., § 157.

54 Ibid., §§ 158–159.

of the interference. EU data protection law is either the sole or the most significant argument to consider the aim of the interference legitimate, and it is the sole legal source used – aside from domestic laws that transpose EU law. Both the objectives of EU legislation and the interpretation given to them by the CJEU are mentioned. The ECtHR seems to refer to the objectives of EU data protection law because domestic law is based on and incorporates these objectives. It therefore takes into account the EU objectives to assess the legitimacy of the goals at domestic level. The use of EU data protection law is data-protection-friendly, as data protection concerns – as developed in EU law – are deemed legitimate purposes. However, this finding also leads to restrictions of other Convention provisions, particularly freedom of religion and freedom of expression.

II. Lawfulness

The ECtHR has taken into account EU data protection law to determine the lawfulness of an interference. Specifically, the ECtHR has considered that the requirement of foreseeability – part of the lawfulness criterion – is met when domestic courts rely on findings from a CJEU's preliminary ruling related to the ECtHR's case. This is a recent development arising from a specific context.

In the past, the ECtHR had declined to consider EU data protection law in assessing the lawfulness of an interference. In *Romet v. the Netherlands* (2012), the applicant contended that the interference with private life was not prescribed by law as it contravened Article 7(1) Data Protection Directive (95/46/EC).[55] The ECtHR dismissed this argument succinctly and ambiguously, stating that 'the Court notes that for purposes of the Convention, it binds domestic authorities only in the form in which it has been transposed into domestic law.'[56] In doing so, the ECtHR declined to oversee the interpretation and compliance with EU law by national authorities. In *Delfi v. Estonia* [GC] (2015), the applicant argued that the interference was not prescribed by law since both domestic and European legislation on Internet service providers prohibited holding service providers liable for third-party content.[57] The ECtHR refused to examine whether domestic authorities had correctly applied EU law.[58]

The recent case-law, particularly in *Satakunnan v. Finland* [GC](2017) and *Jehova's Witness* (2023), signals a discernible shift. The ECtHR dealt with cases originating from applicants which were involved in proceedings before the CJEU, and where the latter had issued preliminary rulings on analogous data

55 ECtHR, *Romet v. the Netherlands*, no. 7094/06, § 35, 14 February 2012.
56 Ibid.
57 ECtHR, *Delfi AS v. Estonia* [GC], no. 64569/09, § 123, ECHR 2015.
58 Ibid., § 127.

protection issues. Given the importance of EU data protection law in these judgments, it is useful to delve into them in greater detail.

The *Satakunnan* case concerns companies in Finland which published information on the taxable income and assets of Finish taxpayers. The Data Protection Ombudsman requested the Data Protection Board to prohibit the applicant companies from processing taxation data.[59] The Data Protection Board dismissed the Ombudsman's request, asserting that the exemption enshrined in the Finnish Personal Data Act (which transposed Data Protection Directive (95/46/EC)) regarding journalism was applicable to the current situation.[60] The case reached the Supreme Administrative Court, which decided to seek a preliminary ruling from the CJEU concerning the interpretation of the notion of journalism enshrined in the Data Protection Directive (95/46/EC).[61] The preliminary questions related to the interpretation of Article 9 of the said Directive, which incorporates a specific provision related to data processing for journalistic purposes, mandating EU States to institute exemptions or derogations for the processing of data solely for these purposes.

The CJEU deemed that the processing of personal data from documents which are in the public domain under national legislation, must be considered as activities involving the processing of personal data carried out 'solely for journalistic purposes', within the meaning of Article 9 of Data Protection Directive (95/46/EC), if the sole object of those activities is the disclosure to the public of information, opinions or ideas.[62] In light of this ruling, the Supreme Administrative Court requested the Data Protection Board to prohibit the processing of taxation data as it deemed that Article 9 of Data Protection Directive (95/46/EC) was inapplicable, given that the activities of the companies could not be regarded as journalistic activity.[63] The companies contended before the ECtHR that their right to impart information safeguarded under Article 10 ECHR, had been infringed.

It is against this EU law background that the ECtHR examined whether the interference with the applicant companies' right to freedom of expression was 'prescribed by law'. The primary inquiry pertains to whether the applicant companies could reasonably have anticipated that their publishing activities would be contrary to existing legislation, taking into account the existence of the derogation for journalistic purposes.[64] The ECtHR reminded that

---

59 ECtHR, *Satakunnan Markkinapörssi Oy and Satamedia Oy v. Finland* [GC], no. 931/13, § 14, 27 June 2017.

60 Ibid., § 15.

61 Ibid., §§ 18–19.

62 Case C-73/07, *Tietosuojavaltuutettu v. Satakunnan Markkinapörssi Oy and Satamedia Oy*, ECLI:EU:C:2008:727, para. 62.

63 ECtHR, *Satakunnan Markkinapörssi Oy and Satamedia Oy v. Finland* [GC], no. 931/13, §§ 21–22, 27 June 2017.

64 Ibid., § 148.

the requirement of foreseeability implies that a law must be formulated with sufficient precision to enable individuals to regulate their conduct.[65] The ECtHR considered that the condition of foreseeability was met based – to a significant extent – on the following reasons:

> For the Court, the terms of the relevant data protection legislation and the nature and scope of the journalistic derogation on which the applicant companies sought to rely were sufficiently foreseeable and those provisions were applied in a sufficiently foreseeable manner *following the interpretative guidance provided to the Finnish court by the CJEU.* [...]
>
> Even if the applicant companies' case was the first of its kind under the Personal Data Act, that would not render the domestic courts' interpretation and application of the journalistic derogation *arbitrary or unpredictable* [...], nor would the fact that the Supreme Administrative Court sought guidance from the CJEU on the interpretation of the derogation in Article 9 of the Data Protection Directive. *Indeed, as regards the latter, the Court has regularly emphasised the importance, for the protection of fundamental rights in the EU, of the judicial dialogue conducted between the domestic courts of EU Member States and the CJEU in the form of references from the former for preliminary rulings by the latter.*[66]

This reasoning, which we discuss below, is also present in *Jehovah's Witness v. Finland* (2023). The case pertains to the incompatibility with data protection laws of the activities of Jehovah's Witnesses which consisted in collecting and processing personal data during door-to-door preaching without consent of data subjects.[67] The Data Protection Board prohibited to do such activities without the unambiguous consent of the data subject.[68] The case was brought before the Helsinki Administrative Court, which deemed this prohibition unlawful.[69] The matter went to the Supreme Administrative Court, which decided to seek a preliminary ruling from the CJEU regarding the interpretation of the Data Protection Directive (95/46/EC).[70]

The CJEU held that the collection of personal data by members of a religious community engaged in door-to-door preaching did not fall within the exception for the processing of personal data carried out by a natural person in the course of a purely personal or household activity.[71] Jehovah's Witnesses could be considered a 'controller' within the meaning of the

---

65 Ibid., § 143.
66 Ibid., §§ 149–150. Emphasis added.
67 ECtHR, *Jehovah's Witnesses v. Finland*, no. 31172/19, § 5, 9 May 2023.
68 Ibid., § 8.
69 Ibid., §§ 12–14.
70 Ibid., § 17.
71 Case C-25/17, *Jehovan todistajat*, ECLI:ECLI:EU:C:2018:551, § 51.

Data Protection Directive (95/46/EC) in the context of their door-to-door preaching activities.[72] In light of this judgment, the Supreme Administrative Court overturned the Administrative Court's decision to the extent that it had annulled the Board's decision.[73] The applicant community alleged that the Board's decision, forbidding Jehovah's Witnesses from taking notes during door-to-door preaching without the data subject's consent, infringed their rights under Articles 9 (freedom of thought, conscience, and religion) and 10 (freedom of expression) ECHR.[74]

Once again, the ECtHR considered that the interference was 'prescribed by law', here within the meaning Article 9(2) ECHR. Despite the applicant community's contention that the Supreme Administrative Court had incorrectly applied domestic law to the case's particulars, the ECtHR disagreed:

> The Court observes that the Personal Data Act transposed the Data Protection Directive into Finnish law [. . .]. *Before the Supreme Administrative Court reached its final conclusion on the matter, it sought guidance from the CJEU on the interpretation of the Data Protection Directive. The Court has regularly emphasised the importance, for the protection of fundamental rights in the EU, of the judicial dialogue conducted between the domestic courts of EU member States and the CJEU in the form of references from the former for preliminary rulings by the latter* [...].
>
> In the judgment of 10 July 2018, *the CJEU gave an authoritative interpretation of the Data Protection Directive relevant for the main legal issues* contested by the applicant community. [...]
>
> *Following the CJEU's guidance, the Supreme Administrative Court provided a similar interpretation of the relevant provisions of the Personal Data Act and applied them taking account of the established facts relevant for the present case* [...]. Even if the applicant community's case was the first of its kind under the Personal Data Act, that would not render the interpretation and application by the domestic authorities arbitrary or unpredictable [...]. Having regard to its limited jurisdiction as regards the interpretation of the domestic law by the national courts [...] and the available material in its possession, the Court does not consider that the manner in which the Supreme Administrative Court interpreted the Personal Data Act was arbitrary and unreasonable.[75]

What can we infer from these two judgments? First, it appears that if national courts seek a preliminary ruling from the CJEU and rely on its findings, the ECtHR will consider the requirement of foreseeability to be satisfied in a related

---

72 Ibid., § 75.
73 ECtHR, *Jehovah's Witnesses v. Finland*, no. 31172/19, §§ 23–29, 9 May 2023.
74 Ibid., § 59.
75 Ibid., §§ 85–87. Emphasis added.

case. EU data protection law – particularly CJEU's preliminary rulings – as interpreted by domestic authorities is crucial in assessing the requirement of foreseeability. EU data protection law is the sole legal source mentioned, and the manner in which national authorities engage with it is a central argument in determining the foreseeability of the interference. The importance of EU law seems to result from the deeply integrated nature of EU law within domestic legal systems. The ECtHR seems to treat it as a component of national law, and takes into consideration the procedures established between national courts and the CJEU. It shows a significant degree of deference to the preliminary ruling procedure.

Second, the ECtHR's scrutiny of the interpretation of EU law by national courts is limited to examining if the interpretation and application of EU law by domestic authorities are not arbitrary or unpredictable. The ECtHR exercises a certain level of scrutiny but this oversight is marginal and viewed through the lens of the Convention. This stance aligns with its case-law asserting that the ECtHR does not have the authority to assess the validity or correct interpretation of EU law.[76]

Third, examining not only these judgments but also cases explored in our equality case study – in particular *Moraru v. Romania* (2022) and *Moraru and Marin v. Romania* (2022) – highlights the importance of national authorities' engagement with EU law at the level of justification.

These three points are revisited in Part IV of this research project, but let us already express a few words of caution here. The ECtHR judgments concerning the engagement of national authorities with EU law are recent, and a significant number of them are Chamber's judgments. Several of them have been rendered against two States, namely Finland[77] and Romania.[78] The 'human factor' should not be underestimated, wherein some lawyers or judges at the ECtHR involved in these cases may have played a significant role to these new trends. Hence, let us stress that such developments may not reflect a consensus within the entire ECtHR, and the trajectory of this trend in the future remains uncertain. Therefore, this is an area that will demand close scrutiny in the coming years.

---

[76] E.g. ECtHR, *K.I. v. France*, no. 5560/19, § 123, 15 April 2021; ECtHR, *Jeunesse v. the Netherlands* [GC], no. 12738/10, § 110, 3 October 2014.

[77] ECtHR, *Jehovah's Witnesses v. Finland*, no. 31172/19, 9 May 2023; ECtHR, *Satakunnan Markkinapörssi Oy and Satamedia Oy v. Finland* [GC], no. 931/13, 27 June 2017.

[78] ECtHR, *Moraru and Marin v. Romania*, nos. 53282/18 and 31428/20, 20 December 2022; ECtHR, *Moraru v. Romania* case, no. 64480/19, 8 November 2022.

III. Necessary in a Democratic Society

The ECtHR has used EU data protection law to assess whether an interference was necessary in a democratic society, meaning that it meets a 'pressing social need' and is not disproportionate to the aims pursued.[79]

EU data protection law has been used to determine the level of scrutiny when the ECtHR reviews the necessity of an interference. It has used EU data protection law to argue for both a low and a high level of scrutiny of interferences with Convention's rights. This is the case of *Breyer v. Germany* (2020), which concerns the storing of personal data of users of prepaid mobile-telephone SIM-cards which the applicants considered to be contrary to their right to privacy. The ECtHR found that there was no violation of Article 8 ECHR. One significant element in the ECtHR's reasoning regarding proportionality was the degree of interference caused by the national measure. Despite the applicants asserting that the interference was severe,[80] the ECtHR considered that the interference was limited. The ECtHR drew an analogy with a judgment from the CJEU, the *Ministerio Fiscal* (2018) case, concerning public authorities' access to data for the purpose of identifying SIM card owners:

> Lastly, in so far as *the applicants argued that the interference was severe*, because section 111 of the Telecommunications Act created a register of all users of mobile SIM cards, and in that sense *was comparable to the data retention at issue in Digital Rights Ireland and Seitlinger and Others, as well as Tele2 Sverige and Tom Watson and Others* [...], the Court notes that the Directive at issue in those cases applied to traffic and location data on both legal entities and natural persons and to the related data necessary to identify the subscriber or registered user.
>
> Indeed, *the data at issue in the present case bear greater resemblance to those at issue in a different preliminary reference, Ministerio fiscal* [...]. As the CJEU stated in that case, the data in question 'do not make it possible to ascertain the date, time, duration and recipients of the communications made with the SIM card or cards in question, nor the locations where those communications took place or the frequency of those communications with specific people during a given period. Those data do not therefore allow precise conclusions to be drawn concerning the private lives of the persons whose data is concerned'. The CJEU therefore concluded that the access to the data at issue could not be defined as a serious interference with the fundamental rights of the persons whose data were concerned [...].

---

79 E.g. ECtHR, *Z v. Finland*, 25 February 1997, § 94, Reports of Judgments and Decisions 1997-I.

80 ECtHR, *Breyer v. Germany*, no. 50001/12, § 93, 30 January 2020.

> In sum, the Court concludes that the interference was, while not trivial, of a rather limited nature.[81]

Not only did the ECtHR reject the EU-based argument presented by the applicants, which relied on *Digital Rights Ireland* and *Tele2 Sverige*,[82] but it also leaned on another specific judgment of the CJEU to take an opposing direction. The *Ministerio Fiscal* case as interpreted by the ECtHR is a significant argument in the examination of the proportionality of the measure, and it is the sole legal source to assert that the level of interference is limited. We will come back to this case as the ECtHR's interpretation is not self-evident, and the significance attributed to one CJEU's judgement may appear questionable.[83]

Instances where EU law is used for a stringent level of scrutiny are diverse. The ECtHR has, for instance, referred to EU data protection law to consider certain personal data as falling under the special categories of sensitive data, attracting a heightened level of protection. This has been the cases with regard to data related to criminal proceedings[84] and political opinions.[85] Another example of using EU data protection for strict scrutiny can be found in *Szabo v. Hungary* (2016) which related to legislation on secret surveillance:

> However, given the particular character of the interference in question and the potential of cutting-edge surveillance technologies to invade citizens' privacy, the Court considers that the requirement "necessary in a democratic society" must be interpreted in this context as requiring 'strict necessity' in two aspects. A measure of secret surveillance can be found as being in compliance with the Convention only if it is strictly necessary, as a general consideration, for the safeguarding the democratic institutions and, moreover, if it is strictly necessary, as a particular consideration, for the obtaining of vital intelligence in an individual operation. In the Court's view, any measure of secret surveillance which does not correspond to these criteria will be prone to abuse by the authorities with formidable technologies at their disposal. *The Court notes that both the CJEU of the European Union and the United Nations Special Rapporteur require secret surveillance measures to answer to strict necessity (see paragraphs 23 and 24 above) – an approach it considers convenient to endorse.*[86]

The CJEU's stance is one of the key elements to justify the ECtHR's strict necessity approach. The ECtHR also cites the United Nations Special Rapporteur, both of which are central to establishing the strict necessity test. The ECtHR does not explicitly refer to the CJEU's cases but rather cites

81 Ibid., §§ 93–95. Emphasis added.

82 Case C-203/15 *Tele2 Sverige AB*, ECLI:EU:C:2016:970; Joined Cases C-293/12 and C-594/12, *Digital Rights Ireland*, ECLI:EU:C:2014:238.

83 See below Part III (case study on data protection), Chapter 3, Section V, §3. Contextualisation.

84 ECtHR, *Biancardi v. Italy*, no. 77419/16, § 67, 25 November 2021.

85 ECtHR, *Catt v. the United Kingdom*, no. 43514/15, §§ 67–71 and 112, 24 January 2019.

86 ECtHR, *Szabó and Vissy v. Hungary*, no. 37138/14, § 73, 12 January 2016. Emphasis added.

paragraphs of the relevant legal documents which refer to CJEU's case-law. This frequently used technique of 'use by reference' will be discussed below.[37]

The ECtHR has used EU data protection law when assessing the necessity criterion in case where the balance between data protection and other interests stems from EU law. This seems to flow from the fact that domestic law integrates the EU balance; EU law is thus the starting point for evaluating the proportionality of national measures with ECHR standards. A rather hands-off approach can be seen in *Jehovah's Witness v. Finland* (2023), where the ECtHR observed that the obligation of consent comes from EU law.[88] In a short reasoning, the ECtHR explained that 'the requirement of consent by the data subject is to be considered an appropriate and necessary safeguard with a view to preventing any communication or disclosure of personal and sensitive data inconsistent with the guarantees in Article 8 of the Convention in the context of door-to-door preaching by individual Jehovah's Witnesses.'[89] Relatedly, the ECtHR shows a rather deferential approach when assessing whether domestic courts have struck a fair balance between Convention rights or other interests and the right to respect for the private life of data subjects. The ECtHR has held that 'where the balancing exercise has been undertaken by the national authorities in conformity with the criteria laid down in the ECtHR's case-law, the ECtHR would require strong reasons to substitute its view for that of the domestic courts.'[90] This deferential approach is applied when national authorities act in light of EU data protection law, which operates the balance between data protection and other interests.

Even if the ECtHR takes into account the balance struck by EU law,[91] it applies its own criteria to assess whether a fair balance has been achieved. This is clear in the case of *Satakunnan v. Finland* [GC](2017), where the ECtHR examines a series of criteria for balancing the right to freedom of expression and the right to privacy.[92] While the balance between rights and interests, including data protection, originating from EU law is considered by the ECtHR, the interference is evaluated under the criteria set out by the ECtHR.

A final observation is that EU data protection law has been very limitedly used to shape the ECtHR's safeguards to prevent the abuse of personal data. The key source for developing these safeguards has been Convention 108, not EU law. Only in *Surikov v. Ukraine* (2017) is EU data protection law – indirectly

87 See below Part III (case study on data protection), Chapter 3, Section V, §1. Transparency.

88 ECtHR, *Jehovah's Witnesses v. Finland*, no. 31172/19, § 92, 9 May 2023.

89 Ibid., § 95.

90 ECtHR, *Satakunnan Markkinapörssi Oy and Satamedia Oy v. Finland* [GC], no. 931/13, § 164, 27 June 2017.

91 ECtHR, *Satakunnan Markkinapörssi Oy and Satamedia Oy v. Finland*, no. 931/13, §§ 68–71, 21 July 2015.

92 ECtHR, *Satakunnan Markkinapörssi Oy and Satamedia Oy v. Finland* [GC], no. 931/13, §§ 165 and following, 27 June 2017.

– referred to in this context. The ECtHR observed that there is a 'certain level of consensus on the international level and, in particular, between the Council of Europe member States has been achieved as regards the fundamental data protection principles and the corresponding basic procedural safeguards to be included in the national legislative frameworks in order to justify the necessity of any possible interference. *These principles were formulated in a number of treaties and other legal instruments, including the Council of Europe Data Protection Convention no. 108 and other documents (see paragraphs 53–60 above).* The ECtHR has previously referred to the relevant international instruments, most notably the Data Protection Convention, in assessing data processing and protection practices in individual cases brought under Article 8 of the Convention.'[93] Under the term 'other documents', by cross-referencing, we can find EU data protection law together with OECD guidelines.[94]

IV. Intermediary Conclusions

As in our equality case study, the justification function of EU data protection law is notable. It has been used to assess whether an interference pursued a legitimate aim,[95] whether it was lawful[96] and necessary in a democratic society.[97] The impact has been significant on the conditions of lawfulness and necessity. For the former, recent case-law shows that the ECtHR takes into account EU data protection law for the requirement of foreseeability.[98] For the latter, EU data protection law is used either to determine the level of scrutiny[99] or is considered when the ECtHR reviews whether a fair balance has been achieved,[100] but not for developing its appropriate safeguards to prevent data abuses,[101] for which the ECtHR has relied on Convention 108.[102] When used at the level of justification, the ECtHR uses sometimes

---

93 ECtHR, *Surikov v. Ukraine*, no. 42788/06, § 74, 26 January 2017.

94 Ibid., §§ 53–60.

95 ECtHR, *Jehovah's Witnesses v. Finland*, no. 31172/19, §§ 39–41 and 89, 9 May 2023; ECtHR, *Satakunnan Markkinapörssi Oy and Satamedia Oy v. Finland* [GC], no. 931/13, §§ 158–159, 27 June 2017.

96 ECtHR, *Jehovah's Witnesses v. Finland*, ibid., §§ 85–87; ECtHR, *Satakunnan Markkinapörssi Oy and Satamedia Oy v. Finland* [GC], ibid., §§ 149–150.

97 E.g. ECtHR, *Breyer v. Germany*, no. 50001/12, §§ 93–95, 30 January 2020; ECtHR, *Szabó and Vissy v. Hungary*, no. 37138/14, § 73, 12 January 2016.

98 ECtHR, *Jehovah's Witnesses v. Finland*, no. 31172/19, §§ 85–87, 9 May 2023; ECtHR, *Satakunnan Markkinapörssi Oy and Satamedia Oy v. Finland* [GC], no. 931/13, §§ 149–150, 27 June 2017.

99 E.g. ECtHR, *Breyer v. Germany*, no. 50001/12, §§ 93–95, 30 January 2020; ECtHR, *Szabó and Vissy v. Hungary*, no. 37138/14, § 73, 12 January 2016.

100 E.g. ECtHR, *Jehovah's Witnesses v. Finland*, no. 31172/19, §§ 92 and 95, 9 May 2023.

101 With the limited exception of ECtHR, *Surikov v. Ukraine*, no. 42788/06, §§ 53–60 and 74, 26 January 2017.

102 See below Part III (case study on data protection), subsection 3.2.5: *Comparative insights*.

EU data protection law as a central argument;[103] in other instances, it serves as one argument among many to support the ECtHR's justification.[104] Often, EU data protection law is used in conjunction with Convention 108, though it sometimes appears as the sole legal source.[105] References at the stage of justification are often to CJEU case-law.[106] EU data protection law has mostly been used in a 'data protection-friendly' manner: it has been mobilised to consider a data protection interest as a legitimate aim as just mentioned, to deem a balance that includes data protection concerns acceptable,[107] and to apply a high level of scrutiny in certain data protection cases.[108] However, this protection of data protection has sometimes come at the expense of other fundamental rights, such as freedom of religion and expression.[109] Conversely, there are instances where EU data protection law is used to justify a low level of scrutiny when reviewing measures which is detrimental to data protection.[110]

§ 3. DISTINGUISHING

The ECtHR has distinguished its stance from that of EU data protection law. This has occurred in a limited manner, with only a few cases where the ECtHR has done so, but it appears that EU data protection law is the sole legal source used in a distinguishing perspective.

The ECtHR has highlighted contextual differences between its own case-law and that of the CJEU, which may account for divergent legal outcomes, as seen in the *Breyer v. Germany* (2020) case. Whereas the applicants had argued that 'the interference was severe, because section 111 of the Telecommunications Act created a register of all users of mobile SIM cards, and in that sense was comparable to the data retention at issue in Digital Rights Ireland and Seitlinger and Others, as well as Tele2 Sverige and Tom Watson and Others

103 E.g. ECtHR, *Jehovah's Witnesses v. Finland*, no. 31172/19, §§ 85–87, 9 May 2023; ECtHR, *Satakunnan Markkinapörssi Oy and Satamedia Oy v. Finland* [GC], no. 931/13, §§ 149–150, 27 June 2017.

104 ECtHR, *Surikov v. Ukraine*, no. 42788/06, §§ 53–60 and 74, 26 January 2017.

105 E.g. ECtHR, *Jehovah's Witnesses v. Finland*, no. 31172/19, §§ 39–41 and 89, 9 May 2023; ECtHR, *Satakunnan Markkinapörssi Oy and Satamedia Oy v. Finland* [GC], no. 931/13, §§ 158–159, 27 June 2017.

106 This is very clear in both ECtHR, *Jehovah's Witnesses v. Finland* and *Satkunnan v. Finland* (ibid.) but also in e.g. ECtHR, *Szabó and Vissy v. Hungary*, no. 37138/14, § 73, 12 January 2016.

107 E.g. ECtHR, *Jehovah's Witnesses v. Finland*, no. 31172/19, §§ 92 and 95, 9 May 2023.

108 E.g. ECtHR, *Szabó and Vissy v. Hungary*, no. 37138/14, § 73, 12 January 2016.

109 E.g. ECtHR, *Jehovah's Witnesses v. Finland*, no. 31172/19, §§ 83–90 and 95, 9 May 2023. For instance, in *Jehovah's Witnesses*, the ECtHR takes into account EU data protection law to justify an interference with the freedom of religion.

110 E.g. ECtHR, *Breyer v. Germany*, no. 50001/12, §§ 93–95, 30 January 2020.

(see paragraphs 51-52 above)',[111] the ECtHR dismissed this EU-law based argument[112] and observed that 'the data at issue in the present case bear greater resemblance to those at issue in a different preliminary reference, Ministerio fiscal (see paragraph 54 above) [...] The CJEU therefore concluded that the access to the data at issue could not be defined as a serious interference with the fundamental rights of the persons whose data were concerned (see paragraph 55 above).'[113] In other words, the ECtHR rejected the comparison proposed by the applicants with some CJEU's judgments and instead drew a parallel with another judgment.

One notable instance of distinguishing has occurred in the context of the right to be forgotten where the ECtHR has drawn on the case-law of the CJEU. The latter has stood out as a front-runner in this field, with its *Google Spain* ruling of 13 May 2014. This case concerned a complaint filed by a Spanish national against a Spanish newspaper as well as Google Inc., and Google Spain. The individual asked for links to the newspaper pages, which announced a real estate auction following a seizure against him, to be removed from Google's search results.

Significantly for our purposes, the CJEU drew a distinction between the activities of a web page publisher and those of a search engine operator. It observed that the processing carried out by the publisher, involving the publication of information about an individual, might be considered as 'solely for journalistic purposes' and thus eligible for derogations under Article 9 of the Data Protection Directive (95/46/EC). This does not appear to be the case for the processing carried out by the operator of a search engine.[114] The CJEU highlighted that the grounds justifying the publication of personal data on a website may not necessarily align with those applicable to search engine activities.[115] It also stressed that the inclusion of a web page in search results, particularly when related to a person's name, significantly facilitates access to information, playing a decisive role in its dissemination and posing a potentially more substantial interference with the data subject's fundamental right to privacy than the publication on the web page itself.[116]

It is on this distinction drawn by the CJEU between the activities of a web page publisher and a search engine operator, that the ECtHR relied upon in its right to be forgotten cases to differentiate the specifics from those considered in the CJEU's cases. This began with the case of *ML and WW v. Germany*

[111] Ibid., § 93.
[112] Ibid.
[113] Ibid., § 94.
[114] Ibid., § 85.
[115] Ibid., § 86.
[116] Ibid., § 87.

(2018).[117] The applicants were convicted of murdering an actor and sentenced to life imprisonment; as their release neared, they initiated legal action against various media organisations, seeking the anonymisation of archive documents from the time of the trial that were accessible on the organisations' Internet sites.[118] They claimed a violation of their right to respect for private life, asserting that the denial to compel the media to anonymise online archive material constituted an infringement.[119] When starting its analysis of the case's specificities, the ECtHR observed that:

> [t]he balancing of the interests at stake may result in different outcomes depending on whether a request for deletion concerns the original publisher of the information, whose activity is generally at the heart of what freedom of expression is intended to protect, or a search engine whose main interest is not in publishing the initial information about the person concerned, but in particular in facilitating identification of any available information on that person and establishing a profile of him or her (*in this connection, see also the CJEU judgment of 13 May 2014, No C-131/12, paragraphs 59-62 above*).[120]

While the reference to the *Google Spain* judgment is brief, the distinction made by the CJEU, and relied upon by the ECtHR, assumes a notable role in the latter's reasoning. The ECtHR concluded, among other considerations, based on the nature of web page publisher activity but also the margin of appreciation, that there is no violation of Article 8 ECHR.[121] If conclusion diverges somewhat from the CJEU's stance, it is partly rooted in the CJEU's case-law which itself draws a distinction between the activities of web page publishers and search engine operators.

In subsequent cases, the ECtHR continued to rely on this distinction. This was evident in *Hurbain v. Belgium* [GC](2023), which involved a newspaper publisher ordered to anonymise the online archived version of a lawful article.[122] Despite the fact that the case concerned web page publishers, the ECtHR did not side with freedom of expression. It analysed several criteria in the context of balancing the right to freedom of expression and the right to respect for private life, while considering the margin of appreciation of States.[123] The ECtHR found that the national courts had carefully balanced the rights at

117 This case is often regarded as the inaugural right-to be forgotten ECtHR's case, see S. O'Leary, 'The EU Charter Ten Years On: A View from Strasbourg', in M. Bobek and J. Adams-Prassl (eds.), *The EU Charter of Fundamental Rights in the Member States*, Oxford, Hart Publishing, 2020, pp. 51–52.

118 ECtHR, *M.L. and W.W. v. Germany*, nos. 60798/10 and 65599/10, §§ 7–9, 28 June 2018.

119 Ibid., § 65.

120 Ibid., § 97. Emphasis added.

121 Ibid., § 116.

122 ECtHR, *Hurbain v. Belgium* [GC], no. 57292/16, § 207, 4 July 2023.

123 Ibid., §§ 200–211.

stake in accordance with the requirements of the Convention. Specifically, the interference with Article 10 ECHR, due to the anonymisation of the electronic version of the article on the newspaper's website, was deemed to be limited to what was strictly necessary, and therefore, there was no violation of Article 10 ECHR.[124] Thus, while the CJEU's distinction is taken into account, it is only part of a broader assessment made by the ECtHR.

If there are limited cases where the ECtHR distinguishes its stance from CJEU case-law, the latter appears the only source with which the ECtHR differentiates its stance. One possible explanation is that the ECtHR seeks to articulate its approach with the CJEU's case-law to ensure coherence between EU and ECHR data protection laws, as in our equality case study.

§ 4. INFORMATION

EU data protection law serves a significant informative function, with the ECtHR referencing it as relevant information in the context of its judgments or in its relevant legal materials. In our equality case study, we observed that EU equality law was often cited as the sole relevant information. In data protection cases, both EU data protection law and Convention 108 are often mentioned together as relevant legal standards.

The ECtHR has referred to EU data protection law as part of the contextual framework in the cases it handles. EU data protection law occasionally plays a limited contextual role, with the ECtHR noting that applicants,[125] domestic courts,[126] or both have referenced it,[127] although it is not key to contextualise the case. In several instances, EU data protection law features prominently in the background of ECHR cases, with the ECtHR extensively discussing EU law as part of the case's context. The significant presence of EU law can be attributed to the fact that it is an integral part of the context of national cases where it sometimes occupies an important place, particularly when national courts refer to the CJEU for a preliminary ruling before the case reaches the ECtHR.[128]

EU data protection law is frequently cited as relevant legal standards. Whereas EU equality law is often cited as the sole legal source alongside domestic laws, in the data protection context, both EU data protection law and Convention 108 emerge as the two primary relevant legal standards.

---

124 Ibid., § 256.

125 ECtHR, *Liebscher v. Austria*, no. 5434/17, § 9, 6 April 2021.

126 ECtHR *L.B. v. Hungary* [GC], no. 36345/16, §§ 15–17, 9 March 2023.

127 ECtHR, *Hurbain v. Belgium* [GC], no. 57292/16, §§ 23 and 28, 4 July 2023.

128 Examples include *Satakunnan v. Finland* [GC](2017) and *Jehova's Witness v. Finland* (2023), where the CJEU addressed relevant preliminary questions and where domestic courts adjudicated on the matter in light of CJEU's judgment. See above Part III (case study on data protection), Chapter 3, Section II, §2, II. Lawfulness.

They are frequently cited as the sole sources in relevant legal materials.[129] The ECtHR rarely provides extensive descriptions of comparative law materials.[130] In recent cases, EU law increasingly appears as the most prominent source, with Convention 108 still mentioned but EU law being more significant. This trend is due to the ECtHR's detailed descriptions of CJEU cases.[131]

The ECtHR increasingly presents the relevant EU data protection law in an exhaustive, precise, and up-to-date manner. The initial references to EU data protection law show that instruments were cited either in a general manner[132] or only with specific provisions.[133] The references have become more specific and thorough. This is evident not only in the ECtHR referring to the preambles of EU data protection instruments[134] but also in a heightened reliance on the CJEU case-law.[135] The ECtHR refers at times to a particular CJEU case relevant to the matter at hand,[136] while in other instances, it provides an extensive description of all relevant CJEU cases. The latter practice became particularly pronounced in recent years.[137]

The high degree of specificity and exhaustivity is also illustrated by references to soft law associated with EU instruments. In the employment context, the ECtHR has cited opinions and working documents from the Working Party on Data Protection.[138] In cases related to the right to be forgotten, it has referred to specific guidelines from the European Data Protection Board.[139] All in all, this demonstrates an effort to obtain a comprehensive overview of relevant EU data protection law in related ECtHR cases. While it does not mean that

129 ECtHR, *Drelon v. France*, nos. 3153/16 and 27758/18, § 29 (Convention 108) and §§ 30–36 (EU data protection law), 8 September 2022.

130 ECtHR, *S. and Marper v. the United Kingdom* [GC], nos 30562/04 and 30566/04, §§ 45–49, ECHR 2008.

131 E.g. ECtHR, *Big Brother Watch and Others v. the United Kingdom* [GC], nos. 58170/13 and 2 others, §§ 192–194 (Convention 108) and 202–241 (EU data protection law), 25 May 2021.

132 ECtHR, *Mosley v. the United Kingdom*, no. 48009/08, § 64, 10 May 2011; ECtHR, *S. and Marper v. the United Kingdom* [GC], nos. 30562/04 and 30566/04 § 50, ECHR 2008.

133 ECtHR, *Romet v. the Netherlands*, no. 7094/06, § 26, 14 February 2012.

134 E.g. ECtHR, *Breyer v. Germany*, no. 50001/12, § 47, 30 January 2020; ECtHR, *Benedik v. Slovenia*, no. 62357/14, § 54, 24 April 2018; ECtHR, *Wasmuth v. Germany*, no. 12884/03, § 34, 17 February 2011.

135 This is very clear in ECtHR, *Delfi AS v. Estonia* [GC], no. 64569/09, §§ 52–57, ECHR 2015.

136 E.g. ECtHR, *Szabó and Vissy v. Hungary*, no. 37138/14, § 23, 12 January 2016 which refers to Case C-293/12 and C-594/12, *Digital Rights Ireland*, 8 April 2014, ECLI:EU:C:2014:238.

137 This was the case for instance in the *Big Brother Watch v. the United Kingdom* [GC](2021) case where the ECtHR extensively described eight CJEU cases related to the access and retention of data in surveillance contexts, see ECtHR, *Big Brother Watch and Others v. the United Kingdom* [GC], nos. 58170/13 and 2 others, §§ 209–241, 25 May 2021.

138 ECtHR, *López Ribalda and Others v. Spain* [GC], nos. 1874/13 and 8567/13, §§ 64–65, 17 October 2019; ECtHR, *Bărbulescu v. Romania* [GC], no. 61496/08, §§ 46–49, 5 September 2017.

139 ECtHR, *Hurbain v. Belgium* [GC], no. 57292/16, § 70, 4 July 2023; ECtHR, *Biancardi v. Italy*, no. 77419/16, § 29, 25 November 2021.

EU law is used in the ECtHR's reasoning, it underscores that decisions of the ECtHR are often made with a careful consideration of relevant information related to EU data protection law.

To illustrate the extensive references to EU data protection law, the field of surveillance appears as a good example. Nearly forty years ago, the ECtHR was given the opportunity to pioneer in this domain, and since then has developed limits and safeguards to prevent abuses.[140] One decade ago, the CJEU rendered several significant judgments on surveillance, starting with *Digital Rights Ireland* in 2014.[141] It has expanded its jurisprudence and shed light on the contours of national data retention and access regimes in key judgments.[142] In the meantime, the ECtHR has encountered new important cases in the realm of surveillance. How has the ECtHR taken into account the new wave of CJEU's judgments?

The ECtHR has mentioned the relevant CJEU's case-law into its own judgments, demonstrating a robust awareness and comprehension of the EU legal framework. This is evident in the case of *Centrum for Rättvisa v. Sweden*. The Chamber's judgment refers to three articles of the Charter (7, 8, and 11); to the Data Protection Directive (95/46/EC), noting that as the activities of Member States regarding public safety, defence, and State security fall outside the scope of Community law, the Directive did not apply to these activities (Article 3(2)); to the Directive (2002/58/EC) on privacy and electronic communications, referencing both two specific recitals and two articles; to the Data Retention Directive (2006/24/EC); to the CJEU's case-law, summarising key findings from *Digital Rights Ireland* and *Tele2 Sverige AB* by citing several relevant paragraphs of these judgments; and finally, mentioning the GDPR.[143]

In the Grand Chamber's judgment, the ECtHR not only mentioned all of the above but also expanded its references to include other judgments from the CJEU, citing decisions that were not yet referenced in the Chamber's judgment (*Schrems I*) and those rendered since the Chamber's judgment (*Ministerio Fiscaal, Schrems II, Privacy International, La Quadrature du Net and Others*).[144] In a nutshell, the ECtHR is meticulous in ensuring that its references to EU data protection law reflect the latest and most relevant CJEU's case-law.

These cases underscore the close scrutiny of EU law developments at ECtHR level. An insight into the practice revealed that numerous internal mechanisms are in place to ensure that lawyers and judges at the ECtHR

140 See above Part III (case study on data protection), Chapter 3, Section I, §3. Frequency per Area.

141 Case C-293/12 and C-594/12, *Digital Rights Ireland*, ECLI:EU:C:2014:238.

142 Among others in Case C-203/15, *Tele2 Sverige AB*, ECLI:EU:C:2016:970 and Joined Cases C-511/18, 512/18 and C-520/18, *La Quadrature du Net and Others*, ECLI:EU:C:2020:791.

143 ECtHR, *Centrum för rättvisa v. Sweden*, no. 35252/08, §§ 75–81, 19 June 2018.

144 ECtHR, *Centrum för rättvisa v. Sweden* [GC], no. 35252/08, §§ 92–130, 25 May 2021.

maintain an updated and precise understanding of EU law. While specifics cannot be delved into, this practice involves continuous monitoring of EU law developments. It encompasses tools that enable judges and legal experts at the ECtHR, in the context of ongoing proceedings, to stay informed about the current state of EU law, as we will further discuss in Part IV of our study.[145]

§ 5. COMPARATIVE INSIGHTS

Looking at comparative data on the functions of Convention 108,[146] this instrument largely serves similar functions to those of EU data protection law, yet with some notable differences. Starting with the interpretative function, the influence of Convention 108 is limited and, to a large extent, similar to that of EU data protection law. Convention 108 is used to determine whether a given situation falls within the scope of Article 8 ECHR. The ECtHR has relied on the notion of 'personal data' enshrined in Convention 108 to support a broad interpretation of private life in the context of personal data. This first occurred in *Z v. Finland* (1997) and has taken place a number of times since.[147] Convention 108 is most often the sole legal source, albeit not the sole argument to consider whether the matter falls within the ambit of private life.[148]

The difference in the use of EU data protection law and Convention 108 becomes more significant with regard to the justification function. While the latter has not been used to assess the legitimacy criterion and has been very limitedly used for the lawfulness criterion[149] the ECtHR has used it significantly for the necessity criterion. The ECtHR has significantly relied on the principles enshrined in Convention 108 to develop its safeguards to avoid data abuses. *Z. v. Finland* (1997) was the first case where it occurred. The ECtHR mentioned that: '[t]he domestic law must [...] afford appropriate safeguards to prevent any such communication or disclosure of personal health data as may be inconsistent with the guarantees in Article 8 of the Convention (Art. 8) *(see, mutatis mutandis, Articles 3 para. 2 (c), 5, 6 and 9 of the Convention for the Protection of Individuals with Regard to Automatic Processing of Personal*

---

145 Part IV, Chapter 1, Section III. A Shift in the Infrastructure.

146 Our focus is on Convention 108, as it is the instrument most frequently used, alongside EU data protection law, as we have seen above.

147 ECtHR, *Z v. Finland*, § 64, 25 February 1997, Reports of Judgments and Decisions 1997-I.

148 The ECtHR recognised this practice *inter alia* in ECtHR, *Satakunnan Markkinapörssi Oy and Satamedia Oy v. Finland* [GC], no. 931/13, § 133, 27 June 2017, where it stated: 'In the particular context of data protection, the Court has, on a number of occasions, referred to the Data Protection Convention (see paragraph 80 above), which itself underpins the Data Protection Directive applied by the domestic courts in the present case. That Convention defines personal data in Article 2 as "any information relating to an identified or identifiable individual.'

149 ECtHR, *M.M. v. the United Kingdom*, no. 24029/07, §§ 194–196, 13 November 2012.

Data, European Treaty Series no. 108, Strasbourg, 1981).'[150] In following cases, the ECtHR has drawn heavy inspiration from Convention 108 to flesh out its safeguards.[151] The ECtHR has acknowledged its reliance on Convention 108. In *Drelon v. France* (2023), for instance, the ECtHR observed that:

> The domestic law must also afford 'appropriate safeguards' to prevent any such use of personal data as may be inconsistent with the guarantees of Article 8 (ibid., § 103). In this connection, *the Court takes into account the stipulations of the Convention for the Protection of Individuals with regard to Automatic Processing of Personal Data* ('the 1981 *Convention') (see Z v. Finland, 25 February 1997, § 95, Reports of Judgments and Decisions 1997 I, and S. and Marper, cited above, §§ 103 and 107). To verify whether a measure infringing the principle of personal data protection is 'necessary in a democratic society', the Court examines whether it meets any of the requirements listed in Article 5 of that Convention, including minimising stored data, ensuring data are accurate, restricting data use and limiting data retention periods.* In particular, the domestic law should ensure that processed data are relevant and not excessive in relation to the purposes for which they are stored; and preserved in a form which permits identification of the data subjects for no longer than is required for the purpose for which those data are stored (ibid., § 103). Such considerations are especially valid as regards the protection of special categories of more sensitive data referred to in Article 6 of the 1981 Convention (ibid.).[152]

Regarding the information function, the use of Convention 108 is notable but less significant than that of EU data protection law. Convention 108 has not been used as contextual information but only as relevant legal standards. Convention 108 is often mentioned in conjunction with EU data protection law, with the latter becoming more prominent in recent cases, as we have seen above. When cases concern non-EU States, the ECtHR often mentions Convention 108 on its own.[153] Similar to our findings for EU data protection law, there is a high level of precision, comprehensiveness, and up-to-dateness for Convention 108, with the ECtHR mentioning not only the preambles and provisions of the Convention[154] but also its additional Protocol,[155] the modernised Convention,[156] and related explanatory reports.[157] One key

---

150 ECtHR, *Z v. Finland*, § 95, 25 February 1997, Reports of Judgments and Decisions 1997-I. Emphasis added

151 E.g. *Gardel v. France*, no. 16428/05, § 62, ECHR 2009; ECtHR, *Peck v. the United Kingdom*, no. 44647/98, § 78, ECHR 2003-I.

152 ECtHR, *Drelon v. France*, nos. 3153/16 and 27758/18, § 82, 8 September 2022. Emphasis added.

153 E.g. ECtHR, *N.F. and Others v. Russia*, nos. 3537/15 and 8 others, §§ 26–28, 12 September 2023.

154 ECtHR, *Centrum för rättvisa v. Sweden* [GC], no. 35252/08, § 82, 25 May 2021.

155 E.g. ECtHR, *Roman Zakharov v. Russia* [GC], no. 47143/06, § 142, ECHR 2015.

156 ECtHR *L.B. v. Hungary* [GC], no. 36345/16, § 43, 9 March 2023.

157 ECtHR, *Hurbain v. Belgium* [GC], no. 57292/16, § 62, 4 July 2023.

difference is that the ECtHR has referred to the outputs of the Consultative Committee in only one case, whereas it has heavily referred to CJEU case-law.[158]

SECTION III. ACTORS

Next to the ECtHR, there are various actors that engage with EU data protection law, including the parties, third-party interveners, national courts, and individual judges at the ECtHR, on which we will focus now. We demonstrate that there is a strong engagement with EU data protection law by these actors, which stands in contrast to the very limited engagement with international instruments. There are strong similarities in the way actors use EU data protection and equality laws, with one key difference: there is a stronger engagement with EU data protection law in separate opinions.

§ 1. QUANTITATIVE OVERVIEW

Let us begin by examining the frequency of references per actor.[159] Our investigation reveals a notable engagement with EU data protection law by different actors, largely similar to our equality case study. In contrast with the latter, however, there is a significantly stronger engagement with EU data protection law than international instruments.

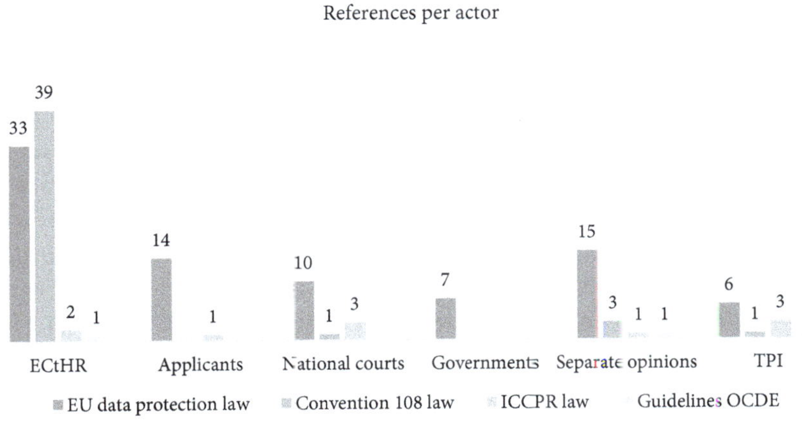

158 ECtHR, *Gluhkin v. Russia*, no. 11519/20, § 37, 4 July 2023.

159 We looked at the number of ECtHR cases in which a given actor has referred to EU data protection law and international instruments. This includes references to EU data protection law, Convention 108 law, ICCPR law, and the OECD guidelines.

The bar chart displays the frequency with which different actors have referred to EU data protection law and several international instruments. As in our equality case study, an important disclaimer should be made here: when the ECtHR refers to EU data protection law, it might be based on references made by parties and national courts, either before national courts or the ECtHR itself, which are not mentioned in the judgment. There might also be references by various actors before the ECtHR which are not reflected in the ECtHR's judgments. This necessitates caution in interpreting these data.

Focusing on EU data protection law, the ECtHR emerges as the key actor, referring to it in 33 instances. Judges in separate opinions demonstrate notable engagement with 12 cases. National courts, governments, and judges in separate opinions display slightly lower but still significant levels of involvement, referencing EU data protection law in 10, 7, and 6 instances. This highlights the diverse engagement with EU data protection law, paralleling our findings in the equality case study. A major difference is the strong engagement with EU data protection law in separate opinions, contrasting with the limited engagement observed in our equality case study.

When we compare these data with those from international instruments, a striking observation emerges: the various actors rely much more significantly on EU data protection law. Convention 108 is referenced 39 times by the ECtHR, three times in separate opinions, and once by third-party interveners. In contrast, the ICCPR is referenced three times by national courts, twice by the ECtHR, and once by applicants, judges in separate opinions, and third-party interveners. The OECD guidelines are referenced only once by the ECtHR and once in a separate opinion. This limited engagement with international law contrasts with our equality case study, where nearly all actors refer to all international instruments, albeit in varying proportions.

As highlighted in our equality case study, it is important to contextualise the involvement of these actors by considering the overall number of cases on data protection, which totals 121 cases. Although the proportion of cases in which actors refer to EU data protection law is higher than for our equality case study, EU data protection law is still mentioned in only a limited proportion of cases before the ECtHR. However, it should be noted that some references made by the actors may not be reflected in the final judgments, which adds a layer of complexity and makes it difficult to draw definitive conclusions from the data.

§ 2. ZOOMING IN ON THE ACTORS

The above highlights that parties, third-party interveners, national judges, and individual judges at the ECtHR rely notably on EU data protection law. When we examine the specific use of EU data protection, we find that it mirrors the usage patterns observed in our equality case study to a large extent. The exception relates to judges in separate opinions, who exhibit more engagement with EU data protection law. We begin with the perspective of parties and third parties, for which EU law is used as an argumentative resource.

I. Applicants

Similar as to what we observed in our equality case study, applicants use EU data protection law as a 'sword' in the sense that they use it when challenging the legality of a national practice or measure. Applicants invoke EU data protection law either before the ECtHR or national courts.[160] Sometimes, they invoke EU data protection law both before both national courts and the ECtHR.[161] The use of EU data protection law can vary, serving as an ancillary element at times[162] and taking a central role in the applicants' arguments at others.[163] There are two main types of arguments: applicants either use EU law to neutralise national courts' decisions based on EU law that are unfavourable to them, or they invoke EU data protection law that supports their claims. Within the first category, applicants sometimes challenge the interpretation of EU law by domestic courts.[164] In other instances, applicants argue that the use of EU law by domestic courts lacked proper contextualisation.[165]

Within the second category, where applicants invoke EU data protection law that is advantageous to them, we observe various sub-arguments. First,

---

160 E.g. at national level: ECtHR, *Hurbain v. Belgium* [GC], no. 57292/16, § 23, 4 July 2023.

161 An example is the case of *Oddone and Pecci v. San Marino* (2019), where the applicants argued before domestic courts that the acquisition of their mobile phone records was illegitimate, citing the *Digital Rights Ireland* case from the CJEU. They reiterated this argument before the ECtHR (ECtHR *Oddone and Pecci v. San Marino*, nos. 26581/17 and 31024/17, §§ 43 and 117, 17 October 2019).

162 ECtHR, *Bărbulescu v. Romania*, no. 61496/08, § 30, 12 January 2016.

163 ECtHR, *Romet v. the Netherlands*, no. 7094/06, § 35, 14 February 2012. In *Romet v. The Netherlands* (2012), concerning the registration of a vehicle in the applicant's name based on his stolen driving license, a pivotal argument was that the registration of the vehicle in his name contradicted Article 7 §1 of Data Protection Directive (95/46/EC), contending that it was therefore not 'in accordance with the law' within the meaning of the ECHR.

164 In *Delfi v. Estonia* [GC](2015), domestic courts had considered that the relevant EU law – which could beneficial to the applicant – was not applicable. The applicants argued that 'the domestic courts had clearly misinterpreted [EU] law.' (ECtHR *Delfi AS v. Estonia* [GC], no. 64569/09, § 80, ECHR 2015).

165 In *Hurbain v. Belgium* (2021), the applicants contended that 'the Court of Appeal had drawn an analogy with the CJEU judgment in the case of Google Spain, transposing the principles established in that judgment regarding a search engine to a newspaper publisher. It had equated newspaper publishers with search engines without taking into account that they were not subject to the same obligations, as newspaper publishers were granted exemptions 'for journalistic purposes' within the meaning of Article 9 of Directive 95/46/EC, or the fact that the CJEU had expressly distinguished between these two types of activities.' (ECtHR, *Hurbain v. Belgium*, no. 57292/16, § 55, 22 June 2021).

there is the argument of comparability: applicants contend that the situation at hand is comparable to those in EU data protection law, particularly CJEU cases, which are favourable to them.[166] There is the argument of compatibility: applicants assert that EU law is not being complied with and, as a consequence, either implicitly or explicitly, argue that the ECtHR should consider it a breach of the Convention.[167] There is the argument of coherence: applicants aim to demonstrate that if the ECtHR were to deem a practice or measure illegal under the ECtHR while it is legal under EU law, this could lead to inconsistencies.[168]

Are the applicants successful in invoking their EU law-based arguments? The answer appears to be negative, which contrasts with our equality case study. Our analysis shows only cases of explicit and implicit rejections. On the explicit side, we can refer to the *Breyer v. Germany* (2020) case, where the applicants argued that the situation of data retention was comparable to the CJEU's cases, which were favourable to them. The ECtHR not only dismissed this comparison but also found that the case was more comparable to another CJEU's case, leading the ECtHR to conclude that the interference was limited, as previously discussed.[169] On the implicit side, there are several cases where the ECtHR does not address the EU law-based arguments.[170] This indicates a reluctance or differing perspective in the incorporation of EU law arguments in data protection cases compared to equality law cases. This may be linked to the fact that, in contrast with EU equality law, EU law-based arguments by the applicants seem to be less prominent in data protection cases. In our view, there are more instances in equality law where EU arguments are central in the applicants' reasoning.[171]

166 In *Breyer v. Germany* (2020), the applicants argued 'that the interference was severe, because section 111 of the Telecommunications Act created a register of all users of mobile SIM cards, and in that sense was comparable to the data retention at issue in *Digital Rights Ireland and Seitlinger and Others*, as well as *Tele2 Sverige* and *Tom Watson and Others*.' (ECtHR, *Breyer v. Germany*, no. 50001/12, § 93, 30 January 2020).

167 E.g. ECtHR *Oddone and Pecci v. San Marino*, nos. 26581/17 and 31024/17, § 117, 17 October 2019.

168 This is well illustrated by the *Delfi v. Estonia* [GC](2015) case, where the applicants submitted that 'the Chamber judgment had created a collision of obligations and legal uncertainty since adhering to EU law on the issue of liability for host service providers would render the State liable under the Convention, whereas adhering to the test set out in the judgment would not be in conformity with EU law.' (ECtHR, *Delfi AS v. Estonia* [GC], no. 64569/09, § 80, ECHR 2015)

169 See above Part III (case study on data protection), Chapter 3, Section II, §2, III. Necessary in a Democratic Society.

170 E.g. ECtHR, *Oddone and Pecci v. San Marino*, nos. 26581/17 and 31024/17, §§ 107–108, 17 October 2019.

171 See above Part III (case study on equality), Chapter 3, Section III, §2, I. Applicants.

II. Governments

If we examine how governments use EU data protection law, we observe, as in our equality case study, that this law serves a 'shield' function, with governments referring to it in defense against alleged breaches of the Convention. Governments use arguments either to neutralise the use of EU data protection law when it is unfavourable to them or to mobilise it when it is favourable to them. In the first category, one of the neutralisation's techniques is that governments assert that it is not the task of the ECtHR to interpret or ensure the compliance with EU law.[172] They have also argued that the CJEU has not ruled on the issue or that the circumstances differ from CJEU case-law.[173]

In the second category, where governments mobilise positively EU data protection law, various arguments are developed. Two arguments that were found in our equality case study are also present. First, the argument of legality or compatibility: governments emphasise that their policies or measures are legal or conform to EU data protection law, for instance, by highlighting that the interference with the right to privacy was permitted under EU law.[174] Second, the argument of discretion: governments argue that EU law grants States discretionary power to regulate the issue.[175]

III. Third-Party Interveners

Third-party interveners also use EU data protection law strategically. They rarely refer to EU data protection law to support Article 8 ECHR's violations or to advocate for a high level of data protection. Instead, EU data protection law is most often used to shape arguments in favour of freedom of expression. There are numerous interventions by organisations defending freedom of expression and media rights in cases that balance these freedoms against data protection. This is seen in interventions by organisations such as Guardian

172 ECtHR, *Delfi AS v. Estonia* [GC], no. 64569/09, § 81, ECHR 2015.

173 Ibid., § 85.

174 E.g. ECtHR, *Margari v. Greece*, no. 36705/16, § 40, 20 June 2023.

175 In *Ekimdzhiev and others v. Bulgaria* (2022), the Government stressed that 'there was no European consensus about the need to retain communications data or its modalities. Even after the CJEU's judgments in Digital Rights Ireland and Others and Tele2 Sverige and Watson and Others, many member States of the European Union had not fully repealed their laws providing for the generalized retention of communications data, since that was a valuable instrument for combatting serious crime. A more restrictive approach could prevent the proper operation of that instrument. *The CJEU had not altogether dismissed the importance of retaining communications data, and the matter remained within the States' margin of appreciation*.' Emphasis added (ECtHR, *Ekimdzhiev and Others v. Bulgaria*, no. 70078/12, § 390, 11 January 2022).

News & Media Ltd,[176] Media Legal Defence Initiative,[177] and the Reporters Committee for Freedom of the Press.[178] These organisations mention EU data protection law to support arguments favouring freedom of expression, often presenting diverse strategies. For instance, they argue that EU law does not impose certain requirements that would restrict freedom of expression.[179] Another argument is that they underline the specificities of the Convention system when there is a data protection right enshrined in EU law.[180]

Among the various freedom of expression's organisations one of the most active to refer to EU data protection law is 'Article 19'.[181] Article 19 has referred to EU data protection law in three third-party interventions and, in one case, was representing the joint position of sixteen third-party interveners.[182] Article 19 has invoked EU data protection, for instance, to argue that the CJEU has adopted a broad interpretation of journalism[183] or to assert that there is no international standard on the right to be forgotten. The latter can be seen in the case of *Hurbain v. Belgium* [GC](2023), where the ECtHR summarised Article 19's argument:

> The third-party interveners stressed that the 'right to be forgotten' was not an international legal standard. Initially, with the CJEU ruling in *Google Spain* (C-131/12), that right had been established in the context of personal data protection and its scope had been limited in a number of ways, applying only to search engines. While the 'right to be forgotten' had subsequently been formalised in the GDPR, Article 17 of that Regulation nevertheless provided for an exception to the right to erasure in respect of data processed for journalistic purposes, an exception whose implementation varied in national legislation. Outside the European Union, the 'right to be forgotten' was not expressly recognised in any international instruments or national constitutions. [...][184]

Beyond the content of the arguments themselves, it is important to emphasise the 'human factor' here: the influence of EU data protection law may depend on specific individuals and actors, such as Article 19, involved before or within the ECtHR. The extent to which these individuals and actors develop their

176 ECtHR, *Mosley v. the United Kingdom*, no. 48009/08, § 93, 10 May 2011.
177 ECtHR, *Delfi AS v. Estonia* [GC], no. 64569/09, § 103, ECHR 2015.
178 ECtHR, *Biancardi v. Italy*, no. 77419/16, § 40, 25 November 2021.
179 ECtHR, *Mosley v. the United Kingdom*, no. 48009/08, § 93, 10 May 2011.
180 ECtHR, *Biancardi v. Italy*, no. 77419/16, § 40, 25 November 2021.
181 See more on this organisation at the following link: https://www.article19.org.
182 ECtHR, *Hurbain v. Belgium* [GC], no. 57292/16, § 164, 4 July 2023; ECtHR, *Breyer v. Germany*, no. 50001/12, § 72, 30 January 2020; ECtHR, *Satakunnan Markkinapörssi Oy and Satamedia Oy v. Finland* [GC], no. 931/13, § 118, 27 June 2017.
183 ECtHR, *Satakunnan Markkinapörssi Oy and Satamedia Oy v. Finland* [GC], no. 931/13, § 118, 27 June 2017.
184 ECtHR, *Hurbain v. Belgium* [GC], no. 57292/16, § 164, 4 July 2023.

arguments based on EU law can play a role in the influence of EU law on ECtHR case-law.

IV. National Judges

Similar to equality law, there is a notable number of references to EU data protection law by national courts, either in the reasoning of their judgments or in dissenting opinions. The relatively high number of references arises because these courts frequently adjudicate on matters involving EU data protection law. Sometimes, EU data protection law is a key aspect of discussions at the national level.[185] The significance of EU data protection law in national courts' decisions may result from the fact that a preliminary question was referred to the CJEU in a related ECtHR's case.[186] Sometimes, EU data protection law is rather ancillary in national courts' decisions.[187]

V. Individual Judges at the ECtHR

We observe a robust engagement with EU data protection in separate opinions of ECtHR's judges, which contrasts with our finding on international instruments and in our equality case study. Some references are informative, highlighting that EU law holds some relevance in the matter at hand.[188] Other references are argumentative in nature, leveraging EU law to argue that the ECtHR's adopted reasoning is correct or flawed If, on occasions, EU data protection law has been used to support the findings of the majority,[189] it is more frequently used to oppose or diverge from the majority's view. In some instances, separate judges argue that the ECtHR has misinterpreted EU data protection law, as we will see in detail in the *Breyer v. Germany* (2020) case.[190] In other instances, judges assert that the ECtHR's reasoning does not align with EU law or on a consensus based on EU law.[191] Some judges have expressed dissatisfaction with the ECtHR's insufficient engagement with EU

185 This was the case in *Delfi v. Estonia* [GC] (2015), where the County Court, the Court of Appeal, and the Supreme Court all considered whether EU law was applicable and/or complied with (ECtHR, *Delfi AS v. Estonia* [GC], no. 64569/09, §§ 23, 24, 31, 43, ECHR 2015).

186 See above Part III (case study on data protection), Chapter 3, Section II, §2, II. Lawfulness.

187 ECtHR, *Hristozov and Others v. Bulgaria*, nos. 47039/11 and 358/12, § 37, ECHR 2012 (extracts).

188 E.g. Separate opinion of Judges Raimondi, Dedov, Kjolbro, Mits, Mourou-Vikstrom in ECtHR, *Bărbulescu v. Romania* [GC], no. 61496/08, § 9, 5 September 2017.

189 Separate opinion of Judge Pinto de Albuquerque in ECtHR, *Centrum för rättvisa v. Sweden* [GC], no. 35252/08, § 22, 25 May 2021.

190 See below Part III (case study on data protection), Chapter 3, Section V, §3. Contextualisation.

191 E.g. Separate opinion of Judges Nussberger and Keller in ECtHR, *Magyar Helsinki Bizottság v. Hungary* [GC], no. 18030/11, § 2, 8 November 2016.

law.[192] There are also coherence arguments where judges highlight that the reasoning of the ECtHR cannot be reconciled with,[193] or is in contrast to,[194] EU data protection law. Finally, judges have expressed the view that the ECHR is lagging behind EU law, a situation they find unacceptable.[195]

The 'human factor' should be emphasised again in this context. The engagement with EU data protection law varies among judges, and not every judge makes references to it to the same extent. There are notable differences in the level of activity among judges. A prime example is Judge Pinto de Albuquerque, who exhibited a high level of engagement with EU data protection law. In several cases, the Judge relied on EU data protection, showcasing a distinct emphasis on this legal framework.[196] This underscores the individual perspectives and preferences of judges within the ECtHR, adding a nuanced layer to the overall dynamics of how EU data protection law is incorporated into the ECtHR's decisions.

§ 3. COMPARATIVE INSIGHTS

As is evident from the quantitative data presented above, the use of international instruments by the actors under scrutiny has been much less frequent than the use of EU data protection law. Governments have not mentioned these instruments (at least as reflected in the ECtHR's judgments), whereas applicants have referenced these instruments only very limitedly.[197] The use of these instruments by third-party interveners is also very restrained. One of the sparse instances is in the Chamber and Grand Chamber's cases *Big Brother Watch* case, where Access Now submitted that the surveillance's measures at

192 See e.g. Separate opinion of Judges Sajo and Tsotsoria in ECtHR, *Delfi AS v. Estonia* [GC], no. 64569/09, § 17, ECHR 2015, *Delfi v. Estonia* [GC][2015] where they pointed out that '[n]either the domestic authorities nor the Court explain why the provision of binding European law that is part of the national legal system is immaterial, except to say that the present case concerns a matter of publication rather than data storage. It is, of course, not for this Court to interpret European Union law as such. This does not mean that we should not regard it as part of the domestic system, attributing to it its proper constitutional weight.'

193 E.g. Separate opinion of Judge Spano joined by Judge Kjolbro in ECtHR, *Magyar Helsinki Bizottság v. Hungary* [GC], no. 18030/11, § 41, 8 November 2016.

194 Separate opinion of Judges Pardalos and Eicke in ECtHR, *Big Brother Watch and Others v. the United Kingdom*, nos. 58170/13 and 2 others, § 22, 13 September 2018.

195 Separate opinion of Judge Pinto de Albuqerque in ECtHR, *Big Brother Watch and Others v. the United Kingdom* [GC], nos. 58170/13 and 2 others, §§ 9, 11 and 59, 25 May 2021.

196 Ibid. See also e.g. Separate Opinion in ECtHR, *Szabó and Vissy v. Hungary*, no. 37138/14, §§ 13, 15–16 and 18, 12 January 2016.

197 E.g. ECtHR, *Big Brother Watch and Others v. the United Kingdom* [GC], nos. 58170/13 and 2 others, §§ 253 and 258, 25 May 2021.

issue failed to comply with the ICCPR in a rather general manner.[198] There are very few cases where national courts engage with international instruments.[199] There are slightly more references in the separate opinions of judges, particularly concerning Convention 108 law, but these instances remain very limited. These references are either informative[200] or argumentative[201] but are always developed in a restricted manner. Overall, there is a strong discrepancy between the use of EU data protection law and international instruments by the actors, with the former standing out.

SECTION IV. STATES

As in our equality case study, we zoom in on the type of respondent States involved in cases where EU data protection law is used. Our primary interest lies in investigating whether EU law is used in cases involving non-EU respondent States, which can raise sensitive issues of institutional balance, as we have observed in Part I of our study.[202]

EU data protection law is most frequently mentioned in cases involving EU States. EU law is employed more often in cases involving EU States than other international instruments. There is very limited – direct or indirect – use of EU data protection law against non-EU States. However, this limited use against non-EU States is implicit, mirroring the patterns seen in the equality case study.

§ 1. QUANTITATIVE OVERVIEW

Looking at the frequency of references per respondent State, the references to EU data protection law occur across a wide array of States. There are notable disparities, with references being much more frequent in cases involving EU States.

---

198 Ibid., § 315; ECtHR, *Big Brother Watch and Others v. the United Kingdom*, nos. 58170/13 and 2 others, § 96, 13 September 2018.

199 One of the few exceptions is the GC case in *Big Brother*, see ibid., §§ 253–258.

200 Separate opinion of Judge Pinto de Albuqerque in ECtHR, *Szabó and Vissy v. Hungary*, no. 37138/14, §§ 3–5, 12 January 2016.

201 Separate opinion of Judge Pinto de Albuqerque in ECtHR, *Centrum för rättvisa v. Sweden* [GC], no. 35252/08, § 22, 25 May 2021.

202 See above Part I, Chapter 2, Section III. Navigating between Fragmentation and Marginalisation.

Frequency per respondent State

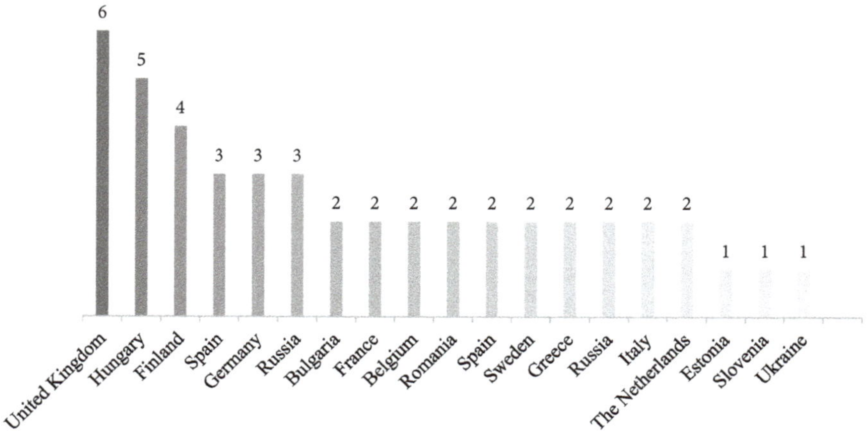

This bar chart shows the distribution of ECtHR cases that refer to EU data protection law per respondent State. The United Kingdom is the most frequently involved country, with 6 out of 46 cases. Following the UK, Croatia, Romania, Russia, and Spain form a middle group with 4 to 5 cases each. Spain, Germany, and Russia each have 3 references, and many other States have 2 references. A few States have one reference. Concerning the distinction between EU and non-EU states, there are a total of six cases involving non-EU States: three against Russia,[203] one against San Marino,[204] one against Ukraine,[205] and one in post-Brexit UK.[206] This results in 13% of cases against non-EU States and 87% against EU States. The vast majority of references to EU data protection law occur in cases involving EU States, highlighting a significant disparity in the use of EU law between EU and non-EU respondent States.

---

[203] ECtHR, *Podchasov v. Russia*, no. 33696/19, 13 February 2024; ECtHR, *Gluhkin v. Russia*, no. 11519/20, 4 July 2023; ECtHR, *Roman Zakharov v. Russia* [GC], no. 47143/06, ECHR 2015.

[204] ECtHR, *Oddone and Pecci v. San Marino*, nos. 26581/17 and 31024/17, 17 October 2019.

[205] ECtHR, *Surikov v. Ukraine*, no. 42788/06, 26 January 2017.

[206] ECtHR, *Big Brother Watch and Others v. the United Kingdom* [GC], nos. 58170/13 and 2 others, 25 May 2021.

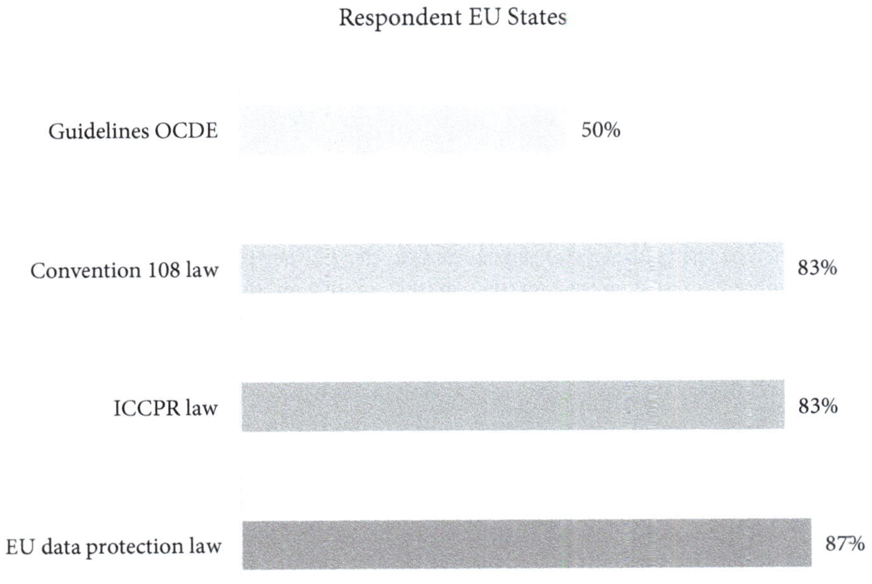

This bar chart indicates the percentage of cases involving EU respondent States for those referencing EU data protection law and international instruments. The data shows limited differences: 87% of the cases referencing EU data protection law involve EU States, which is followed by ICCPR law and Convention 108 law, both at 83%. The references to EU law for the OECD Guidelines represent 50% of the cases, but with only two cases, it is difficult to infer any trends. As in our equality case study, EU law is most frequently referenced in cases involving EU States. In our equality case study, the proportion of cases involving EU States vis-à-vis other instruments was even higher.

§ 2. QUALITATIVE ANALYSIS

The impact of EU data protection law on the ECtHR's reasoning in cases involving non-EU States is very limited, as in our equality case study. EU data protection law is mostly used in an informative way, mentioned within the relevant legal materials. For example, in *Zakharov* (2015), the ECtHR referred to Council Resolutions on the lawful interception of telecommunications and on law enforcement operational needs with respect to public telecommunication networks and services as well as the CJEU's *Digital Rights Ireland* (2014) case in the relevant legal materials.[207] In *Oddone v. San Marino* (2019), the applicants argued that the acquisition of phone records was invalid in light of CJEU's case-law. This argument was discarded by the ECtHR in an implicit and summary manner.[208] Only in *Surikov v. Ukraine* (2017) is EU data protection law used in the ECtHR's reasoning, but even then, it is ancillary as we have seen above.[209] This limited use of EU data protection law in cases involving non-EU States underscores the ECtHR's conscious or unconscious avoidance of using these standards outside the EU context. As in our equality case study, EU data protection law has barely been used in cases involving non-EU respondent States. The frequent mention of EU data protection law in EU States' cases at the ECtHR seems rather logical, as this body of law is akin to domestic law within these States. The integration of EU law into their domestic legal framework makes its use and reference almost inherent in relevant data protection cases involving EU States.

The ECtHR is not explicit about its differential use of EU data protection law. It almost never mentions whether EU data protection law binds the respondent State, with a few exceptions. In *Mosley v. the United Kingdom* (2011), the ECtHR mentioned that the Data Protection Directive (95/46/EC) is applicable to the 27 EU States.[210] Another noteworthy observation comes from Judge Koskelo in the concurring opinion in the *Orlandi v. Italy* (2017) case, where the Judge mentioned that Italy, as a EU State, is subject to EU data protection law.[211] In *Lopez Ribalda* [GC](2019), the ECtHR distinguished the legal regimes applicable to EU and non-EU States in its relevant legal materials.[212]

These instances highlight the few occasions where the ECtHR referred to the binding nature of EU data protection law on EU States, contrasting with its implicit approach. These cases serve as commendable practices that could provide a model for future cases as we explain in Part IV of this research project.[213] The lack of acknowledgement of the binding EU law's status contrasts with the use of international instruments. In numerous judgments, the ECtHR mentions whether the respondent State has ratified the international

---

207 ECtHR, *Roman Zakharov v. Russia* [GC], no. 47143/06, § 147, ECHR 2015.

208 ECtHR, *Oddone and Pecci v. San Marino*, nos. 26581/17 and 31024/17, § 118, 17 October 2019.

209 See above Part III (case study on data protection), Chapter 3, Section II, §2, III. Necessary in a Democratic Society.

210 ECtHR, *Mosley v. the United Kingdom*, no. 48009/08, § 64, 10 May 2011.

211 Separate opinion of Judge Koskelo in ECtHR, *Orlandi and Others v. Italy*, nos. 26431/12 and 3 others, § 21, 14 December 2017.

212 ECtHR, *López Ribalda and Others v. Spain* [GC], nos. 1874/13 and 8567/13, §§ 68–69, 17 October 2019.

213 See below Part IV, Chapter 2, Section II, §3. Contextualisation.

instrument and at what time. This occurs in cases involving both States that have ratified the instrument and those that have not.[214]

The question arises whether the use of EU data protection law in cases involving EU States can have spill-over effects into cases involving non-EU States through precedents.[215] The difficulty here lies in the fact that the influence of EU data protection law has been less structural than that of EU equality law, where specific concepts (such as discrimination by association, indirect discrimination) where inspired by EU law – this is thus more difficult to trace elements on which EU data protection law has influenced ECHR law. Looking at the 'strict necessity' which had been applied in surveillance cases[216] and the distinction between web page publisher and the operator of a search engine,[217] both elements on which the ECtHR had relied on EU data protection law, we found no cases where the ECtHR uses these elements in cases involving non-EU States.

As a last observation, the ECtHR have not used tools (e.g. margin of appreciation or Article 53 ECHR) with a view to modulating the influence of EU data protection law. Yet the use of EU data protection law is sometimes limited to the specific circumstances of the cases. This is, for instance, the case in scenarios where EU data protection law is used when assessing the necessity criterion, particularly when the balance between data protection and other interests stems from EU law. Here, the balance operated by EU law is taken into account as part of the necessity assessment but is not meant to replace the criteria which the ECtHR uses to assess the balance. Similarly, the fact that the ECtHR considers the requirement of foreseeability – part of the lawfulness criterion – to be met when national courts rely on findings from a CJEU's preliminary ruling related to the case, is limited to specific EU cases.

SECTION V. METHODOLOGY OF THE ECTHR WHEN USING EU DATA PROTECTION LAW

Alongside the growing significance of EU data protection law in ECtHR case-law, an overall improvement in the methodological use of EU data protection law can be observed. Despite these advancements, there are still areas that require improvement, whether in terms of transparency, justification, or

214 E.g. ECtHR, *N.F. and Others v. Russia*, nos. 3537/15 and 8 others, § 26, 12 September 2023; ECtHR, *Drelon v. France*, nos. 3153/16 and 27758/18, § 29, 8 September 2022.

215 This is further explained above in Part III (case study on equality), Chapter 3, Section IV, §2.Qualitative Analysis.

216 See above Part III (case study on data protection), Chapter 3, Section II, §2, III. Necessary in A Democratic Society.

217 See above Part III (case study on data protection), Chapter 3, Section II, §3. Distinguishing.

contextualisation. The methodological approach appears more developed concerning international instruments than for EU data protection law, yet the difference is less pronounced than in our equality case study.

§ 1. TRANSPARENCY

There are several situations where the transparency in the use of EU data protection law is limited, potentially due to valid reasons, but this lack of transparency can lead to problematic issues.

As in our equality case study, the phenomenon of 'use by reference' is present. When the ECtHR uses EU data protection law into its reasoning, it often does so in a summarised manner, while referring to EU data protection law in the relevant legal materials. Two instances have been highlighted above. In *Szabo v. Hungary* (2016), the ECtHR refers to EU data protection law to justify its strict necessity approach for surveillance measures. The ECtHR states that '[t]he Court notes that both [the CJEU] and the United Nations Special Rapporteur require secret surveillance measures to meet strict necessity (see paragraphs 23 and 24 above) – an approach it considers convenient to endorse.'[218] In *Jehovah's Witnesses v. Finland* (2023), the ECtHR acknowledged that the aims of EU data protection law are legitimate but did not elaborate on them in the reasoning, simply noting: 'Taking into account the aims of the Personal Data Act [...] and the Data Protection Directive as interpreted by the CJEU (see paragraph 20 above, paragraph 35 of the CJEU's judgment), as well as the established case-law of the Court [...], it is clear that the interference with the applicant community's right to freedom of religion pursued the legitimate aim of protecting 'the rights and freedoms of others', data subjects in the present case, within the meaning of Article 9 § 2 of the Convention.'[219] In both cases, the relevant legal materials provide detailed insights into the content of EU data protection law, whether concerning the approach pursued by the CJEU (*Szabo v. Hungary*)[220] or the aims pursued by EU data protection law (*Jehovah's Witnesses v. Finland*).[221]

By using this approach, the ECtHR encourages the reader to consult EU law within the relevant legal materials. While this strategy makes sense for readability purposes, preventing an overload of information in the reasoning, the ECtHR's concise references to EU law in its reasoning may fall short of elucidating the significance of EU law. In addition, the ECtHR deduces elements from EU law without explicitly fleshing out its way of achieving this.

218 ECtHR, *Szabó and Vissy v. Hungary*, no. 37138/14, § 73, 12 January 2016.
219 ECtHR, *Jehovah's Witnesses v. Finland*, no. 31172/19, § 89, 9 May 2023.
220 ECtHR, *Szabó and Vissy v. Hungary*, no. 37138/14, §§ 23 and 25, 12 January 2016.
221 ECtHR, *Jehovah's Witnesses v. Finland*, no. 31172/19, §§ 39–41, 9 May 2023.

This leaves room for ambiguity, making it challenging to gauge the extent of the influence of EU law or determine whether the ECtHR has deviated from EU law in its reasoning.

There are also counter-examples where the ECtHR provided a more detailed exposition of EU data protection law in its reasoning. A good example is when the ECtHR observed that data in the public domain can be protected in *Jehova's Witness* (2023):

> The Court concurs with the Supreme Administrative Court that data subjects had a reasonable expectation of privacy with regard to personal and sensitive data being collected and processed in the course of door-to-door preaching. The fact that some personal data might be already in the public domain neither reduces this expectation nor does it mean that such data need less protection (see Satakunnan Markkinapörssi Oy and Satamedia Oy, cited above, § 134). This approach finds support in the relevant jurisprudence of the CJEU. In the case Satakunnan Markkinapörssi Oy and Satamedia Oy (C-73/07, ECLI:EU:C:2008:727, 16 December 2008), the Grand Chamber of the CJEU held that "a general derogation from the application of the [Data Protection Directive] in respect of published information would largely deprive the directive of its effect" and that "[i]t would be sufficient for the Member States to publish data in order for those data to cease to enjoy the protection afforded by the directive" (see paragraph 48 of the judgment). This finding was confirmed and reinforced in the case Google Spain and Google (C-131/12, ECLI:EU:C:2014:317, judgment of 13 May 2014), in which the CJEU argued that "the operations referred to in Article 2(b) of Directive 95/46 [had to] also be classified as [data] processing where they exclusively concern[ed] material that [had] already been published in unaltered form in the media" (see paragraph 30 of that judgment).[222]

The ECtHR refers to the reasoning of the CJEU to bolster its approach. Encouraging such a practice is important as it promotes transparency and legal clarity, especially if EU law plays a significant role in the ECtHR's reasoning. It enables an assessment of whether the ECtHR has appropriately used EU data protection law and helps to prevent situations involving inadequate transplants or misinterpretation of EU data protection law, as further explained in Part IV.[223]

A second concern, which is strongly present in EU data protection law, is that the ECtHR often refers to EU data protection law only within the relevant legal materials. While this approach allows the ECtHR to make well-informed decisions, it may become an issue when the ECtHR's reasoning appears to be impacted by EU law without acknowledgement. In the realm of surveillance, the ECtHR has issued two significant cases around 2015 *Zakharov v. Russia*

[222] Ibid., § 94.

[223] See below Part IV, Chapter 2, Section II, §1. Transparency.

[GC](2015) and *Szabo and Vissy v. Hungary* (2016). These cases scrutinised the secret surveillance systems in Russia and Hungary. Authors such as Cole and Vandendriessche have observed that the ECtHR has adopted a more assertive position regarding domestic surveillance in these judgments, indicating a trend toward aligning standards between Luxembourg and Strasbourg.[224] Both cases referred to EU data protection law, and in particular the *Digital Rights Ireland* [GC](2014) case, in the relevant legal materials,[225] yet it is only in *Szabo and Vissy v. Hungary* that the CJEU's approach is mentioned in the reasoning to justify a test of strict necessity.[226] Although it is plausible that EU law impacted the ECtHR's stricter stance in *Zakharov v. Russia* [GC](2015), it is not mentioned in the reasoning.[227]

There is also a phenomenon that might be described as an influence of EU data protection law through the national backdoor. In these instances, the ECtHR mentions that national law transposes EU data protection law in its relevant legal materials. It uses only national law in its reasoning, without reference to EU data protection law. This is well illustrated by *S and Marper v. the United Kingdom* [GC](2008). In the relevant legal documents, the ECtHR noted that the United Kingdom's adoption of the Data Protection Act aimed to implement the provisions of Data Protection Directive (95/46/EC). The ECtHR highlighted that the Data Protection Act defines sensitive personal data in accordance with this Directive.[228] In its reasoning, the ECtHR observed concerning sensitive personal data that:

> [...] it is not disputed by the Government that the processing of DNA profiles allows the authorities to assess the likely ethnic origin of the donor and that such techniques are in fact used in police investigations [...]. The possibility the DNA profiles create for inferences to be drawn as to ethnic origin makes their retention all the more sensitive and susceptible of affecting the right to private life. This conclusion is consistent with the principle laid down in the Data Protection Convention and *reflected in the Data Protection Act* that both list personal data

224 M. Cole and A. Vandendriessche, 'From Digital Rights Ireland and Schrems in Luxembourg to Zakharow and Szabo/Vissy in Strasbourg', *Eur. Data Prot. L. Rev.*, 2016, p. 129.

225 ECtHR, *Szabó and Vissy v. Hungary*, no. 37138/14, §§ 23 and 25, 12 January 2016; ECtHR, *Roman Zakharov v. Russia* [GC], no. 47143/06, §§ 145–147, ECHR 2015.

226 ECtHR, *Szabó and Vissy v. Hungary*, no. 37138/14, § 73, 12 January 2016.

227 M. Cole and A. Vandendriessche, 'From Digital Rights Ireland and Schrems in Luxembourg to Zakharow and Szabo/Vissy in Strasbourg', *Eur. Data Prot. L. Rev.*, 2016, p. 129. It is important to acknowledge a certain degree of speculation here, as there might have been various factors influencing the ECtHR in its choice to adopt a rigorous approach when scrutinising the Russian secret surveillance system and in its decision not to reference EU data protection law. For instance, the fact that Russia is not an EU State may have played a role.

228 ECtHR, *S. and Marper v. the United Kingdom* [GC], nos. 30562/04 and 30566/04, § 30, ECHR 2008.

> revealing ethnic origin among the special categories of sensitive data attracting a heightened level of protection [...].[229]

The ECtHR cites the transposition act of EU law, not EU law itself, when justifying the heightened level of protection for data revealing ethnic origin. A comparable approach is noticeable in the case of *Lopez Ribalda and Others v. Spain* [GC](2019), which pertained to video surveillance in the work context. The ECtHR noted that the Spanish Data Protection Act transposed Data Protection Directive (95/46/EC)[230] and observed that the Spanish Data Protection Act included provisions concerning the information and consent of individuals affected by the collection of their personal data.[231] The right to information, which is transposed from EU law, played a notable role in the ECtHR's reasoning.[232] The ECtHR only mentions the Spanish Data Protection Act and not EU law.

This practice poses a risk of losing track of the influence of EU data protection law. By relying on the transposition of EU data protection law into national legislation without referencing the EU legal framework in its reasoning, the ECtHR may obscure the impact of EU law, potentially overlooking the context and specificities of EU data protection law.

§ 2. JUSTIFICATION

As in our equality case study, there is a lack of justification for the selection and use of EU data protection law as well as a lack of use of the methods of interpretation to justify the use of EU data protection law. The ECtHR does not explain why it considers it is relevant to refer to EU law, with only a very limited number of exceptions in recent cases. One of them is *Benedik v. Slovenia* (2018), where, as noted earlier, the ECtHR began its reasoning by taking note 'of the extensive legislation and of the case-law concerning personal data protection and privacy of electronic communication within the European Union' and mentioning that it 'will rely on them and on other relevant comparative-law material in assessing some of the technical matters applicable to the present case. It will also have regard, where appropriate, to the legal doctrines established therein.'[233] In other words, the ECtHR stated

229 Ibid., § 76. Emphasis added.

230 ECtHR, *López Ribalda and Others v. Spain* [GC], nos. 1874/13 and 8567/13, § 46, 17 October 2019.

231 Ibid., § 47.

232 Ibid., § 133. The ECtHR referred to it to assert that only an overriding requirement related to the protection of significant public or private interests could justify the absence of prior information.

233 Ibid.

that it would refer to EU law due to its relevance in this area. This justification remains very limited: the ECtHR neither refers to the fact that EU law is part of the domestic law of the respondent State nor to its interpretative techniques to justify its use.

The interpretations techniques – such as contextual interpretation, dynamic and evolutive interpretation, or the European consensus – are almost never used to justify the use of EU data protection law, as in our equality case study. One of the rare exceptions concerns the European consensus, where the ECtHR has stated that there is a consensus on a certain element, partly based on EU data protection law, but has provided only a summary reasoning on its technique of European consensus. This was in *Hurbain v. Belgium* [GC](2023):

> The Court also notes the emergence over the past decade of a consensus regarding the importance of press archives. Hence, in the specific context of the processing of personal data at European Union level, the GDPR makes express provision for an exception to the right to the erasure of personal data where the processing of the data is necessary for the exercise of the right of freedom of expression and information (Article 17(3)(a)). Like Directive 95/46/EC which preceded it, the GDPR requires EU member States to provide in their legislation for exemptions or derogations for processing carried out for journalistic purposes if they are necessary to reconcile the right to the protection of personal data with freedom of expression and information (Article 85(2)). According to recital 153 of the GDPR, particular attention is to be paid to the processing of personal data "in news archives and press libraries" (see paragraph 69 above). In the same vein, in the Council of Europe context, the explanatory report to Convention 108+ specifies that the exceptions and restrictions provided for in Article 11 of that Convention should apply "in particular to processing of personal data... in news archives and press libraries" (see paragraph 62 above).[234]

The use of EU law to justify the existence of a consensus on the importance of press archives appears to be more of an exception than a rule. In certain instances, third-party interveners[235] and judges in separate opinions[236] have drawn on EU data protection law to assert the existence or the absence of a consensus. Yet, the ECtHR has not responded to these calls, at least as regards the use of EU law.

While there might be valid reasons for cautiously employing interpretative methods – including the European consensus – when using EU law, these

[234] ECtHR, *Hurbain v. Belgium* [GC], no. 57292/16, § 183, 4 July 2023.

[235] In *Mosley v. the United Kingdom* (2011), the Guardian, as a third-party intervener, argued that there was an absence of European consensus that a pre-notification duty existed by relying on the Data Protection Directive (95/46/EC) (ECtHR, *Mosley v. the United Kingdom*, no. 48009/08, § 93, 10 May 2011).

[236] Separate opinion of Judge Pinto de Albuquerque in ECtHR, *Big Brother Watch and Others v. the United Kingdom* [GC], nos. 58170/13 and 2 others, § 11, 25 May 2021.

methods may offer a more robust and justifiable foundation for using data protection law into the ECtHR's case-law. This topic will be explored in the last part of this research project.[237]

§ 3. CONTEXTUALISATION

A final methodological point concerns how the ECtHR contextualises EU law when it is referenced, namely whether the ECtHR takes into account the context and limits of EU data protection law. Similar to our equality case study, there is a discernible trend toward increased contextualisation, but there are instances where this remains limited. This occurs either because the ECtHR does not mention the context of EU data protection law or neglects to consider its limits.

From a temporal point of view, the ECtHR increasingly mentions the temporal dimension of EU data protection law, to a greater extent than what we observed in the equality case study. Steadily more, the ECtHR notes when EU instruments enter into force and take effect.[238] The ECtHR increasingly mentions when a specific EU data protection instrument replaces or will replace another one from a certain date.[239] The approach taken by the ECtHR on the temporal aspects of EU data protection law is commendable as it ensures a nuanced understanding of the EU legal landscape. If the ECtHR does not take into account the temporal limits of EU data protection law, it could lead to legal misinterpretations and outdated analyses.

From a geographical point of view, as in our equality case study, the ECtHR most often does not specify to whom EU data protection law applies and whether the respondent State is bound by it, as we have seen above.[240]

From a material point of view, as in our equality case study, there are strong signs of improvement over the past few years. The ECtHR increasingly presents the relevant EU data protection law in its judgments in an exhaustive, precise, and up-to-date manner. We have already touched upon this dimension in detail above when discussing the informative function.[241]

When considering whether the ECtHR takes into account the material limits of EU data protection law (e.g., content, scope), the overall trend from

---

237 See below Part IV, Chapter 2, Section II, §2. Justification.

238 This can be seen, for instance, in the case of *Big Brother v. United Kingdom* [GC](2021) case, where the ECtHR mentioned that the GDPR was adopted in April 2016 and became enforceable on 25 May 2018. See ECtHR, *Big Brother Watch and Others v. the United Kingdom* [GC], nos. 58170/13 and 2 others, § 204, 25 May 2021.

239 E.g. ECtHR, *Benedik v. Slovenia*, no. 62357/14, § 59, 24 April 2018.

240 See above Part III (case study on data protection), Chapter 3, Section IV, §2. Qualitative Analysis.

241 See above, Part III (case study on data protection), Chapter 3, Section II, §4. Information.

our analysis suggests that it does. There are cases where the ECtHR arguably neglects the material limits of EU data protection law, however. An example is *Breyer v. Germany* (2020), which relates to the storing of personal data of users of prepaid mobile-telephone SIM-cards, which we have already discussed above.

Let us recall that the ECtHR drew an analogy with a judgment from the CJEU, specifically the *Ministerio Fiscal* [GC](2018) case, which concerned the access of data belonging to SIM card owners.[242] The ECtHR noted that the data bore a resemblance to those in the *Ministerio Fiscal* case and observed that the CJEU had concluded that access to the data in question could not be classified as a serious interference.[243] In light of these observations, the ECtHR concluded that the interference, while not trivial, was of a rather limited nature.[244] This consideration plays a significant role in its assessment that the interference was proportionate. The ECtHR's reasoning is questionable. While it is true that the CJEU held in *Ministerio Fiscal* that access to the data specified in the request not to be a serious interference with the fundamental rights of the individuals involved, it stated that this determination was made in the given circumstances of the case.[245] These circumstances differ from those in the *Breyer v. Germany* (2020) case, as highlighted by Judge Ranzoni:

> However, when comparing [the *Ministerio Fiscal* case] with the present case, some major differences need to be emphasised The CJEU accepted the interference as justified 'in the circumstances' of its case. That case concerned the SIM cards of one stolen mobile telephone that was linked during a period of 12 days with the identity of owners of those SIM cards. The request sought access only to the telephone numbers corresponding to those SIM cards and to the data relating to the identity of the owners of those cards. Only in these circumstances the Luxembourg Court held that access to that specific data could not be defined as 'serious' interference.
>
> The present case, however, is quite different. First, it does not directly concern access to data, but rather the storage of data. Secondly, it does not relate to a specific criminal investigation with concrete investigative measures to be examined Thirdly, it is – in contrast to Ministerio Fiscal – neither about very specific data (SIM cards from one telephone) nor a limited duration (12 days), but rather about the data sets of millions of people stored for a much longer period. Fourthly, access to data in the present case is not limited for the purpose of combating criminal offences, whether serious crimes or not.[246]

---

242 See above Part III (case study on data protection), Chapter 3, Section II, §3. Distinguishing.
243 ECtHR, *Breyer v. Germany*, no. 50001/12, § 94, 30 January 2020.
244 Ibid., § 95.
245 Case 207/16, *Ministerio fiscal*, ECLI:EU:C:2018:788, para. 61.
246 Separate opinion of Judge Ranzoni in ECtHR, *Breyer v. Germany*, no. 50001/12, §§ 13–14, 30 January 2020.

Judge Ranzoni relied significantly on this difference in view on EU data protection law with the ECtHR to arrive at a different conclusion from that of the ECtHR, asserting a violation of Article 8 ECHR. We share this difference in view: the ECtHR made a significant leap from the similarity of the data to the conclusion that the interference was limited. This is despite notable differences in the context, such as the scale, objective, type, and duration of data processing in the CJEU and ECtHR's rulings. In Part IV of this research project, we advocate for a more contextualised approach when the ECtHR relies on EU law.[247]

§ 4. COMPARATIVE INSIGHTS

The methodological approach appears more developed concerning international instruments than for EU data protection law. However, the difference is less pronounced than in the equality case study, as there is a lack of justification for both the use of both EU data protection law and international instruments. Moreover, the ECtHR seldom refers to the outputs of the related bodies.

To begin with transparency, as with EU data protection law, the ECtHR frequently uses the technique of 'use by reference'.[248] In several cases, the ECtHR only refers to the provisions of Convention 108 in a summary manner in its reasoning, without even mentioning them in the relevant legal materials.[249] A notable difference compared to EU data protection law, similar as what we observed in our equality case study, is that the ECtHR is often clearer when it uses international instruments and acknowledges the influence these instruments have had in following related cases.[250]

[247] Part IV, Chapter 2, Section II, §3. Contextualisation.

[248] E.g. ECtHR, *M.M. v. the United Kingdom*, no. 24029/07, § 196, 13 November 2012.

[249] E.g. ECtHR, *Peck v. the United Kingdom*, no. 44647/98, § 78, ECHR 2003-I.

[250] A good example relates to the safeguards the ECtHR has developed to avoid data abuses. *In Z v. Finland* (1997), the ECtHR mentioned that domestic law must afford appropriate safeguards to prevent any such communication or disclosure of personal data, referring to Convention 108. In *Peck v. the United Kingdom* (2003), the ECtHR mentioned *Z v. Finland* to assert that domestic law must afford appropriate safeguards and referred again to Convention 108 (ECtHR, *Peck v. the United Kingdom*, no. 44647/98, § 78, ECHR 2003-I). In recent judgments, the ECtHR has been even more explicit about its use of Convention 108. In *Drelon v. France* (2022) for instance, the ECtHR stated that '[t]he domestic law must also afford 'appropriate safeguards' to prevent any such use of personal data as may be inconsistent with the guarantees of Article 8 (ibid., § 103). In this connection, the Court takes into account the stipulations of the Convention for the Protection of Individuals with regard to Automatic Processing of Personal Data ('the 1981 Convention') (see *Z v. Finland*, 25 February 1997, § 95, *Reports of Judgments and Decisions* 1997-I, and *S. and Marper*, cited above, §§ 103 and 107)' (ECtHR, *Drelon v. France*, nos. 3153/16 and 27758/18, § 82, 8 September 2022).

Looking at the justification for the use of international instruments, it is very similar to what we found for EU data protection law: the ECtHR rarely justifies why it refers to these instruments, except to note that it has used them in previous cases and therefore must do so. This stands in contrast to our equality case study, where there was often strong justification by the ECtHR when referring to international instruments. For international data protection instruments, there is a lack of use of interpretative techniques, with the exception of the *Hurbain v. Belgium* [GC] (2023) case, where Convention 108 was used to assert the consensus on the importance of press archives, alongside EU law, as discussed earlier.[251]

We observe strong contextualisation from both temporal and geographical perspectives. The ECtHR often mentions whether and when the respondent State have signed and ratified Convention 108 laws and when the latter enter into force in the said State.[252] From a material point of view, we see notable contextualisation of Convention 108 laws, especially in more recent years.[253] The key difference with EU data protection law is that, as we have already noted, there is very limited reference to the outputs from the Consultative Committee of Convention 108, whereas there are significant and increasing references to CJEU case-law.[254]

251 ECtHR, *Hurbain v. Belgium* [GC], no. 57292/16, § 183, 4 July 2023.
252 E.g. ECtHR, *Drelon v. France*, nos. 3153/16 and 27758/18, § 29, 8 September 2022.
253 E.g. ECtHR, *Centrum för rättvisa v. Sweden* [GC], no. 35252/08, §§ 82–84, 25 May 2021.
254 See above Part III (case study on data protection), Chapter 3, Section I, §1. Frequency per Standards.

CHAPTER 4
INTERMEDIARY CONCLUSION

Before moving to the general conclusions for our two case studies, let us take an intermediary step to revisit some key findings from our data protection case study.

Section 2 has shown that both the EU and ECHR data protection frameworks are well-established and highly developed, sharing common roots in Convention 108, which has had a profound influence on the principles underlying ECHR data protection law. While the EU and ECHR systems overlap, they are driven by distinct rationales. These factors are important to understanding the dynamics of EU data protection law's influence on ECtHR case-law, which were examined in Section 3.

EU data protection law and Convention 108 serve as the primary external sources in the ECtHR's data protection case-law. The ECtHR has referred to these sources far more frequently than to other instruments and has applied them consistently across various areas of its case-law. EU law is notable for its multifaceted use, with the ECtHR citing not only the Charter and legislative texts but also making significant reference to CJEU case-law. Both EU data protection law and Convention 108 have played important roles in the ECtHR's judgments. Although their functions overlap in some areas – especially in interpretation and information – there are key differences. EU law alone has been used from a distinguishing perspective, and in terms of justification, the two sources perform distinct sub-functions, although both have considerable impact.

Next to the ECtHR itself, EU data protection law has attracted strong engagement from various actors, including parties, third-party interveners, national judges, and individual judges at the ECtHR through separate opinions. EU data protection law has primarily been used in cases concerning EU States, with very limited use against non-EU States. Alongside the growing significance of EU law in ECtHR case-law, there has been a noticeable improvement in the ECtHR's methodological approach to using EU data protection law. Nonetheless, certain aspects still require further improvement.

CONCLUSION: ARE EU FUNDAMENTAL RIGHTS A SOURCE OF SPECIAL SIGNIFICANCE?

The expression 'source of special significance' originates from the CJEU. Although it did not explicitly define it, this expression highlights the distinct role and influence of ECHR law in shaping its jurisprudence on fundamental rights. This distinctiveness is evident in the language of the CJEU: what was once considered just another source among many has evolved into one that must be taken into account, becoming even a source of particular or special significance. This elevated status was reflected in the numbers, as references to ECHR law increased exponentially. And if this source was – and still is – special, it is because it stands apart from other sources. The CJEU has placed the ECHR in a class of its own, distinct from the common constitutional traditions of Member States and international human rights treaties. The same holds true for ECtHR case-law. Referenced later than the ECHR, it has gradually infiltrated CJEU jurisprudence, whereas references to the case-law of other human rights bodies have been scarce, to say the least. The extent of ECHR law's influence has even raised the question of whether it held binding legal force within EU law. While this question has been answered in the negative in the post-Lisbon era, the impact of ECHR law is such that, for a long time, EU fundamental rights were largely inspired by those of the ECHR. The ECHR becoming the main source of inspiration for the CJEU in shaping EU fundamental rights was a relatively natural process. It serves both as a set of shared values among European States and a key instrument for ensuring the coherence of the European architecture of fundamental rights.

The EU's growing role as a standard-setter has invited us to turn upside down the issue: Are EU fundamental rights a source of special significance, and if so, in what sense? The drafting of the Charter, which became binding after the Lisbon Treaty, along with an increasing number of sector-specific EU legislative instruments on fundamental rights, has the potential to reshape the dynamics between EU and ECHR laws. This is true regarding the use of ECHR law by the CJEU, which has declined in favour of an autonomous interpretation of EU fundamental rights. This is also, and perhaps especially, true for the use of these rights by the ECtHR, which may grow due to their special nature. EU fundamental rights appear as both a privileged source of inspiration, owing to their high level of sophistication and their application across 27 Convention States, a source which is part of the background in cases involving EU States, and a source that accentuates the need for articulation between the EU and ECHR layers.

Equality and data protection were selected as case study as they are key areas where the EU has left its mark. Characterised by an array of legislative tools, Charter's provisions, and CJEU case-law, they are highly sophisticated areas of EU fundamental rights. As the domains where the EU has arguably developed its most advanced fundamental rights policies, drawing conclusions from them should be done with caution. They might present a picture of influence that is more significant than in other fields where rights are less developed or still emerging; yet they can be enlightening to understand the dynamics that have occurred or may occur in other areas.

If we focus on the language the ECtHR uses to describe EU fundamental rights, one might quickly conclude that these rights are merely one source among many that the ECtHR refers to in its case-law. Far from consistently describing them as 'special' or 'particular', the cases in which the ECtHR refers to them as privileged sources can be counted on one hand. Such is the case in *Stec v. United Kingdom* [GC](2006) and subsequent cases, where CJEU jurisprudence is regarded as having a 'strong persuasive value'. It is also seen in *Breyer v. Germany* (2020), where the ECtHR notes that there is extensive EU legislation and CJEU case-law on the matter, which should be taken into account. These cases, which are exceptions rather than the norm, highlight that the ECtHR does not recognise a special character to EU law 'on paper'. This point is further supported by the fact that it almost never mentions that these rights are binding on EU States, nor does it reference, when using interpretative techniques like consensus, that this law binds the majority of Convention States. To be frank, when considering form alone, EU fundamental rights appear as just another source in ECtHR case-law. But beyond the form, there is substance, and that substance reveals that they indeed constitute a source of special significance, as we will now explain.

This special significance first manifests itself quantitatively. To begin with, the ECtHR makes a diversified used of EU fundamental rights: it refers to EU legislation, the Charter, and CJEU case-law in a balanced manner. References to EU law instruments outnumber those to other external sources. In data protection, the difference between the number of references to EU law instruments and those to Convention 108 is small, but in equality, the prominence of EU equality law instruments is more pronounced. This trend between our case studies reverses when we look at the number of references to the outputs of related bodies: the ECtHR makes substantially more references to CJEU case-law than to the outputs of the Consultative Committee of

Convention 108, while the disparity between CJEU equality case-law and the outputs of bodies related to external equality sources is limited. In any case, whether we consider instruments or outputs, EU fundamental rights emerge as the most prominent source. This special quantitative character is also evident from a temporal perspective: they represent the first or second external source that the ECtHR has referenced, and since then, the ECtHR has consistently referred to them for over twenty or twenty-five years. Around 2015, there was an intensification in the references to EU fundamental rights, which outpaces that of other external sources. In addition, the ECtHR invokes them across a wide range of areas. While this can also be observed for other external sources, certain international equality instruments tend to apply primarily within areas linked to their specific scope, such as gender or disability discrimination.

The quantitative prominence of EU fundamental rights is mirrored in their qualitative impact. These rights are either the most prominent external source in equality law or one of the two primary external sources, alongside Convention 108, in data protection law. EU fundamental rights have played a wide variety of functions, and while international instruments also perform similar functions to those of EU fundamental rights, they do so to a lesser extent.

First of all, there is one function performed by EU fundamental rights that is not by other external sources: the distinguishing function. The ECtHR has sought to distinguish its stance from that of EU fundamental rights. This has taken various forms: it has emphasised that EU rights were not applicable, pointed out the absence of relevant CJEU cases, noted factual or contextual differences between its own case-law and that of the CJEU, and even relied on a distinction made by the CJEU itself. Although the instances in which the ECtHR distinguishes its stance from EU law are limited, EU fundamental rights are (almost) the sole legal source used in a distinguishing manner.

There is also one function that, in our two case studies, is performed more by EU fundamental rights than by other external sources: the informative function. EU fundamental rights serve a significant informative role, with the ECtHR referencing them as relevant information in the context of cases or within its relevant legal materials. EU fundamental rights are increasingly presented in an exhaustive, precise, and up-to-date manner, with a growing description of CJEU case-law. While EU equality law is clearly more often cited as relevant information than other external sources, in data protection cases, both EU data protection law and Convention 108 are frequently mentioned together. Yet, Convention 108 has not been used as contextual information and EU data protection law is increasingly emerging as the most prominent relevant legal standard information.

When we explore the other two functions – interpretation and justification – significant distinctions arise depending on the case study. In equality, EU law clearly plays a more prominent role in these functions compared to other external sources. In data protection, the situation is more nuanced, with Convention 108 either standing on equal footing or playing a notable but distinct role alongside EU law.

EU equality law has played a notable role in shaping the interpretation of ECHR equality law. Its influence has permeated all aspects of ECHR equality law, leading to some significant transformations. In comparison, international equality instruments, while serving a similar function, have had a less significant impact, with only a few instances where their influence has been notable. The situation is quite different when it comes to data protection. The role of EU law in interpreting the Convention has been very limited, primarily focused on determining whether a given situation falls within the scope of Article 8 ECHR. This function has also been performed by Convention 108, and somewhat more prominently, with the ECtHR frequently referencing the concept of 'personal data' as defined in this Convention.

EU equality law has played a notable role when assessing the justification of an interference, being used in several cases to either support or refute that a difference in treatment is based on an objective and reasonable justification. In contrast, international instruments have rarely been used for this purpose, and when they have been, the ECtHR has only used them to support that a difference in treatment is not proportionate. When it comes to data protection, both EU law and Convention 108 have played notable roles, although they have had distinct impacts. EU law has been relevant in assessing whether an interference pursued a legitimate aim, whether it was lawful, and whether it was necessary in a democratic society. In comparison, Convention 108 has had a more significant impact on the necessity condition, yet it has not been used to assess the legitimacy of an interference and has only been limitedly referenced in evaluating its lawfulness.

All in all, EU fundamental rights have either fulfilled functions that other external sources have not, or have performed similar functions but in a more significant manner. However, there is one exception: in the context of equality law, reports from monitoring bodies of international instruments serve an evidentiary function that EU equality law does not. The ECtHR relies on these reports as evidence of the factual situation in the respondent State.

While there are similarities between our two case studies, the dynamics are markedly different. If the ECtHR has notably drawn from EU equality law to shape some of the key principles of its equality case-law, this is not the case with EU data protection law. The latter has had minimal impact on the interpretation of the Convention and played a very limited role in developing the ECtHR's safeguards to prevent the abuse of personal data.

These distinct dynamics can largely be explained by the distinct normative environments of our two case studies. On one hand, there is a factor related to the established nature of the protected interest within ECHR law. While the ECtHR has developed extensive case-law on data protection since the late 1980s, the protection of equality has historically been considered underdeveloped. It is within this context that the ECtHR has sought to enrich its equality case-law by turning to external sources. On the other hand, there is a factor related to the presence of other external sources in the field. In data protection law, the principles of Convention 108 – being the key and foundational instrument for data protection – have emerged as the main source of inspiration for the ECtHR in shaping its safeguards against data abuse. This reliance on Convention 108 has made it less necessary for the ECtHR to turn to EU law, which also incorporates these principles. In equality, EU equality law has emerged as a more attractive source of inspiration than other external sources. This can be explained by the fact that EU equality law offers a highly sophisticated framework, deeply integrated within the domestic legal systems of EU States, and has a broad scope of application, which differs from other international instruments which often have a more limited and targeted scope.

If EU fundamental rights are of special significance, the primary source of this significance lies in the CJEU case-law. Beyond the fact that the ECtHR refers to it more frequently than the outputs of bodies related to international instruments, in particular in the realm of data protection, it is often the CJEU's case-law that plays a pivotal role in the ECtHR's rulings. When EU fundamental rights are used to interpret the ECHR, the references are most often to the Charter or CJEU case-law. At the justification stage, CJEU case-law is most commonly cited. Distinguishing between the stances of EU and ECHR laws frequently involves CJEU case-law. When identifying relevant legal standards, the ECtHR relies significantly on CJEU case-law. There is thus a kind of triangular relationship in the dynamics of influence of EU fundamental rights on the ECtHR case-law: the standards are adopted at EU primary and secondary levels, then interpreted by the CJEU, and eventually the ECtHR references the latter jurisprudence. The ECtHR, though it has occasionally done so, is cautious in directly using fundamental rights enshrined in the Charter and expressed in EU secondary laws. This caution reflects a certain deference to the CJEU and a willingness not to interpret EU law itself.

EU fundamental rights hold special significance not only for the ECtHR, but also for other actors involved prior to, before, and within the ECtHR. Parties (including applicants, governments, and third-party interveners), national judges, and judges in separate opinions have notably referred to EU fundamental rights, whether before a case reaches the ECtHR or while it is before the ECtHR. In general, they refer to EU fundamental rights more significantly than other external sources. This is particularly evident in data protection law, where there is a notable engagement with the EU framework by the various actors, in contrast to the very limited engagement with international instruments. In equality law, this is true for applicants, governments, and national judges, but not for third-party interveners and judges in separate opinions where other external sources are more often referred to. Both applicants and governments use them to defend their interests, either by seeking to neutralise them when they are unfavourable or by leveraging them positively when they are advantageous. Third-parties also strategically use these rights according to their interests, with certain organisations being particularly inclined to do so. Judges in separate opinions also make use of these rights, especially in data protection cases, often to oppose the majority view. The use of EU fundamental rights by various actors highlights the 'human factor' in their influence: their impact may depend on specific individuals and actors involved prior to, before, or within the ECtHR who rely on these rights, potentially leading to the incorporation of their EU law-based arguments in the ECtHR's reasoning.

The ECtHR's special use of EU law has not led to compromise the fundamental aspects of its human rights system. The ECtHR appears to be careful to use EU fundamental rights without integrating the specific dynamics of EU fundamental rights. The ECtHR has preserved the human rights logic which underpins ECHR law. EU fundamental rights have mostly been used in a 'human rights-friendly' manner: they have been used to enhance the protection of equality and personal data without incorporating an economic rationale, with only a few exceptions such as *Stec v. United Kingdom* [GC] (2006). However, this has sometimes come at the expense of other fundamental rights, such as freedom of religion and expression, as illustrated by *Jehova's Witness v. Finland* (2023). The ECtHR has also maintained the structure of its own fundamental rights system. It has not incorporated the specific set of rules contained within EU secondary law but continues to operate according to general principles, allowing it to maintain flexibility. The ECtHR has not integrated the specific characteristics of EU law, such as its horizontal applicability or its high degree of proceduralisation.

When examining the specific dynamics of our case studies, certain differences emerge. EU equality law have contributed to a more substantive version of equality under ECHR law, through the incorporation of concepts such as indirect discrimination and discrimination by association. Arguably, EU equality law has also influenced the shift from an open to a closed system of protected grounds, though there is limited case-law explicitly supporting this view and this shift remains uncertain. The underlying dynamics of data protection under ECHR law have not been altered: the ECHR system remains focused on privacy, as illustrated by the fact that categorising data as personal data alone is not sufficient to bring it within the scope of Article 8 ECHR. Overall, the ECtHR and the ECHR system have not been marginalised by the use of EU fundamental rights, yet certain dynamics of ECHR equality law have evolved under the influence of EU law.

The special significance of EU fundamental rights seems to be largely confined to cases involving EU States. The ECtHR has referred to them in cases concerning a wide variety of States, most frequently those within the EU. EU rights are proportionally more often invoked than other external sources in cases involving EU States. There are only a few instances where the ECtHR has referred to EU fundamental rights in cases involving non-EU States, and these have had a very limited impact on the ECtHR's reasoning. EU fundamental rights have a limited indirect impact on non-EU States through precedents; there are only a few cases (in the field of equality law) where the ECtHR has mentioned elements inspired by EU law in cases involving non-EU States. While the ECtHR generally avoids using EU fundamental rights in cases involving non-EU States, it does so implicitly. The ECtHR rarely refers to whether EU law binds the respondent State, seldom employs techniques, such as the margin of appreciation, to modulate the influence of EU fundamental rights based on the respondent State, and does not acknowledge the influence of EU law in subsequent cases. All in all, despite the increasing use of EU fundamental rights, the risk of marginalisation of non-EU States does not appear to have materialised, yet there is room for more transparency.

Thus far, we have seen that EU fundamental rights hold special significance in our two case studies, both qualitatively and quantitatively, for the ECtHR as well as for other actors involved prior to, before, and within the ECtHR, particularly in cases involving EU States. But what explains this special significance? Arguably, this results from the fact that these fundamental rights are both highly sophisticated and deeply integrated within the legal systems of EU States. EU fundamental rights exhibit features of comprehensiveness, specificity, and innovation, and are subject to increasingly autonomous interpretation by the CJEU. They enjoy primacy and direct effect, and are applicable within the EU States in both vertical and horizontal situations. These characteristics make these rights a valuable source of inspiration not only for the ECtHR but also for other actors who may draw upon them. They constitute a unique body of law that is highly developed and applicable to 27 Convention States, making it a persuasive means to argue that there is (or is not) common ground at a pan-European level. Additionally, EU law appears akin to domestic law in cases involving EU States: the ECtHR appears more and more inclined to treat EU fundamental rights as a component of national law, considering their objectives, procedures, the balances they establish between fundamental rights protection and other interests, and increasingly, how national authorities engage with them. Their close proximity with domestic laws also explains the significant use of EU law in the context of ECtHR's cases, including by various actors involved in domestic proceedings. Because these rights permeate domestic systems yet are increasingly autonomous from ECHR law, they also create a greater need for coherence. This is reflected in the ECtHR's case-law, which attempts to articulate the EU and ECHR layers, particularly evident when it differentiates its stance from EU law.

Considering the special use of EU fundamental rights through the lens of legitimacy – as we suggested in Part I of our study[1] – offers a dual perspective. When focusing on so-called substantive legitimacy, the picture is positive: EU fundamental rights have contributed to enhancing the legitimacy of the ECtHR's rulings. Firstly, EU fundamental rights have been increasingly referenced in the contextual and informative sections of ECtHR judgments. By adopting this approach, the ECtHR demonstrates that its rulings are made with comprehensive awareness of relevant standards. Secondly, EU fundamental rights have been used in the reasoning of ECtHR judgments to support its stance. In doing so, they contribute to substantiate the ECtHR's decisions and can persuade various stakeholders of the soundness of these decisions.

However, when focusing on so-called procedural legitimacy, the picture is more negative: While there has been some improvement in the methodological use of EU fundamental rights, a series of issues persists. First, there are several situations where transparency in the use of EU fundamental rights is limited (such as references made only in legal materials, by reference, or even no reference at all) which may lead to problematic situations (such as implicit influence, erroneous use of EU law, or diffuse influence). Second, the ECtHR almost never explains what justifies its references to EU fundamental rights and very rarely uses its methods of interpretation to justify these references. Third, while there is a discernible trend toward increased contextualisation, it remains limited from a temporal and geographical point of views in our equality case study. The methodological approach is more developed with regard to international instruments than for EU fundamental rights especially concerning EU equality law, despite the fact that the latter is the most important external source used by the ECtHR.

1 See above Part I, Chapter 2, Section IV. The Double-Edged Sword of Legitimacy.

PART IV.

Future and Recommendations: A Special Method for a Special Source

INTRODUCTION

The discussion above has demonstrated that EU fundamental rights hold a special significance in ECtHR case-law. This significance is likely to endure and may even grow in the future, driven by factors such as the potential for more EU fundamental rights to emerge, the increasing number of Convention States that incorporate EU fundamental rights, and the prospect of EU accession to the ECHR. This special significance should be accompanied by a special method consisting of three key components. Firstly, it should be guided by principles of complementarity, coherence, and dialogue. Secondly, the method should incorporate clear methodological principles that enhance transparency, provide robust justification, and ensure contextualisation. Lastly, this approach must be supported by an appropriate infrastructure, designed to improve the use of EU fundamental rights within the ECtHR's fabric.

CHAPTER 1

GROWING SIGNIFICANCE: THE FUTURE OF EU FUNDAMENTAL RIGHTS

The special significance of EU fundamental rights has been observed in the areas of equality and data protection. It is likely that this significance will remain. This is because the ECtHR can still use EU equality and data protection standards as a source of inspiration and these standards continue to form part of the background in cases involving EU States and must be articulated with ECHR standards. The significance of EU fundamental rights could extend beyond these areas in the future and even increase. Three factors could contribute to, and strengthen, the special significance of EU fundamental rights in ECtHR case-law.

SECTION I. MORE EU FUNDAMENTAL RIGHTS

The first is that more EU fundamental rights are emerging and are likely to emerge in the future. In the fields of equality and data protection, where EU fundamental rights hold special significance, the CJEU continues to deliver judgments interpreting standards developed at primary and secondary law levels with sometimes increasing frequency. This can be seen in data protection; over the last five years, there have been 61 cases on data protection, including 21 in 2023 and 11 in 2022. This year, there have already been 19 cases on data protection before the CJEU.[1] These cases, as well as those forthcoming, will be highly relevant in cases involving EU States and will need to be articulated with ECtHR case-law. Yet, it is not only the EU judiciary that is active; the EU legislator has also shown notable activity in recent years. Initiatives have multiplied to enhance the effectiveness of the fundamental rights to equality and data protection. This includes the Pay Transparency Directive, which aims to strengthen the principle of equal pay between men and women through pay

[1] We use the subject-matter 'data protection' from 1 January 2024 to 15 August 2024 on Curia.

transparency and reinforced enforcement mechanisms.[2] Instruments have been developed to lay down minimum requirements for the functioning of equality bodies, improving their effectiveness and guaranteeing their independence to strengthen the application of the principle of equal treatment.[3] The proposal for a Regulation laying down additional procedural rules related to the enforcement of the GDPR is also noteworthy.[4] It should be noted that these new laws primarily focus on procedural aspects. Given this procedural nature, we believe that the ECtHR should exercise caution when considering incorporating concepts of these laws into ECHR law, as we explain below.[5] Let us also take note of the long-standing proposal for a Council Directive on implementing the principle of equal treatment between persons irrespective of religion or belief, disability, age, or sexual orientation which remains on the table.[6] This proposal aims to combat discrimination beyond the field of employment.[7] While the EU Parliament approved the Commission's proposal in 2009, it has remained blocked at the Council level due to the fact that the unanimity requirement imposed by Article 19 TFEU cannot be reached.

Beyond equality and data protection, there are other domains where the EU legislator has intervened over the past decade, and where the EU standards could gain significance in ECtHR case-law as they mature within CJEU case-law. EU procedural rights in the field of criminal law are a prime example.[8] In this domain, the EU has adopted a series of instruments, rooted partly in the 2009 Roadmap for strengthening the procedural rights of suspected or accused

---

2 Article 1 Pay Transparency Directive (2023/970/EU) (Directive (2023/970/EU) of 10 May 2023 to strengthen the application of the principle of equal pay for equal work or work of equal value between men and women through pay transparency and enforcement mechanisms, [2023] OJ L132/21; hereafter 'Pay Transparency Directive (2023/970/EU)).

3 Article 1 Directive 2024/1499/EU of 7 May 2024 on standards for equality bodies in the field of equal treatment between persons irrespective of their racial or ethnic origin, equal treatment in matters of employment and occupation between persons irrespective of their religion or belief, disability, age or sexual orientation, equal treatment between women and men in matters of social security and in the access to and supply of goods and services, and amending Directives 2000/43/EC and 2004/113/EC, [2024] OJ L2024/1499; Article 1 Directive 2024/1500/EU of 14 May 2024 on standards for equality bodies in the field of equal treatment and equal opportunities between women and men in matters of employment and occupation, and amending Directives 2006/54/EC and 2010/41/EU, [2024] OJ L2024/1500.

4 Proposal for a Regulation laying down additional procedural rules relating to the enforcement of Regulation 2016/679/EU, COM(2023) 348 final.

5 See below Part IV, Chapter 2, Section I, §1, I. Preserving.

6 Proposal for a Directive on implementing the principle of equal treatment between persons irrespective of religion or belief, disability, age or sexual orientation, COM(2008) 426 final.

7 Ibid., Article 1.

8 Please note that the following two paragraphs are inspired by or strem from a joint work (I. Gambardella and V. Davio, 'Introduction to the Special Issue: EU Directives on Procedural Rights in Criminal Matters: 15 Years After the Roadmap, Where do We Stand, Where do We Go?', *EU Law Live*, 2023) as well as the introduction from a joint research event co-organised in June 2023 between the Centre for European Law of ULB, the Institute of Criminology of KU Leuven and the Institute for European Law of KU Leuven

persons in criminal proceedings. The Roadmap laid out a step-by-step approach, requiring the EU Commission to submit proposals for measures related to various fundamental procedural rights.[9] This Roadmap was endorsed by the European Council in the Stockholm Programme of 11 December 2009. In that programme, the European Council emphasised that the protection of the rights of suspected and accused persons in criminal proceedings is a fundamental value of the Union, 'which is essential in order to maintain mutual trust between the Member States and public confidence in the European Union'.[10] In the same year, the Lisbon Treaty entered into force, providing a specific legal basis (Article 82(2)(b) TFEU) that empowers the EU to adopt minimum rules on the rights of individuals in criminal procedures.[11] The decision to establish common minimum rules on a set of procedural fundamental rights was made with the aim of strengthening mutual trust between EU States and thereby facilitating mutual recognition.[12] The fact that all EU States are parties to the ECHR was deemed insufficient to ensure mutual trust in each other's criminal justice systems, due to varying, and sometimes inadequate, levels of respect for the fundamental rights enshrined in the ECHR in some EU States.[13]

The Roadmap gave birth to six directives which have been adopted on the basis of Article 82(2)(b) TFEU. They seek to harmonise the rights of suspects and defendants across the EU and to facilitate the application of these rights. They relate for instance to the right to interpretation and translation[14] and the right to information.[15] While these directives are intended to enhance cross-border cooperation between EU States, they are applicable in purely

(https://cde.ulb.be/wp-content/uploads/2023/05/Closing-Academic-Year-Event-on-the-EU-Directives-on-Procedural-Rights-in-Criminal-Matters_final50.pdf) which led to the above-mentioned special issue.

9 Resolution of the Council of 30 November 2009 on a Roadmap for strengthening procedural rights of suspected or accused persons in criminal proceedings, [2009] OJ C 295/1.

10 Stockholm Programme – An open and secure Europe serving and protecting the citizens, December 2009.

11 In particular Article 82(2)(b) TFEU empowers the European Parliament and the Council to adopt, by means of directives in accordance with the ordinary legislative procedure, such rules to facilitate mutual recognition of judgments and judicial decisions and police and judicial cooperation in criminal matters having a cross-border dimension.

12 See above Part II, Chapter 2, Section II, §1. The Diverse and Evolving Dynamics behind EU Legislative Action.

13 See e.g. Recital 7 of Directive 2012/13/EU of 22 May 2012 on the right to information in criminal proceedings, [2012] OJ L142/1.

14 Directive 2010/64/EU of 20 October 2010 on the right to interpretation and translation in criminal proceedings, [2010] OJ L280/1.

15 Directive 2012/13/EU of 22 May 2012 on the right to information in criminal proceedings, OJ L 142/1.

national situations: they apply to all criminal proceedings conducted in EU States without requiring a transnational element.[16]

Increasingly, these instruments are reaching not only the CJEU but also the ECtHR.[17] There is a growing body of ECtHR case-law where EU procedural rights directives are mentioned, yet this remains fairly limited.[18] This is not entirely surprising as these instruments are recent, with some only requiring implementation as late as June 2019.[19] While the CJEU has growingly interpreted the EU procedural rights directives, often relying on ECHR law,[20] the Luxembourg case-law itself remain fairly restricted. It can be assumed that as the CJEU continues to interpret these directives, there will be more references to EU procedural rights in ECtHR case-law. If EU equality law and data protection can be seen as mature fields within EU law, EU procedural rights are more akin to an advanced teenager.[21]

Beyond the limited number of ECtHR cases referencing EU procedural rights directives, their use does not appear yet to be very fertile. In many instances, the ECtHR only mentions the instruments in the relevant legal materials without integrating them into its reasoning.[22] Some references are made in passing,[23] while others are more detailed, including comprehensive summaries of the relevant preambles and provisions of the directives.[24] At this stage, there are (arguably) only two key cases where the ECtHR has made notable use of these directives. The first is *Ibrahim and Others v. UK* [GC] (2016), where the ECtHR has relied on them to reinforce its case-law on

16 In this respect, see I. Wieczorek, 'The emerging role of the EU as a primary normative actor in the EU Area of Criminal Justice', *European Law Journal: Review of European Law in Context*, 2023, pp. 378–407.

17 N. Daminova, 'The European Court of Human Rights on the 'Stockholm's Roadmap Directives': the Quest for a Coherent Application of 'Due Process' Rights in Europe?', in I. Gambardella and V. Davio (eds.), *EU Directives on Procedural Rights in Criminal Matters: 15 Years After the Roadmap, Where do We Stand, Where do We Go?*, EU Law Live, 2023, pp. 15–16.

18 Ibid., pp. 16-17.

19 This is the case of Directive 2016/800/EU of 11 May 2016 on procedural safeguards for children who are suspects or accused persons in criminal proceedings, [2016] OJ L 132, 21 May 2016.

20 E.g. Case C-348/21, *HYA and Others*, ECLI:EU:C:2022:965, paras. 29, 39–42, 53, 55–58. See more examples in J. Callewaert, 'The Recent Luxembourg Case-Law on Procedural Rights in Criminal Proceedings: Towards Greater Convergence with Strasbourg?', *EU Law Live*, 2023.

21 I. Gambardella and V. Davio, 'Introduction', in *EU Directives on Procedural Rights in Criminal Matters: 15 Years After the Roadmap, Where do We Stand, Where do We Go?*, EU Law Live, 2023, p. 3.

22 E.g. ECtHR, *A.T. v. Luxembourg*, no. 30460/13, § 37, 9 April 2015.

23 ECtHR, *Zachar and Čierny v. Slovakia*, nos. 29376/12 and 29384/12, § 49, 21 July 2015.

24 ECtHR, *Simeonovi v. Bulgaria* [GC], no. 21980/04, § 74, 12 May 2017.

the right to information in criminal proceedings.[25] The second is *Vizgirda v. Slovenia* (2018), where the ECtHR has drawn upon the EU directives to establish that there is a duty to assess the interpretation needs of suspects or accused persons.[26] Nonetheless, EU procedural rights have the potential to reflect a consensus at European level, as observed by Daminova.[27]

While the ECtHR's case-law is still fairly limited, it will be important to closely monitor this development. This area is subject to specific dynamics, partly distinct from those in equality and data protection. On one hand, they largely codify ECHR rights.[28] As such, it is unlikely that these EU instruments will alter the key dynamics of procedural rights protection under ECHR law. Instead, the focus will likely be on how these directives are articulated in cases involving EU States. It is also likely that the flow of influence will be more from Strasbourg to Luxembourg, rather than the opposite, in this field.[29] On the other hand, the directives are based on a legal basis which provides that the EU can only adopt minimum rules in this field.[30] The question is how and whether the ECtHR will use these 'minimum' requirements and the extent to which it will draw inspiration from them.

There are also even more recent areas where the EU legislator is regulating aspects of fundamental rights that could, in the medium term, become significant for the ECtHR. The EU is placing particular emphasis on fundamental rights in the digital age, as reflected in the European Declaration on Digital Rights and Principles.[31] There are a growing number of digital fields where the EU regulates the balance between digital and internal market interests as well as fundamental rights, sometimes even taking the lead on a global scale.

---

25 ECtHR, *Ibrahim and Others v. the United Kingdom* [GC], nos. 50541/08 and 3 others, § 271, 13 September 2016.

26 ECtHR, *Vizgirda v. Slovenia*, no. 59868/08, §§ 78 and following, 28 August 2018.

27 N. Daminova, 'The European Court of Human Rights on the 'Stockholm's Roadmap Directives': the Quest for a Coherent Application of 'Due Process' Rights in Europe?', in I. Gambardella and V. Davio (eds.), *EU Directives on Procedural Rights in Criminal Matters: 15 Years After the Roadmap, Where do We Stand, Where do We Go?*, EU Law Live, 2023, pp. 18–19.

28 E.g. Recitals 8, 14, 21, 40 and 42 of Directive 2012/13/EU of 22 May 2012 on the right to information in criminal proceedings, [2012] OJ L142/1.

29 See the speech of the Former President of the ECtHR, S. O'Leary, 'Judicial Dialogue: Fundamental Rights Issues in National Court Judgments. Trilateral Meeting with the CJEU of the European Union and the Network of the Presidents of the Supreme Judicial Courts of the European Union', 10 November 2023, available here https://www.echr.coe.int/documents/d/echr/speech-20231110-oleary-trilateral-meeting-vienna-eng, pp. 3–4.

30 Article 82(2) TFEU. This is also reflected in the EU procedural rights directives, see e.g. Recital 20 of Directive 2012/13/EU of 22 May 2012 on the right to information in criminal proceedings, [2012] OJ L 142/1.

31 European Declaration on Digital Rights and Principles for the Digital Decade 2023/C 23/01, [2023] OJ C23/1.

For instance, consider the Media Freedom Act, which establishes common rules for the proper functioning of the internal market for media services, including the creation of the European Board for Media Services, while ensuring the quality of media services.[32] As noted in the preparatory work, this instrument aims to 'facilitate the provision of independent and quality media services across borders, thereby promoting media freedom and pluralism.'[33] The EU has also adopted a significant instrument in the field of artificial intelligence, the Artificial Intelligence Act, aimed at improving 'the functioning of the internal market and promote the uptake of human-centric and trustworthy artificial intelligence, while ensuring a high level of protection of health, safety, fundamental rights enshrined in the Charter, including democracy, the rule of law and environmental protection, against the harmful effects of AI systems in the Union and supporting innovation.'[34] A final example is the Digital Services Act, which regulates aspects of fundamental rights related to online platforms.[35]

It is highly likely that, as these instruments become more embedded within EU law, they will soon find their place in ECtHR case-law, particularly in cases involving EU States. This has already been the case, for example, in *Sanchez v. France* [GC](2023), where the applicant, who is a politician, was fined in criminal proceedings for not deleting racist comments posted by third parties on his Facebook wall during an election campaign, and where the applicant argued that there was a violation of Article 10 ECHR. Although the ECtHR did not mention EU digital instruments in its reasoning, it did note in the relevant legal materials that the Digital Services Act was adopted and entered into force in 2022.[36] While the facts in this case predated the Digital Services Act, the ECtHR may need to take this instrument into account in the future.

Outside the digital sphere, whistleblower protection offers a strong example. In 2019, the EU adopted a directive that establishes common minimum standards for the protection of whistleblowers reporting breaches of EU law, the Whistleblower Directive,[37] thereby safeguarding their freedom

---

32 Article 1 of Regulation 2024/1083/EU of 11 April 2024 establishing a common framework for media services in the internal market and amending Directive 2010/13/EU (hereafter: 'European Media Freedom Act'), [2024] OJ L2024/1083.

33 Explanatory Memorandum of the Proposal for a Regulation establishing a common framework for media services in the internal market (European Media Freedom Act) and amending Directive 2010/13/EU, COM(2022) 457 final, p. 13.

34 Article 1 of Regulation 2024/1689/EU of 13 June 2024 laying down harmonised rules on artificial intelligence and amending Regulations No 300/2008/EU, No 167/2013/EU, No 168/2013/EU, 2018/858/EU, 2018/1139/EU and 2019/2144/EU and Directives 2014/90/EU, 2016/797/EU and 2020/1828/EU, [2024] OJ L2024/1689 (hereafter: 'Artificial Intelligence Act (2024/1698/EU)').

35 Article 1 of the Digital Services Act (2022/2065/EU).

36 ECtHR, *Sanchez v. France* [GC], no. 45581/15, § 83, 15 May 2023.

37 Article 2 of the Whistleblower Directive (2019/1937/EU).

of expression and information as guaranteed by Article 11 Charter.[38] It has been suggested that whistleblower protection offered by EU law is higher than that provided under ECHR law, and that the ECtHR should align its case-law with the directive to ensure the same level of protection across all Convention States.[39] The ECtHR delivered a judgment in *Halet v. Luxembourg* [GC](2023) after the adoption and transposition deadline of the Whistleblower Directive, although the facts of the case predated these events. While the ECtHR itself referenced the EU instrument to a limited extent,[40] various parties – applicants, governments, and third parties – have referred to the Whistleblower Directive in their arguments before the ECtHR.[41] When the ECtHR will face a case where the facts occur after the transposition deadline of the Whistleblower Directive and the CJEU's case-law on the matter has developed, it seems almost inevitable that the ECtHR will need to consider both the directive and the case-law, particularly if it concerns an EU State.

SECTION II. MORE CONVENTION STATES INCORPORATING EU FUNDAMENTAL RIGHTS

Next to the increase in EU fundamental rights, it is also likely that an increasing number of Convention States will incorporate these rights into their domestic legal systems. It is noteworthy that several non-EU Convention States have already adopted certain EU fundamental rights. This is particularly true for the EEA States – Norway, Iceland, and Liechtenstein – with respect to the GDPR. Whereas this instrument does not enjoy primacy and direct effect in these States,[42] they have incorporated large part of GDPR rules into their national law as a result of the EEA Agreement.[43]

Moreover, all nine candidate States to the EU accession are Convention States.[44] To join the EU, they must comply with EU fundamental rights, as

38 Recital 31 of the Whistleblower Directive (2019/1937/EU).

39 D. Kafteranis and R. Brockhaus, 'Time to Reconsider Strasbourg's Whistleblower Case-law', *European Law Blog*, 2020.

40 ECtHR, *Halet v. Luxembourg* [GC], no. 21884/18, § 58, 14 February 2023.

41 Ibid., § 73 (applicant), § 95 (government) and §§ 99, 101, 106 (third-party interveners).

42 In this vein, ECtHR, *Norwegian Confederation of Trade Unions (LO) and Norwegian Transport Workers' Union (NTF) v. Norway*, no. 45487/17, § 106, 10 June 2021.

43 See Decision of the EEA Joint Committee No 154/2018 of 6 July 2018 amending Annex XI (Electronic communication, audiovisual services and information society) and Protocol 37 (containing the list provided for in Article 101) to the EEA Agreement [2018/1022], [2018] OJ L 183/23.

44 These States are Albania, Bosnia and Herzegovina, Georgia, Moldova, Montenegro, North Macedonia, Serbia Türkiye and Ukraine.

respect for these rights has been made a prerequisite for accession. In the 1973 Declaration on European Identity, the Heads of State or Government of the nine Member States of the Community declared that the construction of a united Europe is 'open to other European nations which share the same ideals and objectives',[45] thus implicitly referring to respect for fundamental rights, which was described as a component of the European identity. The respect of fundamental rights would then be qualified as an 'essential element' of the membership of the European Communities in the declaration on democracy of the European Council of Copenhagen of April 1978.[46] Fifteen years later, in 1993, the European Council fleshed out the Copenhagen criteria, according to which membership requires 'that the candidate country has achieved stability of institutions guaranteeing democracy, the rule of law, human rights and respect for and protection of minorities, the existence of a functioning market economy and the capacity to cope with competitive pressure and market forces within the Union.'[47] The Treaty of Amsterdam explicitly conditioned accession to the EU to the respect of fundamental rights,[48] a requirement now enshrined in Article 49 TEU, which states that 'any European State which respects the values referred to in Article 2 and is committed to promoting them' can apply to become a member of the EU.

Respect for fundamental rights is not only an eligibility condition to become a candidate State, but it is also an integral part of the EU acquis that the candidate State must fully adopt for accession negotiations to conclude.[49] A specific chapter, Chapter 23, on 'Judiciary and Fundamental Rights,' is included in the list of accession negotiation chapters.[50] This implies that as candidate States implement EU fundamental rights throughout the accession process, these rights may already form the backdrop of ECtHR's cases involving these States. After accession, EU fundamental rights acquire primacy and direct effect within their legal orders, just as they do in all EU States. This means that they form part of the context of cases involving the new EU States, but also that as more non-EU states accede to the EU, the more weight EU law can carry in discerning a consensus at pan-European level.

---

45 Declaration on European Identity (Copenhagen, 14 December 1973).

46 Declaration on democracy at the Copenhagen European Council (7 and 8 April 1978).

47 Presidency Conclusions at the Copenhagen European Council, 21–22 June, 1993.

48 C. Hillion, 'Enlarging the European Union and deepening its fundamental rights protection', *European Policy Analysis*, 2013, p. 2.

49 Ibid., pp. 2–7.

50 Ibid., p. 4.

SECTION III. THE PROSPECT OF EU'S ACCESSION TO THE ECHR

The EU's accession to the ECHR could influence how the ECtHR uses EU fundamental rights. Given that accession has been widely debated in the past, including previous unsuccessful attempts and discussions on its desirability,[51] our focus is on the current state of play and the potential impact of accession on the use of EU fundamental rights. It is important to recall that accession is a legal obligation under EU law and is possible under ECHR law.[52] Accession has been the subject of several negotiations, leading to draft agreements that ultimately did not succeed, largely due to opinions from the CJEU. The most recent is Opinion 2/13, in which the CJEU found that accession was incompatible with the autonomy of EU law.[53] Following this opinion there was a prolonged period of inactivity, but negotiations resumed in 2020 between the Council of Europe and the EU. They are now close to an agreement, though a pending issue remains regarding jurisdiction in CFSP matters.[54] The future of accession remains uncertain, as all Convention States and the EU will need to ratify the accession agreement, and it is likely that the CJEU will be asked to deliver an Opinion on the compatibility of the draft agreement with EU law.

At first glance, accession may appear not to have any significant impact on the use of EU fundamental rights by the ECtHR. This is because its primary aim is to allow any person, non-governmental organisation, or group of individuals the right to submit the acts, measures, or omissions of the EU to the external scrutiny of the ECtHR.[55] The underlying dynamic is thus about ensuring the

---

51 E.g. T. Lock, 'The Future of EU Human Rights Law: Is Accession to the ECHR Still Desirable?', *Journal of International and Comparative Law*, 2020 pp. 428–447; S. Peers, 'The EU's Accession to the ECHR: The Dream Becomes a Nightmare', *German Law Journal*, 2015, pp. 213–222; C. Eckes, 'EU accession to the ECHR: between autonomy and adaptation', *The Modern Law Review*, 2013, pp. 254–285.

52 Article 6(2) TEU and Article 59 ECHR.

53 Opinion 2/13 of 18 December 2014, ECLI:EU:C:2014:2454, para. 258. See more in D. Halberstam, 'It's the Autonomy, Stupid! A Modest Defense of Opinion 2/13 on EU Accession to the ECHR, and the Way Forward', *German Law Journal*, 2015, pp. 105–146; T. Lock, 'Walking on a tightrope: the draft ECHR accession agreement and the autonomy of the EU legal order', *Common Market Law Review*, 2011, pp. 1025–1054.

54 A draft Accession Agreement is available as from 2 January 2023 (https://rm.coe.int/consolidated-version-of-the-draft-accession-instruments-as-of-2-februa/1680aa3443). It is noteworthy that the CJEU has recently delivered the *KS and KD* judgment on its jurisdiction in CFSP matters, which appear to facilitate the EU's accession to the ECHR (Case C-29/22 P, *KS and KD v. Council of the European Union and Others*, ECLI:EU:C:2024:725). In this vein, J. Krommendijk, 'One step closer after KS and KD: EU accession to the ECHR', *Review of European Administrative Law Blog*, 2024, available here: https://realaw.blog/2024/10/01/one-step-closer-after-ks-and-kd-eu-accession-to-the-echr-by-jasper-krommendijk/.

55 Recital 5 of the Draft Accession Agreement.

compliance of EU law with ECHR law, rather than using EU fundamental rights as a potential source of enrichment for the ECtHR.

However, there are ways in which accession could lead to EU fundamental rights playing a more significant role in ECtHR case-law. First, EU fundamental rights would form the backdrop in cases involving EU institutions. As such, it is likely that the ECtHR will consider whether EU fundamental rights have been taken into account in the EU decision-making process or judicial proceedings and will examine the objectives and content of EU fundamental rights instruments, as well as their implementation at domestic level.

Second, EU fundamental rights could become a more persuasive source for interpreting the Convention or determining whether an interference is justified. These rights would not only be the laws of 27 EU States but would also become directly the law of a Convention Party. Consequently, EU fundamental rights would become more entrenched within the Convention system, thereby strengthening their persuasive value to find common ground at pan-European level.

Third, there might be an increase in references to EU fundamental rights aimed at ensuring coherence between these rights and ECHR law.[56] The ECtHR could, in particular, consider that the protection provided by EU fundamental rights exceeds that offered by ECHR law. Similarly, it could also point out situations where the protection falls below the ECHR threshold. However, this would only be the case to the extent that the current draft agreement includes a clause of mutual trust, which could limit the ECtHR's ability to rule when EU standards fall below ECHR standards when mutual trust is at stake.[57]

Fourth, accession would likely foster a stronger dialogue on the interactions between EU fundamental rights and ECHR law, particularly between the ECtHR and the CJEU.[58] This dialogue could occur when the ECtHR refers to and considers EU fundamental rights as interpreted by the CJEU in cases involving EU States and/or EU institutions. It could also take place in a more direct manner through the prior involvement mechanism, when the CJEU is involved beforehand to assess the compatibility of domestic measures with EU fundamental rights.[59]

---

56 See on the likely increased coherence brought about by EU's accession to the ECHR, T. Lock, 'EU Accession to the ECHR: when, how and implications', 2024, available here: https://ssrn.com/abstract=4766356, p. 4; J. Krommendijk, 'EU Accession to the ECHR: Completing the Complete System of EU Remedies?', 2023, available here: https://ssrn.com/abstract=4418811; J. Callewaert, 'No More Common Understanding of Fundamental Rights ?', *La revue des jurists de Sciences Po*, 2022, p. 25.

57 Article 5b of the Draft Accession Agreement: 'Accession of the European Union to the Convention shall not affect the application of the principle of mutual trust within the European Union. In this context, the protection of human rights guaranteed by the Convention shall be ensured.'

58 In this vein, J. Krommendijk, 'EU Accession to the ECHR: Completing the Complete System of EU Remedies?', 2023, available here: https://ssrn.com/abstract=4418811.

59 Article 3(6) of the Draft Accession Agreement.

CHAPTER 2
A SPECIAL METHOD FOR THE USE OF EU FUNDAMENTAL RIGHTS

We have observed that EU fundamental rights carry particular significance in the realms of equality and data protection. The significance of EU fundamental rights could extend beyond equality and data protection in the future and even increase. If this appears to be the current state of the law regarding EU fundamental rights in the ECtHR's case-law, another important question is how the ECtHR should or should not use EU fundamental rights. We argue that the ECtHR should develop a special method that matches the special significance of EU fundamental rights. Our approach aligns with a movement aimed at developing method-based approaches when a court relies on external sources, particularly in human rights matters.[1] For instance, Tulkens, Van Droogenbroeck, and Krenc have observed that the debate has shifted away from the principle of borrowing from soft law to focus instead on the methodology

---

1 See E. Brems, 'Smart human rights integration', in *Fragmentation and Integration in Human Rights Law*, Cheltenham, Edward Elgar Publishing, 2018, pp. 192–194. Reflecting on dialogue in the field of fundamental rights, Brems argues for a method-based approach: 'It is submitted that smart human rights integration does not point to particular outcomes of human rights protection, but is *instead primarily a matter of process*. Smart human rights integration requires a certain mind-set in - supranational as well as domestic - human rights monitoring bodies, in which each body is conscious of being part of a broader human rights project, and reflects upon its role in that project. The central feature of smart human rights integration is thus a global human rights conversation. *The idea is not that any particular human rights monitoring body acts in the same way or comes to the same conclusions as another body on the same issue, but rather that it is informed about what others do or have done, and that it reflects upon the desirability of adopting the same approach* [...] The imperative of the global human rights conversation would expect a monitoring body in the first place to be systematically informed of the relevant work of other human rights monitoring bodies. In the second place, it would be expected to explain why it is (not) aligning itself with the relevant work of other human rights bodies. In the current system, such information and explanation is far from systematic. What is particularly remarkable is that motivated dismissive references to other monitoring bodies are extremely rare.' See also in favour of the use of a method-based approach, e.g. A. von Bogdandy and I. Venzke, *In Whose Name? A Public Law Theory of International Adjudication*, Oxford, Oxford University Press, 2014.

of the reasoning that leads to such borrowing.[2] As they noted, when a judge applies a legally binding norm, there is no need to justify its use, as the norm's intrinsic binding nature provides sufficient justification.[3] When a judge turns to other sources, the judge must justify this approach.[4]

Our approach aims to move beyond a binary approach to the use of external sources, where the choice is either that human rights found in other instruments or related case-law can always be used by a court from another legal system or that they can never be used. The focus shifts from 'whether' to 'how' a court can use an external source. The development and use of a method is neither a mathematical exercise nor a one-size-fits-all approach.[5] Each method should take into account the specific context of the court engaging with external law, the context of the external law itself, and the broader context in which both operate. In concreto, consideration should be given to the normative environments of the ECHR legal system, EU fundamental rights and the broader European fundamental rights architecture of which they are a part.

The fact that the method we advocate is 'special' means that it is specifically designed for the use of EU fundamental rights by the ECtHR. However, many of the principles we promote would also be applicable when the ECtHR uses another source of external law, or when another court (such as the CJEU) engages with human rights enshrined in a different instrument (such as the ECHR).

Our suggested method encompasses three key elements. At an abstract level, we argue for guiding principles that should steer the ECtHR's approach to EU fundamental rights, emphasising complementarity, coherence, and dialogue. At a more concrete level, we advocate for methodological principles to be applied when the ECtHR uses EU fundamental rights, including transparency, justification, and contextualisation. Last but not least, we call for an infrastructure shift to improve the use of EU fundamental rights within the ECtHR's fabric.

SECTION I. GUIDING PRINCIPLES

Three principles should guide the ECtHR's approach to EU fundamental rights. First, the use of EU fundamental rights should be driven by a logic of complementarity, which takes into account the strengths and limits of both the

2 F. Tulkens, S. Van Drooghenbroeck and F. Krenc, 'Le soft law et la Cour européenne des droits de l'Homme. Questions de légitimité et de méthode', in I. Hachez (ed.), *Les sources du droit revisitées. Normes internationales et constitutionnelles*, Paris, Anthemis, 2012, p. 384.
3 Ibid., p. 408.
4 Ibid.
5 Ibid., p. 487.

EU and ECHR legal systems. Second, the ECtHR should be guided by a logic of coherence, which is essential given that the ECHR and EU legal systems operate within a shared European space. Third, the use of EU fundamental rights should be part of a broad dialogue, not only between the ECtHR and the CJEU but also involving domestic courts and the EU legislator.

§ 1. COMPLEMENTARITY

The EU and ECHR legal systems are interdependent and should collaborate to protect fundamental rights at European level. There are instances where EU law offers stronger protection, while in other cases, ECHR law provides better safeguards. It is crucial to consider the complementarity between the two systems when assessing the desirability and appropriateness of using EU fundamental rights into ECtHR case-law. By recognising their respective strengths and limits, these systems can work together to ensure a high level of fundamental protection across Europe. The search for complementarity in deciding whether and how to use EU fundamental rights can be broken down into three elements. First, the ECtHR must avoid incorporating aspects of the EU fundamental rights system that could undermine the distinct characteristics of the ECHR legal system and should instead preserve the complementary strengths of its own regime. Second, the ECtHR can enhance the effectiveness of the EU regime without integrating EU fundamental rights. Third, the ECtHR can enrich its case-law in light of EU fundamental rights, provided this does not compromise the core principles of ECHR law

I. Preserving

As we have seen, although the EU and ECHR fundamental rights systems share similarities and overlap, they are distinct. Their rationales, structures, and content differ, with each system characterised by its own specificities. The EU system is distinguished in several ways. First, it stands out due to the coexistence of fundamental rights objectives alongside other goals related to European integration. Second, the legislative framework plays a central role in establishing specific rules that determine case outcomes in fundamental rights cases. Third, EU fundamental rights can apply not only in vertical situations but also in horizontal situations. Fourth, these rights have a strong procedural orientation, which, in certain areas, involves institutional actors responsible for enforcing EU fundamental rights and provides individuals with procedural rights.

Our case studies have revealed that the ECtHR has avoided integrating the specificities of the EU fundamental rights system into the ECHR legal system. The ECtHR has preserved the human rights logic that underpins ECHR law.

It has not adopted the rule-based approach of EU fundamental rights but has assessed interferences with human rights according to general principles such as legitimacy, lawfulness, and proportionality. The use of EU law has not led to the 'horizontalisation' of the ECHR legal system and has contributed to a stronger 'proceduralisation' to a very limited extent.

While not incorporating the EU fundamental rights' distinctive features in the ECHR legal system may seem like a missed opportunity, there are compelling reasons to avoid their incorporation. First, such integration could lead to the distortion of the ECHR legal system, both in its objectives and its fundamental structures. Second, significant changes, such as creating enforcement authorities or making human rights applicable in horizontal situations, arguably require amendments to the ECHR and fall outside the scope of judicial power. Third, incorporating the EU's specificities could undermine the distinctive features of the ECHR legal system, which are beneficial for the protection of human rights. One might consider, for example, the fully human rights-focused logic of the ECHR system, the broad scope of application for certain Convention rights, and the flexibility inherent in the ECHR legal framework. In this vein, while a rule-based system may offer detailed rules that can be advantageous to individuals and provide more foreseeability, it can also be rigid and may not always provide adequate protection for fundamental rights. In contrast, a principle-based system, like that of the ECHR, is more flexible and can be adapted to the specific circumstances of each case, allowing for a more context-sensitive approach. Fourth, if the specific features of EU fundamental rights are not incorporated into the ECHR legal system, they remain available within the context of EU law. This allows individuals to invoke these rights, albeit within a more limited framework than that of the Convention, yet still applicable in 27 Convention States.

Focusing on our case studies, the ECtHR has preserved its privacy-focused approach while using certain elements of EU law, such as the notion of personal data, into its reasoning and balancing tests. This approach is convincing as data are most often protected under the right to private life, and there is no autonomous right to data protection enshrined in the Convention. The strong emphasis on data protection within the EU legal system has not been fully integrated into the ECHR framework; however, it remains available under EU law, allowing it to address data-related situations where the Convention system may not be able to intervene.

In the field of equality, EU equality law has contributed to a shift from a formal to a more substantive approach to equality under ECHR law, through the incorporation of concepts such as indirect discrimination and discrimination by association. This evolution enables the ECtHR to address some issues which cannot be tackled by a formal approach to equality. There is also an ongoing evolution in ECHR law, where a shift from an equality to a non-discrimination rationale has become apparent. This shift involves moving from an open to a closed system of protected grounds as well as the use of the very weighty reasons test for specific grounds There are strong arguments for the ECtHR to avoid turning into a closed model of protected grounds and combine both an equality and a non-discrimination rationale. There seems to be limited textual reasons which would limit the ECtHR from providing an equality framework where all forms of unjustified unequal treatment are prohibited. From a complementary perspective, this would be beneficial for the protection of equality at European level, since EU law does not offer such a comprehensive system and focuses instead on specific, albeit growing, protected grounds.[5] Maintaining an equality rationale would not preclude the ECtHR to adopt a discrimination approach which emphasises the need for specific protection for certain grounds, for instance through the use of the very weighty reasons test.

II. Contributing to the Effectiveness

Both the ECHR and EU legal systems can reinforce the effectiveness of the other. While EU law can bolster ECHR law,[7] our focus here is on how the ECtHR can contribute to strengthening the effectiveness of EU fundamental rights without incorporating its rules. This is particularly promising from a perspective of complementarity, as it allows the ECtHR to contribute to the protection of fundamental rights across Europe while maintaining the distinctiveness of its own legal system.

Historically, situations where the ECtHR sanctioned the lack of, or poor, application of EU law were restrained.[8] The most well-known example relates to the preliminary ruling procedure. The ECtHR has reinforced the effectiveness of this mechanism by imposing an obligation to state reasons when a domestic court refuses to refer a question to the CJEU.[9] In *Ullens*

---

6 Yet, there are some exceptions such as Article 20 Charter, see above Part III (case study on equality), Chapter 2, Section II, §1, II. Equality v. Non-Discrimination.

7 See the speech of F. Ronkes Agerbeek, 'The tale of two cities continues: the Convention and the expanding scope of EU law' at the ECtHR's seminar *The articulation between the European Convention of Human Rights and the European Law: past, present and future*, 14 June 2024, available here: https://www.echr.coe.int/documents/d/echr/speech-20240614-seminar-echr-eulaw-felix-ronkes-agerbeek-eng, p. 1.

8 Please note that some paragraphs of this sub-section are inspired by or stem from V. Davio, 'Le droit de l'Union européenne dans la jurisprudence de la Cour européenne des droits de l'homme', *Journal des Tribunaux - Droit Européen*, 2023, pp. 46–50.

9 In this respect, it is worth recalling that a court of one of the EU States may refer a question to the CJEU for a preliminary ruling on the interpretation of the EU Treaties and the validity and interpretation of the acts of the institutions, bodies, offices or agencies of the Union, where such a question is raised before it and where it considers that a decision on the matter is necessary to enable it to give judgment (Art. 267(2) TFEU). This *faculty* becomes an *obligation* when such a question is raised by a national court whose decisions

de Schooten v. Belgium (2011), the ECtHR pointed out that the refusal of a national court to refer a question for a preliminary ruling may, in certain circumstances, affect the fairness of the proceedings, in particular where the refusal is arbitrary.[10] From this it deduced that Article 6(1) ECHR imposes an obligation on national courts to give reasons for decisions to refuse a reference for a preliminary ruling.[11] In particular, national courts whose decisions are not subject to judicial remedy under national law must give reasons for their refusal in the light of the exceptions provided for in the CJEU case-law.[12] This obligation to state reasons, which has been shaped on a case-by-case basis, has been the subject of numerous elaborations in subsequent cases, which are to a large extent summarised in the *Sanofi Pasteur* (2020).[13] The ECtHR does not adopt a formalistic approach and attaches importance to the fact that the applicants have been able to understand the reasons for the refusal to submit a preliminary question.[14] More recently, the ECtHR has suggested that, when the obligation to state reasons has been breached, domestic proceedings should be reopened if requested, so that the request for a preliminary reference can be properly examined.[15]

Aside from the line of cases related to the preliminary ruling procedure, there were also some specific, albeit limited cases where the ECtHR had sanctioned national authorities for failing to apply EU law in the past. In *Hornsby v. Greece* (1998), the ECtHR ordered Greece to pay damages to the applicants for not complying with a decision of the CJEU.[16] In *Dangeville*

are not subject to judicial remedy under national law (Art. 267(3) TFEU). According to established case-law of the CJEU, a national court or tribunal against whose decisions there is no judicial remedy under national law cannot be relieved of that obligation unless it has established (i) that the question raised is irrelevant or (ii) that the EU law provision in question has already been interpreted by the Court or (iii) that the correct interpretation of EU law is so obvious as to leave no scope for any reasonable doubt (Case C-561/19, *Consorzio Italian Management*, ECLI:EU:C:2021:799, para. 33).

10 ECtHR, *Ullens de Schooten and Rezabek v. Belgium*, nos. 3989/07 and 38353/07, § 57, 20 September 2011.

11 Ibid., § 60.

12 Ibid., § 62.

13 After recalling the above principles concerning the obligation to state reasons, the ECtHR pointed out that it may be acceptable under Article 6 of the Convention not to deal explicitly with a referral for a preliminary ruling when the request (i) has been rejected with summary reasoning because it raised no fundamentally important legal issues or had no prospects of success (ii) is declared inadmissible for failure to comply with the admissibility requirements. In addition, the ECtHR underlines that the reasons the rejection of the request for a preliminary ruling under the *Cilfit* criteria can be deduced from the reasoning of the remainder of the decision given by the court in question or from reasons considered implicit in the decision rejecting the request (ECtHR, *Sanofi Pasteur v. France*, no. 25137/16, § 70, 13 February 2021).

14 ECtHR, *Quintanel v. France*, no. 12528/17, § 90, 17 June 2021.

15 ECtHR, *Georgiou v. Greece*, no. 57378/18, § 33, 14 March 2023.

16 ECtHR, *Hornsby v. Greece*, no. 18357/91, §§ 13–19, 1 April 1998.

v. France (2002), the ECtHR sanctioned the French authorities for failing to correctly transpose directives into national law. The ECtHR found that, due to the French legislature's failure to align domestic law with a Community directive,[17] the interference with the applicant company's right to the peaceful enjoyment of its possessions was not justified in the general interest.[18]

In recent years, the ECtHR has increasingly found ways to sanction the lack of, or inadequate application of, EU fundamental rights, and more generally EU law, by national authorities, thereby contributing to the effectiveness of EU law.

First, the ECtHR has sanctioned violation of EU law by national authorities as they correspond to a violation of a specific obligation arising from an ECHR right. An illustration is provided by the *Romeo Castano v. Belgium* (2019) with regard to the duty to cooperate flowing from Article 2 ECHR. The applicants had complained, on the basis of the right to life protected by Article 2 ECHR, about the refusal of the Belgian authorities to execute a European arrest warrant issued by the Spanish authorities against an individual allegedly involved in the death of their father, thereby preventing the criminal proceedings against him. The decision to refuse was based on the risk that the individual's fundamental rights would be infringed if he were handed over to Spain, in particular in that his detention could lead to a risk of inhuman and degrading treatment.[19] Although such a justification could constitute a legitimate ground for refusing to execute the European arrest warrant, the ECtHR found that the examination carried out by the Belgian courts in the course of the surrender procedure was not sufficiently thorough to enable them to find that there was a sufficient factual basis for the ground on which they refused surrender. Due to the insufficiency of this factual basis, it concluded that Belgium failed in its obligation to cooperate arising under the procedural limb of Article 2 ECHR.[20] In doing so, the ECtHR is in line with the case law of the CJEU, which requires the executing judicial authority to base itself on objective, reliable, precise and duly updated elements in order to refuse the execution of a European arrest warrant where there is a risk of violation of the prohibition of inhuman and degrading treatment.[21]

Second, the ECtHR has examined the compliance of measures taken by domestic authorities with EU law through the lens of the concept of 'law' which is mentioned in several ECHR provisions. For instance, Article 5(1) ECHR provides that everyone has the right to liberty and security of person and that no one shall be deprived of their liberty except in specified cases

17 ECtHR, *S.A. Dangeville v. France*, no. 36677/97, § 57, ECHR 2002-III.

18 Ibid., § 58.

19 ECtHR, *Romeo Castaño v. Belgium*, no. 8351/17, §§ 12–15, 9 July 2019.

20 Ibid., §§ 90–92.

21 Cases C-404/15 and C-659/15 PPU, *Aranyosi*, ECLI:EU:C:2016:198, paras. 89 and 94.

and in accordance with a 'procedure prescribed by law'. In assessing whether the decision to detain an asylum seeker had been taken 'in accordance with a procedure prescribed by law', the ECtHR has held that the national rules referred to by that expression could include provisions stemming from EU law, and that it has the competence to ensure that States comply with their domestic law, including EU law, as we shall further see below.[22]

Third, the ECtHR has taken into account the lack of engagement by national authorities with EU fundamental rights when examining whether an interference is proportionate. This was evident in *Moraru v. Romania* (2022) and *Moraru and Marin v. Romania* (2022), which we analysed above, where the ECtHR found that the domestic authorities failed to engage meaningfully with CJEU case-law and took it into account, contributing to the conclusion that the differences in treatment were disproportionate.[23]

Fourth, the ECtHR held in *Spasov v. Romania* (2022) that the applicant's conviction based on domestic law provisions manifestly contrary to EU regulations constituted a 'denial of justice' in violation of Article 6(1) ECHR. The applicant had argued that he had been subjected to an arbitrary sentence as it was in breach of the rules of EU law on the Common Fisheries Policy. The ECtHR decided that the Romanian Court of Appeal had committed a manifest error of law based on two reasons. First, the ECtHR made its own interpretation of the EU regulations and implicitly rejects the interpretation made by the Romanian authorities.[24] Second, the ECtHR insisted on the fact that the Commission initiated infringement proceedings for violation of the EU rules and that it only terminated them after Romania had amended its internal legislation in order to bring it into line with EU law. In case of doubt the Romanian Court of Appeal should have referred the matter to the CJEU on the interpretation of EU law.[25]

Across these various lines of cases, a common thread emerges: the ECtHR is prepared to sanction domestic authorities if they breach EU law under the prism of ECHR law. While this trend may seem new, it is perhaps less so when viewed in light of the ECtHR's approach towards national law and its previous jurisprudence. The ECtHR has addressed the lack of, or inadequate implementation of, domestic laws, for instance through the lawfulness condition. However, the ECtHR has observed that it has only limited power to review compliance with domestic laws.[26] Similarly, when conducting a procedural

22 ECtHR, *Thimothawes v. Belgium*, no. 39061/11, §j70, 4 April 2017; ECtHR, *Muzamba Oyaw v. Belgium* (dec.), no. 23707/15, § 35, 28 February 2017. See below Part IV, Chapter 2, Section II, §2, II. EU Law as A Condition for Lawfulness.

23 See above Part III (case study on equality), Chapter 3, Section II, §2, II.B. Dismissive.

24 ECtHR, *Spasov v. Romania*, no. 27122/14, § 97, 6 December 2022.

25 Ibid., § 95.

26 ECtHR, *Beyeler v. Italy* [GC], no. 33202/96, §§ 108–109, 5 January 2000.

review, the ECtHR may consider whether domestic fundamental rights were taken into account during the judicial or legislative decision-making process.[27] Regarding *Spasov v. Romania* that may appear as a novelty, the ECtHR held in *Moreira Ferreira v. Portugal (no. 2)* (2017) that a domestic judicial decision could be incompatible with Article 6 ECHR if it was so arbitrary as to prejudice the fairness of proceedings. This is particularly the case when no reasons are provided for the decision, or if the reasons given are based on a manifest factual or legal error by the domestic court, resulting in a 'denial of justice'.[28] It is quite logical for the ECtHR to extend these approaches to EU fundamental rights, especially as these rights become increasingly integrated into domestic law.

Sanctioning breaches of EU law through the prism of the Convention can have positive consequences. This approach fosters coherence between EU and ECHR law, ensuring that what is deemed wrongful under EU law is also recognised as such under ECHR law. This method enhances the effectiveness of EU law without directly incorporating it into the ECHR legal system, thereby avoiding its imposition on non-EU States. Moreover, it offers added value for individuals by providing an additional avenue for redress when satisfaction cannot be obtained through EU channels.[29]

That being said, several points warrant careful consideration when examining this line of cases. First, many of the judgments concerning the engagement of national authorities with EU law are relatively recent, with a significant number being Chamber's judgments. Notably, several of these cases have been rendered against just two States, Finland[30] and Romania.[31] We should not underestimate the 'human factor', where the involvement of particular lawyers or judges at the ECtHR may have played a role in shaping these new trends. As such, these developments may not reflect a consensus within the entire ECtHR, and the future trajectory of this trend remains uncertain.

Second, there remains ambiguity regarding the criteria used by the ECtHR to sanction the lack of, or inadequate, application of EU law by national authorities. The various lines of cases discussed above are still quite blurry. For instance, in the *Moraru v. Romania* (2022) and *Moraru and Marin v. Romania* (2022) cases, the causal link between the lack of engagement with

27 See e.g. on procedural review by the ECtHR, J. Gerards, 'Procedural Review by the ECtHR: A Typology', in J. Gerards and E. Brems (eds.), *Procedural Review in European Fundamental Rights Cases*, Cambridge, Cambridge University Press, 2017, pp. 127–160.

28 ECtHR, *Moreira Ferreira (No. 2) v. Portugal*, no. 19867/12, § 85, 11 July 2017.

29 J. Krommendijk, 'Straatsburg als hoeder van het EU-recht', *Nederlands Juristenblad*, 2023, p. 2469.

30 ECtHR, *Jehovah's Witnesses v. Finland*, no. 31172/19, 9 May 2023; ECtHR, *Satakunnan Markkinapörssi Oy and Satamedia Oy v. Finland* [GC], no. 931/13, 27 June 2017.

31 ECtHR, *Spasov v. Romania*, no. 27122/14, 6 December 2022; ECtHR, *Moraru and Marin v. Romania*, nos. 53282/18 and 31428/20, 20 December 2022; ECtHR, *Moraru v. Romania* case, no. 64480/19, 8 November 2022.

EU law and the finding of non-proportionality is not fully explained, nor is it clear what the ECtHR considers to constitute a failure to engage 'meaningfully' with EU law. Similarly, in *Spasov v. Romania*, it is unclear what exactly is meant by a manifest breach of EU law by domestic authorities. Third, there is a thin line between sanctioning the lack or poor application of EU law and interpreting or applying EU law itself.[32] While the ECtHR has affirmed that it cannot assess the conformity of national measures with EU law nor interpret it,[33] there is a risk that by sanctioning breaches of EU law, it may encroach upon the competence of the CJEU and domestic courts. In *Spasov v. Romania* for instance, there was no judgment from the CJEU and the ECtHR proposed its own assessment of the EU rules.[34]

In our view, it may be advisable for the ECtHR to sanction the lack of, or incorrect implementation of, EU law only in exceptional cases of manifest insufficiency, and preferably when the CJEU has already ruled on the matter. We consider that the test for assessing manifest insufficiency should be procedural rather than substantive, focusing on how EU fundamental rights are taken into account by domestic authorities rather than whether those authorities correctly apply EU fundamental rights standards. This approach would help the ECtHR avoid overstepping into the jurisdiction of the CJEU and domestic authorities. The ECtHR would also need to clearly substantiate how domestic authorities have failed to adequately take into account fundamental rights. It would be preferable for the ECtHR to use existing channels, such as the concept of 'law' and procedural review, to justify its examination of the lack of, or inadequate application of, EU fundamental rights by national authorities.[35] This would provide a solid foundation to justify such an approach.

III. Enriching

The complementarity approach is not intended to prevent cross-influence; there is ample room for the ECHR system to learn from the highly sophisticated EU fundamental rights system, without compromising the core principles of the ECHR legal framework.

---

32 J. Krommendijk and M. Timmerman, 'The Slippery Slope of a Snooping Strasbourg: The erroneous application of EU law as an ECHR breach', *VerfBlog*, 2022, available here: https://verfassungsblog.de/the-slippery-slope-of-a-snooping-strasbourg/.

33 E.g. ECtHR, *K.I. v. France*, no. 5560/19, § 123, 15 April 2021; ECtHR, *Diallo v. the Czech Republic*, no. 20493/07, § 76, 23 June 2011.

34 J. Krommendijk and M. Timmerman, 'The Slippery Slope of a Snooping Strasbourg: The erroneous application of EU law as an ECHR breach', *VerfBlog*, 2022, available here: https://verfassungsblog.de/the-slippery-slope-of-a-snooping-strasbourg/. See for another view the comment made by J. Callewaert on this blogpost.

35 Part IV, Chapter 2, Section II, §2. Justification.

The Charter can serve as a valuable source for enriching and fine-tuning ECHR law. As we have seen in Part II of this project, the Charter encompasses several generations of fundamental rights within a single comprehensive instrument. Additionally, it is an enriched and updated version of the ECHR for certain rights.[36] Beyond the judgments discussed in our case studies,[37] the ECtHR has already made significant use of the Charter's innovations.[38] Examples of the influence of the Charter are manifold and concern notably the right of civil servants to form trade unions,[39] the right of conscientious objection to military service,[40] the right to a fair trial in the case of a dispute between civil servant and State,[41] the extension of the right to a fair trial to interim measures,[42] and the principle of retroactivity of the most lenient criminal law.[43] The Charter has played a multiplicity of functions, such as being used to determine whether there is a European consensus, following which the ECHR occasionally reverses its case-law, as we will see below.[44] If the ECtHR has already relied significantly on the Charter,[45] there remains ample room for the ECtHR to learn from it. This is true for specific Charter provisions that have no equivalent in the ECHR. In the field of equality, the Charter includes provisions that protect specific groups, such as the elderly and persons with disabilities, which the ECtHR could potentially rely on as a source to support a higher degree of protection for these groups under ECHR equality law.

Next, EU secondary laws on fundamental rights are a relevant source of learning. These legislations are often highly sophisticated, as they typically define the scope, clarify key concepts, and provide guidance on balancing fundamental rights against competing legitimate interests. A good example is the recent Whistleblower Directive. This instrument defines notions such as 'internal reporting', 'external reporting', 'reporting person', and 'retaliation'

---

36 See above Part II, Chapter , Section III, §1. Highly Sophisticated

37 E.g. ECtHR, *Christine Goodwin v. the United Kingdom* [GC], no. 28957/95, § 100, ECHR 2002-VI; ECtHR, *I. v. the United Kingdom* [GC], no. 25680/94, § 30, 11 July 2002.

38 See for a study devoted to the use of the Charter by the ECtHR, B. Dickson, 'The EU Charter of Fundamental Rights in the Case-law of the European Court of Human Rights', *European Human Rights Law Review*, 2015, pp. 27–40.

39 ECtHR, *Demir and Baykara v. Turkey* [GC], no. 34503/97, §§ 105–107, ECHR 2008.

40 ECtHR, *Bayatyan v. Armenia* [GC], no. 23459/03, § 106, 7 July 2011.

41 ECtHR, *Vilho Eskinen v. Finland* [GC], no. 63235/00, § 60, 19 April 2007.

42 ECtHR, *Micallef v. Malta* [GC], no. 17056/06, §§ 32 and 78, 15 October 2009.

43 ECtHR, *Scoppola v. Italy (no. 2)* [GC], no. 10249/03, §§ 105–109, 17 September 2009.

44 See below Part IV, Chapter 2, Section II, §2, III. EU Law as Part of A European Consensus.

45 See for different analyses of the use of the Charter by the ECtHR, P. Lemmens and M. Piret, 'The Charter of Fundamental Rights of the European Union and the European Convention on Human Rights, from the Perspective of the European Court of Human Rights', *Cahiers de droit européen*, 2021, pp. 183–210; S. O'Leary, 'The EU Charter Ten Years On: A View from Strasbourg', in M. Bobek and J. Adams-Prassl (eds.), *The EU Charter of Fundamental Rights in the Member States*, Oxford, Hart Publishing, 2020, pp. 37–68; T. Lock, 'The Influence of EU Law on Strasbourg Doctrines', *European Law Review*, 2016, pp. 804–825.

which are key to understand the protection offered to whistleblowers.[46] It establishes a well-defined scope, both material and personal,[47] and lays out the conditions under which reporting persons qualify for protection.[48] Additionally, it details how reporting persons should use internal and external reporting channels and how authorities must ensure that these channels are available.[49] Furthermore, it specifies the protection measures that EU States must implement to protect reporting persons.[50] The high degree of precision in this instrument makes it a valuable source of inspiration for the ECtHR, especially since 27 Convention States have implemented it into their domestic law.

Last, the ECtHR can benefit from the insights provided by CJEU cases related to fundamental rights, not only by drawing on the concepts developed by the CJEU but also by considering cases where the CJEU has intervened before the ECtHR. Often, the CJEU intervenes before the ECtHR since the ECtHR acts as a court of last resort.[51] In the context of the EU's potential accession to the ECHR, this could take place through the prior involvement mechanism, whereby the CJEU would have the first say on the compatibility of EU law with EU fundamental rights before the ECtHR intervenes.[52] This dynamic offers a precious opportunity for the ECtHR to get inspiration from the CJEU's reasoning and contribute to a more cohesive and harmonised approach to fundamental rights protection across Europe, while maintaining its approach and role as a court that ensures that a minimum threshold of human rights is respected at pan-European level.

EU fundamental rights hold significant potential to enhance the substantive legitimacy of ECtHR's decisions. Substantial legitimacy, as discussed in Part I of this project, refers to the ECtHR's ability to make decisions that are informed by all relevant circumstances and based on persuasive sources to ensure that these decisions are accepted and respected.[53] EU law is arguably one of the most persuasive external sources available to the ECtHR, as it is deeply embedded within the legal frameworks of 27 Convention States, making it almost akin to domestic law in these jurisdictions. The persuasive value of

---

46 Article 5 of Whistleblower Directive (2019/1937/EU).

47 Ibid., Articles 2 and 4.

48 Ibid., Article 6.

49 Ibid., Articles 7 to 14.

50 Ibid., Articles 19 to 24.

51 This can be seen in cases such as ECtHR, *Jehovah's Witnesses v. Finland*, no. 31172/19, 9 May 2023; and ECtHR, *Satakunnan Markkinapörssi Oy and Satamedia Oy v. Finland* [GC], no. 931/13, 27 June 2017 (which we have previously analysed), where a case begins at the domestic level, reaches the CJEU through the preliminary ruling procedure, returns to the domestic level, and finally reaches the ECtHR. See above Part III (case study on data protection), Chapter 3, Section II, §2,II. Lawfulness.

52 Article 3(6) of the Draft Accession Agreement.

53 See above Part I, Chapter 2, Section IV. The Double-Edged Sword of Legitimacy.

EU law could grow even further if more Convention States incorporate EU fundamental rights into their legal systems. While the integration of EU law can bolster the legitimacy of ECtHR's decisions, it is essential that the ECtHR adheres to sound methodological principles, as we will further explain below.[54]

§ 2. COHERENCE

Coherence between the ECHR and EU legal systems is essential since both operate within a shared European space. Within this space, domestic courts play a central role as they must ensure that ECHR law is respected and that EU law is applied. As much as they are 'central actors and driving force behind human rights protection' in the ECHR legal system,[55] they are also at the heart of the implementation of EU law.[56] Being mandated by the two systems, they 'have to identify in each individual case the applicable standards and accommodate the various legal sources which will exist wholly independently from each other.'[57]

The effective application of both sets of rights, making them meaningful for individuals, requires a certain level of coherence between the systems. As the EU and ECHR systems become increasingly autonomous, the need for coherence between these two legal systems grows. As interpreters of these two sets of laws, the CJEU and ECtHR share part of the responsibility for ensuring that their layers are articulated coherently. That is why we argue that the ECtHR should be guided by a logic of coherence when (considering) using EU fundamental rights. Coherence can be achieved through convergence, and there are many areas that show convergence between the EU and ECHR

54 See below Part IV, Chapter 2, Section II. Methodological Principles.

55 See the speech of the Former President of the ECtHR, S. O'Leary, 'Judicial Dialogue: Fundamental Rights Issues in National Court Judgments. Trilateral Meeting with the CJEU of the European Union and the Network of the Presidents of the Supreme Judicial Courts of the European Union', 10 November 2023, available here https://www.echr.coe.int/documents/d/echr/speech-20231110-oleary-trilateral-meeting-vienna-eng, p 2.

56 See above Part II, Chapter 2, Section III, §2. Deeply Integrated within EU States.

57 Speech of J. Polakiewicz, 'EU accession to the ECHR: How to square the circle?', 2020, available here: https://www.coe.int/en/web/dlapil/-/eu-accession-to-the-echr-how-to-square-the-circle-. In other words, as observed by Callewaert, '[n]ational judges play an essential role in the protection of fundamental rights today, as they are the ones entrusted with the difficult task of combining and translating into viable solutions the multiple sources of such rights which are being produced by today's complex multipolar and multilayer legal world. They are the ones who, at the end of the day, apply these multiple legal sources to the citizens in the most coherent possible way. In other words, the proof of the pudding, i.e. the real interaction between those sources takes place at domestic level, nowhere else.' (J. Callewaert, 'Convention Control Over the Application of Union Law by National Judges: The Case for a Wholistic Approach to Fundamental Rights', *European Papers*, 2023, p. 332).

systems of fundamental rights protection in recent years. However, there are good reasons not to opt for convergence of ECHR law with EU law, or to do so only in specific circumstances. Coherence can also be maintained without this type of convergence.

I. Coherence through Convergence

One way to achieve coherence is through alignment between the EU and ECHR legal systems. In recent years, many areas have shown significant convergence between the EU and ECHR standards. This has occurred partly as a result of the ECHR legal system aligning with the EU legal system. Our equality case study provides a good example. Indeed, the ECtHR has drawn notable inspiration from EU equality law, aligning its stance with concepts from EU equality law and approaches developed by the CJEU. In other instances, it is the EU legal system that tends to align with the ECHR legal system. This is the case with the EU procedural rights directives, where the flow of influence has been pronounced from Strasbourg to Luxembourg.[58] There can also be a mutual alignment, where through dialogue, the European Courts adjust their jurisprudence in harmony with one another.[59]

Alignment of ECHR law with EU law should however not always be welcomed. Such alignment may result in 'levelling down' the protection of human rights at European level. This is illustrated, for instance, by the *Stec* saga, where the ECtHR followed the approach found in EU equality law, leading to a low level of equality protection under ECHR law.[60] The issue can also be raised in the context of reconciling the principle of mutual trust under EU law with the protection of human rights. Recent cases have demonstrated signs of increased alignment on both the CJEU and ECtHR sides.[61] The ECtHR has recognised the legitimacy of the mutual trust mechanisms[62] and has sanctioned the inadequate enforcement of mutual trust mechanisms.[63] However, one must bear in mind that if the ECtHR would follow the two-step approach of the CJEU which the latter often uses (that is, there should be both

58 See above Part IV, Chapter , Section I. More EU Fundamental Rights. See also S. O'Leary, ibid. pp. 3–4.

59 See below Part IV, Chapter 2, Section I, §3, I.B. Virtuous Circles.

60 See above Part III (case study on equality), Chapter 3, Section II, §2, II.A. Supportive.

61 On the CJEU's side, see Case C-699/21, *EDL*, ECLI:EU:C:2023:295 where the CJEU does not use a two-step test. See more in L. van der Meulen, 'Another Exception to The Rule: The E.D.L Case On EAW Surrenders Of Seriously Ill Persons', *Common Market Law Review*, 2024, pp. 223–238.

62 ECtHR, *Avotiņš v. Latvia* [GC], no. 17502/07, § 113, 23 May 2016.

63 See above Part IV, Chapter 2, Section I, §1, II. Contributing to the Effectiveness.

a systemic test and an individual test),[64] there is a risk of moving away from an approach that focuses on individual violations of fundamental rights.[65]

In addition, aligning on the EU standards carries the risk of marginalising non-EU Convention States. Although this issue has not materialised in our case studies, as EU fundamental rights are mostly used in cases involving EU States, the ECtHR must remain vigilant to the potential effects of convergence with EU law. Specifically, this could result in non-EU States being obliged to adhere to rules they have not participated in shaping. While this possibility cannot and should not be excluded, it should be justified with solid reasoning. Furthermore, by converging with the EU system, the ECtHR itself might risk marginalisation and deviation from its role as the guarantor of a minimum standard of fundamental rights protection for 46 diverse States.

If convergence between the EU and ECHR legal systems is not pursued, a certain degree of fragmentation must be accepted – be it between EU and non-EU States or within EU States where both EU and ECHR laws apply. However, fragmentation is not inherently problematic. First, it creates a sphere of experimentation where EU and ECHR legal systems can learn from each other,[66] and individuals can strategically use various legal pathways.[67] Second, the purpose of fundamental rights is not to achieve uniformity, but rather 'about the empowerment of individuals and the protection of liberty primarily against state authorities'[68] Indeed, '[u]niformity in fundamental rights protection is neither required nor desirable in a Europe composed of nation states, each of which with its own distinctive traditions of fundamental rights protection.'[69] Third, in the specific context of the ECHR, its aim is not to harmonise fundamental rights but rather to guarantee a minimum standard of human rights above which States can go.[70]

---

64 E.g. Case C-158/21, *Puig Gordi*, ECLI:EU:C:2023:57, paras. 102 and 106.

65 See for an argument in favour of replacing the two-step test with a one-step test that focuses on the risk faced by the person affected by the measure that implements mutual trust, C. Rizcallah, 'The principle of mutual trust and the protection of fundamental rights in the Area of Freedom, Security and Justice: A critical look at the Court of Justice's stone-by-stone approach', *Maastricht Journal of European and Comparative Law*, 2023, pp. 255–272.

66 See E. Brems, 'Smart human rights integration', in *Fragmentation and Integration in Human Rights Law*, Cheltenham, Edward Elgar Publishing, 2018, pp. 186–187.

67 Ibid., p. 188.

68 J. Callewaert et al., 'The EU Fundamental Rights Landscape after Opinion 2/13', *Maastricht Faculty of Law Working Paper No. 2016/3*, available here: https://papers.ssrn.com/sol3/papers.cfm?abstract_id=2799100, p. 67.

69 Ibid.

70 E.g. J. Callewaert, 'No More Common Understanding of Fundamental Rights ?', *La revue des juristes de Sciences Po*, 2022, p. 25.

II. Coherence without Aligning with EU Standards

There are various ways to achieve coherence without the ECtHR converging with the EU standards. First of all, the ECtHR can recognise situations where EU law provides higher protection than ECHR law without incorporating EU standards. One avenue for this is Article 53 ECHR, which allows the ECtHR to consider EU law as a source of protection that exceeds ECHR standards, without using it as a benchmark for assessing violations of ECHR law. We will return to this in more detail.[71]

Where EU – fundamental rights – standards are potentially lower than ECHR law, coherence can be guaranteed by ensuring that the EU standards comply with ECHR law.[72] As the EU is not a party to the ECHR, it cannot be held responsible for measures adopted by its institutions before the ECtHR. In concrete terms, this implies that applications directly against these institutions are declared inadmissible.[73] Yet, EU States remain responsible regarding EU primary law, as established in the *Matthews v. United Kingdom* case of 18 February 1999.[74] Moreover, the ECtHR exercises indirect control when EU States implement EU law. While the ECHR does not prohibit the transfer of sovereign powers from the Contracting Parties to an international organisation, they remain responsible for all acts and omissions of their organs, including those arising from the need to comply with international legal obligations.[75] However, a measure seeking to implement these obligations must be considered justified if the international organisation in question is found to offer protection of fundamental rights at least equivalent to that provided by the ECHR.[76]

The presumption of equivalent protection, which is applied with regard to EU law, helps to ensure coherence between the EU and ECHR systems.[77] Let us recall that if the ECtHR finds that this presumption applies and that there is no manifest deficiency in the protection of the rights guaranteed by the ECHR, it concludes that there is no violation of the Convention without

---

71 See below Part IV, Chapter 2, Section II, §2, I. Article 53 ECHR.

72 Please note that some paragraphs of this sub-section are inspired by or stem from V. Davio, 'Le droit de l'Union européenne dans la jurisprudence de la Cour européenne des droits de l'homme', *Journal des Tribunaux - Droit Européen*, 2023, pp. 46–50.

73 ECtHR, *Matthews v. UK* [GC], no. 24833/94, § 32, CEDH 1999-I.

74 Ibid., § 33.

75 ECtHR, *Bosphorus Hava Yolları Turizm ve Ticaret Anonim Şirketi v. Ireland* [GC], no. 45036/98, §§ 152–153, CEDH 2005-VI.

76 Ibid., § 155.

77 See for a critical view on the presumption of equivalent protection and its contribution to coherence, C. Rizcallah, 'The Systemic Equivalence Test and the Presumption of Equivalent Protection in European Human Rights Law – A Critical Appraisal', *German Law Journal*, 2023, pp. 1062–1077.

further examination.[78] Where the presumption does not apply, States remain fully responsible under the ECHR.[79] The presumption is subject to two well-established conditions.[80] The first is the absence of any margin of manoeuvre on the part of the domestic authorities.[81] The second is the deployment of the full potential of the supervisory mechanism provided for by EU law.[82] Where the presumption of equivalence is established, it can only be rebutted if the protection of ECHR rights is manifestly insufficient.[83]

In other words, the Bosphorus presumption allows the EU system to address potential fundamental rights issues, with ECtHR intervention occurring only in exceptional circumstances. When a domestic measure implementing EU law has been fully reviewed within the EU supervisory system, the ECtHR intervenes only if the protection remains manifestly insufficient. This means that, when the presumption applies, there will be limited cases where a measure deemed legal under EU law will not be considered legal under ECHR law. However, such situations can occur, as evidenced by *Bivolaru v. France* (2021).[84]

The EU's accession to the ECHR may bring coherence between EU and ECHR standards when EU standards are lower than those of the ECHR. This is primarily because the ECtHR would be able to directly review acts from EU institutions. However, several questions remain. First, there is the issue of how the ECtHR would control acts emanating from EU institutions and/or EU States in cases related to mutual trust and CFSP matters.[85] Second,

---

[78] ECtHR, *Bosphorus Hava Yolları Turizm ve Ticaret Anonim Şirketi v. Ireland* [GC], no. 45036/98, § 166, CEDH 2005-VI.

[79] Ibid., § 157.

[80] ECtHR, *Avotiņš v. Latvia* [GC], no. 17502/07, § 105, 23 May 2016.

[81] See for an illustration of the first condition, ibid., §§ 106–107.

[82] See for an illustration of the second condition, ibid., § 109.

[83] ECtHR, *Bosphorus Hava Yolları Turizm ve Ticaret Anonim Şirketi v. Ireland* [GC], no. 45036/98, § 156, CEDH 2005-VI.

[84] ECtHR, *Bivolaru and Moldovan v. France*, nos. 40324/16 and 12623/17, § 126, 25 March 2021.

[85] Some insights can be gleaned from the draft agreement but it remains somewhat unclear. Regarding mutual trust, Article 5b of the Draft Accession Agreement mentions that: 'Accession of the European Union to the Convention shall not affect the application of the principle of mutual trust within the European Union. In this context, the protection of human rights guaranteed by the Convention shall be ensured' Regarding CFSP matters, the CJEU has recently delivered the *KS and KD* judgment on its jurisdiction in CFSP matters, which appear to facilitate the EU's accession to the ECHR (Case C-29/22 P, *KS and KD v. Council of the European Union and Others*, ECLI:EU:C:2024:725), as mentioned above (Part IV, Chapter 1, Section III. The Prospect of EU's Accession to the ECHR). Should accession occur, it remains to be seen whether the jurisdiction of the ECtHR over CFSP matters will align with that of the CJEU.

it is unclear whether the Bosphorus presumption would continue to apply post-accession.[86]

While divergences between CJEU and ECtHR case-law are often temporary,[87] some are more lasting as they are linked to the specificities and constraints of the legal system in which they operate.[88] An example relates to the principle of ne bis in idem. In recent cases, the CJEU has aligned its approach with the ECtHR's case-law.[89] Despite this increasing convergence, differences still persist between the approaches of the two European Courts. First, ne bis in idem applies only within the jurisdiction of a single Convention State in the ECHR context, whereas under EU law, it extends to proceedings involving multiple EU States.[90] Second, the two Courts adopt slightly different methodological approaches.[91] The divergences in the protection of ne bis in idem by the CJEU and the ECtHR are linked to differences in how this principle is shaped in EU and ECHR laws.

In cases of lasting divergence, the European Courts should clearly indicate the existence of such divergence and the reasons behind it, to assist national courts in their work.[92] This can be achieved, for example, by indicating when EU law offers higher protection, where feasible.[93] This can also be done by highlighting the structural differences between the protection offered by EU and ECHR laws. *Krombach v. France* (2018) provides an elegant example. The applicant's position was that the principle of ne bis in idem in ECHR law should be interpreted as prohibiting a person who has been acquitted or convicted by a final judgment in accordance with the law and procedure of one State Party from being prosecuted or punished for the same offence not only

86 The Draft Accession Agreement does not mention the Bosphorus presumption, leaving some uncertainty as to whether it will remain applicable post-accession. See for an argument in favor of abandoning the presumption post-accession, S. Imamović, 'Post-EU Accession to the ECHR: The Argument for Why the ECtHR Should Abandon the Bosphorus Doctrine', *Utrecht Journal of International and European Law*, 2024, pp. 17–29.

87 In this vein, V. Davio, 'Detention in the Hungarian transit zones: A case of higher fundamental rights protection by EU law vis-à-vis the ECHR', *European Law Review*, 2022, p. 403 (fn. 99).

88 In this vein, see the speech of the Former President of the ECtHR, S. O'Leary, 'Judicial Dialogue: Fundamental Rights Issues in National Court Judgments. Trilateral Meeting with the CJEU of the European Union and the Network of the Presidents of the Supreme Judicial Courts of the European Union', 10 November 2023, available here https://www.echr.coe.int/documents/d/echr/speech-20231110-oleary-trilateral-meeting-vienna-eng, p. 7.

89 Please note that this paragraph on ne bis idem is inspired by or stem from V. Davio and I. Gambardella, 'Greater Coherence for the Ne Bis in Idem Principle, at Last: The Bpost Judgment (C-117/20)', *EU Law Analysis*, 2022.

90 See more on the transnational character of ne bis idem in EU law, M. Wasmeier, 'The principle of ne bis in idem', *Revue internationale de droit pénal*, 2006, p. 121.

91 See for an illustration in V. Davio and I. Gambardella, 'Greater Coherence for the Ne Bis in Idem Principle, at Last: The Bpost Judgment (C-117/20)', *EU Law Analysis*, 2022.

92 S. O'Leary, 'Courts, Charters and Conventions', *The Irish Jurist*, 2016, p. 40.

93 See below Part IV, Chapter 2, Section II, §2, I. Article 53 ECHR.

by the courts of that State but also by the courts of any other State Party to the Convention.[94] In this regard, the ECtHR observed that 'the fact that France and Germany are members of the [EU] and that EU law gives the principle of ne bis in idem a transnational dimension within the European Union [...] is irrelevant to the question of the applicability of Article 4 of Protocol No. 7 in this case.'[95] The ECtHR further noted that 'the Convention does not prevent State Parties from granting broader legal protection to the rights and freedoms it guarantees, whether through domestic law, other international treaties, or EU law. As it has previously emphasised, by its system of collective guarantee of the rights it enshrines, the Convention reinforces, in accordance with the principle of subsidiarity, the protection offered at the national level, without ever imposing limitations on it (Article 53 of the Convention) [...].'[96] Thus, the ECHR not only highlights structural differences with EU law but also explains that EU law can provide a higher level of protection than ECHR law.

Coherence can be achieved not only by identifying divergences in standards but also by pointing out divergences in the facts or contexts of cases handled by the CJEU and the ECtHR. As shown in our case studies, the ECtHR has shed light on some differences between its own cases and those of the CJEU. The ECtHR has also noted instances where the CJEU had not yet addressed certain issues. However, these distinctions have often been made only in a limited number of cases and frequently addressed in a brief or peripheral manner.[97] There is room for a more robust distinguishing approach, where the ECtHR would more explicitly outline the differences in facts or contexts between cases decided by the CJEU and those by the ECtHR, and clearly explain how these differences account for differences in reasoning and legal outcomes.

§ 3. DIALOGUE

If the use of EU fundamental rights by the ECtHR is to be guided by complementarity and coherence, it must also be part of a dialogue – whether through case-law or other forums such as informal meetings – among the various actors active within the European space of fundamental rights. It should be noted from the outset that human rights are particularly prone to be subject of dialogue. Human rights are indeed in network.[98] As Dubout and Touze have observed, fundamental rights serve as vectors of communication, both by

94 ECtHR, *Krombach v. France* (dec.), no. 67521/14, § 34, 20 February 2018.
95 Ibid., § 38 (own translation)
96 Ibid., § 39 (own translation)
97 See above the conclusion of Part III: Are EU Fundamental Rights A Source of Special Significance?
98 A. Bailleux, 'Human Rights in Network', *Journal européen des droits de l'homme*, 2014, pp. 293–325.

need and nature. By need, firstly, of security and legitimacy. Security because with the multiplication of systems for the protection of fundamental rights, there must be a minimum of substantive convergence in the interpretation of fundamental rights, especially when the geographical scope of the systems overlaps.[99] Legitimacy as human rights courts, especially supranational ones, have to maintain their authority, which can be done by using comparative law to support their findings.[100] By nature, secondly, because of their universality and their common origin. The claim of human rights to universality, regardless of whether it is a tangible reality, leads to a tendency to cross legal barriers and to dialogue among judges.[101] In addition, modern human rights instruments are rooted in a common instrument, the Universal Declaration of Human Rights, which implies commonality between the different instruments, thus facilitating communication between human rights texts.

The quality of the judicial dialogue in the shared European space is crucial for ensuring the coherence and effectiveness of fundamental rights protection across Europe. The dialogue between the CJEU and ECtHR is the first to come to mind, as these two Courts give flesh to the Convention and to EU fundamental rights. While the dialogue between them is long-standing and generally of very high quality, there are situations where a lack of dialogue has occurred that can be detrimental to national courts and, ultimately, to individuals. Such situations should be avoided; on the contrary, dialogue between them can create 'virtuous circles' within the European fundamental rights space. While the dialogue between these two Courts is important, it should also be part of a broader dialogue involving other key actors involved in the shared European space – most notably, domestic courts, which make fundamental rights a tangible reality. This dialogue should also extend to the EU legislator, who plays an increasing role in shaping the landscape of fundamental rights protection across Europe.

I. A Dialogue between the CJEU and the ECtHR

The dialogue between the CJEU and the ECtHR is long-standing and considerable. An emblematic illustration is the *Roquettes Frères* (2000) judgment, where the CJEU revisited its *Hoechst* (1989) judgment in light of new developments in Strasbourg. In the latter, the CJEU ruled that the inviolability of the home as guaranteed by Article 8 ECHR did not apply to

---

99 E. Dubout and S. Touze, 'La fonction des droits fondamentaux dans les rapports entre ordres et systèmes juridiques', in E. Dubout and S. Touze (eds.), *Les droits fondamentaux: charnières entre ordres et systèmes juridiques*, Paris, Pedone 2009, p. 17.

100 Ibid.

101 Ibid., pp. 18–19.

business premises,[102] whereas the ECtHR stated in subsequent case-law that the protection of Article 8 ECHR could be invoked by businesses[103] – and referred on that occasion to the case law of the CJEU.[104] In *Roquettes Frères* (2000) judgment, the CJEU considered that 'for the purposes of determining the scope of that principle in relation to the protection of business premises, regard must be had to the case-law of the European Court of Human Rights subsequent to the judgment in Hoechst.'[105] Such type of dialogue has been key to ensuring the coherence and effectiveness of fundamental rights protection in Europe. Generally speaking, the dialogue between the two Courts is of very high quality, whether through their judgments or informal meetings.[106]

A. Missed Judicial Dialogue

However, there are situations of 'missed dialogue' between the CJEU and the ECtHR. A compelling example relates to the judicial saga related to the Hungarian transit zones.[107] Let us recall that amidst the rise of asylum applications in Europe in 2015, Hungary established so-called transit zones. Located on the southern border between Hungary and Serbia, these no-man's-lands were not only the place where asylum seekers had to apply for asylum but also where they were accommodated during their asylum application. It did not last long before the legality of stay in these transit zones was contested before the CJEU and the ECtHR.

One of the core issues was whether these stays should be considered as 'detention'. The ECtHR was the first to rule in 2019 and considered, in *Ilias and Ahmed v. Hungary* [GC], that the stay in one of these transit zones did not constitute a deprivation of liberty and that, therefore, the right to liberty and security enshrined in Article 5 ECHR was not applicable.[108] One year later, the CJEU took a distinct stance: in *FMS and Others* (C-924/19 PPU and C-925/19

102 Joined Cases C-46/87 and C-227/88, *Hoechst*, ECLI:EU:C:1989:337, paras. 17–18; ECtHR, *Niemitz v. Germany*, no. 13710/88, §§ 27–33, 16 December 1992.

103 Joined Cases C-46/87 and C-227/88, *Hoechst*, ECLI:EU:C:1989:337, paras. 17–18; ECtHR, *Niemitz v. Germany*, no. 13710/88, §§ 27–33, 16 December 1992.

104 ECtHR, *Niemitz v. Germany*, ibid., § 22.

105 Case C-94/00, *Roquette Frères*, ECLI:EU:C:2002:603, para. 29.

106 In this vein, S. O'Leary, 'The EU Charter Ten Years On: A View from Strasbourg', in M. Bobek and J. Adams-Prassl (eds.), *The EU Charter of Fundamental Rights in the Member States*, Oxford, Hart Publishing, 2020, p. 56: 'In terms of judicial dialogue, the Strasbourg-Luxembourg report card in recent years would probably read 'satisfactory/working hard'. Informal, bilateral meetings between the two courts take place and are open and constructive. Cross-referencing continues apace and, in the main, is done with care.'

107 Please note that the following paragraphs on the judicial saga related to the Hungarian transit zones are inspired by or stem from V. Davio, 'Detention in the Hungarian transit zones: A case of higher fundamental rights protection by EU law vis-à-vis the ECHR', *European Law Review*, 2022, pp. 393–409.

108 ECtHR, *Ilias and Ahmed v. Hungary* [GC], no. 47287/15, § 249, 21 November 2019.

PPU) and *Commission v. Hungary* (C-808/18),[109] the CJEU concluded that the stay in the Hungarian transit zones constituted detention under both the Return Directive (2018/115)[110] and the Receptions Conditions Directive (2013/33).[111] The divergence between the case-law of the two Courts was partially resolved a few months later when the question arose again in Strasbourg. In *R.R. and Others v. Hungary* (2021), the ECtHR concluded that the confinement of an Iranian-Afghan family in the transit zones, including three minor children, constituted a deprivation of liberty.[112] While the ECtHR came to the same conclusion as the CJEU, the reasoning of the ECtHR is different and, arguably, provides lower protection than that offered under EU law.[113]

One of the striking features of this judicial saga was the quasi-silence of the two European Courts regarding their respective case-law despite the close proximity of their cases. As for the ECtHR, it noted in *R.R. and Others*, in its 'relevant legal framework and practice' section, that the CJEU held in *FMS and Others* that the stay in transit zones constituted detention, but did not engage substantively with the latter judgment.[114] As for the CJEU, it only mentioned in passing the ECtHR's Grand Chamber judgment in *Ilias and Ahmed* in *FMS and Others*,[115] while it did not even refer to the latter in *Commission v. Hungary* (C-808/18). If the CJEU does not engage explicitly with the judgment of the ECtHR's Grand Chamber judgment in *Ilias and Ahmed*, it is apparent that the CJEU has, implicitly but firmly, rejected the latter's position on the threshold at which a situation should be considered a detention by not taking into account its interpretation of Article 5 ECHR.[116]

Such an implicit position by the two European Courts vis-à-vis each other's case-law may be detrimental to national courts.[117] Indeed, how should national courts understand the silence of the CJEU on the *Ilias and Ahmed* case, despite the strong factual similarities and the fact that the CJEU appears to adopt a position that diverges from that of the ECtHR? Conversely, how should they understand that the ECtHR in *R.R. and Others* mentioned the CJEU's

---

109 Case C-808/18, *Commission v. Hungary*, ECLI:EU:C:2020:1029, para. 166; Joined Cases C-924/19 PPU and 925/19 PPU, *FMS and Others*, ECLI:EU:C:2020:367, para. 231.

110 Directive 2008/115 on common standards and procedures in Member States for returning illegally staying third-country nationals, [2008] OJ L348/98.

111 Directive 2013/33 laying down standards for the reception of applicants for international protection (recast), [2013] OJ L180/96.

112 ECtHR, *R.R. and Others v. Hungary*, no. 36037/17, § 56, 2 March 2021.

113 V. Davio, 'Detention in the Hungarian transit zones: A case of higher fundamental rights protection by EU law vis-à-vis the ECHR', *European Law Review*, 2022, pp. 402–404.

114 ECtHR, *R.R. and Others v. Hungary*, no. 36037/17, § 28, 2 March 2021.

115 Joined Cases C-924/19 PPU and 925/19 PPU, *FMS and Others*, ECLI:EU:C:2020:367, para. 71.

116 Opinion of Advocate General Pikamäe, 25 June 2020 in Case C-808/18, *Commission v. Hungary*, ECLI:EU:C:2020:493, para. 131.

117 S. Imamovic, *The Architecture of Fundamental Rights in the European Union*, Oxford, Hart Publishing, 2022, p. 3.

position in the relevant legal materials, but did not refer to it in the rest of the judgment?[118] Not only can the approaches of the two European Courts create ambiguous and confusing signals for national judges who are bound to apply both EU law and the ECHR, but they can also serve as a 'false excuse' for recalcitrant States to refuse to comply with the judicial decision unfavourable to them, (erroneously) arguing that they are respecting the other decision.

The fact that a different approach is possible is illustrated by the Opinion of Advocate General Pikamäe in the *FMS and Others* case. Not only did Advocate General Pikamäe recall the ECtHR's Grand Chamber judgment in *Ilias and Ahmed* and underline its relevance to the preliminary questions at stake, but he explained *how* – on the basis of an autonomous interpretation of the Charter – and *why* – in the light of the definition of detention provided by EU secondary law – the CJEU should offer a higher level of protection than the ECHR.[119]

B. Virtuous Circles

If the lack of dialogue can be damaging, fostering dialogue can, on the other hand, create 'virtuous circles' within the shared European space.[120] This is perhaps most well illustrated by the extensive dialogue amidst the rule of law crisis that has taken place over the last few years in Europe.[121] In this context, the CJEU and the ECtHR have increasingly dealt with issues related to the organisation of national judicial legal systems. With the growing number of cases on the matter, the European Courts has been led to clarify the contours of the requirement of an independent and impartial tribunal established by law. For that purpose, both Courts have been referring extensively to the case-law of their counterpart.

A telling example relates to the requirement that tribunals must be established by law.[122] This concept has seen a resurgence in the case-law of both Courts. On 1 December 2020, the Grand Chamber of the ECtHR has

118 In this vein, S. O'Leary, 'Courts, Charters and Conventions: Making Sense of Fundamental Rights in the EU', *The Irish Jurist*, 2016, p. 25.

119 Opinion of AG Pikamäe, 23 April 2020 in Joined Cases C-924/19 PPU and 925/19 PPU, *FMS and Others*, ECLI:EU:C:2020:367, paras. 148–174.

120 See the speech of the Former President of the ECtHR, S. O'Leary, 'Judicial Dialogue: Fundamental Rights Issues in National Court Judgments. Trilateral Meeting with the CJEU of the European Union and the Network of the Presidents of the Supreme Judicial Courts of the European Union', 10 November 2023, available here https://www.echr.coe.int/documents/d/echr/speech-20231110-oleary-trilateral-meeting-vienna-eng, p. 5.

121 On the 'rule of law crisis', see e.g. M. Smith, 'Staring into the abyss: A crisis of the rule of law in the EU', *European Law Journal*, 2019, pp. 561–576.

122 Please note that the following paragraphs on the requirement of a tribunal established by law are inspired by or stem from C. Rizcallah and V. Davio, 'The Requirement that Tribunals be Established by Law: A Valuable Principle Safeguarding the Rule of Law and the Separation of Powers in a Context of Trust', *European Constitutional Law Review*, 2021, pp. 581–606.

rendered a landmark judgment in the *Guðmundur Andri Ástráðsson v. Island* case, in which it has provided detailed guidance on the right of a tribunal established by law enshrined in Article 6 ECHR.[123] At EU level, the requirement of a tribunal established by law was brought into the spotlight in *Simpson v. Council* and *HG v. Commission*, which concerned the irregular appointment of judges at the Civil Service Tribunal. In its judgment in the *Simpson and HG* case of 26 March 2020,[124] the Grand Chamber of the CJEU relied extensively on the Chamber judgment of the ECtHR in the case *Ástráðsson*,[125] to define the contours of the requirement of a tribunal established by law at EU level.[126] Since then, many cases have been brought before the CJEU on this requirement and the CJEU has often referred to the Strasbourg case-law on the matter.[127]

Yet the process of influence between the two legal systems has also gone in the other direction with regard to the requirement of a tribunal established by law, and more generally on the rule of law.[128] In *Ástráðsson* for instance, the Grand Chamber discussed at length no less than four CJEU rulings, from those relating to the *Simpson* saga to Case C-619/18.[129] As a result of the interaction between the two Courts, we can observe a genuine process of mutual enrichment on the requirements flowing from the rule of law.

---

123 ECtHR, *Guðmundur Andri Ástráðsson v. Island* [GC], no. 26374/18, 1 December 2020.

124 Cases C-542/18 RX-II and 543/18 RX-II, *Erik Simpson and HG v. Council of the European Union and European Commission*, ECLI:EU:C:2020:232.

125 ECtHR, *Guðmundur Andri Ástráðsson v. Iceland*, no. 26374/18, 12 March 2019.

126 Among other things, the CJEU relied on the *Ástráðsson* Chamber judgment to consider that the right to be judged by a court established by law encompasses the process of appointment of judges (Joined Cases C-542/18 RX-II and 543/18 RX-II, *Erik Simpson and HG v. Council of the European Union and European Commission*, ECLI:EU:C:2020:232, para. 74) and that a certain threshold of gravity must be reached for an irregularity to amount to a violation of this right (ibid., paras. 71–74).

127 For instance, in *Commission v. Poland* (C-791/19) of 15 July 2021, the CJEU relied on the ECtHR's *Miracle Europe* judgment (ECtHR, *Miracle Europe KFT v. Hungary*, no. 57774/13, 12 January 2016) to consider that the Polish law which gives the President of the Chamber the discretionary power to designate the disciplinary court of first instance competent in cases concerning judges of ordinary courts, without providing any criteria for designation, does not meet the requirements of the court established by law in the sense of Article 19(1)(2) TEU (Case C-791/19, *Commission v. Poland*, ECLI:EU:C:2021:596, paras. 164–177).

128 See e.g. the Speech of the Former President to the ECtHR, R. Spano for the Opening of the 2021 ECtHR's judicial year (available here: https://www.echr.coe.int/documents/d/echr/Annual_report_2021_ENG, 18): 'It is not just the Strasbourg Court which has been grappling with crucial rule of law questions over the last few years. The Court of Justice of the European Union has delivered a number of important judgments on judicial independence. Why do I mention this? It is because of the symbiotic relationship between Strasbourg and Luxembourg on this question. The jurisprudential core of many of the Luxembourg Court's rulings rely on Strasbourg case-law, and Strasbourg case-law itself relies on the findings of the Luxembourg Court.'

129 ECtHR, *Guðmundur Andri Ástráðsson v. Island* [GC], no. 26374/18, §§ 131–140, 1 December 2020.

II. Opening up the Dialogue

If dialogue between the CJEU and the ECtHR is essential for the functioning of the shared European space, the dialogue should not be limited to just these two Courts. It should also extend to other key actors involved in implementing or shaping European fundamental rights. Particularly, there should be significant dialogue between the ECtHR and domestic courts. The ECtHR should consider how domestic courts understand and apply EU fundamental rights. As observed above, the ECtHR has been willing to sanction cases where there is a lack of, or inadequate, engagement with these rights.[130] Conversely, the ECtHR has also shown a degree of deference when domestic courts actively engage with EU fundamental rights and the supervisory mechanisms available under EU law.

This was evident in the cases of *Satakunnan v. Finland* [GC](2017) and *Jehovah's Witnesses* (2023) we have explored above.[131] As we may recall, domestic courts sought preliminary rulings from the CJEU and subsequently relied on the answers provided by the latter. The applicants then challenged the decisions before the ECtHR. The ECtHR found that the requirement of foreseeability, as part of the test of lawfulness, was met when national courts sought a preliminary ruling from the CJEU and relied on its findings. The ECtHR shows deference to the preliminary ruling procedure, stressing the importance of judicial dialogue between domestic courts and the CJEU.[132] Additionally, the ECtHR's scrutiny of the interpretation and application of EU law by national courts is limited to examining whether the domestic authorities' actions are not arbitrary or unpredictable. While the ECtHR exercises a certain level of scrutiny, this oversight remains marginal and is primarily viewed through the lens of the Convention.[133] We can thus observe the emergence of a 'trilogue'[134] involving national courts, the CJEU, and the ECtHR, where a case starts at the national level, moves to the CJEU, and finally reaches the ECtHR. The deference shown by the ECtHR is appropriate as it allows EU supervisory mechanisms to function and grants national authorities some discretion in their interpretation of EU fundamental rights.

---

130 See above Part IV, Chapter 2, Section I, §1, II. Contributing to the Effectiveness.

131 See above Part III (case study on data protection), Chapter 3, Section II, §2, II. Lawfulness.

132 E.g. ECtHR, *Jehovah's Witnesses v. Finland*, no. 31172/19, § 85, 9 May 2023; ECtHR, *Satakunnan Markkinapörssi Oy and Satamedia Oy v. Finland* [GC], no. 931/13, § 150, 27 June 2017.

133 See above Part III (case study on data protection), Chapter 3, Section II, §2, II. Lawfulness.

134 See for another type of 'trilogue' within EU fundamental rights law (between the EU legislator, the CJEU and domestic courts): P. Aertgeerts, 'Between Unity and Diversity: EU Data Protection Legislation as a Catalyst for a Constitutional Trilogue', in M. Sahadžić et al. (ed.), *Accommodating Diversity in Multilevel Constitutional Orders: Legal Mechanisms of Divergence and Convergence*, London, Routledge, 2023, pp. 70–90.

This kind of trilogue is also evident in the recent line of cases on the ban on ritual slaughter of animals without prior stunning. Both European Courts demonstrated significant openness and understanding toward each other's perspectives, ultimately benefiting national courts, which had to apply both EU and ECHR laws. The CJEU, which intervened before the ECtHR following a preliminary ruling request, referred to its own legal framework to assess the legality of the ban. However, it referred to the ECHR as a 'minimum threshold of protection'[135] and relied extensively on ECHR law, including on ECHR doctrines such as the margin of appreciation and the living instrument doctrine in its reasoning.[136] When the issue was later examined under the ECHR, particularly in light of Article 9 ECHR, the ECtHR demonstrated openness and considered the CJEU's perspective and how it was implemented by national authorities in its analysis.[137] However, rightly so, the ECtHR did not merely replicate the reasoning of the CJEU. Instead, it provided its own analysis based on the standards of the Convention, thus acting as a safety net for the protection of human rights in Europe.

If we can speak of trilogue, there is maybe also room to speak of a quadrilogue. The conversion on shaping European rights should not only include the CJEU, the ECtHR and domestic courts, but also the EU legislator. As we have seen, the EU legislator has become a key player in the protection of fundamental rights in Europe, particularly through the development of increasingly sophisticated standards. It is important that the EU legislator and the ECtHR engage with each other and consider each other's perspectives. The ECtHR has shown a willingness to incorporate elements from EU fundamental rights legislation and to consider the objectives and balances these laws establish between fundamental rights and other interests, while continuing to rely on its own principles.[138] It would also be appropriate for the ECtHR to consider how fundamental rights have been taken into account in the EU decision-making process when assessing whether the Convention has been breached, as we will argue below.[139]

For the EU legislator, there are strong reasons to legislate on fundamental rights at the EU level: harmonising standards to make the common EU space function more effectively, enhancing the protection of specific fundamental rights, and allowing these rights to benefit from unique features of EU law,

---

135 Case C-336/19, *Centraal Israëlitisch Consistorie van België and Others*, ECLI:EU:C:2020:1031, para. 56.

136 Ibid., paras. 67 (on the margin of appreciation doctrine) and 77 (on the living instrument doctrine).

137 ECtHR, *Executief van de Moslims van België and Others v. Belgium*, nos. 16760/22 and 8 others, §§ 97–99 and 109–116, 13 February 2024.

138 See above Part III (case study on data protection), Chapter 3, Section II, §2, III. Necessary in A Democratic Society.

139 See below Part IV, Chapter , Section II, §2, IV. Procedural Review.

such as primacy and direct effect, which can make them particularly effective. Additionally, the legislator can make fundamental rights apply horizontally and create specific procedural rights or enforcement mechanisms. However, the EU legislator must be mindful of the fact that new standards add complexity to the European multi-layered architecture and may create coherence issues between the EU and the ECHR. Therefore, it would be beneficial for the legislator to provide clarity and carefully consider how to articulate the relationship between EU and ECHR standards, which could facilitate the work of both the CJEU and the ECtHR.

SECTION II. METHODOLOGICAL PRINCIPLES

Alongside guiding principles, we argue that there should be methodological principles that the ECtHR ought to follow when it engages with EU fundamental rights. Such an approach would enhance the procedural legitimacy of its decisions, which we introduced in Part I of our study. As we have seen, procedural legitimacy refers to the belief that a process is legitimate if it adheres to established rules and principles.[140] In our case studies we have observed that while there has been overall improvement in the ECtHR's methodological approach, certain areas still require enhancement. The substantive legitimacy derived from the use of EU law to support the ECtHR's decisions should not come at the cost of procedural legitimacy. The use of EU law should be transparent, ensuring that its use is clear and accessible. Moreover, the ECtHR must provide solid justifications for why EU law has been used. This also includes the careful contextualisation of EU law, taking into account its context and limits.

§ 1. TRANSPARENCY

Several situations emerged where there was limited transparency in the use of EU fundamental rights in our case studies. First, numerous cases demonstrated a phenomenon of 'use by reference', where the ECtHR used EU fundamental rights in its reasoning in a summary manner, cross-referring the relevant legal materials where these rights are described in detail.[141] Second, instances of 'use through the national backdoor' were noted, where the ECtHR mentioned that domestic law transposes EU fundamental rights in its relevant legal materials

140 See above Part I, Chapter 2, Section IV. The Double-Edged Sword of Legitimacy.

141 See above Part III (case study on equality and data protection), Chapter 3, Section V, §1. Transparency (in each case study).

but relied solely on domestic law in its reasoning.[142] Third, the ECtHR often referenced EU fundamental rights only within the relevant legal materials, without using them as part of its reasoning.[143] Fourth, in some cases, no reference to EU fundamental rights was made at all, despite the close proximity of EU and ECHR laws on the matter.[144] Finally, it was observed that the ECtHR rarely acknowledged the influential role that EU fundamental rights may have played in its subsequent judgments.[145]

These instances of limited transparency are, in many cases, not problematic and can even offer advantages, contributing to the clarity and robustness of ECtHR's decisions. The use by reference, for example, can enhance the concision of the ECtHR's reasoning, preventing an overload of information. When the ECtHR mentions EU fundamental rights within the relevant legal materials, it shows that the ECtHR considered all relevant circumstances under EU law. However, certain situations may lead to potential issues.

These situations can lead to the incorrect application of EU fundamental rights. This was evident in certain 'use by reference' instances where there were detailed references to EU fundamental rights in the relevant legal materials and brief, arguably erroneous, use of these rights by the ECtHR in its reasoning, with sometimes important consequences. Such situations can also result in the decontextualised use of EU fundamental rights. For example, the approach of 'use through the national backdoor' may obscure the impact of EU fundamental rights, potentially overlooking the context and specificities of these rights. Moreover, instances of limited transparency can create scenarios of implicit influence, where EU law appears to have affected the ECtHR's reasoning but is only mentioned in the relevant legal materials, or cases of diffuse influence, where EU law is not mentioned at all, yet there is a suspicion that it played a role in shaping ECHR law.

There are several ways in which the ECtHR could improve transparency in its use of EU fundamental rights. First, at a more general level, it is necessary or desirable for the ECtHR to refer to EU fundamental rights in certain instances. Such references are necessary when EU fundamental rights law plays a role in the ECtHR's reasoning and desirable when the ECtHR faces cases that are comparable or analogous to those considered by the CJEU. Second, it would be beneficial to encourage a practice where the ECtHR provides more detailed exposition of EU fundamental rights in its reasoning. The more significant the role of EU law in the ECtHR's reasoning, the more important it is for this to be thoroughly explained. This approach allows for a proper assessment of whether

142 See above Part III (case study on data protection), Chapter 3, Section V, §1. Transparency.
143 See above Part III (case study on equality and data protection), Chapter 3, Section V, §1. Transparency (in each case study).
144 See above Part III (case study on equality), Chapter 3, Section V, §1. Transparency.
145 See above Part III (case study on equality), Chapter 3, Section IV, §2. Qualitative Analysis.

the ECtHR has correctly applied EU fundamental rights and helps prevent issues related to the inadequate or decontextualised use of EU fundamental rights. Third, the ECtHR should be encouraged to identify divergences in standards or context between EU and ECHR laws, a practice it appears increasingly inclined to adopt.[146] Fourth, it would be beneficial if the ECtHR recognised more explicitly the influence of EU law in its subsequent cases.

Enhanced transparency in the ECtHR's use of EU fundamental rights would offer several advantages. First, it would ensure the proper use of EU law. Second, clear and transparent legal standards are essential for national courts, which play a central role in the European fundamental rights landscape. By clarifying what standards should be applied and how the EU and ECHR standards relate to one another, national courts can more effectively uphold these standards. Third, greater transparency would also benefit non-EU States. By acknowledging the influence of EU law in subsequent decisions, the ECtHR could avoid situations where EU fundamental rights are imposed on non-EU States through precedents.

§ 2. JUSTIFICATION

Among the most striking methodological observations from our case studies was the lack of justification for the use of EU fundamental rights. The ECtHR almost never mentions what justifies its reference to EU fundamental rights and very rarely uses its methods of interpretation, such as contextual, dynamic, and evolutive interpretation, or the European consensus, to justify its use of EU fundamental rights. Additionally, the ECtHR rarely uses tools to modulate the influence of EU fundamental rights based on whether the respondent State is an EU State or not. This contrasts with the justification for the use of international instruments, especially in the field of equality law, where the ECtHR often provides strong justifications when referring to them or situates their use within its interpretation techniques.

The hybrid nature of EU law, which combines features of both domestic and international law, makes it a source of law that can be particularly well-supported by both the text of the Convention and the ECtHR's adjudicative and interpretation techniques. Without discussing all possible justifications, let us focus on a series of fertile grounds: Article 53 of the Convention, the concept of 'law', procedural review, and the European consensus technique. By using them, the ECtHR could offer a more robust foundation for using EU fundamental rights in its case-law. It should be noted that the goal is not to

[146] E.g. ECtHR, *K.I. v. France*, no. 5560/19, §§ 122–123, 15 April 2021; ECtHR, *Krombach v. France* (dec.), no. 67521/14, § 34, 20 February 2018.

cover each of these grounds in exhaustive detail, but rather to consider how they can be used to justify the ECtHR's use of EU law.

I. Article 53 ECHR

Article 53 ECHR is a textual provision on which the ECtHR can rely in cases of divergence between EU and ECHR laws, particularly when EU fundamental rights offer a higher level of protection than those under the ECHR. This provision provides that: 'Nothing in this Convention shall be construed as limiting or derogating from any of the human rights and fundamental freedoms which may be ensured under the laws of any High Contracting Party or under any other agreement to which it is a party.' It reflects the nature of the ECHR as a minimum standard that can be exceeded by higher standards at national and international level.[147] This type of provision is found in many international conventions,[148] and aims to ensure that the highest level of fundamental rights protection serves as the benchmark standard when multiple standards are present.[149] Although Article 53 ECHR does not mention EU law, it offers a promising avenue for cases where EU fundamental rights provide a higher level of protection than ECHR standards.

Several interpretations of Article 53 have been proposed in the context of situations of higher fundamental rights protection by EU law. One of them is to read it as an 'optimising provision'. In cases involving EU States, the ECtHR should not adopt a more restrictive interpretation of a Convention's right than that is guaranteed by EU law. This approach is exemplified in the third-party intervention by the AIRE Centre and ILGA Europe in the pending *A.B. and K.V. against Romania*, where they argue that: '[…] where a High Contracting Party (and an EU Member State) is refusing to comply with explicit and unambiguous laws by which it is bound (under its own legal system through the application of EU law) guaranteeing certain human rights protections, it is clear from Article 53 ECHR that the Convention will not afford the relevant High Contracting Party with any justification for such non-compliance. […] The interveners submit that the Strasbourg Court can optimally supervise a Contracting Party's compliance with Article 53 of the ECHR by adopting an approach that guarantees at least the protection required under the applicable EU law, and that such an approach is consistent with the

147 Separate opinion of Judge Wojtyczek in ECtHR, *The National Union of Rail, Maritime and Transport Workers v. The United Kingdom*, no. 31045/10, § 3, 8 April 2014.

148 J. Gerards, 'Article 53 ECHR and Minimum Protection by the European Court of Human Rights', *European Convention on Human Rights Law Review*, 2022, pp. 456–457.

149 Ibid., p. 453.

Convention, its case-law and the letter and the spirit of Article 53.'[150] The AIRE Centre and ILGA Europe claim that if the ECtHR fails to align with EU law, it would undermine its long-standing principle of interpreting the Convention as a living instrument for human rights protection, consistent with other international obligations.[151] Additionally, this would create fragmentation, incoherence, and legal uncertainty if the ECtHR leaves unresolved whether an EU State is meeting its Convention obligations while violating overlapping EU law rights.[152]

While this position has gained some support in separate opinions,[153] the ECtHR has not adopted this interpretation of Article 53 ECHR. At most, the ECtHR adopts a reading whereby if a State provides a higher level of protection for a fundamental right, it is required to uphold the principles of non-discrimination and guarantees of procedural fairness for that higher level of protection.[154] Although the idea of ensuring compliance with the highest level of fundamental rights protection is appealing, this approach is not without challenges. First, it would require the ECtHR to interpret and apply EU fundamental rights, potentially encroaching the competences of the CJEU and domestic courts. Second, guaranteeing a higher level of protection for one EU fundamental right could lead to a weaker protection of another ECHR's right in cases of conflict, such as between data protection and freedom of expression.[155]

Another interpretation of Article 53 ECHR is to view it as a 'coherence provision'. This provision allows for the possibility that a higher level of protection than that provided by the ECHR can be ensured at national or international level, without requiring the ECtHR to align with these higher standards. This perspective is clearly expressed and argued in the concurring Opinion of Judge Wojtyczek in *National Union of Rail, Maritime and Transport Workers v. the United Kingdom* (2014) in which the Judge observed that: 'It should be stressed that the Convention establishes a minimum standard for

[150] See written comments submitted jointly by the AIRE Centre and ILGA-Europe in *A.B. and K.V. v. Romania*, no. 17816/21, available here: https://www.ilga-europe.org/case-law/a-b-and-k-v-v-romania/, point 6.

[151] Ibid.

[152] Ibid.

[153] Separate opinion of Judges Yudkivska, Pinto de Albuquerque and Chanturia in ECtHR, *Georgia v. Russia (II)* [GC], no. 38263/08, § 24, 21 January 2021; Separate opinion of Judges Sicilianos, Ravarani and Serghides in ECtHR, *Gestur Jónsson and Ragnar Halldór Hall v. Iceland* [GC], nos. 68273/14 and 68271/14, § 13, 22 December 2020.

[154] ECtHR, *M.H. and Others v. Croatia*, nos. 15670/18 and 43115/18, §231, 18 November 2021; ECtHR, *A.H. and Others v. Russia*, nos. 6033/13 and 15 others § 381, 17 January 2017; ECtHR, *E.B. v. France* [GC], no. 43546/02, § 49, 22 January 2008. See more in J. Gerards, 'Article 53 ECHR and Minimum Protection by the European Court of Human Rights', *European Convention on Human Rights Law Review*, 2022, pp. 470–479.

[155] Ibid., p. 457.

a selective catalogue of rights. In this context, it is interesting to note the content of Article 53 of the Convention [...]. The Convention clearly envisages in this provision a situation in which different instruments may provide a higher level of protection than the Convention itself. Such a situation cannot be seen as an example of fragmentation, let alone of incoherence, of international law. The nature of the Convention as a minimum standard for a limited catalogue of rights limits the risk of contradictions with other treaties. A situation in which other treaties guarantee broader rights or offer a higher standard of protection of the same rights cannot be seen as a conflict of treaties. Nor does it change per se the scope of the rights protected under the Convention. While there is no doubt that the Convention has to be interpreted in the context of other rules of international law, the scope of its protection does not automatically align on the highest standard set by other rules of international law binding the Parties to the Convention. [...]'[156] Thus, Article 53 ECHR allows for coherence between the ECHR and another instrument which guarantees a higher level of protection, without precluding any evolutive interpretation of the Convention in light of international law.

EU law can be considered as one of the sources that can provide higher protection than the ECHR under Article 53 ECHR.[157] This possibility is also recognised under EU law in Article 52(3) Charter. Its first sentence includes a principle of 'homogeneity' or 'equivalence' with the ECHR, according to which the Charter rights shall have the same meaning and scope as those of the corresponding rights guaranteed by the ECHR.[158] Its second sentence provides that: 'this provision shall not prevent Union law providing more extensive protection'. This sentence allows EU law to guarantee a higher level of protection of fundamental rights than the ECHR. The ECHR is a floor, but not a ceiling, beyond which EU law can go to offer better protection.[159]

By referencing these provisions in their case-law, the ECtHR and the CJEU can assist EU domestic judges in understanding how EU and ECHR laws interact, both of which they are required to apply. If EU law offers higher standards than ECHR law, national judges should apply the higher standards. The ECtHR appears inclined to use Article 53 to bring coherence in recent cases,

156 Separate opinion of Judge Wojtyczek in ECtHR, *The National Union of Rail, Maritime and Transport Workers v. The United Kingdom*, no. 31045/10, § 3, 8 April 2014.

157 In this vein, O. de Schutter, 'The Two Europes of Human Rights: the Emerging Division of Tasks between the Council of Europe and the European Union in Promoting Human Rights in Europe', *Columbia Journal of European Law*, 2008, p. 528. See also V. Davio, 'Detention in the Hungarian transit zones: A case of higher fundamental rights protection by EU law vis-à-vis the ECHR', *European Law Review*, 2022, p. 406.

158 See above Part II, Chapter 1, Section III, §2. *The special significance of ECHR law*.

159 Separate opinion of Judge Pinto de Albuquerque in ECtHR, *GIEM SRL and Others* [GC], no. 1828/06, § 86, 28 June 2018.

as we have seen in *Krombach v. France* (2018) above.[160] If using Article 53 can help achieving some coherence between EU and ECHR standards, there are limitations. First, there are instances where it is unclear whether EU standards offer a higher level of protection, as the ECtHR and CJEU and use different methodologies to assess fundamental rights.[161] Second, Article 53 seems ill-suited when they are conflicts between rights: if EU standards are higher for one fundamental right but result in a lower level of protection for another. The possibility of EU law to go beyond the ECHR floor should not be achieved at the expense of the protection of another ECHR right.[162] In the words of Advocate General Kokott in the *Puškár* case with regard to Article 52(3) ECHR, the deviation of the CJEU from the ECtHR case-law is 'only permitted provided that it does not also cause another fundamental right in the Charter corresponding to a right in the ECHR to be accorded less protection than in the case-law of the ECtHR'.[163]

II. EU Law as a Condition for Lawfulness

Continuing into the textual foundations within the Convention, another avenue to justify the use of EU fundamental rights is the concept of 'law', which is enshrined in several provisions of the ECHR, as we have already observed above.[164] It is often stipulated that restrictions on Convention rights can only occur if they are provided by 'law' or exercised according to a procedure prescribed by 'law'.[165] Increasingly, the ECtHR equates EU law, and in particular EU fundamental rights, with this concept of 'law'. This is especially true in the areas of asylum and migration, in particular as regards the detention of asylum-seekers. In assessing whether the decision to detain an asylum-seeker has been taken 'in accordance with a procedure prescribed by law', the ECtHR consider that the national rules to which that expression referred can stem from EU law.[166] Yet, the ECtHR has made clear that it is primarily for the national authorities, in particular the courts, to interpret and

---

160 See above Part IV, Chapter 2, Section I, §2, II. Coherence without Aligning with EU Standards.

161 Ibid.

162 This sentence – as well as the following – stem from V. DAVIO, 'Detention in the Hungarian transit zones: A case of higher fundamental rights protection by EU law vis-à-vis the ECHR', *European Law Review*, 2022, p. 404. See also S. VAN DROOGHENBROECK, 'Vérité à Luxembourg, erreur à Strasbourg', *Annuaire de droit de l'Union européenne 2020*, Paris, Editions Panthéon-Assas, 2021, p. 178.

163 Opinion of Advocate General Kokott, 30 March 2017 in Case C-73/16, *Puškár*, ECLI:EU:C:2017:253, para. 123.

164 See above Part IV, Chapter 2, Section I, §1, II. Contributing to the Effectiveness.

165 E.g. Articles 5(1), 8(2) and 9(2) ECHR.

166 ECtHR, *Thimothawes v. Belgium*, no. 39061/11, § 70, 4 April 2017; ECtHR, *Muzamba Oyaw v. Belgium* (dec.), no. 23707/15, § 35, 28 February 2017.

apply domestic law.[167] The ECtHR's role is limited to examining whether the interpretation of the legal provisions relied on by the domestic authorities is not arbitrary or manifestly unreasonable as to render the applicant's detention unlawful.[168]

Aside from detention cases, there are an increasing number of cases where the ECtHR refers to EU law when assessing whether an interference is made in accordance with the law. This is what we have seen in our data protection cases where in *Satakunnan v. Finland* [GC](2017) and *Jehova's Witness* (2023), the ECtHR has considered that the requirement of foreseeability – part of the lawfulness criterion – is met when domestic courts rely on findings from a CJEU's preliminary ruling related to the ECtHR's case.

Another recent example can be found in the field of the rule of law. *Tuleya v. Poland* (2023) concerns a Polish judge against whom there were investigations for disciplinary proceedings, notably as the latter asked a preliminary question to the CJEU on the compatibility of the Polish disciplinary system with EU law. The ECtHR observed that the CJEU had found that the interference in the form of a preliminary inquiry into the reference for a preliminary ruling was contrary to EU law.[169] In light of this, the ECtHR found that '[t]his conclusion is equivalent to the finding that section 114(1) of the 2001 Act, as applied to the applicant's case, was incompatible with Article 267 TFEU, while Article 91 § 2 of the Polish Constitution provides that an international agreement ratified upon prior consent granted by statute, like the TFEU, takes precedence over statutes if such an agreement cannot be reconciled with their provisions. It follows that the interference with the applicant's right to respect for his private life in this part was not 'in accordance with the law' within the meaning of Article 8 of the Convention.'[170] In other words, because the Polish law was contrary to EU law, it was not considered to be in accordance with the law within the meaning of Article 8 ECHR.

That the ECtHR considers EU law, and particularly EU fundamental rights, to fall within the concept of 'law' appears logical. This is due to the profound integration of EU fundamental rights into the legal systems of EU States, making them comparable to domestic law in cases involving these States. The use of the term 'law' provides a valuable justification for the use of EU fundamental rights. It allows the ECtHR to assess whether national authorities have complied with EU fundamental rights or if the EU procedures have been followed. This can foster coherence between EU and ECHR laws and enhance

---

167 ECtHR, *Jehovah's Witnesses v. Finland*, no. 31172/19, § 84, 9 May 2023; ECtHR, *Muzamba v. Belgium*, ibid., § 37.

168 ECtHR, *Thimothawes v. Belgium*, no. 39061/11, § 71, 4 April 2017; ECtHR, *Muzamba Oyaw v. Belgium* (dec.), ibid., § 37.

169 ECtHR, *Tuleya v. Poland*, nos. 21181/19 and 51751/20, § 436, 6 July 2023.

170 Ibid., § 438.

the effectiveness of EU law, while restricting its use to cases involving EU States. Thus far, the oversight of whether domestic law complies with EU 'law' has been relatively limited, with the ECtHR confining it to situations where the use of EU fundamental rights by domestic authorities is arbitrary or manifestly unreasonable. As we argued above, there are valid reasons to restrict the oversight of EU law to cases of manifest insufficiency and to favour a procedural approach in this matter.[171]

It is important to recall that legality under EU law does not equate to legality under ECHR law. In other words, a measure that is legal under EU law, even from a fundamental rights perspective, will not necessarily be legal under ECHR law, as the test carried out under ECHR law is different and can lead to other outcomes. This was evident in our data-protection case study, where, in some instances, after finding that domestic judgments aligned with CJEU decisions, the ECtHR assessed whether the interference was necessary in a democratic society. Even if the ECtHR considers the balance struck by EU law, it applies its own criteria to determine whether a fair balance has been achieved.[172] The ECtHR plays a role as a guardian of a minimum safeguard of human rights; it must ensure that EU law does not lead to fall below this floor of human rights. Such an approach can be seen in *M.B. v. the Netherlands* (2024), which concerned the detention of an asylum-seeker on the grounds of the protection of national security or public order, a ground stemming from EU law. In this case, the ECtHR observed that: 'Although Article 8(3)(e) of the Reception Conditions Directive permits, from an EU-law standpoint, detention when national security or public order so requires, this has no bearing on the fact that Article 5 § 1 (f) of the Convention only allows for immigration detention to prevent unauthorised entry or to effect deportation.'[173] For this reason, inter alia, the ECtHR found that there was a breach of Article 5 ECHR, even though the detention was permitted under EU law.[174]

III. EU Law as Part of a European Consensus

Apart from the textual foundations that are Article 53 ECHR and the concept of 'law', we can also consider the interpretive techniques used by the ECtHR to justify the use of EU fundamental rights. In this context, EU fundamental

[171] See above Part IV, Chapter 2, Section I, §1, II. Contributing to the Effectiveness.

[172] See above Part III (case study on data protection), Chapter 3, Section II, §2, III. Necessary in A Democratic Society.

[173] ECtHR, *M.B. v. the Netherlands*, no. 71008/16, § 72, 23 April 2024.

[174] Ibid., § 75. See for a comment of this case, J. Callewaert, 'The Convention and the Reception Conditions Directive: judgment of the ECtHR in the case of M.B. v. the Netherlands', *Blog Johan Callewaert*, 2024, available here: https://johan-callewaert.eu/fr/the-convention-and-the-reception-conditions-directive-judgment-of-the-ecthr-in-the-case-of-m-b-v-the-netherlands/.

rights can contribute to shaping a European consensus, which, in turn, offers strong justification for a dynamic and evolutive interpretation of the Convention. The dynamic and evolutive interpretation has its origins in the *Tyrer v. United Kingdom* (1978) case and has been extensively applied by the ECtHR across a wide range of rights.[175] Essentially, it involves viewing the Convention as a flexible tool that adapts to 'present-day conditions and of the ideas prevailing in democratic States'.[176] This approach ensures a key principle underlying the Convention, as developed by the ECtHR: the principle of effectiveness which requires that the protection of Convention's rights should not be merely theoretical or illusory, but rather practical and effective.[177] However, the dynamic and evolutive interpretation is subject to criticism. First, it can undermine legal certainty and predictability, as it may introduce changes that are not foreseeable by the States.[178] Second, it may bypass the consent of States by introducing new concepts and interpretations that were not initially envisaged when the States ratified the Convention.[179] Finally, the ECtHR is often criticised for not sufficiently substantiating its use of the evolutive interpretation.[180]

The European consensus helps to provide a rationale for the dynamic and evolutive interpretation. It can be defined in the ECtHR case-law 'as a general agreement among the majority of Member States of the Council of Europe about certain rules and principles identified through comparative research of national and international law and practice.'[181] To objectify the evolving trends, the ECtHR now considers not only domestic laws but also increasingly international and European laws.[182] European consensus provides a significant foundation for the evolutive interpretation as it helps avoid arbitrariness

---

175 ECtHR, *Tyrer v. the United Kingdom*, 25 April 1978, § 31, Series A no. 26. See more in G. Letsas, 'The ECHR as a living instrument: its meaning and legitimacy', in A. Føllesdal B. Peters and G. Ulfstein (eds.), *Constituting Europe: The European Court of Human Rights in a National, European and Global Context. Studies on Human Rights Conventions*, Cambridge, Cambridge University Press, 2013, pp. 106–141.

176 E.g. ECtHR, *Bayatyan v. Armenia* [GC], no. 23459/03, § 102, 7 July 2011.

177 E.g. ECtHR, *Svinarenko and Slyadnev v. Russia* [GC], no. 32541/08, § 138, 17 July 2014; ECtHR, *Chassagnou and Others v. France* [GC], no. 25088/94, § 100, 29 April 1999.

178 E.g. on the tension between dynamic interpretation and legal certainty, ECtHR, *Cossey v. the United Kingdom*, 27 September 1990, § 35, Series A no. 184. See K. Dzehtsiarou, 'European Consensus and the Evolutive Interpretation of the European Convention on Human Rights', *German Law Journal*, 2011, pp. 1735 and references.

179 K. Dzehtsiarou, ibid., p. 1734.

180 Ibid., p. 1735.

181 Ibid., p. 1734

182 See for a synthesis of the different types of consensus, K. Dzehtsiarou, 'Does Consensus Matter? Legitimacy of European Consensus in the Case-law of the European Court of Human Rights', *Public Law*, 2011, p. 548.

and takes seriously the consent of States.[183] European consensus creates a rebuttable presumption in favour of the solution adopted by the majority of the Convention Parties.[184] European consensus and margin of appreciation function in an 'accordion-like manner': as the level of consensus increases, the margin of appreciation for the respondent State decreases.[185]

EU fundamental rights, and more broadly EU law, emerge as (one of) the most persuasive source(s) for determining the existence of a European consensus. This is due to their unique characteristics. EU fundamental rights share similarities with domestic laws but have a broader scope of application, given that 27 Convention States must respect these rights. As a result, EU fundamental rights represent a more readily identifiable common point than consensus among the (other) domestic laws of the Convention States.[186] Because of the hybridity of EU law – which has features of both domestic and international laws –, EU law can be considered not only as part of an international consensus but also of domestic consensus.[187]

Although our case studies show that EU law is rarely used to determine European consensus, there are several instances where the ECtHR has used the Charter for this purpose. For example, it has used this instrument to feed a European consensus concerning the principle of retroactive leniency in criminal law,[188] the right to conscientious objection,[189] and the application

---

183 K. Dzehtsiarou, 'European Consensus and the Evolutive Interpretation of the European Convention on Human Rights', *German Law Journal*, 2011, p. 1745. In this vein, Dzehtsiarou observes that: 'Evolutive interpretation faces serious legitimacy challenges. If evolutive interpretation utilizes the approach of European consensus, greater overall credibility is accomplished because European consensus has at its heart a strong emphasis on commonality between states thereby reflecting the traditional approach of international law. European consensus is the mechanism used to assess post-drafting consent, which avoids burdensome international negotiations over new Protocols. European consensus provides the ECtHR with the evidence that the Contracting Parties have accepted a particular rule in their own law and practice.' See for an example of the use of consensus to justify a dynamic interpretation of the Convention, ECtHR, *Bayatyan v. Armenia* [GC], no. 23459/03, §§ 108–109, 7 July 2011.

184 Ibid., p. 1733.

185 E.g. ECtHR, *Hämäläinen v. Finland* [GC], no. 37359/09, § 75, 16 July 2014; ECtHR, *Vo v. France* [GC], no. 53924/00, § 82, 8 July 2004. S. O'Leary, 'The EU Charter Ten Years On: A View from Strasbourg', in M. Bobek and J. Adams-Prassl (eds.), *The EU Charter of Fundamental Rights in the Member States*, Oxford, Hart Publishing, 2020, p. 46.

186 For an argument along these lines, T. Lock, 'The Influence of EU Law on Strasbourg Doctrines', *European Law Review*, 2016, p. 821. See also C. Dautricourt, 'A Strasbourg Perspective on the Autonomous Development of Fundamental Rights in EU Law: Trends and Implications', *Jean Monnet Working Paper Series*, 2020, p. 31.

187 Ibid. Lock noted that: 'As such it would be appropriate to consider [EU law] part of the domestic consensus rather than international consensus, which implies a high persuasive value.'

188 ECtHR, *Scoppola v. Italy (no 2)* [GC], no. 10249/03, §§ 104–109, 17 September 2009.

189 ECtHR, *Bayatyan v. Armenia* [GC], no. 23459/03, §§ 102–109, 7 July 2011.

of freedom of association to public officials.[190] There is potential for the ECtHR to use also fundamental rights as expressed in EU legislation to determine whether there is a European consensus. With the prospect of the EU's enlargement and the EU's accession to the ECHR, EU fundamental rights could gain even greater significance in determining European consensus.[191]

However, caution is necessary when the ECtHR uses EU fundamental rights to determine a European consensus. EU fundamental rights should not be equated with European consensus, contrary to what some authors have suggested.[192] While EU fundamental rights apply in the majority of Convention States, they do not apply to all of them. Additionally, EU fundamental rights sometimes have a limited scope that challenge their value as a consensus.[193] For example, the Charter is binding on EU States only when they are implementing EU law; EU States did not consent to being bound by the Charter in all situations.[194] Furthermore, many articles of the Charter specify that the protection of a right is determined by national laws and practices, which demonstrates that there is no common agreement on the right at the EU level.[195] The case of *Bayatyan v. Armenia* (2011) provides an interesting illustration. The ECtHR interprets Article 10(2) Charter, which states that '[t]he right to conscientious objection is recognised, in accordance with the national laws governing the exercise of this right', as reflecting 'the unanimous recognition of the right to conscientious objection by the member States of the European Union, as well as the weight attached to that right in modern European society.'[196] In doing so, the ECtHR appears to overestimate

190 ECtHR, *Demir and Baykara v. Turkey* [GC], no. 34503/97, §§ 96–107, ECHR 2008.

191 See above Part IV, Chapter 1, Section I. More EU Fundamental Rights and Chapter 1, Section II. More Convention States Incorporating EU Fundamental Rights.

192 C. Rozakis, 'A View from the ECHR', in V. Kosta, N. Skoutaris and V. Tzevelekos (eds.), *The EU Accession to the ECHR*, Oxford, Hart Publishing, 2014, p. 331. The Former Judge Rozakis observed that: 'It is undeniable that evidence of the existence of a European consensus in situations where an advanced protection is offered by the EU legal order is easily detectable. The evidence that the EU Member States consent to an advanced protection suffices, I think, to prove the existence of a European consensus since the Member States of the EU constitute the majority of the states parties to the ECHR, and given that the real meaning of consensus is not identical to a unanimous consent of all states participating in the ECHR system.'

193 In this vein See also C. Dautricourt, 'A Strasbourg Perspective on the Autonomous Development of Fundamental Rights in EU Law: Trends and Implications', *Jean Monnet Working Paper Series*, 2020, p. 31; T. Lock, 'The Influence of EU Law on Strasbourg Doctrines', *European Law Review*, 2016, pp. 822–824.

194 Ibid., p. 822. See Article 51(1) Charter on its scope. See for an example where the scope of the Charter is taken into account, separate opinion of Judge Wojtyczek in ECtHR, *The National Union of Rail, Maritime and Transport Workers v. The United Kingdom*, no. 31045/10, § 6, 8 April 2014.

195 E.g. Articles 16, 27, 28, 30, 35 Charter.

196 ECtHR, *Bayatyan v. Armenia* [GC], no. 23459/03, § 106, 7 July 2011.

the consensus value of this provision; it did not mention that it refers to national laws and does not consider the scope of application of the Charter.

The ECtHR should assess the consensus value of EU fundamental rights on a case-by-case basis. Besides, while EU fundamental rights can serve as a significant source for determining whether a European consensus exists, they should be considered alongside other national or international legal sources. While this was done in the *Bayatyan v. Armenia* (2011) case and other cases,[197] *Baykara v. Turkey* (2008) provides a mixed picture. The ECtHR uses Article 12 of the Charter as one source among others to find consensus on the applicability of the right to freedom of association to public servants.[198] However, Article 28 Charter is (arguably) used predominantly to establish that the right to bargain collectively is part of the right to form and join trade unions for the protection of one's interests.[199] This is particularly questionable, as Article 28 Charter refers to the right of collective bargaining 'in accordance with Union law and national laws and practices', which limits its scope and raises concerns about its use as a basis for a broader consensus.

The ECtHR should in particular exercise caution when using EU fundamental rights in cases involving non-EU States. As Lock observed, the ECtHR should not rely solely on a numbers game when determining consensus.[200] While it should not be excluded that EU fundamental rights may contribute to establishing consensus in cases involving non-EU States, the ECtHR must remain mindful that doing so could lead to impose standards on these States without their participation in the decision-making process. One way to incorporate EU fundamental rights into consensus without imposing them outright is through the margin of appreciation. The greater the consensus, including through EU fundamental rights, the narrower the margin of appreciation. This margin could also be differentiated depending on whether the State involved is an EU or non-EU State. In cases involving EU States, it seems reasonable that the margin of appreciation be particularly limited, as these States are bound by these rights.

---

197 Ibid., §§ 102–109.

198 ECtHR, *Demir and Baykara v. Turkey* [GC], no. 34503/97, §§ 96–107 (in particular §103 on the use of the Charter), ECHR 2008.

199 Ibid., §§ 147–154. See in particular separate opinion of Judge Zagrebbelsky, ibid., § 2: 'The Court has thus expressly departed from its case-law, taking into account 'the perceptible evolution in such matters, in both international law and domestic legal systems' (see paragraph 153 of the judgment). In reality, the new and recent fact that may be regarded as indicating an evolution internationally appears to be only the proclamation (in 2000) of the European Union's Charter of Fundamental Rights. The evolution of legislation in the various States (see paragraphs 52 and 151 of the judgment) is a more difficult basis on which to assess the time or period from which a significant change became perceptible.'

200 T. Lock, 'The Influence of EU Law on Strasbourg Doctrines', *European Law Review*, 2016, p. 823.

IV. Procedural Review

Beyond the textual foundations and interpretation techniques, a notable adjudicative approach of the ECtHR holds potential to justify the consideration of EU fundamental rights, namely procedural review. While the ECtHR has often stressed the importance of substantively reviewing the reasonableness of limitations on Convention rights, the ECtHR's focus has expanded.[201] It now not only evaluates the reasonableness of the balance struck by national authorities but also examines the fairness and diligence observed in the national procedures leading to such limitations.[202] In this vein, the ECtHR has expressed that 'where the balancing exercise has been undertaken by the national authorities in conformity with the criteria laid down in the Court's case-law, the Court would require strong reasons to substitute its view for that of the domestic courts'.[203] This procedural approach takes into account the way in which decisions has been taken and can be challenged to assess whether a measure is proportionate.[204]

As Gerards has explained, the ECtHR engages in different types of procedural review. One type focuses on the quality of the legislative process, examining whether it was open, transparent, and whether fundamental rights were properly considered.[205] The second type looks at the quality of national judicial and administrative decisions. In these cases, the ECtHR assesses whether the national courts have explicitly taken the ECtHR's case-law into account, applied the substantive standards it has developed, and paid sufficient attention to the fundamental rights involved.[206] In both situations, the ECtHR evaluates the quality of decision-making, whether legislative or judicial, which can influence its rulings either positively (i.e. leading to non-violation of a Convention's right) or negatively (leading to a violation of a Convention's right), depending on the diligence shown by the national authorities.[207] The

---

201 J. Gerards, 'Procedural Review by the ECtHR: A Typology', in J. Gerards and E. Brems (eds.), *Procedural Review in European Fundamental Rights Cases*, Cambridge, Cambridge University Press, 2017, p. 128.

202 Ibid.

203 E.g. ECtHR, *Satakunnan Markkinapörssi Oy and Satamedia Oy v. Finland* [GC], no. 931/13, § 164, 27 June 2017.

204 See for an analysis of the 'proceduralisation' of the ECtHR's case-law, N. Le Bonniec, *La procéduralisation des droits substantiels par la Cour européenne des droits de l'homme*, Brussels, Bruylant, 2017.

205 J. Gerards, 'Procedural Review by the ECtHR: A Typology', in J. Gerards and E. Brems (eds.), *Procedural Review in European Fundamental Rights Cases*, Cambridge, Cambridge University Press, 2017, pp. 141–149.

206 Ibid., pp. 149–155.

207 Ibid., pp. 141–155.

procedural review is most often supportive, rather than decisive, in reaching the ECtHR's outcomes.[208]

Adopting a procedural review approach in cases involving EU States can be fruitful. The ECtHR can assess the quality of judicial decision-making, both at the EU and domestic levels, and the extent to which domestic courts or the CJEU have considered EU fundamental rights when taking their decisions. The ECtHR already applies this approach to some degree through the *Bosphorus* presumption: one of the conditions for its application is the full use of the supervisory mechanisms provided by EU law. When a domestic measure implementing EU law has been thoroughly reviewed within the EU's supervisory system (including in light of EU fundamental rights), the ECtHR intervenes only if the protection is manifestly inadequate. Furthermore, the ECtHR has increasingly considered whether domestic authorities, including national courts, have taken into account for EU fundamental rights in their decisions, as we have seen above.[209] This can be framed within a procedural review approach, where the failure to consider EU fundamental rights could support the conclusion that an interference is disproportionate.

The ECtHR can also take into the quality of the EU legislative process which lead to domestic measures and the extent to which EU fundamental rights were taken into account. As we have seen, the Commission, the Council and the European Parliament have increasingly developed mechanisms to ensure that fundamental rights are taken into account during the decision-making process.[210] It may be argued that the extent to which the EU institutions make use of the ex-ante mechanisms for ensuring compliance with fundamental rights may have an impact on the validity of these acts both before the CJEU and ECtHR.[211]

While cases where the ECtHR considers the quality of the legislative process at EU level may be difficult to identify, the recent *Executief van de Moslims van België v. Belgium* (2024) case provides a offers a good example of the ECtHR taking the quality of judicial decision-making at EU level into account. The ECtHR conducted a procedural review to assess whether the ban on ritual slaughter without stunning in Flanders and Wallonia was compatible with Article 9 ECHR. The ECtHR first examined the quality of the parliamentary process, noting that regional legislators had made a genuine effort to balance competing rights and interests through a thoughtful legislative

208 Ibid., p. 159.

209 See above Part IV, Chapter 2, Section I, §1, II. Contributing to the Effectiveness.

210 See above Part II, Chapter 2, Section I. The Emergence of the Charter and EU Fundamental Rights Legislation.

211 See for an example at CJEU level, Joined Cases C-92/09 and C-93/09, *Volker and Eifert*, ECLI:EU:C:2010:662, para. 81.

process.[212] The ECtHR then evaluated the judicial review process, observing that the case had undergone a double level of scrutiny before reaching the ECtHR at domestic and EU level. The ECtHR noted that both the CJEU and the Belgian Constitutional Court had carefully considered the requirements of Article 9 ECHR, as interpreted by the ECtHR.[213] While the ECtHR continued its substantive analysis, the high quality of the legislative and judicial decision-making processes (both at domestic and EU level) contributed to the conclusion that there had been no breach of Article 9 ECHR.[214]

There are compelling reasons to favour a procedural review approach in relation to EU law. First, this ensures a degree of coherence between EU law and the ECHR, since, to the extent that fundamental rights have been duly considered within the EU system, this serves as an argument (even if not decisive) in favour of legality under ECHR law. Furthermore, this approach can enhance the EU system by encouraging a robust decision-making process without undermining its substantive choices.[215] It may prompt the EU legislature to consider fundamental rights at the earliest stage and consistently throughout its decision-making process. Simultaneously, this promotes a democratic approach to fundamental rights, leaving space for political institutions to ensure that these rights are taken into account.[216] At the same time, it allows the ECtHR to refrain from ruling on the substance of EU law, focusing instead on the quality of the legislative and judicial decision-making process, thus avoiding encroachment on the competences of the EU legislator, CJEU and domestic courts. Procedural review appears particularly appropriate when the ECtHR faces sensitive or ethical questions, such as in the case of ritual slaughter, and/or complex and novel issues,[217] as in the digital domain, where the EU is increasingly active.[218]

Nonetheless, some caution should be exercised regarding a procedural review approach in relation to EU law. First, it should support the reasoning of the ECtHR rather than be decisive, as the quality of the decision-making process alone cannot ensure that minimum standards of fundamental rights will always be upheld.[219] Second, the procedural approach must clearly demonstrate how the quality of the legislative or judicial process was inadequate

---

212 ECtHR, *Executief van de Moslims van België and Others v. Belgium*, nos. 16760/22 and 8 others, § 109, 13 February 2024

213 Ibid., §§ 112–115.

214 Ibid., §§ 123–124.

215 In this vein, see K. Lenaerts, 'The European Court of Justice and Process-Oriented Review', *Research Paper in Law College of Europe*, 2012, p. 2.

216 Ibid.

217 R. Spano, 'The Future of the European Court of Human Rights – Subsidiarity, Process-Based Review and the Rule of Law', *Human Rights Law Review*, 2018, vol. 18, p. 491.

218 See above Part IV, Chapter 1, Section I. More EU Fundamental Rights.

219 S. Van Drooghenbroeck and X. Delgrange, 'Le principe de proportionnalité : retour sur quelques espoirs déçus', *Revue du droit des religions*, 2019, p. 6.

in considering fundamental rights. This also necessitates transparency from the EU legislator, the CJEU, and national courts regarding how they have incorporated fundamental rights into their processes.

§ 3. CONTEXTUALISATION

A last issue is whether the ECtHR contextualises EU fundamental rights when it uses it, namely whether it takes into account the context and limits of EU fundamental rights. While the ECtHR has made significant progress in contextualising EU fundamental rights in its judgments, there remains room for further improvement on temporal, geographical, and material levels.

The temporal dimension of EU fundamental rights has often been overlooked by the ECtHR, especially in equality law cases. The ECtHR seldom specifies when EU equality laws come into force, when they become binding, or whether they have been repealed. In contrast, the ECtHR has shown a greater awareness of the temporal aspects of EU data protection law. In recent judgments, the ECtHR has increasingly noted when specific EU instruments enter into force, take effect, or replace older instruments. This approach is commendable as it promotes a nuanced understanding of the evolving EU legal landscape. Failure to consider the temporal scope of EU data protection law risks leading to legal misinterpretations and outdated analyses.

Similarly, the ECtHR does not always take (explicitly) the geographical dimension of EU fundamental rights into account. Most often, the ECtHR does not explicitly clarify to whom EU fundamental rights applies or whether the respondent State is bound by it. Yet, EU law is applied mostly in cases involving EU States, but the approach is implicit. This contrasts with the ECtHR's use of international instruments, where it frequently notes whether the respondent State has ratified the instrument and specifies the time of ratification, even in cases involving non-EU States. Failing to specify and take into account the geographical (and temporal) dimension of EU law can lead to criticisms. For example, in *Vizgirda v. Slovenia* (2018), Judges Bianku and Vucinic observed in a separate opinion that:

> In terms of methodology, we similarly cannot subscribe to the way in which the majority have taken European Union law into consideration. In introducing new criteria and positive obligations under Article 6 § 3 (e), the majority have partly built upon the developments in EU law described in paragraphs 52-61 of the judgment and relied upon in the general principles part of the Court's assessment in paragraphs 82, 83, 84 and 86, which form the core of the newly set standards. While EU law may, in a certain context, be used as a source of inspiration in the case-law of the Court, its task is not to assess whether the respondent State complied with it in a particular case (see, mutatis mutandis, Ullens de Schooten and Rezabek

> v. Belgium, nos. 3989/07 and 38353/07, 20 September 2011). *This notwithstanding, one should bear in mind that at the material time Slovenia was not yet a member of the EU.* Furthermore, all the EU standards relied upon by the majority were adopted well after the events in question took place. Consequently, the domestic courts can hardly be blamed for not acting in conformity with those subsequent standards.[220]

Yet, there are increasingly more examples where the ECtHR takes the geographical dimension of EU law into account. A notable example is found in *Biao v. Denmark* (2016), where the ECtHR observed that: 'The rules for family reunification under EU law did not apply to the applicants' case in August 2004 [...]. However, it is instructive to view the contested Danish legislation in the light of relevant EU law.'[221] Thus, the ECtHR stresses that EU law is not directly applicable to the case in question, yet EU law can still provide valuable guidance. Similarly, in *S.E. v. Serbia* (2023), the ECtHR explicitly mentioned that Serbia is not an EU State, while also noting its candidate status and accession negotiations.[222] These practices, which take into account whether EU law is binding on respondent States, are commendable. They show a sensitivity and awareness that using EU standards can lead to imposing them on non-EU States, which have not participated in the EU's decision-making processes. While EU fundamental rights can be used in cases involving non-EU States (for example, when they contribute to identifying of consensus at pan-European level), this should be approached with care.[223] One needs to bear in mind the risk of marginalisation of these States within the Council of Europe system, as well as the task of the ECHR, which is not to provide uniformity for human rights, but rather a minimum standard of rights across Europe.

From a material point of view, the ECtHR has shown significant improvement in the contextualisation of EU fundamental rights in recent years. The ECtHR increasingly presents relevant EU fundamental rights in its judgments with high precision, thoroughness, and up-to-date references, as we have seen.[224] However, there are still instances where the ECtHR overlooks or misapplies the material limits of EU fundamental rights. Some cases show distortions, where the ECtHR seems to overstretch the interpretation of EU fundamental rights, and others involve inadequate legal transplants, where

---

220 Separate opinion of Judges Bianku and Vucinic in ECtHR, *Vizgirda v. Slovenia*, no. 59868/08, § 8, 28 August 2018. Emphasis added.

221 ECtHR, *Biao v. Denmark* [GC], no. 38590/10, § 134, 24 May 2016.

222 ECtHR, *S.E. v. Serbia*, no. 61365/16, § 39, 11 July 2023.

223 In this vein, S. O'Leary, 'The EU Charter Ten Years On: A View from Strasbourg', in M. Bobek and J. Adams-Prassl (eds.), *The EU Charter of Fundamental Rights in the Member States*, Oxford, Hart Publishing, 2020, p. 55.

224 See above the conclusion of Part III: Are EU Fundamental Rights A Source of Special Significance?

the ECtHR uses aspects of EU fundamental rights to inform different aspects of ECHR law, without considering that they are distinct elements and not necessarily compatible.[225] The ECtHR must exercise caution when integrating EU law into its reasoning, as ECHR and EU laws differ significantly in their concrete protection of fundamental rights. To address this, the ECtHR should ensure clarity on the scope and content of EU law being used, assess its relevance within the ECHR context, and maintain transparency in its reasoning to avoid misapplying EU standards.

SECTION III. A SHIFT IN THE INFRASTRUCTURE

Throughout this research project, we have aimed to underscore the 'human factor' in the influence of EU fundamental rights on ECtHR case-law, meaning that the impact of these rights may hinge on specific individuals and actors involved either before or within the ECtHR. We now turn our attention to another important aspect to end our study: the 'institutional factor'. This refers to how the use of EU fundamental rights in ECtHR's decisions is influenced by the ECtHR's organisation of its internal work and the resources dedicated to this issue.[226]

Several mechanisms exist within the ECtHR relating to the nexus between EU and ECHR laws. There are mechanisms for monitoring and sharing information as well as mechanisms enabling the ECtHR to take EU law into account during the proceedings. While these mechanisms help ensuring that EU law is appropriately considered within the ECtHR, there are some limits. This is why we advocate for a shift in the infrastructure concerning the use of EU law within the ECtHR. This shift, which is already underway, requires a rethinking of the current mechanisms to ensure the proper consideration of EU law, along with an allocation of greater resources to the issue.

As this section is informed by first-hand observations made during a research stay at the ECtHR, we ask for the reader's understanding regarding the level of abstraction we may occasionally use. While some information about the mechanisms is publicly available, other details remain confidential or are not easily accessible. Consequently, to respect confidentiality, we will sometimes present our analysis in general terms.

---

225 See above Part III (case study on equality and data protection), Chapter 3, Section V, §3. Contextualisation (in each case study).

226 See more on the organisation of the internal work of the ECtHR, E. Penninckx, 'The organisation of the internal work of the ECtHR', in E. Muir, S. Garben and I. Govaere (eds.), *Activating the Protection of Fundamental and Human Rights at European Level*, Oxford, Hart Publishing, forthcoming in 2025–2026.

§ 1. CURRENT TOOLBOX

The ECtHR has developed a growing number of mechanisms aimed at monitoring and sharing information related to the interplay between EU and ECHR laws. These mechanisms are often the result of initiatives within the ECtHR, but there are also efforts to monitor and share information that come from private initiatives.[227] The ECtHR's Registry has developed a comprehensive *Guide on European Union Law in the Court's case-law*, which was finalised on 29 February 2024. Spanning nearly fifty pages, it is the only guide dedicated exclusively to a body of law external to the ECHR, in line with our findings that EU (fundamental rights) law holds special significance for the ECtHR.[228] This guide has been created as a key reference tool for the ECtHR's jurisprudence related to EU law,[229] starting from the premise that '[t]wenty-seven of the States Parties to the Convention are also member States of the European Union.'[230] It addresses not only the issue of cases that directly or indirectly involve EU acts or national measures implementing EU law but also examines the ECtHR's approach to issues related to proceedings before the CJEU. Furthermore, it explores broader contexts in which the ECtHR has invoked EU law in its reasoning.[231] The guide is marked by its systematic and comprehensive approach, identifying key judgments and fundamental principles across these various dimensions.

The Registry has also launched a 'ECHR/EU' page on its Knowledge-Sharing platform on 14 June 2024.[232] This platform is meant to 'share Convention case-law knowledge, complementing the existing information tools such as HUDOC'.[233] It provides case-law knowledge either on a particular provision of the Convention or on a transversal theme. Here again, EU law is the only external law that has a dedicated page on the platform. This page refers to the aforementioned guide, provides a selection of significant ECtHR cases on EU

---

227 See in particular Johan Callewaert's blog, which is dedicated to the interplay between EU and ECHR laws. It encompasses an analysis of recent case-law on the matter, along with more general articles or overviews of cases (https://johan-callewaert.eu). See also Steve Peers' blog which has a significant focus on European fundamental rights law (http://eulawanalysis.blogspot.com).

228 The guide is available here: https://ks.echr.coe.int/documents/d/echr-ks/guide_eu_law_in_echr_case-law_eng.

229 Ibid., p. 6.

230 Ibid.

231 Ibid.

232 The 'ECHR/EU' page is available here: https://ks.echr.coe.int/web/echr-ks/echr-eu. See more on the KS platform, E. Penninckx, 'The organisation of the internal work of the ECtHR', in E. Muir, S. Garben and I. Govaere (eds.), *Activating the Protection of Fundamental and Human Rights at European Level*, Oxford, Hart Publishing, forthcoming in 2025–2026.

233 See: https://ks.echr.coe.int/web/echr-ks#:~:text=Introduction,does%20not%20bind%20the%20Court.

law, and offers access to specific materials on EU/ECHR laws (such as books, articles, and fact sheets), as well as relevant links on the theme. This page therefore allows access to the most important recent judgments on the matter, as well as a range of sources and recommendations for further exploration of EU/ECHR laws.

Information monitoring and sharing on EU and ECHR laws has also been a collaborative effort between the Council of Europe and the EU Agency for Fundamental Rights (FRA). Together, they have produced five handbooks that cover specific themes from both the EU and ECHR perspectives. These handbooks, regularly updated, address non-discrimination law, the rights of the child, asylum, borders and immigration, access to justice, and data protection law.[234] Designed for legal practitioners, they offer guidance on standards from both the EU and the Council of Europe, including CJEU and ECtHR case-law.[235] These handbooks are particularly thorough, providing insights and comparisons on specific aspects of these topics.

There are also other mechanisms for information sharing and monitoring that go beyond written information. One example is the regular meetings between members of the CJEU and the ECtHR, during which judges discuss key topics on which both Courts have intervened. In addition, a specific course called the 'Interplay Between the ECHR and the EU Charter of Fundamental Rights' was launched in 2023 as part of the Human Rights Education for Legal Professionals project.[236] This course is 'primarily addressed at legal/justice professionals (judges, prosecutors, lawyers, court staff)'[237] and stems from 'the need of training on fundamental rights issues within the scope of both the ECHR and EU Charter, focusing on the interplay between the two systems.'[238]

Next to the information monitoring and sharing mechanisms, there are also specific mechanisms within the ECtHR that allow taking into account and being informed about EU law during the proceedings, on which we cannot go into great details.[239] The Jurisconsult of the ECtHR and its Directorate, which is tasked to assist the ECtHR for the purposes of ensuring the quality

---

[234] The handbooks are available here: https://ks.echr.coe.int/web/echr-ks/echr-/-fra-handbooks.

[235] See FRA and Council of Europe, *Overview of the cooperation between the European Union Agency for Fundamental Rights and the Council of Europe, 2023 Report*, available here: https://fra.europa.eu/sites/default/files/fra_uploads/fra-coe-cooperation-report-2023_en.pdf, pp. 6–7.

[236] See more on the project here: https://www.coe.int/fr/web/help/help-in-the-eu#{%22251055000%22:[0]}.

[237] See the course brief, available here: https://rm.coe.int/interplay-course-brief-english/1680ac3177, p. 3.

[238] Ibid.

[239] This is because there is not much information on them available in the public domain.

and consistency of its case-law,[240] plays an important role in this regard. First, the Jurisconsult's primary mandate is to ensure the quality and consistency of case-law. In this capacity, the Jurisconsult provides observations on draft judgments and decisions that are placed on a Chamber's agenda.[241] These observations may address the consistency of ECtHR case-law with EU law. Second, the Jurisconsult offers legal support to the ECtHR and the case-lawyers by preparing research reports, which can take three different forms: reports on ECHR case-law, reports on international and/or European law, and comparative law reports.[242] As such, a number of reports have been prepared on specific issues in EU law, which explains why some judgments of the ECtHR are particularly thorough and precise regarding the state of EU law on the matter.

Overall, there is a wide range of mechanisms related to EU and ECHR laws, which have significantly expanded in recent times. This development is not so surprising given the increasing presence of EU law within ECtHR case-law and the prospect of EU accession to the ECHR. The existence of these mechanisms is highly beneficial for the effective functioning of the shared European space. For the ECtHR, these mechanisms are valuable as they provide insights into EU law, which can serve as an interpretative resource, is part of the background in cases involving EU States, and must be articulated with ECHR law. These mechanisms also benefit other actors, such as parties and third parties, who can strategically leverage EU law before the ECtHR. For national judges, this information is also important as they are responsible for applying both EU and ECHR laws. Additionally, these mechanisms foster dialogue between the CJEU and the ECtHR, as well as with other related institutions like the Council of Europe and the FRA.

§ 2. LIMITS AND PROSPECTS

While these mechanisms contribute to the fact that EU law is appropriately considered within the ECtHR, they are not without limitations. Three key limitations can be highlighted, though we will remain at general level. First, there appears to be a certain lack of awareness of EU law within the ECtHR and among the parties appearing before it. Despite notable engagement by the parties with EU law in our case studies, this engagement remains relatively

240 See Rule 18B of the Rules of ECtHR. See more on the Jurisconsult, E. Penninckx, 'The organisation of the internal work of the ECtHR', in E. Muir, S. Garben and I. Govaere (eds.), *Activating the Protection of Fundamental and Human Rights at European Level*, Hart, forthcoming in 2025–2026.

241 E. Penninckx, ibid.

242 Ibid.

limited at this stage, even though EU law often forms the backdrop in cases involving EU States.[243] Second, the mechanisms intended to take into account EU law within the ECtHR's proceedings are not always used systematically and coherently. Third, there seems to be a limited number of specialists within the ECtHR to manage a substantial workload related to the interplay between EU and ECHR laws.

This is why we believe that a shift in the infrastructure regarding the use of EU law within the ECtHR would be beneficial. In fact, such a shift appears to be underway, as many of the mechanisms described above are relatively new, and additional mechanisms are expected to be introduced soon.

Let us offer some general thoughts on this evolving infrastructure. We have observed that numerous initiatives have recently been launched. There may be further developments in the future. Recently, the ECtHR's Registry and the FRA initiated the preparation of factsheets 'as part of a collaborative effort to highlight jurisprudence in selected areas where [EU] law and the [ECHR] interact.'[244] The first factsheet, which covers the European Arrest Warrant and fundamental rights in ECtHR and CJEU case-law, is now available, with more expected to follow.[245] Regarding information monitoring and sharing mechanisms, the challenge may be less about the quantity of available information and more about ensuring that these resources reach the targeted audience. Therefore, initiatives like the recent course on EU/ECHR laws aimed at legal practitioners should be particularly welcomed. Additionally, sharing information and fostering close cooperation among various institutional actors is also beneficial. In this context, it is noteworthy and commendable that the ECtHR will begin regular exchanges with the Legal Service of the Commission to 'improve knowledge of EU law at the Court's Registry level and enhance the EU Commission's understanding of Convention law.'[246]

If it is crucial to ensure that information on EU/ECHR law is effectively disseminated, it is equally important for actors such as parties and third-party organisations to actively engage with this information and use it before the ECtHR. This proactive engagement can help the ECtHR in dealing with cases with an EU-related dimension. In this vein, it should be noted that

243 See the opening words of Former President of the ECtHR, S. O'Leary for the Seminar 'The articulation between the European Convention of Human Rights and the European Law: past, present and future', 14 June 2014, available here: https://www.echr.coe.int/documents/d/echr/speech-20240614-seminar-echr-eulaw-siofra-oleary-eng, p. 1.

244 Registry of the ECtHR and FRA, 'Factsheet on the European Arrest Warrant and fundamental rights in ECtHR and CJEU case-law', available here: https://ks.echr.coe.int/documents/d/echr-ks/european-arrest-warrant-and-fundamental-rights, p. 1.

245 Ibid. See also the opening words of Former President of the ECtHR, S. O'Leary for the Seminar 'The articulation between the European Convention of Human Rights and the European Law: past, present and future', 14 June 2014, available here: https://www.echr.coe.int/documents/d/echr/speech-20240614-seminar-echr-eulaw-siofra-oleary-eng, p. 3.

246 Ibid.

the European Commission has rarely intervened before the ECtHR,[247] but increased intervention, possibly spurred by the EU accession to the ECHR, could be valuable.

Regarding the mechanisms that allow EU law to be considered during proceedings, it could be beneficial to establish systematic processes for taking into account EU law in certain cases. This could include cases involving issues already addressed by the CJEU or questions concerning the compatibility of EU law with ECHR law. Additionally, ad hoc mechanisms could be strengthened to address specific requests related to EU law when such issues arise in individual cases.

Overall, the ongoing shift in the infrastructure represents a significant and positive development. To ensure that EU law is properly considered within the ECtHR and that mechanisms operate effectively, it is important that there are sufficient human resources that can deal with EU law matters. Today, it seems that there are only a few lawyers and judges specialised in EU law matters, despite the growing importance of this law for the ECtHR. In this regard, it is worth noting the recent decision to hire additional Registry lawyers with expertise in EU law.[248] It may be beneficial to have more lawyers whose primary focus is on EU law. They could handle specific cases related to EU law, such as admissibility cases or those involving EU institutions if accession occurs. They could also provide advice on specific EU law matters and offer general training on the subject. The more resources that are available, and the better organised the process of integrating EU law within the ECtHR's fabric, the more effectively EU law is likely to be used in its judgments.

---

247 This has occurred in ECtHR, *Duarte Agostinho and Others v. Portugal and 32 Others* [GC], no. 39371/20, § 142, 9 April 2024; ECtHR, *Avotiņš v. Latvia* [GC], no. 17502/07, §§ 89–93, 23 May 2016; ECtHR, *Bosphorus Hava Yolları Turizm ve Ticaret Anonim Şirketi v. Ireland* [GC], no. 45036/98, §§ 122–128, ECHR 2005-VI.

248 See the opening words of Former President of the ECtHR, S. O'Leary for the Seminar *The articulation between the European Convention of Human Rights and the European Law: past, present and future*, 14 June 2014, available here: https://www.echr.coe.int/documents/d/echr/speech-20240614-seminar-echr-eulaw-siofra-oleary-eng, p. 3.

EPILOGUE

ON THE BRIDGE(S): OPENING, BROADENING AND STRENGTHENING

It has been a long way since we began the story of this book with a photograph. That photograph depicts a bridge connecting the right and left banks of the Ill canal in Strasbourg, which we used as a symbol of the interactions between two Europes and the legal sources born under their auspices. The beginnings of our story are well-known. In the aftermath of the horrors of war that ravaged the European continent, two Europes emerged, driven by a shared intention to build lasting peace in Europe and strengthen the bonds between European States. These two Europes took different paths: one dedicated to the promotion and protection of the rule of law, democracy, and human rights – the Council of Europe – and the other fostering the emergence of a European market, carrying within it a broader political project that would unfold step by step – the European Union.

Under the auspices of the first emerged the European Convention on Human Rights and the European Court of Human Rights, and under the second, EU law, which was originally developed through the three Community Treaties. Despite the adoption of the Universal Declaration of Human Rights in 1948, the EU's foundational structure remained largely silent on human rights. A political EU project that aimed to place them at its core was abandoned, and a sectoral and economic approach to EU integration prevailed. It was under the impetus of the EU judiciary that fundamental rights were introduced by means of general principles, under pressure from litigants and also from the highest courts of certain States, which would not give precedence to EU law unless it protected fundamental rights.

It is in this context that the bridge of human/fundamental rights between EU law and ECHR law *opened*. Lacking sources of fundamental rights within the EU legal framework, the CJEU had to look elsewhere to give flesh to EU fundamental rights. It turned to common constitutional traditions and international treaties, eventually making ECHR law its privileged source of inspiration. The flow of human rights from ECHR law to EU law became particularly significant: it increased over time, with references made to both the Convention and ECtHR case-law, far more than to any other human rights sources or outputs of related body. ECHR law appeared as a set of common European values, since all EU States adhere to the ECHR. Drawing from ECHR law also allowed for relative harmony within the European fundamental rights architecture – a necessary harmony, as EU and ECHR laws operate within a shared space where EU national judges must apply both bodies of law.

For a long time, the flow across the EU/ECHR bridge was a one-way street, crossing from ECHR law to EU law. The EU political institutions, far from developing a bill of rights for the EU, supported the development of the EU's fundamental rights regime as one infused with ECHR law. From the late 1970s, these institutions focused on the EU's accession to the ECHR, despite some judicial turbulence. The situation differed from one side of the bridge to the other: EU law was not a source of inspiration for ECHR law, but rather a source whose compliance with ECHR law had to be ensured. Until the 2000s, there was no significant flow of fundamental rights from EU law to ECHR law.

At the turn of the 2000s, however, significant developments occurred on the right bank: EU political institutions, sometimes in concert with EU States, increasingly developed EU fundamental rights standards. The Charter of Fundamental Rights caught much of the (academic) attention, and rightly so: it is a comprehensive bill of rights that includes many innovations and was created through a transparent and open process with unprecedented parliamentary participation.

However, the emergence of the Charter should not overshadow what is perhaps one of the most important shifts for the protection of fundamental rights in the EU: the growing role of the EU legislator in this area, with two dimensions. First, passively, EU political institutions established mechanisms to comply with fundamental rights when developing EU norms. Second, actively, the EU legislator increasingly developed laws that give substance to, or are linked to, fundamental rights. While the EU legislator had previously acted somewhat in this area based on general competences, the real game changer was the attribution of specific competences to this legislator, initiated by the Treaty of Amsterdam and reinforced by the Treaty of Lisbon.

The combination of these competences and the political will to use them led to an intensification and diversification of EU legislative fundamental rights standards. Although the EU's fundamental rights competences remain fragmented, numerous sectoral laws have blossomed – whether in asylum, data protection, equality, or criminal law – that the CJEU would qualify as 'giving expression' to the Charter. Moreover, the CJEU made EU fundamental rights, as enshrined in the Charter and expressed in EU secondary laws, the focal point of its fundamental rights jurisprudence, to some extent at the expense of ECHR law, whose role in Luxembourg's case-law has diminished. Nevertheless, ECHR law continues to be a significant source of inspiration for the CJEU, and remains by far the most frequently used external source in its fundamental rights case-law.

If this renewed EU context has affected the flow of human rights from ECHR law to EU law, it has also *broadened* the bridge with a new flow of fundamental rights, this time from EU law to ECHR law. From the early 2000s, the bridge evolved from a one-way to a two-way bridge, with increasingly frequent references to EU fundamental rights by the ECtHR. It is this flow of fundamental rights – whether from the Charter, EU legislation, or related CJEU case-law – that has been at the heart of our research and which we have studied through two case studies: equality and non-discrimination, and data protection. We will not revisit in detail all the conclusions we have drawn about the influence of EU fundamental rights on Strasbourg's case-law in these fields, as they are largely summarised in the conclusion of our case studies. However, we can recall some key elements.

First, the flow of fundamental rights from EU law to ECHR law is significant. The ECtHR has long and consistently referred to various EU fundamental rights standards in a wide range of areas, with an intensification around 2015. Second, this flow of EU fundamental rights is impactful. These rights have notably been used to interpret the scope and meaning of Convention's rights and to assess whether an interference can be justified. They also constitute an important source of information and contextualisation for ECtHR judgments, and the ECtHR has at times sought to distinguish its stance from that of EU fundamental rights. Both quantitatively and qualitatively, the flow of EU fundamental rights is more significant than other international sources, leading us to conclude that EU fundamental rights hold a special significance.

What has also become clear throughout our research is that our story is not just about one bridge between EU and ECHR laws, but about many interconnected bridges. The EU/ECHR bridge cannot be considered in isolation; we must take into account the pluralistic space of interactions between human rights sources. These sources interact increasingly through the case-law of their adjudicators, creating network effects. In the field of data protection, for example, the impact of Convention 108 on the development of safeguards against data abuse at the ECHR level allows to understand the limited role of EU law in shaping these safeguards.

As much as this is a story of a plurality of bridges, it is also a story of a plurality of actors. The EU/ECHR bridge cannot be limited to the interactions between the CJEU and the ECtHR. As we have seen, there is a growing engagement by several actors with fundamental rights on the EU side, where the CJEU is one actor among many, alongside the EU legislator, for example. It is also not only the ECtHR that engages with EU fundamental rights, but a multitude of actors involved prior to, before or within the ECtHR. Before the ECtHR for instance, applicants, governments, and third parties often use

EU fundamental rights as an argumentative resource to defend their interests. Within the ECtHR itself, there are divergences among judges on the use of EU law. This highlights that the influence of EU fundamental rights is not a monolithic process shaped solely by the ECtHR, but rather a process involving multiple actors with diverging views and interests regarding EU law.

If there is a plurality of bridges (and actors), how can we explain the special importance of the EU/ECHR bridge, and in particular the flow of EU fundamental rights into ECHR law? While there is no single answer, it is likely related to several characteristics of EU fundamental rights. First, they are highly sophisticated standards, often comprehensive and specific, and frequently innovative compared to ECHR rights. Second, they are deeply integrated within the laws of EU States, notably through the principles of primacy and direct effect. Third, there is the hybrid nature of EU fundamental rights, and of EU law more broadly. EU law borrows characteristics from national law, making it almost akin to domestic law for the 27 EU States, while also borrowing characteristics from international law, such as its broad scope, which applies to the majority of Convention States. As a result, EU fundamental rights form part of the background in cases involving EU States before the ECtHR; they offer significant value in finding common ground at a pan-European level and are a source that must be articulated with ECHR law, as EU national judges are required to apply both EU and ECHR laws.

If the flow of EU fundamental rights into ECHR law is particularly strong, we believe the EU/ECHR bridge could be further *strengthened* through a method-based approach to the use of EU fundamental rights by the ECtHR. While our method primarily relates to the ECtHR, given our research focus, it could also resonate significantly for the use of ECHR law by the CJEU. The aim is to shift from the question of whether there should be flows of human/fundamental rights across the Ill canal – which is already a reality – to how to ensure that these flows strengthen and maintain the coherence of the European shared space of fundamental rights. The way the ECtHR uses EU fundamental rights matters: if they are used to transform the foundational principles of the ECHR system, it could denaturalise this system; if their use is not justified or transparent, it could undermine the (procedural) legitimacy of ECtHR's judgments.

This method-based approach becomes even more needed as the flow of EU fundamental rights into ECHR law could intensify in the future. This is because, first, it is likely that more EU fundamental rights will emerge, either in fields where the EU has already intervened for years, with the CJEU's case-law maturing and the development of new legislative standards, or in more recent areas like the digital sphere, where the EU is increasingly emerging as a global leader. Additionally, more Convention States are likely to incorporate EU fundamental rights. The 27 EU States are already somewhat closer to 27+

States, with several non-EU States, such as the EEA States, having incorporated specific EU fundamental rights. Moreover, the nine candidate States for EU membership are all Convention States and are required to integrate EU fundamental rights as part of the accession process. The more Convention States that incorporate EU fundamental rights, the greater their significance in the ECtHR case-law will probably be. Finally, the potential accession of the EU to the ECHR, which seems increasingly likely in light of recent CJEU judgments on CFSP matters, could further strengthen the use of EU fundamental rights by the ECtHR, for instance through enhanced dialogue on these rights between the CJEU and the ECtHR.

The method should first be rooted in an approach based on the complementarity between the EU and ECHR legal systems of fundamental rights. One clear insight from our study is that while these two systems have overlaps in substance and scope, they remain fundamentally distinct, whether in the rationales behind the protection of fundamental/human rights or the structure of their protection. These differences, which require articulation, can also serve as a strength for the European fundamental rights architecture, as what one system does not offer can sometimes be found under the other system. It is essential that both systems retain their complementary strengths, such as the flexibility and human rights-focused logic of the ECHR system. Additionally, the European Courts can enhance the effectiveness of the other system without necessarily incorporating its standards. In this vein, the ECtHR has increasingly sanctioned the lack or poor application of EU law by national authorities. However, there is a delicate balance between strengthening the effectiveness of EU law and leaving the interpretation and enforcement of EU law to the CJEU and national courts, to which the ECtHR must be careful. Complementarity does not mean the systems cannot enrich each other; the ECHR legal system can learn from the innovations of the Charter, the specific requirements in EU legislative instruments, and the ways in which the CJEU applies EU fundamental rights in concrete cases, in so far as the key tenets of the ECHR system are respected.

Second, coherence between the two sides of the bridge – the two systems of fundamental rights protection – is crucial. This coherence is especially needed because EU national judges are tasked with applying both EU and ECHR laws. Incoherence between the two systems complicates their role, which can ultimately hinder the protection of fundamental rights for individuals. Convergence between EU and ECHR laws can contribute to achieve coherence, and we see many areas, such as equality and the rule of law, where the CJEU and ECtHR's case-law have converged in recent years. However, convergence is a means, not an end in itself – the ultimate goal is harmony between the systems, not harmonisation. Aligning ECHR standards too closely with those of EU law could marginalise non-EU Convention States and undermine the

ECtHR's role as the guarantor of a safety net for human rights across Europe. Coherence can be achieved without convergence, especially through greater clarity on the differences in standards and contexts between cases handled by the two European Courts.

Third, there is a need for enhanced dialogue between the two sides of the river. This dialogue should first involve the CJEU and the ECtHR, which must remain open to the case-law of their counterpart. Although this dialogue is often of high quality, its absence – for instance, through silence on the counterpart's case-law – can negatively impact the protection of fundamental rights in Europe. Conversely, fostering this dialogue can create virtuous circles where both courts reinforce and legitimise each other's case-law. While dialogue between the CJEU and ECtHR is essential, it should not be limited to them. It should also involve key actors in the protection of fundamental rights in Europe, allowing for the emergence of trilogues or even quadrilogues in this domain. This includes national judges, whose application of EU fundamental rights must be taken into account by the ECtHR, as well as the EU legislator, who must consider ECHR law when enacting new EU standards.

Alongside these guiding principles, the ECtHR must demonstrate methodological rigour when using EU fundamental rights. This approach avoids the beneficial effects of using EU law – such as enhancing the persuasiveness of ECtHR's judgments – being overshadowed by questionable use of EU law. An open and transparent approach when the ECtHR uses EU fundamental rights is essential, for instance by clearly referencing EU law and explaining its relevance when it is used. This also requires a stronger justification for the use of EU law. There are many ways to justify EU law within the ECHR law's palette, whether within the text of the ECHR (e.g., Article 53 or the concept of law) or through the ECtHR's interpretative and adjudicative techniques (e.g., European consensus or procedural review). Additionally, it is crucial for the ECtHR to take into account the context and limits of EU law – whether material, temporal, or geographical. In this respect, the ECtHR has primarily used EU fundamental rights in cases involving EU States, but this approach is often implicit. Making this approach more explicit would prevent the unintended spill-over of EU law in cases involving non-EU States without sufficient justification.

For these guiding and methodological principles to become a reality, a shift in the infrastructure concerning the use of EU law within the ECtHR's fabric is also necessary. We are beginning to see movement in this direction, with a growing number of mechanisms aimed at monitoring and sharing information on EU/ECHR laws, as well as informing ECtHR's judgments in light of EU law. However, there are still limitations, such as a general lack of awareness on the interactions between EU and ECHR laws among various actors inside and outside the ECtHR. These mechanisms must be strengthened, supported by specialists on the interplay between EU and ECHR laws to ensure their smooth operation. Indeed, for the bridge to function well, we need bridge-makers.

Before concluding our project, let us recall the wise words of Alfred Korzybski: 'The map is not the territory.' This phrase serves as a reminder that representation is never the reality itself, allowing us to reflect on the limitations of this work and the potential for future research.

Our EU/ECHR bridge is a simplified representation of a reality that has become increasingly complex, with a growing number of human rights actors and sources of human rights law in Europe, the so-called 'crowded house of rights'. We focused on one specific aspect – the flow of EU fundamental rights into ECHR law – which is only one aspect of the complex legal reality between EU and ECHR laws. Another dimension of this reality is that the EU can pose threats to human rights. As a powerful policy actor, the EU can violate the rights enshrined in the Convention. This dimension cannot be ignored and is also sometimes linked to the more positive role that the EU can play in the field of fundamental rights. The Bosphorus presumption, for instance, rests on the high level of protection for fundamental rights in the EU legal system. It would be valuable to study these dimensions together in the future, such as by examining the impact of EU accession to the ECHR – should it happen – on the influence of EU fundamental rights on ECtHR case-law.

Even within the flow of EU fundamental rights to ECHR law that we have studied, we have only shed light on part of the reality. We have mapped out the influence for two case studies: equality and non-discrimination, and data protection. Even between them, significant disparities emerge, with EU equality law having a deeper impact on Strasbourg case-law. We must therefore be cautious not to overextend the conclusions drawn from these case studies; one side of the territory may not resemble the other. In each field, there are different dynamics regarding how a fundamental right is protected at the EU level, at the ECHR level, and within the broader normative environments. Thus, in each area studied, one must consider the particular dynamics of these fields, identifying the points of tension, influence, and convergence.

Our analysis has been primarily based on an examination of the ECtHR's case-law. This case-law analysis retains its significance because courts remain central actors in the development of fundamental rights in Europe. However, it is also important to turn attention to other actors who play significant roles, such as the EU legislator, national courts, and the States that must comply with EU fundamental rights. Studies that focus on how domestic courts address the rise of autonomous EU standards alongside those of the ECHR are particularly welcome. Beyond what can be explicitly detected in court's judgments, there are also subtleties that occur between the lines: the silences, the rejections, or the implicit incorporations. Here, researchers have an important role to play in identifying them and confronting the institutional actors with them. Finally, there are processes that happen behind the scenes: EU and ECHR laws result in part from the internal structures of the institutions. Focusing on these internal structures and the actors working within them allows us to shed light on how the actors shape the legal reality. Among many interesting questions for future research is to understand who are the actors (such as legal clerks) who operate behind the scenes of the European Courts and how they influence the shaping of human rights in Europe.

Annexes

1. ANNEX I

Key questions and sub-questions
Quantitative analysis: what is the quantitative significance of EU fundamental rights in the ECtHR's case-law?
– What is the frequency per category of EU standards? – What is the cumulative frequency of references to EU fundamental rights? – What is the frequency over time? – What is the frequency per area? – What is the frequency per respondent State? – What is the frequency per actor? – How do the quantitative data on EU fundamental rights compare to quantitative data on international instruments and the overall evolution of ECtHR's case-law?
Functions: what are the functions performed by EU fundamental rights?
– Are there other arguments which are used in fulfilling the function? – Are there other legal sources which are used in fulfilling the function? – Which sources of EU fundamental rights contribute to the function? – Does the use of EU fundamental rights enhance the protection of fundamental rights? – How do the functions performed by EU fundamental rights compare to the functions of international instruments?
Actors: who are the other actors than the ECtHR who use EU fundamental rights and for what purpose do they use them?
– Do parties and third-party interveners refer to EU fundamental rights and to what end? – Do national courts refer to EU fundamental rights and to what end? – Do ECtHR's judges refer to EU fundamental rights in separate opinions and to what end? – What is the role of actors involved in the process prior to the decision in the use of EU fundamental rights? – How does the use of EU fundamental rights by the various actors compare to their use of international instruments?
States: who are the respondent States when the ECtHR uses EU fundamental rights?
– To what extent are EU fundamental rights used in cases involving EU States? – To what extent are EU fundamental rights used in cases involving non-EU States? – Are there tools which are used to modulate EU fundamental rights based on the respondent State?

Methodology: what is the methodology when the ECtHR uses EU fundamental rights?
– Is the use of EU fundamental rights transparent? – Is the use of EU fundamental rights justified? – Is the use of EU fundamental rights contextualised? – How does the methodology used for EU fundamental rights compare to the methodology used for international instruments?

2. ANNEX II

EU legislation giving expression to the equality fundamental rights
Council Directive 75/117/EEC of 10 February 1975 on the approximation of the laws of the Member States relating to the application of the principle of equal pay for men and women
Council Directive 76/207/EEC of 9 February 1976 on the implementation of the principle of equal treatment for men and women as regards access to employment, vocational training and promotion, and working conditions
Council Directive 79/7/EEC of 19 December 1978 on the progressive implementation of the principle of equal treatment for men and women in matters of social security
Council Directive 86/378/EEC of 24 July 1986 on the implementation of the principle of equal treatment for men and women in occupational social security schemes
Council Directive 96/97/EC of 20 December 1996 amending Directive 86/378/EEC on the implementation of the principle of equal treatment for men and women in occupational social security schemes
Council Directive 97/80/EC of 15 December 1997 on the burden of proof in cases of discrimination based on sex
Council Directive 98/52/EC of 13 July 1998 on the extension of Directive 97/80/EC on the burden of proof in cases of discrimination based on sex to the United Kingdom of Great Britain and Northern Ireland
Directive 2002/73/EC of the European Parliament and of the Council of 23 September 2002 amending Council Directive 76/207/EEC on the implementation of the principle of equal treatment for men and women as regards access to employment, vocational training and promotion, and working conditions
Council Directive 2000/43/EC of 29 June 2000 implementing the principle of equal treatment between persons irrespective of racial or ethnic origin
Council Directive 2000/78/EC of 27 November 2000 establishing a general framework for equal treatment in employment and occupation
Council Directive 2004/113/EC of 13 December 2004 implementing the principle of equal treatment between men and women in the access to and supply of goods and services
Directive 2006/54/EC of the European Parliament and of the Council of 5 July 2006 on the implementation of the principle of equal opportunities and equal treatment of men and women in matters of employment and occupation (recast)

Directive 2010/41/EU of the European Parliament and of the Council of 7 July 2010 on the application of the principle of equal treatment between men and women engaged in an activity in a self-employed capacity and repealing Council Directive 86/613/EEC

3. ANNEX III

	EU equality law	ECHR equality law
Central v. marginal	Equality is a fundamental and ubiquitous principle in the EU legal order	Equality protection historically considered underdeveloped or inadequate, yet undergoing a process of autonomy and enrichment
Rule-based v. principle-based	Rule-based	Principle-based
Fundamental v. economic	Co-existence of market and fundamental rights rationales	Fundamental rights
Equality v. non-discrimination	Features both equality and non-discrimination rationales, with the latter predominant	Features both equality and non-discrimination rationales, with the former predominant
Formal v. substantive	From formal to a more substantive version of equality	From formal to a more substantive version of equality
Material scope	Primarily confined to the economic sphere	Potentially unlimited but application is limited to its accessory nature
Personal scope	Specific feature of horizontalisation	Vertical nature but indirect horizontal application through positive obligations
Protected grounds	Features of both open and closed systems	Traditionally an open system, arguably getting closer to a closed system
Substantive elements	Definition of the forms of discrimination and the grounds of justification in legislative instruments	Assessment if a difference in treatment has an objective and reasonable justification, combined with the model of suspected grounds
Procedural elements	Strong proceduralisation	Growing proceduralisation

4. ANNEX IV

EU legislation giving expression to the data protection fundamental right
Directive 95/46/EC of the European Parliament and of the Council of 24 October 1995 on the protection of individuals with regard to the processing of personal data and on the free movement of such data
Directive 2002/58/EC of the European Parliament and of the Council of 12 July 2002 concerning the processing of personal data and the protection of privacy in the electronic communications sector (Directive on privacy and electronic communications)
Directive 2006/24/EC of the European Parliament and of the Council of 15 March 2006 on the retention of data generated or processed in connection with the provision of publicly available electronic communications services or of public communications networks and amending Directive 2002/58/EC
Regulation (EC) No 45/2001 of the European Parliament and of the Council of 18 December 2000 on the protection of individuals with regard to the processing of personal data by the Community institutions and bodies and on the free movement of such data
Council Framework Decision 2008/977/JHA of 27 November 2008 on the protection of personal data processed in the framework of police and judicial cooperation in criminal matters
Regulation (EU) 2016/679 of the European Parliament and of the Council of 27 April 2016 on the protection of natural persons with regard to the processing of personal data and on the free movement of such data, and repealing Directive 95/46/EC
Directive (EU) 2016/680 of the European Parliament and of the Council of 27 April 2016 on the protection of natural persons with regard to the processing of personal data by competent authorities for the purposes of the prevention, investigation, detection or prosecution of criminal offences or the execution of criminal penalties, and on the free movement of such data, and repealing Council Framework Decision 2008/977/JHA
Regulation (EU) 2018/1725 of the European Parliament and of the Council of 23 October 2018 on the protection of natural persons with regard to the processing of personal data by the Union institutions, bodies, offices and agencies and on the free movement of such data, and repealing Regulation (EC) No 45/2001 and Decision No 1247/2002/EC

5. ANNEX V

	EU data protection law	ECHR data protection law
Fundamental v. economic	Co-existence of market and fundamental rights rationales	Fundamental rights
Data protection v. Privacy	Data protection	Privacy
Rule-based v. principle-based	Rule-based	Principle-based
Material scope	Data oriented	Privacy oriented

Personal scope	Specific feature of horizontalisation	Vertical nature but indirect horizontal application through positive obligations
Protected grounds	Features of both open and closed systems	Traditionally an open system arguably getting closer to a closed system
Substantive elements	Rights and principles largely fleshed out in EU secondary law	Assessment if an interference pursues a legitimate aim is lawful and necessary, with safeguards developed under the last two criteria
Procedural elements	Strong proceduralisation	Growing proceduralisation

SELECTED BIBLIOGRAPHY

1. EU Primary Law

Treaty establishing the European Coal and Steel Community, not published

Treaty establishing the European Economic Community, not published

Treaty establishing the European Atomic Energy Community, not published

Single European Act, [1987] OJ L169/1.

Treaty establishing the European Community, [1992] OJ C224/6.

Treaty on the European Union (consolidated version 2012), [2012] OJ C326/13.

Treaty on the Functioning of the European Union (consolidated version 2012), [2012] OJ C326/47.

Charter of Fundamental Rights of the European Union, [2012] OJ C326/391.

2. Council of Europe Instruments

Council of Europe, European Convention for the Protection of Human Rights and Fundamental Freedoms, *European Treaty Series No. 5*, 4 November 1950.

Council of Europe, Convention for the Protection of Individuals with regard to Automatic Processing of Personal Data, *European Treaty series No. 108*, 28 January 1981.

Council of Europe, Framework Convention for the Protection of National Minorities, *European Treaty Series No. 157*, 1 February 1995.

Council of Europe, Additional Protocol to the Convention for the Protection of Individuals with regard to Automatic Processing of Personal Data regarding supervisory authorities and transborder data flows, *European Treaty Series No. 181*, 8 November 2001.

Council of Europe, Protocol No. 14 to the Convention for the Protection of Human Rights and Fundamental Freedoms, amending the control system of the Convention, *European Treaty Series No. 194*, 13 May 2005.

Council of Europe, Convention on Preventing and Combating Violence Against Women and Domestic Violence, *European Treaty Series No. 210*, 11 May 2011.

Council of Europe. Amending Protocol to the Convention for the Protection of Individuals with regard to Automatic Processing of Personal Data (Convention 108+), *European Treaty Series No. 223*, 10 October 2018.

3. Case-Law

3.1. European Court of Human Rights

Case 'relating to certain aspects of the laws on the use of languages in education in Belgium' (merits), 23 July 1968, Series A no. 6. 2.

European Commission of Human Rights, *Confédération française démocratique du travail v. European Communities* (dec.), no. 8030/77.

Tyrer v. the United Kingdom, 25 April 1978, Series A no. 26.

Klass and Others v. Germany, 6 September 1978, Series A no. 28.

Marckx v. Belgium, 13 June 1979, Series A no. 31.

X and Y v. the Netherlands, 26 March 1985, Series A no. 91.

Leander v. Sweden, 26 March 1987, Series A no. 116.

European Commission of Human Rights, *M & Co v. Germany*, no. 13258/87, 9 January 1990.

Cossey v. The United Kingdom, no. 10843/84, 27 September 1990.

Niemitz v. Germany, no. 13710/88, 16 December 1992.

European Commission of Human Rights, *Heinz v. The Contracting States Parties to the European Patent Convention* (dec.), no. 21090/92, 10 January 1994.

López Ostra v. Spain, 9 December 1994, Series A no. 303-C.

Z v. Finland, 25 February 1997, Reports of Judgments and Decisions 1997-I.

X, Y and Z v. the United Kingdom, 22 April 1997, Reports of Judgments and Decisions 1997-II.

Hornsby v. Greece, no. 18357/91, 1 April 1998.

Sheffield and Horsham v. the United Kingdom, 30 July 1998, Reports of Judgments and Decisions 1998-V.

Pafitis and Others v. Greece, 26 February 1998, Reports of Judgments and Decisions 1998-I.

Chassagnou and Others v. France [GC], no. 25088/94, 29 April 1999.

Lustig-Prean and Beckett v. the United Kingdom, nos. 31417/96 and 32377/96, 27 September 1999.

Pellegrin v. France [GC], no. 28541/95, 8 December 1999.

Matthews v. the United Kingdom [GC], no. 24833/94, ECHR 1999-I.

Smith and Grady v. the United Kingdom, nos. 33985/96 and 33986/96, ECHR 1999-VI.

Beyeler v. Italy [GC], no. 33202/96, 5 January 2000.

Amann v. Switzerland [GC], no. 27798/95, ECHR 2000-II.

Thlimmenos v. Greece [GC], no. 34369/97, ECHR 2000-IV.

Chapman v. the United Kingdom [GC], no. 27238/95, ECHR 2001-I.

I. v. the United Kingdom [GC], no. 25680/94, 11 July 2002.

Beck and Others v. the United Kingdom, nos. 48535/99 and 2 others, 22 October 2002.

Perkins and R. v. the United Kingdom, nos. 43208/98 and 44875/98, 22 October 2002.

S.A. Dangeville v. France, no. 36677/97, ECHR 2002-III.

Christine Goodwin v. the United Kingdom [GC], no. 28957/95, ECHR 2002-VI.

Posti and Rahko v. Finland, no. 27824/95, CEDH 2002-VII.

Wessels-Bergervoet v. the Netherlands, no. 34462/97, ECHR 2002-IV.

Van Kück v. Germany, no. 35968/97, ECHR 2003-VII.

Peck v. the United Kingdom, no. 44647/98, ECHR 2003-I.

Vo v. France [GC], no. 53924/00, 8 July 2004.

Senator Lines GmbH v. Austria, no. 56672/00, ECHR 2004-IV.

Hoogendijk v. The Netherlands (adm. decision), no. 58641/00, 6 January 2005.

Nachova and Others v. Bulgaria, nos. 43577/98 and 43579/98, 6 July 2005.

Bosphorus Hava Yolları Turizm ve Ticaret Anonim Şirketi v. Ireland [GC], no. 45036/98, ECHR 2005-l.

Barrow v. the United Kingdom, no. 42735/02, 22 August 2006.

Pearson v. the United Kingdom, no. 8374/03, 22 August 2006.

Walker v. the United Kingdom, no. 37212/02, 22 August 2006.

Hobbs, Richard, Walsh and Geen v. the United Kingdom, nos. 63684/00 and 3 others, 14 November 2006.

Coopérative des agriculteurs de la Mayenne and Coopérative laitière Maine-Anjou v. France (dec.), no. 16931/04, ECHR 2006-XV.

Stec and Others v. the United Kingdom [GC], nos. 65731/01 and 65900/01, ECHR 2006-VI.

D.H. and Others v. the Czech Republic [GC], no. 57325/00, ECHR 2007-IV.

Vilho Eskelinen and Others v. Finland [GC], no. 63235/00, ECHR 2007-II.

E.B. v. France [GC], no. 43546/02, 22 January 2008.

Hugh Jordan v. the United Kingdom, no. 24746/94, 4 June 2008.

Demir and Baykara v. Turkey [GC], no. 34503/97, ECHR 2008.

S. and Marper v. the United Kingdom [GC], nos. 30562/04 and 30566/04, ECHR 2008.

Beganović v. Croatia, no. 46423/06, 25 June 2009.

Scoppola v. Italy (no. 2) [GC], no. 10249/03, 17 September 2009.

G.N. and Others v. Italy, no. 43134/05, 1 December 2009

Bosnia and Herzegovina [GC], nos. 27996/06 and 34836/06, ECHR 2009.

Cooperatieve Producentenorganisatie van de Nederlandse Kokkelvisserij U.A. v. the Netherlands (dec.), no. 13645/05, ECHR 2009.

Glor v. Switzerland, no. 13444/04, ECHR 2009.

Micallef v. Malta [GC], no. 17056/06, ECHR 2009.

Muñoz Díaz v. Spain, no. 49151/07, ECHR 2009.

Opuz v. Turkey, no. 33401/02, ECHR 2009.

Sejdić and Finci v. Bosnia and Herzegovina [GC], nos. 27996/06 and 34836/06, ECHR 2009.

Sergey Zolotukhin v. Russia [GC], no. 14939/03, ECHR 2009.

Peterka v. Czech Republic (adm. decision), no. 21990/08, 4 May 2010.

Clift v. the United Kingdom, no. 7205/07, 13 July 2010.

Saltynite v. Lithuania, no. 32934/19, 26 October 2010.

Milanović v. Serbia, no. 44614/07, 14 December 2010.

Wasmuth v. Germany, no. 12884/03, 17 February 2011.

Diallo v. the Czech Republic, no. 20493/07, 23 June 2011.

Bayatyan v. Armenia [GC], no. 23459/03, ECHR 2011.

Carson and Others v. the United Kingdom [GC], no. 42184/05, ECHR 2010.

M.S.S. v. Belgium and Greece [GC], no. 30696/09, ECHR 2011.

Schalk and Kopf v. Austria, no. 30141/04, ECHR 2010.

Neulinger and Shuruk v. Switzerland [GC], no. 41615/07, ECHR 2010.

Uzun v. Germany, no. 35623/05, ECHR 2010.

Mosley v. the United Kingdom, no. 48009/08, 10 May 2011.

Ullens de Schooten and Rezabek v. Belgium, nos. 3989/07 and 38353/07, 20 September 2011.

Romet v. the Netherlands, no. 7094/06, 14 February 2012.

M.M. v. the United Kingdom, no. 24029/07, 13 November 2012.

Hristozov and Others v. Bulgaria, nos. 47039/11 and 358/12, ECHR 2012 (extracts).

Michaud v. France, no. 12323/11, ECHR 2012.

I.B. v. Greece, no. 552/10, ECHR 2013.

Vallianatos and Others v. Greece [GC], nos. 29381/09 and 32684/09, ECHR 2013.

Abdu v. Bulgaria, no. 26827/08, 11 March 2014.

The National Union of Rail, Maritime and Transport Workers v. The United Kingdom, no. 31045/10, 8 April 2014.

Hämäläinen v. Finland [GC], no. 37359/09, 16 July 2014.

Svinarenko and Slyadnev v. Russia [GC], no. 32541/08, 17 July 2014.

Jeunesse v. the Netherlands [GC], no. 12738/10, 3 October 2014.

Klausecker v. Germany (dec.), no. 415/07, 6 January 2015.

A.T. v. Luxembourg, no. 30460/13, 9 April 2015.

Satakunnan Markkinapörssi Oy and Satamedia Oy v. Finland, no. 931/13, 21 July 2015.

Oliari and Others v. Italy, nos. 18766/11 and 36030/11, 21 July 2015.

Zachar and Čierny v. Slovakia, nos. 29376/12 and 29384/12, 21 July 2015.

Delfi AS v. Estonia [GC], no. 64569/09, ECHR 2015.

Ebrahimian v. France, no. 64846/11, ECHR 2015.

Roman Zakharov v. Russia [GC], no. 47143/06, ECHR 2015.

Bărbulescu v. Romania, no. 61496/08, 12 January 2016.

Miracle Europe KFT v. Hungary, no. 57774/13, 12 January 2016.

Szabó and Vissy v. Hungary, no. 37138/14, 12 January 2016.

Çam v. Turkey, no. 51500/08, 23 February 2016.

Pajić v. Croatia, no. 68453/13, 23 February 2016.

Guberina v. Croatia, no. 23682/13, 22 March 2016.

Avotiņš v. Latvia [GC], no. 17502/07, 23 May 2016.

Biao v. Denmark [GC], no. 38590/10, 24 May 2016.

Aldeguer Tomás v. Spain, no. 35214/09, 14 June 2016.

Baka v. Hungary [GC], no. 20261/12, 23 June 2016.

Taddeucci and McCall v. Italy, no. 51362/09, 30 June 2016.

Ibrahim and Others v. the United Kingdom [GC], nos. 50541/08 and 3 others, 13 September 2016.

Magyar Helsinki Bizottság v. Hungary [GC], no. 18030/11, 8 November 2016.

A.H. and Others v. Russia, nos. 6033/13 and 15 others, 17 January 2017.

Khamtokhu and Aksenchik v. Russia [GC], nos. 60367/08 and 961/11, 24 January 2017.

Muzamba Oyaw v. Belgium (dec.), no. 23707/15, 28 February 2017.

Talpis v. Italy, no. 41237/14, 2 March 2017.

Ilias and Ahmed v. Hungary, no. 47287/15, 14 March 2017.

Thimothawes v. Belgium, no. 39061/11, 4 April 2017.

Simeonovi v. Bulgaria [GC], no. 21980/04, 12 May 2017.

Bălşan v. Romania, no. 49645/09, 23 May 2017.

Satakunnan Markkinapörssi Oy and Satamedia Oy v. Finland [GC], no. 931/13, 27 June 2017.

Moreira Ferreira (No. 2) v. Portugal, no. 19867/12, 11 July 2017.

Carvalho Pinto de Sousa Morais v. Portugal, no. 17484/15, 25 July 2017.

Bărbulescu v. Romania [GC], no. 61496/08, 5 September 2017.

Orlandi and Others v. Italy, nos. 26431/12 and 3 others, 14 December 2017.

Enver Şahin v. Turkey, no. 23065/12, 30 January 2018.

Krombach v. France (dec.), no. 67521/14, 20 February 2018.

Benedik v. Slovenia, no. 62357/14, 24 April 2018.
Centrum för rättvisa v. Sweden, no. 35252/08, 19 June 2018.
GIEM SRL and Others [GC], no. 1828/06, 28 June 2018.
M.L. and W.W. v. Germany, nos. 60798/10 and 65599/10, 28 June 2018.
Vizgirda v. Slovenia, no. 59868/08, 28 August 2018.
Big Brother Watch and Others v. the United Kingdom, nos. 58170/13 and 2 others, 13 September 2018.
Molla Sali v. Greece, no. 20452/14, 19 December 2018.
Catt v. the United Kingdom, no. 43514/15, 24 January 2019.
Volodina v. Russia, no. 41261/17, 9 July 2019.
Romeo Castaño v. Belgium, no. 8351/17, 9 July 2019.
López Ribalda and Others v. Spain [GC], nos. 1874/13 and 8567/13, 17 October 2019.
Oddone and Pecci v. San Marino, nos. 26581/17 and 31024/17, 17 October 2019.
Ilias and Ahmed v. Hungary [GC], no. 47287/15, 21 November 2019.
Breyer v. Germany, no. 50001/12, 30 January 2020.
Sanofi Pasteur v. France, no. 25137/16, 13 February 2020.
Beeler v. Switzerland [GC], no. 78630/12, 20 October 2020.
Napotnik v. Romania, no. 33139/13, 20 October 2020.
Guðmundur Andri Ástráðsson v. Iceland [GC], no. 26374/18, 1 December 2020.
Gestur Jónsson and Ragnar Halldór Hall v. Iceland [GC], nos. 68273/14 and 68271/14, 22 December 2020.
Georgia v. Russia (II) [GC], no. 38263/08, 21 January 2021.
Jurčić v. Croatia, no. 54711/15, 4 February 2021.
R.R. and Others v. Hungary, no. 36037/17, 2 March 2021.
Bivolaru and Moldovan v. France, nos. 40324/16 and 12623/17, 25 March 2021.
Liebscher v. Austria, no. 5434/17, 6 April 2021.
K.I. v. France, no. 5560/19, 15 April 2021.
Caamaño Valle v. Spain, no. 43564/17, 11 May 2021.
Centrum för rättvisa v. Sweden [GC], no. 35252/08, 25 May 2021.
Big Brother Watch and Others v. the United Kingdom [GC], nos. 58170/13 and 2 others, 25 May 2021.
Jessica Marchi v. Italy, no. 54978/17, 27 May 2021.
Norwegian Confederation of Trade Unions (LO) and Norwegian Transport Workers' Union (NTF) v. Norway, no. 45487/17, 10 June 2021.
Quintanel v. France, no. 12528/17, 17 June 2021.
Hurbain v. Belgium, no. 57292/16, 22 June 2021.
Reczkowicz v. Poland, no. 43447/19, 22 July 2021.
Toplak and Mrak v. Slovenia, nos. 34591/19 and 42545/19, 26 October 2021.
Biancardi v. Italy, no. 77419/16, 25 November 2021.
Dolińska-Ficek and Ozimek v. Poland, nos. 49868/19 and 57511/19, 8 November 2021.
Willems v. the Netherlands (dec.), no. 57294/16, 9 November 2021.
Ekimdzhiev and Others v. Bulgaria, no. 70078/12, 11 January 2022.
Jivan v. Romania, no. 62250/19, 8 February 2022.
Grzęda v. Poland [GC], no. 43572/18, 15 March 2022.

Y and Others v. Bulgaria, no. 9077/18, 22 March 2022.
Arnar Helgi Lárusson v. Iceland, no. 23077/19, 31 May 2022.
Drelon v. France, nos. 3153/16 and 27758/18, 8 September 2022.
Pinkas and Others v. Bosnia and Herzegovina, no. 8701/21, 4 October 2022.
Muhammad v. Spain, no. 34085/17, 18 October 2022.
Basu v. Germany, no. 215/19, 18 October 2022.
Moraru v. Romania, no. 64480/19, 8 November 2022.
Spasov v. Romania, no. 27122/14, 6 December 2022.
Moraru and Marin v. Romania, nos. 53282/18 and 31428/20, 20 December 2022.
Fedotova and Others v. Russia [GC], nos. 40792/10 and 2 others, 17 January 2023.
Duğan v. Türkiye, no. 84543/17, 7 February 2023.
Halet v. Luxembourg [GC], no. 21884/18, 14 February 2023.
L.B. v. Hungary [GC], no. 36345/16, 9 March 2023.
Georgiou v. Greece, no. 57378/18, 14 March 2023.
Jehovah's Witnesses v. Finland, no. 31172/19, 9 May 2023.
Sanchez v. France [GC], no. 45581/15, 15 May 2023.
A.E. v. Bulgaria, no. 53891/20, 23 May 2023.
Margari v. Greece, no. 36705/16, 20 June 2023.
Hurbain v. Belgium [GC], no. 57292/16, 4 July 2023.
Gluhkin v. Russia, no. 11519/20, 4 July 2023.
Tuleya v. Poland, nos. 21181/19 and 51751/20, 6 July 2023.
S.E. v. Serbia, no. 61365/16, 11 July 2023.
N.F. and Others v. Russia, nos. 3537/15 and 8 others, 12 September 2023.
Valiullina and Others v. Latvia, nos. 56928/19 and 2 others, 14 September 2023.
Luca v. the Republic of Moldova, no. 55351/17, 17 October 2023.
Podchasov v. Russia, no. 33696/19, 13 February 2024.
Executief van de Moslims van België and Others v. Belgium, nos. 16760/22 and 8 others, 13 February 2024.
Duarte Agostinho and Others v. Portugal and 32 Others [GC], no. 39371/20, 9 April 2024.
M.B. v. the Netherlands, no. 71008/16, 23 April 2024.

3.2. Court of Justice of the European Union

Case C-1/58, *Stork*, 4 February 1959, ECLI:EU:C:1959:4.
Cases C-36, 37, 38–59 and 40–59, *Geitling*, 15 July 1960, ECLI:EU:C:1960:36.
Case C-26/62, *Van Gend & Loos*, 5 February 1963, ECLI:EU:C:1963:1.
Case C-6/64, *Costa v. Enel*, 15 July 1964, ECLI:EU:C:1964:66.
Case C-40/64, *Sgarlata*, 1 April 1965, ECLI:EU:C:1965:36.
Case C-29/69, *Stauder*, 12 November 1969, ECLI:EU:C:1969:57.
Case C-11/70, *Internationale Handelsgesellschaft*, 17 December 1970, ECLI:EU:C:1970:114.
Case C-80/70, *Defrenne I*, 25 May 1971, ECLI:EU:C:1971:55.
Case C-4/73, *Nold*, 14 May 1974, ECLI:EU:C:1974:51.
Case C-36/75, *Rutili*, 28 October 1975, ECLI:EU:C:1975:137.
Case C-43/75, *Defrenne II*, 8 April 1976, ECLI:EU:C:1976:56.
Case C-106/77, *Simmenthal*, 9 March 1978, ECLI:EU:C:1978:49.

Case C-149/77, *Defrenne III*, 15 June 1978, ECLI:EU:C:1978:130.

Case C-44/79, *Hauer*, 13 December 1979, ECLI:EU:C:1979:290.

Case C-125/79, *Bernard Denilauler v. SNC Couchet Frères*, 21 May 1980, ECLI:EU:C:1980:130.

Case C-14/83, *Von Colson*, 10 April 1984, ECLI:EU:C:1984:153.

Case C-170/84, *Bilka*, 13 May 1986, ECLI:EU:C:1986:204.

Case C-222/84, *Marguerite Johnston*, 15 May 1986, ECLI:EU:C:1986:206.

Case C-12/86, *Demirel*, 30 September 1987, ECLI:EU:C:1987:400.

Case C-24/86, *Blaizot*, 2 February 1988, ECLI:EU:C:1988:43.

Case C-5/88, *Wachauf*, 13 July 1989, ECLI:EU:C:1989:321.

Joined Cases C-46/87 and 227/88, *Hoescht*, 21 September 1989, ECLI:EU:C:1989:337.

Case, C-374/87, *Orkem*, 18 October 1989, ECLI:EU:C:1989:387.

Case C-260/89, *ERT*, 18 June 1991, ECLI:EU:C:1991:254.

Case C-271/9, *Marshall*, 2 August 1993, ECLI:EU:C:1993:335.

Case C-127/92, *Enderby*, 27 October 1993, ECLI:EU:C:1993:859.

Case C-450/93, *Kalanke*, 17 October 1995, ECLI:EU:C:1995:322.

Case *Opinion 2/94*, 28 March 1996, ECLI:EU:C:1996:140.

Case C-13/94, *P v. S and Cornwall County Council*, 30 April 1996, ECLI:EU:C:1996:170.

Case C-299/95, *Kremzow*, 29 May 1997, ECLI:EU:C:1997:254.

Case C-249/96, *Grant*, 17 February 1998, ECLI:EU:C:1998:63.

Case T-347/94, *Mayr-Melnhof*, 14 May 1998, EU:T:1998:101.

Case C-185/95 P, *Baustahlgewebe*, 17 December 1998, ECLI:EU:C:1998:608.

Case C-50/96, *Schröder*, 10 February 2000, ECLI:EU:C:2000:72.

Case C-196/98, *Hepple*, 23 May 2000, ECLI:EU:C:2000:278.

Case C-376/98, *Tobacco Advertising*, 5 October 2000, ECLI:EU:C:2000:544.

Case T-112/98, *Mannesmannröhren-Werke*, 20 February 2001, ECLI:EU:T:2001:61.

Case C-94/00, *Roquette Frères*, 22 October 2002, ECLI:EU:C:2002:603.

Case C-112/00, *Schmidberger*, 12 June 2003, ECLI:EU:C:2003:333.

Case C-482/01, *Orfanopoulos*, 29 April 2004, ECLI:EU:C:2004:262.

Case C-36/02, *Omega Spielhallen*, 14 October 2004, ECLI:EU:C:2004:614.

Case C-387/02, *Berlusconi*, 3 May 2005, ECLI:EU:C:2005:270.

Case C-144/04, *Mangold*, 22 November 2005, ECLI:EU:C:2005:709.

Case C-540/03, *Parliament v. Council*, 27 June 2006, ECLI:EU:C:2005:517.

Case T-404/06 P, *Pia Landgren*, 26 October 2006, ECLI:EU:T:2009:313.

Case C-450/06, *Varec*, 14 February 2008, ECLI:EU:C:2008:91.

Case T-99/04, *Treuhand*, 8 July 2008, ECLI:EU:T:2008:256.

Case C-303/06, *S. Coleman v. Attridge Law and Steve Law*, 17 July 2008, ECLI:EU:C:2008:415.

Joined Cases C-402/05 P and C-415/05 P, *Kadi*, 3 September 2008, ECLI:EU:C:2008:461.

Case C-73/07, *Tietosuojavaltuutettu v. Satakunnan Markkinapörssi Oy and Satamedia Oy*, 16 December 2008, ECLI:EU:C:2008:727.

Case C-465/07, *Elgafaji*, 17 February 2009, ECLI:EU:C:2009:94.

Case C-237/09, *Belgium v. De Fruytier*, 3 June 2010, ECLI:EU:C:2010:316.

Joined Cases C-92/09 and C-93/09, *Volker and Eifert*, 9 November 2010, ECLI:EU:C:2010:662.

Opinion 1/09 of 8 March 2011, ECLI:EU:C:2011:123.

Joined Cases C-3989/07 and 38353/07, *Ullens de Schooten and Rezabek v. Belgium*, 20 September 2011.

Case C-617/10, *Åkerberg Fransson*, 26 February 2013, ECLI:EU:C:2013:105.

Joined Cases C-335/11 and C-337/11, *HK Danmark*, 11 April 2013, ECLI:EU:C:2013:222.

Case C-291/12, *Schwarz*, 17 October 2013, ECLI:EU:C:2013:670.

Case C-293/12 and C-594/12, *Digital Rights Ireland*, 8 April 2014, ECLI:EU:C:2014:238.

Case C-510/11, *Kone*, 5 June 2014, ECLI:EU:C:2013:696.

Case C-166/13, *Mukarubega*, 5 November 2014, ECLI:EU:C:2014:2336.

Case C-131/12, *Google Spain*, 13 May 2014, ECLI:EU:C:2014:317.

Case *Opinion 2/13*, 18 December 2014, ECLI:EU:C:2014:2454.

Case C-83/14, *CHEZ*, 16 July 2015, ECLI:EU:C:2015:480.

Joined Cases C-404/15 and C-659/15 PPU, *Aranyosi*, 5 April 2016, ECLI:EU:C:2016:198.

Case C-362/14, *Schrems I*, 6 October 2015, ECLI:EU:C:2015:650.

Case C-582/14, *Breyer*, 19 October 2016, ECLI:EU:C:2016:779.

Case C-203/15, *Tele2 Sverige AB*, 21 December 2016, ECLI:EU:C:2016:970.

Case C-174/16, *H.*, 7 September 2017, ECLI:EU:C:2017:637.

Case C-64/16, *Associação Sindical dos Juíes Portugueses*, 27 February 2018, ECLI:EU:C:2018:117.

Case C-414/16, *Egenberger*, 17 April 2018, ECLI:EU:C:2018:257.

Case C-25/17, *Jehovan todistajat*, 10 July 2018, ECLI:ECLI:EU:C:2018:551.

Case C-207/16, *Ministerio fiscal*, 2 October 2018, ECLI:EU:C:2018:788.

Case C-55/18, *Federación de Servicios de Comisiones Obreras*, 14 May 2019, ECLI:EU:C:2019:402.

Case C-573/17, *Polawski II*, 24 June 2019, ECLI:EU:C:2019:530.

Case C-467/18, *Rayonna prokuratura Lom*, 19 September 2019, ECLI:EU:C:2019:765.

Case C-136/17, *GC and others*, 24 September 2019, ECLI:EU:C:2019:773.

Case C-507/17, *Google*, 24 September 2019, ECLI:EU:C:2019:772.

Joined Cases C-542/18 RX-II and 543/18 RX-II, *Erik Simpson and HG v. Council of the European Union and European Commission*, 26 March 2020, ECLI:EU:C:2020:232.

Case C-507/18, *Associazione Avvocatura per i diritti LGBTI*, 23 April 2020, ECLI:EU:C:2020:289.

Joined Cases C-924/19 PPU & 925/19 PPU, *FMS and Others*, 14 May 2020, ECLI:EU:C:2020:367.

Case C-311/18, *Schrems II*, 16 June 2020, ECLI:EU:C:2015:650.

Case C-264/19, *Constantin Film*, 9 July 2020, ECLI:EU:C:2020:542.

Case C-223/19, *YS v. NK*, 24 September 2020, ECLI:EU:C:2020:753.

Case C-623/17, *Privacy International*, 6 October 2020, ECLI:EU:C:2020:790.

Joined Cases C-511/18, 512/18 & C-520/18, *La Quadrature du Net and Others*, 6 October 2020, ECLI:EU:C:2020:791.

Case C-336/19, *Centraal Israëlitisch Consistorie van België and Others*, 17 December 2020, ECLI:EU:C:2020:1031.

Case C-808/18, *Commission v. Hungary*, 17 December 2020, ECLI:EU:C:2020:1029.

Case C-589/19, *Academia de Studii Economice din București Judgment*, 17 March 2021, ECLI:EU:C:2017:637.

Joined Cases C-804/18 and C-341/19, *WABE*, 15 July 2021, ECLI:EU:C:2021:594.

Case C-791/19, *Commission v. Poland*, 15 July 2021, ECLI:EU:C:2021:596.

Case C-350/20, *O.D.*, 2 September 2021, ECLI:EU:C:2021:659.

Case C-561/19, *Consorzio Italian Management*, 6 October 2021, ECLI:EU:C:2021:799.

Case C-564/19, *IS*, 23 November 2021, ECLI:EU:C:2021:949.

Case C-282/19, *MIUR*, 13 January 2022, ECLI:EU:C:2022:3.

Case C-242/22 PPU, *Criminal proceedings against TL*, 1 August 2022, ECLI:EU:C:2022:611.

Case C-348/21, *HYA and Others*, 8 December 2022, ECLI:EU:C:2022:965.

Case C-699/21, *EDL*, 18 April 2023, ECLI:EU:C:2023:295.

Case C-29/22 P, *KS and KD v. Council of the European Union and Others*, 10 September 2024, ECLI:EU:C:2024:725.

4. Literature

Aertgeerts, P., 'Between Unity and Diversity: EU Data Protection Legislation as a Catalyst for a Constitutional Trilogue', in M. Sahadžić et al. (ed.), *Accommodating Diversity in Multilevel Constitutional Orders: Legal Mechanisms of Divergence and Convergence*, London, Routledge, 2023, pp. 70–90.

Alston, P. and Weiler, J., 'An "Ever Closer Union" in Need of a Human Rights Policy: The European Union and Human Rights', in P. Alston (ed.), *The EU and Human Rights*, Oxford, Oxford University Press, 1999, pp. 3–68.

Ambrus, M., 'Comparative Law Method in the Jurisprudence of the European Court of Human Rights in the Light of the Rule of Law', *Erasmus Law Review*, 2009, pp. 353–371.

Arnardottir, O.M., *Equality and non-discrimination under the European Convention on Human Rights*, Nijhoff, 2003.

Arnardóttir, O.M., 'The differences that make a difference: recent developments on the discrimination grounds and the margin of appreciation under Article 14 of the European Convention on Human Rights', *Human Rights Law Review*, 2014, pp. 647–670.

Arnardottir, O.M, 'Cross-fertilisation, Clarity and Consistency at an Overburdened European Court of Human Rights-the Case of the Discrimination Grounds under Article 14 ECHR', *Nordic Journal of Human Rights*, 2015, pp. 220–242.

Arnadóttir, O. and Guðmundsdóttir, A., 'Speaking the Same Language? Comparing Judicial Restraint at the ECtHR and the ECJ', in O. Arnadóttir and A. Buyse (eds.), *Shifting Centres of Gravity in Human Rights Protection, Rethinking relations between the ECHR, EU and national legal orders*, London, Routledge, 2016, pp. 161–182

Arnadóttir, O. and Buyse, A. (eds.), *Shifting Centres of Gravity in Human Rights Protection, Rethinking Relations Between the ECHR, EU and National Legal Orders*, London, Routledge, 2016, p. 222.

Bailleux, A. and Van Meerbeeck, J., 'Droits de l'homme, droit pénal et droit communautaire à Luxembourg : Enjeux, difficultés et paradoxes d'un ménage à trois', in Y. Cartuyvels, H. Dumont, F. Ost, M. Van de Kerchove and S. Van Drooghenbroeck (eds.), *Les droits de l'homme, bouclier ou épée du droit pénal?*, Brussels, FUSL, 2007, pp. 111–174.

Bailleux, A., Cartuyvels Dumont, Y.-H. and Ost, F., *Traduction et droits européens – Enjeux d'une rencontre, Hommage au recteur Michel Van de Kerchove*, Brussels FUSL, 2009.

Bailleux, A., 'Human Rights in Network', *Journal européen des droits de l'Homme*, 2014, pp. 293–325.

Bailleux, A. and Bribosia, E., 'La protection des droits fondamentaux', in A. Bailleux (ed.), *Actualités du contentieux européen*, Louvain-la-Neuve, Anthemis, 2020, pp. 107–155.

Barkhuysen, T. and Emmerik, M.L., 'Legitimacy of European Court of Human Rights Judgments: Procedural aspects', in N. Huls, M. Adams and J. Bomhoff (eds.), *The legitimacy of Highest Courts' rulings: judicial deliberations and beyond*, The Hague, T.M.C. Asser Press, 2008, pp. 437–449.

Barnard, C. and Deakin, S., 'In Search of Coherence: Social Policy, the Single Market and Fundamental Rights', *Industrial Relations Journal*, 2000, pp. 341–345.

Beijer, M., *The Limits of Fundamental Rights Protection by the EU. The Scope for the Development of Positive Obligations*, Brussels, Intersentia, 2017.

Bell, B., 'The principle of equal treatment: widening and deepening', in P Craig and G de Búrca (ed), *The evolution of EU law*, Oxford, Oxford University Press, 2011, pp. 611–639.

Bell, M., *Anti-Discrimination Law and the European Union*, Oxford, Oxford University Press, 2002.

Besselink, L., 'The European Union and the European Convention on Human Rights: From Sovereign Immunity in Bosphorus to Full Scrutiny Under the Reform Treaty?', in I. Boerefijn and J. Goldschmidt (eds.), *Changing Perceptions of Sovereignty and Human Rights, Essays in Honour of Cees Flinterman*, Brussels, Intersentia, 2008, pp. 295–309.

Besson, S., 'Gender Discrimination under EU and ECHR Law: Never Shall the Twain Meet?', *Human Rights Law Review*, 2008.

Bobek, M and Adams- Prassl, J. (eds.), *The EU Charter of Fundamental Rights in the Member States*, Oxford, Hart Publishing, 2020.

von Bogdandy, A., 'The European Union as a Human Rights Organization? Human Rights and the Core of the European Union', *Common Market Law Review*, 2000, pp. 1307–1338.

von Bodgdandy, A. and Venzke, I., *In Whose Name? A Public Law Theory of International Adjudication*, Oxford, Oxford University Press, 2014.

Bradford, A. 'The Brussels Effect', *Northwestern University Law Review*, 2012, pp. 1–64.

Bradford, A., *The Brussels effect: How the European Union rules the world*, Oxford, Oxford University Press, 2020.

Brems, E., 'Smart Human Rights Integration', in E. Brems and S. Ouald Chaib (eds.), *Fragmentation and Integration in Human Rights Law: Users' Perspectives*, Cheltenham, Edward ElgarPublishing, 2018, pp. 165–194.

Bribosia, E. and Van Drooghenbroeck, S., 'Emprunts et migrations entre le droit de l'Union européenne et celui du Conseil de l'Europe', in A. Bailleux, Y. Cartuyvels, H. Dumont and F. Ost (eds.), *Traduction et droits européens: enjeux d'une rencontre*, Brussels, FUSL, 2009, pp. 133–179.

Butler, I., 'Ensuring Compliance with the Charter of Fundamental Rights in Legislative Drafting: The Practice of the European Commission', *European Law Review*, 2012, pp. 397–418.

Callewaert, J., 'Convergences et divergences dans la protection européenne des droits fondamentaux', *Journal de droit européen*, 2016, pp. 166–174.

Callewaert, J, Do we still need Article 6(2) TEU? Considerations on the absence of EU accession to the ECHR and its consequences', *Common Market Law Review*, 2018, pp. 1685–1716.

Callewaert, J., 'Interactions migratoires entre Strasbourg et Luxembourg', *Journal de droit européen*, 2020, pp. 310–318.

Callewaert, J., 'Convention Control Over the Application of Union Law by National Judges: The Case for a Wholistic Approach to Fundamental Rights', *European Papers*, 2023, pp. 331–347.

Carozza, P., 'Uses and Misuses of Comparative Law in International Human Rights: Some Reflections on the Case-law of the European Court of Human Rights', *Notre Dame Law Review*, 1998, pp. 1217–1238.

COLEMAN, J.S., 'Comment on "On the Concept of Influence"', *Public Opinion Quarterly*, 1963, pp. 63–82.

MC CRUDDEN, C., 'Common Law of Human Rights? Transnational Judicial Conversations on Constitutional Rights', *Oxford Journal of Legal Studies*, 2000, pp. 499–532.

DAVIO, V., 'Le droit fondamental à la protection des données personnelles : illustrations, principes et limites', in B. DOCQUIR (ed.), *Le RGPD dans la pratique : un exercice d'équilibre*, Brussels, Larcier, 2021, pp. 9–40.

DAVIO, V., 'Detention in the Hungarian transit zones: A case of higher fundamental rights protection by EU law vis-à-vis the ECHR', *European Law Review*, 2022, pp. 393–409.

DAVIO, V. and MUIR, E.,'Introduction. The ECHR in the CJEU's Case-law Post-Charter: A Dual Perspective', *European Papers*, 2023, pp. 317–322.

DAVIO, V., 'Le droit de l'Union européenne dans la jurisprudence de la Cour européenne des droits de l'homme', *Journal des Tribunaux - Droit Européen* 2023, 2023, pp. 46–50

DAUTRICOURT, C., 'A Strasbourg Perspective on the Autonomous Development of Fundamental Rights in EU Law: Trends and Implications', *Jean Monnet Working Paper Series*, 2010, pp. 1–70.

DAUSES, A., 'The Protection of Fundamental Rights in the Community Legal Order', *European Law Review*, 1985, pp. 398–419.

DAWSON, M., *The Governance of EU Fundamental Rights*, Cambridge, Cambridge University Press, 2017.

DZEHTSIAROU, K., 'Comparative Law in the Reasoning of the European Court of Human Rights', *University College Dublin Law Review*, 2010, pp. 109–140

DZEHTSIAROU, K., 'Does Consensus Matter? Legitimacy of European Consensus in the Case-law of the European Court of Human Rights', *Public Law*, 2011, pp. 534–555.

DZEHTSIAROU, K. and LUKASHEVICH, V., 'Informed Decision-Making: The Comparative Endeavours of the Strasbourg Court', *Netherlands Quarterly of Human Rights*, 2012, pp. 272–298.

DZEHTSIAROU, K., KONSTADINIDES, T., LOCK, T. and O'MEARA, N. (eds.), *Human Rights Law in Europe: The Influence, Overlaps and Contradictions of the EU and the ECHR*, London, Routledge, 2014.

DZEHTSIAROU, K., *European Consensus and the Legitimacy of the European Court of Human Rights*, Cambridge, Cambridge University Press, 2015.

DZEHTSIAROU, K. 'What Is Law for the European Court of Human Rights?', *Georgetown Journal of International Law*, 2017, pp. 89–134.

DE BÚRCA, G., 'The Drafting of the EU Charter of Fundamental Rights', *European Law Review*, 2001, pp. 126–138.

DE BÚRCA, G. and ASCHENBRENNER, J., 'The Development of European Constitutionalism and the Role of the EU Charter of Fundamental Rights', *Columbia Journal of European Law*, 2003, pp. 355–382.

DE BÚRCA, G., 'The Road not Taken: the European Union as a Global Human Rights Actor', *The American Journal of International Law*, 2011, pp. 649–693.

DE BÚRCA, G., 'The Evolution of EU Human Rights Law', in P. CRAIG and G. DE BÚRCA (eds.), *The Evolution of EU Law*, Oxford, Oxford University Press, 2011, pp. 465–497.

DE BÚRCA, G., 'The Trajectories of European and American Antidiscrimination Law', *The American Journal of Comparative Law*, 2012, pp. 1–22.

DE BÚRCA, G., 'After the EU Charter of Fundamental Rights: The Court of Justice as a Human Rights Adjudicator?', *Maastricht Journal of European and Comparative Law*, 2013, pp. 168–184.

Deftou, M.-L., *Exporting the European Convention on Human Rights*, Oxford, Hart Publishing, 2022.

de Hert, P. and Gutwirth, S., 'Data Protection in the Case Law of Strasbourg and Luxemburg: Constitutionalisation in Action', in S. Gutwirth et al. (ed.), *Reinventing Data Protection*, Springer, 2009, pp. 3–44.

de Schutter, O., 'Les droits fondamentaux dans le projet européen. Des limites à l'action des institutions à une politique des droits fondamentaux', in O. De Schutter and P. Nihoul (eds.), *Une constitution pour l'Europe. Réflexions sur les transformations du droit de l'Union européenne*, Brussels, Larcier, 2004, pp. 81–117.

de Schutter, O., 'Fundamental Rights and the Transformation of Governance in the European Union', *Cambridge Yearbook of European Legal Studies*, 2007, pp. 133–175.

de Schutter, O., 'L'influence de la Cour européenne des droits de l'homme sur la Cour de justice des Communautés européennes', *CRIDHO Working Paper*, 2007, pp. 3–27.

de Schutter, O., 'The two Europes of Human Rights: the Emerging Division of Tasks Between the Council of Europe and the European Union in Promoting Human Rights in Europe', *Columbia Journal of European Law*, 2008, pp. 509–561.

de Witte, B., 'From a "Common Principle of Equality" to "European Antidiscrimination Law"', in *American Behavioral Scientist*, 2010, pp. 1715–1730.

de Witte, B., 'The Use of the ECHR and Convention Case-Law by the European Court of Justice', in P.C. Popelier Van de Heyning and P. Van Nuffel (eds.), *Human Rights Protection in the European legal Order: The Interaction Between the European and the National Courts*, Brussels, Intersentia, 2011, pp. 17–34.

de Witte, B. 'New Institutions for Promoting Equality in Europe: Legal Transfers, National Bricolage and European Governance', *The American Journal of Comparative Law*, 2012, pp. 49–74.

de Vries, S., Bernitz, U. and Weatherill, S. (eds.), *The EU Charter of Fundamental Rights as a Binding Instrument: Five Years Old and Growing*, Oxford, Hart Publishing, 2015.

Dickson, B., 'The EU Charter of Fundamental Rights in the Case-law of the European Court of Human Rights', *European Human Rights Law Review*, 2015, pp. 27–40.

di Federico, G. (ed.), *The EU Charter of Fundamental Rights: From Declaration to Binding Instrument*, Dordrecht, Springer Netherlands, 2011.

Douglas-Scott, S., 'The EU Charter of Fundamental Rights as a Constitutional Document', *European Human Rights Law Review*, 2004, pp. 1–10.

Douglas-Scott, S., 'A Tale of two Courts: Luxembourg, Strasbourg and the Growing European Human Rights Acquis', *Common Market Law Review*, 2006, pp. 629–665.

Douglas-Scott, S., 'The European Union and Human Rights after the Treaty of Lisbon', *Human Rights Law Review*, 2011, pp. 645–682.

Dubout, E. and Touze, S. (eds.), *Les droits fondamentaux: charnières entre ordres et systèmes juridiques*, Paris, Pedone 2009.

Dubout, E., 'The Protection of Fundamental Rights and the Allocation of Competences in the EU. A Clash of Constitutional Logics', in L. Azoulai (ed.), *The Question of Competence in the European Union*, Oxford, Oxford University Press, 2014, pp. 193–212.

Dubout, E., 'Une approche comparative du principe de non-discrimination dans le cadre européen : Convention européenne des droits de l'homme et droit de l'Union européenne', in M. Balboni (ed.), *The European Convention of Human Rights and the Principle of Non-Discrimination,* Naples, Editoriale Scientifica, 2017, pp. 63–120.

Duxbury, N. 'The Dynamics of Influence', in N. Duxbury (ed.), *Jurists and Judges: An Essay on Influence*, Oxford, Hart Publishing, 2001, pp. 5–22.

Eckes, C., 'EU accession to the ECHR: between autonomy and adaptation', *The Modern Law Review*, 2013, pp. 254–285.

Eeckhout, P., 'The EU Charter of Fundamental Rights and the Federal Question', *Common Market Law Review*, 2002, pp. 945–994.

Feyen, S., *Beyond Federal Dogmatics. The Influence of EU Law on Belgian Constitutional Case Law Regarding Federalism*, Leuven, Leuven University Press, 2013.

Forowicz, M., *The Reception of International Law in the European Court of Human Rights*, Oxford, Oxford University Press, 2010.

Fredman, S., 'Foreign Fads or Fashions? The Role of Comparativism in Human Rights Law', *International and Comparative Law Quarterly*, 2015, pp. 631–660.

Fredman, S., 'Emerging from the Shadows: Substantive Equality and Article 14 of the European Convention on Human Rights', *Human Rights Law Review*, 2016, pp. 273–301.

Frese, A. and Olsen, H., 'Spelling It Out-Convergence and Divergence in the Judicial Dialogue between CJEU and ECtHR', *Nordic Journal of International Law*, 2019, pp. 429–458.

Gambardella, I. and Davio, V., Introduction', in *EU Directives on Procedural Rights in Criminal Matters: 15 Years After the Roadmap, Where do We Stand, Where do We Go?*, EU Law Live, 2023.

Gellert, R. and Gutwirth, S., 'The legal construction of privacy and data protection', *The Computer Law and Security Report*, 2013, pp. 522–530.

Gerards, J., 'The Discrimination Grounds of Article 14 of the European Convention on Human Rights', *Human Rights Law Review*, 2013, pp. 99–124.

Gerards, J., 'Procedural Review by the ECtHR: A Typology', in J. Gerards and E. Brems (eds.), *Procedural Review in European Fundamental Rights Cases*, Cambridge, Cambridge University Press, 2017, pp. 127–160.

Gerards, J., 'Non-Discrimination, the European Court of Justice and the European Court of Human Rights: Who Takes the Lead?', in T. Giegerich (ed.), *The European Union as Protector and Promoter of Equality*, Cham, Springer, 2020, pp. 135–163.

Gerards, J., 'Systeemverklaringen voor verschillen tussen de gelijkebehandelingsrechtspraak van het HvJ EU en het EHRM', *SEW*, 2021, pp. 571–581.

Gerards, J., 'Article 53 ECHR and Minimum Protection by the European Court of Human Rights', *European Convention on Human Rights Law Review*, 2022, pp. 451–480.

Gless, S. and Martin, J., 'The Comparative Method in European Courts: A Comparison Between the CJEU and ECtHR?', *Bergen Journal of Criminal Law and Criminal Justice*, 2013, pp. 36–52.

Gonzalez Fuster, G. et Gellert, R., 'The Fundamental Right of Data Protection in the European Union: In Search of an Uncharted Right', *International Review of Law, Computers & Technology*, 2012, pp. 73–82.

Gonzalez Fuster, G., *The Emergence of Personal Data Protection as a Fundamental Right of the EU*, Brussels, Springer, 2014.

Gonzalez, G. and Gutwirth, S., 'Opening up personal data protection: A conceptual controversy', *The Computer Law and Security Report*, 2013, pp. 531–539.

Gragl, P., 'An Olive Branch from Strasbourg? Interpreting the European Court of Human Rights' Resurrection of Bosphorus and Reaction to Opinion 2/13 in the Avotiņš Case: ECtHR 23 May 2016, Case No. 17502/07, Avotiņš v Latvia', *European Constitutional Law Review*, 2017, pp. 551–567.

GREER, S. and WILLIAMS, A., 'Human Rights in the Council of Europe and the EU: Towards 'Individual', 'Constitutional' or 'Institutional' Justice?', *European Law Journal*, 2009, pp. 462–481.

GROUSSOT, X., AROLD LORENZ, N. and PETURSSON, G., 'The Paradox of Human Rights Protection in Europe: Two Courts, One Goal?', in O. ARNADOTTIR and A. BUYSE (eds.), *Shifting Centres of Gravity in Human Rights Protection, Rethinking Relations between the ECHR, EU and National Legal Orders*, London, Routledge, 2016, pp. 8–25.

HALBERSTAM, D., 'It's the Autonomy, Stupid! A Modest Defense of Opinion 2/13 on EU Accession to the ECHR, and the Way Forward' in *German Law Journal*, 2015, pp. 105–146.

HARPAZ, G., 'The European Court Of Justice And Its Relations With The European Court Of Human Rights: The Quest For Enhanced Reliance, Coherence And Legitimacy', *Common Market Law Review*, 2009, pp. 105–141.

HELFER,L., 'Consensus, Coherence and the European Convention on Human Rights', *Cornell International Law Journal*, 1993, pp. 133–165.

HENDRICKX, F., 'Article 8 – Protection of Personal Data.', in F.K. DORSSEMONT LÖRCHER, S. CLAUWAERT and M. SCHMITT (eds.), *The Charter of Fundamental Rights of the European Union and the Employment Relation*, Oxford, Hart Publishing, 2019, pp. 249–272.

HENNEBEL, L., 'Les références croisées entre les juridictions internationales des droits de l'Homme', in P. MARTENS et al. (ed.), *Le dialogue des juges*, Brussels, Bruylant, 2007, pp. 31–76.

HERMEREN, G., *Influence in Art and Literature*, Princeton, Princeton University Press, 2015.

IPPOLITO, F. and VELLUTI, S., 'The Relationship between the ECJ and the ECtHR: the Case of Asylum', in K. DZEHTSIAROU, T. KONSTADINIDES, T. LOCK and N. O'MEARA (eds.), *Human Rights Law in Europe: the Influence, Overlaps and Contradictions of the EU and ECHR*, London, Routledge, 2014, pp. 156–187.

JACQUÉ, J.-P., 'La charte des droits fondamentaux et le législateur de l'Union', in P. ILIOPOULOU and L. XENOU (eds.), *La Charte des droits fondamentaux, source de renouveau constitutionnel européen?*, Brussels, Bruylant, 2020, pp. 139–148.

KERIKMÄE, T. (ed.), *Protecting Human Rights in the EU. Controversies and Challenges of the Charter of Fundamental Rights*, Berlin, Springer, 2013.

KOKOTT, J. and SOBOTTA, C., 'The distinction between privacy and data protection in the jurisprudence of the CJEU and the ECtHR', *International Data Privacy Law*, 2013, pp. 222–228.

KRANENBORG, H., 'Article 8', in S.T. PEERS, J. HERVEY KENNER and A. WARD (eds.), *The EU Charter of Fundamental Rights. A Commentary*, Oxford, Hart Publishing, 2014, pp. 228–265.

KROMMENDIJK, J., 'The Use of ECtHR Case-law by the Court of Justice of the European Union: The View of Luxembourg Insiders', *Maastricht Journal of European and Comparative Law*, 2015, pp. 812–835.

LARCHÉ, M., *Les fonctions du droit international dans la jurisprudence de la Cour européenne des droits de l'Homme*, Paris, Pedone, 2025.

LAWSON, R., 'Confusion and Conflict? Divergent Interpretations of the ECHR in Strasbourg and Luxembourg', in R. LAWSON and M. DE BLOIJS (eds.), *The Dynamics of the Protection of Human Rights in Europe*, Dordrecht, Nijhoff, 1994, pp. 219–251.

LECONTE, C. and MUIR, E., 'Understanding Resistance to the EU Fundamental Rights Policy', *Human Rights Review*, 2014, pp. 13–24.

LEACH, P., 'Injunctive relief at the European Court of Human Rights – progress and push-back', in E. MUIR, S. GARBEN and I. GOVAERE (eds.), *Activating the Protection of Fundamental and Human Rights at European Level*, Oxford, Hart Publishing, forthcoming in 2025–2026.

LEMMENS, P., 'The Relations between the Charter of Fundamental Rights of the European Union and the European Convention on Human Rights. Substantive Aspects', *Maastricht Journal of European and Comparative Law*, 2001, pp. 49–67.

LEMMENS, P., 'The right to a fair trial and its multiple manifestations. Article 6(1) ECHR. Shaping Rights in the ECHR', in E. BREMS and J. GERARDS (eds.), *The Role of the European Court of Human Rights in Determining the Scope of Human Rights*, Cambridge, Cambridge University Press, 2013, pp. 294–314.

LEMMENS, P. and PIRET, M., 'The Charter of Fundamental Rights of the European Union and the European Convention on Human Rights, from the Perspective of the European Court of Human Rights', *Cahiers de droit européen*, 202_, pp. 13_–210.

LENAERTS, K., 'Respect for Fundamental Rights as a Constitutional Principle of the European Union', *Columbia Journal of European Law*, 2000, pp. 1–26.

LENAERTS, K. and DE SMIJTER, E., 'A 'Bill of Rights' for the European Union', *Common Market Law Review*, 2001, pp. 273–300.

LENAERTS, K.,'Exploring the Limits of the EU Charter of Fundamental Rights', *European Constitutional Law Review*, 2012, pp. 375–403.

LENAERTS, K., 'EU Values and Constitutional Pluralism: The EU System of Fundamental Rights Protection', *Polish Yearbook of International Law*, 2014, pp. 135–160.

LENAERTS, K. and GUTIÉRREZ-FONS, J., 'The Place of the Charter in the EU Constitutional Edifice', in S.T. PEERS, J. HERVEY KENNER and A. WARD (eds.), *The EU Charter of Fundamental Rights: A Commentary*, Oxford, Hart Publishing, 2014, pp. 1559–1594.

LENAERTS, K., 'La vie après l'avis: Exploring The Principle of Mutual (Yet Not Blind) Trust', *Common Market Law Review*, 2017, pp. 805–840.

LOCK, T., 'The ECJ and the ECtHR: The Future Relationship between the Two European Courts,' *Law and Practice of International Courts and Tribunals*, 2009, pp. 375–398.

LOCK, T., 'Beyond Bosphorus: The European Court of Human Rights' Case-law on the Responsibility of Member States of International Organisations under the European Convention on Human Rights', *Human Rights Law Review*, 2010, pp. 529–545

LOCK, T., 'EU Accession to the ECHR: Implications for the Judicial Review in Strasbourg', *European Law Review*, 2010, pp. 777–798.

LOCK, T., 'Walking on a tightrope: the draft ECHR accession agreement and the autonomy of the EU legal order', *Common Market Law Review*, 2011.

LOCK, T., *The European Court of Justice and International Courts*, Oxford, Oxford University Press, 2015.

LOCK, T., 'The Influence of EU law on Strasbourg Doctrines', *European Law Review*, 2016, pp. 804–825.

LOCK, T., 'The Future of EU Human Rights Law: Is Accession to the ECHR Still Desirable?', *Journal of International and Comparative Law*, 2020, pp. 428–447.

LOENEN, T. and VICKERS, L., 'More is Less? Multiple Protection of Human Rights in Europe and the Risks of Erosion of Human Rights Standards', in S. MORANO-FOADI and L. VICKERS (eds.), *Fundamental Rights in the EU. A Matter for Two Courts*, Oxford, Hart Publishing, 2015, pp. 159–178.

LORANS, Y., 'Le législateur européen et la protection des droits fondamentaux dans l'Union : vers une concrétisation législative de la Charte', *Revue trimestrielle de droit européen*, 2021, pp. 59–86.

LORANS, Y., *Le juge et le législateur de l'Union européenne. Étude d'une protection collaborative des droits fondamentaux*, PhD thesis, forthcoming.

LYNSKEY, O., 'Deconstructing data protection: the "added-value" of a right to data protection in the EU legal order, *International and Comparative Law Quarterly*, 2013, pp. 569–597.

LYNSKEY, O., *The foundations of EU data protection law*, Oxford, Oxford University Press, 2015.

LYNSKEY, O., 'Article 8: The Right to Data Protection', in M. BOBEK and J. ADAMS-PRASSL (eds.), *The EU Charter of Fundamental Rights in the Member States*, Oxford, Hart Publishing, 2020, pp. 353–370.

MAHONEY, P., 'The Comparative Method in Judgments of the European Court of Human Rights: Reference back to National Law' in G.M. Canivet Andenas, and F. Duncan (ed), *Comparative Law Before the Courts, British Institute of International and Comparative Law*, 2004, pp. 135–150.

MEGURO, M., 'Tracing Influence in International Law: Beyond the Antagonism between Doctrine of Law and Social Science', *Amsterdam Law School Research Paper*, 2020, pp. 1–27.

VAN DER MEULEN, L., *National Courts as EU Fundamental Rights Courts: An analysis of Dutch, German and Belgian adjudication on fundamental rights exceptions to transfer decisions under the Dublin Regulation and the European Arrest Warrant*, PhD thesis, forthcoming.

VAN DER MEULEN, L., 'Another Exception to The Rule: The E.D.L Case on EAW Surrenders Of Seriously Ill Persons', *Common Market Law Review*, 2024, pp. 223–238.

MITSILEGAS, V. et al., 'Data retention and the future of large-scale surveillance: The evolution and contestation of judicial benchmarks', *European Law Journal*, 2022, pp. 1–36.

MOONEN, T., 'Special Investigation Techniques, Data Processing and Privacy Protection in the Jurisprudence of the European Court of Human Rights', *Pace International Law Review Online Companion*, 2010, pp. 97–136.

MORANO-FOADI, S.and VICKERS, L. (eds.), *Fundamental Rights in the EU. A Matter for Two Courts*, Oxford, Hart Publishing, 2015.

MORE, G., 'The Principle of Equal Treatment: From Market Unifier to Fundamental Right?', in P. Craig and G. De Burca (ed), *The Evolution of EU law*, 1st Edition, Oxford, Oxford University Press, 1999, 517-553.

MORIJN, J., 'Kissing Awake a Sleeping Beauty? The Charter of Fundamental Rights in EU and Member States' Policy Practice', in V.N. KOSTA SKOUTARIS and V. TZEVELEKOS (eds.), *EU Accession to the ECHR*, Oxford, Hart Publishing, 2014, pp. 123–139.

MORIJN, J., 'Post-Lisbon Civil Rights Protection by the EU's Political Institutions' in S. DE VRIES, H. DE WAELE and M.-P. GRANGER (eds.), *Civil Rights and EU Citizenship*, Cheltenham, Edward Elgar Publishing, 2018, pp. 14–42.

MÖSCHEL, M., 'European Convention of Human Rights/Council of Europe', in M. MERCAT-BRUNS, D. OPPENHEIMER and C. SARTORIUS (eds.), *Comparative Perspectives on the Enforcement and Effectiveness of Antidiscrimination Law. Ius Comparatum - Global Studies in Comparative Law*, Cheltenham, Edward Elgar Publishing, 2018.

MÖSCHEL, M., 'Comparing the activist claim between Strasbourg and Luxembourg in the field of non-discrimination', in B. DE WITTE, M. DAWSON and E. MUIR (eds.), *Revisiting*

Judicial Politics in the European Union, Cheltenham, Edward Elgar Publishing, 2024, pp. 334–351.

Muir, E., 'The transformative function of EU equality law', *European Review of Private Law* 2013, pp. 1231–1254.

Muir, E., Dawson, M. and Claes, M., 'A tool-box for legal and political mobilisation in European equality law', in *Rights in pursuit of social change- legal mobilisation in the multi-level European system*, Oxford, Hart Publishing, 2014, pp. 105–126

Muir, E., 'Fundamental Rights: an Unsettling EU Competence', *Human Rights Review*, 2014, pp. 25–37.

Muir, E., 'The Fundamental Rights Implications of EU Legislation: Some Constitutional Challenges', *Common Market Law Review*, 2014, pp. 219–245.

Muir, E., *EU Equality Law as the 'First' Fundamental Rights Policy of the EU*, Oxford, Oxford University Press, 2018, p. 256.

Muir, E., *EU Fundamental Rights Legislation: The Constitutional Imbroglio. Critical Reflections on Constitutional Democracy in the European Union*, Oxford, Hart Publishing, 2019, pp. 93–114.

Muir, E., 'Reshuffling our understanding of fundamental rights law in Europe: an EU lawyer's research agenda', *European Human Rights Law Review*, 2021, pp. 142–148.

Muir, E., Davio, V. and Van der Meulen, L., 'The Horizontal Clauses (arts 8 & 10 TFEU and Their Contribution to the Course of EU Equality Law: Still an Empty Vessel', *European Papers*, 2022, pp. 1381–1403.

Müller, A. (ed.), *Judicial Dialogue and Human Rights*, Cambridge, Cambridge University Press, 2017.

Murray, J., 'The Influence of the European Convention on Fundamental Rights on Community Law', *Fordham International Law Journal*, 2011, pp. 1388–1422.

Nagel, J., *The Descriptive Analysis of Power*, Yale University Press, 1975.

Nusserberg, A., 'La prise en compte de la Charte des droits fondamentaux par la Cour européenne des droits de l'homme', in P. Iliopoulou and L. Xenou (eds.), *La Charte des droits fondamentaux, source de renouveau constitutionnel européen?*, Brussels, Bruylant, 2020, pp. 69–75.

O'Connell, R., 'Cinderella Comes to the Ball: Art 14 and the Right to Non-discrimination in the ECHR', *Legal Studies*, 2009, pp. 211–229.

O'Leary, S., 'The Relationship Between Community Citizenship and the Protection of Fundamental Rights in Community Law', *Common Market Law Review*, 1995, pp. 519–554.

O'Leary, S., 'Courts, Charters and Conventions', *The Irish Jurist*, 2016, pp. 4–41.

O'Leary, S., 'A tale of two Cities: fundamental rights protection in Strasbourg and Luxembourg', *Cambridge Yearbook of European Legal Studies*, 2018, pp. 3–31.

O'Leary, S., '*Balancing Rights in a Digital age*', Irish Jurist, 2018, pp. 59–92.

O'Leary, S., 'The EU Charter Ten Years On: A View from Strasbourg', in M. Bobek and J. Adams-Prassl (eds.), *The EU Charter of Fundamental Rights in the Member States*, Oxford, Hart Publishing, 2020, pp. 37–68.

Ost, F., *Le droit comme traduction*, Presses de l'université de Laval, 2009.

Ost, F., *Traduire. Défense et illustration du multilinguisme*, Paris, Fayard, 2009.

Parsons, T., 'On the concept of influence', *Public opinion quarterly*, 1963, pp. 52–53.

Peers, S., 'Bosphorus – European Court of Human Rights: Limited responsibility of European Union member states for actions within the scope of Community law.

Judgment of 30 June 2005, Bosphorus Airways v. Ireland, Application No. 45036/98', *European Constitutional Law Review*, 2006, pp. 443–455.

Peers, S., Hervey, T, Kenner, J. and Ward, A. (eds.), *The EU Charter of Fundamental Rights: A Commentary*, Oxford, Hart Publishing, 2014.

Peers, S., 'The EU's Accession to the ECHR: The Dream Becomes a Nightmare', *German Law Journal*, 2015, pp. 213–222.

Penninckx, E., 'The organisation of the internal work of the ECtHR', in E. Muir, S. Garben and I. Govaere (eds.), *Activating the Protection of Fundamental and Human Rights at European Level*, Oxford, Hart Publishing, forthcoming in 2025–2026.

Pescatore, P., 'Les droits de l'homme et l'intégration européenne', *Cahiers du droit européen*, 1968, pp. 629–673.

Pescatore, P., 'Fundamental Rights and Freedoms in the System of the European Communities', *American Journal of Comparative Law*, 1970, pp. 343–351

Pescatore, P. 'The Context and Significance of Fundamental Rights Law of the European Communities', *Human Rights Journal*, 1981, pp. 295–308.

Psychogiopoulou, E., 'The European Court of Human Rights, Privacy and Data Protection in the Digital Era', in E. Psychogiopoulou and (ed.), *Courts, Privacy and Data Protection in the Digital Environment*, 2017, pp. 32–62.

Psychogiopoulou, E., 'Judicial Dialogue and Digitalization: CJEU Engagement with ECtHR Case Law and Fundamental Rights Standards in the EU', *JIPITEC*, 2022, pp. 145–159.

Psychogiopoulou, E. and. de la Sierra, S. (eds.), *Digital Media Governance and Supranational Courts: Selected Issues and Insights from the European Judiciary*, Cheltenham, Edward Elgar Publishing, 2022.

Quinn, G., 'The European Union and the Council of Europe on Human Rights Issues: Twins Separated at Birth', *McGill Law Journal*, 2001, pp. 849–874.

Rodota, S., 'Data Protection as a Fundamental Right', in S. Gutwirth et al. (ed.), *Reinventing Data Protection*, Springer, 2009, pp. 77–83.

Rosas, A., 'Fundamental Rights in the Luxembourg and Strasbourg Courts', in C. Baudenbacher, P. Tresselt and T. Orlygsson (eds.), *The EFTA Court: Ten Years On*, Oxford, Hart Publishing, 2005, pp. 163–178.

Scarcello, O., *Contestatory Federalism and Rights: Incorporation and Contestation in the US, Canada, and the EU*, forthcoming.

Scheeck, L., 'Solving Europe's Binary Human Rights Puzzle: The Interaction between Supranational Courts as a Parameter of European Governance', *Questions de recherche/ Research Questions, Centre d'études et de recherches internationales Sciences Po*, 2005, pp. 1–64.

Schermers, H., 'The European Communities Bound by Fundamental Human Rights', *Common Market Law Review*, 1990, pp. 249–258.

Schütze, R., 'Three 'Bills of Rights' for the European Union', *Yearbook of European Law*, 2011, pp. 131–158.

Scruton, R., *A Dictionary of Political Thought*, New York, Macmillan, 1996.

Simon, D., 'Des influences réciproques entre CJCE et CEDH: "Je t'aime, moi non plus"?', *Pouvoirs*, 2001, pp. 31–49.

Spielmann, D., 'Human Rights Case-Law in the Strasbourg and Luxembourg Courts: Conflicts, Inconsistencies and Complementarities', in P.M. Alston Butselo and J. Heenan (eds.), *The EU and Human Rights*, Oxford, Oxford University Press, 1999, pp. 757–780.

van der Sloot, B., 'Wij zijn twee vriendjes, jij en ik: De innige tango van de twee Europese hoven op het gebied van privacy en gegevensbescherming', *S.E.W.*, 2021, pp. 582–594.

Rizcallah, C. and Davio, V. 'The Requirement that Tribunals be Established by Law: A Valuable Principle Safeguarding the Rule of Law and the Separation of Powers in a Context of Trust', *European Constitutional Law Review*, 2021, pp. 581–606.

Rizcallah, C., 'The principle of mutual trust and the protection of fundamental rights in the Area of Freedom, Security and Justice: A critical look at the Court of Justice's stone-by-stone approach', *Maastricht Journal of European and Comparative Law*, 2023, pp. 255–272.

Rizcallah, C., 'The Systemic Equivalence Test and the Presumption of Equivalent Protection in European Human Rights Law – A Critical Appraisal', *German Law Journal*, 2023, pp. 1062–1077.

Rizcallah, C., *The European Union and Human Rights. Unlocking the opportunities and challenges of a singular regional player*, forthcoming.

Rizcallah, C. and Davio, V., 'L'article 19 du Traité sur l'Union européenne : sésame de l'Union de droit - Analyse de la jurisprudence récente de la Cour de justice de l'Union européenne relative à l'indépendance des juges nationaux', *Revue trimestrielle des droits de l'homme*, 2009, pp. 155–185.

Tinière, R., 'Article 8. Protection des données à caractère personnel' in F. Picod, C. Rizcallah and S. Van Drooghenbroeck (eds.), *Charte des droits fondamentaux de l'Union européenne. Commentaire article par article*, 2nd ed, Brussels, Larcier, 2020.

Tinière, R., 'The Use of ECtHR Case-law by the CJEU: Instrumentalisation or Quest for Autonomy and Legitimacy', *European Papers*, 2023, pp. 323–330.

Tinière, R. and Vial, C., *Manuel de droit de l'Union européenne des droits fondamentaux*, Brussels, Larcier, 2023.

Tridimas, T., 'Fundamental Rights, General Principles of EU Law, and the Charter', *Cambridge Yearbook of European Legal Studies*, 2014, pp. 361–392.

Tulkens, F., Van Drooghenbroeck, S. and Krenc, F., 'Le soft law et la Cour européenne des droits de l'Homme. Questions de légitimité et de méthode', in I. Hachez (ed.), *Les sources du droit revisitées. Normes internationales et constitutionnelles*, Limal, Anthemis, 2012, pp 433–489.

Turgis, S., 'La Convention européenne des droits de l'homme et la protection des droits et libertés à l'ère du numérique', *Civitas Europa*, 2023, pp. 263–272.

Van Der Haegen, M. 'Building a Legal Citation Network: The Influence of the Court of Cassation on the Lower Judiciary', *Utrecht Law Review*, 2017, pp. 65–76.

Van Drooghenbroeck, S. and Delgrange, X., 'Le principe de proportionnalité : retour sur quelques espoirs déçus', *Revue du droit des religions*, 2019, pp. 41–61.

Van Drooghenbroeck, S., 'Vérité à Luxembourg, erreur à Strasbourg' in *Annuaire de droit de l'Union européenne 2020*, Paris, Editions Panthéon-Assas, 2021, pp. 173–192.

Villalon, P., 'Rights in Europe The Crowded House ?', *KCL Working Papers in European Law*, 2012, pp. 1–20.

Waddington, L. and Bell, M., 'Reflecting on Inequalities in European Equality Law, in *European law review*, 2003, pp. 349–369.

Waddington, L. and Bell, M. 'More Equal than Others: Distinguishing European Union Equality Directives', *Common Market Law Review*, 2001, pp. 587–612.

Walter, J.,'La Convention 108, un complément nécessaire à l'article 8 de la CEDH à l'heure du numérique', *Civitas Europa*, 2023, pp. 251–261.

WILDHABER, L., 'The European Convention on Human Rights and International Law', *The International and Comparative Law Quarterly*, 2007, pp. 217–232.

WILLIAMS, A., *EU Human Rights Policies: a Study in Irony*, Oxford, Oxford University Press, 2004.

XENIDIS, R., 'Shaking the Normative Foundations of EU Equality Law: Evolution and Hierarchy between Market Integration and Human Rights Rationales', 2017, EUI Department of Law Research Paper No. 2017/04.